Criminal Justice in America

Theory, Practice, and Policy

Second Edition

Barry W. Hancock

Social Science Department
Southwest State University
Marshall, Minnesota

Paul M. Sharp

Department of Sociology
Auburn University at Montgomery

Prentice Hall
Upper Saddle River, NJ 07458

OCT 0 5 2000

Library of Congress Cataloging-in-Publication Data

Criminal justice in America : theory, practice, and policy / [edited
by] Barry W. Hancock, Paul M. Sharp. -- 2nd ed.
   p.   cm.
  Includes bibliographical references.
  ISBN 0-13-083229-4
  1. Criminal justice, Administration of--United States.   2. Law
enforcement--United States.   3. Criminal courts--United States.
4. Corrections--United States.   5. Juvenile justice, Administration
of Crime--United States.   I. Hancock, Barry W., 1954--   . II. Sharp,
Paul M.
HV9950.C746   2000
364.973--dc21

99-35854
CIP

Editorial/Production Supervision,
   Interior Design, and Electronic Paging: *Naomi Sysak*
Director of Manufacturing and Production: *Bruce Johnson*
Managing Editor: *Mary Carnis*
Manufacturing Buyer: *Ed O'Dougherty*
Acquisitions Editor: *Neil Marquardt*
Cover Designer: *Joe Sengotta*
Marketing Manager: *Shannon Simonsen*
Editorial Assistant: *Susan Kegler*
Marketing Assistant *Adam Kloza*

Printed in the United States of America

10 9 8 7 6 5 4 3 2 1

ISBN 0-13-083229-4

Prentice-Hall International (UK) Limited, *London*
Prentice-Hall of Australia Pty. Limited, *Sydney*
Prentice-Hall Canada Inc., *Toronto*
Prentice-Hall Hispanoamericana, S.A., *Mexico*
Prentice-Hall of India Private Limited, *New Delhi*
Prentice-Hall of Japan, Inc., *Tokyo*
Simon & Schuster Asia Pte. Ltd., *Singapore*
Editora Prentice-Hall do Brasil, Ltda., *Rio de Janeiro*

Contents

Part II
Law Enforcement   71

Part III
The Courts   157

Part IV
Corrections   245

Part V
Juvenile Justice   311

Part VI
Current Issues and Policy   365

Preface

We had several goals in creating this second edition of *Criminal Justice in America: Theory, Practice, and Policy.* First and foremost, we wanted to produce an anthology that contained superior primary source materials covering the major components of the justice system in America. We believe that there is no substitute for reading in an area rather than reading about an area of study. The standard textbook approaches that dominate undergraduate classes in criminal justice are in dramatic transition. The need for new ideas and approaches dealing with crime has never been greater. It will take great effort by millions of people to change the current justice system toward a more effective and efficient whole. To begin to achieve these changes, all persons interested in solutions to the nation's social problems, especially crime, must continually strive to do and be just a little better. We believe that this process begins with instructors and students expanding the envelope of possibilities rather than perpetuating the status quo. This collection of readings represents change toward the margins of possibility rather than the center of stagnation.

Our second goal was to create pedagogical materials that integrate the information in each reading with vocabulary, discussion, and application exercises at the end of each reading or in the glossary of key terms. These materials are designed to help students learn information through review, discussion, and application. The inclusion of these materials can be used as assignments or to facilitate debate and are especially useful for instructors and students in these regards. Due to the inclusion of these pedagogical materials, the anthology can be used as a primary text or as a supplement. Students should consider these pedagogical materials as devices that help them integrate vocabulary and information found in the readings, and in improving their performance on examinations.

Our last major goal was to produce a well-integrated anthology with articles divided into such parts as law enforcement, courts, corrections, juvenile justice, and policy. This traditional division adds continuity, congruence, and flow to the anthology and makes it easier to use for both students and instructors. Additionally, this organization makes the anthology easily adaptable as a supplement or primary text. The combination of organization and pedagogical materials is unique to this work and enhances the impact of the work in the classroom.

This second edition of *Criminal Justice in America: Theory, Practice, and Policy* consists of twenty-eight articles organized into six parts. At the end of each article you will find a series of questions for discussion and application that facilitate understanding and debate over issues in criminal justice. A second pedagogical feature is that of boldface terms in the readings that are defined in the glossary of key terms at the end of the book. These materials are especially good at helping you understand each reading in relation to criminal justice issues and concerns. There are only minor changes to this new edition that we believe help streamline the anthology into a more balanced whole. We have deleted several articles and added others that are more relevant to the current debates in criminal justice.

Part I, Criminal Justice in America, presents five articles that contribute to a foundation or overview of criminal justice and some of the more controversial issues in the field. These readings capture not only the major organization of criminal justice but newer ideas concerning direction and emphasis of our agencies of justice. It is with these readings that you come to understand the sheer magnitude and complexities of the criminal justice system in the United States.

In Part II, Law Enforcement, we delve into the challenges, issues, and personal struggles of policing agencies and personnel. Beginning with a brief history of police in the United States, we go on to present readings covering police stress, personality, policing in the community, and the future of law enforcement. Policing agencies will continue to elevate the requirements for personnel in order to have a better educated, better trained workforce and a more professional organization. Without a doubt, computer and other technologies will revolutionize all aspects of law enforcement as we enter the new century.

Part III, The Courts, includes five articles that deal with various aspects of the judiciary system in the United States. Aspects such as the effectiveness of the courts to the priority prosecution of recidivists are presented here. Judicial structure and procedural mechanisms are extremely important to understand if we plan to improve the workings of the courts. The court systems, both federal and state, are often confusing and difficult to understand. The articles presented relieve some of this confusion and difficulty.

We have included five articles in Part IV, Corrections. Perhaps no subject is so hotly debated as how to deal with offenders after conviction. Our goal has been to present articles that cover a wide range of issues and ideas as well as the general structure and workings of correctional institutions and agencies. With correctional populations at the highest levels in history, we must clearly understand our goals and objectives in relation to corrective processes. Rational choice and econometric arguments are becoming more popular in relation to correctional budgets, policy, and outcomes.

Part V, Juvenile Justice, includes four articles geared to cover various aspects of this rather unique system. The structure, organization, and intent of juvenile justice are quite different from the larger adult system but still highly interrelated. What happens in this system often influence entire lives and the larger society. Especially important to understand are the changes in family structure and function, youth culture, changes in education, and socioeconomic status.

In the final section, Part VI, Current Issues and Policy, we present ideas and positions directed at public policy concerns about crime and criminal justice. The structuring, implementation, and effectiveness of crime-related policy must be understood since most citizens are affected by these policies in one way or another. Solutions to the myriad of social problems, of which crime is only one, come only after understanding the multitude of processes that produced our current system.

Acknowledgments

We extend our thanks and gratitude to Neil Marquardt and his staff at Prentice Hall for providing us the opportunity to publish this work. It is a great pleasure to work with professionals who possess vision and positive expectations. We extend thanks and appreciation to the following reviewers for their many helpful critiques of the manuscript: Dr. Wayne Wolf, South Suburban College, South Holland, Illinois; C. Thomas Whitt, Fresno City College, Fresno, California; and Ron Walker, Trinity Valley Community College, Athens, Texas

In addition, we especially feel that our colleagues and students have invariably shaped our ideas for an anthology in criminal justice and we sincerely thank you all. It is our greatest hope that instructors and students squeeze every ounce of benefit from these readings in preparation to contribute to the goal of reducing crime in our great nation.

Barry W. Hancock
Paul M. Sharp

Criminal Justice in America

The system of justice administration in the United States has evolved out of the polemical debates of crime control versus due process. On the one hand, the crime control model argues that controlling crime is the essence of the system and further that the safety of the majority is a mandate. The due process arguments have focused on the fairness of the system and suggest that all persons must be treated equally under the law. The safety and rights of the larger society versus the safety and rights of the individual have been the dialectics of debates that have influenced police, court, correctional, and juvenile justice policies and resources. The rule of law and **habeas corpus** are fundamental to the administration of justice in a democracy whatever the enigmatic nature of the system itself and whatever the current philosophical debates concerning resource allocation or focus.

Historically, the United States has attempted to balance crime control and individual rights through the development of three basic components known collectively as the *criminal justice system*. The police, the courts, and the correctional system are the parts that, ideally, work as a system to control crime in a fair and legal manner. The system has often been reactive to the total crime problem in the country and is held responsible for many social issues outside the purview of the system itself. In other words, the system generally reacts to crime and criminals rather than having a "before the fact" approach to crime and criminals. Additionally, crime and criminals are not the only social issues the system must deal with as a routine part of its very nature. Each component of the system is called upon and held responsible for a multitude of issues that should be handled elsewhere in the society. As if these basic issues are not confounding enough to deal with, the system is often blamed for processes and events that are only remotely related to the system.

The expectations of criminal justice are often based on a nebulous goal of crime control or reduction. This may make sense to those who refer only to openly violent street-level crimes; however, the control and reduction of organized, white-collar, and governmental crimes have proven much more difficult. The system has been called to account for inequities in responding to crime problems based on the status of the **perpetrator** or victim rather than the situation itself. If the system is skewed to be fair only to those who can afford, either economically or politically, to defend themselves, a democratic system of justice fails the litmus test of fairness. Overhauling an unfair or reactive system is much easier said

1

than done. If a student of criminal justice wishes to come to a genuine understanding of this vast system and its underlying strengths and weaknesses, try to change the system. Change agents from within are seen as traders, while change agents from outside are seen as ignorant of the real agenda of the system. Most often, however, change comes slowly and with little serious impact on the volume or amount of crime in our society.

We are not suggesting that the system of criminal justice is a system of failure. There will be crime and criminals in any society, whatever the degree of social control. The establishment of a system of justice in a democracy, however, will always be in the process of becoming. What the system becomes and how it operates is based on the society's expectations of the system, clear and measurable objectives concerning these expectations, resource allocations for succeeding, and leadership in the direction of expected change. The system itself must never be allowed to stagnate but must continue to evolve through the use of modern technology and ideas. No American expects a **utopian** system of criminal justice. Most Americans want freedom from fear and violence and keep expecting the formal agents of social control to achieve these ends. Increasingly, however, Americans are growing weary of a system that often seems overwhelmed by its responsibilities, out of touch with reality, and in jeopardy of failing the public faith despite the highest funding levels in history. We have never spent more as a nation on our police, courts, or correctional systems than at this point in history, nor have we ever experienced as much fear, mistrust, and apathy regarding crime, criminals, and even our own system of justice.

What is right and what is wrong with the system cannot be answered in a simplistic fashion. The system has become as complicated as our own modern existence, and the solutions to the many problems are often as elusive as what the future will look like 10 years from today. One thing is clear in studying criminal justice: We cannot keep doing the same things and expecting different results. This is insanity and it is up to those who become involved professionally in criminal justice to implement the causes that will bring about the changes that will lead to a more effective, efficient, and positive outcome-based system of justice in the United States.

The past century has brought about more social change than any preceding historical period. The United States and our system of justice have undergone profound changes. Most of the changes were undreamed of just a few short decades ago, and most people know that the rate of change has only increased. The U.S. criminal justice system is simply a part of the larger social structure, and any changes in the larger social system will inevitably affect the structure of justice as well. Our society and the world must deal with some of the most serious social problems ever faced by humans as we approach the twenty-first century. The social issues involved in dealing effectively with crime are among the most serious of these social problems. Only we as a nation of people can make our justice system better. We have developed some of the best police procedures and personnel in history, we have a court system that is the envy of the majority of the world, and we have even produced a correctional system that is often criticized but seldom applauded for being progressive. We have succeeded often in walking the fine line between crime control and due process. If we have succeeded, we have also failed. It is the future of the administration of justice that we must now dwell on.

Much of the future system of justice in the United States will be determined by students like you who have decided on a career in criminal justice. We have selected five articles for Part 1 of this anthology to serve as an introductory foundation so that you can more fully understand the organization, history, procedures, and issues involved in the U.S. criminal justice system.

We begin this part with "An Overview of the Criminal Justice System," which graphically indicates the sequence of events that occur in relation to crime in our society. Although simple, this graphic presentation has become a classic demonstrative tool for understanding the total system and how the various parts function in relation to the whole. This article suggests that everything from citizen participation to discretion influences the effectiveness and efficiency of the overall system.

Our second selection, "The Rediscovery of Crime Victims" by Andrew Karmen, delves into the fairness of the system by exploring the recent focus on victims of crime. Criminals have often been the major focus of the system, Karmen claims, and victims have been lost or ignored. Efforts by journalists, criminal justice experts, citizen groups, and others, especially since the late 1950s, have shifted the focus away from the perpetrators and onto the victims. This reawakening has focused significant attention on domestic violence and abuse, alcohol-related deaths, and crimes such as rape. This shift in focus has altered the functioning, organization, and structure of the system of criminal justice.

"Choosing Crime: Close Your Eyes and Take Your Chances" is an excellent piece of research by Kenneth D. Tunnell, who was interested in repetitive offenders in relation to how they make decisions to commit a crime given the possibility of legal punishment. He identifies cognitive and social variables related to criminal decision making in addition to identifying habitual offender characteristics. Interestingly, the fear of being caught and/or punished had little deterrent effect on the habitual offenders in this study. This raises serious questions regarding harsher punishments and how selective incapacitation might be reasonable in neutralizing the criminality of these career criminals.

William Wilbanks and Coramae Richey Mann, in our fourth selection, take opposing views of "Racism in the Criminal Justice System." As you examine this debate, you will notice that much of the controversy has to do with the rule-of-law issue. Is the criminal justice system dealing fairly and equally with various racial groups? Part of the underlying complication of answering this serious question is related to the method used in collecting data and the overall focus of the system on particular types of crime and criminals.

Our final selection, "Crime in the 1990s: A Federal Perspective," is based on excerpts taken from a symposium of criminal justice experts and edited by Magnus J. Seng and Thomas M. Frost. These experts agreed that drug proliferation is the most critical problem facing law enforcement in the 1990s. There was broad agreement that the focus of the drug problem should shift to demand reduction if we are to succeed in our efforts to stop the significant harm caused by drugs. Without serious attention at all levels of our society, the proliferation of drugs could cause a collapse of the criminal justice system. Issues such as political corruption, white-collar crime, and public attitudes toward crime are also addressed in this important article.

chapter 1

An Overview of the Criminal Justice System

Report to the Nation on Crime and Justice

THE RESPONSE TO CRIME IS A COMPLEX PROCESS THAT INVOLVES CITIZENS AS WELL AS MANY AGENCIES, LEVELS, AND BRANCHES OF GOVERNMENT

The Private Sector Initiates the Response to Crime

This first response may come from any part of the private sector: individuals, families, neighborhood associations, business, industry, agriculture, educational institutions, the news media, or any other private service to the public. It involves crime prevention as well as participation in the criminal justice process once a crime has been committed. Private crime prevention is more than providing private security or burglar alarms or participating in neighborhood watch. It also includes a commitment to stop criminal behavior by not engaging in it or condoning it when it is committed by others.

Citizens take part directly in the criminal justice process by reporting crime to the police, by being a reliable participant (for example, witness, juror) in a criminal proceeding, and by accepting the disposition of the system as just or reasonable. As voters and taxpayers, citizens also participate in criminal justice through the policymaking process that affects how the criminal justice process operates, the resources available to it, and its goals and objectives. At every stage of the process, from the original formulation of objectives to the decision about where to locate jails and prisons and to the reintegration of inmates into society, the private sector has a role to play. Without such involvement, the criminal justice process cannot serve the citizens it is intended to protect.

The Government Responds to Crime through the Criminal Justice System

We apprehend, try, and punish offenders by means of a loose confederation of agencies at all levels of government. Our American system of justice has evolved from the

5

English common law into a complex series of procedures and decisions. There is no single criminal justice system in this country. We have many systems that are similar, but individually unique.

Criminal cases may be handled differently in different **jurisdictions**, but court decisions based on the due process guarantees of the U.S. Constitution require that specific steps be taken in the administration of criminal justice (Figure 1). The description of the criminal and juvenile justice systems that follows portrays the most common sequence of events in the response to serious criminal behavior.

Figure 1   What is the Sequence of Events in the Criminal Justice System?

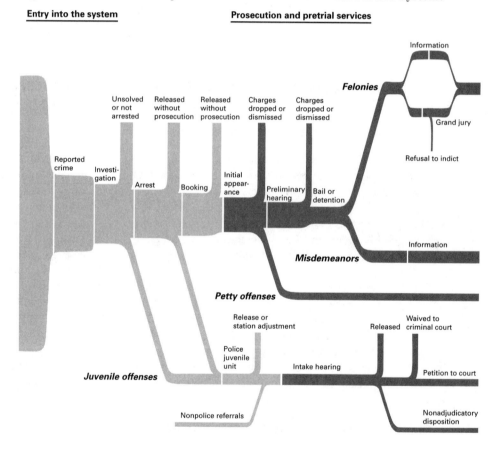

Note: This chart gives a simplified view of caseflow through the criminal justice system. Procedures vary among jurisdictions. The weights of the lines are not intended to show the actual size of caseloads.

ENTRY INTO THE SYSTEM

The justice system does not respond to most crime because so much crime is not discovered or reported to the police. Law enforcement agencies learn about crime from the reports of citizens, from discovery by a police officer in the field, or from investigative and intelligence work. Once a law enforcement agency has established that a crime has been committed, a suspect must be identified and apprehended for the case to proceed through the system. Sometimes, a suspect is apprehended at the scene; however, identification of a suspect sometimes requires an extensive investigation. Often, no one is identified or apprehended.

Figure 1   *Continued*

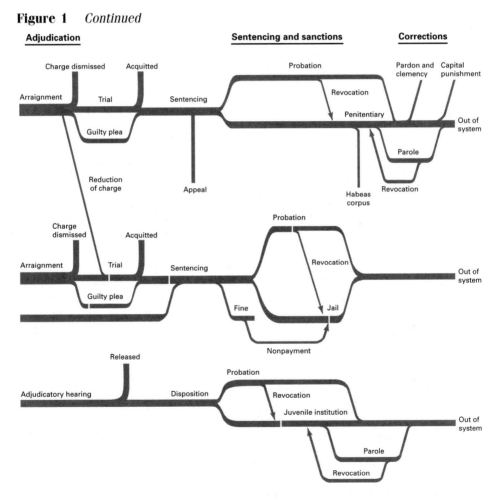

Source: Adapted from *The challenge of crime in a free society.*
President's Commission on Law Enforcement and Administration of Justice, 1967.

Prosecution and Pretrial Services

After an arrest, law enforcement agencies present information about the case and about the accused to the prosecutor, who will decide if formal charges will be filed with the court. If no charges are filed, the accused must be released. The prosecutor can also drop charges after making efforts to prosecute *(nolle prosequi)*.

A suspect charged with a crime must be taken before a judge or magistrate without unnecessary delay. At the initial appearance, the judge or magistrate informs the accused of the charges and decides whether there is probable cause to detain the accused person. Often, the defense counsel is also assigned at the initial appearance. If the offense is not very serious, the determination of guilt and assessment of a penalty may also occur at this stage.

In some jurisdictions, a pretrial release decision is made at the initial appearance, but this decision may occur at other hearings or may be changed at another time during the process. Pretrial release and bail were traditionally intended to ensure appearance at trial. However, many jurisdictions permit pretrial detention of defendants accused of serious offenses and deemed to be dangerous to prevent them from committing crimes in the pretrial period. The court may decide to release the accused on his/her own **recognizance**, into the custody of a third party, on the promise of satisfying certain conditions, or after the posting of a financial bond.

In many jurisdictions, the initial appearance may be followed by a preliminary hearing. The main function of this hearing is to discover if there is probable cause to believe that the accused committed a known crime within the jurisdiction of the court. If the judge does not find probable cause, the case is dismissed; however, if the judge or magistrate finds probable cause for such a belief, or the accused waives his or her right to a preliminary hearing, the case may be bound over to a grand jury.

A *grand jury* hears evidence against the accused presented by the prosecutor and decides if there is sufficient evidence to cause the accused to be brought to trial. If the grand jury finds sufficient evidence, it submits to the court an indictment (a written statement of the essential facts of the offense charged against the accused). Where the grand jury system is used, the grand jury may also investigate criminal activity generally and issue **indictments** called grand jury originals that initiate criminal cases.

Misdemeanor cases and some felony cases proceed by the issuance of an *information* (a formal, written accusation submitted to the court by a prosecutor). *In some jurisdictions,* indictments *may be* required in felony cases. However, the accused may choose to waive a grand jury indictment and, instead, accept service of an information for the crime.

Adjudication

Once an indictment or information has been filed with the trial court, the accused is scheduled for **arraignment.** At the arraignment, the accused is informed of the charges, advised of the rights of criminal defendants, and asked to enter a plea to the charges. Sometimes, a plea of guilty is the result of negotiations between the prosecutor and the defendant, with the defendant entering a guilty plea in expectation of reduced charges or a lenient sentence.

If the accused pleads guilty or pleads *nolo contendere* (accepts penalty without admitting guilt), the judge may accept or reject the plea. If the plea is accepted, no trial is held and the offender is sentenced at this proceeding or at a later date. The plea may be rejected if, for example, the judge believes that the accused may have been coerced. If this occurs, the case may proceed to trial.

If the accused pleads not guilty or not guilty by reason of insanity, a date is set for the trial. A person accused of a serious crime is guaranteed a trial by jury. However, the accused may ask for a bench trial where the judge, rather than a jury, serves as the finder of fact. In both instances the prosecution and defense present evidence by questioning witnesses while the judge decides on issues of law. The trial results in **acquittal** or conviction on the original charges or on lesser included offenses.

After the trial a defendant may request appellate review of the conviction or sentence. In many criminal cases, appeals of a conviction are a maker of right; all States with the death penalty provide for automatic appeal of cases involving a death sentence. However, under some circumstances and in some jurisdictions, appeals may be subject to the discretion of the appellate court and may be granted only on acceptance of a defendant's petition for a **writ of certiorari.** Prisoners may also appeal their sentences through civil rights petitions and writs of habeas corpus where they claim unlawful detention.

SENTENCING AND SANCTIONS

After a guilty verdict or guilty plea, sentence is imposed. In most cases the judge decides on the sentence, but in some states, the sentence is decided by the jury, particularly for capital offenses such as murder.

In arriving at an appropriate sentence, a sentencing hearing may be held at which evidence of aggravating or **mitigating** circumstances will be considered. In assessing the circumstances surrounding a convicted person's criminal behavior, courts often rely on presentence investigations by probation agencies or other designated authorities. Courts may also consider victim impact statements.

The sentencing choices that may be available to judges and juries include one or more of the following:

- The death penalty
- Incarceration in a prison, jail, or other confinement facility
- Probation—allowing the convicted person to remain at liberty but subject to certain conditions and restrictions
- Fines—primarily applied as penalties in minor offenses
- Restitution—which requires the offender to provide financial compensation to the victim

In many States, State law mandates that persons convicted of certain types of offenses serve a prison term. Most States permit the judge to set the sentence length within certain limits, but some States have determinate sentencing laws that stipulate a specific sentence length, which must be served and cannot be altered by a parole board.

CORRECTIONS

Offenders sentenced to incarceration usually serve time in a local jail or a State prison. Offenders sentenced to less than 1 year generally go to jail; those sentenced to more than 1 year go to prison. Persons admixed to a State prison system may be held in prisons with varying levels of custody or in a community correctional facility.

A prisoner may become eligible for parole after serving a specific part of his or her sentence. Parole is the conditional release of a prisoner before the prisoner's full sentence has been served. The decision to grant parole is made by an authority such as a parole board, which has power to grant or revoke parole or to discharge a parolee altogether. The way parole decisions are made varies widely among jurisdictions.

Offenders may also be required to serve out their full sentences prior to release (expiration of term). Those sentenced under determinate sentencing laws can be released only after they have served their full sentence (mandatory release) less any "goodtime" received while in prison. Inmates get such credits against their sentences automatically or by earning it through participation in programs.

If an offender has an outstanding charge or sentence in another State, a **detainer** is used to ensure that when released from prison he or she will be transferred to the other State.

If released by a parole board decision or by mandatory release, the releases will be under the supervision of a parole officer in the community for the balance of his or her unexpired sentence. This supervision is governed by specific conditions of release, and the releases may be returned to prison for violations of such conditions.

THE JUVENILE JUSTICE SYSTEM

The processing of juvenile offenders is not entirely dissimilar to adult criminal processing, but there are crucial differences in the procedures. Many juveniles are referred to juvenile courts by law enforcement officers, but many others are referred by school officials, social services agencies, neighbors, and even parents, for behavior or conditions that are determined to require intervention by the formal system for social control.

When juveniles are referred to the juvenile courts, their *intake* departments, or prosecuting attorneys, determine whether sufficient grounds exist to warrant filing a petition that requests an **adjudicatory hearing** or a request to transfer jurisdiction to criminal court. In some States and at the Federal level prosecutors under certain circumstances may file criminal charges against juveniles directly in criminal courts.

The court with jurisdiction over juvenile matters may reject the petition or the juveniles may be diverted to other agencies or programs in lieu of further court processing. Examples of diversion programs include individual or group counseling or referral to educational and recreational programs.

If a petition for an adjudicatory hearing is accepted, the juvenile may be brought before a court quite unlike the court with jurisdiction over adult offenders. In disposing of cases juvenile courts usually have far more discretion than adult courts. In addition to such options as probation, commitment to correctional institutions, restitution, or fines, State laws grant juvenile courts the power to order removal of children from their homes to foster homes or treatment facilities. Juvenile courts also may order participation in special programs aimed at shoplifting prevention, drug counseling, or driver education. They also may order referral to criminal court for trial as adults.

Despite the considerable discretion associated with juvenile court proceedings, juveniles are afforded many of the due-process safeguards associated with adult criminal trials. Sixteen States permit the use of juries in juvenile courts; however, in light of the U.S. Supreme Court's holding that juries are not essential to juvenile hearings, most States do not make provisions for juries in juvenile courts.

THE RESPONSE TO CRIME IS FOUNDED IN THE INTERGOVERNMENTAL STRUCTURE OF THE UNITED STATES

Under our form of government, each State and the Federal Government has its own criminal justice system. All systems must respect the rights of individuals set forth in court interpretation of the U.S. Constitution and defined in case law.

State constitutions and laws define the criminal justice system within each State and delegate the authority and responsibility for criminal justice to various jurisdictions, officials, and institutions. State laws also define criminal behavior and groups of children or acts under jurisdiction of the juvenile courts.

Municipalities and counties further define their criminal justice systems through local ordinances that proscribe additional illegal behavior and establish the local agencies responsible for criminal justice processing that were not established by the State.

Congress also has established a criminal justice system at the Federal level to respond to Federal crimes such as bank robbery, kidnapping, and transporting stolen goods across State lines.

The Response to Crime Is Mainly a State and Local Function

Very few crimes are under exclusive Federal jurisdiction. The responsibility to respond to most crime rests with the State and local governments. Police protection is primarily a function of cities and towns. Corrections is primarily a function of State governments. More than three-fifths of all justice personnel are employed at the local level (Table 1).

Discretion Is Exercised Throughout the Criminal Justice System

Discretion is "an authority conferred by law to act in certain conditions or situations in accordance with an official's or an official agency's own considered judgment and conscience." Discretion is exercised throughout the government. It is a part of decisionmaking in all government systems from mental health to education, as well as criminal justice.

Concerning crime and justice, legislative bodies have recognized that they cannot anticipate the range of circumstances surrounding each crime, anticipate local **mores,** and enact laws that clearly encompass all conduct that is criminal and all that is not. Therefore,

Table 1   PERCENT OF CRIMINAL JUSTICE EMPLOYMENT BY LEVEL OF GOVERNMENT

	Local	*State*	*Federal*
Police	77	15	8
Judicial (courts only)	60	32	8
Prosecution and legal services	58	26	17
Public defense	47	50	3
Corrections	35	61	4
Total	62	31	8

Source: Justice expenditure and employment, 1985. BJS Bulletin, March 1987.

persons charged with the day-to-day response to crime are expected to exercise their own judgment within *limits* set by law. Basically, they must decide:

• Whether to take action

• Where the situation fits in the scheme of law, rules, and precedent

• Which official response is appropriate

To ensure that discretion is exercised responsibly, government authority is often delegated to professionals. Professionalism requires a minimum level of training and orientation, which guides officials in making decisions. The professionalism of policing discussed later in this chapter is due largely to the desire to ensure the proper exercise of police discretion.

The limits of discretion vary from State to State and locality to locality. For example, some State judges have wide discretion in the type of sentence they may impose. In recent years other States have sought to limit the judges' discretion in sentencing by passing mandatory sentencing laws that require prison sentences for certain offenses.

Who Exercises Discretion?

These criminal justice officials...	must often decide whether or not or how to:
Police	Enforce specific laws
	Investigate specific crimes
	Search people, vicinities, buildings
	Arrest or detain people
Prosecutors	File charges or petitions for adjudication
	Seek indictments
	Drop cases
	Reduce charges

Judges or magistrates	Set bail or conditions for release
	Accept pleas
	Determine delinquency
	Dismiss charges
	Impose sentence
	Revoke probation
Correctional officials	Assign to type of correctional facility
	Award privileges
	Punish for disciplinary infractions
Paroling authority	Determine date and conditions of parole
	Revoke parole

More Than One Agency Has Jurisdiction over Some Criminal Events

The response to most criminal actions is usually begun by local police who react to violation of State law. If a suspect is apprehended, he or she is prosecuted locally and may be confined in a local jail or State prison. In such cases, only one agency has jurisdiction at each stage in the process.

However, some criminal events because of their characteristics and location may come under the jurisdiction of more than one agency. For example, such overlapping occurs within States when local police, county sheriffs, and State police are all empowered to enforce State laws on State highways.

Congress has provided for Federal jurisdiction over crimes that:

- Materially affect interstate commerce
- Occur on Federal land
- Involve large and probably interstate criminal organizations or conspiracies
- Are offenses of national importance, such as the assassination of the President

Bank robbery and many drug offenses are examples of crimes for which the States and the Federal Government both have jurisdiction. In cases of dual jurisdiction, an investigation and a prosecution may be undertaken by all authorized agencies, but only one level of government usually pursues a case. For example, a study of FBI bank robbery investigations during 1978 and 1979 found that of those cases cleared:

- 36% were solved by the FBI alone.
- 25% were solved by a joint effort of the FBI and State and local police.
- 40% were solved by the State and local police acting alone.

In response to dual jurisdiction and to promote more effective coordination, Law Enforcement Coordinating Committees have been established throughout the country and include all relevant Federal and local agencies.

Within States the Response to Crime Also Varies from One Locality to Another

The response differs because of **statutory** and structural differences and differences in how discretion is exercised. Local criminal justice policies and programs change in response to local attitudes and needs. For example, the prosecutor in one locality may concentrate on particular types of offenses that plague the local community while the prosecutor in another locality may concentrate on career criminals.

The Response to Crime Also Varies On a Case-by-Case Basis

No two cases are exactly alike. At each stage of the criminal justice process officials must make decisions that take into account the varying factors of each case. Two similar cases may have very different results because of various factors, including differences in witness cooperation and physical evidence, the availability of resources to investigate and prose-cute the case, the quality of the lawyers involved, and the age and prior criminal history of the suspects.

Differences in Local Laws, Agencies, Resources, Standards, and Procedures Result in Varying Responses in Each Jurisdiction

The outcomes of arrests for serious cases vary among the States as shown by Offender-based Transaction Statistics from nine States (Table 2). Some of this variation can be explained by differences among States. For example, the degree of discretion in deciding whether to prosecute differs from State to State; some States do not allow any police or prosecutor discretion; others allow police discretion but not prosecutor discretion and vice versa.

Table 2   OUTCOMES (%) OF ARRESTS FOR SERIOUS CRIMES

	Prosecution	*Conviction*	*Incarceration*
Virginia	100	61	55
Nebraska	99	68	39
New York	97	67	31
Utah	97	79	9
Virgin Islands	95	55	35
Minnesota	89	69	48
Pennsylvania	85	56	24
California	78	61	45
Ohio	77	50	21

Source: Disaggregated data used in *Tracking Offenders: White-collar crime.* BJS Special Report, November 1986.

Questions for Discussion

1. Discuss the role that individual citizens play in the prevention and reduction of crime.
2. Describe how offenders are processed in the criminal justice system from the initial apprehension of the police through the correctional system.
3. Explain how police, prosecutors, judges, and correctional officials exercise discretion through every phase of the criminal justice system.

Applications

1. Contact a local law enforcement officer. Interview the person as to what he or she likes and dislikes about the profession. Share your findings with others in your class. Are there any similarities in the responses given by the various officers?
2. Have you ever come in contact with the criminal justice system? What is your perception of the system?

chapter 2

The Rediscovery of Crime Victims

Andrew Karmen

INTRODUCTION

Laws create criminals and formally define persons as victims at the same time. The outlawing of specific harmful activities thus always marks, in a sense, the discovery of another set of victims. The laws prohibiting what are now called street crimes are among the very oldest on the books. Victims of murder, rape, robbery, assault, and theft were recognized and placed under the protection of the legal system centuries ago.

Some laws are controversial. People may disagree, for example, over whose interests are genuinely served by tax codes or which groups are actually protected by laws restricting drug use. But laws forbidding interpersonal violence and theft of property appear to be universal—present in all societies and necessary for every social system's survival. Everyone agrees that these kinds of victimizations can't be tolerated. If there is any lack of consensus about the laws governing violence and theft, it concerns how to handle the lawbreakers.

THE DECLINE OF CRIME VICTIMS

In colonial America, victims were the central figures in the criminal justice drama. Police forces and public prosecutors did not yet exist. Criminal acts were viewed primarily as harmful to the individuals involved. Victims conducted their own investigations, paid for warrants to have sheriffs make arrests, and hired private attorneys to indict and prosecute their alleged offenders. Convicts were forced to repay victims up to three times as much as they damaged or stole. The fates of offenders were closely tied to the wishes of their victims. Victims were key decision makers within and direct beneficiaries of the criminal justice process. But after the Revolutionary War and the framing of the Constitution, distinctions

Reprinted by permission of publisher.

arose between offenses against the social order (crimes) and harmful acts inflicted on one individual by another (torts, or civil wrongs). Crimes were considered hostile attacks against the authority of the state, as the representative governing body of the people. Addressing the suffering of the victims was deemed to be less important than dealing with the symbolic threat posed by criminals to the society as a whole. Public prosecutors, as representatives of the government and of society, took over powers and responsibilities formerly assumed by victims. Federal, state, and district attorneys decided whether or not to press charges, what indictments to file, and what sanctions to ask judges to invoke against the guilty parties. Reimbursement of the victims became a minor concern as new priorities in sentencing took hold. The goals of **deterring** crime through punishment, rehabilitating troublemakers through treatment, and protecting society through the incarceration of dangerous persons began to overshadow the demands of victims that they be restored to financial, emotional, and physical health whenever possible. The state undertook the obligation of providing accused and convicted persons with lawyers, food, housing, medical care, recreational opportunities, schooling, job training, and psychological counseling, while leaving victims to fend for themselves. Victims lost control over their cases, and their role was reduced to initiating investigations by complaining to the police and testifying for the prosecution as just another piece of evidence in the state's presentation of damning facts against the accused. When the overwhelming majority of cases came to be resolved through confessions of guilt elicited in negotiated settlements, most victims lost their last opportunity to actively participate in the process—by telling their stories on the witness stand. Victims became so overlooked in criminal justice proceedings that they were rarely asked what actions the prosecution should take, and often were never informed of the outcome or the reasons for it. Many victims concluded that they had been harmed twice, the second time by a system **ostensibly** set up to help them but in reality more intent on satisfying the needs of its constituent agencies and officials (McDonald, 1977; Davis, Kunreuther, and Connick, 1984).

RENEWED INTEREST

Social problems appear to have a natural history of their own and progress through stages in what can be termed a career or even a life-cycle (Fuller and Myers, 1941; Ross and Staines, 1972). In the case of the rediscovery of the plight of crime victims, the cycle was initiated in the late 1950s and early 1960s by a small number of self-help advocates, social scientists, crusading journalists, enlightened criminal justice officials, and responsive lawmakers. They started to make the public aware of what they defined as problematic: the historic and systematic inattention toward victim issues. Through writings, meetings, and events such as petition drives and demonstrations, these activists communicated to a wider audience their message that victims were forgotten persons who needed to be rediscovered. Discussion and debate emerged in the late 1960s and intensified throughout the 1970s and 1980s over why the situation existed and what could be done about it. Various groups with their own distinct interests formed coalitions and mobilized to campaign for changes. As a result, criminal justice policies are being reformed and new laws favorable to victims are being passed.

The major contributors to this process of rediscovery and to this critique of unjusti-fiable neglect have been the following: victims of rape and battering; survivors whose loved ones were murdered, or were killed in car crashes caused by drunk drivers; parents whose children were kidnapped; social scientists such as **victimologists,** criminologists, psychologists, and political scientists; criminal justice professionals such as judges, prose-cutors, other lawyers, and police administrators; care givers such as doctors, nurses, and social workers; legislators on local, state, and federal levels; writers and investigative reporters; and inventors and entrepreneurs.

The leading institutional participants in this reawakening have been the news media, businesses selling security products and services, and the groups comprising the victims' movement in the political arena. Their participation has turned out to be a double-edged sword, however, with both promises and pitfalls. After routinely overlooking the plight of victims for many years, journalists within the news media now risk sensationalizing their descriptions of the impact of crime. After systematically ignoring the needs and wants of victims and of people afraid of being harmed by criminals, profit-oriented enterprises now are tapping a huge market of fearful customers who are vulnerable to commercial **exploitation.** After years of inattention, political figures are now addressing issues raised by the victims' rights movement in self-serving ways that can be manipulative and **cynical** in order to garner votes, campaign contributions, and endorsements.

THE NEWS MEDIA: PORTRAYING THE VICTIM'S PLIGHT

The news media—newspapers, magazines, and radio and television stations—deserve a great deal of credit for contributing to the rediscovery of victims. Running accounts of crimes as front-page items, with prominent headlines and as the lead story in broadcasts, is a long-standing journalistic tradition. Today, everyone is familiar with America's crime problem—not because of firsthand experience but because of secondhand accounts relayed through the news media.

Since the media's historical preoccupation with violence and **mayhem** shows no sign of abating, however, two disturbing questions are being raised with increasing frequency: "How accurate is media coverage of the plight of street crime victims?" and "How ethical are journalists when they report on the harm suffered by victims?"

Questions about Accuracy

At its best, crime reporting can explain in precise detail just what happens to victims—how they are harmed, what losses they incur, what emotions they feel, what helps and hin-ders their recovery. By remaining faithful to the facts, journalists can enable their audiences to transcend their own limited experiences with criminals, and see emergencies, tragedies, triumphs, and dangers through the victims' eyes. Skillfully drafted accounts can convey a full picture of the consequences of lawless acts—from the raw emotion and drama of the situation to the institutional responses that make up the criminal justice process. Accurate information and well grounded, insightful interpretations allow nonvictims to better understand and empathize with the actions and reactions of victims.

The news media's coverage of crime and its impact can be misleading instead of enlightening, however, and a source of fallacies and myths instead of the truth. For example, media reporting practices can create the impression that a particular kind of crime is on the rise. The rediscovery of some group of victims by one news department can inspire competitors to search for additional newsworthy stories on the same theme. As editors and reporters scour the news releases of police departments for still more cases, a "crime wave" takes shape. Law enforcement officials and politicians who favor calling the public's attention to such cases can then use their news-making powers (for example, by holding press conferences or scheduling hearings) to keep the coverage going. The creation of a crime wave can be illustrated by describing events that took place in New York City for about seven weeks in 1976. The three daily newspapers and five local television stations all featured numerous stories describing an upsurge in crimes of violence against the elderly. In response, the mayor criticized lenient judges, the police commissioner beefed up the Senior Citizen's Robbery Squad, local precincts hosted victimization prevention demonstrations, and state legislators introduced bills mandating prison sentences for criminals who used force to subdue elderly victims. Opinion polls revealed that the public believed that assaults against the aged were on the rise; older people told interviewers that they were becoming more fearful. And yet, statistics released a few years later cast doubt on the impression that during the period when this theme was dominating the news media, the older generation was being abused by the younger generation like never before. Police reports of robberies of senior citizens did show a sharp increase, but statistics on the murder of older persons showed just as sharp a decrease. After the coverage of the alleged crime wave peaked, the number of such items per month dropped to levels somewhat higher than before the rediscovery of elderly victims, indicating a continuing interest in and sensitivity to this ongoing problem by news media editorial boards (Fishman, 1978).

Editors and journalists sift through an overwhelming number of real-life tragedies that come to their attention (largely through their contacts with the local police department) and select out the cases they anticipate will shock people out of their **complacency** or sear the public's social conscience. The stories that are featured strike a responsive chord in their audiences because the incidents symbolize some significant theme: for example, the potential for practically anyone to be chosen at random to be brutally victimized (simply for being at the wrong place at the wrong time); the depths to which contemporary society has sunk, especially in anonymous big city settings (as shown by the indifference of bystanders to the plight of a person under attack); or perhaps the potential dangers of interactions with complete strangers (as demonstrated by cases of betrayals of trust, such as those risked by women who frequent the singles-bar scene) (Roberts, 1989).

Unfortunately, the images depicted by the news media are often distortions of reality. Several kinds of obvious as well as subtle biases color most news reports about victimization. First of all, almost by definition, the items considered newsworthy must be attention grabbers; that is, some aspect of the crime, the offender, or the victim must be unusual, unexpected, strange, perverse, or shocking. What is typical, commonplace, or predictable is not news.

As a result, as soon as some pattern of victimization becomes well known, it ceases to be "newsworthy." The media's roving eye has a notoriously short attention span. For example, victims of drive-by shootings who are caught in the crossfire between rival gang members might be the subject of lead stories for a week or so. Then this topic will disappear from the news, and a **spate** of incidents in which motorists get shot on congested highways might seize center stage. After that, a series of mysterious deaths among hospital patients might be featured. These events are then superseded by coverage of a rash of poisonings due to product tampering, or slayings of taxi drivers, or holdups of elderly women by teenage boys, or murders of children by abusive parents, or attacks on teachers by angry students. The procession of grisly, depressing, and infuriating tidbits never ceases, although eventually the subjects begin to be repeated. The question arises whether particular kinds of crime really break out and fade away in such patterns or whether such incidents occur at a fairly consistent rate, constituting a constant presence that news editors can choose to highlight or ignore.

Superficiality of coverage represents another bias within crime reporting. Space and time limitations dictate that items be short and quick, making fast-paced news more entertaining but less informative. Complex issues must be oversimplified, caricatured, reduced to stereotypes, edited out, or simply ignored. As a result, the intricacies of the victim–offender relationship, and the complicated reactions of victims to crimes, are rarely examined in any depth.

The third bias that colors media coverage is a tendency to accentuate the negative. Bad news sells better than good news. However, dwelling on defeat, destruction, and tragedy breeds cynicism, pessimism, even a sense of despair. The public is led to believe that victims suffer endless misery, that extreme reactions are typical responses, that problems are getting worse and worse, that crime is spiraling out of control, and that nothing positive is being done or ever can be done to counteract the damage inflicted by offenders.

At the root of the media's tendency to depart from accurate portrayals of victims' plights is a desire for financial gain. Newspapers, magazines, radio stations, and television networks are profit-oriented businesses. Shocking stories attract readers, listeners, and viewers. Blaring headlines, gripping accounts, colorful phrasing, memorable quotes, and other forms of media "hype" (hyperbole) build the huge audiences that permit media firms to charge sponsors high rates for advertising.

Questions about Ethics

Beneath the headline on the front page of the tabloid is a picture of the victim's smiling face. Next to it is a photo of her father, caught off guard by an enterprising photographer. The caption reads, "The tortured face of _____ displays the anguish of a father over the brutal murder of his 14-year-old daughter _____, who was found raped and bludgeoned to death in Queens [New York] yesterday." ("Queens Girl," 1988)

A woman is found murdered in a housing project. A camera crew arrives and starts as policemen carry the body into an ambulance. That night the six o'clock news shows a teenage girl pounding on the ambulance door, sobbing with disbelief and anguish, "That's my sister in there!" (Greenfield, 1987)

The remains of young women murdered by a serial killer begin to turn up. The cameras are rolling at the crime scene when the medical examiner picks up one of the victims' skulls and lets sand sift from the brain cavity. This footage is aired on all the local TV stations. The families of the missing young women, who have not been warned about the contents of the news broadcast, are horrified to see what has happened to their daughters. (Barker, 1987)

These examples illustrate the kind of insensitivity to victims and survivors that raises questions of ethics and fairness in crime reporting. Overzealous journalists are frequently criticized for maintaining deathwatch vigils at kidnap victims' homes or for shoving microphones in the faces of bereaved, dazed, or hysterical persons. When reporters turn a personal tragedy into a media event, and thus into a public spectacle, their invasion of the victim's privacy represents a dismissal of the seriousness of the incident to the injured party (Briggs-Bunting, 1982; Karmen, 1989).[1]

Victims harbor many grievances against the press for what they consider to be "sensationalism" in the depiction of their plight. The kind of coverage that can be called "scandal-mongering," "pandering," and "yellow journalism" occurs primarily because the news media that employ the journalists are commercial enterprises that seek to attract audiences for sponsors. But other factors are operating as well: considerations of personal gain (getting an "inside story" and "scooping" the competition, for example) and organizational imperatives (meeting inflexible deadlines and space limitations).

Journalistic sensationalism can take either of two forms: understating the victim's plight or overstating it. Understating occurs whenever the effects of the crime on the victim are overlooked, dismissed, minimized, or belittled. Those who understate the plight of victims seem to assume that victims can simply shrug off the emotional repercussions of a brush with disaster, a beating, or the death of a loved one. A more subtle and insidious form of downplaying the victim's plight occurs when reporters use the victim's suffering as a pretext for telling a much more "interesting" tale: the life story of the offender. This reduction of the victim to a minor character overshadowed by a powerful, albeit evil, central figure crops up in movies, plays, novels, and even ballads, as well as in news accounts of notorious arch-criminals.

The other tendency in sensationalism is to distort media coverage in the opposite direction and overstate the victim's plight. This can take several forms: overrating threats to safety and overestimating the risks of being victimized, exaggerating the degree to which the victim suffers, and overdramatizing the victim's reaction to the event.

Sensationalized coverage is exploitative whether the victim's plight is overstated or understated. Either way, certain details are highlighted to heighten interest or advance an argument. What the victim did or did not say or do may be used to prove some point. Any prior relationship the victim might have had with the offender will be scrutinized. The victim's lifestyle may be held up for criticism. Lies or half-truths may be presented as fact. In addition, when a story is splashed across the front page of the local newspaper or featured as the lead item in the evening news broadcast, the victim suffers an invasion of privacy that can damage his or her personal reputation and social standing. The victim experiences a loss of control as others comment on, interpret, draw lessons from, and impose judgments on the case.

And yet, this is a necessary evil. Criminal acts not only harm particular victims but also threaten society as a whole. The public has a right and a need to know about the emergence of dangerous conditions and troublesome developments like outbreaks of theft and violence. The news media has a right, perhaps even a duty, to probe into, disclose fully, and disseminate widely all relevant details regarding significant violations of the law. Reporters and news editors have a constitutional right arising from the First Amendment protection of free speech to present the facts to the public without interference from the government. The problem is that the public's right to know the news and the media's right to report it clash with the victim's right to privacy in the face of unwanted publicity (Karmen, 1989).

Several remedies have been proposed to curb the abusive treatment of victims by insensitive journalists. One approach would be to enact new laws to protect victims from needless publicity, such as the unnecessary disclosure of their names and addresses. An alternative approach would be to rely on editors' self-restraint. The fact that most news accounts of rapes no longer reveal the victims' names is an example of this approach in action. A third remedy would be for the media to adopt a code of professional ethics. Journalists who abide by the code would "read victims their rights" at the outset of interviews just as police officers read suspects their *Miranda* rights when taking them into custody.

Of course, when victims know their rights in advance they can more effectively exercise them to protect their own interests. Empowering victims in this way could be accomplished by people serving as "victim advocates" (either as volunteers or as criminal justice professionals).

Victimologists can play an important role within this conflict between victims and the media, by studying how frequently and how seriously news reporters offend crime victims and by monitoring how successfully the various reform strategies limit and prevent abuses.

BUSINESSES: SELLING PRODUCTS AND SERVICES TO VICTIMS

Businesses have discovered in victims an untapped market for goods and services. After suffering through an unpleasant experience, many victims become willing, even eager, consumers, searching for products that will protect them from any further harm. Potential victims—everyone else—constitute a far larger market, if they can be convinced that the personal security industry can increase their safety.

But the attention paid to the victim's plight by businesses may turn out, like media coverage, to be a mixed blessing. Along with the development of this new personal security market comes the possibility of commercial exploitation. Profiteers can engage in false advertising and fear **mongering** to cash in on the crime problem and capitalize on the legitimate concerns and needs of vulnerable and sometimes panicky customers.

Of equal significance, the development of a personal and home security industry (offering services such as bodyguards for rent and products ranging from guns to bulletproof clothing to burglar alarms) is imposing a commercial and private bias into efforts to reduce crime. Individuals and small groups equipped with the latest in technological gadgetry are becoming the troops in the "war on crime" as responsibility shifts away from the corporate and governmental sources of the problem.

From Crime Prevention to Victimization Prevention

The new interest in victims on the part of businesses has contributed to an evolution in crime prevention strategies. The term *crime prevention* refers to efforts taken to forestall or deter offenders before they strike, as opposed to *crime control* measures, which are taken in response to outbreaks of lawlessness.

Formerly, crime prevention strategies centered on government programs designed to get at the social roots of illegal behavior, such as poverty, unemployment, and discrimination. Crime prevention used to conjure up images of campaigns to improve the quality of education in inner city school systems, to provide decent jobs for all those seeking work, and to develop meaningful recreational outlets for idle youth. Now, however, crime prevention has come to mean "the anticipation, recognition, and appraisal of a crime risk, and the initiation of some action to remove or reduce it" (National Crime Prevention Institute, 1978). Crime prevention strategies are shifting toward individual and small-group actions rather than large-scale, even national, efforts. Perhaps a better term than *crime prevention* for these preemptive measures is *victimization prevention* (Cohn, Kidder, and Harvey, 1978). Victimization prevention is much more modest in intent than crime prevention. Its goal is simply to discourage criminals from attacking particular targets, such as a home, warehouse, store, car, or person. Like defensive driving, victimization prevention hinges on the dictum, "Watch and anticipate the other person's moves."

The first step in victimization prevention is to identify areas of vulnerability and assess all threats. The second step is to take precautions to reduce the risks of becoming a victim. Any measures that make a person look well protected and property well guarded will encourage potential offenders to look elsewhere for easier pickings (Moore, 1985).

Two strategies contribute to the prevention of victimization. The first involves educating likely victims about what they should and should not do to avoid trouble. The second calls for likely victims to enhance their safety through security hardware and protective services.

The shift from crime prevention on a societal and governmental level to victimization prevention on a group and individual level requires potential victims to become crime conscious, or "street smart." The responsibility for personal safety now falls on the would-be victims, who must outmaneuver the would-be offenders. Homeowners who would fend off burglars, for example, must observe certain basic precautions, such as installing security locks on all windows and outside doors and leaving lights on inside and outside the house at night. Of course, this new emphasis on being prepared sets the stage for finding fault with persons who fail to do so and wind up being harmed by offenders.

Clearly, victimization cannot be prevented solely through educational campaigns that simply stress following common sense do's and don'ts. A more comprehensive approach advocates a reliance on security hardware and protective services as well. As a result, the private security industry has come into being.

A major new focus in victimization prevention is on mechanical, or mechanistic, prevention, so named because it seeks to redesign the environment to reduce criminal opportunities, not because the approach necessarily relies on mechanical devices. Methods of mechanical prevention are supposed to reduce crime by increasing the risks of arrest, conviction, and punishment. One strategy is called "crime resistance," or "target hardening." It involves would-be victims (concerned, cautious individuals) in efforts to make the offender's task more difficult (the opposite of facilitating it through carelessness). Two examples of mechanical prevention are installing a burglar alarm in a home and wearing bulletproof clothing. The aim in both cases is to deter criminal attack by making property less vulnerable to theft or a person less subject to harm.

A "valve theory of crime-shifts" predicts that the number of crimes committed will not drop when targets are hardened, but that criminal activity will simply be deflected. If one area of illegal opportunity is "shut-off"—for example, if bus drivers are protected from robbery by the imposition of exact-fare requirements—criminals will shift their attention to more vulnerable targets—such as cabdrivers or storekeepers (National Commission on the Causes and Prevention of Violence, 1969). When crime is displaced, the risk of victimization goes down for some but rises for others, assuming that offenders are intent on committing crimes and that they are flexible in terms of time, place, target, and tactics (Allen, Friday, Roebuck, and Sagarin, 1981).

Whether or not these victimization prevention methods really work, on either an individual or a community-wide level, they lend themselves to commercial exploitation. Many new goods and services are being marketed to direct crime elsewhere.

Cashing in on Crime: Burglar Alarms

Intruders have always posed a threat. In ancient times, cities were surrounded by high walls to ward off invaders. Castles had moats as well as steep sides to keep unwanted visitors out. Fortresses had watchtowers in which lookouts could be posted. Today, electronic sensors warn homeowners if prowlers try to break in.

The FBI estimates that one out of every four residences is likely to be broken into in the next ten years. The average loss suffered by burglary victims approaches $1000 per incident ("U.S. Households," 1986). Worse yet, intruders intent on stealing things may also commit more serious acts of violence against anyone who is home at the time: robbery, assault, rape, or even murder. Even if no one is home, the invasion of one's personal space can be very upsetting. On the other hand, a substantial percentage of household burglaries are less unsettling, being unsuccessful attempts to break in, burglaries that result in minor property loss and damage, or burglaries committed by persons known or related to the victim. All such incidents are grouped together in police statistics (Rand, 1985).

Businesses selling home security hardware and monitoring services have zeroed in on burglary victims. Spokespersons for this industry boast that sales are booming, and predict that the day is fast approaching when alarm systems will be considered standard equipment for residences, stores, cars, and boats (Hager, 1981). Recognizing the considerable potential for growth, some manufacturers are trying to stimulate business by scaring the public with sales hype—overstatements similar to media hype. One company tried to trade on fear by falsely claiming in a full-page newspaper ad that "One Out of Every Four Homes in America Will Be Burglarized This Year" (Vertronix, 1981). Government figures revealed the actual burglary rate that year was closer to one out of every eleven homes (Bureau of Justice Statistics, 1983). A few years later, when government surveys estimated the burglary rate had dropped to about 5 percent—one home in twenty per annum (Bureau of Justice Statistics, 1987)—a security company claimed in a nationwide mail marketing campaign, "You've put a lot in your home. Too much to let it be the one out of six homes that will be hit by crime this year" (ADT Security Systems, 1987). An ad produced by another company cited a meaningless statistic: "The sad truth is that one out of five apartments is broken into sooner or later"—and continued, "Who's watching your apartment when you're not there? You may not like to think about it, but someone could be casing your apartment right now, looking for an easy way in. Chances are he'll find it" (Scandia Telecom, 1986). A competitor advertised its wares through the mail with unnerving messages like "Burglars are looking forward to your vacation as much as you are!" and "There are no safe neighborhoods…but there are safe homes." It portrayed its hardware as being "more than a security system, it's a 'peace of mind' system" (Shelburne, 1982). A mail-order firm opened its pitch to potential customers by reminding them that "In the United State there is now one [burglary] every ten seconds!" and noted that "A few poor souls simply shiver behind locked doors" before it unveiled its product line (Watchdog Security Systems, 1987).

Has the discovery of burglary victims by home security companies been a positive or negative development? Are unsuspecting people being alerted to real dangers, or are businesses exploiting the fears they themselves feed?

Alarm company representatives now call themselves "security engineers"—an effective impression management strategy. Depending on the customer, they draw on one of two different strategies of persuasion to clinch a sale The first is fear accentuation, a sophisticated version of high-pressure scare tactics that plays upon the emotions of someone who might have been a victim in the past. The second is an aura-of-protection approach that stresses mechanical features and electronic wizardry in a more rational and technical vein (Siegel, 1978).

The most sophisticated systems set up an electronic barricade along the perimeter of the property to be protected. Low-light video cameras, electric eyes, heat sensors, and motion detectors warn of the approach of intruders. "Silent alarms" with automatic dialers alert a central monitoring station and the local police precinct with a prerecorded message about a break-in in progress. Infrared, photoelectric, microwave, or ultrasonic detectors also trigger blaring alarms to alert neighbors.

The most likely purchasers of burglar alarm systems are persons who have recently been victimized. Among households that have suffered a break-in, 20 percent invest in an alarm system (Burden, 1984). A U.S. Department of Justice survey revealed that 7 percent of all households in the nation were equipped with alarms. But sharp differences in sales showed up when respondents were broken down into income groups. Only about 5 percent of poor and working class households were guarded by alarms, whereas in more affluent neighborhoods more than three times as many homes, 16 percent, were wired by security firms

(Whitaker, 1986). But according to statistics collected by the FBI, low-income households experience break-ins more often than high-income households, apartments are struck more frequently than private homes, city dwellers are victimized more often than suburbanites or rural folks, and the homes of blacks are burglarized more often than those of whites (Rand, 1985). Hence, the people who need protection the most are less likely to have it.

It is not clear exactly how effective burglar alarms are. Are homes protected by alarm systems less likely to be targeted than comparable homes in comparable neighborhoods that are unprotected? Are homes with alarms ransacked less—do thieves cart off less loot because they are frightened by a blaring alarm? Are burglars more likely to be captured if they attack a home guarded by an alarm? Well-designed, methodologically sound scientific studies have not yet appeared in the professional literature of criminology and victimology. The value of alarm systems has not yet been firmly established (Mayhew, 1984), even though insurance companies encourage homeowners to buy them by offering those that have them discounts on their premiums.

The installation of an alarm (as evidenced by foil tape and decals in windows) does seem to have some value as a deterrent, however. Would-be trespassers and thieves may be warded off by the warning signs, which signal that their intended victims are prepared to detect and perhaps help capture them. Such deterrence is shown by statistics compiled by the police in the affluent, relatively safe, yet crime-conscious suburb of Scarsdale, New York, where over a quarter of the homes are guarded by electronic burglar alarms. From 1976 to 1982, the break-in rate ranged from around 0.5 percent a year to a little more than 2 percent a year for protected homes. During this period, residences without alarms were victimized from two to four times as often ("Alarm Systems," 1982).

A survey conducted in 1983 by the trade magazine of the security industry came up with similar results: only 2 percent of houses protected by alarms suffered losses from break-ins annually over a period of several years (Edersheim, 1986). However, if only deterrence is the goal, then there are much simpler and cheaper ways to scare away burglars. A dummy horn mounted outside the home and a sticker (falsely announcing that an alarm system is in operation) might be sufficient to ward off prowlers. Leaving lights on and a radio playing in strategic places provides an added measure of protection (Moore, 1985). Only about half of a nationwide sample of police chiefs reported (in a survey sponsored by the home security industry) that they had personally encouraged homeowners and business owners to install alarm systems. As many as 15 percent of police officials remain unconvinced that alarms decrease the chances of a residence being burglarized (Stat Resources, 1986). A government study concluded that no evidence could be found that the growing proliferation of security devices and alarms has had any demonstrable effect on the overall rates of either attempted or completed forcible entries. The researchers hypothesized, however, that would-be burglars might be avoiding homes with alarms (especially in communities with neighborhood patrols) and striking unprotected areas. If so, then the target-hardening precautions that some people have undertaken are shifting or deflecting offenders on to others (Rand, 1985).

Clearly, the private solution to the burglary problem promoted by the security hardware industry can cause hardships for neighbors, who might feel compelled to "keep up with the

Joneses" for the sake of self-preservation rather than status seeking. If most nearby residences are protected by alarm systems, a prudent homeowner unwilling to be the only attractively vulnerable target on the block must purchase an alarm system too. The net effect of this "arms race" in security hardware is to deflect predatory street criminals from the well-guarded to the unguarded. To the extent that buying protective devices is more a question of income than of consumer priorities, the overall societal impact may be that the affluent will purchase security at the expense of those who can't afford to keep up with them. As alarm sales soar, the burden of victimization will be displaced, falling even more squarely on families that don't have much to lose but do have a great deal of trouble replacing stolen items.

Up to this point, several problems have been identified: alarm companies may be taking advantage of fears they stir up through their advertising slogans; alarm systems may not deliver all that the manufacturers promise, in terms of deterring intruders, limiting losses, and capturing burglars red-handed; and, if visible signs of protection do have a deterrent effect, the effect on society may be to deflect burglars from preying on the privileged to preying on the underprivileged. One further problem deserves attention: false alarms.

When burglar alarm sales began to take off, police departments enthusiastically agreed to coordinate their efforts with private security monitoring stations. The police anticipated increased opportunities to halt crimes in progress. But serious flaws in this scenario quickly became evident. Most of the time—in over 90 percent of all responses, in fact—the police find that they are answering false alarms. Investigating alarms that have malfunctioned or been tripped off innocently and accidentally wastes police officers' time and taxpayers' money. For example, one district covered by the Metro-Dade County police in Florida reported that 229 out of 230 alarm calls were false (Clark, 1988). The Los Angeles Police Department estimated that 10 percent of all calls for assistance were responses to burglar alarms, of which 98 percent were false alarms, costing police two hundred thousand hours that could have been used for other services. In New York City, some midtown precincts waste more than 30 percent of their patrol car runs checking out false alarms. Local governments and law enforcement agencies have been forced to crack down on "alarm abusers" by adopting various measures: requiring a permit to own a home alarm system, requiring a license to install alarm devices, fining owners of chronically false alarm systems, and ignoring alarms that have "cried wolf" too many times in the past. Since these measures discourage people from purchasing alarm systems, the security hardware industry has set up a foundation to research ways of reducing false alarms (Duncan, 1985; "L.A. Police," 1982; Buder, 1981).

Clearly, the attention directed at burglary victims by businesses that sell alarm systems has had mixed effects. The proliferation of security devices has not yet been matched by a decrease in break-ins or alarm-related problems. Surely some intended victims have been spared from harm because blaring alarms frightened intruders away (these incidents would be classified as attempts, as opposed to successfully completed break-ins). A smaller number of victims have lost less because the commotion of the alarm drove burglars to rush through the premises and overlook valuables. An even smaller number of victims have enjoyed the satisfaction of knowing that the thieves who targeted them were caught red-handed by the police, thanks to alert neighbors or monitoring services or passing patrol officers. But these benefits must be weighed by policymakers (using studies conducted by criminologists and victimologists) against the social costs of this private solution to the crime problem: the unrealistically heightened fears due to exploitative advertising campaigns, the geographical and **socioeconomic** redistribution of the burden of burglary, and the wasting of scarce police resources.

SOCIAL MOVEMENTS: TAKING UP THE VICTIM'S CAUSE

Aside from having been harmed by criminals, victims have very little in common. They differ in age, gender, race, class, political orientation, and in many other important ways. Yet, as various kinds of victims gain recognition, sustained efforts are being made to organize them into self-help groups and to recruit these groups into a larger social movement. This victims' rights movement is now a large and diverse coalition of activists, self-help groups, and even government-financed organizations that act together to lobby for increased rights and expanded services. The movement's base is composed of over 2,000 private and independent projects, government-funded programs, and support groups that have sprung up across the country since the mid-1970s. The activities of its members include demonstrating at trials; lobbying for new rights; educating the public about the victim's plight; training criminal justice professionals and care givers; setting up research institutes and information clearinghouses; initiating experiments to improve **advocacy,** counseling, and emergency help; and meeting together at conferences to share ideas and experiences. The guiding principle holding this coalition together is that victims who otherwise would feel powerless, guilty, and enraged can regain a sense of control over their lives through practical assistance, mutual support, and involvement in the criminal justice process (Friedman, 1985). But, like any other social movement, this one has had its share of successes, defeats, rivalries, and factional fighting.

The emergence, growth, and development of the victims' rights movement has been fostered by campaigns conducted by members of other social movements whose aims coincided with the goals of particular groups of victims. The most important contributions to the progress of the victims' rights movement are being made by those in the law-and-order movement, the women's movement, and the civil rights and civil liberties movements.

The Law-and-Order Movement

The first social movement to rediscover crime victims was the conservative, hard-line law-and-order movement. Alarmed by an upsurge in street crime, the groups in this coalition launched a political campaign to convince public officials to support "get tough" policies toward offenders. The strength of this movement grows as people worry more about becoming a victim than about being falsely accused and unjustly punished (Hook, 1972). Law-and-order groups are particularly opposed to Supreme Court decisions that have restrained the state's (that is, the criminal justice system's) power to take action against individuals (as suspects, defendants, and prisoners). The rediscovery of crime victims provides the law-and-order movement with a symbolic lone individual (as a replacement for the government) to counterpose against the figure of the accused or convicted person when discussing questions of fairness and rights. Instead of arguing about the powers of the government versus the rights of the individual, law-and-order advocates equate the rights of the victim with the rights of the criminal. They charge that the scales of justice are unfairly tilted in favor of the wrongdoer at the expense of the innocent injured party. Once the victim of theft or violence is substituted for the government in the formulation, the issue appears to be one of undeserving offenders enjoying privileges while sympathetic figures must endure needless hardships, neglect, and restrictions.

In the victim-oriented criminal justice system that this movement seeks, punishment would be more heavily emphasized, and permissiveness—unwarranted leniency—rooted out. The imprisonment of convicted persons would be more certain, swift, and severe, and the granting of bail, probation, and parole would be restricted. Police, prosecutors, and prison officials would exercise greater power over offenders, to ensure that they would be punished more harshly as a way of vindicating victims.

Advocates of law-and-order policies that would enhance the government's ability to lock up troublemakers denounce their opponents as "pro-criminal" and "anti-victim" (see Carrington, 1975). At the same time, their opponents accuse them of seeking to undermine the fundamental principles of criminal justice within a democratic framework: the presumption that the accused is innocent unless proven guilty; the need for **corroboration** beyond the complainant's testimony in order to convict; and the exclusion of illegally obtained evidence from consideration in court. The assumption made by law-and-order advocates that all victims want harsh penalties to be imposed on their behalf also draws fire. Forcing the perpetrator to suffer does not really alleviate the victim's distress, nor does degrading the wrongdoer erase the humiliation felt by the injured party. Actually, under the guise of granting victims more rights to pursue what law-and-order advocates consider justice, the law-and-order movement extends the degree of control exercised by the administrators of the state machinery over all citizens (Fattah, 1986; Henderson, 1985).

The Women's Movement

The feminists of the 1800s and early 1900s fought primarily for the rights of women to own property, participate in political affairs, and vote. The contemporary movement began in the late 1960s by challenging the discrimination that women faced in education and employment. By the early 1970s, its focus had grown to encompass demands by women to control their own bodies. The silence that had shrouded the taboo subjects of abortion and rape (and later wife beating, sexual harassment, and incest) was shattered at consciousness-raising gatherings called "speak-outs," where victims shared their experiences with sympathetic audiences.

Both the anti-rape and the anti-battering movements were inspired by the feminist insight that all forms of violence unleashed by males against females are tools of domination intended to preserve the privileges males enjoy at the expense of females. The anti-rape movement originated when radical feminists set up the first crisis centers for victims in Berkeley, California, and Washington, DC, in 1972. The volunteers who staffed the centers were often former victims of sexual assaults themselves. The centers offered a wide selection of services: hot lines for emergency advice, escorts to accompany victims to police stations and hospitals, peer counseling and support groups, self-defense classes, and referrals to other projects and agencies. But the centers were not only places of aid and comfort, they were also rallying sites for outreach efforts—public education campaigns and political organizing. Movement activists sought to counter the widely held notions that many used to try to justify the indifference or even hostile treatment to which sexual assault victims were subjected: the myths that women secretly longed to be raped, that females really meant "Yes" when they emphatically said "No!" and that rapists were merely misled by the allegedly provocative clothing, acts, words, and gestures of their victims. In fact sheets and pamphlets, anti-rape groups argued that rape ought to be reconceptualized: the act was not an impulsive outburst of uncontrollable desire and passion but rather a sign of contempt and an expression of a need to **subjugate.** Rape expresses violation rather than lust, and victims are innocent of any blame. Yet those who sought help from the criminal justice system were often accused of improper behavior, and in effect were put on trial and compelled to prove their innocence. To try to correct this injustice, anti-rape activists petitioned, lobbied, and demonstrated for reforms in laws and in police and court procedures. They achieved victories in nearly all states when certain ant-victim features were eliminated from rape statutes, especially double standards (compared to other crimes) concerning testimony (about the victim's past sexual experiences), evidence (requiring independent corroboration of the victim's testimony), and appropriate conduct (requiring the victim to prove that she physically resisted the rapist). Anti-rape activists also successfully pressured police departments to set up specialized and sensitized sex crimes squads, and hospitals to improve emergency room evidence-gathering procedures. A federally funded National Center for the Prevention and Control of Rape was established in 1976. A National Coalition against Sexual Assault facilitates communication between crisis centers and guides efforts to improve and coordinate services (Rose, 1977; Largen, 1981; Schecter, 1984).

Some anti-rape activists and groups went on to protest street harassment, uniting behind the slogan "Take back the night." This phrase expressed women's determination to regain the freedom to walk about without being considered "fair game" by men inclined toward verbal abuse or physical assault. Demonstrations were organized to discourage theaters from showing pornographic "snuff" films and horror movies that coupled graphic violence with explicit sex; to promote the boycotting of record companies that put out albums with covers glamorizing women in pain; and to protest other instances of the commercial exploitation of women's suffering. Activists argued that images that present violence against women as "entertainment" contribute to a climate in which too many people are indifferent to the ordeals endured by molested children, battered wives, and victims of rape. The prevalence of themes of sexual violence in popular culture—manifest in everything from cartoons and fairy tales to murder mysteries—is interpreted as evidence of the depth of woman hating in society as a whole. Marchers who want to "Take back the night" reject the well-meant advice that women should restrict their activities and observe self-imposed curfews to avoid harassment or sexual assault. They argue that any strategy that calls for women to rely on men to accompany them for protection is a self-defeating one that guarantees continued subordination (see Burgess, 1983; Lederer, 1980).

The movement to shelter battered women paralleled the pro-victim anti-rape movement in a number of ways. Both were initiated for the most part by former victims. Both developed a political position that rape and battering are societal and institutional problems rather than personal troubles and instances of individual failings. Both sought to empower victims by confronting established authority, challenging existing procedures, providing peer support and advocacy, and establishing alternative places to go for assistance. The "refuges," or "safe houses," for victims of wife beating provided services similar to those offered to rape victims at crisis centers: hotlines, advocates, consciousness-raising groups, counseling, and referrals, plus food and shelter. A federal Office on Domestic Violence coordinates activities, and a National Coalition against Domestic Violence, begun in 1978, lobbies for new administrative policies and legislation to assist battered women and their children (Capps and Myhre, 1982).

Activists in the battered women's movement argued that the time had come to reject the notion that the problem of wife beating was a family matter best handled behind closed doors. They traced the neglect and indifference shown women who have been beaten by their husbands back to beliefs about a husband's "right" to chastise, "correct," or "discipline" his wife, expressed throughout history, and in contemporary culture, religious teachings, and legal codes. As in cases of rape, those injured in domestic disturbances are often blamed for provoking their spouses' wrath, either by acting too aggressively or by acting too submissively. Like rape victims, battered women found the criminal justice system unresponsive to their needs, even though every state had laws against assault and battery long before activists focused attention on the problem. Activists groups argued that battered women were entitled to the same considerations as any other victim of violent crime: the police should respond, and make arrests, when called; prosecutors, recognizing the seriousness of the infractions, should press charges; and judges should grant orders of protection (called temporary injunctions or restraining orders in some jurisdictions) to prohibit further contacts that might endanger the victim. The movement also exposed that probation officers and family court judges were so concerned about keeping the marriage intact that they routinely sacrificed the victim's interests in regard to matters of marital counseling, mandatory therapy for the abuser, separation, divorce, child custody, visitation privileges, support payments, and attorney's fees. Through demonstrations, court-monitoring activities, and lawsuits, anti-battering advocates were able to change some policies and introduce new legal remedies and options. Yet some activists concluded from bitter experience that the problems victims of domestic battery had with criminal justice and social welfare agencies reflected deep-rooted sexist, racist, and classist features of the lager society. Attempts to bring about reform were necessary to alleviate needless suffering and even save lives, but consumed enormous amounts of time, energy, and money, and usually were either co-opted and rendered ineffective or abandoned and reversed when movement activists relaxed their vigilance and political pressure dissipated (Schecter, 1984).

Despite the prevalence of an **ideology** that blames victims of rape, battering, and harassment for their own plight, it is the fundamental institutions on which this social system is built that are the root causes of the crime problems women face. Offenses committed by men against women reflect a stubborn and pervasive sexism deeply embedded in the culture. With the bureaucratization and professionalization of anti-rape and anti-battering projects, however, much of the original impetus—the feminist critique that inspired these movements—has been lost: the recognition that preventing male violence against females requires profound changes in the ways boys and girls are raised, so that boys would no longer be socialized to be domineering and contemptuous of girls and women, nor girls to be passive and accommodating.

The Civil Rights and Civil Liberties Movements

For many years, the leading civil rights and civil liberties organizations have been working together to pursue common goals. The main focus of the civil rights movement has been a quest for racial equality and fair treatment in the face of deeply entrenched discriminatory practices. The central thrust of the civil liberties movement has been to preserve and extend constitutional rights and due process guarantees to all people, especially those who are poor, powerless, and unpopular.

As far as crime victims are concerned, the greatest achievements of the civil rights movement have been gained in the struggle against racist violence. In the past, the major problem was that the thousands of lynchings of minority males by racist mobs largely went unsolved and unpunished. Since local and state officials were ineffective in preventing lynchings or prosecuting the ringleaders, civil rights organizations campaigned for federal intervention. At present, their main concern centers upon hate-motivated *bias crimes*. These acts range from minor instances of vandalism and harassment (such as cross burnings) to major acts of violence (such as bombings and assassinations) that have the potential to foment intense racial and ethnic divisions. In a few jurisdictions across the country, civil rights groups have been instrumental in setting up anti-bias task forces and human rights commissions and in establishing special police squads and prosecutorial teams to deter or solve crimes that otherwise would polarize communities along racial and ethnic lines (Governor's Task Force, 1988).

Civil rights groups argue that a discriminatory double standard still infects the operations of the criminal justice system. Crimes by perpetrators who are black against victims who are white are handled as high-priority cases and are punished severely, whereas crimes by whites against blacks are routinely assigned a lower priority (unless the offenders were obviously motivated by bias and the incidents are likely to cause interracial conflict). "Black on black crime" also is apparently taken less seriously by the media, the general public, and criminal justice officials. For example, a gang rape and nearly fatal beating of a young white woman as she jogged through New York's Central Park one night by a group of teenage boys from minority backgrounds was the subject of headline stories for a week. Yet, during that same time period, the city's police were notified about 28 other first-degree rapes (those involving either violence or the threat of force). But nearly all of these attacks were committed against poor black or Hispanic women by poor minority males and therefore went largely unnoticed by the media and unsolved by the police (Terry, 1989). "Black on black crime" was rediscovered during the 1970s, when representatives of minority communities pointed out that blacks were victimized more often than whites in nearly every category of serious street crime; that fear levels were higher in minority ghettos than in more affluent neighborhoods; that intra-racial victimization was undermining the solidarity needed for progress; and that the problem of street crime and arson was destroying housing, driving away jobs, and closing down services (see *Ebony,* 1979).

Activists in the civil rights movement also point out that minority suspects may become victims of official misconduct, in the form of police brutality (or even worse, the unjustified use of deadly force), false accusations, frame-ups, and other miscarriages of justice.

Civil liberties organizations focus on the way government officials and agencies exercise their authority. The major contributions of the civil liberties movement to the welfare of crime victims has reformed the way in which complainants are handled by the criminal justice system.

Law-and-order groups calling for tougher measures against offenders have severely criticized civil rights and civil liberties groups for supporting policies that they claim "handcuff" the police and "coddle" criminals. What law-and-order groups call "loopholes" and "technicalities" that allow streetwise offenders to "beat the rap" are viewed by **civil libertarians** as procedural safeguards (for example, in obtaining confessions and physical evidence) that restrain the tendency of the government to overreact against individuals. Conservatives within the law-and-order movement condemn liberals and radical leftists within the civil liberties movement for allegedly showing excessive concern for the rights of suspects, defendants, and convicts at the expense of innocent victims and law-abiding citizens. Civil libertarians retort that the victims of official misconduct (like beatings) and abuses of authority (like unauthorized spying) by law enforcement agents, prosecutors, and prison administrators must be defended in court, not because they are sympathetic figures deserving of support but in order to prevent the development of a **dictatorial** police state, such as exists in many other countries.

Other Social Movements

Other social movements, besides those concerned with law and order, women's equality, civil rights, and civil liberties, have contributed to public awareness of the victim's plight. Most notable among the social movements that have rallied to the defense of specific kinds of street crime victims, starting in the 1960s and 1970s and continuing through the 1980s, are those that champion the causes of children's rights, senior citizens' rights, homosexual rights, and self-help.

Members of the children's rights movement campaign against the physical abuse, sexual abuse, and neglect of children. Their successes include more effective parenting programs; stricter reporting requirements; less stringent requirements for arrest, prosecution, and conviction; greater sensitivity to the needs of victimized children as complaining witnesses; and enhanced protection and prevention services.

Activists in the senior citizens' movement are concerned about the abuse of older persons by caregivers as well as street crimes committed against elderly victims. As a result of their campaigns in some jurisdictions, special police squads have been formed to protect older persons from younger persons, stiffer penalties apply when victims are over sixty, and extra benefits and forms of assistance are available to those who are harmed financially and physically.

The gay rights movement has called attention to the vulnerability of homosexuals and lesbians to robbery, blackmail, mobster exploitation, and police harassment. Gay anti-violence task forces have pointed out that street attacks against suspected homosexuals and lesbians have escalated since the outbreak of the AIDS epidemic and should be counted and prosecuted as serious bias-motivated crimes.

Groups loosely affiliated around the theme of self-help can be credited with some of the most dramatic advances on behalf of crime victims. They unite the participatory spirit of the grass roots protest movements of the 1960s and the self-improvement ideals of the human-potential movement of the 1970s. Self-help groups tend to be impatient with and distrustful of large distant bureaucracies and detached professional caregivers. Their simple organizing principle is to bring together individuals who share the same problems. The groups provide mutual assistance and dependable support networks. Their underlying assumption is that the most-effective aid and insights come from people who have directly experienced and overcome similar hardships themselves. By accepting the role of helper and caring for others, victims facilitate their own recoveries. They empower themselves to cope with the distressing situations that arise in everyday life, and they engage in political activism to spare others such anguish in the future (Gartner and Riessman, 1980).

Victims' rights organizations, like any organization, risk losing sight of their original purposes. Further, within the movement itself, as in any movement, charismatic persons may wield disproportional influence. "Moral entrepreneurs" may lead crusades to enhance their own statuses, and in some situations, victims may end up exploited by the very persons who claim to champion their interests. Finally, as in all struggles for power, the gains won by groups and coalitions within the victims' movement might later be coopted or erased by those with **antagonistic** (or simply different) interests, including administrators and professionals within the criminal justice system.

The social movements that have stimulated the growth of the victims' rights movement, and the self-help groups that comprise its base, need to be studied more closely by victimologists. The **demographic** characteristics of their membership and backers, and their alliances and rivalries, must be analyzed objectively, and their effectiveness as advocates for their constituents assessed. In addition, the meaningfulness of the changes they have brought about in terms of public consciousness of victims' plights and in the exercise of new rights by victims within the criminal justice process has to be evaluated (Smith, 1985).

THE CONTINUING PROCESS OF REDISCOVERY

There is no end in sight to the process of discovering and rediscovering victims. All kinds of victims are beginning to receive the attention, concern, care, and assistance they deserve. They are being rediscovered by investigative journalists who put together feature stories, **entrepreneurs** who put out new lines of personal safety products, social scientists who explore their plight at conferences, legislators who introduce new laws to benefit them, and self-help groups that organize support networks to overcome the isolation that has divided them.

Since the late 1960s, and accelerating throughout the 1970s and 1980s, both in the United States and in other countries, victims of street crimes like murder, rape, robbery, assault, burglary, and auto theft have received most of the attention. Also in the public eye have been battered women, physically abused and sexually molested children, and neglected and frail elderly persons. During the 1980s, tremendous outpourings of concern were directed at missing and presumably kidnapped children, motorists injured or killed by drunk divers, innocent persons singled out for attack because of their race or ethnicity, and hostages seized by terrorists.

A steady stream of fresh revelations appears daily in the popular press, on radio and TV talk shows, and in the professional literature about groups of people whose suffering has traditionally been overlooked, such as victims of crank phone calls, and college students, police officers wounded in the line of duty, or victims of credit card fraud. In this sense, it can be said that the process of rediscovering victims goes on and on.

NOTES

1. To avoid exploiting victims in this way, the names of the victims will not be disclosed.

REFERENCES

ADT SECURITY SYSTEMS. 1987. *For Under $30 a Month You Can Protect Something Priceless.* North Amityville, NY: Author.

"Alarm Systems Cut Burglary Rate in Scarsdale, N.Y." 1982. *Alarm Signal,* March, p. 26.

BARKER, L. 1987. "Quotes from the Symposium." In T. Thomason and A. Babbili (Eds.), *Crime Victims and the News Media* (p. 23). Fort Worth, TX: Texas Christian University Department of Journalism.

BRIGGS-BUNTING, J. 1982. "Behind the Headlines: News Media Victims." In J. Scherer and G. Shepherd (Eds.), *Victimization of the Weak: Contemporary Social Reactions* (pp. 80–97). Springfield, IL: Charles C Thomas.

BUDER, L. 1981. "New York Police Moving to Curb False Automatic Burglar Alarms." *New York Times,* February 12, pp. Al, B6.

BURDEN, O. 1984. "Home Security: A Mixed Bag of Blessings?" *Law Enforcement News,* May 21, p. 9.

BUREAU OF JUSTICE STATISTICS. 1983. *Technical Report: Criminal Victimization in the United States, 1981.* Washington, DC: U.S. Department of Justice.

———. 1987. *Bulletin: Households Touched by Crime, 1986.* Washington, DC: U.S. Department of Justice.

BURGESS, C. 1983. "Battered Chic: Fashion's Latest Assault." *Newsreport: Women Against Pornography,* 5(1) (Spring–Summer), p.9.

CAPPS, M. AND D. MYHRE. 1982. "Safe Space: A Strategy." *Aegis* 34(Spring): pp. 8–13.

CARRINGTON, F. 1975. *The Victims.* New Rochelle, NY: Arlington House.

CLARK, J. 1988. "Use of 'Force' Analyzed in Dade County." *Law Enforcement News,* June 30, pp. 1, 7.

COHN, E., L. KIDDER AND J. HARVEY. 1978. "Crime Prevention vs. Victimization Prevention: The Psychology of Two Different Reactions." *Victimology,* 3(3), pp. 285–296.

DAVIS, R., F. KUNREUTHER AND E. CONNICK. 1984. "Expanding the Victim's Role in the Criminal Court Dispositional Process: The Results of an Experiment." *Journal of Criminal Law and Criminology,* 75(2), pp. 491–505.

DUNCAN, J. 1985. "False Alarms Prove There Is No 'Free Lunch.'" *Police Chief,* May, p. 67.

Ebony Magazine. 1979. *Black on Black Crime* (Special issue, August).

EDERSHEIM, P. 1986. "Making Sense of Alarms." *U.S. News and World Report,* August 4, pp. 49–50.

FATTAH, E. A. (Ed.). 1986. *From Crime Policy to Victim Policy.* New York: St. Martin's Press.

FISHMAN, M. 1978. "Crime Waves as Ideology." *Social Problems* 25(5) (June), pp. 531–542.

FRIEDMAN, L. 1985. "The Crime Victim Movement at Its First Decade." *Public Administration Review,* 45(November), pp. 790–794.

FULLER, R. AND R. MYERS. 1941. "The Natural History of a Social Problem." *American Sociological Review,* 6(June), pp. 320–328.

GARTNER, A. AND F. RIESSMAN. 1980. "Lots of Helping Hands." *New York Times,* February 19, p. A22.

Governor's Task Force on Bias-Related Violence. 1988. *Final Report.* Albany, NY: Author.

GREENFIELD, J. 1987. "TV: The Medium Determines Impact of Crime Stories." In T. Thomason and A. Babbili (Eds.), *Crime Victims and the News Media* (pp. 19–23). Fort Worth, TX: Texas Christian University Department of Journalism.

HAGER, S. 1981. "Do Be Alarmed." *New York Daily News,* July 15, p. 37.

HENDERSON, L. 1985. "The Wrongs of Victim's Rights." *Stanford Law Review,* 37(April), pp. 937–1021.

HOOK, S. 1972. "The Rights of the Victims: Thoughts on Crime and Compassion." *Encounter,* April, pp. 29–35.

KARMEN, A. 1989. "Crime Victims and the News Media: Questions of Fairness and Ethics." In J. Sullivan and J. Victor (Eds.), *Annual Editions: Criminal Justice 1988–1989* (pp. 51–57). Guilford, CT: Dushkin Publishing Group.

"L.A. Police Imposing Fines for Excessive False Burglar Alarms." 1982. *Law Enforcement News,* January 25, p. 3.

LARGEN, M. 1981. "Grassroots Centers and National Task Forces: A Herstory of the Anti-rape Movement." *Aegis* 32(Autumn), pp. 46–52.

LEDERER, L. 1980. *Take Back the Night.* New York: Morrow.

MAYHEW, P. 1984. "Target Hardening: How Much of an Answer." In R. Clarke and T. Hope (Eds.). *Coping with Burglary* (pp. 29–44). Boston: Kluwer-Nijhoff.

MCDONALD, W. 1977. "The Role of the Victim in America." In R. Barnett and J. Hagel III (Eds.), *Assessing the Criminal: Restitution, Retribution, and the Legal Process* (pp. 295–307). Cambridge, MA: Ballinger.

MOORE, L. 1985. "Your Home: Make It Safe." *Security Management,* March, pp. 115–116.

NATIONAL COMMISSION ON THE CAUSES AND PREVENTION OF VIOLENCE. 1969. *Crimes of Violence.* Washington, DC: U.S. Government Printing Office.

NATIONAL CRIME PREVENTION INSTITUTE. 1978. *Understanding Crime Prevention.* Louisville, KY: Author.

"Queens Girl, 14, Slain." 1988. *New York Post,* February 8, p. 1.

RAND, M. 1985. *BJS Bulletin: Household Burglary.* Washington, DC: U.S. Department of Justice.

ROBERTS, S. 1989. "When Crimes Become Symbols." *New York Times,* March 7, Section 4, pp. 1, 28.

ROSE, V. 1977. "Rape as a Social Problem: A By-product of the Feminist Movement." *Social Problems,* 25(October), pp. 75–89.

ROSS, R. AND G. STAINES. 1972. "The Politics of Analyzing Social Problems." *Social Problems,* 20(Summer), pp. 18–40.

SCANDIA TELECOM. 1986. *Who's Watching Your Apartment When You're Not There?* Cambridge, MA: Author.

SCHAFER, S. 1968. *The Victim and His Criminal.* New York: Random House.

SCHECTER, S. 1984. *Women and Male Violence.* Boston: South End Press.

SHELBURNE. 1982. *There Are No Safe Neighborhoods...But There Are Safe Homes.* Owings Mills, MD: Author.

SIEGAL, G. 1978. "Cashing in on Crime: A Study of the Burglar Alarm Business." In J. Johnson and J. Douglas (Eds.), *Crime at the Top: Deviance in Business and the Professions* (pp. 69–89). Philadelphia: Lippincott.

SMITH, B. 1985. "Trends in the Victims' Rights Movement and Implications for Future Research." *Victimology,* 10(1–4), pp. 34–43.

STAT RESOURCES. 1986. *Ninety Percent of Police Believe Security Systems Slow Down Burglars.* Boston: Author.

TERRY, D. 1989. "A Week of Rapes: The Jogger and 28 Not in the News." *New York Times,* May 29, p. 25.

"U.S. Households Lost About $13 Billion to Burglars So Far in the 1980s, FBI Report Says." 1986. *Crime Control Digest,* September 8, p. 1.

VERTRONIX. 1981. "One Out of Every Four Homes in America Will Be Burglarized This Year." *New York Times,* August 4, p. A20.

WATCHDOG SECURITY SYSTEMS. 1987. *Watchdog, Now...Man's Best Friend.* Hauppauge, NY: Author.

WHITAKER, C. 1986. *Special Report: Crime Prevention Measures.* Washington, DC: U.S. Department of Justice.

QUESTIONS FOR DISCUSSION

1. Discuss several ways in which the news media have encouraged the "rediscovery of crime victims." Cite specific examples to support your answer.

2. How have businesses capitalized on victims of crime? Provide examples.

3. Is the fear of crime in the United States justified? Why?

4. How are the women's movement and the civil rights movement related to issues of crime and victims of crime? Provide examples to support your answer.

APPLICATIONS

1. How has news, particularly television news, affected your view of crime? Discuss with other class members the impact of media on crime in your community. Are the media giving a fair appraisal of the extent of crime and the impact on victims?

2. Some experts believe that we live in a "society of victims," where every person claims to be systematically abused by some other person or group, which hampers everyone's ability to obtain a higher quality of life. Do you agree or disagree with this observation?

c h a p t e r   3

Choosing Crime
Close Your Eyes and Take Your Chances

Kenneth D. Tunnell

INTRODUCTION

Previous research on property crimes shows that a small group of repetitive offenders is responsible for a substantial percentage of index crimes (Blumstein 1986). One study found that 25 percent of a sample of 624 California inmates were "career criminals" who committed 60 percent of armed robberies and burglaries (Peterson, Braiker, and Polich 1980). A more recent study of **recidivists** informs us that at least "80 percent of the men and women held in local jails in 1983 had a prior criminal conviction. About two-thirds had served time before in a jail or prison, and about a third had served a prior sentence at least twice" (Beck and Shipley, 1987, p. 1).

This group of chronic offenders is labeled a "problem population" because during their "careers" in crime they are responsible for the majority of thefts, burglaries, armed robberies, and forgeries. Still, little is known about the *nature* and the *incidence* of their offending and the way in which they incorporate the threat of punishment into their decisions to commit crimes. Researchers and policy makers have not determined "whether those individuals who habitually make criminal decisions think in different ways from other people" (Clarke and Cornish 1985, p. 161). Despite calls for greater understanding of this population, little is known about what makes them tick (e.g., Clarke and Cornish 1985; Feeney 1986; Glassner and Carpenter 1985; Paternoster 1987).

Previous research on crime neglected to examine criminals' explanations and elaborations of their perceptions of the risks and rewards from crime commission, how they make decisions to engage in crime, and how they conceptualize the threat of sanction. This weakness remains despite the recognized need for studies that employ personal and qualitative measures of deterrent effects and of the offender's perspective (e.g., Clarke and

Cornish 1985; Glassner and Carpenter 1985; Jacob 1979; Jensen, Erickson, and Gibbs 1978; Paternoster, Saltzman, Waldo, and Chiricos 1982; Piliavin, Thornton, Gardner, and Matsueda 1986; Tuck and Riley 1986).

Attempts have been made to learn the offender's perspective, but these attempts have suffered from certain limitations. Previous studies of individual criminals engaged in decision-making about crime focused only on *target selection* for various crimes rather than on the decision to commit a crime—a decision that precedes both target selection and the criminal act (e.g., Akerstrom 1985; Bennett and Wright 1984a, 1984b; Maguire 1980; and Bennett 1982; Rengert and Wasilchick 1985). These studies ignore the individual's assessment of behavioral options, namely to commit or not to commit a crime. Doubtless these decisions are interrelated, but they involve different assessments of different decision-making problems.

In light of the recent research on target selection and the calls for further inquiry, I designed this research, in which the central objective was to learn how repetitive criminals make decisions about committing typical property crimes and how they incorporate the various sanction threats into their assessment of various behavioral options. As a way of situating this study within a broader theoretical explanation and of relying on previous research, I used deterrence and decision-making theories for theoretical and **empirical** guidance. This study is not a test of these theories; rather, it incorporates some of the theoretical suppositions into the types of questions posed to the individual respondents. As a result, the findings from this study have implications for these theories and for public policy.

The social science community has developed a greater understanding of minor illegality and of the decision-making processes among individuals facing risky legitimate decisions than among repetitive property criminals (e.g., Grasmick 1985; Grasmick and Milligan 1976; Jensen and Stitt 1982). In recent years, deterrence theorists have emphasized the importance of the psychological processes of individual criminals' decision making, which includes their perceptions of the risks and rewards of crime commission (e.g., Brown 1981; Carroll 1982; Cornish and Clarke 1987; Feeney 1986; Jacob 1979). This shift in focus has resulted in the development and use of perceptual deterrence theory—a rational-choice model of criminal decision making. It highlights the importance of the actor's assessment of the potential costs and benefits of various choices of behavior.

Perceptual deterrence and decision-making theories inform us that individuals, before acting, think about the potential positive and negative consequences of their actions (e.g., Cook 1980; Cornish and Clarke 1987). The decision whether to engage in a particular act is a product of the individual's rational calculation of the expected benefits and risks associated with that act. The logic of the theories, then, informs us that if the action is believed to produce greater positive than negative results, the actor is more than likely to proceed. In such a case it can be said that the rewards are believed to outweigh the risks. On the other hand, if the actor believes that the act will produce greater negative than positive consequences, he or she is more than likely not to engage in the act. In this case, the risks are believed to outweigh the benefits. Individual behavior is considered the product of *rational* deliberation about the expected risks and benefits of a particular course of action, compared to those of alternative courses of action (e.g., Brown and Reynolds 1973; Carroll 1978; Clarke and Cornish 1985).

Perceptual deterrence and decision-making theories emphasize the actor's ability to relate action to consequence, which is of the utmost importance in understanding how "risky" decision problems are resolved (e.g., Paternoster et al. 1983; Rettig and Rawson 1963; Rim 1984; Sullivan 1973; Tversky and Kahneman 1981). Relating action to consequence is a result of the actor's *perceptions* of the likely outcome of actions, which propel him or her to act in one way or another.

RESEARCH METHODS

The objective of this study was to obtain an insider's description of decision making among this overlooked and very important problem population (Petersilia, Greenwood, and Lavin 1978; Peterson et al. 1980)—repetitive property criminals—and to determine how they incorporate sanction threats into their **criminal calculus.**

To this end, I selected a sample of 60 "ordinary" repetitive male property offenders incarcerated in a state prison system, in cooperation with the State's Department of Corrections and Board of Parole (see Table 1 for demographics). I used this particular sample of offenders to learn how they decide to commit a crime and how the possibility of legal punishment is processed cognitively and socially in a problem population. Certainly repetitive property criminals are undeterred by the threat of legal and extralegal sanctions. They may not represent the average street criminal and certainly do not represent the average citizen, but they belong to a population that society would like most to see deterred (see Table 2 for numbers of self-reported crimes).

I used three criteria in the sample selection. First, each respondent must have been serving at least his second prison incarceration for felony property crimes. Second, one of these incarcerations must have been for either burglary or armed robbery. Because these offenses represent the most "serious" types of index property crimes, it was important to select a sample of criminals who had histories of committing such crimes frequently. Third, each respondent had to be at least 25 years of age. I used this minimum age to eliminate younger participants from the sample for two reasons. First, this research depended on individual self-reflection of the kind that often eludes young adults. In addition, because sample members were required to be serving at least their second incarceration, they would have had opportunities to commit many more crimes than individuals below age 25.

Table 1   Demographics of the Sample (N=60)

	Mean
Age	34
Years of education	10
Age at first arrest	11

Racial composition: 38 white, 22 black

Table 2   Total Number of Self-Reported Crimes by Type and Number of Offenders

Crime Type	Number of Offenders	Total Number Committed[a]
Armed robbery	29	1,080
Strong-armed robbery	17	907
Residential burglary	43[b]	5,011
Business burglary	43[c]	2,441
Auto theft	37	3,400
Shoplifting	40	4,040
Dealing stolen goods	43	13,946
Forgery	24	6,441
Grand theft	41	7,581
Petty theft	38	3,879
Total number of crimes committed		48,626

[a]These figures represent self-report data. The participants were asked whether they had committed each of these crimes. If the answer was affirmative, they were asked how many they had committed as a juvenile, as a young adult, and as an adult. I also asked them about the frequency with which they had committed each of the self-reported crimes. The only possible validity check was to compare the types of crimes they reported committing with their official arrest and incarceration records. If they reported committing several burglaries, I expected to find some indication of burglary among their official arrest records. Again, such a method of data collection presents problems.

[b]Nine of the 43 reported that they had committed no business burglaries.

[c]Eight of the 43 reported that they had committed no residential burglaries.

The sample was limited to males because they represent ordinary property offenders more fully. Research shows that males account for the great majority of all serious property crimes and that females traditionally have not been involved actively in such crimes as burglary and armed robbery (Mann 1984; Morris 1987).

I contacted each of the 60 by letter, told him of the research, and said that I would visit him soon in prison. After agreeing to participate in the project, each respondent was interviewed in a private conference room that had been arranged by prison officials. Each participant and I had complete privacy; on those rare occasions when a prison official entered the room, we ceased our conversation immediately. This privacy further assured the participants of confidentiality. Each interview lasted from one to three hours. Much of the interview focused on one specific crime, the events leading up to that crime, the individual's description of his thoughts and conversations during the actual decision, and his thoughts of arrest and confinement. The crime itself and the target were only of peripheral interest. I asked each respondent to recall the most recent and most typical crime he had committed and could remember clearly. At that point we reconstructed in temporal order all events that occurred both before and during the crime. The emphasis, however, was on the individual's *decision* to commit the crime.

Because this research was informed by decision-making and deterrence theories, I gave attention to **variables** indicative of decision-making processes, namely the individual's knowledge and perceptions of the likely positive and negative consequences of his actions, the alternatives he considered in resolving the decision problem, and the neutralization technique (if applicable) that facilitated his decision to participate in the risky decision or event. The interviews were audiotaped and later were transcribed Then I subjected the interview transcripts to qualitative analysis whereby I sought out patterns and constructed typologies from the in-depth descriptions.

The interviews produced 60 detailed descriptions of how the offenders reached the decision to commit a crime. In other words, they yielded a retrospective description of the offenders' *criminal calculus.* I accomplished this by asking the participants to describe specifically (1) the most recent and most typical crime they had committed, (2) the context within which they reached the decision to commit the crime, and (3) their method of assessing the perceived risks and rewards of committing the crime. These three lines of inquiry produced the nucleus of the data for this study.

FINDINGS AND THEORETICAL IMPLICATIONS

Until this point in their lives, these offenders certainly had been undeterred by the threat of legal sanction. Only after having served at least two prison sentences and after suffering serious extralegal consequences did the majority claim that they would desist from committing property crimes. What aspect of the nature of their decision making and of their perceptions of legal punishment explains why the deterrent effect was lacking until now?

Three themes were most common in explaining the absence of deterrent effects on these respondents' actions. First, they believed that they would not be caught for their crimes (the most active criminals, high-rate offenders, knew from personal experience that the probability was low). Second, they believed that if they were caught, they would be imprisoned for a relatively short time. Third, they considered prison to be a nonthreatening environment. Each of these themes is explicated below; they suggest that the most active property offenders operate beyond the reach of the law and of policies designed to deter criminal behavior.

Getting Caught: Fat Chance

All 60 respondents reported that they (and nearly every thief they knew) simply do not think about the possible legal consequences of their criminal actions before committing crimes. This is especially true for criminals of grave concern to deterrence-minded policy makers—those who commit crimes at a very high rate. Rather than thinking of the possible negative consequences of their actions, those offenders reported thinking primarily of the anticipated positive consequences.

Deterrence and decision-making theories inform us that "risk" ideally is **conceptualized** and evaluated before acting. Again, however, contrary to decision-making theories, those few participants who conceptualized the possible negative consequences of their actions when deciding to commit a crime reported that they did not evaluate them. They managed to put thoughts of negative consequences out of their minds to complete the crime. Their fear was neutralized as they turned away from signs of danger. This finding suggests that the use of fear to influence behavior through punitive policies for repeat property criminals may be misplaced and may lack empirical support.

Even more important, the respondents reported that they rarely thought of the prison environment or their incarceration. Fifty-two reported that they simply believed they would not be caught and refused to think beyond that point. One 29-year-old rural burglar, who fancied himself an outlaw in the fashion of John Dillinger, reported the following during our conversation:

> Come on, now. You're not saying you didn't think about getting caught, are you?
>
> I never really thought about getting caught until, pow, you're in jail, you're in juvenile or something. That's when you go to think about it.

An inner-city hustler reported similar thoughts.

> So how much do you think you feared getting caught?
>
> I didn't. I never did think about it really. Not to a point that it would make me undecided or anything like that. I knowed I wasn't supposed to get caught. I just figured every time I wouldn't get caught. I never thought that I would get caught for nothing that I did.

During the crime, thinking of risks was distracting and interfered with performing well. I asked a 33-year-old burglar who specialized in stealing kitchen appliances from newly built apartment complexes about his thoughts of risks before committing a crime.

> As you did burglaries, what came first—the crime or thinking about getting caught for the crime?
>
> The crime comes first because it's enough to worry about doing the actual crime itself without worrying about what's going to happen if you get caught.

Even those who knew the possible consequences of their actions functioned with the belief that they would not be apprehended or suffer. The following conversation with a 29-year-old armed robber illustrates how he made the decision to commit a crime even though he was aware of the potential negative consequences.

> So, it sounds like as you were approaching an armed robbery you thought about going to prison.
>
> Yeah.
>
> And you said you also knew that your mama knew what you were into, and you said that bothered you.
>
> Yeah.
>
> And you also just now said you were worried about getting killed or killing somebody. So knowing all those things…how did you manage to go ahead and do the armed robberies?
>
> I was doing it just to get money. I didn't really…think about all the trouble…I'd end up in or anything.

Nearly all offenders claimed to have thought rarely of the potential legal consequences of criminality. Table 3 illustrates not only that thoughts of legal consequences were considered rarely, but that such thoughts changed with age (see, e.g., Shover 1985).

The decision-making process appears *not* to be a matter of rational evaluation or calculation of the benefits and risks that these criminals perceive as possible. Rather, they consider only the benefits; risks (1) are thought about only rarely or (2) are considered minimally but are put out of their minds. Risk was a distraction to those individuals. The decision was a matter of how to commit the crime. It was predicated on the anticipated benefits, *not* on the calculated expected outcome of the benefits versus the risks. The offenders put the possible negative consequences out of their minds; such perceptions of consequences distracted them from the act itself. A few reported that they could not commit a crime if negative thoughts lingered in their minds. If they were unable to rid themselves of these perceptions, they would not go through with the act. Thus in this sample, risk does not appear in the calculus of typical crimes. When perception of risk surfaces, it is evaluated (e.g., the individual asks whether it is instinctive or real) and acted upon. Typically the offender casts it aside and considers it a nuisance. Because this sample of repetitive property offenders believed that they would not be apprehended or punished for their crimes, they were undeterred.

Getting Caught: No Time

Many of the offenders had unrealistic or erroneous perceptions of the severity of the punishment for their crimes. Each participant reported that he knew his actions were illegal, and therefore did his best to avoid capture. Yet, a surprising number (N=32) did not know the severity of the punishment for their offenses before their arrest. Most learned the "going rate" *after* arrest (Walker 1985).

Table 3   THOSE WHO REPORTED NOT WORRYING ABOUT ARREST AND INCARCERATION BY PERCENTAGE AND AGE CATEGORY

Response	*Juvenile*[a]	*Young Adult*[b]	*Adult*[c]
Never or occasionally worried about arrest	60	56.7	21.7
Never or occasionally worried about going to jail	66.7	60	28.3
Chances of arrest[d]	61.7	51.7	21.7
Chances of incarceration[d]	60	50	18.3

[a]Younger than age 18.
[b]Ages 18 through 26.
[c]Ages 27 and older.
[d]Responses are based on an eight-point Likert scale: 1 represents the belief that they had no chance of being arrested or incarcerated, and 8 represents a certain chance. The respondents were asked to state their perceptions of their chances for the three age periods. These figures represent cumulative percentages for numbers 1 through 4 on the eight-point scale.

The respondents' perceptions of the severity of legal sanction were unrealistic. Therefore risk carried less weight than ideally it should have carried. One-armed robber (the same as mentioned above) thought that his first conviction would yield a probationary sentence rather than a lengthy prison term. He never considered his chances of going to prison for a long time.

> So, before you learned the penalty for armed robbery, did you know that you could go to the penitentiary for it?
>
> I hadn't never got caught for robbery or nothing. I thought I'd go to jail and they'd put me on probation or something the first two times. So I really didn't pay too much attention to the penalty because I knew if I got caught that first time I might spend a few days in jail and I knew that my first time…I could get probation since it was my first offense. After my first conviction, five years for robbery, I really found out the penalty.

The offenders typically believed that the prison sentence for their actions would be less than the actual **prescriptive punishment.** I posed the following question to an inner-city offender who typically committed both armed robbery and strong-armed robbery.

> Did you have knowledge of the potential penalty for doing [strong-armed robbery]?
>
> In the state of _____, absolutely not. This Class X crime penalty that's supposed to be a deterrent…I wasn't aware of any Class X. I wasn't aware of any penalties whatsoever.

The rationality of the respondents' decisions is debatable because they could not have considered realistically the possible outcomes of their actions. They were predisposed to calculate erroneously because they assessed the degree of punishment unrealistically.

> I asked a participant who "specialized" in burglary about his worries of incarceration as a juvenile.
>
> Did you know you could get some time as a juvenile for burglary?
>
> Everybody told me, said, 'Hey, all they're going to do is give you probation.'

These offenders resolved problems about criminal decisions with less than full knowledge of the real possible outcomes of various decisions and actions.

Going to Prison: No Threat

Before their first incarceration, when considering a prison environment, these men thought of the same types of threats as nearly every other individual (e.g., physical and verbal abuse, threats of sexual assault, no contact with the outside world). During their first incarceration, however, they reached the conclusion that the state's punishment for committing property crimes was not as severe as they had feared. The worst punishment that the state could impose on them could be endured relatively easily; from that time on they viewed it as no great threat. The following dialogue with a 28-year-old burglar with a tenth-grade education illustrates how he came to define prison as a fairly insignificant threat and also to believe that it contributed to his manhood.

Prison must not be much of a threat to you.

It's not. Prison wasn't what I thought it was.

What do you mean by that?

When I went in…well, at that point in time it was kind of an awful thing to go to prison. That's what I had always heard, but when I got there and then found out the "Well hell, look who is here"…"I didn't know he was here or they was here"…And then I seen that I'm a man just like they are and I can make it, and I went and come back so quick.

These individuals learned the ins and outs of the correctional system (e.g., sentence reduction for "good and honor time"). They could rationalize their sentences more easily by knowing that actually they would not serve the full term. While committing crimes after they had learned the system, they calculated another prison sentence as a fairly insignificant threat. I held the following conversation with a 42-year-old who had committed dozens of residential burglaries and who also had served six prison sentences.

When I asked you how much time you did, you said "Nothing, 18 months." Did that not seem like much time to you?

I always thought it wasn't nothing because I went and did it and come on back here. But it really wasn't eighteen months, it was thirteen months and something. See they give me eighteen months…they give me so much off for good behavior. Just like this time I'm doing now. To you fifteen years would be a lot of time because you don't quite understand it, but after you get into the system here then they give you so many points for this and so many points for that…and when you get through looking at that you really don't have to stay as long as you might think.

Incarceration was no threat to many of these individuals (N=36), who calculated it as a less than serious negative consequence. Even those few who did consider the potential for legal punishment and those who had encountered it previously perceived it as not a great threat.

While serving their first prison sentence, these offenders acquired a typical education about prison lifestyles and learned for the first time about prison sentences. For most of them this knowledge was new. Afterward some offenders desisted from crime for a while. They attributed this decision to (1) their new knowledge of legal punishment and the threat it imposed and (2) extralegal factors in their lives (e.g., new family commitments, abstinence from drugs and alcohol, legitimate employment). During this period, some claimed to have considered and pursued legitimate alternatives to crime for the first time since they began to commit crimes frequently. They also reported going through phases of **desistance** which were not related to the threat of legal sanction. Rather, these phases were related to periods when conditions in their lives were positive and rewarding.

According to these findings, the most significant argument against deterrence theory and deterrence-guided policy is that the majority who desisted temporarily did so for reasons other than the threat of legal sanction. These findings give some support to "temporary deterrence," since the offenders desisted for a while because of the threat of legal punishment. Recent research suggests that desistance "is not necessarily permanent and may simply be part of a continuing process of lulls in the offending of persistent criminals" (Clarke and Cornish 1985, p. 173). Thus these respondents could be labeled cyclical or temporary desisters.

Those who did *not* desist for a time and who continued to commit crimes after their first incarceration changed their decision making in one of two ways. Some thought about the possibility of legal sanction much more than in the past. This thinking often led, at best, to a minimal increase in planning a crime. Others claimed that they simply chose not to think about the legal consequences of their actions. Such a choice was one of several **neutralization** techniques used by the participants to enable them to commit a crime even in the face of real consequences.

While committing crimes, most of the respondents (N=51) considered themselves immune from arrest and incarceration, although they believed that every habitual criminal eventually would be arrested. In their "profession" they internalized and exhibited what Tom Wolfe (1979) referred to among test pilots as the "right stuff." Their belief in their own immunity disallowed adequate consideration of the likelihood of legal consequences.

Although these participants had served several cumulative years in prison, few had served many years in a single prison term. Now, however, because of their habitual criminal involvement and their histories of repetitive incarcerations, they were faced with the threat of reincarceration as habitual criminals if they should be convicted of further property crimes. (States with "habitual criminal" statutes mandate that habitual criminal convictions result in a lifetime prison sentence.) Fifty-five percent of the sample (N=33) reported that they had been threatened with trial as habitual criminals. The respondents also said that they believed their chances of rearrest were greater now than at any point in their lives, and that their arrest on new criminal charges certainly would result in another prison sentence. This finding is similar to those of previous research efforts with chronic offenders (e.g., Petersilia et al. 1978; Shover 1985).

The participants also reported that they believed any future prison sentence would be long—given their age, too long for them at this point in their lives. (Table 3 illustrates the dynamics of their perceptions of the chance of arrest and imprisonment in relation to aging and the realities of long prison sentences.) All of those previously threatened with the "bitch" claimed that the severity of punishment posed too great a risk to justify continued commission of property crimes. This very severe penalty may act as a deterrent to these repetitive property offenders, who already have served several years in prison, who now perceive the threat of being tried as habitual criminals as real and consequential, and who realize that age is creeping up on them.

Even so, these responses may not indicate a deterrent effect. Prisoners, when talking of their plans for life after release from prison, construct such events rather questionably. They actually may believe that they will go straight until they are released and encounter the tribulations of being a two-time losing ex-con (e.g., stigma, reduced job marketability, loss of family trust). Again, when predicting their post-release behavior, they may be unable to separate the researcher from other members of "legitimate society" with whom they have had contact during their imprisonment, even if they can do so at other times. In other words, they may convey to researchers the same assertions that they make to prison counselors, parole board members, prison administrators, prospective employers, and family members—assertions that their life of crime is finished and that they are willing and eager to make a contribution to society. They may be telling us what they believe we want to hear, or they actually may be deterred by this severe punishment at this point in their lives; such a punishment would rob them of the remainder of their quickly passing years (see, e.g., Shover 1985). Although only 33 of these respondents have been threatened with this possibility, all now are potentially eligible for habitual criminal status and punishment—the most severe penalty the state can levy on property offenders.

CONCLUSION

For this sample of very active repeat offenders, deterrence theory and policy lack an adequate explanation. This sample represents a criminal population that commits a disproportionate number of street crimes, and does so with little concern for the law, arrest, or imprisonment. The implementation of harsher penalties may be adequate to deter those populations who either do not commit crime or do so infrequently, but it appears to be dubious when applied to frequent offenders. They view themselves as immune from criminal sanction, and hence are undeterred. They tend to believe that they simply will not be apprehended for their criminal actions; if they are caught, they will be imprisoned for a very short amount of time. Those who actually consider the possibilities of brief imprisonment view prison as a nonthreatening environment.

Further research using larger samples of active criminals would inform us further about perceptions of legal punishment and would allow generalizations to be made to other populations of offenders. Better yet, a participant observational research design (which may be impossible) using a sample of active property criminals would contribute invaluable insight on decision making in this problem population. Such research would allow data to be collected at the moment when decisions are made rather than retrospectively.

REFERENCES

AKERSTROM, MALIN. 1985. *Crooks and Squares*. New Brunswick, NJ: Transaction.

BECK, ALLEN J. AND BERNARD E. SHIPLEY. 1987. "Recidivism of Young Parolees." *Criminal Justice Archive and Information Network.*

BENNETT, TREVOR AND RICHARD WRIGHT. 1984a. "What the Burglar Saw." *New Society*, 2: 162–163.

———. 1984b. *Burglars on Burglary*. Hampshire, England: Cower.

BERK, RICHARD A. AND JOSEPH M. ADAMS. 1970. "Establishing Rapport with Deviant Groups." *Social Problems*, 18: 102–118.

BLUMSTEIN, ALFRED. 1986. *Criminal Careers and Career Criminals*. Washington, DC: National Academy Press.

BORCHERDING, K. AND R. E. SCHAEFER. 1982. "Aiding Decision-Making and Information Processing." In Martin Irle (ed.), *Studies in Decision-Making*. Berlin: Walter de Gruyter, pp. 627–673.

BROWN, IVAN D. 1981. "The Traffic Offense as a Rational Decision." In Sally Lloyd-Bostock (ed.), *Psychology in Legal Contexts*. London: Macmillan, pp. 203–222.

BROWN, WILLIAM AND MORGAN REYNOLDS. 1973. "Crime and Punishment Risk Implications." *Journal of Economic Theory*, 6: 508–514.

CARROLL, JOHN S. 1978. "A Psychological Approach to Deterrence: The Evaluation of Crime Opportunities." *Journal of Personality and Social Psychology*, 36: 1512–1520.

——. 1982. "Committing a Crime: The Offender's Decision." In Vladimir J. Konecni and Ebbe B. Ebbesen (eds.), *The Criminal Justice System: A Social-Psychological Analysis*. San Francisco: Freeman, pp. 49–67.

CLARKE, RONALD V. AND DEREK B. CORNISH. 1985. "Modeling Offenders' Decisions: A Framework for Research and Policy." In Michael Tonry and Norval Morris (eds.), *Crime and Justice: An Annual Review of Research*, Volume 6. Chicago: University of Chicago Press, pp. 147–185.

COOK, PHILIP J. 1980. "Research in Criminal Deterrence: Laying the Groundwork for the Second Decade." In Norval Morris and Michael Tonry (eds.), *An Annual Review of Research*. Chicago: University of Chicago Press, pp. 211–268.

CORNISH, DEREK B. AND RONALD V. CLARKE. 1987. "Understanding Crime Displacement: An Application of Rational Choice Theory." *Criminology*, 25: 933–947.

FEENEY, FLOYD. 1986. "Robbers as Decision-Makers." In Derek B. Cornish and Ronald V. Clarke (eds.), *The Reasoning Criminal*. New York: Springer-Verlag, pp. 53–71.

GLASSNER, BARRY AND CHERYL CARPENTER. 1985. *The Feasibility of an Ethnographic Study of Adult Property Offenders*. Washington, DC: U.S. Department of Justice.

GRASMICK, HAROLD G. 1985. "The Application of a Generalized Theory of Deterrence to Income Tax Evasion." Paper presented to the Law and Society Conference.

GRASMICK, HAROLD G. AND HERMAN MILLIGAN. 1976. "Deterrence Theory Approach to Socioeconomic/Demographic Correlates of Crime." *Social Science Quarterly*, 57: 608–617.

JACOB, HERBERT. 1979. "Rationality and Criminality." *Social Science Quarterly*, 59: 584–585.

JENSEN, GARY F., MAYNARD L. ERICKSON AND JACK P. GIBBS. 1978. "Perceived Risk of Punishment and Self-Reported Delinquency." *Social Forces*, 57: 57–78.

JENSEN, GARY AND B. GRANT STITT. 1982. "Words and Misdeeds: Hypothetical Choices versus Past Behavior as Measures of Deviance." In John Hagan (ed.), *Deterrence Reconsidered*. Beverly Hills, CA: Sage, pp. 33–54.

MAGUIRE, MIKE. 1980. "Burglary as Occupation." *Home Office Research Bulletin*, 10: 6–9.

MAGUIRE, MIKE AND TREVOR BENNETT. 1982. *Burglary in a Dwelling*. London: Heinemann.

MANN, CORAMAE. 1984. *Female Crime and Delinquency*. Birmingham, AL: University of Alabama Press.

MORRIS, ALLISON. 1987. *Women, Crime, and Criminal Justice*. Oxford: Basil Blackwell.

PATERNOSTER, RAYMOND. 1987. "The Deterrent Effect of the Perceived Certainty and Severity of Punishment: A Review of the Evidence and Issues." *Justice Quarterly*, 4: 173–217.

PATERNOSTER, RAYMOND, L. E. SALTZMAN, G. P. WALDO AND T. G. CHIRICOS. 1982. "Causal Ordering in Deterrence Research." In John Hagan (ed.), *Deterrence Reconsidered*. Beverly Hills, CA: Sage, pp. 55–70.

——. 1983. "Perceived Risk and Social Control: Do Sanctions Really Deter?" *Law and Society Review*, 17: 457–479.

PETERSILIA, JOAN, PETER W. GREENWOOD AND MARVIN LAVIN. 1978. *Criminal Careers of Habitual Felons*. Washington, DC: National Institute of Law Enforcement and Criminal Justice.

PETERSON, MARK A., H.B. BRAIKER AND SUZANNE M. POLICH. 1980. *Doing Crime: A Survey of California Prison Inmates*. Santa Monica, CA: Rand.

PILIAVIN, IRVING, C. THORNTON, R. GARTNER AND R.L. MATSUEDA. 1986. "Crime, Deterrence and Rational Choice." *American Sociological Review*, 51: 101–119.

RENGERT, GEORGE AND JOHN WASILCHICK. 1985. *Suburban Burglary*. Springfield, IL: Charles C Thomas.

RETTIG, S. AND H.E. RAWSON. 1963. "The Risk Hypothesis in Predictive Judgments of Unethical Behavior." *Journal of Abnormal and Social Psychology*, 66: 243–248.

RIM, YESHAYAHU. 1964. "Social Attitudes and Risk Taking." *Human Relations*, 17: 259–265.

SHOVER, NEAL. 1985. *Aging Criminals*. Beverly Hills, CA: Sage.

SULLIVAN, RICHARD F. 1973. "The Economics of Crime: An Introduction to the Literature." *Crime and Delinquency*, 19: 138–149.

SYKES, GRESHAM M. AND DAVID MATZA. 1957. "Techniques of Neutralization: A Theory of Delinquency." *American Sociological Review*, 22: 664–670.

TUCK, MARY AND DAVID RILEY. 1986. "The Theory of Reasoned Action: A Decision Theory of Crime." In Derek B. Cornish and Ronald V. Clarke (eds.), *The Reasoning Criminal*. New York: Springer-Verlag, pp. 156–169.

TVERSKY, AMOS AND DANIEL KAHNEMAN. 1981. "The Framing of Decisions and the Psychology of Choice." *Science*, 211: 453–458.

WALKER, SAMUEL. 1985. *Sense and Nonsense about Crime: A Policy Guide*. Monterey, CA: Brooks/Cole.

WOLFE, TOM. 1979. *The Right Stuff*. New York: Farrar, Strauss, and Giroux.

QUESTIONS FOR DISCUSSION

1. Discuss the rational-choice model of criminal decision making. How is this decision making supposed to effect deterrence?

2. What were Tunnell's findings with regard to property offenders' perceptions of "getting caught"?

3. What conclusions were presented with regard to harsher punishments for property offenders?

APPLICATIONS

1. Consider your own behavior. Do you conscientiously consider the rewards and costs of everything you do? Explain?

2. An assumption made about rational-choice decision making is that people think rationally. Do human beings always think rationally? Can a person make a rational choice if he or she is thinking irrationally? Are people deterred from committing crime if they are irrational (e.g., angry, upset, vengeful, psychotic)? Discuss.

chapter 4

Racism in the Criminal Justice System

Two Sides of a Controversy

*I*n this article, the authors present alternate viewpoints with respect to the issue of racism. Mann argues that racial prejudice and discrimination pervade the criminal justice system and social structure of America. Wilbanks argues the opposite, suggesting that the system discriminates for blacks. He posits that blacks are, on a per capita basis, 8 times more likely than whites to be in prison because of an 8:1 black/white level of offenses. Mann then points out a series of flaws in this argument.

The Myth of a Racist Criminal Justice System*

William Wilbanks

White and black Americans differ sharply over whether their criminal justice system is racist. The vast majority of blacks appear to believe that the police and courts do discriminate against blacks, whereas a majority of whites reject this charge. A sizable minority of whites even believe that the justice system actually discriminates for blacks in "leaning over backward" for them in reaction to charges of racism from the black community and the media.

*This is a summary of the book by the same name.

The Reality of a Racist Criminal Justice System

Coramae Richey Mann

I first heard of Bill Wilbanks' *The Myth of a Racist Criminal Justice System* at the Academy of Criminal Justice Sciences' annual meeting in Orlando during a panel discussion of urban crime in Black communities where the book rapidly became the focus of attention and outrage expressed by the panel and participants. The discussion clearly suggested that *The Myth* was the antithesis of the book I am writing, *Minorities, Crime and Public Policy.* Two subsequent readings of Wilbanks' book confirmed my original impression; therefore, when Editor

The contrasting views of blacks and whites as to the fairness of the criminal justice system are of more than academic interest as research indicates that the higher level of offending by blacks may be due in part to the belief that "the system" is unfair. The belief produces a "justification for no obligation" or the attitude that "I don't respect a system that is racist, and so I don't feel obliged to abide by the laws of that system." This view in the collective has led to riots in Miami and other cities. Furthermore, the hostility to police generated by the belief has led to a mutual expectation of violence between police and blacks that has produced more violence as part of a self-fulfilling prophecy. Finally, the white backlash to affirmative action programs may be due in part to the perception that blacks complain about racism in a society that actually practices reverse discrimination (favoritism toward blacks).

THE THESIS

I take the position that the perception of the criminal justice system as racist is a myth. This overall thesis should not be misinterpreted. I do believe that there is a racial prejudice and discrimination *within* the criminal justice system, in that there are individuals, both white and black, who make decisions, at least in part, on the basis of race. I do not believe that *the system* is characterized by racial prejudice or discrimination *against* blacks. At every point from arrest to parole there is little or no evidence of an overall racial effect, in that the percentage outcomes for blacks and whites are not very different. There is evidence, however, that some individual decision makers (e.g., police officers, judges) are more likely to give "breaks" to whites than to blacks. However, there appears to be an *equal* tendency for other individual decision makers to favor blacks

Frank Williams invited me to present an alternative view to *The Myth*, I strongly agreed that another perspective was demanded.

In the two years that I have taught my undergraduate course on race and crime, the classes were fraught with anxiety and frustration in the face of the students' personal misconceptions, ignorance about American minorities, and reliance on racial stereotypes, particularly as applied to crime. There clearly was a need for a text which could present the "minority" side. With the arrival of *The Myth,* the need increased for a more balanced presentation of the topic.

As I view it, there are two major issues involved which must be definitively addressed. First, that Wilbanks is mistaken and that there *is* racial prejudice and discrimination in the criminal justice system (and throughout the United States' social system) which is *rooted* in racism. And second, the linchpin of his thesis not only relies on a simplistic and rather naive view of what takes place in the "real world" of criminal justice—out in the trenches so to speak—but also Wilbanks' complete dependence on **quantitative data** for his "proof" results in his dismissal of the rich qualitative data available which he erroneously describes as "anecdotal" or as reported by "lay persons." It is this latter **elitism** that is most problematic.

DEFINITIONS

Despite the use of the eye-catching and inflammatory term *racist* in the title of his book, Wilbanks quickly and inexplicably abandons the term *racism* and substitutes *racial prejudice* and *racial discrimination* in its stead. It is my contention that all terms are applicable when the plight of minorities in the criminal justice system is examined. Although Wilbanks limited his thesis to Blacks, in this alternative view, I over whites. This "canceling-out effect" results in studies that find no *overall* racial effect.

The assertion that the criminal justice system is not racist does not address the reasons why blacks appear to offend at higher rates than whites before coming into contact with the criminal justice system. It may be that racial discrimination in American society has been responsible for conditions (e.g., discrimination in employment, housing and education) that lead to higher rates of offending by blacks, but that possibility does not bear on the question of whether the criminal justice system discriminates against blacks. Also, the thesis that racism is not systematic and pervasive in the criminal justice system does not deny that racial prejudice and discrimination have existed or even been the dominant force in the design and operation of the criminal justice system in the past.

DEFINING RACISM

One of the main barriers in the discussion and resolution of the issue of racism in the criminal justice system involves the multiple uses and meanings of the term "racism." Definitions of this term range from a conscious attitude by an individual to an unconscious act by an institution or even to the domination of society by white culture. I have suggested that the term "racism" be abandoned in favor of the terms "racial prejudice" (an attitude) and "racial discrimination" (an act).

Any discussion of the **pervasiveness** of racism in the justice system is clouded by the tendency of Accusers (e.g., those who claim the system is racist) to use a double standard in that the term is used only to apply to whites. For example, it is often pointed out that 50% of the victims of police killings are black and that this fact alone presents a prima

refer to all racial minorities, since racial prejudice, racial discrimination, and racism are directed at non-whites in this country.

Wilbanks cited, but glossed over, the impressive, in-depth, objective national assessment of the impact of the criminal justice system on minorities by the National Minority Advisory Council on Criminal Justice (1980:1) which used five study methods (literature review, public hearings, commissioned specific issue studies, field studies, and critical analyses of criminal justice programs and policies) to reach the conclusion that "...for minorities all over the nation, the issues, above all others, are political and economic exploitation and *racism,* the basic causes of conflict and disorder in the American criminal justice system." (Emphasis added.) Racism **connotes** power, thus, by definition, in only very few limited instances can a minority person have a quantum of power; and since they lack institutional power, it is definitionally impossible for American minorities to be identified as racist.

An Afro-American does not need to go to Brighton Beach (New York) to find out about racial prejudice and violence, an American Vietnamese need not travel to Boston or Florida to be insulted and violently attacked, nor does a Mexican American have to go to Los Angeles or a Native American (Indian) anywhere in the continental United States to experience differential treatment simply because of their color. All any of these persons have to do to face racial prejudice and discrimination is to be non-white in America today. As a minority who for a lifetime has experienced prejudicial treatment because of my race (and gender) I totally disagree with Wilbanks' contention that racial prejudice against minorities "appears to be declining" (p. 146). More in accord with our urbane times, racial prejudice has not declined but has simply "gone underground" and become facie case of racism. But it is seldom pointed out that 50% of the police officers who are killed are victimized by blacks. If the first fact indicates racism by white police officers, why does not the second fact indicate racism by black killers of police?

At times the use of the term racism appears to constitute a "non-falsifiable thesis" in that any result is deemed as racist. For example, in *McCleskey v. Georgia* (a case before the U.S. Supreme Court this term) the petitioner claims that he received the death penalty because he (a black) killed a white whereas those who kill blacks seldom receive the death penalty. Thus lenient treatment given to black killers (or those who kill black victims) is defined as racism. But if black killers had been more likely to be sentenced to death, that result would also be (and has been) viewed as racist. Thus the term is defined so that any result is indicative of racism (i.e., a non-falsifiable thesis). The double standard of racism is also seen in this case in that the death penalty statistics actually indicate harsher treatment of white than black killers, but this result is not seen as racism (against whites).

In a similar fashion a lower percentage of blacks (than whites) being convicted has been interpreted by Accusers as racist in that this result indicates that charges against blacks were often without substance. On the other hand, if more blacks were convicted, this result would also be viewed by Accusers as being indicative of racism since black defendants were treated more harshly.

THE DATA

The book was undertaken to explain why blacks in the U.S. are 8 times more likely, on a per capita basis, to be in prison than are whites. The major point of the book is that the

much more subtle. That is, it has become institutionalized—the process that "institutionalized racism" connotes.

THE REALITY: AN ALTERNATIVE VIEW

Aside from the observation that Wilbanks often contradicts his own thesis throughout the book and adopts a **chauvinistic** approach by consistently reporting research to substantiate his position and skimming over contrary views (particularly qualitative studies), such detailed critique is left to book reviewers. The focus of this alternative view is therefore best served through analyses and comments that respond to Wilbanks' challenges to the discrimination thesis, or DT as he calls it, which is contrasted with NDT or a nondiscrimination thesis (pp. 144–147).

1. After repeatedly stating that the research is "sparse," Wilbanks is chagrined that with or without controls, "a sizable race effect" cannot be demonstrated at decision points throughout the criminal justice system. Aside from not defining "sizable," "substantial," or even "race effect," Wilbanks uses his aggregate study in two states (California and Pennsylvania) for one year (1980) as the exemplar. This is curious, since in his later recommendations for future research, Wilbanks states that aggregate studies of decision making should be abandoned in favor of studies concentrating on individual decision makers (a point I strongly endorse), since research "attempting to validate the DT or the NDT has been seriously deficient" (p. 147). Thus we find that aggregate studies should not be used, yet such studies are an integral part of Wilbanks' thesis, notably his own California/Pennsylvania

approximate 8:1 per capita ratio of blacks to whites in prison is the result of an approximately 8:1 black to white level at offending and not the result of racial selectivity by the police and the courts. In other words, the 8:1 black to white ratio at offending is not increased as offenders are brought into and processed by the criminal justice system.

Some original data are presented in an appendix to the book on the black vs. white gap from arrest to incarceration in prison for two states—California and Pennsylvania. In 1980 felony cases, blacks in California were arrested 5.2 times as often as whites. This black/white gap increased to 6.2 at incarceration. Thus the black/white "gap" increased by 20% from arrest to prison. However, the reverse occurred in Pennsylvania where the 8.1 gap at arrest decreased to 7.4 at incarceration (a decline of 9%). Overall, it would appear that the black/white gap does not increase from arrest to prison. Thus there is no evidence overall that black offenders processed by the criminal justice system fare worse than white offenders.

But perhaps the black/white gap at arrest is a product of racial bias by the police in that the police are more likely to select and arrest black than white offenders. The best evidence on this question comes from the National Crime Survey which interviews 130,000 Americans each year about crime victimization. Those who are victimized by violent crime are asked to describe the offenders (who were not necessarily caught by the police) as to age, sex and race. The percentage of offenders described by victims as being black is generally consistent with the percentage of offenders who are black according to arrest figures. For example, approximately 60% of (uncaught) robbers described by victims were black and approximately 60% of those arrested for robbery in the U.S. are black. This would not be the case if the police

aggregate data (Appendix). Interestingly, in California Wilbanks' data revealed a 19 percent increase in the black/white "gap" from arrest to incarceration, whereas Pennsylvania showed a slight decrease in the black/white gap (p. 145). Nonetheless, the "gaps" continued to exist which is the major concern of a DT position. Unfortunately, the value of this effort is diminished since Wilbanks did not use any controls in the study. Wilbanks comments that "no study has examined the racial gap for all the decision points from arrest to incarceration" (p. 151). However, Petersilia (1983) reports such a study and the same has been reported for women felons (Mann, forthcoming). Petersilia (1983:93) found that minorities were "less likely to be given probation, more likely to receive prison sentences, more likely to get longer sentences, and more likely to serve a longer time in prison than whites after controlling for offense seriousness, prior record and prison violence."

2. A perplexing tactic that Wilbanks uses throughout *The Myth,* in addition to the "blaming the victim" approach, is the frequent use of an "apples and oranges" argument by the constant introduction of reverse sexism and reverse racism. The theoretical debate on whether female offenders are treated more leniently or more harshly by the criminal justice system is about as divided as that on race discrimination, but it is not the issue the book purports to address. Thus, the constant reference to "sexism" and "white discrimination" in *The Myth* tends to detract from the major thesis.

3. Wilbanks wonders why there is an overrepresentation of blacks in both arrests and incarcerations and the racial gap does

were "picking on" black robbers and ignoring white robbers.

Given the above figures, those who claim that racism is systematic and pervasive in the criminal justice system should explain why the black/white gap does not cumulatively increase from arrest to prison. Furthermore, those who claim racism is pervasive should be asked to specify the number of black offenders who are thought to receive harsher treatment (e.g., whether 10%, 50% or 100%) and the extent of that "extra" harshness in cases where "it" is given. For example, at sentencing do those mistreated black offenders receive on the average of 10%, 50% or 100% harsher sentence?

There is large body of research on the alleged existence of racial discrimination at such points as arrest, conviction and sentencing. The bibliography of my book lists over 80 sentencing studies which examined the impact of race on outcome. A number of scholars have examined this large body of research and concluded that there is no evidence of systematic racial discrimination. James Q. Wilson, the most prominent American criminologist, asserts that the claim of discrimination is not supported by the evidence as did a three-volume study of the sentencing literature by the National Academy of Sciences.

METHODOLOGICAL PROBLEMS

However, some studies do claim to have found evidence of racial discrimination. However, as Wilson and others have pointed out, most of these studies are marked by flaws in design or interpretation. One chapter of *The Myth of a Racist Criminal Justice System* is devoted to seven models of design and/or interpretation which have been utilized in studies of the possible existence of racial discrimination. Many of the studies claiming to have found racial

not increase cumulatively. Again, he bases this interpretation of the black/white gap on his two-state study where in one state, it *did* increase. It should also be noted that an examination of the Uniform Crime Reports (UCR) for the past seven years (1979–1985) indicates that there is also an overrepresentation of arrests of Hispanic Americans, Asian Americans and Native Americans disproportionate to their numbers in the population (Mann, forthcoming). Also, contrary to Wilbanks' incitive and untrue statement that according to the UCR, 50 percent of those arrested in 1984 for sex offenses were black, for the period 1979–1985, black arrests for sex offenses showed little variation from 1979 (20.2 percent) to 1985, which was also 20.2 percent (U.S. Department of Justice, 1980, Table 25; 1986, Table 38).

4. A point stressed throughout the book is that the dropping of charges against blacks by the police or prosecutor, and less convictions, are interpreted as "more lenient treatment" than that received by whites, although harsher treatment is realized by blacks at the "back end" of the system. As Joan Petersilia's (1983:92) highly respected study of racial disparity in the criminal justice system clearly notes: minority suspects were more likely to be released after arrest because the police did not have strong cases! This is not more lenient treatment, but contrarily, could be viewed as discriminatory treatment since they were arrested without sufficient evidence in the first place.

5. Similar to other questionable figures cited throughout the book, Wilbanks challenges the DT by offering 1979 figures alleging that the southern (prejudiced) states (e.g., Mississippi) have the lowest black/white

discrimination utilized a model of analysis that ensured such a result.

But many readers will be thinking at this point that "one can prove anything with statistics" and thus that the validity of the claim for a racist criminal justice system should be determined by what one knows by personal experience or observation. However, the layperson's confidence in and reliance upon "common sense" in rejecting the statistical approach to knowledge in favor of what one knows by personal experience and observation is misplaced. The layperson does not take into account the impact of bias (and in some cases racial prejudice) in personal experience and observation.

Let us take, for example, the question as to whether there is racial discrimination in the use of force by the police. Those who reject studies of large numbers of "use of force" incidents which do not show evidence of racial discrimination by race of victim suggest that "unbiased" observation will reveal racism. But suppose that several people see a white police officer hit a black youth. There are a multitude of explanations (e.g., the youth hit the officer first, the youth resisted authority, the officer was the macho type who would hit any victim who was not properly deferential, the officer was a racist) for such an act. The tendency is for those with a particular bias to select that explanation which is consistent with their bias. For example, other police officers or white citizens might select the explanation which is consistent with their bias. For example, other police officers or white citizens might select the explanation that the youth resisted authority while black citizens might select the explanation that the officer was a racist. In either case the observer simply infers the explanation that is most consistent with his/her bias and thus knowledge via observation is anything but unbiased. Large-scale statistical

incarceration gap while those less racially prejudiced states (Minnesota, Wisconsin, Iowa, New Hampshire) have higher gaps (p. 146). However, it appears that the interpretation is in error since this would be the expected finding to support a discrimination thesis. Furthermore, according to *Prisoners in State and Federal Institutions* (U.S. Department of Justice, 1982, Table 6, p.18), totaling *all* known incarcerated minorities yields the following minority/white percentages by race: Mississippi (54.5./27.1) or 2: 1, Minnesota (26.7/72.3) or 1:2.7, Iowa (19.9/80) or 1:4, Wisconsin (42.9/58.8) or 1:1.4, New Hampshire (4.9/95.1) or 1:19.4, which are not as dramatic as the figures reported by Wilbanks for these same states a year earlier.

6. As with the erroneous charges of disproportionate black sex offense arrests (see comment 3 above), Wilbanks asserts that blacks are more likely to choose white victims to attack, rape, and rob, than black victims. The 1983 Bureau of Justice Statistics publication (U.S. Department of Justice, 1985:5) he cites supports all other victimization findings that violent crime is predominantly *intraracial* by stating:

> Violent crime had intraracial as well as interracial aspects. On the other hand, most violent crimes against whites were committed by white offenders (78%); most violent crimes against blacks were committed by black offenders (87%); and most violent crimes committed by white offenders were against white victims (98%). On the other hand, 55% of the violent crimes committed by black offenders were against white victims.

It is the last sentence that concerns Wilbanks and leads to his charge of black racism, when he emphasizes "choice" of studies allow one to control for factors (other than race) which might impact on a decision or act. Without such studies those who disagree on the impact of racism will simply be trading **anecdotes** ("I know a case where…") to "prove" their case.

CONCLUSION

Racial prejudice, in my view, is the process by which people assign positive traits and motives to "them" (the other race). Blacks tend to see the beating of a black youth by a white police officer as being indicative of racism (an evil motive or trait attributed to the "out-group") while whites (or police officers) tend to see the beating as being the result of some improper action by the black youth. The white view is also influenced by the assigning of evil motives or traits to the out-group (to the black youth). In both cases the observers, whether black or white, have been influenced by racial prejudice in their assigning of blame or cause for the incident.

My basic position is that both the black and white views on the extent of racism in the criminal justice system are "ignorant" in that personal knowledge is gained primarily via observation and experience—methods which are heavily influenced by bias and racial prejudice. In other words, racial prejudice keeps the races polarized on this issue since each race sees the "facts" which "prove" its thesis. Statistical studies of large numbers of blacks and whites subjected to a particular decision (e.g., the use of force) are a safeguard against personal bias and are far more valid as a means to "truth" than personal observation and experience. It is my view that an examination of those studies available at various points in the criminal justice system fails to support the view that racial discrimination is pervasive. It is in this sense that the belief in a racist criminal justice system is a myth.

victim. Two possible explanations come to mind with this statistic. First, victimization surveys which report *perceived* offenders have specific limitations where blacks are concerned. With rape, for example, white rape victims tend to report black offenders more than white rape offenders (Hindelang, 1978), while conversely, black rape victims have a tendency to under-report white male rapists (Weis and Borges, 1973); rapists of Spanish heritage are often reported as black; other racial characteristics and stereotypes may influence the victims' accounts (Hindelang, 1978); false accusations based on discovery with a black lover (Baughman, 1966) or racial prejudice (see Mann, forthcoming).

Second, the issue is not necessarily "choice" of a white victim, but availability. Whites have little hesitancy to enter segregated minority communities to undertake business and/or socialize with non-whites. On the other hand, a minority, particularly a black, is not only conspicuous in an all-white community, but also is rarely welcomed and more frequently subject to attack. In sum, more "integration" in minority communities yields disproportionately more potential white victims than there are available black victims in white areas.

7. In his conclusion Wilbanks states, "My basic position is that both black and white views on the extent of racism in the criminal justice system are 'ignorant' in that personal knowledge is gained primarily via observation and experience—methods which are heavily influenced by bias and racial prejudice." Such a statement is an affront to careful researchers who use observational methods and practitioners who rely upon and report their experience in the field. The accusation that they cannot

The Myth of a Racist Criminal Justice System examines all the available studies that have examined the possible existence of racial discrimination from arrest to parole. For example, the chapter on the police examines the evidence for and against the charge that police deployment patterns, arrest statistics, the use of force ("brutality") and the use of deadly force reflect racism. The chapter on the prosecutor examines the evidence for and against the charge that the bail decision, the charge, plea bargaining, the provision of legal counsel, and jury selection are indicative of racism. The chapter on prison looks at evidence concerning the possibility of racism as reflected through imprisonment rates for blacks vs. whites, in racial segregation, in treatment programs, in prison discipline and in the parole decision. In general, this examination of the available evidence indicates that support for the "discrimination thesis" is sparse, inconsistent, and frequently contradictory.

be objective demonstrates a bias as well as a paucity of knowledge about qualitative research methods.

Clearly, one method is insufficient to explore such a sensitive issue as racism in the criminal justice system. As Wilbanks suggests, future research on this question should concentrate on individual decision-makers (p. 147). This cannot be fully accomplished without qualitative methods such as observation, interviews, biographical, analyses, testing, card sorts, and similar techniques. It is the melding of the micro and macro levels of data gathering and analysis where we will hopefully come together for meaningful answers to the provocative questions Wilbanks raises. *The Myth of a Racist Criminal Justice System* introduces more questions than it provides answers, which makes it a long overdue catalyst for all social scientists interested in racial injustice.

REFERENCES

BAUGHMAN, LAURANCE E. ALAN (1966) *Southern Rape Complex: One Hundred Year Psychosis.* Atlanta, GA: Pendulum Books.

HINDELANG, MICHAEL J. (1978) "Race and Involvement in Common Law Personal Crimes." *American Sociological Review.* 43:93–109.

MANN, CORAMAE R. (Forthcoming) *Minorities, Crime, and Public Policy.*

NATIONAL MINORITY ADVISORY COUNCIL ON CRIMINAL JUSTICE (1980) *The Inequality of Justice: A Report on Crime and the Administration of Justice.* Washington, DC: U.S. Government Printing Office.

PETERSILIA, JOAN (1983) *Racial Disparities in the Criminal Justice System.* Santa Monica, CA: The Rand Corporation.

U.S. DEPARTMENT OF JUSTICE (1980) *Crime in the United States, 1979.* Washington, DC: U.S. Government Printing Office.

———. (1982) *Prisoners in State and Federal Institutions on December 31, 1980.* Washington, DC: U.S. Government Printing Office.

———. (1985) *Criminal Victimization in the United States, 1983.* Washington, DC: U.S. Government Printing Office.

———. (1986) *Crime in the United States 1985.* Washington, DC: U.S. Government Printing Office.

WEIS, KURT AND SANDRA S. BORGES (1973) "Victimology and Rape: The Case of the Legitimate Victim," *Issues in Criminology* 8:71–115.

Questions for Discussion

1. Discuss the evidence presented that racism is a myth in the criminal justice system.
2. What evidence is presented that racism is a reality in the criminal justice system?
3. Do you believe that there is racism in the criminal justice system? Why?

Applications

1. Contact a local criminal justice official. This may be a law enforcement officer, judge, probation officer, attorney, or corrections officer. Ask the person the following questions:
   a. In your opinion, is the criminal justice system racist?
   b. Does the economic status of an offender affect the way that he or she is processed through the criminal justice system?
   c. What is the current population of the county or city jail? What is the racial makeup of this population? With what are most of these offenders charged? What is your guess as to the income level of those presently in jail?

   Discuss your findings with other members of your class.

2. Identify someone in your class or on your campus who is of a different race or ethnicity than yours. Ask the person if he or she believes that the criminal justice system is racially biased. Discuss your findings with the members of your class.

chapter 5

Crime in the 1990s
A Federal Perspective

Magnus I. Seng • Thomas M. Frost

INTRODUCTION

During the last decade, law enforcement appears to have both won and lost the battle against crime. In the 1980's we have seen significant success in the nation's fight against organized crime, yet it reappears, often with a complete new identity. Likewise, law enforcement agencies have launched a major attack on dangerous drugs, but drug **proliferation** continues to fester as a national plague.

Also in the 1980's, law enforcement enjoyed continued advances in technology, enhanced professionalism at all levels, and a more active, determined community effort. But at the same time crime continued to increase.

As we prepare to enter the next decade, we felt it prudent and necessary to engage in some preliminary examination of the variety and depth of crime we may anticipate over the next 10 years and to explore what must be done within the law enforcement community to successfully contain both old and new forms of criminal activity.

In general we wanted to take an anticipatory look at crime in the 1990's. As part of this effort we invited a Federal judge, a Federal prosecutor, and special agents from the Federal Bureau of Investigation (FBI) and the Drug Enforcement Administration (DEA) to independently develop and present their views of crime in the 1990s at a symposium on this topic held at Loyola University of Chicago in February 1989. Each of these men brought a wealth of knowledge and distinguished experience to this task.

They included the Honorable William Bauer, chief judge, Seventh U.S. Court of Appeals, Northern District of Illinois; Mr. Anton Valukas, U.S. attorney, Northern District of Illinois; Mr. James MacKenzie, agent-in-charge, Chicago Office, Federal Bureau of

Reprinted by permission of the publisher.

Investigation; and Mr. Luther Cooke, assistant special agent-in-charge, Chicago Field Division, Drug Enforcement Administration.

Although each of the presenters, by virtue of his function, deals with crime and its effects at different points in the criminal justice process, all four made strikingly similar predictions about crime and law enforcement in the coming decade. Each in their own way, often with passion and eloquence, identified drugs as the central, most compelling, and most critical problem for law enforcement in the 1990's, and there was an air of pessimism in their comments which offered little hope that the drug problem in this nation would be solved even by the end of the next decade. There was frank and open admission that law enforcement has not and will not solve the drug problem through **interdiction** and that the emphasis has to shift to demand reduction.

They also agreed that the Federal effort against white-collar crime and official corruption would see large-scale expansion in the 1990's. The greed and total disregard for ethical and lawful behavior by some prominent members of the private and public sectors, uncovered in the 1980's, simply must be stopped.

All four speakers also maintained that the single most significant development in law enforcement in the 1980's which would continue into the 1990's was real interagency cooperation among law enforcement agencies at all levels. Previously, cooperation and coordination among Federal, state, and local law enforcement agencies, while receiving rhetorical support, rarely emerged in practice. However, the intercity, interstate, and international dimensions of the drug trade in the 1980's have compelled such cooperation. As a result, law enforcement will become more unified in the coming decade.

This article elaborates on these (and other) points in the belief that the opinions expressed are vital and deserve a wider audience than was possible through symposium participation. Judge Bauer, Mr. Valukas, Mr. MacKenzie, and Mr. Cooke not only serve in one of the nation's more important jurisdictions (the Northern District of Illinois) but also bring years of outstanding law enforcement experience to bear on their predictions about crime in the 1990's.

It is not feasible, in this short format, to report all of the comments presented. Therefore, we have taken the liberty of selecting from the audiotape of the symposium proceedings those statements which we believe best reflect the views expressed on a particular topic. We have further deviated from the actual order of presentations by rearranging certain comments in order to maintain topical consistency. Finally, in a number of instances we have rephrased portions of specific comments for the purpose of clarity. But in no instance have we changed the meaning of any statement.

DRUGS IN THE 1990S

As noted earlier, all four of the symposium panelists identified drug proliferation as the most critical problem law enforcement will face in the coming decade. Their comments were passionate and unequivocal.

The single word that describes what drove law enforcement in the eighties and will also drive law enforcement in the nineties is DRUGS. (Mr. Valukas)

In the U.S. today approximately 23 million people used an illegal drug within the last month; 6 million use cocaine regularly; one-fourth of the babies born in one hospital in Chicago in 1988 were cocaine or heroin addicted at birth; two-thirds of the people arrested test positive for drugs. (Mr. Cooke)

The drug problem will have to be solved in the early part of the nineties. If we are lucky as a nation, if we do everything that can be done and do it well…a total commitment…we may be able to address the drug problem by the end of the 1990's. (Mr. Valukas)

When a community feels threatened by crime it is more willing to act.…The middle and upper class community in the U.S. is going to have to feel threatened by the drug traffic before it acts. (Judge Bauer)

The people who engage in the drug business (the drug cartels) have more money than the local law enforcement agencies which seek to combat it. This has forced us to change our approach. We can no longer simply look at investigations as "buy and bust" or as some-thing that will have results in 6 months…now we must be prepared to commit resources for investigations where we anticipate results only in 2 or 3 years…a longterm and costly com-mitment of resources made well in advance. The "buy and bust" days are gone. (Mr. Valukas)

The only way to handle the drug problem is to take the profit out of it. (Judge Bauer)

We'll see an internationalization of law enforcement efforts devoted to the drug problem. Emphasis will be upon the drug organizations as organizations, not simply upon the top leaders or even those in between, but upon the whole organization and everyone involved in it. This will take time and resources but will characterize the federal effort in the nineties. (Mr. Valukas)

Over the past 4 or 5 years we have made admissions that I have never heard law enforcement officers make before…we have acknowledged that we cannot solve the drug problem. We have stood up and said our seizure of 5,000 pounds of cocaine should not lull us into the belief that we have solved the drug problem because we know that right behind that 5,000 pounds of coke is another 5,000 we will not succeed in seizing. (Mr. Valukas)

On November 3rd, 1981, Federal agents seized 10,000 pounds of hashish and felt pretty good about their efforts until they learned that on the same night 110,000 pounds got by undetected. One bust does not make a dent. We are not stopping much. As we got better, they got better, and shipments got bigger. As we became more sophisticated, so did the opposition. They used to ship 350 pounds of drugs; now it's into the tons. The quantities per shipment are enormous. Our seizing one enormous shipment now and then makes good press, but we must not lose sight of the fact that many other enormous shipments get through. (Mr. Cooke)

Law enforcement has improved technology, videotape, sophisticated listening devices, even computers. But criminals will also increase their use of these tools. Hi-tech is available to both sides…drug dealers use instant worldwide communications, and they can and do wiretap at will. The war on crime is a real war, but only one side has to follow rules. (Judge Bauer)

Law enforcement must not give false assurances that we are dealing with the problem. Rather, we must become committed to and involved in making the public aware of the need to reduce demand because law enforcement has not been able to control supply. (Mr. Valukas)

The U.S. is not a large-scale drug-producing nation, but it is a large-scale drug-consuming nation. Most of the drugs that are consumed are illegally imported, and the simple fact is that we can do little to stop this importation. The obvious point of attack is on consumption. (Mr. Cooke)

We keep on giving speeches about demand reduction, and we don't do anything about it We need to get serious about drugs in the 1990's. We need to get the people to demand...reduction. (Mr. MacKenzie)

There is no such thing as recreational drug use. Whatever we call it, however we spell it, it's deadly. We must reduce demand, and we must understand that demand is related to attitude. Demand that started in the sixties, continued into the seventies, and now into the eighties, must stop dead in the nineties. (Mr. Cooke)

We have allowed our public schools to become distribution points for narcotics. That's ridiculous. It is the only place where hundreds of thousands of kids get together every day, yet we have some kids wearing beepers and some selling drugs out of their lockers. This simply has to stop. Each parent has to say, "The school that my kid goes to must be drug free." We used to resent **magnetometers** at airports but now with awareness of terrorism the public expects and even demands security procedures. We need to develop the same attitudes about drugs in school. We need people to demand "walking magnetometers," i.e., dogs, to get rid of drugs on school property. (Mr. MacKenzie)

The average age at which drug consumption starts is 12. Trying to stop initial drug use by talking to high school kids is too late. We need to start in the elementary grades. We can talk to all the civic groups we want to, all the community groups and community leaders we want to. We can go to all the luncheons we want to, but if we don't get the message to the kids we're going to lose this battle. A significant number of drug dealers started dealing as young as 8 years old. We have to arouse the public's attitude. An 8-year-old selling drugs must be seen by everyone as **abhorrent.** (Mr. Cooke)

We need to get the public mad about the drug problem. (Judge Bauer)

There are some unmistakable trends in these comments. It is clear from these views that the drug problem in the United States is enormous and equally clear that these seasoned criminal justice practitioners do not believe that law enforcement either has or will solve this problem. Such public admission from law enforcement officials is both noteworthy and sobering. That this admission comes simultaneously from the judicial, prosecutorial, investigatory, and control levels as represented by these commentators is astounding.

If this view is indeed shared by law enforcement generally, the public should know. Otherwise, we will feel safe or at least take some comfort in the illusion that law enforcement will eventually solve the problem. We somehow expect that the cavalry will arrive to save us. If they aren't coming—they had better let us know.

Another clear trend in these comments is the emphasis upon demand reduction and the allied idea that this is tied to attitudes. These commentators do not, however, spell out law enforcement's role in this aspect but they do identify some key directions the demand reduction approach must take. The first is to place great emphasis upon reducing consumption and distribution in the preteen population. The second and in our view perhaps the most effective method is to get the public sufficiently angry and motivated to destroy this plague.

WHITE COLLAR CRIME AND OFFICIAL CORRUPTION

Federal investigations of white-collar crime and official corruption have resulted in some spectacular cases in the later part of the 1980's. Insider trading on Wall Street and illegal commodities trading in Chicago, nationwide mismanagement and fraud in the savings and loan industry, judicial misconduct in Illinois and Ohio, contract bribes and kickback schemes in Chicago, New York, and other cities and states, and even illegal congressional and executive branch behavior represent just a few of the complex and comprehensive situations investigated.

The symposium presenters, particularly Judge Bauer and Mr. Valukas, left no doubt that white collar crime and official corruption will continue to receive very close attention in the 1990's.

> White-collar crime is not really the subject of public fear. Nobody ever felt threatened by someone embezzling a bank. We will need to get the public mad about white-collar crime, as well. (Judge Bauer)

> I think, or at least I hope, there is a growing intolerance with official corruption. It is no longer thought of as something cute or quaint or something that's okay and not real crime. The present Attorney General doesn't see it that way and we can expect strong emphasis on prosecution of official corruption. (Mr. Valukas)

> In the 1990's there will be a greater recognition that white collar crime is not something that should be envied. (Judge Bauer)

> There have been more bank failures in the past 4 years than occurred throughout all the years of the depression. A significant difference between the bank and savings and loan failures that are occurring today and those that occurred during the depression is this: there were virtually no failures during the depression which were due to misconduct by bank officers or those associated with them. White collar crime cases require extremely sophisticated, labor-intensive investigations which in turn will require significant resources on a long-term basis well into the nineties. (Mr. Valukas)

> We can anticipate more private and public sector cooperation in the 1990's. For example, it is possible that in bank fraud cases the banks may do the investigations, and the FBI may take the cases to court. (Mr. MacKenzie)

> I anticipate an extension of the statute of limitations on bank fraud cases in the nineties. (Mr. Valukas)

> The white-collar criminal responds about equally to 2 months in jail or 2 years in prison, provided you take all of his money away. (Judge Bauer).

> This is not simply a law enforcement problem but one that affects all of us. The amount of money involved in white-collar crime is immense. (Mr. Valukas)

Again we note some themes in these comments. The idea that the public must become angry about white-collar crime and official corruption emerges just as it did for drugs. The need for unequivocal public support is clear from these remarks. The unvoiced **admonition** in Judge Bauer's comment that "no one ever felt threatened by someone embezzling a bank" is that we should all feel threatened. The nature of white collar crime is that the public eventually ends up paying the bill.

Another theme, also mentioned in regard to drugs, was that investigations of white collar crime and official corruption cases are long-term, very complex, and costly. Similar to drug cases, they require commitment of significant resources well in advance of results that may be years away. One measure of public support for the effort required in the 1990's is the degree to which new dollars are allocated to Federal law enforcement despite Federal budget reductions. On Monday, May 16, 1989, President Bush announced specific plans to address this nation's crime problem and included, among many other things, recommendations for significant increases in the number of FBI agents and Federal prosecutors. It remains to be seen whether the public through its elected representatives will provide the necessary funding.

INTERAGENCY COOPERATION

Speaking with refreshing candor, the symposium presenters clearly acknowledged that law enforcement was not particularly well served by interagency cooperation in the past. Federal agencies in particular were aloof and unwilling to share information with local agencies and sometimes even with each other. But the war on drugs has dramatically changed all that as the following remarks demonstrate.

All this [drug proliferation] has compelled a spirit of cooperation among law enforcement agencies that never existed before. Drugs in one city come to other cities...drugs that enter this country in New York wind up in Chicago and vice versa. We are all in this together. It is no longer possible for the FBI to take the position that when they uncover a state crime they fail to tell the state officials of it, yet they want state officials to tell them of uncovered federal crimes. One-way communication between agencies is simply no longer possible. (Judge Bauer)

Within this country drug proliferation has led to real federal, state, and local cooperation. In many instances we have integrated the command. In order to do this, each agency has had to give up some **semblance** of control. That way, all law enforcement agencies can work together. It's the only way we can combat drugs. Nothing generates cooperation like giving money to each other. The Chicago Police Department makes a drug arrest; the Feds seize the house under the Federal Forfeiture Statute, then sell it and return the proceeds to Chicago. We didn't work with the Chicago Police Department in the seventies. The Department of Justice contacted the Chicago Police Department in the seventies when we were holding Christmas parties, and they contacted us to invite us to the annual ball. Today there isn't a significant case in this area where we don't work together on a day-to-day basis. (Mr. Valukas)

Law enforcement agencies now really do more than cooperate with each other...we collaborate. We decide together how we will attack a problem. Science and technology are essential and important but they cannot replace quality people at all levels. (Mr. MacKenzie)

One of the more dramatic changes in interagency relationships is that they are now international. Investigations that in the seventies began with the state now begin not only in other states but also in other countries. A recent seizure of 5,200 pounds of cocaine in Chicago was due to law enforcement cooperation and relationships which begin in Peru, then Colombia, the Caribbean Islands, Panama, and Miami. To detect, track, and eventually seize this load required intensive cooperation of Federal and local law enforcement agencies in various countries. Such cooperation, while limited in the seventies, became the norm in the eighties and will continue in the nineties. (Mr. Valukas)

Law enforcement is one single team. (Judge Bauer)

There is really only one central theme here, but it is an important one. Drug proliferation has compelled law enforcement, kicking and screaming, to do something long overdue. Born of necessity and enticed by dollar rewards, as Mr. Valukas notes, law enforcement is finally putting the job before individual agency pride. These comments also confirm that, like so much in society today, crime has become international. The world has shrunk economically, and crime simply followed the trend. Law enforcement has finally recognized that in unity there is strength.

ADDITIONAL OBSERVATIONS

A number of important comments and observations about crime in the 1990s do not fit neatly under the topic areas so far discussed. However, they reflect the perceptions and wisdom of the symposium speakers and are reported below.

The wave of the future in criminal activities includes continued trafficking in drugs, terrorism, computer crime, and new weapons. We have to take advantage of every possible advancement in science, every possible device that is available to law enforcement, and the law should permit their use. The '90's will present a threat but also a challenge to get us all working together in fighting crime. (Judge Bauer)

We see the civil seizure as a significant part of law enforcement's effort today, totally different from the '70's, and think it will become the trend that we will see in the next decade. There will be an increased use of other professionals in law enforcement…accountants, computer specialists, noncriminal lawyers. We are just now learning how to deal with computer crime. During the 1990's there will be increased application of discoveries in basic science research to law enforcement—for example, use of laser technology for fingerprint identification from surfaces untestable before (wood, human bodies, Styrofoam cups), DNA research applied to genetic identification in criminal cases, and use of artificial intelligence computers in violent crime pattern identification. (Mr. MacKenzie)

We can no longer afford the luxury of thinking that we don't have to worry about somebody else's problems, because the problems that the world faces today in terms of the assaults by criminals, by terrorists, by drug dealers, affect all of us adversely and we have to work together to solve them. (Judge Bauer)

These comments make reference to new types of crime and new technologies that emerged in the 1980's, which will be the focus of scientific law enforcement in the next 10 years. They reflect law enforcement's realization that to modernize means we must use the most advanced tools we have, and Judge Bauer encourages legal flexibility in allowing their use. But Judge Bauer's other remarks in this section as well as those of Mr. Valukas, Mr. MacKenzie, and Mr. Cooke call attention to the central point which is that in the long run, people—both the public at large and law enforcement personnel—are the key to winning the fight against crime.

SUMMARY COMMENTS

This brief article has reported on the views about crime in the 1990's expressed by four very knowledgeable, experienced, and respected professionals. Their message is simple, straightforward, and urgent: The drug problem in this nation is beyond the control of law enforcement. Unless and until there is a dramatic reduction in demand, supply will continue to outstrip law enforcement's ability to deal with it.

Demand reduction, of course, starts with attitudinal change. As a nation we must rise up and in unmistakable terms "Say NO to drugs." But we must all say no: not just junkies or school kids or ghetto dwellers but account executives and lawyers and doctors and butchers and bakers and candlestick makers. All of us at all levels of society should say no to drugs and mean it.

This will require the complete commitment of every segment of society as well as: law enforcement in all its dimensions—police, courts, and corrections; education—all the way from elementary to graduate school; business—beginning with top management to the lowest position within the corporation or foundation. The message in the business community must be zero tolerance.

Because of its potent influence the entertainment industry, including the advertising segment of that industry, must seriously engage in deglamorizing substance abuse in all its forms. In addition, the print and broadcast media must lend their considerable weight to this effort. Religious and political and community organizations should continue to work against drug proliferation. Finally, treatment programs and drug treatment research must be sharply increased, and we must be willing to pay for both.

We really have no choice. Unless we deal effectively with the drug problem in this nation, our criminal justice system, which is already in serious trouble, will simply collapse.

The need for attitude change was really the common element in the remarks presented by all four panelists and is clearly the key in the war on drugs. It is also important in terms of white collar crime and official corruption. The public, i.e., all of us, must recognize that white collar crime affects everyone in society because we eventually pay for it through higher prices and/or higher taxes. Therefore, we should recognize that the ramifications of some financial scam in New York are not limited to New York but are national and even international. These crimes involve enormous sums of money and eventually impact financial institutions and business enterprises throughout the country. We are all being ripped off, and as Judge Bauer said, the public has to get mad about white-collar crime as well.

On a perhaps more meaningful level, there has to be a change in or greater emphasis upon ethical values. Crimes involving official corruption, such as white-collar crimes, are committed by individuals who, in varying degrees, are bearers of the public trust. Such individuals must develop and maintain a personal ethic which abhors the violation of public trust. Although there will be increased Federal emphasis on official corruption and white-collar crimes in the 1990's, investigations in these areas are complex and lengthy. Therefore, we are not as likely to significantly curb such crimes. For that, we will need public support, and, ultimately, it will come down to individual ethics.

The fact of genuine interagency coordination within the law enforcement community is also attitudinal. There is a new spirit of cooperation. Law enforcement is becoming more unified and beginning to like it that way.

When all is said and done, the central message presented at this symposium by these men is that crime in the 1990's will be influenced not only by what we do but also by what we think—by public attitude and action.

QUESTIONS FOR DISCUSSION

1. What is meant by law enforcement winning and losing the battle against crime during the 1980s?
2. Discuss the issues surrounding the continuing problem of drug use. What is meant by shifting law enforcement efforts to "demand reduction"? How might demand reduction be accomplished?
3. Explain why white collar crime does not typically cause the same concern among the public as violent street crime.
4. What role will a change in individual ethics play in the prevention and reduction of crime?

APPLICATIONS

1. Contact a local law enforcement officer in your community and ask him or her to describe how local citizens help in the crime control effort. Compare your results with those of other members of your class.
2. Let us assume that a change in individual ethics can produce improvements in the crime problem. What specific changes in ethics need to be made? How might these changes be implemented? Discuss your ideas with those of other class members and try to identify any similarities in your ideas.

Law Enforcement

Law enforcement agencies and personnel are required to respond to the ever-increasing complexities of policing in a democratic society. Major academic and training programs at universities and police academies have helped professionalize law enforcement in the direction of better understanding and in responding to these complexities. Research continues to identify the challenges faced by policing agencies as we enter the new century. Technology, for example, has greatly enhanced the abilities of law enforcement but has also made the enforcement task more complicated. The mass media alone have had more impact on law enforcement than perhaps any other single **phenomenon** in our modern world. Police personnel are under constant scrutiny, and what may require split-second decision making by a police officer is examined in minute detail by the press.

Besides technology, the applicability of particular laws and rules has been greatly refined, with the Fourth, Fifth, Sixth, and Eighth Amendments at the center of much of the controversy regarding the rights of a person suspected of criminal behavior. In many ways, law enforcement has become more effective, due to internal and external changes in the nature of the enforcement. Police work stands as perhaps the most stressful, complicated, and critical job in our society. The rate of social and cultural change is continuing to accelerate, and the major task of the enforcement profession must be to stay abreast of these changes.

Perhaps the greatest changes in law enforcement are related to the larger social changes that have occurred over the last several decades. Most important has been the loss of confidence in government and, **concomitantly,** the loss of confidence in the criminal justice system to protect citizens from those who will not conform to the rules of order in a civilized society. The sheer diversity of the U.S. population is often overlooked when searching for solutions to societal problems. Crime is a critical social problem, and any thinking person realizes that it took decades to get to the current crises concerning solutions to this problem. There are no **panaceas,** no short-term solutions, no easy answers about how to improve the policing side of criminal justice. Solutions often involve major paradigmatic shifts in our thinking to see real progress toward less crime and more effective enforcement procedures. The avalanche of illegal drugs into the United States, for example, has been the most serious assault on our society in this century. Debates may continue regarding solutions to our drug problems, but the relationship between illegal drugs and other criminality, even police corruption, is undeniable. The total costs of drugs on our society are immeasurable. The United States appears weak in its efforts to control the importation of illegal drugs. Perhaps the best question to ask is: Who benefits from the current supply of drugs entering the country? Drugs and the underlying economic problems in the inner cities have produced huge gaps in the trust we have in our own country and those who are charged with protecting our citizens. The profits from illegal drugs are now second only to the profits from the trade of weapons. One should not conclude that illegal drugs are the only serious crime problems faced by enforcement personnel, but that the continued supply must be extricated before real progress can be made in solving our nation's most serious problem.

No matter the level of frustration, we would destroy our democracy if we attempted to carry out social control measures aimed at preventing all crimes. Most Americans realize this, but they are demanding that our streets and neighborhoods become safe. Fear of crime and violence is so pervasive that it appears to be the principal concern of our nation as a whole. As formal control agents and direct political authority representatives, the police cannot be effective without community assistance. In fact, the transference of responsibility away from individuals, small communities, neighborhood organizations, and other primary groups to the formalized authority of the police has been at the basis of many problems. In most respects it is our responsibility to create the sense of community lost by the processes of modernity, urbanization, and other forms of change. To create better law enforcement, people must demand more involvement at every level of our society and begin with ourselves. Perhaps the best solutions begin with understanding clearly where we are now and then planning our future enforcement efforts based on what is effective. As in medicine, the diagnosis is half the cure.

"The Development of the American Police: An Historical Overview" by Craig D. Uchida establishes a historical foundation that presents a coherent understanding of the complexities of law enforcement. Uchida divides the historical development of police into seven sections that suggest major shifts in the history of policing. He is especially interested in the changes in policing over the past 300 years. The professionalization of the police force in the United States is very interesting, and the crises of the 1960s, especially civil rights, Uchida contends, placed more demands on law enforcement and resulted in a tainted image. Professionalization itself resulted in latent consequences that are still being assessed. This article simplifies a deeper understanding of the social and cultural background of policing in the United States that spawned the current system of law enforcement.

In "A Sketch of the Police Officer's 'Working Personality,'" Jerome Skolnick shares his classic work on the police subculture, analyzing the outstanding elements of the police milieu—danger, authority, and efficiency—as they combine to generate distinctive cognitive and behavioral responses in police. Danger and authority often combine to frustrate procedural regularity and may undermine the rule of law. Skolnick enlightens us with his great insights into police culture and deals with such subjects as isolation, solidarity, and the role of police in society.

In "The Dark Side of the Force," John Dorschner opens the Pandora's box of police corruption in the Miami police department. He claims that disorganization and corruption within the department are related to the larger changes that have occurred in Miami since

1950. Miami has gone from being a small southern town to being a large metropolitan area and was especially affected by newer forms of immigration. Lowered public confidence in the police happened because of a department caught off guard in terms of demographic and social changes. Miami serves as a glaring example of how complicated enforcing the law has become in the modern world and how difficult social and cultural change can be for traditional institutions.

George L. Kelling takes us back in history with "Police and Communities: The Quiet Revolution." Although many both inside and outside the police community may not realize it, the new trend toward community policing is as old as formal policing itself. Police work does not happen in a social vacuums; it happens in our communities. Street by street, block by block, and neighborhood by neighborhood, police work happens and succeeds. We are successful to the degree to which we can get citizens involved, reduce neighborhood disorganization, and increase concern for our neighborhoods. Police are only the formally organized crime fighters; citizens are the foundation of dynamic and safe communities. Sociologists have argued for decades that the social organization of a community influences crime rates and the subsequent responses of citizens. These surprisingly simple findings have been ignored or subverted by economic or political agendas that have little concern for crime and effect on our nation. Ignoring great research and the desire of citizens to have safe communities is simply political malfeasance.

We conclude Part II with "The Future of Diversity in America: The Law Enforcement Paradigm Shift," by Charles M. Bozza, who focuses on American racial and cultural diversity as it relates to law enforcement. Bozza argues, as do many others, that we are extremely diverse and that law enforcement must consider these issues to be effective. We have become a "salad bowl" or mosaic: The various ingredients or parts exist together, but rather than melting, the components remain intact and distinguishable while contributing to a whole that is richer than the sum of its parts alone. This change calls for a paradigmatic shift in our thinking about our society, especially about policing in our society. The future of the United States is toward more diversity, not less. The larger social changes require law enforcement to carry out change and to advocate continuous change in the methods of policing. Any modern police department that refuses to change will soon be replaced by a department that will.

chapter 6

The Development of the American Police

A Historical Overview

Craig D. Uchida

INTRODUCTION

During the past 20 years, scholars have become fascinated with the history of police. A **plethora** of studies have emerged as a result. Early writings were concerned primarily with descriptions of particular police agencies. Roger Lane (1967) and James F. Richardson (1970) broke new ground in describing the origins of policing in Boston and New York, respectively. Since that time, others have followed suit with narratives of police organizations in St. Louis (Maniha, 1970; Reichard, 1975), Denver (Rider, 1971), Washington, DC (Alfers, 1975), Richmond (Cei, 1975), and Detroit (Schneider, 1980).

Other authors have focused on issues in policing. Wilbur R. Miller (1977) examined the legitimation of the police in London and New York. Samuel Walker (1977) and Robert Fogelson (1977) concentrated on professionalism and reform of errant police in the 19th and 20th centuries. Eric Monkkonen (1981) took an entirely different approach by using **quantitative methods** to explain the development of policing in 23 cities from 1860 to 1920.[1]

Overall these histories illustrate the way in which police have developed over time. They point out the origins of concepts like crime prevention, authority, professionalism and discretion. In addition, these historical analyses show the roots of problems in policing, such as corruption, brutality, and inefficiency.

The major purpose of this selection is to examine the development of the police since 900 A.D. and more specifically, to determine whether the role of the police has changed in American society over a period of about 300 years. This is not an easy task. The debate over the "true" or "proper" police function is an ongoing one and cannot itself be resolved in a selection such as this.[2] However, by describing the various roles, activities, and functions of law enforcement over time, we can at least acquire a glimpse of what the

Reprinted by permission of Waveland Press, Inc., from Dunham-Alpert, *Critical Issues in Policing: Contemporary Readings*, 3rd ed. (Prospect Heights, IL: Waveland Press, Inc., 1997). All rights reserved.

police do and how their activities have varied over time. To do so, we rely on a number of important contributions to the study of the history of police.

The selection is divided into seven parts and basically covers the history of law enforcement and the role of the police from colonial America to the present. Part I examines the English heritage of law enforcement and its effect on colonial America. The colonists relied heavily on the mother country for their ideas regarding community involvement in law enforcement.

Part II examines the problems of urban centers in the 18th and 19th centuries and turns to the development of the full-time uniformed police in England and America. The preventive approach to law enforcement became central to the police role in both London and American cities. Part III is concerned with police activity in 19th century American cities. Patrol work and officer involvement in corruption are discussed.

In Part IV the reform movement of the Progressive Era is examined. From 1890 to 1920 reformers attempted to implement social, economic, and political change in the cities. As part of city government, police departments were targets of change as well.

In Part V we study a second reform era. From 1910 to 1960 chiefs became involved in a movement to professionalize the police. Part VI covers the riots and disorders of the 1960s and their immediate effect on policing across the country. Finally, in Part VII, we discuss the long-term legacy of the 1960s. That is, we examine the developments of the police since 1969 in terms of research and public policy.

I. COMMUNITIES, CONSTABLES, AND COLONISTS

Like much of America's common-law tradition, the origins of modern policing can be linked directly to its English heritage. Ideas concerning community policing, crime prevention, the posse, constables, and sheriffs developed from English law enforcement. Beginning at about 900 A.D., the role of law enforcement was placed in the hands of common, everyday citizens. Each citizen was held responsible for aiding neighbors who might be victims of outlaws and thieves. Because no police officers existed, individuals used state-sanctioned force to maintain social control. Charles Reith, a noted English historian, refers to this model of law enforcement as "kin police" (Reith, 1956). Individuals were considered responsible for their "kin" (relatives) and followed the adage, "I am my brother's keeper." Slowly this model developed into a more formalized "communitarian," or community-based police system.

After the Norman Conquest of 1066, a community model was established, which was called frankpledge. The frankpledge police system required that every male above the age of twelve form a group with nine of his neighbors called a tything. Each tything was sworn to apprehend and deliver to court any of its members who committed a crime. Each person was pledged to help protect fellow citizens and, in turn, would be protected. This system was "obligatory" in nature, in that tythingmen were not paid salaries for their work, but were required by law to carry out certain duties (Klockars, 1985:21). Tythingmen were required to hold suspects in custody while they were awaiting trial and to make regular appearances in court to present information on wrong-doing by members of their own or other tythings. If any member of the tything failed to perform his required duties, all members of the group would be levied severe fines.

Ten tythings were grouped into a hundred, directed by a constable (appointed by the local nobleman) who, in effect, became the first policeman. That is, the constable was the first official with law enforcement responsibility greater than simply helping one's neighbor. Just as the tythings were grouped into hundreds, the hundreds were grouped into shires, which are similar to counties today. The supervisor of each shire was the shire reeve (or sheriff), who was appointed by the king.

Frankpledge began to disintegrate by the 13th century. Inadequate supervision by the king and his appointees led to its downfall. As frankpledge slowly declined, the parish constable system emerged to take its place. The Statute of Winchester of 1285 placed more authority in the hands of the constable for law enforcement. One man from each parish served a one-year term as constable on a rotating basis. Though not paid for his work, the constable was responsible for organizing a group of watchmen who would guard the gates of the town at night. These watchmen were also unpaid and selected from the parish population. If a serious disturbance took place, the parish constable had the authority to raise the "hue and cry." This call to arms meant that all males in the parish were to drop what they were doing and come to the aid of the constable.

In the mid-1300s the office of justice of the peace was created to assist the shire reeve in controlling his territory. The local constable and the shire reeve became assistants to the justice of the peace and supervised the night watchmen, served warrants, and took prisoners into custody for appearance before justice of the peace courts.

The English system continued with relative success well into the 1700s. By the end of the 18th century, however, the growth of large cities, civil disorders and increased criminal activity led to changes in the system.

Law Enforcement in Colonial America

In colonial America (17th and 18th centuries), policing followed the English systems. The sheriff, constable, and watch were easily adapted to the colonies. The county sheriff, appointed by the governor, became the most important law enforcement agent particularly when the colonies remained small and primarily rural. The sheriff's duties included apprehending criminals, serving subpoenas, appearing in court and collecting taxes. The sheriff was paid a fixed amount for each task he performed. Since sheriffs received higher fees based on the taxes they collected, apprehending criminals was not a primary concern. In fact, law enforcement was a low priority.

In the larger cities and towns, such as New York, Boston, and Philadelphia constables and the night watch performed a wide variety of tasks. The night watch reported fires, raised the hue and cry, maintained street lamps, arrested or detained suspicious persons, and walked the rounds. Constables engaged in similarly broad tasks, such as taking suspects to court, eliminating health hazards, bringing witnesses to court, and so on.

For the most part, the activities of the constables and the night watch were "reactive" in nature. That is, these men responded to criminal behavior only when requested by victims or witnesses (Monkkonen, 1981). Rather than preventing crime, discovering criminal behavior, or acting in a "proactive" fashion, these individuals relied on others to define their work. Public health violations were the only types of activity that required the officers to exercise initiative.

II. PREVENTIVE POLICE: COPS AND BOBBIES

The development of a "new" police system has been carefully documented by a number of American and English historians. Sir Leon Radzinowicz (1948–1968), Charles Reith (1956), and T.A. Critchley (1967) are among the more notable English writers. Roger Lane (1967), James F. Richardson (1970), Wilbur R. Miller (1977), Samuel Walker (1977), and Eric Monkkonen (1981) represent a rather diverse group of American historians who describe and analyze a number of early police departments. Taken together these works present the key elements of the activities of the first English and American police systems that used the preventive model.

During the mid to late 1700s the growth of industry in England and in Europe led to rapid development in the cities. London, in particular, expanded at an unprecedented rate. From 1750 to 1820 the population nearly doubled (Miller, 1977) and the urban economy became more complex and specialized. The Industrial Revolution led to an increase in the number of factories, tenements, vehicles, and marketplaces. With industrial growth came a breakdown in social control, as crime, riots, disorder, and public health problems disrupted the city. Food riots, wage protests, poor sewage control, pickpockets, burglars, and vandals created difficulties for city dwellers. The upper and middle classes, concerned about these issues sought more protection and preventive measures. The constable-watch system of law enforcement could no longer deal successfully with the problems of the day, and alternative solutions were devised.

Some of the alternatives included using the militia; calling out the "yeomanry" or cavalry volunteers for assistance; swearing in more law-abiding citizens as constables; or employing the army to quell riot situations (Richardson, 1974:10). However, these were short-term solutions to a long-term problem.

Another proposal was to replace the constable-watch system with a stronger, more centralized police force. Henry and John Fielding (magistrates in the 1750s), Patrick Colquhoun (a magistrate from 1792 to 1818), and philosopher Jeremy Bentham and his followers advocated the creation of a police force whose principal object was the prevention of crime. A preventive police force would act as a deterrent to criminals and would be in the best interests of society. But the idea of a uniformed police officer was opposed by many citizens and politicians in England. An organized police too closely resembled a standing army, which gave government potentially **despotic** control over citizens and subjects. The proponents of a police force eventually won out, based primarily on the disorder and fear of crime experienced by London residents. After much debate in the early 1800s, the London Metropolitan Police Act was finally approved by Parliament in 1829 (see Critchley, 1967; Reith, 1956).

The London Metropolitan Police Act established a full-time, uniformed police force with the primary purpose of patrolling the city. Sir Robert Peel, Britain's Home Secretary, is credited with the formation of the police. Peel synthesized the ideas of the Fieldings, Colquhoun and Bentham into law, convinced Parliament of the need for the police, and guided the early development of the force.

Through Peel and his two police commissioners, Charles Rowan and Richard Mayne, the role of the London Police was formulated. Crime prevention was the primary function, but to enforce the laws and to exert its authority, the police had to first gain legitimacy in the eyes of the public. According to Wilbur R. Miller (1977) the legitimation of the London police was carefully orchestrated by Peel and his associates. These men recognized that in order to gain authority police officers had to act in a certain manner or the public would reject them. To gain acceptance in the eyes of the citizen, Peel and his associates selected men who were even-tempered and reserved; chose a uniform that was unassuming (navy blue rather than military red); insisted that officers be restrained and polite; meted out appropriate discipline; and did not allow officers to carry guns. Overall, the London police emphasized their legitimacy as based on *institutional* authority—that their power was grounded in the English Constitution and that their behavior was determined by rules of law. In essence, this meant that the power of the London "bobby" or "Peeler" was based on the institution of government.

American cities and towns encountered problems similar to those in England. Cities grew at phenomenal rates; civil disorders swept the nation, and crime was perceived to be increasing. New York, for example, sprouted from a population of 33,000 in 1790 to 150,000 in 1830. Foreign immigrants, particularly Irish and Germans, accounted for a large portion of the increase. Traveling to America in search of employment and better life-styles, the immigrants competed with native-born Americans for skilled and unskilled positions. As a result, the American worker saw the Irishman and German as social and economic threats.

Other tensions existed in the city as well. The race question was an important one in the northern cities as well as on the Southern plantations. In fact, historians have shown that hostility to blacks was just as high in the North as in the South (Litwack, 1961). Those opposed to slavery (the abolitionists) were often met by violence when they attempted to speak out against it.

Between the 1830s and 1870s, numerous conflicts occurred because of ethnic and racial differences, economic failures, moral questions, and during elections of public officials. In New York, 1834 was designated the "Year of the Riots" (Miller, 1977). The mayoral election and anti-abolitionist sentiment were the two main reasons for the disorders. Other cities faced similar problems. In Philadelphia, the Broad Street Riot of 1837 involved almost 15,000 residents. The incident occurred because native-born volunteer firemen returning from a fire could not get by an Irish funeral procession. In St. Louis in 1850, a mob destroyed the brothels in the city in an attempt to enforce standards of public decency. To quell most of these disturbances, the local militia was called in to suppress the violence, as the constables and the night watch were ineffectual.

At the same time that the riots occurred, citizens perceived that crime was increasing. Homicides, robberies, and thefts were thought to be on the rise. In addition, **vagrancy,** prostitution, gambling, and other vices were more observable on the streets. These types of criminal activities and the general deterioration of the city led to a sense of a loss of social control. But in spite of the apparent immediacy of these problems, replacements for the constable-watch police system did not appear overnight.

The political forces in the large industrial cities like New York, Philadelphia. Boston, and others precluded the immediate acceptance of a London-style police department. City councils, mayors, state legislatures, and governors debated and wrangled over a number of questions and could not come to an immediate agreement over the type of police they wanted. In New York City for example, although problems emerged in 1834, the movement to form a preventive police department did not begin until 1841; it was officially created in 1845, but officers did not begin wearing uniforms until 1853.

While the first American police departments modeled themselves after the London Metropolitan Police, they borrowed selectively rather than exactly. The most notable carry-over was the adoption of the preventive patrol idea. A police presence would alter the behavior of individuals and would be available to maintain order in an efficient manner. Differences, however, between the London and American police abounded. Miller (1977), in his comparative study of New York and London police, shows the drastic differences between the two agencies.

The London Metropolitan Police was a highly centralized agency. An extension of the national government, the police department was purposely removed from the direct political influence of the people. Furthermore, as noted above, Sir Robert Peel recruited individuals who fit a certain mold. Peel insisted that a polite, aloof officer who was trained and disciplined according to strict guidelines would be best suited for the function of crime prevention. In addition, the bobbies were encouraged to look upon police work as a career in professional civil service.

Unlike the London police, American police systems followed the style of local and municipal governments. City governments, created in the era of the "common man" and democratic participation, were highly decentralized. Mayors were largely figureheads; real power lay in the wards and neighborhoods. City councilmen or aldermen ran the government and used political patronage freely. The police departments shared this style of participation and decentralization. The police were an extension of different political factions, rather than an extension of city government. Police officers were recruited and selected by political leaders in a particular ward or precinct.

As a result of the democratic nature of government, legal intervention by the police was limited. Unlike the London police which relied on formal institutional power, the American police relied on informal control or individual authority. That is, instead of drawing on institutional legitimacy (i.e., parliamentary laws), each police officer had to establish his own authority among the citizens he patrolled. The personal, informal police officer could win the respect of the citizenry by knowing local standards and expectations. This meant that different police behavior would occur in different neighborhoods. In New York, for example, the cop was free to act as he chose within the context of broad public expectations. He was less limited by institutional and legal restraints than was his London counterpart, entrusted with less formal power, but given broader personal discretion.

III. POLICE ACTIVITY IN THE 19TH CENTURY

American police systems began to appear almost overnight from 1860 to 1890 (Monkkonen, 1981). Once large cities like New York, Philadelphia, Boston, and Cincinnati had adopted the English model, the new version of policing spread from larger to smaller cities rather quickly. Where New York had debated for almost ten years before formally adopting the London-style, Cleveland, Buffalo, Detroit, and other cities readily accepted the innovation. Monkkonen explains that the police were a part of a growing range of services provided by urban administrations. Sanitation, fire, and health services were also adopted during this period and the police were simply a part of that natural growth.

Across these departments, however, differences flourished. Police activity varied depending upon the local government and political factions in power. Standards for officer selection (if any), training procedures, rules and regulations, levels of enforcement of laws, and police–citizen relationships differed across the United States. At the same time, however, there were some striking similarities.

Patrol Officers

The 19th century patrolman was basically a political operative rather than a London-style professional committed to public service (Walker, 1977). Primarily selected for his political service, the police officer owed his allegiance to the ward boss and police captain that chose him.

Police officers were paid well but had poor job security. Police salaries compared favorably with other occupations. On average in 1880, most major cities paid policemen in the neighborhood of $900 a year. Walker (1977) reports that a skilled tradesman in the building industry earned about $770 a year, while those in manufacturing could expect about $450 a year. A major drawback, however, was that job security was poor, as their employment relied on election day events. In Cincinnati, for example, in 1880, 219 of the 295 members of the force were dismissed, while another 20 resigned because of a political change in the municipal government. Other departments had similar turnover rates.

New officers were sent out on patrol with no training and few instructions beyond their rule books. Proper arrest procedures, rules of law, and so on were unknown to the officers. Left to themselves, they developed their own strategies for coping with life in the streets.

Police Work

Police officers walked a beat in all types of weather for two to six hours of a 12-hour day. The remaining time was spent at the station house on reserve. During actual patrol duty, police officers were required to maintain order and make arrests, but they often **circumvented** their responsibilities. Supervision was extremely limited once an officer was beyond the station house. Sergeants and captains had no way of contacting their men while they were on the beat, as communications technology was limited. Telegraph lines linked district stations to headquarters in the 1850s, but call boxes on the beat were not introduced until late in the 19th century, and radio and motorized communications did not appear until the 1900s (Lane, 1980). Police officers, then, acted alone and used their own initiative.

Unfortunately, little is known about ordinary patrol work or routine interactions with the public. However, historians have pieced together trends in police work based on arrest statistics. While these data have their limitations, they nonetheless provide a view of police activity.

Monkkonen's work (1981) found that from 1860 to 1920 arrests declined in 23 of the largest cities in the United States. In particular, crimes without victims, such as vice, disturbances, drunkenness, and other public order offenses, fell dramatically. Overall, Monhkonen estimated that arrests declined by more than 33% during the 60-year period. This trend runs contrary to "common sense notions about crime and the growth of industrial cities, immigration and social conflict" (p. 75). Further analysis showed that the decline occurred because the police role shifted from one of controlling the "dangerous class" to one of controlling criminal behavior only. From 1860 to 1890, Monkkonen argues, the police were involved in assisting the poor, taking in overnight lodgers, and returning lost children to their parents or orphanages. In the period of 1890 to 1920, however, the police changed their role, structure and behavior because of external demands upon them. As a result, victimless arrests declined, while assaults, thefts, and homicide arrests increased slightly. Overall, however, the crime trend showed a decrease.

Police Corruption and Lawlessness

One of the major themes in the study of 19th century policing is the large-scale corruption that occurred in numerous departments across the country. The lawlessness of the police—their systematic corruption and nonenforcement of the laws—was one of the paramount issues in municipal politics during the late 1800s.

Police corruption was part of a broader social and political problem. During this period, political machines ran municipal governments. That is, political parties (Democrats and Republicans) controlled the mayor's office, the city councils and local wards. Municipal agencies (fire departments, sanitation services, school districts, the courts, etc.) were also under the aegis of political parties. As part of this system, political patronage was rampant. Employment in exchange for votes or money was a common procedure. Police departments in New York, Chicago, Philadelphia, Kansas City, San Francisco, and Los Angeles were filled with political appointees as police officers. To ensure their employment, officers followed the norms of the political party, often protecting illicit activities conducted by party favorites.

Corrupt practices extended from the chief's office down to the patrol officer. In New York City, for example, Chief William Devery (1898–1901) protected gambling dens and illegal prize fighting because his friend, Tim Sullivan (a major political figure on the Lower East Side) had interests in those areas. Police captains like Alexander "Clubber" Williams and Timothy Creeden acquired extensive wealth from protecting prostitutes, saloonkeepers, and gamblers. Williams, a brutal officer (hence, the nickname Clubber), was said to have a 53-foot yacht and residences in New York and the Connecticut suburbs. Since a captain's salary was about $3,000 a year in the 1890s, Williams had to collect from illegal enterprises in order to maintain his investments.

Because police officers worked alone or in small groups, there were ample opportunities to shake down peddlers and small businesses. Detectives allowed con men, pickpockets, and thieves to go about their business in return for a share of the proceeds. Captains often established regular payment schedules for houses of prostitution depending upon the number of girls in the house and the rates charged by them. The monthly total for police protection ranged between $25 and $75 per house plus $500 to open or re-open after being raided (Richardson, 1970).

Officers who did not go along with the nonenforcement of laws or did not approve of the graft and corruption of others found themselves transferred to less than desirable areas. Promotions were also denied; they were reserved for the politically astute and wealthy officer (promotions could cost $10,000 to $15,000).

These types of problems were endemic to most urban police agencies throughout the country. They led to inefficiency and inequality of police services.

IV. REFORM, REJECTION, AND REVISION

A broad reform effort began to emerge toward the end of the 19th century. Stimulated mainly by a group known as the Progressives, attempts were made to create a truly professional police force. The Progressives were upper middle class, educated Protestants who opposed the political machines, sought improvements in government, and desired a change in American morality. They believed that by eliminating machine politics from government, all facets of social services, including the police, would improve.

These reformers found that the police were without discipline, strong leadership, and qualified personnel. To improve conditions, the progressives recommended three changes: (1) the departments should be centralized; (2) personnel should be upgraded; and (3) the police function should be narrowed (Fogelson, 1977). Centralization of the police meant that more power and authority should be placed in the hands of the chief. Autonomy from politicians was crucial to centralization. Upgrading the rank and file meant better training, discipline, and selection. Finally, the reformers urged that police give up all activities unrelated to crime. Police had run the ambulances, handled licensing of businesses, and sheltered the poor. By concentrating on fighting crime, the police would be removed from their service orientation and their ties to political parties would be severed.

From 1890 to 1920 the Progressive reformers struggled to implement their reform ideology in cities across the country. Some inroads were made during this period, including the establishment of police commissions, the use of civil service exams, and legislative reforms.

The immediate responses to charges of corruption were to create police administrative boards. The reformers attempted to take law enforcement appointments out of the hands of mayors and city councilmen and place control in the hands of oversight committees. The Progressives believed that politics would be eliminated from policing by using this maneuver. In New York, for example, the Lexow Committee, which investigated the corrupt practices of the department, recommended the formation of a bipartisan Board of Police Commissioners in 1895. Theodore Roosevelt became a member of this board, but to his dismay found that the commissioners were powerless to improve the state of policing. The bipartisan nature of the board (two Democrats and two Republicans) meant that consensus could not be reached on important issues. As a result, by 1900 the New York City police were again under the influence of party politics. In the following year the board of commissioners was abolished and the department was placed under the responsibility of a single commissioner (Walker, 1977). Other cities had similar experiences with the police commission approach. Cincinnati, Kansas City, St. Louis, and Baltimore were among those that adopted the commission, but found it to be short-lived. The major problem was still political—the police were viewed as an instrument of the political machine at the neighborhood level and reformers could not counter the effects of the Democratic or Republican parties.

Civil service was one answer to upgrading personnel. Officers would be selected and promoted based on merit, as measured by a competitive exam. Moreover, the officer would be subject to review by his superiors and removal from the force could take place if there was sufficient cause. Civil service met with some resistance by officers and reformers alike. The problem was that in guarding against the effects of patronage and favoritism, civil service became a rigid, almost inflexible procedure. Because it measured abstract knowledge rather than the qualities required for day-to-day work, civil service procedures were viewed as problematic. Eventually, the program did help to eliminate the more blatant forms of political patronage in almost all of the large police departments (Walker, 1977).

During this 30-year period, the efforts of the Progressive reformers did not change urban departments drastically. The reform movement resulted, in part, in the elimination of the widespread graft and corruption of the 1890s, but substantive changes in policing did not take place. Chiefs continued to lack power and authority, many officers had little or no education, training was limited, and the police role continued to include a wide variety of tasks.

Robert Fogelson (1977) suggests several reasons for the failure of reform. First, political machines were too difficult to break. Despite the efforts by the Progressives, politicians could still count on individual supporters to undermine the reforms. Second, police officers themselves resented the Progressives' interventions. Reformers were viewed by the police as individuals who knew little about police work and officers saw their proposals for change as ill conceived. Finally, the reforms failed because the idea of policing could not be divorced from politics. That is, the character of the big-city police was interconnected with policymaking agencies that helped to decide which laws were enforced, which public was served, and whose peace was kept (Fogelson, 1977). Separating the police completely from politics could not take place.

V. THE EMERGENCE OF POLICE PROFESSIONALISM

A second reform effort emerged in the wake of the failure of the Progressives. Within police circles, a small cadre of chiefs sought and implemented a variety of innovations that would improve policing generally. From about 1910 to 1960 police chiefs carried on another reform movement, advocating that police adopt the professional model.

The professional department embodied a number of characteristics. First, the officers were experts. They applied knowledge to their tasks and were the only ones qualified to do the job. Second, the department was autonomous from external influences, such as political parties. This also meant that the department made its own rules and regulated its personnel. Finally, the department was administratively efficient, in that it carried out its mandate to enforce the law through modern technology and businesslike practices. These reforms were similar to those of the Progressives, but because they came from within police organizations themselves, they met with more success.

Leadership and technology assisted the movement to professionalize the police. Chiefs like Richard Sylvester, August Vollmer, and O. W. Wilson emphasized the use of innovative methods in police work. Samuel Walker (1977) notes that Sylvester, the chief of the Washington, D.C. police, helped to establish the idea of professionalism among police chiefs. As president of the International Association of Chiefs of Police (IACP), Sylvester inculcated the spirit of reform into the organization. He stressed acceptance of technological innovations, raised the level of discussion among chiefs to include crime control ideas, and promoted professionalism generally.

The major innovator among the chiefs was August Vollmer, chief of the Berkeley, California police. Vollmer was known for his pioneering work in developing college-level police education programs, bicycle and automobile patrols, and scientific crime detection aids. His department was the first to use **forensic science** in solving crimes.

Vollmer's emphasis on the quality of police personnel was tied closely to the idea of the professional officer. Becoming an expert in policing meant having the requisite credentials. Vollmer initiated intelligence, psychiatric, and neurological tests by which to select applicants. He was the first police chief to actively recruit college students. In addition, he was instrumental in linking the police department with the University of California at Berkeley. Another concern of Vollmer's dealt with the efficient delivery of police services. His department became the first in the nation to use automobiles and the first to hire a full-time forensic scientist to help solve crimes (Douthit, 1975).

O. W. Wilson, Vollmer's student, followed in his mentor's footsteps by advocating efficiency within the police bureaucracy through scientific techniques. As chief in Wichita, Kansas, Wilson conducted the first systematic study of one-officer squad cars. He argued that one-officer cars were efficient, effective, and economical. Despite arguments from patrol officers that their safety was at risk, Wilson claimed that the public received better service with single-officer cars.

Wilson's other contributions include his classic textbook, *Police Administration* which lays out specific ideas regarding the use of one-man patrol cars, deployment of personnel on the streets, disciplinary measures, and organizational structure. Later in his career, Wilson accepted a professorship at the University of California at Berkeley where he taught and trained law enforcement officers. In 1947 he founded the first professional school of criminology.

Other chiefs contributed to the professional movement as well. William Parker changed the Los Angeles Police Department (LAPD) from a corrupt, traditional agency to an innovative, professional organization. From 1950 to his death in 1966, Parker served as chief. He was known for his careful planning, emphasis on efficiency, and his rigorous personnel selection and training procedures. His public relations campaigns and adept political maneuvers enabled him to gain the respect of the media and community. As a result, the LAPD became a model for reform across the country.

Technological changes also enabled the police to move toward professionalism. The patrol car, two-way radio, and telephone altered the way in which the police operated and the manner in which citizens made use of the police. Motorized patrol meant more efficient coverage of the city and quicker response to calls for service. The two-way radio dramatically increased the supervisory capacity of the police; continuous contact between sergeant and patrol officer could be maintained. Finally, the telephone provided the link between the public and the police. Though not a new invention, its use in conjunction with the car and two-way radio meant that efficient responses to calls for service could be realized.

Overall, the second reform movement met with more success than the Progressive attempt, though it did not achieve its goal of professionalization. Walker (1977) and Fogelson (1977) agree that the quality of police officers greatly improved during this period. Police departments turned away the ill-educated individual, but at the same time failed to draw college graduates to their ranks. In terms of autonomy, police reformers and others were able to reduce the influence of political parties in departmental affairs. Chiefs obtained more power and authority in their management abilities, but continued to receive input from political leaders. In fact, most chiefs remained political appointees. In terms of efficiency, the police moved forward in serving the public more quickly and competently. Technological innovations clearly assisted the police in this area, as did streamlining the organizations themselves. However, the innovations also created problems. Citizens came to expect more from the police—faster response times, more arrests, and less overall crime. These expectations, as well as other difficulties, led to trying times for the police in the 1960s.

VI. RIOTS AND RENEWAL

Policing in America encountered its most serious crisis in the 1960s. The rise in crime, the civil rights movement, anti-war sentiment, and riots in the cities brought the police into the center of a **maelstrom.**

During the decade of the 1960s crime increased at a phenomenal rate. Between 1960 and 1970 the crime rate per 100,000 persons doubled. Most troubling was the increase in violent crime—the robbery rate almost tripled during these ten years. As crime increased, so did the demands for its reduction. The police, in emphasizing its crime fighting ability, had given the public a false expectation that crime and violence could be reduced. But with the added responsibility of more crime, the police were unable to live up to the expectation they had created. As a result, the public image of the police was tarnished.

The civil rights movement created additional demands for the police. The movement, which began in the 1950s, sought equality for black Americans in all facets of life. Sit-ins at segregated lunch counters, boycotts of bus services, attempts at integrating schools, and demonstrations in the streets led to direct confrontations with law enforcement officers. The police became the symbol of a society that denied blacks equal justice under the law.

Eventually, the frustrations of black Americans erupted into violence in northern and southern cities. Riots engulfed almost every major city between 1964 and 1968. Most of the disorders were initiated by a routine incident involving the police. The spark that ignited the riots occurred on July 16, 1964, when a white New York City police officer shot and killed a black teenager. Black leaders in the Harlem ghetto organized protests demanding disciplinary action against the officer. Two days later, the demonstrators marched on precinct headquarters, where rock throwing began. Eventually, looting and burning erupted during the night and lasted for two full days. When the riot was brought under control one person was dead, more than 100 injured, almost 500 arrested, and millions of dollars worth of property destroyed. In the following year, the Watts riot in Los Angeles led to more devastation. Thirty-four persons died, a thousand were injured, and 4000 arrested. By 1966, 43 more riots broke out across the country and in 1967 violence in Newark and Detroit exceeded the 1965 Watts riot. Disorders engulfed Newark for five days, leaving 23 dead, while the Detroit riot a week later lasted nearly seven days and resulted in 43 deaths with $40 million in property damages.

On the final day of the Detroit riot, President Lyndon Johnson appointed a special commission to investigate the problem of civil disorder. The National Advisory Commission on Civil Disorders (the Kerner Commission) identified institutional racism as the underlying cause of the rioting. Unemployment, discrimination in jobs and housing, inadequate social services, and unequal justice at the hands of the law were among the problems cited by the commission.

Police actions were also cited as contributing to the disorders. Direct police intervention had sparked the riots in Harlem, Watts, Newark, and Detroit. In Watts and Newark the riots were set off by routine traffic stops. In Detroit a police raid on an after-hours bar in the ghetto touched off the disorders there. The police thus, became the focus of national attention.

The Kerner Commission and other investigations found several problems in police departments. First, police conduct included brutality, harassment, and abuse of power. Second, training and supervision was inadequate. Third, police–community relations were poor. Fourth, the employment of black officers lagged far behind the growth of the black population.

As a means of coping with these problems in policing (and other agencies of the criminal justice system) President Johnson created a crime commission and Congress authorized federal assistance to criminal justice. The President's crime commission produced a final report that emphasized the need for more research, higher qualifications of criminal justice personnel, and greater coordination of the national crime-control effort. The federal aid program to justice agencies resulted in the Office of Law Enforcement Assistance, a forerunner of the Law Enforcement Assistance Administration (LEAA).

VII. THE LEGACY OF THE 60S

The events of the 1960s forced the police, politicians, and policymakers to reassess the state of law enforcement in the United States. For the first time, academicians rushed to study the police in an effort to explain their problems and crises. With federal funding from LEAA and private organizations, researchers began to study the police from a number of perspectives. Sociologists, political scientists, psychologists, and historians began to scrutinize different aspects of policing. Traditional methods of patrol deployment, officer selection, and training were questioned. Racial discrimination in employment practices, in arrests, and in the use of deadly force was among the issues closely examined.

In addition, the professional movement itself came into question. As Walker notes, the legacy of professionalization was "ambiguous" (Walker, 1977:167). On one hand, the police made improvements in their level of service, training, recruitment, and efficiency. On the other hand, a number of problems remained and a number of new ones emerged. Corruption scandals continued to present problems. In New York, Chicago, and Denver systematic corruption was discovered. Political parties persisted in their links to policing.

The professional movement had two unintended consequences. The first involved the development of a police subculture. The second was the problem of police–community relations. In terms of the subculture, police officers began to feel alienated from administrators, the media and the public and turned inward as a result. Patrol officers began to resent the police hierarchy because of the emphasis on following orders and regulations. While this established uniformity in performance and eliminated some abuses of power, it also stifled creativity and the talents of many officers. Rather than thinking for themselves (as professionals would) patrol officers followed orders given by sergeants, lieutenants, or other ranking officers. This led to morale problems and criticism of police administrators by the rank and file.

Patrol officers saw the media and the public as foes because of the criticism and disrespect cast their way. As the crime rate increased, newspaper accounts criticized the police for their inability to curtail it. As the riots persisted, some citizens cried for more order, while others demanded less oppression by the police on the streets. The conflicting messages given to the patrol officers by these groups led to distrust, alienation, and frustration. Only by standing together did officers feel comfortable in their working environment.

The second unintended consequence of professionalism was the problems it generated for police–community relations. Modern technology, like the patrol car, removed the officer from the street and eliminated routine contact with citizens. The impersonal style of professionalism often exacerbated police–community problems. Tactics such as aggressive patrol in black neighborhoods, designed to suppress crime efficiently, created more racial tensions.

These problems called into question the need for and effectiveness of professionalism. Some police administrators suggested abandoning the movement. Others sought to continue the effort while adjusting for and solving the difficulties. For the most part, the goal of professionalization remains operative. In the 1970s and 1980s, progressive police chiefs and organizations continue to press for innovations in policing. As a result, social science research has become an important part of policymaking decisions. By linking research to issues like domestic violence repeat offenders, use of deadly force, training techniques, and selection procedures, police executives increase their ability to make effective decisions.

CONCLUDING REMARKS

This chapter has examined the history of American police systems from the English heritage through the 20th century. Major emphasis has been placed on the police role, though important events that shaped the development of the police have also been discussed. As can be seen through this review, a number of present-day issues have their roots in different epochs of American history. For example, the idea of community policing can be traced to the colonial period and to medieval England. Preventive patrol, legitimacy, authority, and professionalism are 18th and 19th century concepts. Riots, disorders, and corruption are not new to American policing; similar events occurred in the 19th century. Thus, by virtue of studying history, we can give contextual meaning to current police problems, ideas, and situations. By looking at the past, present-day events can be better understood.

NOTES

1. This list of police histories is by no means a comprehensive one. A vast number of journal articles, books and dissertations have been written since the 1960s.
2. A number of scholars have examined the "police function," particularly in the last 20 or so years. Among the most well known are Wilson (1968), Skolnick (1966), Bittner (1970), and Goldstein (1977). Each of these authors prescribes to a different view of what the police should and should not do.

REFERENCES

ALFERS, KENNETH G. 1975. "The Washington Police: A History, 1800–1886." Ph.D. dissertation. George Washington University.

BITTNER, EGON. 1970. *The Functions of the Police in Modern Society*. Chevy Chase, MD: National Institute of Mental Health.

CEI, LOUIS B. 1975. "Law Enforcement in Richmond: A History of Police Community Relations, 1937–1974." Ph.D. dissertation. Florida State University.

CRITCHLEY, T. A. 1967. *A History of Police in England and Wales*. Montclair. NJ: Patterson Smith.

DOUTHIT, NATHAN. 1975. "August Vollmer: Berkeley's First Chief of Police and the Emergence of Police Professionalism." *California Historical Quarterly* 54 Spring: 101–124.

FOGELSON, ROBERT. 1977. *Big-City Police*. Cambridge, MA: Harvard University Press.

GOLDSTEIN, HERMAN. 1977. *Policing a Free Society.* Cambridge, MA: Ballinger Press.

KLOCKARS, CARL. 1985. *The Idea of Police.* Beverly Hills, CA: Sage Publications.

LANE, ROGER. 1967. *Policing the City: Boston, 1822–1885.* Cambridge, MA: Harvard University Press.

———. 1980. "Urban Police and Crime in Nineteenth-Century America," in Michael Tonry and Norval Morris (eds.), *Come and Justice: An Annual Review of Research, Vol. 2.* Chicago: University of Chicago Press.

LITWACK, LEON. 1961. *North of Slavery.* Chicago: University of Chicago Press.

MANIHA, JOHN K. 1970. "The Mobility of Elites in a Bureaucratizing Organization: The St. Louis Police Department, 1861–1961." Ph.D. dissertation. University of Michigan.

MILLER, WILBUR R. 1977. *Cops and Bobbies: Police Authority in New York and London, 1830–1870.* Chicago: University of Chicago Press.

MONKKONEN, ERIC H. 1981. *Police in Urban America, 1860–1920.* Cambridge: Cambridge University Press.

RADZINOWICZ, LEON. 1948–1968. *History of the English Criminal Law, Vols. 1–4.* New York: Macmillan.

REICHARD, MAXIMILIAN I. 1975. "The Origins of Urban Police: Freedom and Order in Antebellum St. Louis." Ph.D. dissertation. Washington University.

REITH, CHARLES. 1956. *A New Study of Police History.* Edinburgh.

RICHARDSON, JAMES E. 1970. *The New York Police: Colonial Times to 1901.* New York: Oxford University Press.

———. 1974. *Urban Police in the United States.* Port Washington, NY: Kennikat Press.

RIDER, EUGENE F. 1971. "The Denver Police Department: An Administrative, Organizational, and Operational History, 1858–1905." Ph.D dissertation. University of Denver.

SCHNEIDER, JOHN C. 1980 *Detroit and the Problems of Order, 1830–1880.* Lincoln, NE: University of Nebraska Press.

SKOLNICK, JEROME. 1966. *Justice without Trial: Law Enforcement in Democratic Society.* New York: John Wiley and Sons.

WALKER, SAMUEL. 1977. *A Critical History of Police Reform: The Emergence of Professionalism.* Lexington, MA: D.C. Heath and Company.

WILSON, JAMES Q. 1968. *Varieties of Police Behavior: The Management of Law and Order in Eight Communities.* Cambridge, MA: Harvard University Press.

QUESTIONS FOR DISCUSSION

1. Summarize the development of full-time uniformed policing in England and America.

2. The nineteenth century is characterized as a period of police corruption. What contributed to this corruption?

3. Discuss the emergence of police professionalism. What contributions did August Vollmer and O. W. Wilson make in the move toward police professionalism? Cite specific examples.

4. List and discuss two unintended consequences of police professionalization.

APPLICATIONS

1. What are the requirements for becoming a law enforcement officer in your community? Who or what group sets the standards for police professionalism? Are the standards set at the federal, state, or local level?
2. Assign three class members to interview the chief of police in your community. Ask the police chief to describe what is meant by *police professionalism*. Additionally, inquire as to what programs and/or policies the department has to further professionalism.

A Sketch of the Police Officer's "Working Personality"

Jerome Skolnick

INTRODUCTION

A recurrent theme of the sociology of occupations is the effect of people's work on their outlook on the world.[1] Doctors, janitors, lawyers, and industrial workers develop distinctive ways of perceiving and responding to their environment. Here we shall concentrate on analyzing certain outstanding elements in the police milieu—danger, authority, and efficiency—as they combine to generate distinctive cognitive and behavioral responses in police: a "working personality." Such an analysis does not suggest that all police are alike in working personality, but that there are distinctive cognitive tendencies in police as an occupational grouping. Some of these tendencies may be found in other occupations sharing similar problems. So far as exposure to danger is concerned, police officers may be likened to soldiers. The police officers' problems as an authority bear a certain similarity to those of school-teachers, and the pressures the police feel to prove themselves efficient are not unlike those felt by industrial workers. The combination of these elements, however, is unique to police officers. Thus, the police, as a result of the combined features of their social situation, tend to develop ways of looking at the world that are distinctive to themselves, cognitive lenses through which to see situations and events. The strength of the lenses may be weaker or stronger depending on certain conditions, but they are ground on a similar axis.

Analysis of the police officer's cognitive propensities is necessary to understand the practical dilemma faced by police required to maintain order under a democratic rule of law. We discussed earlier how essential a conception of order is to the resolution of this dilemma. It was suggested that the paramilitary character of police organization naturally leads to a high evaluation of similarity, routine, and predictability. Our intention is to emphasize features of the police officer's environment interacting with the paramilitary police organization to generate a working personality. Such an intervening concept should aid in explaining how the social environment of police affects their capacity to respond to the rule of law.

We also stated earlier that emphasis would be placed on the division of labor in the police department, that "operational law enforcement" could not be understood outside these special work assignments. It is therefore important to explain how the **hypothesis** emphasizing the generalizability of the police officer's working personality is compatible with the idea that police division of labor is an important analytic dimension for understanding operational law enforcement. Compatibility is evident when one considers the different levels of analysis at which the hypotheses are being developed. Janowitz stated, for example, that the military profession is more than an occupation; it is a "style of life" because the operational claims over one's daily existence extend well beyond official duties. Janowitz was quick to point out that any profession performing a crucial life-and-death task, such as medicine, the ministry, or the police, develops such claims.[2] A conception like "working personality" of police should be understood to suggest an analytic breadth similar to that of "style of life." That is, just as the professional behavior of military officers with similar styles of life may differ notably depending on whether they command an infantry battalion or participate in the work of an intelligence unit, so too does the professional behavior of police officers with similar working personalities vary with their assignments.

The police officer's working personality is most highly developed in the constabulary role of the "cop on the beat." For analytical purposes that role is sometimes regarded as an enforcement specialty, but in this general discussion of police officers as they comport themselves while working, the uniformed "cop" is seen as the foundation for the police officer's working personality. There is a sound organizational basis for making this assumption. The police, unlike the military, draw no caste distinction in socialization, even though their order of ranked titles approximates the military's. Thus, one cannot join a local police department as a lieutenant the way a West Point graduate joins the army. Every officer of rank must serve an apprenticeship as a patrol officer. This feature of police organization means that the constabulary role is the primary one for all police officers, and that whatever the special requirements of roles in enforcement specialties, they are carried out with a common background of constabulary experience.

The process by which the police officer's "personality" is developed may be summarized: The police officer's role contains two principal variables, danger and authority, that should be interpreted in the light of a "constant" pressure to appear efficient.[3] The element of danger seems to make the police officer especially attentive to signs indicating a potential for violence and lawbreaking. As a result, the officer is generally a "suspicious" person. Furthermore, the character of police work makes an officer less desirable than others as a friend, because norms of friendship implicate others in the officer's work. Accordingly, the element of danger isolates the police socially from that segment of the citizenry that they regard as symbolically dangerous and also from the conventional citizenry with whom they identify.

The element of authority reinforces the element of danger in isolating the police. Typically, the police are required to enforce laws representing **puritanical morality,** such as those prohibiting drunkenness, and also laws regulating the flow of public activity, such as traffic laws. In these situations, the police direct the citizenry, whose typical response denies recognition of the officers' authority and stresses their obligation to respond to danger. The kinds of people who respond well to danger, however, do not normally subscribe to codes of puritanical morality. As a result, the police are unusually liable to the charge of hypocrisy. That the whole civilian world is an audience for the police further promotes police isolation and, in consequence, solidarity. Finally, danger undermines the judicious use of authority. Where danger, as in Britain, is relatively less, the judicious application of authority is facilitated. Hence, British police may appear to be somewhat more attached to the rule of law, when, in fact, they may appear so because they face less danger, and they are as a rule better skilled than American police in creating the appearance of conformity to procedural regulations.

THE SYMBOLIC ASSAILANT AND POLICE CULTURE

In attempting to understand the police officer's view of the world, it is useful to raise a more general question: What are the conditions under which police, as authorities, may be threatened?[4] To answer this, we must look to the situation of the police in the community. One attribute of the many that characterize the officer's role stands out: The police officer is required to respond to assaults against persons and property. When a radio call reports an armed robbery and gives a description of the person involved, every police officer, regardless of assignment, is responsible for the criminal's apprehension. The **raison d'être** of the police officer and the criminal law, the underlying collectively held moral sentiments that justify penal sanctions, arises ultimately and most clearly from the threat of violence and the possibility of danger to the community. Police who "lobby" for severe narcotics laws, for instance, justify their position on grounds that the addict is a harbinger of danger. It is maintained that addicts require one hundred dollars a day to support their habit, and they must steal to get it. Even though the addict is not typically a violent criminal, criminal penalties for addiction are supported on grounds that the addict may become one.

Police officers, because their work requires them to be occupied continually with potential violence, develop a perceptual shorthand to identify certain kinds of people as symbolic assailants, that is, as persons who use gesture, language, and attire that the police have come to recognize as a prelude to violence. This does not mean that violence by a symbolic assailant is necessarily predictable. On the contrary, the police officer responds to the vague indication of danger suggested by appearance. Like the animals of the experimental psychologist, the officer finds the threat of random damage more compelling than a predetermined and inevitable punishment. Something of the flavor of the police officer's attitude toward the symbolic assailant comes across in a recent article by a police expert. In discussing the problem of selecting subjects for field interrogation, Thomas F. Adams wrote:

A. Be suspicious. This is a healthy police attitude, but it should be controlled and not too obvious.

B. Look for the unusual:

   1. Persons who do not "belong" where they are observed.
   2. Automobiles which do not "look right."
   3. Businesses opened at odd hours, or not according to routine or custom.

C. Subjects who should be subjected to field interrogations:

1. Suspicious persons known to the officer from previous arrests, field interrogations, and observations.
2. **Emaciated** appearing alcoholics and narcotics users who invariably turn to crime to pay for cost of habit.
3. Person who fits description of wanted suspect as described by radio, teletype, daily bulletins.
4. Any person observed in the immediate vicinity of a crime very recently committed or reported as "in progress."
5. Known trouble-makers near large gatherings.
6. Persons who attempt to avoid or evade the officer.
7. Exaggerated unconcern over contact with the officer.
8. Visibly "rattled" when near the policeman.
9. Unescorted women or young girls in public places, particularly at night in such places as cafes, bars, bus and train depots, or street corners.
10. "Lovers" in an industrial area (make good lookouts).
11. Persons who loiter about places where children play.
12. Solicitors or peddlers in a residential neighborhood.
13. Loiterers around public rest rooms.
14. Lone male sitting in car adjacent to schoolground with newspaper or book in his lap.
15. Lone male sitting in car near shopping center who pays unusual amount of attention to women, sometimes continuously manipulating rearview mirror to avoid direct eye contact.
16. Hitchhikers.
17. Person wearing coat on hot days.
18. Car with mismatched hubcaps, or dirty car with clean license plate (or vice versa).
19. Uniformed "deliverymen" with no merchandise or truck.
20. Many others. How about your own personal experiences?[5]

Nor, to qualify for the status of symbolic assailant, need an individual ever have used violence. For example, a woman backing out of a jewelry store with a gun in one hand and jewelry in the other would qualify even if the gun were a toy and the woman had never in her life fired a real pistol. To the police officer in the situation, the woman's personal history is momentarily immaterial. There is only one relevant sign: a gun signifying danger. Similarly, a young man may suggest the threat of violence to the police by his manner of walking or "strutting," the insolence in the demeanor being registered by the police as a possible preamble to later attack.[6] Signs vary from area to area, but a youth dressed in a black leather jacket and motorcycle boots is sure to draw at least a suspicious glance from a police officer.

Police officers themselves do not necessarily emphasize the peril associated with their work when questioned directly and may even have well-developed strategies of denial. The element of danger is so integral to an officer's work that explicit recognition might induce emotional barriers to work performance. Thus, one patrol officer observed that more police have been killed and injured in automobile accidents in the past ten years than from gunfire. Although this assertion is true, the officer neglected to mention that the police are the only peacetime occupational group with a systematic record of death and injury from gunfire and other weaponry. Along these lines, it is interesting that of the 224 working Westville police officers (not including the 16 juvenile officers) responding to a question about which assignment they would like most to have in the police department,[7] 50 percent selected the job of detective, an assignment combining elements of apparent danger and initiative. The next category was adult street work, that is, patrol and traffic (37 percent). Eight percent selected the juvenile squad,[8] and only 4 percent selected administrative work. Not a single police officer chose the job of jail guard. Although these findings do not control for such factors as **prestige**, they suggest that confining and routine jobs are rated low on the **hierarchy** of police preferences, even though such jobs are least dangerous. Thus, the police officer, as a personality, may well enjoy the possibility of danger, especially its associated excitement, while fearing it at the same time. Such "inconsistency" is easily understood. Thanks to Freud, it is now an axiom of personality theory that logical and emotional consistency are by no means the same phenomenon.

However complex the motives aroused by the element of danger, its consequences for sustaining police culture are unambiguous. This element requires the police officer, like the combat soldier, the European Jew, the South African (white or black), to live in a world straining toward duality, and suggesting danger when "they" are perceived. Consequently, it is in the nature of the police officers' situation that their conception of order emphasizes regularity and predictability. It is, therefore, a conception shaped by persistent suspicion. The English "copper," often portrayed as a courteous, easygoing, rather jolly sort of chap, on the one hand, or as a devil-may-care adventurer, on the other, was differently described by Colin MacInnes:

> The true copper's dominant characteristic, if the truth be known, is neither those daring nor vicious qualities that are sometimes attributed to him by friend or enemy, but an ingrained conservatism, and almost desperate love of the conventional. It is untidiness, disorder, the unusual, that a copper disapproves of most of all: far more, even than of crime which is merely a professional matter. Hence his profound dislike of people loitering in streets, dressing extravagantly, speaking with exotic accents, being strange, weak, eccentric, or simply any rare minority—of their doing, in fact, anything that cannot be safely predicted.[9]

The police are indeed specifically *trained* to be suspicious, to perceive events or changes in the physical surroundings that indicate the occurrence or probability of disorder. A former student who worked as a patrol officer in a suburban New York police department described this aspect of the police officer's assessment of the unusual:

> The time spent cruising one's sector or walking one's beat is not wasted time, though it can become quite routine. During this time, the most important thing for the officer to do is notice the *normal*. He must come to know the people in his area, their habits, their automobiles

> and their friends. He must learn what time the various shops close, how much money is
> kept on hand on different nights, what lights are usually left on, which houses are
> vacant…only then can he decide what persons or cars under what circumstances warrant
> the **appellation** "suspicious."[10]

The individual police officer's sensitivity to "suspiciousness" does not hang on whether the officer has personally undergone an experience that could objectively be described as hazardous. Personal experience of this sort is not the key to the psychological importance of exceptionality. Each, in the routine performance of police work, will experience situations that threaten to become dangerous. Like the American Jew who contributes to "defense" organizations such as the Anti-Defamation League in response to Nazi brutalities that the Jew has never experienced personally, the police officer identifies with a colleague who has been beaten, perhaps fatally, by a gang of young thugs.

SOCIAL ISOLATION

The patrol officer in Westville, and probably in most communities, has come to identify the African-American man with danger. James Baldwin vividly expressed the isolation of the ghetto police officer:

> …The only way to police a ghetto is to be oppressive. None of the Police Commissioner's
> men, even with the best will in the world, have any way of understanding the lives led by
> the people they swagger about in twos and threes controlling. Their very presence is an
> insult, and it would be, even if they spent their entire day feeding gumdrops to children.
> They represent the force of the white world, and that world's criminal profit and ease, to
> keep the black man corralled up here, in his place. The badge, the gun in the holster, and
> the swinging club make vivid what will happen should his rebellion become overt…
>
> It is hard, on the other hand, to blame the policeman, blank, good-natured, thoughtless,
> and insuperably innocent, for being such a perfect representative of the people he serves.
> He, too, believes in good intentions and is astounded and offended when they are not
> taken for the deed. He has never, himself, done anything for which to be hated—which of
> us has?—and yet he is facing, daily and nightly, people who would gladly see him dead,
> and he knows it. There is no way for him not to know it: there are few things under heaven
> more unnerving than the silent, accumulating contempt and hatred of a people. He moves
> through Harlem, therefore, like an occupying soldier in a bitterly hostile country; which is
> precisely what, and where he is, and is the reason he walks in twos and threes.[11]

Although Baldwin's observations on police–African-American relations cannot be disputed seriously, there is greater social distance between police and "civilians" in general, regardless of their color, than Baldwin considered. Thus, Colin MacInnes had his English hero, Mr. Justice, explaining:

> …The story is all coppers are just civilians like anyone else, living among them not in bar-
> racks like on the Continent, but you and I know that's just a legend for mugs. We are cut
> off; we're not like everyone else. Some civilians fear us and play up to us, some dislike us

and keep out of our way but no one—well, very few indeed—accepts us as just ordinary like them. In one sense, dear, we're just like hostile troops occupying an enemy country. And say what you like, at times, that makes us lonely.[12]

MacInnes' observation suggests that by not introducing a white control group, Baldwin failed to see that the police officer may not get on well with anybody, regardless (to use the hackneyed phrase) of race, creed, or national origin. Police officers whom one knows well often express their sense of isolation from the public as a whole, not just from those who fail to share their color. Westville police were asked, for example, to rank the most serious problems police have (Table 1). The category most frequently selected was not racial problems, but some form of public relations: lack of respect for the police, lack of cooperation in enforcement of the law, lack of understanding of the requirements of police work.[13] One respondent answered:

> As a policeman my most serious problem is impressing on the general public just how difficult and necessary police service is to all. There seems to be an attitude of "law is important, but it applies to my neighbor—not to me."

Of the 282 Westville police who rated the prestige police work receives from others, 70 percent ranked it as only fair or poor, whereas less than 2 percent ranked it as "excellent" and another 29 percent as "good." Similarly, in Britain, two-thirds of a sample of police interviewed by a royal commission stated difficulties in making friends outside the force; of those interviewed, 58 percent thought members of the public to be reserved, suspicious, and constrained in conversation; and 12 percent attributed such difficulties to the requirement that police officers be selective in associations and behave circumspectly.[14]

A Westville police officer related the following incident:

> Several months after I joined the force, my wife and I used to be socially active with a crowd of young people, mostly married, who gave a lot of parties where there was drinking and dancing, and we enjoyed it. I've never forgotten, though, an incident that happened

Table 1   WESTVILLE POLICE RANKING OF NUMBER ONE PROBLEM FACED BY POLICE

	Number	Percent
Relations with public	74	26
Racial problems and demonstrations	66	23
Juvenile Delinquents and Delinquency	23	8
Unpleasant police tasks	23	8
Lack of cooperation from authorities (D.A., legislature, courts)	20	7
Internal departmental problems	17	6
Irregular life of police officer	5	2
No answer or other answer	56	20
	284	100

on one Fourth of July party. Everybody had been drinking, there was a lot of talking, people were feeling boisterous, and some kid there—he must have been twenty or twenty-two—threw a firecracker that hit my wife in the leg and burned her. I didn't know exactly what to do—punch the guy in the nose, bawl him out, just forget it. Anyway, I couldn't let it pass, so l walked over to him and told him he ought to be careful. He began to rise up at me, and when he did, somebody yelled, "Better watch out, he's a cop." I saw everybody standing there, and I could feel they were all against me and for the kid, even though he had thrown the firecracker at my wife. I went over to the host and said it was probably better it my wife and I left because a fight would put a damper on the party Actually, I'd hoped he would ask the kid to leave, since the kid had thrown the firecracker. But he didn't, so we left. After that incident, my wife and I stopped going around with that crowd and decided that if we were going to go to parties where there was to be drinking and boisterousness, we weren't going to be the only police people there.

Another reported that he seeks to overcome his feelings of isolation by concealing his police identity:

> I try not to bring my work home with me, and that includes my social life. I like the men I work with, but I think it's better that my family doesn't become a police family. I try to put my police work into the background, and try not to let people know I'm a policeman. Once you do, you can't have normal relations with them.[15]

Although the police serve a people who are, as Baldwin said, the established society, the white society, these people do not make the police feel accepted. As a result, they develop resources within their own world to combat social rejection.

POLICE SOLIDARITY

All occupational groups share a measure of inclusiveness and identification. People are brought together simply by doing the same work and having similar career and salary problems. As several writers have noted, however, police show an unusually high degree of occupational solidarity.[16] It is true that the police have a common employer and wear a uniform at work, but so do doctors, mail carriers, and bus drivers. Yet it is doubtful that these workers have so close-knit an occupation or so similar an outlook on the world as do police. Set apart from the conventional world, the police officer experiences an exceptionally strong tendency to find a social identity within the occupational milieu.

Compare the police with another skilled craft (Table 2). In a study of the International Typographical Union, the authors asked printers the first names and jobs of their three closest friends. Of the 1,236 friends named by the 412 printers in their sample, 35 percent were printers.[17] Similarly, among the Westville police, of 700 friends listed by 250 respondents, 35 percent were police officers. The police officers, however, were far more active than printers in occupational social activities. Of the printers, more than half (54 percent) had never participated in any union clubs, benefit societies, teams, or organizations composed mostly of printers, or attended any printers' social affairs in the past five years. Of the

Westville police, only 16 percent had failed to attend a single police banquet or dinner in the past year (as contrasted with the printers' *five years*); and of the 234 officers answering this question, 54 percent had attended 3 or more such affairs *during the past year.*

These findings are striking in light of the interpretation made of the data on printers. Lipset, Trow, and Coleman did not, as a result of their findings, see printers as an unintegrated occupational group. On the contrary, they ascribed the democratic character of the union in good part to the active social and political participation of the membership. The point is not to question their interpretation, because it is doubtlessly correct when printers are held up against other manual workers. However, when seen in comparison to police, printers appear a minimally participating group; put positively, police emerge as an exceptionally socially active occupational group.

POLICE SOLIDARITY AND DANGER

There is still a question, however, as to the process through which danger and authority influence police solidarity. The effect of danger on police solidarity is revealed when we examine a chief complaint of police: lack of public support and public apathy. The complaint may have several referents, including policy pay, police prestige, and support from the legislature. But the repeatedly voiced broader meaning of the complaint is resentment at being taken for granted. The police do not believe that their status as civil servants should relieve the public of responsibility for law enforcement. The officers feel, however, that payment out of public coffers somehow obscures their humanity and, therefore, their need for help.[18] As one police officer put it:

> Jerry, a cop, can get into a fight with three or four tough kids, and there will be citizens passing by, and maybe they'll look, but they'll never lend a hand. It's their country, too, but you'd never know it the way some of them act. They forget that we're made of flesh and blood, too. They don't care what happens to the cop so long as they don't get a little dirty.

Although police officers see themselves as specialists in dealing with violence, they do not want to fight alone. They do not believe that their specialization relieves the general public

Table 2   Closest Friends of Printers and Police, by Occupation

	Punters N = 1236 (%)	Police N = 700 (%)
Same occupation	35	35
Professionals, business executives, and independent business owners	21	30
White-collar or sales employees	20	12
Manual workers	25	22

of citizenship duties. Indeed, if possible, they would prefer to be the managers rather than the workers in the battle against criminals.

The general public, of course, does withdraw from the workaday world of the police officer. The officer's responsibility for controlling dangerous and sometimes violent persons alienates the average citizen perhaps as much as does the officer's authority over the average citizen. If the police officer's job is to ensure that public order is maintained, the citizen's inclination is to shrink from the dangers of maintaining it. The citizen prefers to see the police officer as an automaton, because once the officer's humanity is recognized, the citizen necessarily becomes implicated in the officer's work, which is, after all, sometimes dirty and dangerous. What police officers typically fail to realize is the extent they become tainted by the character of the work they perform. The dangers of their work not only draws police together as a group but separates them from the rest of the population. Banton, for instance, commented:

> ...patrolmen may support their fellows over what they regard as minor infractions in order to demonstrate to them that they will be loyal in situations that make the greatest demands upon their fidelity....
>
> In the American departments I visited it seemed as if the supervisors shared many of the patrolmen's sentiments about solidarity. They too wanted their colleagues to back them up in an emergency, and they shared similar frustrations with the public.[19]

Thus, the element of danger contains seeds of isolation that may grow in two directions. In one, a stereotyping perceptual shorthand is formed through which the police come to see certain signs as symbols of potential violence. The police probably differ in this respect from the general middle-class white population only in degree. This difference, however, may take on enormous significance in practice. Thus, the police officer works at identifying and possibly apprehending the symbolic assailant; the ordinary citizen does not. As a result, the ordinary citizen does not assume the responsibility to become implicated in the police officer's required response to danger. The element of danger in the role of police officers alienates them not only from populations with a potential for crime but also from the conventionally respectable (white) citizenry, in short, from that segment of the population from which friends would ordinarily be drawn. As Janowitz noted in a paragraph suggesting similarities between the police and the military, "...any profession which is continually preoccupied with the threat of danger requires a strong sense of solidarity if it is to operate effectively. Detailed regulation of the military style of life is expected to enhance group cohesion, professional loyalty, and maintain the martial spirit. "[20]

SOCIAL ISOLATION AND AUTHORITY

The element of authority also helps to account for the police officer's social isolation. Police officers themselves are aware of their isolation from the community and are apt to weight authority heavily as a causal factor. When considering how authority influences rejection, police officers typically single out their responsibility for the enforcement of traffic violations.[21] Resentment, even hostility, is generated in those receiving citations, in part because such contact is often the only one citizens have with police, and in part because municipal administrations and courts have been known to utilize police authority primarily to meet budgetary requirements, rather than those of public order. Thus, when a municipality engages in "speed trapping" by changing limits so quickly that drivers cannot realistically slow down to the prescribed speed or, while keeping the limits reasonable, charging high fines primarily to generate revenue, the police officer carries the brunt of public resentment.

That the police officer dislikes writing traffic tickets is suggested by the quota system police departments typically employ. In Westville, each traffic police officer has what is **euphemistically** described as a working "norm." A motorcyclist is supposed to write two tickets an hour for moving violations. It is doubtful that norms are needed because police are lazy. Rather, the employment of quotas most likely springs from the reluctance of police officers to expose themselves to what they know to be public hostility. As a result, as one traffic police officer said:

> You learn to sniff out the places where you can catch violators when you're running behind. Of course, the department gets to know that you hang around one place, and they sometimes try to repair the situation there. But a lot of the time it would be too expensive to fix up the engineering fault, so we keep making our norm.

When meeting "production" pressures, the police officer inadvertently gives a false impression of patrolling ability to the average citizen. The traffic cyclist waits in hiding for moving violators near a tricky intersection, reasonably sure that such violations will occur with regularity. The violator believes he or she has observed a police officer displaying exceptional detection capacities and may have two thoughts, each apt to generate hostility toward the police officer: "I have been trapped," or "They can catch me; why can't they catch crooks as easily?" The answer, of course, lies in the different behavior patterns of motorists and "crooks." The latter do not act with either the frequency or predictability of motorists at poorly engineered intersections.

Although traffic patrol plays a major role in separating police officers from the respectable community, other of their tasks also have this consequence. Traffic patrol is only the most obvious illustration of the police officer's general responsibility for maintaining public order, which also includes keeping order at public accidents, sporting events, and political rallies. These activities share one feature: the officer is called on to direct ordinary citizens and therefore to restrain their freedom of action. Resenting the restraint, the average citizen in such a situation typically thinks something along the lines of, "He is supposed to catch crooks; why is he bothering me?" Thus, the citizen stresses the "dangerous" portion of the police officer's role while belittling the officer's authority.

Closely related to police officers' authority-based problems as *directors* of the citizenry are difficulties associated with their injunction to *regulate public morality*. For instance, police officers are obliged to investigate "lovers' lanes" and to enforce laws pertaining to gambling, prostitution, and drunkenness. Their responsibility in these matters allows them much administrative discretion because they may not actually enforce the law by making an arrest, but instead merely interfere with continuation of the objectionable activity.[22]

Thus, an officer may put the drunk in a taxi, tell the lovers to remove themselves from the back seat, and advise a man soliciting a prostitute to leave the area.

Such admonitions are in the interest of maintaining the proprieties of public order. At the same time, the police officer invites the hostility of the citizen so directed in two respects: the officer is likely to encourage the sort of response mentioned earlier (that is, an antagonistic reformulation of the officer's role), and the officer is apt to cause resentment because of the suspicion that police do not themselves strictly conform to the moral norms they are enforcing. Thus, the police, faced with enforcing laws against fornication, drunkenness, and gambling, are easily liable to charges of hypocrisy. Even when officers are called on to enforce the laws relating to overt homosexual activities, reflecting a sexual orientation for which police are not especially noted, the officers may encounter a charge of hypocrisy on grounds that they do not adhere strictly to prescribed heterosexual codes. Police officers' difficulty in this respect is shared by all authorities responsible for the maintenance of disciplined activity, including industrial line supervisors, political leaders, elementary schoolteachers, and college professors. All are expected to conform rigidly to the entire range of norms they espouse.[23] The police officer, however, as a result of the unique combination of the elements of danger and authority, experiences a special predicament. It is difficult to develop qualities enabling the officer to stand up to danger and to conform to standards of puritanical morality. The element of danger demands that the police officer be able to carry out efforts that are often thought to be by their nature overtly "masculine." Police work, like soldiering, requires an exceptional caliber of physical fitness, agility, toughness, and the like. The person who ranks high on these so-called masculine characteristics is, again like the soldier, not usually disposed to be puritanical about sex, drinking, and gambling.

On the basis of observations, police officers do not subscribe to moralistic standards for conduct. For example, the officers in the morals squad of the police department, when questioned, were unanimously against the statutory rape age limit, on the grounds that as older teenagers they themselves might not have rejected an opportunity for sexual relations with, say, a seventeen-year-old.[24] Neither, from observations, are police officers by any means total abstainers from the use of alcoholic beverages. The police officer who is arresting a drunk has probably been drunk in the past; the officer knows it and the drunk knows it.

More than that, a portion of the social isolation of the police officer can be attributed to the discrepancy between moral regulation and the norms and behavior of police officers in these areas. We have presented data indicating that police engage in a comparatively active occupational social life. One interpretation might attribute this activity to a basic interest in such affairs; another might explain police officers' occupational society activity as a measure of restraint in publicly violating norms they enforce. The interest in attending police affairs may grow as much out of security in "letting oneself go" in the presence of police, and a corresponding feeling of insecurity with civilians, as an authentic preference for police social affairs. Much alcohol is usually consumed at police banquets with all the **melancholy** and boisterousness accompanying such occasions. As Horace Cayton reported on his experience as a police officer:

> Deputy sheriffs and policemen don't know much about organized recreation; all they usually do when celebrating is get drunk and pound each other on the back, exchanging loud insults which under ordinary circumstances would result in a fight.[25]

To some degree the reason for the behavior exhibited on these occasions is the company, because the police officer would feel uncomfortable exhibiting insobriety before civilians. The police may be likened to other authorities who prefer to violate moralistic norms away from onlookers for whom they are routinely supposed to appear as normative models. College professors, for instance, also get drunk on occasion, but they prefer to do so where students are not present. Unfortunately for police officers, such settings are harder for them to come by than they are for college professors. The whole civilian world watches the police. As a result, they tend to be limited to the company of other police officers for whom their police identity is not a stimulus to carping normative criticism.

CORRELATES OF SOCIAL ISOLATION

The element of authority, like the element of danger, is thus seen to contribute to the **solidarity** of police officers. To the extent that police share the experience of receiving hostility from the public, they are also drawn together and become dependent on one another. Trends in the degree to which police may exercise authority are also important considerations in understanding the dynamics of the relation between authority and solidarity. It is not simply a question of how much absolute authority police are given, but how much authority they have relative to what they had, or think they had, before. If, as Westley concluded, police violence is frequently a response to a challenge to the police officer's authority, so too may a perceived reduction in authority result in greater solidarity. Whitaker commented on the British police as follows:

> As they feel their authority decline, internal solidarity has become increasingly important to the police. Despite the individual responsibility of each police officer to pursue justice, there is sometimes a tendency to close ranks and to form a square when they themselves are concerned.[26]

These inclinations may have positive consequences for the effectiveness of police work, because notions of professional courtesy or colleagueship seem unusually high among police.[27] When the nature of the policing enterprise requires much joint activity, as in robbery and narcotics enforcement, the impression is received that cooperation is high and genuine. Police do not appear to cooperate with one another merely because such is the policy of the chief, but because they sincerely attach a high value to teamwork. For instance, there is a norm among detectives that two who work together will protect each other when a dangerous situation arises. During one investigation, a detective stepped out of a car to question a suspect who became belligerent. The second detective, who had remained overly long in the back seat of the police car, apologized indirectly to his partner by explaining how wrong it had been of him to permit his partner to encounter a suspect alone on the street. He later repeated this explanation privately, in genuine **consternation** at having committed the breach (and possibly at having been culpable in the presence of an observer). Strong feelings of empathy and cooperation, indeed almost of "clannishness," a term several police officers themselves used to describe the attitude of police toward one another, may be seen in the daily activities of police. Analytically, these feelings can be traced to the elements of danger and shared experiences of hostility in the police officer's role.

Finally, to round out the sketch, police are notably conservative, emotionally and politically. If the element of danger in the police officer's role tends to make the officer suspicious, and therefore emotionally attached to the **status quo,** a similar consequence may be attributed to the element of authority. The fact that a person is engaged in enforcing a set of rules implies that the person also becomes implicated in *affirming* them. Labor disputes provide the most common example of conditions inclining the police officer to support the status quo. In these situations, the police are necessarily pushed on the side of the defense of property. Their responsibilities thus lead them to see the striking and sometimes angry workers as their enemy and, therefore, to be cool, if not antagonistic, toward the whole conception of labor militancy.[28] If the police did not believe in the system of laws they were responsible for enforcing, they would have to go on living in a state of conflicting cognitions, a condition that a number of social psychologists agree is painful.[29]

This hypothetical issue of not believing in the laws they are enforcing simply does not arise for most police officers. In the course of the research, however, there was one example. An African-American civil rights advocate became a police officer with the conviction that by so doing he would be aiding the cause of impartial administration of law for African Americans. For him, however, this outside rationale was not enough to sustain him in administering a system of laws that depends for its impartiality on a reasonable measure of social and economic equality among the citizenry. This recruit identified with the black community. He challenged directives of the department; the department claimed his efficiency was impaired. He resigned under pressure in his rookie year.[30]

Police are understandably reluctant to appear to be anything but impartial politically. The police are forbidden from publicly campaigning for political candidates. The London police are similarly prohibited and before 1887 were not allowed to vote in parliamentary elections, or in local ones until 1983.[31] It was not surprising that the Westville chief of police forbade questions on the questionnaire that would have measured political attitudes.[32] One police officer, however, explained the chief's refusal on grounds that "a couple of jerks here would probably cut up and come out looking like Commies."

During the course of administering the questionnaire over a three-day period, I talked with approximately fifteen officers and sergeants in the Westville department, discussing political attitudes of police. In addition, during the course of the research itself, approximately fifty officers were interviewed for varying periods of time. Of these, at least twenty were interviewed more than once, some over time periods of several weeks. Furthermore, twenty police were interviewed in Eastville, several for periods ranging from several hours to several days. Most of the time was not spent on investigating political attitudes, but I made a point of raising the question, if possible making it part of a discussion centered around the contents of a right-wing newsletter to which one of the detectives subscribed. One discussion included a group of eight detectives. From these observations, interviews, and discussions, it was clear that a Goldwater type of conservatism was the dominant political and emotional persuasion of police. I encountered only three police officers who claimed to be politically liberal, at the same time asserting that they were decidedly exceptional.

Whether or not the police officer is an "authoritarian personality" is a related issue, beyond the scope of this discussion partly because of the many questions raised about this concept. Thus, in the course of discussing the concept of "normality" in mental health, two psychologists made the point that many conventional people were high scorers on the California F scale and similar tests. The great mass of the people, according to these authors, is not much further along the scale of ego development than the typical adolescent who the authors described as "rigid, prone to think in **stereotypes,** intolerant of deviations, punitive and anti-psychological—in short, what has been called an authoritarian personality."[33] Therefore, it is preferable to call the police officer's a conventional personality.

Writing about the New York police force, Thomas R. Brooks suggested a similar interpretation. He wrote:

> Cops are conventional people....All a cop can swing in a **milieu** of marijuana smokers, interracial dates, and homosexuals is the night stick. A policeman who passed a Lower East Side art gallery filled with paintings of what appeared to be female genitalia could think of doing only one thing—step in and make an arrest.[34]

Despite a fundamental identification with conservative conventionality, however, the police officer may be familiar, unlike most conventional people, with the **argot** of the deviant and the criminal. (The police officer tends to resent the quietly respectable liberal who comes to the defense of the deviant and criminals on principle but who has rarely met such people in practice.) Indeed, the police officer will use a knowledge of the argot to advantage in talking to a suspect. In this manner, the officer *puts on* the suspect by pretending to share the suspect's moral conception of the world through the use of "hip" expressions. The suspect may put on a parallel show for the police officer by using only conventional language to indicate respectability. (In my opinion, neither fools the other.)

A COMPARATIVE GLANCE AT POLICE ROLE AND CULTURE

Must this theory of the police officer's working personality be limited to the police under observation, or can it be generalized to a wider police population? Unfortunately, there are few systematic studies of police for comparison. American studies, as well as reports of police chiefs, indicate that police typically perceive the citizenry to be hostile to them.[35] Thus, for example, a recent survey made by James Q. Wilson of an urban American police force concluded:

> Criticisms of the way a big-city police department was run were largely confined to the younger, most recently promoted sergeants, but alienation—an acute sense of the citizen hostility or contempt toward of officers—as found in almost all age groups. More than 70

percent of the over 800 officers scored high on an index of perceived citizen hostility—more indeed, than thought the force was poorly run (though these were over half the total).[36]

This finding of Wilson's, so close to those reported here, is not surprising, and therefore not forceful in persuading the reader that the findings are generalizable. The common pattern of activities of American urban police—for instance, their enforcement of traffic laws—suggests that findings in one city would be similar to those in another. Furthermore, because the Westville police are high caliber, greater citizen hostility would be anticipated in other American cities where the enforcing authorities are less respected and therefore more likely to generate citizen hostility. Assuming that hostility is correlated with social isolation, this feature of police life also is likely to be more pronounced in other American urban areas.

Suppose, however, we were to consider the "working personality" of police who constitute part of a relatively homogeneous society and who also enjoy an international reputation for honesty, efficiency, and legality. A study of such a police force was completed by Michael Banton, who observed five police departments in Scotland and in the United States.[37] The main object of his inquiry was the urban Scottish constable, roughly the equivalent of the American patrol officer or "cop on the beat." Comparing the social isolation of American and British police, Banton wrote:

> Before my visit to the United States I thought that for a variety of reasons American police officers might well experience more social isolation than their British counterparts. I assumed that the heavier incidence of violent crime, the high proportion of 'cop-haters,' the 'shoot first, ask afterwards' tactics American police have to use on occasion, and the lower prestige of police work, would cause policemen to feel more like outcasts or like troops in occupation of enemy territory. Such an expectation was in accordance with an impression to be gained from a study of Westley's dissertation, where it said: 'The exigencies of the occupation form the police into a social group which tends to be in conflict with and isolated from the community; and in which the norms are independent of the community' (Westley, 1951, p. 294). The locality in which Westley's research was conducted turns out, however, to be far from representative of the present-day situation, and a reconsideration of his evidence from a comparative rather than a purely American perspective reveals a whole series of influences which operate in a contrary fashion. *American police may seem isolated from the community to an American observer because he compares them with other occupational groups in the same society; they may at the same time seem to an outsider much less isolated than policemen in other societies.*[38]

Banton accounted for the relatively greater isolation of British police by emphasizing the consequences of the exemplary character of the British police officer's role. British police, as portrayed by Banton, are reserved, dignified, impersonal, detached. For them, the role is the person, and the example to be set is taken seriously. He wrote:

> Most officers with twenty years' service in a county force can remember the days when a policeman who proposed to marry was required first to submit the name of his fiancée to his superiors so that they could ascertain whether she was a fit and proper person for the role of a policeman's wife.[39]

Although the element of danger is not so ultimate for the British police officer, it never-theless exists. "In Edinburgh," wrote Banton, "violence means to a policeman, I suspect, either fists or stones, or at the worst, assault with sticks or iron bars. It does not mean guns or knives."[40] Furthermore, the theme of the police being a "race apart" is a recurring one in Scotland, which Banton attributed to the requirement that police officers must examine critically every statement made to them.[41] In our interpretation, these reports suggest that the police officer, wherever located, is in a position of vulnerability. Exposure to physical danger represents the height of vulnerability, a situation the British police officer encounters less often than the American. The British officer does, however, experience the possibility of lesser physical danger and of attacks on his or her professional competence. The police officer's role is therefore exceptional insofar as the need to be so often on the defensive. Banton found one of his subjects defining "the police mind" as follows: "…you suspect your grandmother and that's about the strength of it."

Although the elements of authority and danger have similar consequences for British and American police, the processes bringing about social isolation seem different. British police are inclined to take the initiative in separating themselves from society. They tend to internalize authority, to perform an exemplary role, and thereby are instruments of their own isolation. Even in Great Britain, however, there seem to be differences between the Scottish police studied by Banton and the British police in general. Although the 1962 Royal Commission concluded that a social survey conducted by the Home Office consti-tuted an overwhelming vote of confidence in the police, that interpretation has been widely criticized. For example, the survey disclosed that 42.4 percent of the public thought police took bribes, 34.7 percent that the police used unfair methods to get information, 32 percent that the police might distort evidence in court, and 17.8 percent that on occasions the police used too much force.[42] The Royal Commission, however, felt that because almost half of those interviewed did not believe that the police took bribes, used unnec-essary violence, employed unfair means of getting evidence, or gave false evidence in court, it was reasonable to "assert, confidently, on the basis of this survey, that relations between the police and the public are on the whole very good."[43] This interpretation is obviously overoptimistic. Police relations, especially with certain segments of the public, are clearly strained.

In America there has not been a comparable national survey. There have, however, been enough complaints to such groups as the U.S. Civil Rights Commission to suggest that American police are no more beloved or trusted than their English counterparts.[44] The chief difference may be that in America hostile public attitudes isolate police who would prefer to be more friendly. Although the Westville police have been presented as people who are conservative, suspicious, relatively isolated from the community at large, clannish, and resentful of public apathy, this is only part of the portrait of complex beings. Westville police officers see themselves as relatively congenial persons, able to make friends. Police were asked to rank eight qualities in the order they felt these qualities best described them.[45] Here we find the quality of "congeniality and the ability to make friends" ranking high. In Great Britain, also, the social survey finds police ruing their lack of friends, an attitude especially prevalent among the rural police. Of these, 74 percent thought they would have more friends if they had a different job. On the whole, 66.8 percent of police officers said that the job adversely affected their outside friendships.[46]

Unfortunately, the nature of their work often inhibits the police from indulging their **gregariousness** in a personally meaningful way. They would like to be friendlier, but of the public over whom they are authority figures, they must be suspicious of strangeness, oddity, indeed any sort of *change*. The elements of danger and authority in the police officer's work evidently impede gregarious tendencies and, in general, account for similar cognitive inclinations in American and British police. To be sure, differences exist in the salience and character of these elements and in the processes by which danger and authority affect the officer's way of looking at the world. Nevertheless, both elements seem to be present, specific outcomes such as social isolation are similar, and, most importantly, the British and American police seem to see the world similarly.

COGNITIVE SIMILARITY AND THE RULE OF LAW

If the proposition is largely correct that elements of the police officer's role result in broadly similar "working personalities" in British and American police, is the validity of this conclusion affected by observations that British police conform to the rules of legal procedure more closely than American police?[47] Should not the similarity of cognitive inclination manifest itself in the behavior of the police? Although a number of factors, such as relations of the police organization to the community and a less moralistic substantive criminal law, may help to account for such behavioral differences, this final discussion is confined to the effect of the general social environment. The discussion that follows is limited to the question of how differences in general social environment can influence the relation between the elements of danger and authority in the direction of apparently greater compliance with the rule of law.

It is important to note that the actual degree of difference often stated is open to serious question. A reader of memoirs of British police is impressed by the extent to which they described violations of the judges' rules.[48] One officer wrote: "You can see that if we worked according to the strict letter of the Rules we would get nowhere....We have to break the law to enforce it...."[49] Evidently, the British police do not conform to rules so much as know how to present the appearance of conformity. By contrast, when American police vary from **canons** of procedural regularity, their misbehaviors tend to be more visible. Reared in a society with finer social distinctions, the British police officer is schooled in etiquette to a degree unknown to most Americans. Victor Meek, a former inspector of the Metropolitan Police, described how an English police officer investigating a burglary manages to "stop" relatively large numbers of people, at the same time avoiding the appearance of procedural irregularity. Meek wrote:

> You see, when a policeman has stopped a hundred people, which number has included perhaps ten proved guilty persons, he has learned the behaviour of these conditions of ninety innocent people and of ten thieves. In the next hundred stopped he will have twenty thieves, in the next perhaps thirty. Not altogether because thieves are thicker but because

his "Police here," or "Excuse me a moment, Sir," are enough to satisfy him, by the reaction of the person stopped, whether he is dealing with a sheep or a goat, whether chummy is in the clear or loaded. So to the sheep his next remark is, "I am very sorry to bother you but my watch has stopped. Can you please tell me the time?" The answer will naturally be, "If you want to know the time I thought you had to ask another policeman," and the mutual appreciation of this witticism sends chummy away chuckling and quite unaware that Section 66[50] has been tried on him.[51]

The ability of the British police to make fine social discriminations, plus their training in etiquette, enable them to distinguish not only among those who are more likely to commit crimes but also among those who are more likely to report procedural irregularities. As Meek said, "...the names and address of a Section 66 complainer is doubly worth passing on to a good copper of the manor on which chummy lives or works."[52]

Thus, when we envision the "discretion" of the British police, we should certainly keep in mind more than the issue of whether they decide to invoke the law. A key distinction between the English and American police is that the former tend to be more discreet in an interactional sense as well as discrete in an administrative one, thereby avoiding the censure that is often the lot of the American police. Indeed, as the rest of this study of a "professionalized" American police force is read, the reader may find it interesting to speculate as to what constitutes the central elements of professional training. We believe the material to follow will suggest that the training of etiquette, including the ability to make fine social distinctions, is such an element; more, indeed, than the development of an actual regard for the rule of law.

CONCLUSIONS

The combination of *danger* and *authority* found in the task of the police unavoidably combine to frustrate procedural regularity. If it were possible to structure social roles with specific qualities, it would be wise to propose that these two should never, for the sake of the rule of law, be permitted to coexist. Danger typically yields self-defensive conduct, conduct that must strain to be impulsive because danger arouses fear and anxiety so easily. Authority under such conditions becomes a resource to reduce perceived threats rather than a series of reflective judgments arrived at calmly. The ability to be discreet, in the sense discussed above, is also affected. As a result, procedural requirements take on a "frilly" character, or at least tend to be reduced to a secondary position in the face of circumstances seen as threatening.

If this analysis is correct, it suggests a related explanation drawn from the realm of social environment to account for the apparent **paradox** that the elements of danger and authority are universally to be found in the police officer's role, yet at the same time fail to yield the same behavior regarding the rule of law. If the element of danger faced by the British police is less than that faced by their American counterparts, its ability to undermine the element of authority is proportionately weakened. Bluntly put, the American police may have a more difficult job because they are exposed to greater danger. Therefore, we would expect them to be less **judicious,** indeed less discreet, in the exercise of their authority. Similarly, such an explanation would predict that if the element of actual danger or even the perception of such in the job of the British police were to increase, complaints regarding the illegal use of their authority would also rise.

There have been spectacular cases supporting this proposition. One of these, resulting in a government inquiry that suspended two top police officers, took place at Sheffield on March 14, 1963. Several detectives brutally assaulted four men in five successive and separate relays with a **truncheon,** fists, and a rhinoceros whip. The report of the inquiry concludes that the police were undoubtedly guilty of "maliciously inflicting grievous bodily harm of a serious nature on two prisoners."[53] The assaults were described as "deliberate, unprovoked, brutal and sustained…for the purpose of inducing confessions of crime." The detectives had formed into a "Crime Squad," believing the group had the authority to use "tough methods to deal with tough criminals and take risks to achieve speedy results." The leading offender told the inquiry "that criminals are treated far too softly by the Courts, that because criminals break rules, police may and must do so to be a jump ahead, that force is justified as a last resort as a method of detection when normal methods fail, and that a beating is the only answer to turn a hardened criminal from a life of crime."[54]

Perhaps the most interesting feature of the report is the mitigating factors the inquiry took into account. The inquiry found that the detectives were overworked (in a city where crime was on the rise); that the detectives were, and felt, under pressure to obtain results; that the use of violence had been encouraged by hints beforehand from senior officers; that senior officers instituted, witnessed, and joined in the violence and were inadequately dealt with by the chief constable; and that the detectives were told to give a false account in court by a senior officer, who concocted it. The entire report suggested that the detectives who engaged in the beatings were not unusual men. There was no evidence of mental instability on their part, neither of psychosis, psychopathy, nor neurosis. Not one officer on the force reported the incident, although several had learned of it. The report gives the feeling that although the event itself was exceptional, the conditions leading to it, such as overwork, pressure to produce, and encouragement by superiors, were ordinary. Although the report did not use the language of social science, it strongly suggested that the structural and cultural conditions in the police force supported this sort of response.

Also interesting is the evident racial bias of the Sheffield police. One of them testified he carried his rhinoceros whip to deal with "coloured informants." The racial issue is significant for the British police as a whole. *The New York Times* reported on May 3, 1965, that although the London police force is six thousand people short of full strength, not one applicant of color had been accepted, even though fifteen West Indians, six Pakistanis, and six Indians tried to join the force in the preceding three years. The official reason given was that the applicants did not meet the qualifications. Apart from three part-time constables in the Midlands, however, there was, at the time of the report, not one police officer of color in Britain, even though Pakistanis, Indians, and West Indians, all officially classified as "coloured" by the British, account for nearly 2 percent of the population.

Suggestions have been made to enlist police officers of color for neighborhoods having a nonwhite population, or to bring in trained officers of color from the Commonwealth. Others have asked for the introduction of nonwhite police officers in white neighborhoods,

especially in London. *The New York Times* story closed with a suggestion by one critic, Anthony Lester, that British police chiefs take a trip to New York to see how African-American police officers fit in. "Policemen have a different status here than in the States," he is reported to have said. "They are more a father figure, a symbol of authority with their tall helmets and slow walk. It's difficult to get people to accept coloured men in this job. They have had no Negro officers in the Army, no way of getting used to taking orders from coloured men."

To complete the analogy of similarity of police action with similarity of social conditions, problems of police behavior also appear to be correlated with the restriction of marijuana use, a recent police phenomenon in England. Colin MacInnes argued, in a letter published in the fall of 1963, that when the London police began vigorously enforcing the marijuana law:

> ...it looks as if the hallowed myth that English coppers never use violence, perjury, framing of suspects—let alone participate in crimes—is at last being shattered in the public mind. Now, what has been foolish about this legend is not that coppers *do* do these things—as all police forces do and must—but that national vanity led many to suppose that our coppers were far nicer men than any others.[55]

Although MacInnes' statement may be overly strong, it does suggest that those who too clearly contrast American and British police in favor of the British are probably generally wrong. Of course, there are always individual as well as group differences in police behavior. However, even if conduct varies more than MacInnes indicated, and conduct will vary with relations of the police organization to the community, the character of the substantive criminal law being enforced, and the social conditions of the community, it is nevertheless likely that the variables of danger and authority in the police officer's role, combined with a constant pressure to produce, result in tendencies general enough and similar enough to identify a distinctive "working personality" among police. The question becomes one of understanding what the police do with it. Given this conception of the police officer's "working personality" as background, the chapters that follow analyze the sources of police attitudes and conduct as observed in the setting of specific assignments.

NOTES

1. For previous contributions in this area, see the following: Ely Chinoy, *Automobile Workers and the American Dream* (Garden City, NY: Doubleday and Company, 1955); Charles R. Walker and Robert H. Guest, *The Man on the Assembly Line* (Cambridge, MA: Harvard University Press, 1952); Everett C. Hughes, "Work and the Self," in his *Men and Their Work* (Glencoe, IL: The Free Press, 1958), pp. 42–55; Harold L. Wilensky, *Intellectuals in Labor Unions: Organizational Pressures on Professional Roles* (Glencoe, IL: The Free Press, 1956); Wilensky, "Varieties of Work Experience," in Henry Borow, ea., *Man in a World at Work* (Boston: Houghton Mifflin Company, 1964), pp. 125–54; Louis Kriesberg, "The Retail Furrier: Concepts of Security and Success," *American Journal of Sociology* 57 (March 1952), pp. 478–35; Waldo

Burchard, "Role Conflicts of Military Chaplains," *American Sociological Review* 19 (October 1954), pp. 528–35; Howard S. Becker and Blanche Geer, "The Fate of Idealism in Medical School," *American Sociological Review* 23 (1958), pp. 506–56; and Howard S. Becker and Anselm L. Strauss, "Careers, Personality. and Adult Socialization," *American Journal of Sociology* 62 (November 1956), pp. 253–363.

2. Morris Janowitz, *The Professional Soldier: A Social and Political Portrait* (New York: The Free Press of Glencoe, 1964), p. 175.

3. By no means does such an analysis suggest that there are no individual or group differences among police. On the contrary, most of this study emphasizes differences, endeavoring to relate these to occupational specialties in police departments. This chapter, however, explores similarities rather than differences, attempting to account for the police officer's general disposition to perceive and to behave in certain ways.

4. William Westley was the first to raise such questions about the police, when he inquired into the conditions under which police are violent. Whatever merit this analysis has, it owes much to his prior insights, as all subsequent sociological studies of the police must. See his "Violence and the Police," *American Journal of Sociology* 59 (July 1953), pp. 34–41; also his unpublished Ph.D. dissertation *The Police: A Sociological Study of Law, Custom, and Morality*, University of Chicago, Department of Sociology, 1951.

5. From Thomas F. Adams, "Field Interrogation," *Police*, March–April 1963, p. 28.

6. See Irving Pilavin and Scott Briar, "Police Encounters with Juveniles," *American Journal of Sociology* 70 (September 1964), pp. 206–14.

7. A questionnaire was given to all police officers in operating divisions of the police force: patrol, traffic, vice control, and all detectives. The questionnaire was administered at police line-ups over a period of three days, mainly by the author but also by some of the police personnel themselves. Before the questionnaire was administered, it was circulated to and approved by the police officers' welfare association.

8. Indeed, the journalist Paul Jacobs, who has ridden with the Westville juvenile police as part of his own work on poverty, observed in a personal communication that juvenile police appear curiously drawn to seek out dangerous situations, as if juvenile work without danger is degrading.

9. Colin Macinnes, *Mr. Love and Justice* (London: New English Library, 1962), p. 74.

10. Peter J. Connell, "Handling of Complaints by Police," unpublished paper for course in Criminal Procedure, Yale Law School, Fall, 1961.

11. James Baldwin, *Nobody Knows My Name* (New York: Dell Publishing Company, 1962), pp. 65–67.

12. MacInnes, op. cit., p. 20.

13. Respondents were asked, "Anybody who knows anything about police work knows that police face a number of problems. Would you please state—in order—what you consider to be the two most serious problems police have?" On the basis of a number of answers, the writer and J. Richard Woodworth devised a set of categories. Then Woodworth classified each response into one of the categories (see table below). When a response did not seem clear, he consulted with the writer. No attempt was made to independently check Woodworth's classification because the results are used impressionalistically and do not test a hypothesis. It may be, for instance, that "relations with public" is sometimes used to indicate racial problems, and vice versa. "Racial problems" include only those answers having specific reference to race.

14. Royal Commission on the Police, 1962; Appendix IV to Minutes of Evidence, in Michael Banton, *The Policeman in the Community* (London: Tavistock Publications, 1964), p. 198.

15. Similarly, Banton found Scottish police officers attempting to conceal their occupation when on holiday. He quoted one as saying: "If someone asks my wife, 'What does your husband do?' I've told her to say, 'He's a clerk,' and that's the way it went because she found that being a policeman's wife—well, it wasn't quite a stigma, she didn't feel cut off, but that a sort of invisible wall was up for conversation purposes when a policeman was there" (p. 198).

16. An addition to Banton, William Westley and James Q. Wilson noted this characteristic of police. See Westley, op. cit., p. 294; Wilson, "The Police and Their Problems: A Theory," *Public Policy* 12 (1963), pp. 189–216.

17. S.M. Lipset, Martin H. Trow, and lames S. Coleman, *Union Democracy* (New York: Anchor Books, 1962), p. 123.

18. On this issue there was no variation. The statement "the police officer feels" means that there was no instance of a negative opinion expressed by the police studied.

19. Banton, op. cit., p. 114.

20. Janowitz, op. cit.

21. O.W. Wilson, for example, mentions this factor as a primary source of antagonism toward police. See his "Police Authority in a Free Society," *Journal of Criminal Law, Criminology and Police Science* 54 (June 1964), pp. 175–77. In the current study, in addition to the police themselves, other people interviewed, such as attorneys in the system, also attribute the isolation of police to their authority. Similarly, Arthur L. Stinchcombe, in an as-yet-unpublished manuscript, "The Control of Citizen Resentment in Police Work," provides a stimulating analysis, to which I am indebted, of the ways police authority generates resentment.

22. See Wayne R. LaFave, "The Police and Nonenforcement of the Law," *Wisconsin Law Review*, (1962), pp. 104–37, 179–239.

23. For a theoretical discussion of the problems of leadership, see George Homans, *The Human Group* (New York: Harcourt, Brace and Company, 1950), especially the chapter entitled "The Job of the Leader," pp. 415–40.

24. The work of the Westville morals squad was analyzed in detail in an unpublished master's thesis by J. Richard Woodworth, *The Administration of Statutory Rape Complaints: A Sociological Study*, University of California, Berkeley, 1964.

25. Horace R. Cayton, *Long Old Road* (New York: Trident Press, 1965), p. 154.

26. Ben Whitaker, *The Police* (Middlesex, England: Penguin Books, 1964), p. 137.

27. It would be difficult to compare this factor across occupations, because the indications could hardly be controlled. Nevertheless, I felt that the sense of responsibility to police officers in other departments was on the whole quite strong.

28. In light of this, the most carefully drawn lesson plan in the "professionalized" Westville police department, according to the officer in charge of training, is the one dealing with the police officer's demeanor in labor disputes. A comparable concern is now being evidenced in teaching police the appropriate demeanor in civil rights demonstrations. See, e.g., Judy E. Towler, *The Police Role in Racial Conflicts* (Springfield, IL: Charles C Thomas, 1964).

29. Indeed, one school of social psychology asserts that there is a basic drive, a fundamental tendency of human nature, to reduce the degree of discrepancy between conflicting cognitions. For police officers, this tenet implies having to do something to reduce the discrepancy between their personal beliefs and behavior. The officers would have to modify their behavior and beliefs or introduce some outside factor to justify the discrepancy. If the officers modified behavior, so as not to enforce a law that is personally unacceptable, they would not hold their jobs for long. Practically then, the officers may either introduce an outside factor or modify their beliefs. The outside factor would have to be compelling to reduce the pain resulting

from the dissonance between the officers' cognitions. For example, the officers would have to convince themselves that the only way to make a living was by being a police officer or, instead, modify their beliefs. See Leon Festinger, *A Theory of Cognitive Dissonance* (Evanston, IL: Row-Peterson, 1957). For a brief explanation of Festinger's theory, see Edward S. Sampson, ed., *Approaches, Contexts, and Problems of Social Psychology* (Englewood Cliffs, NJ: Prentice-Hall, 1964), pp. 9–15.

30. I thank Gwynne Pierson for pointing out the inaccuracy of the first edition's report of this incident.

31. Whitaker, op. cit., p. 26.

32. The questions submitted to the chief of police were directly analogous to those asked of printers in the study of the I.T.U. See Lipset et al., op. cit., "Appendix II—Interview Schedule," pp. 493–503.

33. Jane Loevinger and Abel Ossono, "Evaluation of Therapy by Self Report: A Paradox," *Journal of Abnormal and Social Psychology* 58 (May 1959), p. 392; see also Edward A. Shils, "Authoritarianism: 'Right' and 'Left'," in R. Christie and M. Jahoda, eds., *Studies in Scope and Method of "The Authoritarian Personality"* (Glencoe, IL: The Free Press, 1954), pp. 24–49.

34. Thomas R. Brooks, "New York's Finest," *Commentary* 40 (August 1965), pp. 29–30.

35. Cf. *Parker on Police*, O. W. Wilson, ed., (Springfield, IL: Charles C Thomas, 1957), pp. 135–46; O. W Wilson, "Police Authority in a Free Society," *Journal of Criminal Law, Criminology and Police Science* 54 (June 1963), pp. 175–77; Michael J. Murphy, "Stereocracy v. Democracy," *The Police Chief* (February 1962), pp. 36, 38.

36. James Q. Wilson, "Police Attitudes and Citizen Hostility," unpublished draft, Harvard University, September 1964, p. 24.

37. Banton, op. cit.

38. Ibid., p. 215 (italics added).

39. Ibid., p. 195.

40. Banton, personal communication, August 24, 1964.

41. Banton, op. cit., pp. 207–208.

42. Whitaker, op. cit., p. 15.

43. Ibid., p. 103.

44. Commission on Civil Rights Report, Book 5, *Justice* (Washington, DC: U.S. Government Printing Office, 1961), pp. 5–44. In New York, a number of civil rights groups have formed an unofficial citizens' board to review charges of police brutality (*New York Times,* May 23, 1964).

45. These categories were taken from an unpublished paper, "Articulated Values of Law Students." The categories were suggested by the eight-value system elaborated by Harold Lasswell. See, e.g., H. D. Lasswell and A. Kaplan, *Power and Society* (New Haven, CT: Yale University Press, 1950).

46. Whitaker, op. cit., p. 127.

47. See Bruce Smith, *Police Systems in the United States* (New York: Harper and Brothers, 1960, second rev. ed.), pp. 3, 11, et passim; and Sir Patrick Devlin, *The Criminal Prosecution in England* (New Haven, CT: Yale University Press, 1958), passim.

48. See, e.g., Victor Meek, *Cops and Robbers* (London: Gerald Duckworth and Company, 1962); William Gosling, *Ghost Squad* (Garden City, NY: Doubleday, 1959); and a "Letter from English Policemen on Use of Judges' Rules," in William Thomas Fryer, ed., *Selected Writings on the Law of Evidence and Trial* (St. Paul, MN: West Publishing Company, 1957), pp. 843–46.

49. Fryer, ibid.

50. "Any constable may stop, search and detain any vessel, boat, cart or carriage in or upon which there shall be reason to suspect that anything stolen or unlawfully obtained may be found, and also any person who may be reasonably suspected of having or conveying in any manner anything stolen or unlawfully obtained."
51. Meek, op. cit., p. 86.
52. Ibid., p. 85.
53. Sheffield Police Appeal Inquiry, Cmnd. 2176, November 1963.
54. Ibid., p. 5.
55. "The Shy Season," *Partisan Review* 30 (Fall 1963), pp. 430, 432.

QUESTIONS FOR DISCUSSION

1. Discuss the two principal variables involved in the process by which the working personality of the police is developed.
2. Describe the relationship between the symbolic assailant and the development of a police culture. Cite examples to support your answer.
3. Explain social isolation and solidarity with respect to the work of police. Cite examples to support your answer.

APPLICATIONS

1. Construct a list of fifteen words to describe the police in your community. Compare your list with the lists of your classmates, identifying similarities and differences. Now see if the class is able to arrive at a consensus of about fifteen words that accurately describe the police. Why may this be difficult?
2. How do you think police officers compare to correctional officers, firefighters, soldiers, and emergency medical technicians with respect to each of the following?
   (a) Danger
   (b) Authority
   (c) Social isolation
   (d) Group solidarity
   (e) Stress

chapter 8

The Dark Side of the Force

John Dorschner

INTRODUCTION

The real problem, the one that *really* rankles Miami cops, is when they knock on doors, and people peer through a window and see the cop from Miami P.D. in his regulation blue uniform, with his regulation silver badge, his regulation black belt, his regulation Smith and Wesson, with the regulation yellow-and-blue city insignia circling the green palm tree—they see all that, and they…*don't…open…the…door.*

This has happened to officers Rene Landa and Rudolfo Hierro and Luis Diazlay, and to a lot of other Miami cops.

Residents peer through the windows and ask: "What do you want?"

They hesitate even when they have just called to report a burglary in their house or a disturbance in the neighborhood. They make the call, and then when the cop shows up, they start thinking, well, this person looks like a cop, and acts like a cop, but is he a cop? And even if he is a cop, how do I know he's an honest cop? How do I know he's not a burglar?

The officers hate this, of course. They became cops because they wanted people to admire them, to sigh thankfully when they arrive on a scene, sirens blaring, lights flashing—and now they face the closed, chained, dead-bolted door, as if they were burglars.

But what really hurts, the thing that makes it hard to be a Miami police officer these days, is that the wildest, most unkind suspicions are not completely unfounded. It has come to this.

"The Dark Side of the Force" by John Dorschner, *Tropic Magazine*, March 8, 1987. Reprinted with permission of *The Miami Herald*.

THE DIVISION

What a mess Miami P.D. is in. The FBI has launched a broad investigation, suspecting pervasive corruption, **subpoenaing** the records of 25 officers. Miami cops have been charged with murder, with shooting up a doper's house, with conspiring to sell police radios and badges, with big-time dope dealing. The elite Special Investigation Section opens its safe and finds $150,000 missing. In the back of the police compound, a simple bicycle padlock is clipped and several hundred pounds of marijuana are reported missing.

Miami P.D. trembles with tension and uncertainty. There have been three chiefs in a little more than three years: One was fired at 2:47 A.M. following a frenzied night of conspiracy and accusations. Another was asked to retire. The current chief, Clarence Dickson, believes that the marijuana theft may have been carried out by rivals inside the department in an attempt to get him fired. There have been persistent rumors that Dickson is about to resign or be shuffled aside in favor of a new deputy administrator.

How bad is it? Consider this memo: "Paranoia and suspicion has run rampant throughout the Police Department and City Hall, to the extent that free verbal expression cannot be exchanged without fear that the halls, telephones, desks, walls and office of everyone who is part of the decision-making process is illegally bugged."

That memo wasn't written by some cowering functionary with a gripe or a grudge.

Its author was the chief himself, Clarence Dickson.

Talk to the cops—colonels and lieutenants and sergeants and just plain cops on the beat—and they paint a portrait of a department confused, chaotic, demoralized, driven by rumor and leaks and fear.

The publicity on the corruption and on the tumultuous politics has been widespread and seemingly unending. There has been plenty of comment on the sad state of the police department, but barely a word on how it got that way. How did one of Miami's most essential institutions suffer such a disastrous breakdown?

There is no shortage of insiders willing to offer their version of the real reasons for the extended nightmare of a police force going wrong. Still, the discussion has not gone public for a good reason: It is dangerous stuff. It is about ethnic tension, racial distrust.

Listen to the cops and you hear disillusioned Anglos, suspicious blacks and defensive Hispanics. Their perspectives are so different that it seems as if they are describing three departments, not one.

The black and Hispanic organizations now have separate but equal bulletin boards outside the first-floor locker rooms. Some Hispanic officers complain that the FBI investigation is really a vendetta against Hispanics, perhaps initiated by angry Anglo or black officers— 18 of the 25 officers named in the subpoenas are Hispanics. Bitter Anglos race to the telephone to call the news media any time there is the slightest embarrassment within the department. (Indeed, news organizations were tipped off about a stripper performing at the station while the event was still going on, before the chief's office knew about it.)

Miami has undergone a more dramatic ethnic transformation in the last two decades than any other American city. With it has come a tidal wave of crime and racial unrest. From the beginning, the Miami police have been in the middle of it. Cops' jobs have been complicated, made more dangerous. The temptations for corruption have poured in with the suitcases full of cash. Two devastating riots in the last 10 years were touched off when white police officers killed blacks under suspicious circumstances.

The city, in its struggling and imperfect way, has attempted to respond to the pressures. At the heart of the response is an affirmative action program, brought about by a federal consent decree, that has revolutionized the police department. Within a two-year stretch, the Miami Police Department went from being a bastion of Anglo males to a force that is 60 percent minorities.

And here is the really awful possibility, the charge too inflammatory to easily make part of public debate: that in the remaking of the Miami Police Department lie the seeds of its destruction. But even if you have not seen that in the newspapers, it is precisely what many police officers are thinking.

Paul Oboz, an Anglo colonel who recently retired: "I attribute our descent from superiority to affirmative action."

Sgt. J. J. Williams, head of the black officers association: "It's not that the consent decree has created a problem. It's the people fighting *against* the consent decree, that's what's wrong."

Sgt. Sebastian Aguirre, leader of the Hispanic Officers Association: "This isn't the '60s. It's the '80s. And we're building the department for the year 2000. If you can't make the change, get out."

It would be painful for any institution as pressurized as a police department in a large, high-crime city to absorb such dissension and change. And it would be even harder if the change had been rushed and mishandled, creating a poisonous atmosphere that forces good cops out and rewards **cronyism** and incompetence—an atmosphere that breeds corruption.

Or has this unprecedented remaking of an urban police department—the ideal of reformers of the previous decade—in fact succeeded remarkably, with serious but inevitable growing pains? Are the problems due more to lingering **bigotry** and **covetous** politicians eager to build personal fiefdoms?

These are difficult and sensitive questions, not often raised because even to raise them can seem racist. But the questions are there, permeating the police department.

As one colonel says, "We are a divided police department because we are a divided city."

THE SERGEANT

It was 7:30 A.M., and he was hunched over a bagel and a cup of coffee in a rear booth of Berney's Restaurant. He had just finished a 10-hour midnight shift, and his eyes had that hooded, exhausted look that put him out of step with a crowd of workers revving up for the start of their day.

This is Sgt. Ed Westpy, a bald man with a solid jaw and dark, heavy eyebrows that give him a look of authority: the perfect look for a cop.

Ken Harms, a former chief, will tell you: "The Ed Westpys represent the supervisory backbone of the police department." There are a lot of people like Westpy in the department, angry middle-echelon Anglos who were trapped when the rules changed in midcareer. Most don't want their names used. Westpy is different.

"I'm a little difficult," Westpy warns, puffing on a Winston Light, "I speak what's on my mind, and I don't pull any punches."

He started the department's SWAT team and the marine patrol unit, but as Westpy tells it, when Chief Harms was fired in January 1984, some people in the hierarchy were concerned because he and Harms were fishing buddies. He was considered a *Harms* man, a loyalist to the old administration. Suddenly he found himself working midnight shifts. After 18 years on the force, he couldn't sink any lower.

"I used to put 50, 60 hours a week in my first 17 years....But when you just get jerked around, you say, 'Hey, wait a minute. What am I doing here?'

"I'm tired, as simple as that. You get kicked in the teeth enough...I am going to do my job, no more, no less."

Westpy has seen some astounding changes since he came down from the North to join the department in 1969. Back then the Police Benevolent Association was still white-only, and he refused to join until it became integrated. "I have my prejudices, same as anyone else," Westpy says. "But if any job ever existed where the color of a man's skin shouldn't matter, this is it."

Then came the hiring frenzy of the early '80s, following Mariel and the Liberty City riots. Westpy was not happy with the result: "They got quantity and they didn't get quality....If you had to go out and hire 100 white Anglos tomorrow, and you had to pick the first 100 of them off the street, I'd hate to think what kind of quality you'd get. And that's what happened."

His supervisors, he said, complained about the written reports of the new recruits. The brass wanted him to smooth out the language before turning the reports in. Westpy shook his head at the idea. "What do they expect? You're hiring people who can't read and write. I mean, I always thought my spelling was bad, but to see these guys. The higher-ups complain, and I say, 'I can't teach English.'..."

At first, Westpy said, he swallowed hard and went on. He understood the goal, he understood why it might be necessary to sacrifice some aptitude in language skills to recruit a Miami police force that better reflected Miami: "That's hard to take at first, but you can live with it."

But then, he says, it became clear that the affirmative action wasn't going to stop at recruitment. The new officers left vertical streaks as they leapfrogged over the old guard— men who had come in at about the same time as Westpy and slowly worked their way up to lieutenant and captain. Overnight, sergeants became majors. "What's that tell all the hard-working lieutenants and captains?"

Since Westpy was put on midnights, he has been offered better assignments, but he's turned them down. On midnights, without the brass around, cops can do their work with a minimum of interference. "I've got seven people working for me on midnights. Three of them are black. We all get along very well. I wouldn't trade any of them."

But his loyalty does not extend to the people at the top. He has some good words to say about Chief Dickson, but of the others he says, "There's some there who I seriously doubt if they can do a policeman's job on the street."

THE FRENZY

Miami police scandals have come one after another, each one generally reported as if it had sprung full blown from nowhere. What seems puzzling and chaotic in freeze-frame makes a lot more sense in the context of the turbulence of recent history. The problem with the Miami police, those who know will tell you, is Miami.

Until 1960, Miami was small and Southern. Police officers were white males. They were dedicated guys, most of them, military vets who fell naturally into law enforcement. They worked hard; they played by the rules; they took the tests for promotion, and if they were bright enough, they could expect regular promotions over the years: sergeant, to lieutenant, to captain. Being a cop provided a good, stable life, and the cops liked it that way.

In the '50s, Hispanics were virtually nonexistent in the city and on the force. There *were* black cops, but the department was segregated. Blacks were classified as "patrolmen," a step lower than "officers." They could not attend the police academy; they had no chance for promotion. And the PBA, which was the union bargaining agent, was limited to white males.

Slowly, the department integrated. In the mid-'60s, blacks and whites were teamed in patrol cars. In 1971, black officers sued for membership in the PBA. The U.S. Supreme Court upheld their request. Another lawsuit alleged that blacks had been unfairly denied promotions. The courts agreed. Several blacks were promoted.

But what about Hispanics? In the '70s, Cubans were becoming a majority of the city's residents, and the police didn't seem to be adjusting. In 1974, Mayor Maurice Ferre pointedly illustrated the problem to 100 spectators by calling the police complaint desk and shouting, *"¡Emergencia! ¡Emergencia!"*

The cop responded: "Speak in English."

The U.S. Justice Department began demanding an "affirmative action" program by threatening to cut off all federal funds unless 56 percent of all new cops be from minority groups. Another condition: All new hires would have to be City of Miami residents. This restriction, it was felt, would force the police department to reflect the demographics of the city.

Without much debate, the affirmative action program was agreed upon by city and feds in 1977. At the time, it didn't seem to mean much because the cops were doing little hiring anyway. And in fact, little changed. Two years later, a newspaper editorial decried the fact that the police force was only 9.6 percent Hispanic in a city where Hispanics had become the majority.

In the fall of 1979, the city commission had a Latin majority for the first time. Mayor Ferre announced that "it's simply not acceptable" that the police force be such an Anglo bastion. He proposed hiring not 56 percent minorities, but 80 percent.

Again, the proposal aroused little debate: It seemed both sensible and academic, since the police department was doing little hiring.

Then came 1980: the flood of new immigrants from Mariel, some of whom were career criminals, followed by the Liberty City riots.

The city was torn and trembling. Crime rates were soaring. Everyone was demanding more cops, and many were frankly tired of Anglo cops. The riots, after all, had been sparked by the acquittal of five white Metro police officers who had been accused of beating to death a black insurance executive. Getting more minority police officers seemed not only a way to fight crime but also a way to reduce the roiling anger of the city's minorities.

So it was that a hiring frenzy began. At the time, it seemed the best possible solution: more cops, more minorities. Things could only get better, or so it seemed.

City personnel officials insisted then, and continue to insist today, that they never lowered standards in the new hiring crunch, but, in retrospect, many observers think that it was this rush for new officers, not affirmative action itself, that was to lead to the department's future problems.

Geoffrey Alpert, head of the criminal justice program at the University of Miami, said recently that there was "absolutely" a connection between the mass hiring and the department's current problems: "We're seeing the consequences of that indiscriminate hiring."

Desperate for new officers, police recruiters found a very small pool of talent within the Miami city limits. In effect, the department was being forced to choose not just from minority groups, but from a particularly small sampling of minority groups—lower income, less educated people who were found in the core city. If recruiters could have concentrated on more affluent areas outside the city, such as Carol City or Richmond Heights for blacks, Kendall or West Dade for Hispanics, say recruiters, they might have been able to find better applicants.

Just as bad, from the veteran police officers' view, the personnel people had taken over the testing of applicants. The theory was that the Anglo police officers were prejudiced against minorities, so it would be better for unbiased outsiders to do the testing. The new tests combined the scores of the educational and psychological parts of the exam. The theory was that if someone wasn't equipped psychologically to be a cop (overly aggressive, too timid), the test would weed him out. But in practice, it meant that an applicant who scored low on the educational portion and high on the psychological could still make it onto the police force.

With dismay, police officials learned that recruits were going through the academy with reading levels as low as the fifth or sixth grade. The city had to initiate remedial reading and writing classes for police officers—classes that are still going on.

Within two years, the force went from 650 officers to 1,050, an unprecedented increase. The department was beginning to reflect the ethnic–racial makeup of the city. Many veteran Anglo officers, seeing little chance for promotion, were quitting. Those Anglos who remained—including the bulk of middle-echelon management, the sergeants and lieutenants and captains—became "disillusioned and discouraged," in the words of ex-chief Harms.

Today, two out of five Miami cops are Hispanic. Almost one in five is black. Women make up 11 percent of the force. And the once-dominant Anglo male now makes up only one-third of the force.

(By contrast, when the Metro-Dade police force started its own massive recruitment drive to redress ethnic imbalance in the early '80s, it sought only the best minority applicants possible, wherever it could find them; it even sent a recruiter to Puerto Rico. The entire hiring operation was carried out without the same sense of urgency; today, one-third of the Metro force is minorities.)

In the early '80s, Miami was hiring at such a fast rate that there wasn't time to train recruits properly. More than affirmative action, more than the hiring limitations, many veteran officers believe, it was this lack of training that was to cause problems. It was "a miracle," Chief Dickson said recently, that this frenzied hiring did not lead to "total catastrophe."

Young officers out of the academy only six months became field training officers for rookies. The results were disastrous: In December 1982, Officer Luis Alvarez, hired just the year before and already the subject of five citizen complaints, was showing a rookie through an Overtown video arcade when he ended up shooting Nevell Johnson Jr., age 20. The shooting sparked disturbances that lasted several days, and created a rift between Hispanics and blacks, both in the community and in the police department.

When Officer Alvarez was put on trial for manslaughter, Hispanic officers contributed money for his defense, sat behind him in the courtroom, and even planned a motorcade on his behalf to City Hall before they were warned that it might spark another race riot.

George Adams, then a sergeant and a leader in the black officers group, was offended: "You don't rub it in the face of the black community by standing up for Alvarez like that. That's insensitive. They're saying, 'We're a group of Alvarezes, and the same thing could happen again tomorrow.'"

Blacks versus whites, Hispanics versus blacks, Anglos versus everybody. The city commission was changing, and the pressures were mounting. This new mixture of politics and law enforcement did not make a healthy concoction. When Chief Harms found that Sgt. Sebastian Aguirre was going with other Hispanic officers to talk to commissioners at Dinner Key about more promotions for Hispanics, the chief accused Aguirre of trying to get him fired. The chief then turned the tables, firing Aguirre, who had to initiate a lawsuit in order to get his job back.

Chief Harms was trapped between warring factions: promoting far more minorities than the old Anglo officers wanted, but not enough to placate Howard Gary, the black city manager. Harms, struggling to survive, was getting into power politics. In January 1984, he lost. During a frenzied night of intrigue and paranoia, Gary ended up firing Harms in a late-night phone call.

The new chief was Herbert Breslow, a steady and taciturn cop. Breslow quickly followed the city manager's suggestion by doubling the number of top brass, including more Hispanics, blacks and a woman in the top echelon. For the first time, the force had an integrated hierarchy that came close to mirroring the community. Some civic leaders praised the promotions, but within the police department, attitudes were decidedly mixed.

The problem was *who* among the minorities were getting the promotions. Seven officers were leapfrogged from sergeant to major, bypassing a large group of lieutenants and captains. Many of these leapfroggers were politically connected: Jack Sullivan, an Anglo who was a former head of the predominantly white Fraternal Order of Police; Mary Stair, an organizer of the women's officer group; George Adams, a leader in the black benevolent association. These three leaped ahead of minority officers who were higher ranked but apparently lacked the political connections.

Former Miami police colonel Richard Witt, now Hollywood's chief of police, says the leapfrog promotions sent "a message loud and clear. The message: 'If you are going to advance your career, you can study, work hard, do well on the tests, or you can become political, standing up for your group, so your group will stand up for you when it comes time for promotions.'"

Racial–ethnic strife, in other words, had become institutionalized in the department. A cop had to stand firm with his group, opposing the appeals of the other groups, or he (or she) would have a rough time getting promoted.

Many of the rank-and-file—blacks, Hispanics and women, as well as Anglo males— thought the promotions were so cynically political that some lost faith in their ability to climb on merit alone.

Officer Rene Landa, a young Hispanic: "Why did they pick the heads of the organizations? Because they assumed that if the leaders of these organizations were happy, then everybody would be happy. But how are the men supposed to feel when they see all these lieutenants and captains passed over?"

Chief Breslow lasted barely a year before being squeezed out by City Hall. On Jan. 9, 1985, a press conference was called to announce the appointment of Clarence Dickson to the post of police chief. Dickson, the first black to hold the title, stood up and immediately displayed the insecurity that went with the job of being Miami's No. I cop: "Even if I'm not here next week," he said, "I reached the top."

Dickson's first act was to promote an Anglo and a Puerto Rican to assistant chief posts, and to retain a Cuban as an assistant. He said he was doing so to promote harmony in Miami. He might as well have added…in the Miami Police Department.

THE GAME

Pig Bowl IV: The annual football game between Miami cops and Metro cops. A beige Mercedes limo delivers two of the fabulous Bee Gees, and a helicopter plops down in the middle of the football field with the fabulous Don Johnson (dressed in no-earth-tone lime-and-white), but for the **cognoscente**, the truly interesting action is taking place on the sidelines.

Over on the Metro side are the "Deputy Dawgs," a good-old-boy cracker kind of name, fitting a department that is still two-thirds Anglo. Pacing behind the Dawgs' bench is Ray Bedal, a squat detective from the Organized Crime Bureau, who's dressed as a perfect "Boss Hawg," in white suit and white cowboy hat, just like the character on the old *Dukes of Hazzard* show. In case one misses the team's country leaning, ol' Boss is being trailed by a young lady in cowboy hat and fringed mini-dress.

But what's most interesting about the Metro side of the field is what's missing: politicians. None of the Metro commissioners are mingling with the team, none are obvious in the stands.

Now, look over at the Miami police side. This team has a nice neutral name, the Force, fitting for a multiethnic, multiracial department. Here the politicians are obvious, and it is here the knowledgeable ones in the stands are watching carefully, much the way observers in Moscow look at the positioning of the top pols on the Red Square podium.

To the right of the bench, Mayor Xavier Suarez roams in a blue Force jersey and designer jeans, chatting with Chief Clarence Dickson, who's wearing an off-white cowboy hat with *his* Force jersey and designer jeans.

Farther down the bench, City Manager Cesar Odio is chatting with Michael Mahoney, an assistant chief whom Dickson recently forced into retirement. The rumor mill has it that Dickson had feared Mahoney was trying to sabotage him and get his job. And here he is, back for the game.

"What is *he* doing here?" several whisper in the stands. Is Cesar Odio smiling at him to be polite? Or does this mean something bad for Dickson, who is staying over on the right-hand side of the bench, 20 yards from Mahoney. And why is nobody talking to Col. Guillermo Zamora, directly behind the bench? Is it because Zamora has fallen out of political favor, or is it because he's supposedly one of the FBI's top targets?

Meanwhile, up in the stands, old J. L. Plummer is holding court. Here's the city commissioner who loves being an amateur cop, patrolling with the cops at night, and who's sitting up there with him? None other than Col. Walter Martinez. What's *that* supposed to mean? Martinez is one of the names on the FBI list, too, but he's also said to be very close to the city manager, and now if he's close to Plummer as well…

The knowledgeable spectators in the stands are watching all this, because they know how much politics influences the Miami Police Department, and to them the political choreography on the sidelines becomes much more important than the game.

"We do feel there is too much politics," Sgt. Williams of the black officers group will explain later. "It's hard to tell who's running the police department when you have that pressure from City Hall."

On this, at least, the different factions of cops agree: There's too much interference from the City Hall at Dinner Key, and too many police officers who try to play politics.

"That's true," says Sgt. Sebastian Aguirre. "There should be only one politician in the department—the chief."

But in fact, there are many politicians, and word spreads quickly through the department when, say, an ambitious captain has breakfast at a Denny's with civic leaders from northeast Miami. So-and-so was seen at a Kiwanis Club meeting with Commissioner such-and-such. Col. X knows a contractor who's a big contributor to Commissioner Y. And so it goes. Rumors abound that even low-ranking officers have frequent contact with city commissioners. "And then," says Franklin Foote, a psychologist at the Urban Studies Institute, which has been hired by the police department as a consultant, "you have your middle echelon saying, 'Well, I better be careful when I supervise him, because he might complain to a commissioner.'"

THE MOOD

How does all of this turmoil and discontent on the police force affect the Miami citizen? Is it making the city a more dangerous place to live? The crime stats, which rise and fall with no clear pattern, prove little. George Kirkham, a criminologist at Florida State, says,

"Crime is an independent kind of thing. It's going to go up and down, regardless of what the police department does. Unemployment, poverty—all sorts of variables affect crime."

A more complicated question is how cops behave in a demoralized force with uncertain leadership such as Miami's. Here we are dealing with speculation, really, because most officers work alone in patrol cars, their hour-by-hour activities unsupervised by anyone.

Leonard Territo, criminologist at the University of South Florida: "It's no different than any other employee who's unhappy with his work....For instance, a patrolman decides not to take action. Most times, when he decides not to do something, he probably won't be discovered."

Ken Nelson, head of Miami's FOP: "If they observe a violation, they're going to do something about it. That's an inner instinct. But let's say nothing is happening, and so if they're feeling down, maybe the officer is patrolling over on Biscayne Boulevard, where he's not going to see anything, rather than on Third Avenue and 13th Street, in Overtown, where a lot more crime takes place. In other words, he's not out aggressively looking for things."

Another sergeant, who doesn't want to be identified: "The anticipated level of service is not as high as it should be. You get the idea, 'Don't make waves, don't do things that could make trouble.' So you go park the car somewhere. You answer the call, but you don't do anything else. The extra patrol, the extra investigation doesn't get done." The officer doesn't check on the hardware store that has been frequently burglarized, or doesn't scare the crack dealers off their typical corner. If he's in a foul mood, adds the sergeant, "he's also more likely to write traffic tickets. "The s--- flows downhill."

Dick Witt, the ex-colonel: "There's a tendency to go through the motions. 'I'll go up one street and down another.' Don't look for things, very brief on reports. You don't go back through alleys. You don't beat the bushes. These guys on the corner—you figure you won't check them out. There's whores on the boulevard, so what?"

THE GRIPE

"Perhaps," the attorney announced, standing at the podium in the semi-circular federal courtroom, "the greatest ally in this case has been history."

Robert Klausner, attorney for the Fraternal Order of Police, was speaking in the courtroom of James W. Kehoe, U.S. district judge. He was offering up facts and figures to show how far the Miami Police Department had come since the 1977 consent decree, the instrument for affirmative action through hiring and rapid promotion of minorities.

Behind him sat an earnest young man: Ken Nelson, the current FOP president. Back in 1981, when he had expressed interest in becoming a Miami cop—as he explained later—"they told me not to apply, I wouldn't make it, because I was a white Anglo male."

Now, he was spearheading the union's fight to get the consent decree abolished.

The battle had begun a year ago, when FOP conducted a vote of all Miami police officers. The majority voted to ask the federal court to set aside the decree. Some officers cried foul. They claimed the ballot had been confusing, that a yes vote meant an officer was saying no to the decree.

A second vote was held, but the result was the same: 307–204 against the decree.

The vote baffled those who had predicted it would be defeated along ethnic lines since two-thirds of the department are minorities. But when you talk to the rank and file, you find the distaste for the consent decree is quite simple. Many young Hispanics and women, as well as white non-Latin males, are fed up with the Byzantine promotion practices.

The rather astounding truth is, nobody in the department—including the chief—really understands who gets promoted and why.

Everyone knows that the highest scores don't always get promoted. Everybody knows that from a list of 40 candidates for sergeant, No. 1 (often an Anglo male) may get picked, plus, say, No. 11 (Hispanic male), No. 19 (a black) and No. 29 (a female). That is an accepted part of affirmative action, the leapfrogging of minorities over higher-scoring Anglo males.

But what confuses virtually everybody in the department is *how* these minorities are selected, a crucial point in a department where the minorities are actually the majority.

Women are considered a minority group for purposes of affirmative action, but on a recent sergeant's exam, one white female officer was shocked to learn that a minority male who scored lower than she was promoted, and she wasn't. "How did they decide?" the officer asked. No one could tell her.

Likewise, sometimes a Hispanic who ranks, say, 22, is promoted, and a Hispanic who ranked 15 is not. What's the rationale in that?

"We don't like jumping numbers," says Officer Rene Landa. "It's unfair."

Chief Dickson laments the number-jumping and says he is trying to control it. But, he says, he has little control over promotion. As strange and misguided as it seems, that's the system.

"The police department does not have enough play in how that system works," he says. The city's personnel department, he says, sends him a list of eight candidates for an opening: the top five scores on the test, plus three minority scores. He doesn't know how the minorities are selected, but he has to select one of the eight, basing his decisions "on an affirmative action goal I have to meet each year."

To the troops, that doesn't sound like much of an explanation, and that's why many of them would like to go to a system in which the highest scores get the promotions. Period. That's true even of many young Hispanics who could expect to be favored by the consent decree.

"It should be based on qualifications," says Officer Jose Bao. "That's it. If you're good, you're good."

THE OUTSIDERS

The Overtown "mini-station" is a glass-windowed storefront in a small mall. Only a half-mile from the main police station, it was opened after Officer Alvarez killed Nevell Johnson in 1982. It is staffed predominantly with black officers, who have acquired a very noticeable "us versus them" attitude toward the rest of the force.

A report had come in that a short guy with a multicolored cap and dreadlocks was selling crack on 12th Street. The officers were waiting for their sergeant to go make the bust. Until he came, they talked, boasting about their mini-station. It was a matter of pride to them that residents will tell them things (and show them stolen property) after refusing to cooperate with cops from the main station.

But as far as the department overall was concerned, the officers didn't quite trust it. The chief, they said, may be black, but the system is still white.

Said Officer C. T. Jones to the white journalist: "You look at 'Anglos' and 'Hispanics.' *We* are looking at *white men*. They can change their name, they can change their accent. I still know what I'm looking at."

Jones may as well have added, "...the oppressors."

Jones has been with the department for 16 years. Walter Byars and Michael Bryant are younger; both were hired after 1980. And both feel that the department is still a tough place for blacks.

Bryant: "Our integrity is constantly challenged, and we feel we're always being suspected."

Byars: "They hired us to be one color. Blue. But as soon as you get out of the police academy, you're different." Byars felt he had been given reprimands and had been "set up" by white supervisors because he was black. He said that when he was a rookie, he called up the station and said he couldn't make his scheduled court appearance because his wife was in the hospital. The guy took the message and hung up. "I did it three times," says Byars, "and I was up for suspension."

It turned out he should have called the court liaison office, too. He had been taught that in the academy, but he had been taught a lot of things in the academy, he said, and he couldn't be expected to remember everything. A sympathetic veteran, he believed, would have helped him out by reminding him to call the liaison office.

His conclusion: "We don't have enough black officers training black officers."

That's one reason why they are angered by the attempts of the FOP to do away with the consent decree.

"We have a lot of catching up to do," said Byars. "How can you make up in 10 years what's been going on for 100 years?"

Under Chief Dickson, Byars added, "things have improved 70, 80 percent. Now I feel I have a voice in things....But you know what scares me: How long is this going to last?"

All three said they believed that the missing marijuana and the stolen $150,000 were not the acts of common crooks.

"These latest episodes," said Jones, "have been to embarrass the chief. It's a conspiracy. It was made to look like they were doing it for the pot, but they were embarrassing the chief."

Byars looked back at a large photo of Chief Dickson that was hanging from the rear wall. Underneath was a caption, more plaintive than commanding:

"Support our chief."

THE CHIEF

Some of the older Anglo officers will grumble about Clarence Dickson, about his not really understanding the department, about his not being a firm enough commander, but most people have much more neutral feelings about Miami's first black police chief. They say he's a nice guy.

Geoffrey Alpert, director of the criminal justice program at the University of Miami, puts it this way: "I don't know anyone who dislikes Clarence Dickson. He's a nice person."

That statement, like most statements about Dickson, seems to beg for an **ellipsis,** an indication that there is a sentence left unsaid, a "but...."

Talk to rank-and-file cops in the department—Anglo, black and Hispanic—and most will say that the problems with the department aren't really his fault. But Dickson is the man at the top, and these days he acts like a besieged man.

So many negative things have happened—the missing $150,000, the missing marijuana, the looming FBI investigation—that he responds sternly to any problem. When a stripper was sneaked into the building for an officer's birthday celebration, it might have been worth a simple reprimand, but when the media learned of the incident, Dickson felt compelled to call for a full-blown Internal Review investigation, as he did again a few days later when a sergeant on the midnight shift was discovered in a van in the parking lot with a secretary.

Dickson's once **jaunty** individualism has disappeared, his broad-brimmed cowboy hat replaced by a no-nonsense chief's-style hat with gold braid on the brim. The sartorial change occurred shortly after the marijuana was reported missing. When told that many young black officers believe the theft was created to embarrass him, he says: "I've thought the same thing. Let me put it this way, whoever did it wasn't trying to endear themselves to me." Taking the pot, he says, was more than a theft. "It violated the department. It *assaulted* the department."

There have been persistent rumors—into the middle of February, as this is being written—that Dickson may be retiring soon, fleeing while a "deputy administrator" is brought in by the city manager, allegedly to help the chief out.

Several weeks ago, a journalist asked Dickson whether he was contemplating retirement. "Almost anyone in my shoes," he said slowly, "would look back at what's happened and wake up one morning and say, 'Who needs this?' That has crossed my mind....But that's just a reactive response that provides some temporary relief....That's why they wrote that song, *Take this Job and Shove It,* I guess. Everybody likes that song, too, but everybody don't do it."

This is a nondenial denial, as it were, and publicly he says he welcomes the new deputy. "Originally, I think the word was out that this person was going to be the interim chief. Or the heir apparent...I don't know what lies behind the green door. In somebody's mind, that may be what the whole thing is about. But, ah, you know, I am dealing with, with honorable men, and with, uh, people who I trust. I know that is not the manager's intent. If it was, he would have told me."

THE BAD EXAMPLE

In a conference room, a half-dozen young Hispanic police officers gathered to talk about being Hispanic and police officers at a time when they are seeing a considerable number of their colleagues being arrested.

They do not like it, they say, not at all. They are especially angry about the seven so-called Miami River Cops, who have faced charges of dope-dealing and murder.

"It gives the perception," said Rene Landa, "that all of us are dirty."

"You can't deny," said officer Luis Diazlay, "that the seven River Cops are Hispanic. But don't forget that the two lead investigators on the case were Latins."

All of them were tired of the negative publicity that the department has been receiving, and two said they are worried that embittered higher-ups in the department are trying to destroy the chief by leaking any negative information to the media. "Someone in control," said Landa, "wants the administration to look like dirt."

The news that the 3½-month River Cops trial had ended with no verdict was a bitter shock to all of these young cops.

"All of us wanted a verdict," said Diaslay. "I was really upset."

Several others nodded. No verdict meant a new trial, and a new trial meant more headlines about corrupt Hispanic cops—a kind of publicity they would rather have behind them. The group shuddered at the idea that acquitted River Cops might someday come back to work.

"They would be completely ostracized," said Landa.

THE RIVER COPS

Though 75 Miami police officers have been arrested since 1980, it is the seven who have been dubbed "the Miami River Cops" who have been the focus of attention. They have been charged with big-time dope dealing, and three of them were charged with murder, which was altered to "violating the civil rights" of the dead victims when the case was moved to federal court.

They have become a central issue to the problems of the department: Were they "bad apples" who were mistakenly hired during the rush to integrate the department at any cost? Were they good guys led astray by the temptations of drug-saturated Miami? Did the department somehow screw up in handling them? Typically, in trying to point to where the mistakes were made, the blame is distributed according to factions.

Let's look at the evidence. All of the River Cops were young and Hispanic, hired during the early '80s.

According to two sources familiar with the River Cops investigation, speaking on condition they not be identified, one of the River Cops, Roman Rodriguez, had admitted on his application form that he had used cocaine and marijuana during high school. That alone would not have disqualified him. But more ominously, Rodriguez had been fired from a previous job at Florida Power & Light—a job he held for only three months—

accused of falsifying meter reports. This rather amazing information appears to have been completely overlooked.

The River Cops, however, weren't exactly dummies. In reading comprehension tests given after they were hired, Roman Rodriguez was shown to be quite bright, reading at the level of a college freshman. Two others, Armando Estrada and Ricardo Aleman, were reading at high-school level, which is respectable for a police recruit. At least one, however, had lower grades: Osvaldo Coello was reading at an eighth-grade level.

A former Miami High student who went to school with Coello and Armando Garcia said they were "dedicated, pretty good guys," clean-cut jock types who didn't do drugs. The former classmate, who didn't want to be named, never would have envisioned that either would be charged with a crime. "I really blame the system," he says. "They give these guys something like 14 or 16 weeks of training, and then they put them out there where they can make twice their salary just by turning their heads the other way."

Once on the police force, the River Cops' reputations varied. Rudy Arias was thought by several of his supervisors to be a great officer, and he had been named an "officer of the month."

Several of the seven gravitated to the midnight shift. Maj. Aniball E. Ibrahim, commander of the midnight shift during some of the period the River cops were there: "They were very productive at one point. I don't think they were hired in error. Very assertive, very aggressive."

Too aggressive, it turned out. Armando Garcia, for one, amassed a series of complaints from citizens about his tough behavior. Garcia, says Maj. Ibrahim, was a particular problem. "His outlook was basically primitive." He had "no tact," and people complained that he could be "rude, discourteous, offensive."

Over time, says Ibrahim, he saw that "these individuals had changed a lot....They had values they lost, for one reason or another."

Ibrahim blamed the change on an Anglo supervisor's philosophy of maintaining ultra-firm discipline by handing out reprimands for the smallest of infractions. "The philosophy existing in that section was very damaging to young officers....I think a lot of their self-pride and self-esteem was lost."

Sgt. Eddie Blanco, who supervised one of the River Cops and knew several others, agrees with Ibrahim that the system of reprimands—the department's efforts to come to grips with the problems brought on by rapid hiring and advancement of less experienced officers—angered these young cops. Garcia, especially, was angry about one complaint against him, brought by a suspended Beach cop, who primly accused him of using a 12-letter word. "He always brought that up," said Sgt. Blanco. "'Can you believe it?' That's what he kept saying."

Other cops, however, think it was lack of supervision that caused problems. In their trials, testimony has revealed that while on duty they would often frequent a couple of bars where dopers hung out, or meet doper contacts in parking lots. At least one cop, according to testimony, used to have sexual intercourse with women in the back seat of his patrol car. And one cop was said to have gone to the station on his day off and borrowed a police car and a police radio to carry out one ripoff.

George Adams, a black retired major: "We have a responsibility to supervise, and when you have supervisors who don't do that, then you run into problems. We depend on Anglo males for most of that supervision. If they feel disenfranchised, they don't care. So they let the officers on the street run amok."

Sgt. Aguirre, head of the Hispanic officers group, says that some of River Cops' supervisors were Hispanic, not Anglo, but he agrees: "Overall, I would have to place some of the blame on the supervisors. If you supervise a person right, you can't do half the s--- those River Cops did, or were alleged to have done."

One ominous note: Testimony at the River Cops trial revealed that, on one ripoff, there were 11 uniformed cops. Only seven were on trial.

THE MIRANDA RITES

During the mass hiring, one of the cops doing background investigations—checking the pasts of applicants to see if they were qualified to be police officers—was named Joaquin "Jack" Miranda. During an undercover drug investigation called "Operation Snow White," Miranda was seen associating with persons who were ultimately arrested on drug charges.

When detectives questioned Miranda about his connections with the alleged dopers, he refused to answer questions. On Jan. 15, 1983, he was fired.

Dick Witt, a colonel with the Miami police before he became chief of the Hollywood force, says that investigators, appalled by the idea that one of the department's gatekeepers may have been a bad cop, went over Miranda's background files. "We uncovered at least six," he says, in which Miranda seemed to have omitted negative information about an applicant that should have been in the file, including information about previous drug usage. Worse, Miranda appeared to be a "gung-ho cop," and often did background checks to help out his associates—checks to which the associate, not Miranda, signed his name. "So we had no idea," says Witt, "what he could have been up to....What we have here is a bunch of time bombs ticking."

Ken Harrison, who worked with Witt during that time and is now a colonel in charge of internal security, says he recalls that Miranda had indeed omitted information from files, but that he doesn't remember the missing facts to have been all that important. "To the best of my recollection," he says, "no one was hired who should not have been hired."

Col. Harrison says he can't check Miranda's internal security file to see exactly what the investigation showed: The file is among those taken by the FBI as part of its probe into corruption.

READING AND RIGHTING

Whether the mass hiring of the early '80s has planted the seeds of corruption in Miami's police is still debatable. But the general degradation of police reading and writing skills is not. Consider Basic Law Enforcement class 106, which went through the police academy last fall. Of 29 students from Miami P.D., 16 flunked the course in Report Writing. All those who flunked must go through the remedial writing course. (Sally Gross-Farina, an administrator at the academy, says that Metro, by contrast, will have only four or five in a class fail Report Writing.)

Mistakes in live field reports are legend. Captain Ivo Alvarez recalls a young officer who reported that a victim had been "bitten on the head," when the person had been beaten. A judge recalls pondering over a report in which the officer said he had "dried fried" a weapon. He meant, "dry fired." Another cop recalls a traffic accident in which one of the cars left "squid marks." An assistant state attorney was asked to prosecute a case of "attempted morder."

Such mistakes can be humorous, unless the case ends up before a jury in court. Call up three circuit court judges, and all three will say (upon the condition that their names not be used) that Miami cops are inferior to Metro cops in the quality of their reports and their testimony on the witness stand.

Judge one: "The quality of cases is poor and very often the police officer is bright enough to know they're poor, and so they gild the lily on the witness stand." Such tactics, he said, often turn off both judge and jury. The reason for Miami P.D.'s problems, according to the judge: "When you take people based on ethnic or racial background, rather than skill, let's face it, hiring standards have been lowered."

Judge two says that he thinks the main reason that Miami cops seem to be inferior witnesses is that many of them lack the experience of Metro's men. "Metro has, without a doubt, a lot more experienced officers."

Judge three: "Affirmative action killed them, without a doubt. They have an awful lot of officers who don't pay attention in court, who don't show up." One example: in a first-degree murder case, a cop came into court on his day off in sneakers, jeans and a T-shirt. He didn't even have his case file. He recited a few thoughts from memory, then stepped down. The judge has also seen cops forget to bring the murder weapon to court, saying they would have to go back to the station to get the weapon. "That happens a lot also."

THE PAYOFF

Now that we have seen the opinions and the evidence, the question remains, what happened to Miami P.D.? How does all of this fit together? How does the corruption connect with the affirmative action programs, the turmoil, the racial–ethnic tensions, the political interference, the abrupt departure of two chiefs and the tenuous existence of a third?

It is the totality of this instability, some observers feel, this lack of firm control over right and wrong, that has led to the department's problems.

Listen to Larry Sherman, a professor of criminology at the University of Maryland and author of two books on police corruption, who believes that all the turmoil at Miami P.D. is linked:

"It fits together in a very coherent way. Faced with the enormous temptation that you have with the drug traffic in Miami, the only way that a police department can withstand that is to have a very strong organization, with very clear values and procedures to control everything....But just at the time when the drug trade and the temptation was substantially increasing, you saw a total revolution within the department....The politicians became involved in a rather chaotic way....The values were changing, and no one was sure to what, and then there was so much cynicism among the police that no one knew who would be in control the next day, and so you had an atmosphere where corruption would flourish."

Dedicated cops, of course, will tell you that there is no excuse for corruption, that you shouldn't be able to blame it on hiring practices, or lack of education, or poor supervision. Thou shalt not be a crook. Period.

Sgt. Aguirre puts it this way: "If you have a problem with the system, you change the system. You don't go around and start ripping people off."

Which is the way that cops are trained to think, for good reason. No one wants a cop who makes little psycho-socio-economic excuses for crime.

Still, it may not be that simple.

Dick Watt, the former colonel who left to become chief of the Hollywood police: "Put yourself in place of a young police officer. He reads at a fifth-grade level. Hard work and merit mean nothing in promotion. All the messages are: There's no reward for being a good guy."

These may be the words of an embittered Anglo—one does not hear blacks and Hispanics talking like this, and several cops point out that the arrested Hispanics, such as the River Cops, actually had the most to gain from the new affirmative action programs. As Leonard Territo, the criminology professor at the University of South Florida, says: "A guy doesn't get a promotion and start stealing money from the property room—it doesn't work that way."

However, George Kirkham, the FSU criminologist, says that the constant gut-churning changes in the department can create "a pervasive demoralizing in the department, which can lead to not caring about doing good police work, and it's a short step from not giving service to the public to not caring about the public to, for those who are prone to it, saying, 'What the hell, I'm going to do some sort of taking.'"

THE FUTURE

With all its problems, this much can be said for the Miami Police Department: In Dade County, we have gone more than four years without a police-inspired riot. That would be a bizarre measure of success in most cities, but in Miami it can be considered something of a triumph. These days, when a cluster of Miami P.D. squad cars gather at a crime scene, it's almost a certainty that some of the officers will be black. The chance of an all-white group of cops chasing a black man in a black neighborhood, à la McDuffie, is virtually nil.

Many cops praise Chief Dickson for getting rid of some of the top-heavy administration and cutting back on the amount of paperwork that was choking the lower levels, though one does occasionally still see such bureaucratic horrors as a 20-page departmental memo sent by a major to recommend a five-page *Reader's Digest* article on how to make your house safe from burglars.

Both City Manager Cesar Odio and Mayor Xavier Suarez concede that there has been too much political interference in the past, but they believe the police department is on the upswing.

"Morale in the department couldn't be much lower than it was," says the mayor. "And it's been getting better. The department has had a succession of catastrophic occurrences. They were overwhelmed by Mariel and then the riots and demonstrations, and then all the new police officers and the consent decree."

Within both the police department and City Hall, there are strong tendencies toward changing the hiring and promotion systems.

The Urban Studies Advisory Committee, a group made up of outside consultants and police officials, has issued a report asking for improved hiring practices. The committee requested that the city's personnel management people, who administer the pre-hiring tests, no longer merge academic and psychological scores into one uncertain number, but instead "identify individuals who possess above average intellectual and academic skills."

Indeed, a survey by city personnel people has shown that applicants from within the city score considerably lower on the application tests than do other applicants. Because of that, the city recently did something it hadn't done since the consent decree was signed a decade ago: It began looking for the best applicants statewide. Recruiting teams have been sent to Tallahassee and Daytona Beach, particularly seeking qualified black males at Florida A&M University and Bethune Cookman.

And the city is moving on the controversy over promotions. City Manager Odio is saying that, because of the widespread dissatisfaction, he would like to find a new system that "makes sense to everybody and would include promotions for minorities." He says he has three assistants trying to come up with a plan, but it seems unlikely they will develop anything that could mollify everyone.

Despite the positive signs, there are some new negatives. Within the department, it seems that the lines of battle have shifted. During the recent court hearings on the consent decree, there was a notable absence: No attorney from the Hispanic Officers Association was present. The traditionally Anglo FOP was on one side, the black group's attorney on the other, but the Hispanics were sitting it out, which in effect meant support for the FOP. As Officer Jones said at the Overtown mini-station, the battle within the police department seems to be returning to a struggle between blacks and whites.

The other problem, says Chief Dickson—the *real* problem—may well be political. In the past four years, there have been four city managers. "Each of these people," says the chief, "were strong and capable city managers and they left their impact on the police department, like all city managers do. And each time one came in, they struck a staggering blow to the police department, and by the time we recovered from that staggering blow, another powerful manager came in to strike a staggering blow to us, and then another. [Chiefs] Harms, Breslow, Dickson—all recipients of staggering blows. And also sending a tremor throughout the department, which reached all the way down to the police officers on the street.

"We've...been trying to deal with this trauma, and trying to steady the organization, and I hope we don't get dealt a staggering blow in the near future, just when we begin to get our feet on the ground...."

QUESTIONS FOR DISCUSSION

1. Discuss the ethnic tension and racial distrust in the Miami police departments. Utilize specific examples from Dorschner's article to augment your discussion.
2. Explain how the corruption in the Miami police department was related to issues of affirmative action, racial tension, and political interference. Cite examples to support your answer.
3. According to the author, the future of the Miami police department looks both positive and negative. Discuss these positive and negative aspects.

APPLICATIONS

1. Dorschner's article states that "no one wants a cop who makes little psycho-socio-economic excuses for crime." What is meant by this statement? Do you agree or disagree? Why?
2. Suppose that you have been asked as an expert to make recommendations as to how a police department such as Miami's might reduce racial and ethnic tension among its officers. What would be your recommendations?

Police and Communities
The Quiet Revolution

George L. Kelling

INTRODUCTION

A quiet revolution is reshaping American policing. Police in dozens of communities are returning to foot patrol. In many communities, police are surveying citizens to learn what they believe to be their most serious neighborhood problems. Many police departments are finding alternatives to rapidly responding to the majority of calls for service. Many departments are targeting resources on citizen fear of crime by concentrating on disorder. Organizing citizens' groups has become a priority in many departments. Increasingly, police departments are looking for means to evaluate themselves on their contribution to the quality of neighborhood life, not just crime statistics. Are such activities the business of policing? In a **crescendo**, police are answering yes.

True, such activities contrast with popular images of police: the "thin blue line" separating plundering villains from peaceful residents and storekeepers, and racing through city streets in high-powered cars with sirens wailing and lights flashing. Yet, in city after city, a new vision of policing is taking hold of the imagination of progressive police and gratified citizens. Note the 1987 report of the Philadelphia Task Force. Dismissing the notion of police as Philadelphia's professional defense against crime, and its residents as passive recipients of police ministrations, the report affirms new police values:

> Because the current strategy for policing Philadelphia emphasizes crime control and neglects the Department's need to be accountable to the public and for a partnership it, the task force recommends: The police commissioner should formulate an explicit mission statement for the Department that will guide planning and operations toward a strategy of *"community"* or *"problem solving"* policing. Such a statement should be developed in consultation with the citizens of Philadelphia and should reflect their views. [Emphases added.]

These themes—problem solving, community policing, consultation, partnership, accountability—have swept through American policing so swiftly that Harvard University's Professor Mark H. Moore has noted that "We in academe have to scramble to keep track of developments in policing." Professor Herman Goldstein of the University of Wisconsin sees police as "having turned a corner" by emphasizing community accountability and problem solving.

THE NEW MODEL OF POLICING

What corner has been turned? What are these changes that are advancing through policing?

Broken Windows

In February 1982, James Q. Wilson and I published an article in *Atlantic* known popularly as "Broken Windows." We made three points.

1. Neighborhood disorders, drunks, panhandling, youth gangs, prostitution, and other urban incivilities—creates citizen fear.

2. Just as unrepaired broken windows can signal to people that nobody cares about a building and lead to more serious vandalism, untended disorderly behavior can also signal that nobody cares about the community and lead to more serious disorder and crime. Such signals—untended property, disorderly persons, drunks, obstreperous youth, etc.—both create fear in citizens and attract predators.

3. If police are to deal with disorder to reduce fear and crime, they must rely on citizens for legitimacy and assistance.

"Broken Windows" gave voice to sentiments felt both by citizens and police. It recognized a major change in the focus of police. Police had believed that they should deal with serious crime, yet were frustrated by lack of success. Citizens conceded to police that crime was a problem, but were more concerned about daily incivilities that disrupted and often destroyed neighborhood social, commercial, and political life. "We were trying to get people to be concerned about crime problems," says Darrel Stephens, former Chief in Newport News and now Executive Director of the Police Executive Research Forum, "never understanding that daily living issues had a much greater impact on citizens and commanded their time and attention."

Many police officials, however, believed the broken windows **metaphor** went further. For them, it not only suggested the focus of police work (disorder, for example), it also suggested major modifications in the overall strategy of police departments. What are some of these strategic changes?

Defense of a Community

Police are a neighborhood's primary defense against disorder and crime, right? This orthodoxy has been the basis of police strategy for a generation. What is the police job? Fighting crime. How do they do this? Patrolling in cars, responding to calls for service, and investigating crimes. What is the role of citizens in all of this? Supporting police by calling them if trouble occurs and by being good witnesses.

But using our metaphor, let us again ask the question of whether police are the primary defense against crime and disorder. Are police the "thin blue line" defending neighborhoods and communities? Considering a specific example might help us answer this question. For example, should police have primary responsibility for controlling a neighborhood youth who, say, is bullying other children?

Of course not. The first line of defense in a neighborhood against a troublesome youth is the youth's family. Even if the family is failing, our immediate answer would not be to involve police. Extended family—aunts, uncles, grandparents—might become involved. Neighbors and friends (of both the parents and youth) often offer assistance. The youth's church or school might become involved.

On occasion police will be called: Suppose that the youth is severely bullying other children to the point of injuring them. A bullied child's parents call the police. Is the bully's family then relieved of responsibility? Are neighbors? The school? Once police are called, are neighbors relieved of their duty to be **vigilant** and protect their own or other neighbors' children? Does calling police relieve teachers of their obligation to be alert and protect children from assault? The answer to all these questions is no. We expect families, neighbors, teachers, and others to be responsible and prudent.

If we believe that community institutions are the first line of defense against disorder and crime, and the source of strength for maintaining the quality of life, what should the strategy of police be? The old view was that they were a community's professional defense against crime and disorder: Citizens should leave control of crime and maintenance of order to police. The new strategy is that police are to stimulate and buttress a community's ability to produce attractive neighborhoods and protect them against predators. Moreover, in communities that are wary of strangers, police serve to help citizens tolerate and protect outsiders who come into their neighborhoods for social or commercial purposes.

But what about neighborhoods in which things have gotten out of hand—where, for example, predators like drug dealers take over and openly and outrageously deal drugs and threaten citizens? Clearly, police must play a leading role defending such communities. Should they do so on their own, however?

Police have tried in the past to control neighborhoods plagued by predators without involving residents. Concerned, for example, about serious street crime, police made youths, especially minority youths, the targets of aggressive field interrogations. The results, in the United States during the 1960's and more recently in England during the early 1980's, were disastrous. Crime was largely unaffected. Youths already hostile to police became even more so. Worst of all, good citizens became estranged from police.

Citizens in neighborhoods plagued by crime and disorder were disaffected because they simply would not have police they neither knew nor authorized whizzing in and out of their neighborhoods "takin' names and kickin' ass." Community relations programs were beside the point. Citizens were in no mood to surrender control of their neighborhoods to remote and officious police who showed them little respect. Police are the first line of defense in a neighborhood? Wrong—citizens are!

Defending Communities—From Incidents to Problems

The strategy of assisting citizens maintain the quality of life in their neighborhoods dramatically improves on the former police strategy. To understand why, one has to understand in some detail how police work has been conducted in the past. Generally, the business of police for the past 30 years has been responding to calls for service.

For example, a concerned and frightened citizen calls police about a neighbor husband and wife who are fighting. Police come and intervene. They might separate the couple, urge them to get help, or, if violence had occurred, arrest the perpetrator. But basically, police try to resolve the incident and get back into their patrol cars so they are available for the next call. Beat officers may well know that this household has been the subject of 50 or 100 calls to the police department during the past year. In fact, they have known intuitively what researchers Glenn Pierce in Boston and Lawrence Sherman in Minneapolis have confirmed through research: fewer than 10 percent of the addresses calling for police service generate over 60 percent of the total calls for service during a given year.

Indeed, it is very likely that the domestic dispute described above is nothing new for the disputing couple, the neighbors, or the police. More likely than not, citizens have previously called police and they have responded. And, with each call to police, it becomes more likely that there will be another.

This **atomistic** response to incidents acutely frustrates patrol officers. Herman Goldstein describes this frustration: "Although the public looks at the average officer as a powerful authority figure, the officer very often feels impotent because he or she is dealing with things for which he or she has no solution. Officers believe this makes them look silly in the eyes of the public." But, given the routine of police work, officers have had no alternative to their typical response: Go to a call, pacify things, and leave to get ready for another call. To deal with the problem of atomistic responses to incidents, Goldstein has proposed what he calls "problem-oriented policing."

Stated simply, problem-oriented policing is a method of working with citizens to help them identify and solve problems. Darrel Stephens, along with Chief David Couper of Madison, Wisconsin, and Chief Neil Behan of Baltimore County, Maryland, has pioneered in problem-oriented policing. Problems approached via problem-oriented policing include sexual assault and drunk driving in Madison, auto theft, spouse abuse, and burglary in Newport News, and street robbery and burglary in Baltimore County.

Stephens's goal is for "police officers to take the time to stop and think about what they were doing." Mark Moore echoes Stephens: "In the past there were a small number of guys in the police chief's office who did the thinking and everybody else just carried out their ideas. Problem solving gets thousands of brains working on problems."

THE DRIVE TO CHANGE

Why are these changes taking place now? There are three reasons:

1. Citizen disenchantment with police services
2. Research conducted during the 1970's
3. Frustration with the traditional role of the police officer.

1. *Disenchantment with police services.* At first, it seems too strong to say "disenchantment" when referring to citizens' attitudes towards police. Certainly citizens admire and respect most police officers. Citizens enjoy contact with police. Moreover, research shows that most citizens do not find the limited capability of police to prevent or solve crimes either surprising or of particular concern. Nevertheless, there is widespread disenchantment with police tactics that continue to keep police officers remote and distant from citizens.

Minority citizens in inner cities continue to be frustrated by police who whisk in and out of their neighborhoods with little sensitivity to community norms and values. Regardless of where one asks, minorities want both the familiarity and accountability that characterize foot patrol. Working- and middle-class communities of all races are demanding increased collaboration with police in the determination of police priorities in their neighborhoods. Community crime control has become a mainstay of their sense of neighborhood security and a means of lobbying for different police services. And many merchants and affluent citizens have felt so vulnerable that they have turned to private security for service and protection. In private sector terms, police are losing to the competition—private security and community crime control.

2. *Research.* The 1970's research about police effectiveness was another stimulus to change. Research about preventive patrol, rapid response to calls for service, and investigative work—the three mainstays of police tactics—was uniformly discouraging.

Research demonstrated that preventive patrol in automobiles had little effect on crime, citizen levels of fear, or citizen satisfaction with police. Rapid response to calls for service likewise had little impact on arrests, citizen satisfaction with police, or levels of citizen fear. Also, research into criminal investigation effectiveness suggested that detective units were so poorly administered that they had little chance of being effective.

3. *Role of the patrol officer.* Finally, patrol officers have been frustrated with their traditional role. Despite pieties that patrol has been the backbone of policing, every police executive has known that, at best, patrol has been what officers do until they become detectives or are promoted.

At worst, patrol has been the dumping ground for officers who are incompetent, suffering from alcoholism or other problems, or simply burned out. High status for police practitioners went to detectives. Getting "busted to patrol" has been a constant threat to police managers or detectives who fail to perform by some standard of judgement. (It is doubtful that failing patrol officers ever get threatened with being busted to the detective unit.)

Never mind that patrol officers have the most important mission in police departments: They handle the public's most pressing problems and must make complex decisions almost instantaneously. Moreover, they do this with little supervision or training. Despite this, police administrators treat patrol officers as if they did little to advance the organization's mission. The salaries of patrol officers also reflect their demeaned status. No wonder many officers have grown cynical and have turned to unions for leadership rather than to police executives. "Stupid management made unions," says Robert Kliesmet, the President of the International Union of Police Associations AFL-CIO.

The Basis for New Optimism

Given these circumstances, what is the basis of current optimism of police leaders that they have turned a corner? Optimism arises from four factors:

1. Citizen response to the new strategy
2. Ongoing research on police effectiveness
3. Past experiences police have had with innovation
4. The values of the new generation of police leaders

1. *Citizen response.* The overwhelming public response to community and problem-solving policing has been positive, regardless of where it has been instituted. When queried about how he knows community policing works in New York City, Lt. Jerry Simpson responds: "The District Commanders' phones stop ringing." Simpson continues: "Commanders' phones stop ringing because problems have been solved. Even skeptical commanders soon learn that most of their troubles go away with community policing." Citizens like the cop on the beat and enjoy working with him/her to solve problems. Crisley Wood, Executive Director of the Neighborhood Justice Network in Boston—an agency that has established a network of neighborhood crime control organizations—puts it this way: "The cop on the beat, who meets regularly with citizen groups, is the single most important service that the Boston Police Department can provide."

Testimonies aside, perhaps the single most compelling evidence of the popularity of community or problem-solving policing is found in Flint, Michigan, where, it will be recalled, citizens have twice voted to increase their taxes to maintain neighborhood foot patrols—the second time by a two-to-one margin.

2. *New research on effectiveness.* Research conducted during the early and mid-1970's frustrated police executives. It generally showed what did not work. Research conducted during the late 1970's and early 1980's was different. By beginning to demonstrate that new tactics did work, it fueled the move to rejuvenate policing. This research provided police with the following guidance: Foot patrol can reduce citizen fear of crime, improve the relationship between police and citizens, and increase citizen satisfaction with police. This was discovered in Newark, New Jersey,

and Flint. In Flint, foot patrol also reduced crime and calls for service. Moreover, in both cities, it increased officer satisfaction with police work.

The productivity of detectives can be enhanced if patrol officers carefully interview neighborhood residents about criminal events, get the information to detectives, and detectives use it wisely, according to John Eck of PERF.

Citizen fear can be substantially reduced, researcher Tony Pate of the Police Foundation discovered in Newark, by police tactics that emphasize increasing the quantity and improving the quality of citizen–police interaction.

Police anti-fear tactics can also reduce household burglaries, according to research conducted by Mary Ann Wycoff, also of the Police Foundation.

Street-level enforcement of heroin and cocaine laws can reduce serious crime in the area of enforcement, without being displaced to adjacent areas, according to an experiment conducted by Mark Kleiman of Harvard University's Program in Criminal Justice Policy and Management.

Problem-oriented policing can be used to reduce thefts from cars, problems associated with prostitution, and household burglaries, according to William Spelman and John Eck of PERF.

These positive findings about new police tactics provide police with both the motive and justification for continued efforts to rejuvenate policing.

3. *Experience with innovation.* The desire to improve policing is not new with this generation of reformers. The 1960's and 1970's had their share of reformers as well. Robert Eichelberger of Dayton innovated with team policing (tactics akin in many ways to problem solving) and public policymaking; Frank Dyson of Dallas with team policing and generalist/specialist patrol officers; Carl Gooden with team policing in Cincinnati; and there were many other innovators.

But innovators of this earlier era were handicapped by a lack of documented successes and failures of implementation. Those who experimented with team policing were not aware that elements of team policing were simply incompatible with preventive patrol and rapid response to calls for service. As a result, implementation of team policing followed a discouraging pattern. It would be implemented, officers and citizens would like it, it would have an initial impact on crime, and then business as usual would overwhelm it—the program would simply vanish.

Moreover, the lessons about innovation and excellence that Peters and Waterman brought together in *In Search of Excellence* were not available to police administrators. The current generation of reformers has an edge: They have availed themselves of the opportunity to learn from the documented successes and failures of the past. Not content with merely studying innovation and management in policing, Houston's Chief Lee Brown is having key personnel spend internships in private sector corporations noted for excellence in management.

4. *New breed of police leadership.* The new breed of police leadership is unique in the history of American policing. Unlike the tendency in the past for chiefs to be local and inbred, chiefs of this generation are **urbane** and **cosmopolitan.**

Chief Lee Brown of Houston received a Ph.D. in criminology from the University of California–Berkeley; Chief Joseph McNamara of San Jose, California, has a Ph.D. from Harvard University, and is a published novelist; Hubert Williams, formerly Director of the Newark Police Department and now President of the Police Foundation, is a lawyer and has studied criminology in the Law School at Harvard University; Benjamin Ward, Commissioner of the New York City Police Department, is an attorney and was Commissioner of Corrections in New York State.

These are merely a sample. The point is, members of this generation of police leadership are well educated and of diverse backgrounds. All of those noted above, as well as many others, have sponsored research and experimentation to improve policing.

Problems

We have looked at the benefits of community policing. What is the down side? What are the risks?

These questions led to the creation of the Executive Session on Community Policing in the Program in Criminal Justice Policy and Management of Harvard University's John F. Kennedy School of Government. Funded by the National Institute of Justice and the Charles Stewart Mott and Guggenheim Foundations, the Executive Session has convened police and political elites with a small number of academics around the issue of community policing. Francis X. Hartmann, moderator of the Executive Session, describes the purpose of the meetings: "These persons with a special and important relationship to contemporary policing have evolved into a real working group, which is addressing the gap between the realities and aspirations of American policing. Community policing is a significant effort to fill this gap."

Among the questions the Executive Session has raised are the following:

1. Police are a valuable resource in a community. Does community policing squander that resource by concentrating on the wrong priorities?
2. How will community policing fit into police departments given how they arc now organized?
3. Will community policing open the door to increased police corruption or other inappropriate behavior by line officers?

Will Community Policing Squander Police Resources?

This question worries police. They understand that police are a valuable but sparse resource in a community. Hubert Williams, a pioneer in community policing, expresses his concern. "Are police now being put in the role of providing services that are statutorily the responsibilities of some other agencies? Los Angeles's Chief Gates echoes Williams: "Hubie's (Williams is) right—you can't solve all the problems in the world and shouldn't try." Both worry that if police are spread too thin, by problem-solving activities for example, that they will not be able to properly protect the community from serious crime.

This issue is now being heatedly debated in Flint. There, it will be recalled, citizens have passed two bills funding foot patrol—the second by a two-to-one majority. A report commissioned by city government, however, concludes: "The Cost of the Neighborhood Foot Patrol Program Exceeds the Benefit It Provides the Citizens of Flint," and recommends abandoning the program when funding expires.

Why, according to the report, should foot patrol be abandoned? So more "effective" police work can be done. What is effective police work? Quick response to calls for service, taking reports, and increased visibility by putting police officers in cars. "It is simply wrong," says Robert Wasserman, noted police tactician and Research Fellow in the Program in Criminal Justice at Harvard, "to propose abandoning foot patrol in the name of short response time and visibility vis-à-vis patrolling in cars. Every shred of evidence is that rapid response and patrolling in cars doesn't reduce crime, increase citizen satisfaction, or reduce fear. Which is the luxury," Wasserman concludes, "a tactic like foot patrol that gives you two, and maybe three, of your goals, or a tactic like riding around in cars going from call to call that gives you none?" Experienced police executives share Wassermann's concerns. Almost without exception, they are attempting to find ways to get out of the **morass** that myths of the **efficacy** of rapid response have created for large-city police departments. It was Commissioner Ben Ward of New York City, for example, who put a cap on resources that can be used to respond to calls for service and is attempting to find improved means of responding to calls. Commissioner Francis "Mickey" Roache expresses the deep frustration felt by so many police: "I hate to say this, but in Boston we run from one call to another. We don't accomplish anything. We're just running all over the place. It's absolutely insane."

A politician's response to the recommendation to end Flint's foot patrol program is interesting. Daniel Whitehurst, former Mayor of Fresno, California, reflects: "I find it hard to imagine ending a program that citizens not only find popular but are willing to pay for as well."

"The overwhelming danger," Mark Moore concludes, "is that, in the name of efficiency, police and city officials will be tempted to maintain old patterns. They will think they are doing good, but will be squandering police resources." "Chips" Stewart emphasizes the need to move ahead: "As comfortable as old tactics might feel, police must continue to experiment with methods that have shown promise to improve police effectiveness and efficiency."

Will Community Policing Fit within Policing as It Is Now Organized?

Many police and academics believe this to be the most serious problem facing cities implementing community policing. Modern police departments have achieved an impressive capacity to respond quickly to calls for service. This has been accomplished by acquiring and linking elaborate automobile, telephone, radio, and computer technologies, by centralizing control and dispatch of officers, by pressing officers to be "in service" (rather than "out of service" dealing with citizens), and by allocating police in cars throughout the city on the basis of expected calls for service.

Community policing is quite different: It is not incident- or technology-driven; officers operate on a decentralized basis, it emphasizes officers being in regular contact with citizens, and it allocates police on the basis of neighborhoods. The question is, how reconcilable are these two strategies? Some (Lawrence Sherman of the University of Maryland is one example) have taken a strong stance that radical alterations will be required if police are to respond more effectively to community problems. Others (Richard Larson of the Massachusetts Institute of Technology, for example) disagree, believing that community policing is reconcilable with rapid response technology—indeed Professor Larson would emphasize that current computer technology can facilitate community policing.

Will the Community Policing Strategy Lead to Increased Police Corruption and Misbehavior?

The initial news from Houston, New York, Flint, Newark, Los Angeles, Baltimore County, and other police departments which have experimented with community policing is good. Community policing has not led to increased problems of corruption or misbehavior.

Why is it, however, that policymakers fear that community policing has the potential to increase the incidents of police running **amok?** The answer? Community policing radically decentralizes police authority; officers must create for themselves the best responses to problems; and, police become intimately involved with citizens.

These ingredients may not sound so troublesome in themselves—after all, many private and public sector organizations radically decentralize authority, encourage creativity, and are characterized by relative intimacy between service providers and consumers. Nevertheless, in police circles such ingredients violate the orthodox means of controlling corruption. For a generation, police have believed that to eliminate corruption it is necessary to centralize authority, limit discretion, and reduce intimacy between police and citizens. They had good reason to: Early policing in the United States had been characterized by financial corruption, failure of police to protect the rights of all citizens, and **zealotry.**

But just as it is possible to squander police resources in the name of efficiency, it is also possible to squander police resources in the quest for integrity. Centralization, standardization, and remoteness may preclude many opportunities for corruption, but they may also preclude the possibility of good policing. For example, street-level cocaine and heroin enforcement by patrol officers, now known to have crime reduction value, has been banned in cities because of fear of corruption. It is almost as if the purpose of police was to be corruption free, rather than to do essential work. If, as it appears to be, it is necessary to take risks to solve problems, then so be it: police will have to learn to manage risks as well as do managers in other enterprises.

Does this imply softening on the issue of police corruption? Absolutely not. Police and city managers will have to continue to be vigilant: community policing exposes officers to more opportunities for traditional financial corruption; in many neighborhoods police will be faced with demands to protect communities from the **incursions** of minorities; and, police will be tempted to become overzealous when they see citizens' problems being ignored by other agencies.

These dangers mean, however, that police executives will have to manage through values, rather than merely policies and procedures, and by establishing regular neighborhood and community institution reporting mechanisms, rather than through centralized command and control systems.

Each of these issues—use of police resources, organizational compatibility, and corruption—is complicated. Some will be the subject of debate. Others will require research and experimentation to resolve. But most police chiefs will begin to address these issues in a new way. They will not attempt to resolve them in the ways of the past: in secret, behind closed doors. Their approach will reflect the values of the individual neighborhoods as well as the community as a whole.

Policing is changing dramatically. On the one hand, we wish policing to retain the old values of police integrity, equitable distribution of police resources throughout a community, and police efficiency which characterized the old model of police. But the challenge of contemporary police and city executives is to redefine these concepts in light of the resurgence of neighborhood vitality, consumerism, and more realistic assessments of the institutional capacity of police.

The quiet revolution is beginning to make itself heard: citizens and police are joining together to defend communities.

QUESTIONS FOR DISCUSSION

1. Explain why communities and neighborhoods, rather than the police, should be the primary defenders against disorder and crime.
2. There are three reasons that have driven the change to problem-solving and community-oriented policing. List and discuss these reasons.
3. Given the renewed community interest in helping the police, there are reasons to be optimistic about curtailing crime. In this article, Kelling lists four reasons. Discuss each of these reasons.
4. Discuss how community policing may lead to more police corruption.

APPLICATIONS

1. Consider the neighborhood where you presently live. What organized activities to dissuade criminal activity exist? What kinds of programs or changes in your neighborhood do you think would have a crime-reducing impact? Why?
2. Many people often view the police as "the enemy," and unfortunately many police often view the public as the enemy. In your opinion, what can be done to change the sentiments of the public and the police?

The Future of Diversity in America

The Law Enforcement Paradigm Shift

Charles M. Bozza

INTRODUCTION

Diversity has become a central issue to most community leaders and law enforcement officers today because of its tremendous impact on the American society. People continue to cry out for help and understanding and at the forefront is the law enforcement officer who provides the ever so needed emergency service. Law enforcement needs to understand how to deal with people from other backgrounds in today's society or be prepared for the results of lack of understanding. The 1990s are a time when the American culture is in a state of flux hurling to the future at warp speed. No longer are the whites of European descent the dominant culture of this country. If one looks out they will see a mosaic of enriched peoples in all shades of color. The first line of defense in dealing with conflicts among people is the police (Trojanowicz and Bucqueroux, 1991).

In the past decade the terms cross-cultural, inter-cultural, multi-cultural, and cultural have become part of popular terminology amongst scholars, politicians, activists, and philanthropists. It appears that being associated with people, groups, or organizations that strive to promote cross-cultural awareness or study people who are ethnically different has become a popular trend and one that must be understood by the law enforcement administrator and officer. Yet, there are few recent empirical studies that address issues concerning many ethnic groups, especially those which have immigrated to the United States in the latter part of the twentieth century. In fact, although there is much confusion about terminologies, there has been little effort in distinguishing the differences between common words like ethnicity, race and culture.

UNDERSTANDING WHAT IS MEANT BY ETHNICITY, CULTURE, AND RACE

The term race was first used in English approximately three hundred years ago and since then it has become one of the most misused and misunderstood words commonly referred to in everyday speech (Rose, 1964). In a universal context, the term race refers to a system by which both plants and animals are classified into subcategories according to specific physical and structural characteristics. When it pertains to the human group, Krogman (1945) defines race as "...a subgroup of peoples possessing a definite combination of physical characteristics, of genetic origin, the combination of which to varying degrees distinguishes the subgroup from other subgroups of mankind." Differences which are physical such as skin pigmentation, head form, facial features, stature, and the color distribution and texture of body hair are among the most commonly recognized factors distinguishing races of people. In the past law enforcement has taken the stereotype position the most people fall into the categories of white, black, brown, or other.

Most people, however, not familiar with the term race also use it in contexts which have social implications and this is the cause for the confusion. Mack (1968) submits that race in the biological sense has no biological consequences. However, people believe that race has very profound social consequences. Therefore, individuals as part of their socialization accept myths and stereotypes regarding skin color, stature, and so forth to be social facts (Atkinson et al., 1989).

Ethnicity refers to a group classification in which the members share a unique social and cultural heritage passed on from one generation to the next (Rose, 1964). Often times, many individuals use the terms race and ethnicity interchangeably because of the erroneous assumption that ethnicity has a biological or genetic foundation. For example, many groups are identified as racial groups although there is no evidence of biological or genetic foundations to support these claims. Jews, for instance, are frequently associated with being of a distinct race but as Thompson and Hughes (1958) point out, "Jews are not a biological race because the people known as Jews are not enough like each other and too much like other people to be distinguished from them." Jews, therefore, comprise what scholars refer to as an ethnic group.

The most confusing relationship is the one involving culture with race and ethnicity. Moore (1974) illustrates this confusion:

> Sometimes we tend to confuse race and ethnic groups with culture. Great races do have different cultures. Ethnic groups within races differ in cultural content. But, people of the same racial origin and some ethnic groups differ in their cultural matrices. All browns, or blacks, or whites, or yellows, or reds, are not alike in the cultures in which they live and have their being.

Culture, then, at the micro level may exist within ethnic groups and within racial groups. Traditionally, the word culture has been identified with the field of anthropology. To this day scholars credit anthropologists for the creation of the study of culture. Anthropologists define culture as patterns acquired and transmitted by symbols, constituting the distinctive achievement of human groups, including their embodiments in artifacts;

the essential core of culture consists of traditional ideas and especially their attached values (Kroeber and Klukhohn, 1952).

Today, the term culture is not only used in many of the social science disciplines, but it is commonly used in the hard sciences and in business as well. For instance, many scholars and business consultants specialize in examining corporate cultures. Lorenz (1991) defines corporate culture as "who we are, what we do, and how things work around here." Needless to say, this definition does not quite parallel the one presented earlier which was synthesized by anthropologists.

Consequentially, culture has developed many new meanings not only to law enforcement but all of society without any significant scholarly work conducted on the formulation of a new universal definition or definitions unique to various disciplines. Thus, the term culture is used in many contexts and individuals define it based on their own professional, sociological, and theoretical orientations.

In order to facilitate the comprehension of goals and/or issues many have developed interesting combinations of the word culture, such as cross-cultural, multi-cultural, inter-cultural, and so on. These terms are sometimes used interchangeably and sometimes to indicate opposite sides of an issue; it all depends on one's theoretical or practical framework. Law enforcement officers of the past have taken it upon themselves to also define culture in the terms of "Blue Humor" without thinking through the implications. An example of this would he referring to people of black origin as "Gorillas of the Mist."

In the 1980s, these combination of terms using the word culture had become so popular in various societal circles that even social scientists began using the terms to grab their audiences. They found these terms useful when writing grant proposals and requesting funds for research projects. Basically, these combination terms became marketing tools. It need not be implied that scholars do not have the right to use marketing terms, however, what happens is that they become so involved with the selling part of their professions that they often forget the purpose of their roles. In their role as scientists, they need to be especially sensitive to the biases and unexamined assumptions that too often wander into scientific concepts. Scholars and law enforcement officers need to devote more time on clarifying the terms that have created so much confusion in lieu of using these new terms to promote their goals.

WHAT IS DIVERSITY

When one thinks about diversity one also thinks about minority groups. Historically, the term minority was formed to represent more Americans, Latinos, East Asians, Pacific Islanders, and Native Americans. Today, although the term is still used by all organizations in the private and public sector, it is an obsolete concept because many cultures, races, and ethnicities are not recognized by the government or corporations as minority groups. They are labeled as immigrant groups. Why? Because minority groups mentioned above are protected by laws and have access to avenues not provided to the so-called "immigrant groups." Thus, the word "minority" does not truly represent all minorities but a selected few. Since this word misrepresents many non-minority groups which are racially, culturally, and ethnically different many scholars have started to use terms like "underrepresented" or "ethnic" to refer to many racial and immigrant groups in the United States.

Recently, the term minority has been abandoned by scholars specializing in the traditional "minority groups" because it has negative implications, and it is misleading since it is not factual. These groups may be minorities individually, however, collectively they will be the clear majority. By the year 2000, it is projected that in California the Hispanics will be the majority. Moreover, today women have also joined other groups and they are also referred to as an underrepresented group (Fateri, 1989).

What seems to be the major variable affecting the slow growth in the understanding of the underrepresented groups is the group of people who label themselves or who are labeled as experts on diversity. Haro (1991) complains that many of the supposed "authorities" at conferences seem to be overnight gurus on minority concerns. He cites several examples to support his argument. He states that a former university president who had originally gained recognition for his research on white executives started appearing on panels as an expert on the future of cultural diversity. This ex-president never appointed or groomed any minority administrators, even though he headed an institution where minorities made up more than half of the student body.

Diversity issues have become so important that even bodies which accredit secondary schools, colleges, and universities have recently commenced serious discussions about their own diversity policies. Jaschik (1992) reported that the Middle States adopted a policy stating that its diversity standards would not be used as a condition for accrediting institutions and that colleges could define for themselves how the standards would be applied. This revelation received a prompt response from the Education Secretary, Alexander, who asked this accrediting body to revise its new policy. Recently, the Western Association of Schools and Colleges decided to examine its policies on diversity. Since colleges and universities set the standard for the society on new societal philosophies, all organizations are monitoring the progress of universities for proper direction in their own training programs. More and more schools today are seeking teachers who have received "multicultural" training in college (Nicklin, 1991a). Moreover, school systems who have realized their diversity training deficiencies are looking up to universities for new curricula guidance (Nicklin, 1991b).

Berkin (1991) explains that the reason for this immense interest in diversity is not only because of the influx of so many immigrant groups into the United States but also because for more than two decades, scholars interested in creating intellectual space for new perspectives such as feminism and the experiences of underrepresented groups have entered universities in increasing numbers. These new entrants to the scholarly circles have voiced doubts about traditional definitions of proper subject matter and interpretive models. Their attempt to redefine and reinterpret, what should be taught and introduce topic areas such as "women's culture," has been met with a counterattack from supporters of the established thought. Tarnas (1991), for instance, made the attempt to illustrate, in his popular document, why the traditional western culture deserves more attention and why the traditional westerners should not reject their heritage.

Perhaps law enforcement has come upon its own answer to cultural dilemma. By using a community-based policing model that solves this problem by direct interaction and communications with its service population, [they learn] firsthand the cultural differences and [work] with them within the framework of the law and community standards.

SOCIETAL THEORIES ON DIVERSITY: A PARADIGM SHIFT

Thomas Kuhn (1970), perhaps one of the intellectual gurus of this century, reported the shift in humankind's pattern of thought. He called it the **paradigm** shift, a term commonly used today not only in the academic fields but also in the business realms. Unfortunately, Kuhn did not spend adequate time writing and clarifying thoughts on the diverse issues law enforcement is now taking time to clarify. Training in many states is currently being prepared to give the law enforcement official a better understanding of what is ahead in the communities where we deliver service.

What has happened in the American society in the past few decades is that there has been a shift in its structure. In the past, many immigrant groups in the U.S. were, for the most part, from European countries or East Asian countries and they came to the United States gradually and for economic reasons. Recently, immigrant groups have been coming from all over the world and for varying reasons (Fateri, 1986). Therefore, the degree of adaptation and adjustments are not comparable since the cultures, races, and ethnicities of the peoples are very different and the quantity of immigrants and the differences of identities are far greater. Thus, the melting pot concept which may have been attractive and possible in the past is no longer a logical alternative in a society with numerous races, ethnicities, and cultures.

In its early stages of development, the United States projected an image of the cultural melting pot, a nation in which all nationalities, ethnicities, and races melted into one culture. Inherent in the melting pot concept was the perspective that a new and unique culture would continually emerge as each new immigrant group affected the existing culture (Krug, 1976). The melting pot philosophy was not subscribed to by many because it was believed that the "heart of the United States" was an American culture that was based primarily on the values and races of early immigrants, principally English, Irish, German, and Scandinavian groups. Opponents of this concept believed that instead of melting all cultures into one, an effort needed to be made to culturally assimilate all immigrant groups (Fairchild, 1926). Later, in the 1950s and 1960s there were growing objections to the **assimilation** theory because it called for relinquishing traditional ethnic values and **norms** in favor of those of the **dominant culture.**

Today, the melting pot theory and the assimilation concept are still in contention although the former is favored more than the latter simply because it is better understood. Although both of these philosophies are acceptable and possibly practical in other societies, they are not functional in the American society. What may work is the "salad bowl" concept, also referred to as the mosaic: the various ingredients or parts exist together, but rather than melting, the components remain intact and distinguishable while contributing to a whole that is richer than its parts alone.

WHAT DOES THE FUTURE HOLD

The United States today is structured like a salad bowl, where ethnic, racial and cultural groups function independently while contributing to the whole society, but it operates as if it was structured like a melting pot. Alvin Toffler (1990) submits that Los Angeles with its Korea town, its Vietnamese suburbs, its strong and growing Chicano population, its roughly 75 ethnically oriented publications, not to mention its Jews, Africans, Japanese, Chinese, and its large Iranian population provides an example of the new and future diversity. The serious question posed is whether we want to operate realistically and effectively as a society in the future? Certainly, all law enforcement organizations want to succeed in implementing their goals and objectives, therefore, we need to accept the reality and organize ourselves in accord with the status quo and not the way society needs to be philosophically or the way the society needs to be structured. Our society is the result of an evolutionary process which is consistently and continually being influenced by rearrangements and introduction of new and different economic, social, political and cultural variables. Few other societies are affected to this degree, therefore, the challenge we face in operating within these boundaries and under these circumstances is rather unique. Toffler (1990) recommends that government will need new legal and social tools they now lack, if they are to referee increasingly complex, potentially violent disputes.

Since law enforcement organizations possess a structure, a mission, and a system of operation, they can effectively learn about and communicate with the many groups that are, or need to be, of interest to them (Bozza and Fateri, 1990), whereas, the ethnic groups within the society may not have such capabilities or motivations. Law enforcement organizations need to be in the **vanguard** of this social and legal change that is occurring now and will continue in the future in our nation. The idea is to learn more about these groups so that the society would operate more effectively by being able to improvise and adapt. Most importantly the interaction with these groups through various policing methods and community service would not only increase tolerance among all groups but increase our appreciation of people who are culturally different. The acquisition of knowledge and information is central to proper and efficient management. The successful law enforcement organization of the future will develop systems to learn about all of the underrepresented ethnic and non-ethnic groups that affect their operation. These organizations will take the initiative to acquire the necessary knowledge which would help them to make intelligent decisions.

Marvin Cetron and Owen Davies (1991), respected futurists, projected with optimism that the guiding theme of the 90s will be to restore peace by the joint effort of the entire world community. This is one forecast which many wish to become a **self-fulfilling prophecy,** and we, as responsible members of society and law enforcement professionals can contribute and support this new ideology by changing our thinking patterns first and then our national policies on how we see others.

REFERENCES

ATKINSON, D. R., MORTEN, G., AND SUE, D. W. (1989). *Counseling American Minorities.* Dubuque, IA: William C. Brown Publishing.

BERKIN, CAROL. (1991). "Dangerous Courtesies Assault Women's History." *The Chronicle of Higher Education,* December 11, A-44.

BOZZA, C. M., AND FATERI, F. (1990). "Methods Dealing with Cross Cultural Concerns: A Case Study of the Iranian New Year." *Journal of California Law Enforcement.* California Peace Officers, Education Research and Training Foundation, Sacramento, CA, Vol. 24. No. 3.

CETRON, M. J., AND DAVIES, O. (1991). *Crystal Globe: The Haves and Haves-Nots of the New World Order.* New York: St. Martin's Press.

FAIRCHILD, H. P. (1926). *The Melting Pot Mistake.* Boston: Little, Brown, & Company.

FATERI, FARDAD. (1986). "The Politics of the Iranian Exiles in Southern California: A Case Study of Political Activists." Master's thesis, California State University, Fullerton.

FATERI, FARDAD. (1989). "Sex Role Orientation and Perceived Leadership Behavior of Male and Female Middle Managers Working for Electronic Firms. A Doctoral Dissertation." U. S. International University, San Diego, CA.

HARO, R. P. (1991). "So Called Experts on Cultural Diversity Need to Be Subjected to Careful Scrutiny." *The Chronicle of Higher Education,* November 13, B-2.

JASCHIK, SCOTT. (1992). "Middle States' Decision on Diversity Standards Seen Enhancing Federal Role in Accreditation." *The Chronicle of Higher Education,* January 8, A36.

KROEBER, A. L., AND KLUCKHOHN, C. (1952). *Culture: A Critical Review of Concepts and Definitions.* New York: Vintage Books.

KROGMAN, W. M. (1945). "The Concept of Race." In R. Linton, *The Science of Man in the World Crisis* (pp. 38–62). New York: Columbia University Press.

KRUG, M. (1976). *The Melting Pot of the Ethnics.* Bloomington, IN: Phi Delta Kappa Educational Foundation.

KUHN, THOMAS. (1970). *The Structure of Scientific Revolutions.* Chicago: University of Chicago Press.

LORENZ, JOHN. (1991). "Shifting the Corporate Culture." *Orange County Business Journals,* December 9, C-5.

MACK, R. W. (1968). *Race, Class, and Power.* New York: American Book Company.

MOORE, B. M. (1974). "Cultural Differences and Counseling Perspectives." *Texas Personnel and Guidance Association Journal,* 3, 39–44.

NICKLIN, J. L. (1991a). "Teacher Education Programs Face Pressure to Provide Multicultural Training." *The Chronicle of Higher Education,* November 27, A-11.

NICKLIN, J. L. (1991b). "School Systems Seek Guidance from Universities in Bringing More Diversity to Curricula." *The Chronicle of Higher Education,* November 27, A-16.

ROSE, P. I. (1964). *They and We: Racial and Ethnic Relations in the United States.* New York: Random House.

TARNAS, RICHARD. (1991). *The Passion of the Western Mind.* New York: Harmony Books.

THOMPSON, E. T., AND HUGHES, E. C. (1958). *Race: Individual and Collective Behavior.* Glencoe, IL: Free Press.

TOFFLER, ALVIN. (1990). *Power Shift.* New York: Bantam Books.

TROJANOWICZ, ROBERT, AND BUCQUEROUX, BONNIE. (1991). *Community Policing and the Challenge of Diversity.* Flint, MI: National Center for Community Policing School of Criminal Justice, Michigan State University.

QUESTIONS FOR DISCUSSION

1. Explain the differences between ethnicity, culture, and race.

2. Bozza states that the issue of diversity will be of major importance in the 1990s. Why? Cite examples to support your answer.

3. With regard to U. S. society and various underrepresented groups, there has been a structural shift over the past few decades. Explain.

4. What are the future implications for policing in a society that is ever-increasingly diverse?

APPLICATIONS

1. There are those who argue that having an ethnically, culturally, and racially diverse society is desirable and will ultimately strengthen the United States. Conversely, there are those who believe that an increasingly diverse country is undesirable and will result in loss of identity and values for the nation as a whole. What is your position on this issue? Why?

2. Some would say that many Americans are intolerant of groups of people other than the groups to which they belong. Rather than learning to appreciate other culturally, ethnically, or racially diverse groups, Americans see most other groups of people as threatening. Do you agree with this appraisal? Why ?

part III

The Courts

The second component in the U. S. system of justice is the various levels of the judiciary. Our country has two court systems that coexist and maintain various jurisdictional responsibilities. The federal court system is responsible for violations of federal laws and is divided into three levels. The first, the U.S. district courts, hears cases involving alleged violations of federal laws and serves as the lowest level of the federal judiciary. The second level involves the twelve U.S. Courts of Appeals or circuits of appeals, which serve as the intermediate level in the federal court system. These courts hear appeals from the district courts and are concerned essentially with the procedural behavior of the lower court. The final level in the federal system is the U.S. Supreme Court, the "court of last resort." The primary functions of this court are the protection of the Constitution and to serve as an appellate court interested mainly in cases involving only substantial federal questions.

The state courts are the second system within the judiciary. This system is also divided into three levels consisting of the trial, appellate, and state supreme courts. The trial courts hear criminal cases involving violations of state law, while state appeals and supreme courts hear appeals involving cases heard in the trial courts. Although variations exist, most state court systems are very similar in both structure and function.

Both federal and state court systems are limited by the type of offender, offense, law, and action sought from the court. These systems are based on the adversarial process, in which the defense and prosecution are adversaries while the judge serves as a referee. The prosecution is expected to prove its case beyond a reasonable doubt while the defense simply counters such evidence or testimony. The state trial or federal district courts hear cases and decide disposition in these cases while protecting the rights of the person accused. Citizens accused of crimes have certain rights guaranteed to them by the Constitution. A defendant's major rights include a speedy public trial in a fair atmosphere in which the defendant can face his or her accusers with the help of counsel. Of course, a person can waive any of his or her rights any time during the judicial proceedings.

The imposition of a criminal sanction after the establishment of guilt is known as sentencing. Although sentencing philosophies often seem to change emphases, there remain five basic models of sentencing in the criminal justice system. Some of the most important and critical issues in the entire system revolve around inconsistent sentencing philosophies. As you learn more about sentencing, you will come to realize that the police, courts, and correctional components must have congruence in sentencing philosophies or the system's effectiveness becomes low. The five sentencing philosophies include (1) retribution or punishment, (2) incapacitation or restraint, (3) deterrence or prevention, (4) rehabilitation or reform, and (5) restitution or victim compensation. In our system of justice, all five philosophies are used in varying degrees with many inconsistent results or outcomes. Often, however, sentencing philosophies are based on the type of offense and offender. The judiciary tends to favor rehabilitative programs for first-time and young offenders, depending on their offenses, while the system tend toward retribution and incapacitation in relation to habitual adult offenders.

In our first selection dealing with judicial issues, Herbert L. Packer presents an excellent overview of judicial philosophy in "Two Models of the Criminal Process." These two models, known historically as the "due process and crime control models," polarize the issues involving the administration of justice in a democracy. On the one hand, supporters of the due process model argue that the rights of the individual are important, especially regarding the issue of equality. The crime control model advocates, most importantly, which crimes are brought under strict control or we as a society risk the loss of public order. Although neither extreme is a complete approach to solving even the judicial problems within our society, the solution most often sought after is compromise. Even the U.S. Supreme Court vacillates between these two polarities in their deliberations concerning the criminal process.

If you were to ask any U.S. citizen about the crime problem, most, if not all, would claim that crime is a serious problem that needs to be dealt with. How to deal with crime would lead to many answers; however, if you were to ask about the effectiveness of police, courts, or correctional systems, most people would claim that the system needs to be over-hauled or redesigned. In "Fighting Crime in a Crumbling System," Steven Brill suggests that the major players in the system must create a totally new mindset to achieve criminal justice. Like most of the American public, Brill thinks the system is so ineffective that it will fail. The sad fact is that the court system is filled with bright spots of achievement but lacks consistent top-to-bottom effectiveness and efficiency. Many believe that the system's major weakness is a lack of clear goals and objectives in terms of criminal processes and procedures.

Do the courts really just want defendants to plead guilty and make way for the next case? Abraham S. Blumberg argues convincingly in "The Practice of Law as a Con Game" that the contextual realities of social structure skew the system in favor of itself and further, that defense lawyers often act as double agents in negotiated pleas. If every defendant were to choose a jury trial, the court system would be so overwhelmed that it could possibly collapse.

Conservatives and liberals may argue about almost every social issue; however, arguments may cease when considering wrongful convictions. If we convict the wrong person, where is the real criminal? The answer is, of course: still free to victimize another person. Huff, Rattner, and Sagarin point out the dilemmas in "Guilty until Proved Innocent: Wrongful Conviction and Public Policy." Even using conservative estimates of wrongful convictions for index crimes alone, our system may produce as many as 6000 erroneous convictions per year. Although the reasons are many, the system can in no way justify itself, and many think that the major actors **rationalize** these mistakes based on the general efficiency of the system.

Marcia R. Chaiken and Jan M. Chaiken delve into one of the more interesting subjects faced by courts in "Priority Prosecution of High-Rate Dangerous Offenders." Many criminologists believe that the justice system and national crime problems would be reduced significantly if we would incarcerate habitual recidivists for long periods. What constitutes a high-rate dangerous offender and how the courts decide and then deal with such persons is clearly shown by these authors.

chapter 11

Two Models of the Criminal Process

Herbert L. Packer

INTRODUCTION

People who commit crimes appear to share the prevalent impression that punishment is an unpleasantness that is best avoided. They ordinarily take care to avoid being caught. If arrested, they ordinarily deny their guilt and otherwise try not to cooperate with the police. If brought to trial, they do whatever their resources permit to resist being convicted. And even after they have been convicted and sent to prison, their efforts to secure their freedom do not cease. It is a struggle from start to finish. This struggle is often referred to as the criminal process, a **compendious** term that stands for all the complexes of activity that operate to bring the **substantive law** of crime to bear (or to keep it from coming to bear) on persons who are suspected of having committed crimes. It can be described, but only partially and inadequately, by referring to the rules of law that govern the apprehension, screening, and trial of persons suspected of crime. It consists at least as importantly of patterns of official activity that correspond only in the roughest kind of way to the prescriptions of procedural rules.

At the same time, and perhaps in part as a result of this new **accretion** of knowledge, some of our lawmaking institutions—particularly the Supreme Court of the United States— have begun to add measurably to the prescriptions of law that are meant to govern the operation of the criminal process. This accretion has become, in the last few years, exponential in extent and velocity. We are faced with an interesting paradox: the more we learn about the Is of the criminal process, the more we are instructed about its Ought and the greater the gulf between Is and Ought appears to become. We learn that very few people get adequate legal representation in the criminal process; we are simultaneously told that the Constitution requires people to be afforded adequate legal representation in the criminal process. We learn that coercion is often used to extract confessions from suspected criminals; we are then told that convictions based on coerced confessions may not be permitted to stand. We discover that the police often use methods in gathering evidence that violate the norms of privacy protected by the Fourth Amendment; we are told that evidence obtained in this way must be excluded from the criminal trial. But these prescriptions about how the process ought to operate do not automatically become part of the patterns of official behavior in the criminal process. Is and Ought share an increasingly uneasy coexistence. Doubts are stirred about the kind of criminal process we want to have....

Two models of the criminal process will let us perceive the **normative antinomy** at the heart of the criminal law. These models are not labeled Is and Ought, nor are they to be taken in that sense. Rather, they represent an attempt to abstract two separate value systems that compete for priority in the operation of the criminal process. Neither is presented as either corresponding to reality or representing the ideal to the exclusion of the other. The two models merely afford a convenient way to talk about the operation of a process whose day-to-day functioning involves a constant series of minute adjustments between the competing demands of two value systems and whose normative future likewise involves a series of resolutions of the tensions between competing claims.

I call these two models the Due Process Model and the Crime Control Model. There is a risk in an enterprise of this sort that is latent in any attempt to polarize. It is, simply, that values are too various to be pinned down to yes-or-no answers. The models are distortions of reality. And, since they are normative in character, there is a danger of seeing one or the other as Good or Bad. The reader will have his preferences, as I do, but we should not be so rigid as to demand consistently polarized answers to the range of questions posed in the criminal process. The weighty questions of public policy that inhere in any attempt to discern where on the spectrum of normative choice the "right" answer lies are beyond the scope of the present inquiry. The attempt here is primarily to clarify the terms of discussion by isolating the assumptions that underlie competing policy claims and examining the conclusions that those claims, if fully accepted, would lead to.

VALUES UNDERLYING THE MODELS

Each of the two models we are about to examine is an attempt to give operational content to a complex of values underlying the criminal law. As I have suggested earlier, it is possible to identify two competing systems of values, the tension between which accounts for the intense activity now observable in the development of the criminal process. The actors in this development—lawmakers, judges, police, prosecutors, defense lawyers—do not often pause to articulate the values that underlie the positions that they take on any given issue. Indeed, it would be a gross oversimplification to ascribe a coherent and consistent set of values to any of these actors. Each of the two competing schemes of values we will be developing in this section contains components that are demonstrably present some of the time in some of the actors' preferences regarding the criminal process. No one person has ever identified himself as holding all of the values that underlie these two models. The models are polarities, and so are the schemes of value that underlie them. A person who subscribed to all of the values underlying one model to the exclusion of all of the values underlying the other would be rightly viewed as a fanatic. The values are presented here as an aid to analysis, not as a program for action....

Crime Control Values

The value system that underlies the Crime Control Model is based on the proposition that the repression of criminal conduct is by far the most important function to be performed by the criminal process. The failure of law enforcement to bring criminal conduct under tight control is viewed as leading to the breakdown of public order and thence to the disappearance of an important condition of human freedom. If the laws go unenforced— which is to say, if it is perceived that there is a high percentage of failure to apprehend and convict in the criminal process—a general disregard for legal controls tends to develop. The law-abiding citizen then becomes the victim of all sorts of unjustifiable invasions of his interests. His security of person and property is sharply diminished, and, therefore, so is his liberty to function as a member of society. The claim ultimately is that the criminal process is a positive guarantor of social freedom. In order to achieve this high purpose, the Crime Control Model requires that primary attention be paid to the efficiency with which the criminal process operates to screen suspects, determine guilt, and secure appropriate dispositions of persons convicted of crime.

The model, in order to operate successfully, must produce a high rate of apprehension and conviction, and must do so in a context where the magnitudes being dealt with are very large and the resources for dealing with them are very limited. There must then be a premium on speed and finality. Speed, in turn, depends on informality and on uniformity; finality depends on minimizing the occasions for challenge. The process must not be cluttered up with ceremonious rituals that do not advance the progress of a case. Facts can be established more quickly through interrogation in a police station than through the formal process of examination and cross-examination in a court. It follows that extra-judicial processes should be preferred to judicial processes, informal operations to formal ones. But informality is not enough; there must also be uniformity. Routine, stereotyped procedures are essential if large numbers are being handled. The model that will operate successfully on these presuppositions must be an administrative, almost a managerial, model. The image that comes to mind is an assembly-line conveyor belt down which moves an endless stream of cases, never stopping, carrying the cases to workers who stand at fixed stations and who perform on each case as it comes by the same small but essential operation that brings it one step closer to being a finished product, or, to exchange the metaphor for the reality, a closed file. The criminal process, in this model, is seen as a screening process in which each successive stage—pre-arrest investigation, arrest, post-arrest investigation, preparation for trial, trial or entry of plea, conviction, disposition—involves a series of routinized operations whose success is gauged primarily by their tendency to pass the case along to a successful conclusion.

What is a successful conclusion? One that throws off at an early stage those cases in which it appears unlikely that the person apprehended is an offender and then secures, as expeditiously as possible, the conviction of the rest, with a minimum of occasions for challenge, let alone post-audit. By the application of administrative expertness, primarily that of the police and prosecutors, an early determination of probable innocence or guilt emerges. Those who are probably innocent are screened out. Those who are probably guilty are passed quickly through the remaining stages of the process. The key to the operation of the model regarding those who are not screened out is what I shall call a **presumption** of guilt. The concept requires some explanation, since it may appear starting to assert that what appears to be the precise converse of our generally accepted ideology of a presumption of innocence can be an essential element of a model that does correspond in some respects to the actual operation of the criminal process.

The presumption of guilt is what makes it possible for the system to deal efficiently with large numbers, as the Crime Control Model demands. The supposition is that the screening processes operated by police and prosecutors are reliable indicators of probable guilt. Once a man has been arrested and investigated without being found to be probably innocent, or, to put it differently, once a determination has been made that there is enough evidence of guilt to permit holding him for further action, then all subsequent activity directed toward him is based on the view that he is probably guilty. The precise point at which this occurs will vary from case to case; in many cases it will occur as soon as the suspect is arrested, or even before, if the evidence of probable guilt that has come to the attention of the authorities is sufficiently strong. But in any case the presumption of guilt will begin to operate well before the "suspect" becomes a "defendant."

The presumption of guilt is not, of course, a thing. Nor is it even a rule of law in the usual sense. It simply is the consequence of a complex of attitudes, a mood. If there is confidence in the reliability of informal administrative fact-finding activities that take place in the early stages of the criminal process, the remaining stages of the process can be relatively **perfunctory** without any loss in operating efficiency. The presumption of guilt, as it operates in the Crime Control Model, is the operational expression of that confidence.

It would be a mistake to think of the presumption of guilt as the opposite of the presumption of innocence that we are so used to thinking of as the **polestar** of the criminal process and that, as we shall see, occupies an important position in the Due Process Model. The presumption of innocence is not its opposite; it is irrelevant to the presumption of guilt; the two concepts are different rather than opposite ideas. The difference can perhaps be **epitomized** by an example. A murderer, for reasons best known to himself, chooses to shoot his victim in plain view of a large number of people. When the police arrive, he hands them his gun and says, "I did it and I'm glad." His account of what happened is corroborated by several eyewitnesses. He is placed under arrest and led off to jail. Under these circumstances, which may seem extreme but which in fact characterize with rough accuracy the evidentiary situation in a large proportion of criminal cases, it would be plainly absurd to maintain that more probably than not the suspect did not commit the killing. But that is not what the presumption of innocence means. It means that until there has been an adjudication of guilt by an authority legally competent to make such an adjudication, the suspect is to be treated, for reasons that have nothing whatever to do with the probable outcome of the case, as if his guilt is an open question.

The presumption of innocence is a direction to officials about how they are to proceed, not a prediction of outcome. The presumption of guilt, however, is purely and simply a prediction of outcome. The presumption of innocence is, then, a direction to the authorities to ignore the presumption of guilt in their treatment of the suspect. It tells them, in effect, to close their eyes to what will frequently seem to be factual probabilities. The reasons why it tells them this are among the animating presuppositions of the Due Process Model.

In this model, as I have suggested, the center of gravity for the process lies in the early, administrative fact-finding stages. The complementary proposition is that the subsequent stages are relatively unimportant and should be truncated as much as possible. This, too, produces tensions with presently dominant ideology. The pure Crime Control Model has very little use for many conspicuous features of the adjudicative process, and in real life works out a number of ingenious compromises with them. Even in the pure model, however, there have to be devices for dealing with the suspect after the preliminary screening process has resulted in a determination of probable guilt. The focal device, as we shall see, is the plea of guilty; through its use, adjudicative fact-finding is reduced to a minimum. It might be said of the Crime Control Model that, when reduced to its barest essentials and operating at its most successful pitch, it offers two possibilities: an administrative fact-finding process leading (1) to **exoneration** of the suspect or (2) to the entry of a plea of guilty.

Due Process Values

If the Crime Control Model resembles an assembly line, the Due Process Model looks very much like an obstacle course. Each of its successive stages is designed to present formidable impediments to carrying the accused any further along in the process. Its ideology is not the converse of that underlying the Crime Control Model. It does not rest on the idea that it is not socially desirable to repress crime, although critics of its application have been known to claim so. Its ideology is composed of a complex of ideas, some of them based on judgments about the efficacy of crime control devices, others having to do with quite different considerations. The ideology of due process is far more deeply impressed on the formal structure of the law than is the ideology of crime control; yet an accurate tracing of the strands that make it up is strangely difficult. What follows is only an attempt at an approximation.

The Due Process Model encounters its rival on the Crime Control Model's own ground in respect to the reliability of fact-finding processes. The Crime Control Model, as we have suggested, places heavy reliance on the ability of investigative and prosecutorial officers, acting in an informal setting in which their distinctive skills are given full sway, to elicit and reconstruct a tolerably accurate account of what actually took place in an alleged criminal event. The Due Process Model rejects this premise and substitutes for it a view of informal, nonadjudicative fact-finding that stresses the possibility of error. People are notoriously poor observers of disturbing events—the more emotion-arousing the context, the greater the possibility that recollection will be incorrect; confessions and admissions by persons in police custody may be induced by physical or psychological coercion so that the police end up hearing what the suspect thinks they want to hear rather than the truth; witnesses may be animated by a bias or interest that no one would trouble to discover except one specially charged with protecting the interests of the accused (as the police are not). Considerations of this kind all lead to a rejection of informal fact-finding processes as definitive of factual guilt and to an insistence on formal, adjudicative, adversary fact-finding processes in which the factual case against the accused is publicly heard by an impartial **tribunal** and is evaluated only after the accused has had a full opportunity to discredit the case against him. Even then, the distrust of fact-finding processes that animates the Due Process Model is not dissipated. The possibilities of human error being what they are, further scrutiny is necessary, or at least must be available, in case facts have been overlooked or suppressed in the heat of battle. How far this subsequent scrutiny must be available is a hotly **controverted** issue today. In the pure Due Process Model the answer would be: at least as long as there is an allegation of factual error that has not received an adjudicative hearing in a fact-finding context. The demand for finality is thus very low in the Due Process Model.

This strand of due process ideology is not enough to sustain the model. If all that were at issue between the two models was a series of questions about the reliability of fact-finding processes, we would have but one model of the criminal process, the nature of whose constituent elements would pose questions of fact not of value. Even if the discussion is confined, for the moment, to the question of reliability, it is apparent that more is at stake than simply an evaluation of what kinds of fact-finding processes, alone or in combination, are likely to produce the most nearly reliable results. The stumbling block is this: how much reliability is compatible with efficiency? Granted that informal fact-finding will make some mistakes that can be remedied if backed up by adjudicative fact-finding, the desirability of providing this backup is not affirmed or negated by factual demonstrations or predictions that the increase in reliability will be x percent or x plus n percent. It still remains to ask how much weight is to be given to the competing demands of reliability (a high degree of probability in each case that factual guilt has been accurately determined) and efficiency (expeditious handling of the large numbers of cases that the process ingests). The Crime Control Model is more optimistic about the improbability of error in a significant number of cases; but it is also, though only in part therefore, more tolerant about the amount of error that it will put up with. The Due Process Model insists on the prevention and elimination of mistakes to the extent possible; the Crime Control Model accepts the probability of mistakes up to the level at which they interfere with the goal of repressing crime, either because too many guilty people are escaping or, more subtly, because general awareness of the unreliability of the process leads to a decrease in the deterrent efficacy of the criminal law. In this view, reliability and efficiency are not polar opposites but rather complementary characteristics. The system is reliable *because* efficient; reliability becomes a matter of independent concern only when it becomes so **attenuated** as to impair efficiency. All of this the Due Process Model rejects. If efficiency demands shortcuts around reliability, then absolute efficiency must be rejected. The aim of the process is at least as much to protect the factually innocent as it is to convict the factually guilty. It is a little like quality control in industrial technology: tolerable deviation from standard varies with the importance of conformity to standard in the destined uses of the product. The Due Process Model resembles a factory that has to devote a substantial part of its input to quality control. This necessarily cuts down on quantitative output.

The combination of stigma and loss of liberty that is embodied in the end result of the criminal process is viewed as being the heaviest deprivation that government can inflict on the individual. Furthermore, the processes that culminate in these highly afflictive sanctions are seen as in themselves coercive, restricting, and demeaning. Power is always subject to abuse—sometimes subtle, other times, as in the criminal process, open and ugly. Precisely because of its potency in subjecting the individual to the coercive power of the state, the criminal process must, in this model, be subjected to controls that prevent it from operating with maximal efficiency. According to this ideology, maximal efficiency means maximal tyranny. And, although no one would assert that minimal efficiency means minimal tyranny, the proponents of the Due Process Model would accept with considerable **equanimity** a substantial **diminution** in the efficiency with which the criminal process operates in the interest of preventing official oppression of the individual.

The most modest-seeming but potentially far-reaching mechanism by which the Due Process Model implements these anti-authoritarian values is the doctrine of legal guilt. According to this doctrine, a person is not to be held guilty of crime merely on a showing that in all probability, based upon reliable evidence, he did factually what he is said to have done. Instead, he is to be held guilty if and only if these factual determinations are made in procedurally regular fashion and by authorities acting within competences duly allocated to them. Furthermore, he is not to be held guilty, even though the factual determination is or might be adverse to him, if various rules designed to protect him and to safeguard the integrity of the process are not given effect: The tribunal that convicts him must have the power to deal with his kind of case ("jurisdiction") and must be geographically appropriate ("**venue**"); too long a time must not have elapsed since the offense was committed ("statute of limitations"); he must not have been previously convicted or acquitted of the same or a substantially similar offense ("double jeopardy"); he must not fall within a category of persons, such as children or the insane, who are legally immune to conviction ("criminal responsibility"); and so on. None of these requirements has anything to do with the factual question of whether the person did or did not engage in the conduct that is charged as the offense against him; yet favorable answers to any of them will mean that he is legally innocent. Wherever the competence to make adequate factual determinations lies, it is apparent that only a tribunal that is aware of these guilt-defeating doctrines and is willing to apply them can be viewed as competent to make determinations of legal guilt. The police and the prosecutors are ruled out by lack of competence, in the first instance, and by lack of assurance of willingness, in the second. Only an impartial tribunal can be trusted to make determinations of legal as opposed to factual guilt.

Beyond the question of predictability this model posits a functional reason for observing the presumption of innocence: By forcing the state to prove its case against the accused in an adjudicative context, the presumption of innocence serves to force into play all the qualifying and disabling doctrines that limit the use of the criminal sanction against the individual, thereby enhancing his opportunity to secure a favorable outcome. In this sense, the presumption of innocence may be seen to operate as a kind of self-fulfilling prophecy. By opening up a procedural situation that permits the successful assertion of defenses having nothing to do with factual guilt, it **vindicates** the proposition that the factually guilty may nonetheless be legally innocent and should therefore be given a chance to qualify for that kind of treatment.

The possibility of legal innocence is expanded enormously when the criminal process is viewed as the appropriate forum for correcting its own abuses. This notion may well account for a greater amount of the distance between the two models than any other. In theory the Crime Control Model can tolerate rules that forbid illegal arrests, unreasonable searches, coercive interrogations, and the like. What it cannot tolerate is the vindication of those rules in the criminal process itself through the exclusion of evidence illegally obtained or through the reversal of convictions in cases where the criminal process has breached the rules laid down for its observance. And the Due Process Model, although it may in the first instance be addressed to the maintenance of reliable fact-finding techniques, comes eventually to incorporate **prophylactic** and deterrent rules that result in the release of the factually guilty even in cases in which blotting out the illegality would still leave an adjudicative fact-finder convinced of the accused person's guilt. Only by penalizing errant police and prosecutors within the criminal process itself can adequate pressure be maintained, so the argument runs, to induce conformity with the Due Process Model.

Another strand in the complex of attitudes underlying the Due Process Model is the idea—itself a shorthand statement for a complex of attitudes—of equality. This notion has only recently emerged as an explicit basis for pressing the demands of the Due Process Model, but it appears to represent, at least in its potential, a most powerful norm for influencing official conduct. Stated most starkly, the ideal of equality holds that "there can be no equal justice where the kind of trial a man gets depends on the amount of money he has."[1] The factual predicate underlying this assertion is that there are gross inequalities in the financial means of criminal defendants as a class, that in an adversary system of criminal justice an effective defense is largely a function of the resources that can be mustered on behalf of the accused, and that the very large proportion of criminal defendants who are, operationally speaking, "indigent" will thus be denied an effective defense. This factual premise has been strongly reinforced by recent studies that in turn have been both a cause and an effect of an increasing emphasis upon norms for the criminal process based on the premise.

The norms derived from the premise do not take the form of an insistence upon governmental responsibility to provide literally equal opportunities for all criminal defendants to challenge the process. Rather, they take as their point of departure the notion that the criminal process, initiated as it is by government and containing as it does the likelihood of severe deprivations at the hands of government, imposes some kind of public obligation to ensure that financial inability does not destroy the capacity of an accused to assert what may be meritorious challenges to the processes being invoked against him. At its most gross, the norm of equality would act to prevent situations in which financial inability forms an absolute barrier to the assertion of a right that is in theory generally available, as where there is a right to appeal that is, however, effectively conditional upon the filing of a trial transcript obtained at the defendant's expense. Beyond this, it may provide the basis for a claim whenever the system theoretically makes some kind of challenge available to an accused who has the means to press it. If, for example, a defendant who is adequately represented has the opportunity to prevent the case against him from coming to the trial stage by forcing the state to its proof in a preliminary hearing, the norm of equality may be invoked to assert that the same kind of opportunity must be available to others as well. In a sense the system as it functions for the small minority whose resources permit them to exploit all its defensive possibilities provides a benchmark by which its functioning in all other cases is to be tested: not, perhaps, to guarantee literal identity but rather to provide a measure of whether the process as a whole is recognizably of the same general order. The demands made by a norm of this kind are likely by their very nature to be quite sweeping. Although the norm's **imperatives** may be initially limited to determining whether in a particular case the accused was injured or prejudiced by his relative inability to make an appropriate challenge, the norm of equality very quickly moves to another level on which the demand is that the process in general be adapted to minimize discriminations rather than that a mere series of **post hoc** determinations of discrimination be made or makeable.

There is a final strand of thought in the Due Process Model that is often ignored but that needs to be candidly faced if thought on the subject is not to be obscured. This is a mood of skepticism about the morality and utility of the criminal sanction, taken either as a whole or in some of its applications. The subject is a large and complicated one, comprehending as it does much of the intellectual history of our times. It is properly the subject of another essay altogether. To put the matter briefly, one cannot improve upon the statement by Professor Paul Bator:

> In summary we are told that the criminal law's notion of just condemnation and punishment is a cruel hypocrisy visited by a smug society on the psychologically and economically crippled; that its premise of a morally autonomous will with at least some measure of choice whether to comply with the values expressed in a penal code is unscientific and outmoded; that its reliance on punishment as an educational and deterrent agent is misplaced, particularly in the case of the very members of society most likely to engage in criminal conduct; and that its failure to provide for individualized and humane rehabilitation of offenders is inhuman and wasteful.[2]

This skepticism, which may be fairly said to be widespread among the most influential and articulate contemporary leaders of informed opinion, leads to an attitude toward the processes of the criminal law that, to quote Mr. Bator again, engenders "a peculiar receptivity toward claims of injustice which arise within the traditional structure of the system itself; fundamental disagreement and unease about the very bases of the criminal law has, inevitably, created acute pressure at least to expand and liberalize those of its processes and doctrines which serve to make more tentative its judgments or limit its power." In short, doubts about the ends for which power is being exercised create pressure to limit the **discretion** with which that power is exercised.

There are two kinds of problems that need to be dealt with in any model of the criminal process. One is what the rules shall be. The other is how the rules shall be implemented. The second is at least as important as the first. The distinctive difference between the two models is not only in the rules of conduct that they lay down but also in the sanctions that are to be invoked when a claim is presented that the rules have been breached and, no less importantly, in the timing that is permitted or required for the invocation of those sanctions.

As I have already suggested, the Due Process Model locates at least some of the sanctions for breach of the operative rules in the criminal process itself. The relation between these two aspects of the process—the rules and the sanctions for their breach—is a purely formal one unless there is some mechanism for bringing them into play with each other. The hinge between them in the Due Process Model is the availability of legal counsel. This has a double aspect. Many of the rules that the model requires are couched in terms of the availability of counsel to do various things at various stages of the process—this is the conventionally recognized aspect; beyond it, there is a pervasive assumption that counsel is necessary in order to invoke sanctions for breach of any of the rules. The more freely available these sanctions are, the more important is the role of counsel in seeing to it that the sanctions are appropriately invoked. If the process is seen as a series of occasions for checking its own operation, the role of counsel is a much more nearly central one than is the case in a process that is seen as primarily concerned with expeditious determination of factual guilt. And if equality of operation is a governing norm, the availability of counsel to some is seen as requiring it for all. Of all the controverted aspects of the criminal process, the right to counsel, including the role of government in its provision, is the most dependent on what one's model of the process looks like, and the least susceptible of resolution unless one has confronted the antinomies of the two models.

I do not mean to suggest that questions about the right to counsel disappear if one adopts a model of the process that conforms more or less closely to the Crime Control Model, but only that such questions become absolutely central if one's model moves very far down the spectrum of possibilities toward the pure Due Process Model. The reason for this centrality is to be found in the assumption underlying both models that the process is an adversary one in which the initiative in invoking relevant rules rests primarily on the parties concerned, the state, and the accused. One could construct models that placed central responsibility on adjudicative agents such as committing magistrates and trial judges. And there are, as we shall see, marginal but nonetheless important adjustments in the role of the adjudicative agents that enter into the models with which we are concerned: For present purposes it is enough to say that these adjustments are marginal, that the animating presuppositions that underlie both models in the context of the American criminal system relegate the adjudicative agents to a relatively passive role, and therefore place central importance on the role of counsel.

One last introductory note before we proceed to a detailed examination of some aspects of the two models in operation. What assumptions do we make about the sources of authority to shape the real-world operations of the criminal process? Recognizing that our models are only models, what agencies of government have the power to pick and choose between their competing demands? Once again, the limiting features of the American context come into play. Ours is not a system of legislative supremacy. The distinctively American institution of judicial review exercises a limiting and ultimately a shaping influence on the criminal process. Because the Crime Control Model is basically an affirmative model, emphasizing at every turn the existence and exercise of official power, its validating authority is ultimately legislative (although proximately administrative). Because the Due Process Model is basically a negative model, asserting limits on the nature of official power and on the modes of its exercise, its validating authority is judicial and requires an appeal to supra-legislative law, to the law of the Constitution. To the extent that tensions between the two models are resolved by deference to the Due Process Model, the authoritative force at work is the judicial power, working in the distinctively judicial mode of invoking the sanction of **nullity.** That is at once the strength and the weakness of the Due Process Model: its strength because in our system the appeal to the Constitution provides the last and the overriding word; its weakness because saying no in specific cases is an exercise in futility unless there is a general willingness on the part of the officials who operate the process to apply negative prescriptions across the board. It is no accident that statements reinforcing the Due Process Model come from the courts, while at the same time facts denying it are established by the police and prosecutors.

NOTES

1. Griffin v. Illinois, 351 U.S. 12, 19 (1956).
2. "Finality in Criminal Law and Federal Habeas Corpus for State Prisoners," 76 *Harvard Law Review* 441, 442 (1963).

QUESTIONS FOR DISCUSSION

1. Describe the value system that undergirds Packer's crime control model of the criminal process. Cite specific examples to support your answer.
2. Describe the value system that undergirds Packer's due process model of the criminal process. Cite specific examples to support your answer.
3. Is it desirable for the justice system to concern itself with crime control and due process simultaneously? Should there be a balance between the two models? Why?

APPLICATIONS

1. Emerging from the due process model of the criminal process is the "ideal of equality." Simply stated, "there can be no equal justice where the kind of trial a man gets depends on the amount of money he has." Consider the recent case involving former football pro O.J. Simpson. Do you believe that other defendants in circumstances similar to those of Mr. Simpson, whose means are significantly less, would receive the same quality of defense or the benefit of full judicial processing? Why? Do your views differ from those of other members of your class?
2. In your opinion, is it possible to ensure that each person receives "equal justice" regardless of his or her monetary means? Why?

Fighting Crime in a Crumbling System

Steven Brill

He picked them up in his yellow cab at about ten to three on a Sunday morning in October as they came out of a nightclub in the Chelsea section of Manhattan.

They were white, so it seemed safe enough, he'd later explain.

They were well-dressed; he'd later remember their designer leather jackets. They were even friendly; like him, they seemed in their thirties and joked pleasantly with him in their Russian-accented English about finding girls in the clubs.

They told him to pull over. He stopped the meter. Then one of them reached across the front seat, turned off the ignition, and yoked him around the neck with his bulky left forearm. "You know what this is," he whispered.

The other burly Russian drew a gun. A gold, shiny, fat nine-millimeter semiautomatic. The cabbie, who says he used to be an art dealer until he lost his business a year ago and has an eye for detail, says he can still see the gold metal barrel of the gun "when I close my eyes."

He begged for his life. "Please, please, please. I'll give you anything you want, all I have," he cried, yanking fives and tens and singles from the various pockets where he hid his money.

"More, more, more," the one with the gun yelled in his thick accent.

Soon there was $267 scattered on the cabbie's lap and front seat.

He turned out his pockets, then offered them his change, which they refused.

"More, more," repeated the gunman, waving the nine-millimeter. The cabbie begged again. He had a 2-year-old daughter whom he wanted to see in the morning, he cried.

They made him spread across the front seat, face down. "I was sure this was the end of my life," he remembers. "I closed my eyes."

They told him he'd be dead if he looked up, but that if he waited three minutes, they wouldn't shoot him and they'd even throw his keys back.

They jumped out and into a waiting getaway car. He stayed down for five minutes before he peered over the dashboard.

They hadn't thrown back the keys.

Four days later, he was out again in the yellow cab, cruising the same neighborhood, determined to find the men who had threatened, he says, "to take me from my daughter." He was certain, he says, that he had figured out that "their M.O. was to hang around that nightclub waiting for a cabbie."

Sure enough, he spotted them. He drove some more and found a group of cops in a van that is part of a special team assigned to this neighborhood because of problems stemming from the nightclubs. He explained excitedly about the robbery four nights before and demanded they chase the suspects. The cops said they'd follow him in his cab. Flash your lights if you see them, they said.

The cab and the van circled the block once. The cabbie didn't spot his Russian robbers.

The cops told him to go home. They'd look without him, they promised. As he was driving away, he saw his Russians and hit the lights. The cops poured out of the van. The cabbie and the cops say that one of the two soon-to-be-defendants reached for the nine-millimeter tucked in his belt.

On television you'd now have one, maybe two, dead perpetrators and a snappy half-hour episode of *Police Story*. Here you have two very much alive defendants (a cop grabbed the guy's gun), and eight months' worth of justice, urban American-style.

Which means not much justice at all.

What you have instead is waiting. Delay. Laziness. Resignation. Judges, court officers, lawyers reading paperbacks, doing crossword puzzles, scanning the sports pages, exchanging jokes, planning lunch, and generally shooting the shit—there's just no other way to describe it—while the American criminal justice system, at least in this city, grinds to a halt.

But what you also have are people like Manhattan assistant-district attorney Elizabeth Karas—who don't seem to understand about the futility of it all. Who care. Who navigate their way through the system, ignoring the indignities and the numbness and the debris around them and do their bit to redeem the rule of law.

Karas, a 32-year-old from a farm town in Western Massachusetts, seems to be a holdout in a system that has captured, beaten down, and bureaucratized almost every-one else. Spend a day with Beth Karas and you realize that restoring the rule of law for that cabdriver isn't about liberals or conservatives—Karas and the cabdriver consider themselves liberals—but about changing the mind-set of the system. It has to become a place where people are brought to justice, not a numbing, grimy bureaucracy where cases are processed.

And what gets ground down most by the processing of justice is, in fact, the sense that justice is what's being delivered. It's not so much that the sentences meted out in the plea bargaining that is at the center of the process are too lenient, though they are, as it is that almost everyone, except the victims and an oddball judge or two and some unhardened defense lawyers and prosecutors like Karas, seem numb to it all.

Spend time with Beth Karas and her 40 or 50 case files—walk with her into the deadened, shooting-the-shit courtrooms—and you want to scream. You want to remind people of the crisis we keep hearing about. You want to remind people that something important is supposed to be going on here.

It is Thursday morning, April 27, and Karas is on the phone explaining to the cabdriver why his case—which she calls "my Russians case"—is going to be delayed for the ninth time. "Oh, you got robbed again?" she asks. "Another gun? Why didn't you report it? You really should."

"He didn't think he could ID this guy," she explains to me. ("This one was just another indistinguishable black face," the driver later tells me. "He could be anyone. There's no point in reporting it.")

She tells the cabbie to stay near the phone, that maybe the case will come on for the afternoon.

Meantime, one of the cops who made the arrest waits in the hall. He'll wait there all day, costing the city one cop on the street and about $25 an hour. But there will be no case. The two defense lawyers and one of the defendants (both are out on $3,500 bail) won't show up.

Karas is spending the day on the second floor of the Manhattan criminal courts building in what's called the Early Case Assessment Bureau, or ECAB. Of the 396 assistant district attorneys in Manhattan District Attorney Robert Morgenthau's office, some 300 are assigned to the trial division, which means they handle cases from arraignment through a plea bargain or verdict. (The others handle appeals or work in special units.) Of these 300, 200, including Karas, handle basic felonies. They pick up new cases by working once every 12 days in ECAB (either on an 8 A.M. to 4 P.M. shift or a 4 P.M. to 12 A.M. shift), where they meet with police who have just made arrests, go over their arrest reports, and process felony complaints that may lead to grand jury indictments.

ECAB, then, is the beginning of the pipeline for the 40 to 50 cases apiece that Karas and the other ADAs will typically be handling at any one time. As a relatively mid-level ADA (she's been there for about three years since graduating from Fordham law school), Karas now gets a mix of serious and not-so-serious crimes.

Such is the general lack of confidence in the court scheduling system that Karas has been assigned to ECAB today even though her Russians case is scheduled to go to trial at 9:30 that morning. Were it to go to trial, she'd be replaced in ECAB by another ADA.

But of course, it won't go to trial, despite the face that she stayed up the night before preparing her opening and her direct examinations, and despite the presence of her lead-off police witness and the standby readiness of her cabbie and five more cops.

Karas's first case in ECAB seems like a yawner. A man was arrested just after midnight in a locker room at *The New York Times* building, after he was allegedly seen by a security guard looking through the lockers of *Times* deliverymen. The arresting officer is a 24-year veteran who stares at Karas's legs whenever she gets up, and who talks so much like Archie Bunker that it's not a cliche to describe him as such. He's vague on the details, despite a self-proclaimed "photogenic mind."

He's also tired, he says, slurping a cup of coffee; he's been waiting since about 2 A.M., earning overtime since his shift ended.

Like all but three of the defendants whose cases Karas will be working on today and during the next two weeks when I will be tracking her, this one is nonwhite. He's a 33-year-old black man.

The purpose of ECAB is for Karas to assess the case, to see if it's worth prosecuting and for what charges. She's skeptical of this one. As she gets the cop to talk more, it turns out that the suspect has worked as a *Times* deliveryman on and off, though he wasn't working that night. It also turns out that no one has reported anything missing from a locker and that the cop didn't get the name of the right person at the *Times* who could tell him, or Karas, this morning if anyone subsequently reported a theft. So the burglary charge will probably have to go. At best, this will be a trespass.

But Karas presses on. "I'll write it up as a burglary because I want to see his sheet," she tells the cop, meaning that she wants to see the defendant's "rap sheet," or arrest and conviction record.

"I had a trespass at Columbia [University] a few months ago," she explains, "[and] it looked like nothing, until I noticed one of the other ADAs had the same guy on a burglary, which he said was a weak case that he was happy to unload on me. Then we got his sheet and saw he had a bunch of trespasses and a burglary." Karas and another ADA have since indicted that defendant, she says, "on four burglaries of dorms up there, with solid cases. So let's see what comes up here."

Nearly half the time in ECAB the ADAs don't yet have the arrest and conviction records back on defendants because, says Karas, "the computer system…bogs down."

"Did you *Miranda* him?" Karas asks the cop.

"Oh yeah, right off of my card."

"When?"

"At the [police] precinct."

"Did you ask him anything before that?"

"Just if he was working that night at the paper, and he said he wasn't."

Which, of course, makes that admission not admissible.

Karas, who has been writing feverishly on a form (that she will ultimately have to turn over to the defense), now reads back a synopsis of the circumstances surrounding the arrest and the alleged crime.

"That's it in a nutshell, my dear," the cop replies, winking at me.

"This case won't be much," says Karas after the cop leaves. "He had to make the arrest because the security guards caught the guy and said they'd seen him looking in lockers, but there's no proof of anything stolen and the guards' descriptions of what happened are sketchy; it's not clear they could really see the guy, just that he was in there when he wasn't authorized to be there."

Within a week, Karas will have determined that although the defendant has a long police record she still cannot make much of this case. So, she will be about to reduce it to a trespass, which is a misdemeanor, and let the defendant off with no jail time. Except that the defendant, released on his own recognizance, will never return to court, and a **bench warrant** will be issued for him.

It's now 9:30 and Karas calls the clerk in state supreme court justice Robert Haft's court to find out about her Russians case. There's no answer.

"This is incredible," she sputters. "There's not even anyone there yet, and my trial's supposed to start."

Ten minutes later, she gets an answer. The clerk tells her that the lawyers and defendants haven't shown up, and that one of the two lawyers has called and said he won't be able to be there until the afternoon.

"This is ludicrous," she mutters.

Since the arrest of the Russians on October 6, the case has been called in court nine times, and rarely has anything gone according to schedule.

On October 28 only one of the two defendants could be arraigned, because the city's Correction Department did not deliver the alleged gunwielder to court. (Both were being held in jail, until they made bail in January.)

On November 16 one of the two defense lawyers failed to show up for motions for pre-trial hearings. Justice Haft adjourned the case until December 14. "I have a busy calendar," Haft says, explaining the near-month delay, "and my guess is that between my calendar and the lawyers' calendars this is the best we could do." (A *Manhattan Lawyer* random survey of all the judges in criminal sections of the state supreme court in Manhattan on May 9, 1989, found that Justice Haft started court at 9:55 A.M. on May 9 and left at 3:45 P.M.; Haft asserts that he generally runs court "from about 10:00 to 4:30," and works in chambers before and after each session.)

On December 14 Haft ruled that the grand jury minutes had been sufficient to establish the indictment. (Defense lawyers routinely make a fruitless motion questioning the indictment on those grounds.) But he adjourned the case until January 11, 1989, to give Karas time to respond to other defense motions having to do with the arrest, the cabbie's identification of the suspects, and the search and confiscation of the gun.

All of these motions are "boilerplate," Karas contends, asserting that "there is nothing in this case at all controversial about the arrest, the ID, or the gun." Asked about that, Jeffrey Granat, a Mineola, New York, solo practitioner who represents the alleged gunman, says, "You always like to file these motions just to see what's going on. You'd be committing malpractice not to. If you don't file these kinds of motions within forty-five days, you lose your right to, and that would be malpractice....Besides," he adds, "you do try to slow things down."

Indeed, in most cases these motions, though thoroughly justified by any lawyer wanting to lodge a competent defense, are nothing more than the dance that precedes the **plea bargain.** "A lot of our deals," says Karas, "don't get made until the hearings are held and even until the defendants and their lawyers see us picking a jury; then they want to deal. They figure if they delay it some of our evidence will go bad—maybe the witness will disappear or something—or something else will happen. But that's no reason," she adds, "for a judge to hold it up a month or two."

By January 11 Karas had filed her response. In court that day, Haft granted the defense motion to hold a hearing on the pre-trial motions that Karas had responded to in writing. He set the hearing for February 1. Meantime, the defendants were able to post their $3,500 bail.

By January Karas had established that the defendant who had not had the gun but had allegedly yoked the cabdriver had a prior conviction for attempted possession of a weapon in 1984. Attempted possession is one of the clumsier plea bargain pleas (one pictures someone lunging for a gun); it means, in this case, that he'd been caught with a loaded gun but had pled down to the attempt charge, which is the lowest-level felony on the books. His sentence: a $250 fine and five years' probation.

However, that conviction could now hurt him. For, as Karas points out, a second felony conviction would make him a **predicate felon**, which, under a state law requiring all repeat felons to serve at least a year and a half in prison for even the lowest-level felony, would mandate a higher sentence on the cab robbery case.

Thus, by January, Karas was prepared to offer the defendant with the felony record a plea that would get him a four-to-eight-year sentence, meaning he would have to serve a minimum of four years before he could be paroled. She was prepared to offer three to nine years to the defendant who allegedly had had the gun.

If they didn't accept these plea bargains and instead went to trial, the first defendant's maximum sentence could be twelve-and-a-half to twenty-five years; the second defendant's could be eight-and-a-third to twenty-five years. Karas could not guarantee the lower sentences she was proposing; sentencing was technically up to the judge. But judges customarily go along with these negotiated deals.

So by January Karas was already talking plea bargains to the defense lawyers, and it was clear, she says, that "they didn't want to go to trial."

On February 1 the alleged gunman didn't show up. His lawyer announced that he was being held in New Jersey on warrants for burglary, car theft, receiving stolen property, and possession of heroin. Karas had not known about the New Jersey arrests because, incredibly, the computer system that New York uses to check criminal records does not tie into the national computer bank that would allow it to access other states' criminal records. "You could have a guy wanted for murder in North Carolina or convicted five times in Connecticut and not know it," Karas says. "I asked this guy if he'd ever been arrested before and, of course, he said no."

Karas also found out that the gun he had had when arrested, which the cabbie says was the same gun that had been pointed at him, had been traced by the police to a burglary in Virginia. "The prints the cops had in Virginia weren't good," Karas says. "So I couldn't connect him to that."

On February 1 Justice Haft told Karas to work with New Jersey prosecutors on producing the alleged gunman, and he adjourned the case until March 2.

On March 2 the alleged gunman, having made bail in New Jersey, showed up. But his co-defendant, also out on bail, didn't appear in the morning. His lawyer, Queens solo practitioner Alan Kudisch, was there in the morning but was not there in the afternoon because, he says, "I had a sentencing hearing in Queens." The alleged gunman's lawyer, Granat, didn't appear all day because, he says, "I had other business." He declined to be more specific.

"I try to get the lawyers to come to court," says Haft. "But they're busy, too, you know. I think these guys had other trials....When you have a case with two defendants and two defense lawyers," he adds, "it's almost impossible to get them there."

Did he ever consider sanctions for them?

"Well, as far as I know," he answers, "they called the court the day they were supposed to be here and said they couldn't come because they had trials."

Haft acknowledges that by not calling until after they were supposed to be in court at 9:30—in fact, according to the judge's clerk and law secretary the two defense lawyers typically called in the late morning or afternoon if at all; and according to Karas, they sometimes didn't call at all—they had caused Karas's police witnesses to waste a day. But, says Haft, "that's a matter of courtesy between counsel. I have nothing to do with that."

"It may be that they didn't call in a few times," Haft concedes. "But what can you do? Everyone is so busy."

Haft, who has been a judge for 18 years, says he has "never felt that any case was so severe that I should impose sanctions on a lawyer for not appearing."

Karas doubts that the two lawyers were on trial all those days. "Their only goal," she asserts, "is to string this out. They just don't want this case to come to trial. Who knows, maybe the Russians owe them money....A couple of times, I even tried to ask them where they were on trial, but got nothing."

Court rules require lawyers to submit affidavits when they can't make a date because of another trial, stating the name of the competing case and where it is being tried. Hart says he didn't require the affidavits (actually, he has no discretion not to require them) because "if a lawyer is a member of the bar, I think I can assume he's telling the truth."

As for why a warrant wasn't issued for the missing defendant's arrest, Haft said first that he thought he had issued warrants, then that "if the lawyers don't show, that's probably why their clients didn't show."

So on March 2 Haft adjourned the case until March 15 for the pre-trial hearings.

On March 15 the alleged gunman didn't show up but the lawyers did. No warrant was issued. The case was adjourned for April 5.

On April 5 both defense lawyers didn't show up. Granat sent a message that he had another trial, according to Karas's case notes. Kudisch says he "doesn't know" if he was there that day, but that "it wouldn't matter, since the other lawyer wasn't there."

April 13 neither defense lawyer showed up but their clients did, though one appeared late in the afternoon. Both lawyers sent word that they were on trial. Justice Haft adjourned the case until today, April 27.

It is now 9:45 on April 27, and Karas picks up another ECAB file and calls the arresting cop's name into a microphone, hoping to fetch him from the police waiting room across from Karas's ECAB cubicle. (The waiting room is so filthy and overcrowded that one has to wonder who got the better of the deal, the arrestee or the arrester.)

"It's a wolfpack case," she explains, using a term that's old hat to her but that had become part of the language of New York only a week before, when a woman jogging in Central Park one evening had been attacked and raped by a roaming group of teenage thugs, called a wolfpack in police parlance.

A young cop who has answered Karas's page sits opposite her and explains that he had arrested a night security guard who'd been attacked by a group of "six or seven black kids." The gang had piled out of a van and went after their prey at about four in the morning a week before at Park Avenue and 49th Street. The guard, who was unarmed and worked at a law firm, had been held at gunpoint and beaten.

But a cabdriver had seen the attack and followed the van long enough to get a license plate number.

"So we put a bulletin out for the van," the cop explains, "and over the weekend the cops in Elmira, upstate [New York], pick it up. Unbelievable.

"Turns out this kid's [the alleged driver of the van] father has a business driving relatives of prisoners up from New York to the prison in Elmira. The van is set up like a bus....So the cops up there see all these blacks and Puerto Ricans—that's who the families are—riding around in a van in this rural area and they check it out, and the license plate comes up that it's wanted on a robbery. So all kinds of cops and sheriffs close in on it with shotguns, and these poor bastards in the van, including the driver, who's the kid's father, spend all night in the lockup until they call us, and we tell them we're looking for a kid....

"They tell us the driver is an older man. So we talk to him on the phone find out he's got a kid who uses the van, and tell them to let him go as long as he promises to bring his son in....You see, we couldn't go up there and arrest him because the captain wouldn't give us the expense money. I say, 'Captain, what if this guy knocks off a gas station on his way home?' But he won't let us go. Can you imagine that? We've got to get this guy to promise to come back to New York and bring in his son.

"Anyway, he brings the kid in with his mother, and the mother faints when we put the cuffs on the kid. She's carrying a Bible with her; these are a good family. The kid has no record until then. But here he's completely screwed up his father's business and all....And you know what, when he gets bailed out, he turns to the old man and says, 'Dad, I need some money to get home.' The father tells him to get lost. I'd have crippled him."

The suspect arrested today, the one whose case Karas now has, is the van owner's son's friend. His name had been mentioned during the van owner's son's arrest.

"[The van owner's son] told us the whole story about how he and his friends got drunk, took the van, and went riding around," the cop explains. "First they went to Forty-Second Street to those machines that take pictures and pumped money into the machines to have pictures taken of themselves with their guns.

"That's right, they take pictures of themselves with their illegal pieces; they get some kind of charge out of it.

"Then, he says, they drove around some more, and that when he was driving, some of his friends, but not him of course, jumped out and might have robbed a guy—but it wasn't him. But he did mention this other guy's name, so we picked him up last night."

This defendant, too, claimed to have no record, but the cop explains that he's just learned that two days after this alleged robbery this defendant had been arrested for the gunpoint theft of a Jaguar. "He pointed a gun at a guy, got in, and drove off. But he got stopped a few minutes later," the cop explains. "In one week he became a two-time loser. Must have just started on crack or something."

The wolfpack robbery victim had now picked this defendant out in what's called a photo array—a group of mug shots of similar-looking young blacks.

Karas writes up the case then calls Haft's court again, only to find that there's still no sign of the Russian defendants or their lawyers.

A month later, the wolfpack case will still be in the early plea bargaining stages.

Karas then takes the information on two drug cases. One involves a young man and woman who were arrested by two undercover cops when they were found allegedly smoking crack in a rental van parked in the rental company's Lower East Side parking lot. Karas says the case is unlikely to stick because it's not clear that the cops actually saw them smoking the crack and it's not certain that the residue in the crack pipe, which was all that was left when the cops reached the defendants after seeing them light up, will test out in the laboratory.

The male defendant has a long drug arrest record that includes three convictions, none of them felonies, but no prison time. His girlfriend has no apparent record, though she has given as her address a drug clinic near where the truck was parked.

A month later the case will be reduced from a drug possession and burglary (entering a commercial vehicle) to a misdemeanor of attempted drug possession. Both defendants will have been given probation.

In the second drug case, a uniformed cop allegedly saw the defendant dispensing vials of crack on 42nd Street at about six that morning. "These people just have no fear anymore," says the cop, a large, athletic type who's slurping coffee to stay awake and looks about 18 years old. "He's standing there with a vial in one hand and ten others in a plastic bag. Then we found ten more in his pocket....They were ten-dollar vials, you know, two hits or two chunks each.

"He told us they were for him, that he wasn't selling," the cop continues, "that that's what he uses in a day. Then he gets mad at us when we call him a crackhead at the precinct."

"The guy's a career criminal," the cop adds.

This is not the cop's assessment of the man's character. The computer has already spit out his record, and at age 29 he's got nine arrests, including three for burglary and four for drugs, and two convictions—but a total of only about two years' prison time. Now, Karas says, "there's enough drugs here to give him some tough time."

"Did you voucher [log in as evidence] the plastic bag?" Karas asks the cop.

"No, just the vials he had."

"Next time voucher it. The defense lawyer will try to make something of it. He'll say you made it up....These days it's hard enough to be a cop in this town and get a jury or judge to believe you. You shouldn't give them any chances to slip you up."

Two months later the case will be awaiting the usual pretrial hearings because the defense lawyer and his client have refused a two-and-a-half-to-five-year plea bargain suggested by the judge. (Karas had wanted a higher sentence.)

"He's out now," says Karas, so he's in no hurry. "The judge told him he won't go below three-and-a-half-to-seven if he didn't take [this] offer. But they're waiting. And I'll probably give in, and so will the judge." (Although judges are not supposed to get involved in plea bargaining, many do. Again, they have the ultimate say on sentences; the ADA can only recommend a sentence to a judge.)

At about 11:30 Karas takes the elevator to Justice Haft's courtroom to find out firsthand about her Russians case. She is by now so accustomed to the elevators in the criminal courts building at 100 Centre Street that she doesn't realize that she's waited about eight minutes until I point it out. Her patience, or oblivious tolerance, seems metaphorical.

Haft's court is a large, 40-foot-ceilinged empty room with long-since-cracked leather chairs for the jurors, a relic of the majesty of the process that once was.

The only people there are four uniformed, armed court officers, all reading newspapers, and a clerk, who cheerfully tells Karas to forget it when she says she's there and ready for trial. "No one's showing up today," he says with a chuckle.

In fact, one of the defendants, the one who allegedly had the gun, is sitting in the back, but his lawyer and his co-defendant are nowhere to be found.

When the clerk sees Karas's frown, he adds, matter-of-factly, that one of the lawyers has phoned in to say he's got a trial today in Queens, and won't be there until late in the afternoon. (Why he hasn't given that news to the defendant who was nice enough to drop by is anyone's guess.)

Just then, the second defendant arrives. The clerk tells them to go out for lunch.

Although Karas will return, as instructed by the clerk, at 4 P.M., they won't come back from lunch until 5:05, whereupon Karas will ask the judge if she can make a record of the fact that she is there and ready but the opposing lawyers aren't. The judge will tell her he'd like to oblige her but that the court reporter has gone home because it is after 5 P.M.

When Karas gets back to the ECAB cubicle at about noon, she's got another wolfpack case, this one involving a 17-year-old defendant (with one prior robbery arrest and one drug arrest but no convictions) who, with his friends, allegedly robbed and beat a man on Madison Avenue and 130th Street in Harlem at about 4 A.M. (The victim hailed a police car, which caught up with the alleged attackers.)

It turns out that the defendant is also a defendant in a wolfpack case that Karas got in ECAB earlier in April. In that case the defendant had allegedly beaten a man who worked at an all-night delicatessen at the same location after having smashed the window of the deli's door.

When I rejoin Karas the next morning, April 28, she's in her office (a ten-by-twenty piece of linoleum that she shares with another ADA on the sixth floor of the criminal courts building) interviewing two witnesses to that earlier wolfpack case involving this defendant.

One witness is the victim, the man who works in the deli. The other is the deli's owner. They are cousins, and both are immigrants from Yemen.

The owner explains that the defendant "always comes in and takes things. A bottle of soda, some chips, and he says to me, 'I'm not going to pay for this, and I don't give a f— what you do about it.'

"But I don't call the cops," he explains, "because these guys are tough. He's very big"—at age 17, he's listed as 6 feet 1 inch and 200 pounds on the arrest report—"and I see his guns all the time."

"When do you see his gun?" Karas asks.

"Well, I don't want to say anything more about it, but he sells crack in the building next door, him and his friends, and they always have guns. If he knows I tell you this, he will come and shoot me."

Karas notes that the defendant's drug dealing would explain why he was carrying a paging beeper when he was arrested; running a drug business is usually the reason 17-year-old high school dropouts need to stay in touch, she explains.

"Do the police know he sells crack?" she asks.

"Yeah. They come by in the morning and board up the hole where he passes it out from, but he and his friends fix it the same day."

"But," he continues, "I don't make trouble. I let him take what he wants. But this time he started to smash my door for no reason. So my cousin goes outside to tell him to stop. That's when he beat my cousin."

While Karas questions the cousin about the beating, the deli owner explains to me that he used to work in a grocery store for his other cousin in another rough neighborhood in Brooklyn, but that a few months ago he had bought this store for $40,000 in cash.

"The owner told me it was safe, a good neighborhood," he says. "He lied....We have to keep the store open twenty-four hours, because if we leave it, everything will be gone when we come back....At night I sell through a window with bars....So my cousin and I and another brother work there and live in the apartment on the second floor....Now, I think we will move. But do you know anyone who would buy a store like this?"

He fidgets, looking at his watch. "Can we go?" he asks Karas. "We have to get back to the store."

"Soon."

"Will we have to come back?"

"Just once, to go to the grand jury, next week," she says, explaining too quickly and too technically about the grand jury being 23 people who will decide to indict. "Then, you won't have to come back again, unless he doesn't accept a plea. Then you'll have a trial."

"Will we see him there?"

"Well, you will, but that's only if he doesn't accept a plea."

Of course, there's always the chance the cousins will see the suspect at their store; he was released on his own recognizance (that is, without bail) in their case, because it was originally listed on the police report only as criminal mischief (the smashing of the gate), rather than an assault. And he's made his $3,000 bail on the new assault and robbery case that Karas picked up in ECAB the afternoon before.

As they leave, Karas promises that she'll call over the weekend to remind them of the details of their grand jury appearance the following Monday, and reminds them to "wear better clothes and no hats" that day.

One of them, apparently thinking the government is the government, turns as he's leaving, pulls a crumpled document out of his pocket, and asks Karas for help with a social security problem. She patiently gets the number and address of a local social security office for him.

"The guy who owns the store is [five years] younger than me and has three children and a wife back in the Middle East that he wants to bring over here after he makes his fortune," Karas says after they leave. "It's sad. He's got no chance up there on Madison Avenue."

A month later, the deli owner will tell me that he's worried about testifying and that the defendant has been to see him to offer to pay for his broken door, an offer he has refused, because Karas, who calls him regularly, has urged him not to take the money. "But I want to take the money," he tells me. "Who else will pay for my door? And I won't go down to testify [at a trial] if he's going to be there....What can I do if he comes after me? Call the police? They already know about him, and look what they do."

Meanwhile, Karas will have presented both of this defendant's cases to the grand jury and gotten indictments.

By early June Karas will be ready to offer the defendant a plea with a sentence of two to six years that will probably cover not only these two cases but a robbery case he has pending in the Bronx (assuming the prosecutor there agrees) stemming from a December arrest.

Why only two years? "Because," Karas explains, "the witnesses aren't that tight for the robberies. Who knows why [the robbery victim] really was out on the street that late? And in the case of the Arabs it was only an assault, not a robbery....And they could go back to Yemen for six months, and where would I be?

"Besides, he's a seventeen-year-old with no felony convictions," she adds, "and no judge is going to give him the maximum for robbery two"—second degree robbery, which is five to fifteen years. "On the scale of things, two-to-six or even one-and-a-half-to-four-and-a-half is what this rates."

Later that morning, April 28, Karas brushes past a woman cop reading a magazine who's been parked outside her office for more than an hour, on overtime, waiting for Karas to get a secretary to type an affidavit that she can sign. Karas takes the 10:40 elevator back up to Haft's courtroom to see if she can get her Russians case going.

A murder defendant in a different case is sitting at the defense table, without his lawyer, who is late; Haft is to begin jury selection for the man's trial. The court officers are finishing the sports pages; the judge is on the clerk's phone making lunch plans.

When the clerk sees Karas, he whispers to the judge, then tells Karas that the lawyers still haven't arrived. One of the two defendants (the one who allegedly wielded the gun) is there again.

Karas takes a seat, and we wait for about a half hour. Then, the courtroom fills with prospective jurors for the murder case. Haft gives them a little speech about the civic duty they are about to perform, then tells them to take an early lunch break because he has other business to transact.

Karas predicts that Granat, the lawyer for the defendant who allegedly had the gun, will want to plea bargain today. "He's told me his guy wants to serve time in New York, not New Jersey," she explains, "and he's about to go in New Jersey. If he's sentenced there first, he'll do his time there."

What's so good about serving time in New York?

"Well, I wondered about that, too," she answers, "but I asked around the office and found out that these Russians have kind of a network in the prisons in New York. There are now a lot of Russian immigrants involved in crime," she adds. "So he probably figures he'll be safer here."

Karas spots Kudisch, the lawyer for the guy who hadn't had the gun. They walk out of the courtroom together.

"What are you offering?" asks Kudisch. "I think my guy's ready."

"He's a predicate [felon]," says Karas, referring to his prior conviction. "And this is a bad case. So I want a plea to the top count." (This means she will not accept a plea to a count one count lower than the charge, which, under a state law intended to limit plea bargaining, is the limit to any ADA's bargaining leeway in cases such as this.)

"What sentence?"

"I'll recommend four-to-eight. He did something really bad here.

"He's got to allocute [admit to the crimes] and testify against the other guy, if I need him," she adds, as they walk through the crowded hall past another defense lawyer explaining to a scowling, tall, thin black who looks to be in his teens that "your problem is that you're a career criminal under the law."

"You really want him to testify?" Kudisch asks incredulously. "You should have your head examined if you want this guy to take the witness stand. No way he's credible about anything."

"What do you want to do?"

"I'll recommend it to him, if he shows."

"I'm going for a warrant if he doesn't show."

Another half hour passes, before Granat, the alleged gunman's lawyer, strolls down the hall.

"I've been tied up," he explains to Karas, as if explaining why he's late for a dental appointment. "Where are we?"

Karas offers him three-to-nine, and also the opportunity for the defendant to serve his time in New York instead of New Jersey where he has the other charges pending. Granat rolls his eyes. "Let's go talk to the judge," he says.

The three lawyers and the one defendant approach the bench, but there's no judge.

Haft comes back in at about 12:30, but one defendant is still missing. Haft announces that "we'll wait a short time." Meanwhile, he goes over the proposed plea bargains with the two defense lawyers and Karas, who at 5 feet 2 inches has to mount a step of sorts and stretch to converse with the judge at the bench.

One court officer points out the view of her legs to another.

Finally, at 12:55, our alleged gunman strolls in, showing no sign that he knows he's late, let alone that he regrets it. His lawyer chats briefly with him. Then the three lawyers approach the bench again.

Haft tells Karas, according to her subsequent account, that he wants her to take two-and-a-half-to-seven-and-a-half years for the alleged gunman in order to close that deal. But now he is also insisting that the men begin to serve their time immediately, rather than come back at some later date for sentencing.

Their lawyers huddle with them, approach the bench with Karas, exchange whispers, then step back.

They've refused the deal, Karas explains to me, "because they don't want to go in today. But the judge is pissed."

Haft announces that because the defendants have repeatedly missed court dates he is now revoking their bail. What he seems most upset about is that they haven't taken his plea bargain.

The defendants seem dumbfounded; they obviously hadn't realized, nor had their lawyers, that by refusing the bargain of the day they'd be put in jail to await their trial (or a new bargaining session).

The court officers lead them away, as Haft sets May 3 (five days from now) for hearings and trial.

On May 3 Karas, who by then will have found out that the accused gunman had been arrested for new alleged crimes in New Jersey (heroin possession and passing phony $20 bills) in March while out on bail, will be ready for trial once again. She'll have again studied her case the night before and have one of her cops there all day, with the other cops and cabbie standing by their phones ready to get the word to come testify. But one of the lawyers won't show up. The case will be adjourned until May 18.

On May 18 Karas will be ready once again with a cop. But both lawyers won't show. Haft will adjourn the case to May 24.

On May 24 Karas will be ready once again with a cop. But both lawyers won't show and neither will either defendant. Haft will adjourn the case to June 7.

The two lawyers, Kudisch and Granat, maintain that they had trials, or in Granat's words, "other business," on all of the days that they missed in this case. Kudisch supplied case names and courtrooms for the days in question; Granat refused.

Granat counted himself as present on two days when he'd shown up in the afternoon for 9:30 calls, explaining "the 9:30 time is a fiction, and it's especially a fiction if"—as happened on April 28 in this case—"your client is locked up, because corrections almost never delivers prisoners on time in the morning." That assessment is echoed by numerous judges, prosecutors, and defense lawyers interviewed for this article. Spokeswoman Ruby Ryles of the city's Department of Correction, which delivers 1,700–1,800 prisoners a day to courtrooms, says that inmates are delivered on time 90 percent of the time, an estimate that everyone else I spoke with laughs at.

"Look," adds Granat, "I'm a solo practitioner practicing out of Long Island, New York, and there are days when I am supposed to be in six courtrooms in six different places around the city at 9:30 in the morning. At my rates, I can't take just one case at a time. So what am I supposed to do?

"Besides, in this case," Granat continues, "I knew my co-counsel wasn't going to be there, because he had a trial, so why should I show?"

Why hadn't he called Karas in advance, so as not to waste the police witnesses' time? "If she's so worried about that, why can't she call me?" he explains. ("That's hardly my burden," says Karas.)

The solution for all the delays and adjournments, Granat explains, sounding a bit like a drunk who wants the bartender to stop serving him, "is for a judge to set a time and a date and mean it, and sanction prosecutors and lawyers who don't show up."

Granat's co-counsel, Kudisch, who also handles cases throughout the city that are scheduled simultaneously, says that he or his secretary "always call the judge's clerk or secretary the day before if I can't be there."

Haft's clerk, Kenneth Kaplan, says, "These two lawyers never called me the day before. Maybe he called the judge's secretary."

Haft's secretary, Laura Held, says that she "believes almost certainly" that neither Granat nor Kudisch "ever called until the late morning or afternoon of the day they were supposed to be here. And sometimes they never called, I think....We were all quite annoyed."

On June 7 both lawyers will show up but the judge will ask, for the first time, that the court find a Russian interpreter. The clerk will report that that will take at least until the afternoon. Karas, who says she remembers that the defendants spoke good English when she interviewed them, will show up at 2 P.M., only to be told that Haft is conducting a trial and that there are no other judges available that afternoon for the hearing and trial on this case. The case is adjourned until 9:30 on July 5, which is the first day Karas will be back from a vacation.

Despite Karas's protests, Haft has set another of Karas's cases for hearings and trial for 9:30 on July 5, which means that at least some witnesses, including police officers in one of the two cases, will be wasting their time.

This is not at all unusual. Most judges set most of their cases for 9:30 rather than stagger them, and they typically schedule more than one case. Thus Karas, despite her protests to each judge involved, has four trials or hearings in three different courtrooms scheduled for 9:30 on July 5, plus six other motions or sentencings scheduled in other courts at that hour of that day.

The generous explanation for this absurd scheduling is that the judges know that most people won't show up most of the time and, therefore, figure that they'll hit it lucky if they have five or ten chances to get a case going. Also, one or more cases could be plea bargained just before a trial is to start, leaving the judge and his courtroom free to take on another one.

The cynical explanation is that judges are too dumb or too lazy to do otherwise, or that they just don't care about keeping lawyers waiting, or giving lawyers the comfort of knowing that they needn't really show up because some other case can replace theirs.

Haft says he routinely schedules everything for 9:30 because "who knows who's going to show or who's going to decide to cut a deal? Maybe if I had a computer we could do it differently....And on a day like July 5," he adds, "which is after a holiday weekend, I really put a lot of cases on because it's not likely too many people will be here."

"If the defense doesn't show up, the judge can't convict the guy and put him away," Karas complains. "But if we don't show up, the judge can dismiss our case or make us look bad with our bosses. So, we have to show up or send someone else from the office."

"I love this job, because I believe in my cases and I get to handle them on my own," Karas declares later over lunch. "I spent two years as a paralegal at Arnold & Porter before law school and did some fun things—they did some work on Nicaragua that I was involved in—and I have a lot of friends now at big firms who like it. But I couldn't see doing that. Here I get to do my own cases, and the cases really count."

According to Karas and her boss, trial division chief John Fried, her independence on individual cases is tempered only by the law that limits plea bargains in serious cases to a discount of one count off the indicted charge, and by office practice that all drafts of indictments are routinely reviewed by a supervisor and that she check any dicey plea bargain or trial questions with her supervisor or with Fried.

But does Karas accomplish anything by putting a violent robber in prison for a year or two or three after she's jumped through all the procedural hoops? "Well, I hope I do. It takes them off the street, and the next time, they'll get even more," she says. "Sure, I wish the sentences were longer; they should be, but that's not my job."

Isn't she frustrated by the trials that are always on the verge but never happen?

"Sure, but I do get some," she answers, her eyes brightening. "I tried nineteen misdemeanor cases, including eleven jury trials in my first two years, and loved it." (Karas says she has won "more than half.")

"When you have to assemble all the witnesses and evidence, it's like being a director of a movie. And when it's all unfolding, when you're making it unfold, the rush of adrenalin is amazing. It's a blast, especially when you believe in your cases."

Karas has now tried two felonies since becoming more senior. She's lost both of them. "The first was a police misconduct case, a low-grade felony, which we had to try," she maintains. "I was devastated to lose it, but if you can believe it, a half hour later my second trial began. The judge was a tough judge, one of the few who doesn't like delays, and he made me go right into it....It was an attempted robbery of a South American [student] at Times Square....I got him to come back for the trial; I'm real good at keeping on top of my witnesses, staying in touch with them, and it worked....My problem was that my victim was twice the size of the defendant, and the jury just didn't believe he'd been threatened....Sometimes I think Manhattan juries want proof beyond all possible doubt, not beyond a reasonable doubt....I was crushed by the two losses, but everyone in the office told me to forget it. It's hard, though.

"You burn out here," Karas continues. "It's a wonderful job, but you can't do it for more than five years. You make a commitment to stay for three years, and I don't think you can do it for much more than two years after that. You get too frustrated by all the delays."

A week later, on May 4, Karas is in her office preparing three policemen for a hearing on an arrest they made in October. It was on a Sunday afternoon, three days after two policemen had been shot and killed by drug dealers in two separate incidents the same night. This time, the cops received a radio dispatch that someone had called the 911 emergency number to report that a man with a gun was walking on 115th Street between Park and Lexington avenues, which is a known drug activity location, according to Karas and subsequent police testimony. The caller said the man was wearing a gray jacket and blue jeans.

Three cops, one Italian, the other two Puerto Rican, are telling Karas about the arrest. The Italian and one of the Puerto Ricans got the radio call while on patrol in a squad car on 106th Street and Park Avenue. They drove over to 115th Street, turned down the block, and saw the defendant walking up the street on the left side of the block.

"When the guy saw us, he turned around and walked the other way," the cop explains.

"No, that's inadmissible. You can't testify to what he saw," Karas interrupts. "Just tell what you saw."

"Okay. As we turned down the block, he was looking our way; then he turned and walked the other way."

"Good."

"So we kept after him, and pulled up alongside him. I got out from the driver's side and my partner got out from the other side....I approached him from the back, and my partner approached him from the front, just as the other guys in the unmarked car were coming up the street from the other direction."

"Isn't it a one-way street?"

"They were driving the wrong way....So he turned again, and I saw him reach for something in his waistband in his back."

"He probably was reaching for the gun to ditch it, not shoot it out with a group of cops," Karas later explains. "But with two cops shot a few days before, who knows? The cops at least had a right to be scared."

After seizing the gun, their subsequent search yielded several hundred empty tiny glassine bags, commonly used for dispensing drugs, a plastic bag full of marijuana, another bag with five-eighths of an ounce of cocaine, and a scale used for weighing drugs. And he'd been wearing a second holster.

Now the cops faced a hearing about whether their arrest and subsequent search had been made with probable cause.

It would seem that Karas's tape recording of the 911 tape, which she carried today in her pocketbook, along with evidence that the defendant had indeed been wearing a gray jacket and jeans and had been walking up 115th Street, constitutes enough cause for the police to have stopped him and, therefore, to have patted him down to make sure he had no gun, and, therefore, to have arrested him and searched him once they found the gun.

But that doesn't prevent defense counsel—nor should it—from raising all kinds of issues and testing the bona fides of all the circumstances related to the search and the evidence.

It's now 9:45 on May 4, but Karas has called the court and found that Justice Richard Andrias isn't there yet.

At 10 Karas and the three cops decide to go to court anyway.

Andrias's court, like Haft's, is a dusty relic of its once-majestic self. At the front bench in the spectator's gallery a Legal Aid Society lawyer waiting for another case reads a romance paperback. Six court officers are sitting around the prosecution table exchanging jokes. One cracks that the state's chief judge—Court of Appeals Judge Sol Wachtler, who has been making headlines asking for more funds to solve the criminal justice crisis by building new courtrooms and hiring more judges—looks like The Fonz. Two other court officers are talking baseball.

The court reporter, tieless and jacketless, is reading a newspaper.

Someone jokes about the two men, ages 71 and 78, who'd been arrested the night before on gambling and assault charges. "Whatta they gonna get," a court officer smirks, "three-to-life?"

What would this place be like with cameras in the courtroom in place and on all the time, I ask myself as I watch the **hijinks.** Things would change in a hurry if the taxpayers could see this.

The clerk acknowledges Karas, whose seriousness makes her seem like the chaperone at a frat party. She takes a seat, and thumbs through her defendant's rap sheet, which runs two-and-a-half pages and recounts five arrests—for petit larceny, possession of stolen property, drug possession, fare-beating on the subway, and another petit larceny. For the first larceny, the record shows, inexplicably, that he failed to appear after making bail but that nothing happened after that. For the stolen property case, the drug case, and the second petit larceny case he was given a total of six months in jail and five years' probation. He received a fine for the fare beat.

The case file also says that he'd been able to post $1,500 in cash bail in this case.

According to the file, the defendant had been arrested on October 23 and indicted on November 4. He hadn't been arraigned until December 9, apparently because the correction department had not delivered him for an earlier date from prison. (He hadn't made bail until January.) At a conference on December 14, defense lawyer Michael Pineiro of the Legal Aid Society of New York asked for a hearing on the arrest and the admissibility of the resulting evidence.

Did Pineiro really believe that the stop and subsequent search had been illegal? "It's my job to make sure that it was legal," he explains, adding: "The police probably had enough cause to go up and question him. But did they have enough to pat him down? The cases go all over the lot on this....The police just can't stop everyone in the community and pat them down. On the other hand, in a situation like this, some judges will say that they don't have to wait until they see the glint of a gun....It's a balancing. And it depends on the judge's view of the police officer's credibility....Remember, these guys are trained at the [police] academy in search and seizure law, so they know what to say after the fact."

"A lawyer who didn't make motions in a case like this would be guilty of malpractice," says Legal Aid Society criminal defense division chief Robert Baum, responding to my description of the case. "You have to make sure they really had a reason to stop him. You want to check out that 911 tape....You want to make sure they really had cause to pat him down. It seems also that they...searched him immediately [which they would not have had probable cause to do], instead of patting him down first."

On December 14 Andrias adjourned the case to allow the two sides to submit papers on the search and evidence issues.

Karas says that at this point, she offered Pineiro a plea which would result in a three-to-six-year sentence, but he turned it down. (Pineiro confirms the offer but says he told Karas he'd consider it and never formally turned it down. "My client, however, was determined to have a hearing on the search," he adds.)

On January 25 Andrias adjourned the case until February 8 to allow Pineiro to submit more papers by March 17. A hearing was then scheduled for March 21.

On March 21 Karas was on trial, and Andrias adjourned the case until March 31, despite a note Karas says she had sent to the judge saying she'd be away that day.

The March 31 date was postponed to April 18, but on April 18 the defendant, now out on bail, failed to show up. Andrias ordered a warrant issued for his arrest, but he was not arrested, which is no surprise since 150 police in New York are in charge of enforcing more than two hundred thousand such warrants each year. The hearing was rescheduled for May 2.

On May 2 Andrias failed to show up for work, telling the lawyers the next time he saw them that he'd had to go to a funeral.

Now it is May 4, and the hearing is to begin.

Except that it doesn't begin. At 10:55, after Karas had been waiting almost an hour, defense lawyer Pineiro arrives.

"Oh, everybody's here," the clerk exclaims, getting up to go get the judge.

As the judge walks in, robeless, the clerk looks up again and realizes that the defendant hasn't yet arrived. "Looks like they can't find the defendant," he tells Andrias.

Unbothered, Andrias engages in some banter with the clerk, then goes to make a phone call.

Karas is obviously angry. "I've got so much to do," she mutters. The three cops, who are waiting outside in the hall, peek in occasionally.

It is now 11:15.

As I sit there watching the operators of our criminal justice system passing the time like retirees at a country filling station, I devise a plan to spot-check the productivity of the entire system. I will pull all of our reporters and editors from *The American Lawyer* and *Manhattan Lawyer,* and even some from our sister paper in New Jersey, into this building one day and sit one reporter or editor in each courtroom—all 45 of them—for the full working day to clock how long each court is in session conducting business.

The result, published in *Manhattan Lawyer* on May 30, would be that on average each court was in session on May 9 for four hours and 27 minutes, with Andrias's court running four hours and seven minutes. The rest of the day in this and most courtrooms— there were notable exceptions of courtrooms run by judges who know how to run things—would be given over to missing lawyers, missing defendants, missing witnesses, and missing jurors, all unsupervised by docile judges.

Andrias would begin court at 9:57 the day of the spot-check, take a one-hour-and-41-minute lunch break, and adjourn court at 3:45. He would later tell me that he regularly gets to court at about 8 A.M. and works in chambers, and typically leaves "sometime after five thirty," though on occasion he has worked until 8 P.M. or later, and that on the day of the *Manhattan Lawyer* survey he worked until after 5 P.M. on a special court task force. He would also report that he writes about "three to six opinions a month" that vary from "one to thirty pages." The problem with the system, he would explain, is that "you have a small pool of lawyers who are overloaded, and I'm not the kind of ego who feels he should impose sanctions on a lawyer because he can't be here because he has other pressing business. I was once a lawyer too, you know.

"Sure, I schedule lots of things at the same time," Andrias would add. "But that's because you have to be flexible and be ready to go when all the lawyers get here."

At 11:20 on May 4 Andrias tells the clerk to call another case. A Puerto Rican woman is brought in from the lockup and sentenced by the judge to a year in prison for what seems (from what can be discerned from the prosecutor's and clerk's muffled tones) to be some kind of crime involving stolen credit cards. "Counsel has been vociferous in your defense and been quite an effective advocate; I now wish you good luck," Andrias lectures the young, bewildered woman, oblivious to the obvious fact that she can't understand words like counsel and vociferous.

It is now 11:40. Andrias announces that he's ready for Karas's case. But Pineiro has now disappeared, and his client still isn't here.

At 11:45 Pineiro appears with his client. Pineiro approaches the bench with Karas and they talk to the judge for about a minute. Then the first cop is called.

Karas, her words tightly clipped, her presentation unflashy but confident, takes him through a recap of his career, eliciting his experience; he's been involved in "sixty to seventy drug arrests" in the last six months, he says, explaining that since November he's been moved off regular patrol to a special drug unit in the same precinct. Then, Karas has him describe the arrest.

When it's his turn, Pineiro asks the judge "for a minute or two." Then he begins by having the cop answer almost exactly the same questions that Karas had asked him about the circumstances of the arrest. His one new question: "About how many blocks' drive was it from 106th on Park Avenue to 115th?"

Pineiro then asks if the dispatcher had described the race or age of the man in the gray jacket and bluejeans, as if that mattered—as if the cop couldn't have stopped everyone with a gray jacket and blue jeans on that particular street once he'd gotten the call.

Though the questioning is pointless, Karas seems nervous. "He's got a witness outside— that woman we saw before," she whispers, referring to a fidgety young Hispanic woman we had seen waiting in the back of the courtroom.

Karas suspects that the witness is the defendant's girlfriend and that she's probably the one who made the 911 call. "Only now," says Karas, "they've made up after having some kind of fight and she's gonna say he was walking with her or something."

As the questioning continues it becomes increasingly clears—and increasingly annoying to the cop in the dock justifying the good faith of his arrest—that Justice Andrias isn't listening to it all. He can be heard discussing lunch plans with his clerk, then whispering about another case. At least three times he asks the cop (who later tells Karas how upset he felt about being ignored) to repeat something; one time Andrias even says, "I wasn't listening." Of course, this pre-trial, prejury hearing is solely for the judge's ear.

("I was taking careful notes, twenty-six pages' worth," Andrias later recalls, noting that he rarely gets a transcript of the proceedings. "And I might have asked him to repeat something because my notes weren't clear, or because I was distracted momentarily.")

After about a half hour, Pineiro finishes his cross-examination, and Karas puts another cop on the stand. After his cross-examination of that cop and a lunch recess, Pineiro calls the mystery witness.

She says that while out walking her dog she saw the arrest and that there had been "fifty people" on the street at the time. (The cops had said there was no one on the street, let alone anyone with a gray jacket and jeans.)

Karas begins her cross-examination at about 3:30. Yes, the defendant is a friend of hers, but she hasn't spoken to him since April, she swears, until the other day when he'd asked her to testify.

At about 4 P.M., Andrias adjourns the hearing until the following Monday, May 8, so he can hear another case.

"All in all, that wasn't a bad day," Andrias says in a later interview. "I booked four cases for trial that day, which is what I usually try to do, and sentenced two of them after pleas [actually it was one defendant sentenced on two pleas], held the hearing with Miss Karas, and held that other hearing, which I took a plea on the next morning after I dictated a decision [on that hearing] from the bench....Sure, there was some chaos, but you have that when you're a judge and under siege with sixty-five or seventy-five cases to handle. But what we got done that day is not half-bad by our standards....I'm not defensive about that day at all; it's fairly illustrative and fairly good....There's a limit within which even the most efficient judge can operate."

As their hearing ends, Pineiro takes Karas aside and asks, according to Karas's later account, if she's still offering a three-to-six deal. She says no, that now that he's seen her case and put her through all this trouble, she wants four-to-eight. Pineiro, according to Karas, says he'll think about it. (Pineiro confirms this account but stresses that he had not gotten his client to agree to any plea at that point.)

Karas tries to reach the defendant's former common law wife the next day to find out about his relationship with the witness, but she is unable to find her.

On May 8 Karas has all six arresting police officers in Andrias's court (the cops from the patrol car and two unmarked cars), but the defendant doesn't show up at all and the witness doesn't arrive until 4:55. At about 5 P.M. Andrias adjourns the case until May 10.

On May 10 the hearing, called for the morning, doesn't begin until 3 P.M., again because the defendant and his witness, who arrive together, don't appear until then.

On cross-examination, Karas establishes that the woman is unemployed, on welfare, and enrolled in a drug clinic. "I was trying to show Andrias that she was doing it to get drugs from [the defendant]," she later explains.

She also gets the woman to admit that her friend had been wearing a gray jacket and jeans and that he'd had a gun that the cops had patted down. "That proves the cops didn't make it up," Karas later asserts.

Nonetheless Andrias sets an oral argument for May 12, which takes place on schedule, after which he promises a decision by June 5.

After the May 10 hearing Pineiro, according to Karas and Pineiro, again asked Karas if she'd go back to the three-to-six offer. She refused.

"Why should I do that?" she later explains to me. "The guy's put me through all this trouble; he's had all these cops here all these days, and his client's a walking drug factory—and he had a loaded gun. Forget it. I'm ready for trial. All these guys want to do is delay, delay, delay. Well, they pay a price for trying that."

On June 5 Andrias's clerk will tell Karas that he still hasn't decided on the arrest and the resulting evidence. So that case, too, will be put off for decision or trial (assuming he decides the obvious, that the case should go forward) on July 5—which is when Karas has the Russians case and another case scheduled for Justice Haft's courtroom.

When I next see Karas, in late May, she's still regularly calling her cabbie witness and the two men from Yemen, telling them to keep the faith. She's been to the Immigration and Naturalization Service and discovered, in reading through one of the Russians' recent immigration filings, that he's lied about whether he's been arrested. "I can get him deported," she explains, "except that they tell me we don't deport people to the Soviet Union....So after he gets out of prison, we can put him in an INS detention center. Not bad."

She is also working that day on a robbery case involving a man with a long criminal record who had accosted and robbed two women window shoppers one evening and been caught after a Good Samaritan had chased him down and held him at bay until the police came.

"It's a relief from all the drug cases we've all been getting," she notes, referring to New York's crack crisis and the recent arrest crackdowns that have clogged the courts. "Yesterday, five of the seven files I worked on were drug cases, which is a little discouraging. But this [robbery] case is great....Right after the victims picked him out in the lineup, he said he had started hearing voices and is now pleading insanity. That ought to be fun, an insanity defense."

Could she ever be the lawyer on the other side, lodging a defense like that, or any other defense for that matter?

"No, and I've thought about that a lot," she says, eager to explain. "After this I don't want to be a defense lawyer....I don't think of myself as prosecution-oriented or conservative"—Karas has told me she voted for Dukakis, supports the exclusionary rule, and is still "squeamish" about the death penalty— "but with all I see here, I just wouldn't want to do that....

"I only make thirty-four thousand dollars a year now [her salary was raised to $39,000 on July 1], and pay seven hundred dollars a month in rent and [several hundred dollars] for student loans, so I'd like more money. But I don't want to do corporate law either....I'll probably do public service law or government work of some kind. And get married and have some babies, too, I hope.

"No, I've thought a lot about it, and defense work isn't for me....There are a lot of defense lawyers around here whom I respect, but by and large defense lawyers here play a game. It's called delay. The more you delay your cases, the weaker they get for the prosecution. And I don't believe that's what lawyers are for."

"It is arguable that stringing out a case is better for us," concedes the Legal Aid Society's Baum. "But we have an obligation to make all the motions we feel are necessary to establish that the evidence is admissible and that our clients' rights are protected. It's not the motions that take so long," Baum adds persuasively, "it's that the judges take three weeks or a month between every event in the process—and that is not our fault."

Karas's more cynical view of defense work is formed in the main by her assessment that "one hundred percent of the people I see are guilty of something and usually what we're charging them with....In twenty or thirty percent of the cases, we may have to change the charges at ECAB, but after that the cases are real. Let's face it, there may be all kinds of root causes for their crimes—and I believe that, and I think we have to do something about it—but these people are guilty.

"I'd have never believed when I was a college liberal"—at Mount Holyoke in Western Massachusetts, near where she grew up in South Deerfield—"that I'd hear myself saying this, but what the cops do is a noble thing," she adds. "Sure, they sometimes embellish and tell us they saw bulges that they didn't see when they pick up guns, but by and large they do great work that they don't get enough credit for with juries. They really do risk their lives going after very guilty people. I guess that sounds pretty conservative but it's not, because you have to consider my victims."

Indeed, if Karas's defendants are mostly nonwhite and poor, so too are her victims. And to watch Karas work in Haft's or Andrias's courtroom is to understand that crime is no longer a liberal or conservative issue. If, as urban politicians like to say, there is no liberal or conservative way to pick up the garbage, there is also no liberal or conservative way to make the courts run better than at a pace of four hours and 27 minutes a day. Of Karas's three favorite judges, two are conservative and one is a flaming liberal. What they have in common is that they work hard to schedule things and discipline lawyers so that the crisis out there on the streets is translated a least into some sense of urgency at the bench—some sense of purpose that gives those who get caught the idea that they're going to be dealt with quickly and sternly.

But the change has to go further than that. New York and other cities are now so riddled with crime that a sense of futility has set in, a capitulation to fear that is eating away at us—and especially at the poor and near-poor (Karas's grocer Yemenites or the cabbie) among us who are most victimized by crime.

The police claim to have solved just 24 percent of the 86,000 (ten an hour) reported robberies in New York last year; 10 percent of the 128,000 (15 an hour) burglaries; and 7 percent of the 110,000 (12 an hour) larcenies. And those percentages of cases solved are drastically overstated because they include thousands of cases that by their nature get "solved" automatically because they involve people who know each other and crimes that really aren't what their labels make them seem. (For example, a man who breaks up with his girlfriend but then comes back to retrieve his stereo is guilty of a burglary if she's not there and a robbery if she is there and he pushes her aside.) Also, crime experts know that as many as half the serious crimes committed may go unreported because the victims, like the cabbie after his second hold-up, sense the futility of it all.

Nor is New York an **anomaly.** New York is hardly the only place where stores now sell "No Radio" signs for people to hang in their car windows to ward off the radio thieves who almost never get caught. (Is there any better testament to the middle class's capitulation to crime?) New York is hardly the only city where kids growing up in the ghettos can see almost as much violence outside their window as they see on television.

So when we're lucky enough to catch criminals, and then lucky enough to get over all the hurdles of our undeniably necessary and valuable safeguards, such as *Miranda* and the exclusionary rule, to convict them, we have to deal with them more harshly. In all 40 cases that involved violence or the threat of violence that Karas was working on during the times we spoke, none seemed likely to result in a prison sentence of more than four years, and almost all seemed destined to yield a year or two. Indeed, I discovered a kind of unwritten rule of thumb that a first violent offense will get a year on average and a second one may get two to three years. And everyone, including Karas, seems so used to—or resigned to—what this outsider-liberal finds to be this undue leniency that they seem to accept it.

Similarly, drug cases, which almost always involve people associated with some violent crime sooner or later, almost never yield a prison sentence the first time around.

The penal law has to be changed to acknowledge the crisis and the simple reality that what we have now just doesn't work. We have to put people away for five or six years for their first violent crime, which means that the minimums and maximums would have to go much higher than they are now so that Karas's plea bargains would yield those results.

And we ought to make the second violent offense with a deadly weapon punishable by a minimum of ten years. This would raise the odds for those who now know they have little chance of being caught, and, more importantly, warehouse them longer when they are caught. For the simple fact is that warehousing is important because, as Karas puts it, "I almost never see a defendant who's over twenty-five who doesn't already have a record."

This would be unfair to some convicts capable of rehabilitation. It's also unfair to kill soldiers during a war who are simply taking orders from their leaders. But we do it because we have to do it.

Again, it's not simply New York's penal law that needs to be overhauled, in fact, New York's sentencing provisions—which, among other things, mandate at least a year and a half in prison for even the lowest-level second felony offender and work up from there—are relatively severe.

The common reaction to suggestions to toughen sentences and eliminate the incentives for plea bargaining is that this would bog down the system in hundreds of trials. But the system is already bogged down in thousands of pseudo pre-trials. We shouldn't worry all that much about whether tougher sentences will cut down on plea bargaining and force more cases to trial. One thing is clear from the way Karas spends her day, not to mention the way her plea-bargained cases now drag on for six to nine months, thereby robbing plea bargaining of its one virtue, swift punishment: It's that trials, which usually last a day or two in common criminal cases, wouldn't add that much to the length of the process, and would add some dignity to it.

As for the drug cases, we ought to force each illegal possession and small-sale first offender to go into a treatment program—and make sure we spend billions to provide programs for everyone in need. But we also ought to lower the boom on them the second time around, sending them to long terms in special prisons, which, would, of course, cost still more money.

But none of the punishment schemes will work if we don't make the system work, and here we have to start acting like we really do have a crisis, indeed, like we are in a war. On the streets there may be a war, but in the courtrooms where the Beth Karases of the world try to fight the war, it's paperback books and sports pages and jokes and, at best, five o'clock good-byes.

The result of all the chaos and delays is a mentality that assumes plea bargaining, that assumes that sentences meted out by judges will fall at the lower end of the spectrum that is within their discretion (even Karas assumes and accepts it), and, in general, assumes that no aspect of bringing people to justice will be swift, dignified, or otherwise consistent with the notion that the defendant has to be dealt with sternly and with credibility.

When we were at war, we operated our munitions factories overtime. We have to do the same with the courts—and run them with competent managers and accountable, competent judges. We should ask court officers, judges, ADAs, and Legal Aid lawyers to work ten hours a day at the same wage. (Most of the ADAs and many of the Legal Aid lawyers seem to put in those hours already.)

Moreover, we should draft prosperous lawyers into the war, the kind who now don't ever step their wing tips into Beth Karas's stalled elevators.

If we really do have an urban crisis in law enforcement, why shouldn't we require all lawyers coming out of law school to help solve that crisis? We could require them to work—at salaries even lower than Karas's—two or three years in either a Legal Aid office or an assistant district attorney's office in a city in the state where they want to practice. (Perhaps we could give them the option of working for Legal Aid offices on the civil side, too.) The manpower from these public service criminal justice internships (which would be akin to the below-wage, forced training, and work that doctors provide as interns) could be used to operate the courts on extended schedules.

Besides, putting so many of the best and brightest into these systems would do wonders to force changes in the dumb, lazy system we now have. Today, the poor worry every day about crime on their doorsteps (so much so that fighting crime ought to be viewed as part of the liberals' agenda). But the middle and upper classes worry about crime only when they read a headline story of some middle- or upper-class white being a victim (which are typically the only headline stories about crime). They never really have to deal with the system, except in the unlikely event that they are victims themselves and a suspect is caught. But if thousands of heavy-hitting future corporate lawyers were exposed to this brazenly ridiculous system for two or three years, it would have to change.

One can quibble, or even laugh at, any of these ideas, because some of the details are missing or impractical, or even because they're bad at their core. But my real point is that we have to think differently, and radically, about what we're doing about crime. And we have to commit enormous resources to doing something about it.

And, of course, the last but most important place where we have to put those resources has to do with the state of our underclass. Crime is committed mostly by poor people; and, although it's not nice to talk about it this way, in this country's cities most of our poor people are non-white, and they commit most of the crimes. (Such is our collective state of sensitivity about this that I couldn't get our *Manhattan Lawyer* editors to print that all but a handful of the hundreds of defendants our reporters saw in those 45 courtrooms that day in May were black or Hispanic.)

Yes, for the sake of our own preservation and especially for the sake of the poor and minorities for whom every night in America is now like a night in Beirut, we need to spend billions to put the system on a war footing that will deal much more toughly with criminals over the short term. But if we don't also spend billions to do something over the longer term about a burgeoning nonwhite underclass, in which for a minority (indeed, a surprisingly tiny minority given the state of the options available to them) crime is sometimes the only opportunity and criminals the only role models, we may do a better job of warehousing criminals, but we'll lose the war because there will always be replacements.

What we need overall, then, is a different mind-set about crime, one that acts on the reality that there really is a crisis that is eating away at us every bit as much as a terrorist guerrilla attack beginning at sundown every night would eat away at us. For amid all the public **rhetoric** about that crisis there is anything but a crisis atmosphere among those who operate the system now.

This is not to say that there are villains in this story. Anyone who's part of the system will read this article and say that I've picked unfairly on the judges, on some of the lawyers, and on the others singled out; and in the sense that there's nothing evil or especially bad about these people they'll be right. But no one will quibble with the facts; they'll just say that I don't "understand" all the problems of the system.

The problem, though, is that all those who run the system and who work in the system—and even the reporters, including our own from *Manhattan Lawyer,* who cover it—"understand" too well. They "understand" it so well that they accept the absurdity, the lunacy, of it all.

Sure, the players are probably worn down by the futility of it all. And it could be argued that any organization this big with this many cases—154,000 felony arrests were processed in New York in 1988 and arrests are up in Manhattan 24 percent so far this year—is destined to become a gray, linoleum, dull-witted, numb-sensed, gallows-humor bureaucracy.

So perhaps the reason that victims like the cabbie-robbery victim feel so frustrated about the system is that for them the arrest and the prospect of a prosecution is a special, rejuvenating event after the horror of the crime—while for everyone else involved (except maybe the as-yet unjaded, like Karas) there's a numbing, bureaucratic routine to it all.

As the cabbie puts it, "I was euphoric after the arrest, because I thought I had really gotten these guys and put them away for a good long time. But then I realized that no one, except maybe Beth, really gave a shit about the case."

We can't let that continue.

The people who run these urban justice systems—mayors, governors, chief judges, prosecutors, defense lawyers—should stop "understanding" the problem and start screaming from the rooftops that we can't let this go on, that we need more resources, more taxes, hard-nosed management, better people, and, above all, a new mind-set to achieve criminal justice.

We can't continue to operate our law enforcement system like a third-rate motor vehicles bureau. We can't continue to process cases rather than redeem the rule of law.

We can't continue to burn out the Beth Karases after five years.

Their work is too important, and they're too good at it.

We have to decide instead to give them a place—a system, a penal code, judges, defense lawyers, colleagues—that they want to work in forever.

QUESTIONS FOR DISCUSSION

1. The attorney this article, Elizabeth Karas, says she would not want to be a defense attorney after having worked as a prosecuting attorney. Why?
2. Describe what elements, presented by the author, cause the processing of cases through the court to slow down to nearly a standstill.
3. What prescriptions does the author provide for improving the justice system? Cite examples to support your answer.

APPLICATIONS

1. The processing of cases through the court, in your community, may be very different from that outlined by the author in New York City. Identify five major criticisms that the author of this article had about the judicial process. Contact a defense attorney, prosecuting attorney, and a judge in your community. Interview each of these officers of the court, independently, about the criticisms you have identified, and compare their responses. Are their perceptions of the problems in judicial processing different?
2. Based on what you have read, what would be your recommendations for improving the efficiency and effectiveness of judicial processing?

The Practice of Law as a Con Game

Abraham S. Blumberg

INTRODUCTION

A recurring theme in the growing dialogue between sociology and law has been the great need for a joint effort of the two disciplines to illuminate urgent social and legal issues. Having uttered fervent public pronouncements in this vein, however, the respective practitioners often go their separate ways. Academic spokesmen for the legal profession are somewhat critical of sociologists of law because of what they perceive as the sociologist's preoccupation with the application of theory and methodology to the examination of legal phenomena, without regard to the solution of legal problems. Further, it is felt that "contemporary writing in the sociology of law...betrays the existence of painfully unsophisticated notions about the day-to-day operations of courts, legislatures and law offices."[1] Regardless of the merit of such criticism, scant attention—apart from explorations of the legal profession itself—has been given to the sociological examination of legal institutions, or their supporting ideological assumptions. Thus, for example, very little sociological effort is expended to ascertain the validity and viability of important court decisions, which may rest on wholly erroneous assumptions about the **contextual** realities of social structure. A particular decision may rest upon a legally **impeccable** rationale, at the same time it may be rendered **nugatory** or self-defeating by contingencies imposed by aspects of social reality of which the lawmakers are themselves unaware.

Within this context, I wish to question the impact of three recent landmark decisions of the United States Supreme Court; each hailed as destined to effect profound changes in the future of criminal law administration and enforcement in America. The first of these, *Gideon v. Wainwright*, 372 U.S. 335 (1963) required states and localities henceforth to furnish

"The Practice of Law as a Confidence Game: Organizational Cooptation of a Profession," by Abraham S. Blumberg in *Law & Society Review*, Vol. 1:2 (1967). Reprinted by permission of the Law and Society Association.

counsel in the case of indigent persons charged with a felony.[2] The *Gideon* ruling left several major issues unsettled, among them the vital question: What is the precise point in time at which a suspect is entitled to counsel?[3] The answer came relatively quickly in *Escobedo v. Illinois,* 378 U.S. 478 (1964), which has aroused a storm of controversy. Danny Escobedo confessed to the murder of his brother-in-law after the police had refused to permit retained counsel to see him, although his lawyer was present in the station house and asked to confer with his client. In a 5-4 decision, the court asserted that counsel must be permitted when the process of police investigative effort shifts from merely investigatory to that of accusatory: "when its focus is on the accused and its purpose is to elicit a confession—our adversary system begins to operate, and, under the circumstances here, the accused must be permitted to consult with his lawyer."

As a consequence, Escobedo's confession was rendered inadmissible. The decision triggered a national debate among police, district attorneys, judges, lawyers, and other law enforcement officials, which continues unabated, as to the value and propriety of confessions in criminal cases.[4] On June 13, 1966, the Supreme Court in a 5–4 decision underscored the principle **enunciated** in *Escobedo* in the case of *Miranda v. Arizona.*[5] Police interrogation of any suspect in custody, without his consent, unless a defense attorney is present, is prohibited by the self-incrimination provision of the Fifth Amendment. Regardless of the relative merit of the various shades of opinion about the role of counsel in criminal cases, the issues generated thereby will be in part resolved as additional cases move toward decision in the Supreme Court in the near future. They are of peripheral interest and not of immediate concern in this paper. However, the *Gideon, Escobedo,* and *Miranda* cases pose interesting questions. In all three decisions, the Supreme Court **reiterates** the traditional legal conception of a defense lawyer based on the ideological perception of a criminal case as an *adversary, combative* proceeding, in which counsel for the defense **assiduously** musters all the admittedly limited resources at his command to *defend* the accused.[6] The fundamental question remains to be answered: Does the Supreme Court's conception of the role of counsel in a criminal case square with social reality?

The task of this paper is to furnish some preliminary evidence toward the illumination of that question. Little empirical understanding of the function of defense counsel exists; only some ideologically oriented generalizations and commitments. This paper is based upon observations made by the writer during many years of legal practice in the criminal courts of a large metropolitan area. No claim is made as to its methodological rigor, although it does reflect a conscious and sustained effort for participant observations.

COURT STRUCTURE DEFINES ROLE OF DEFENSE LAWYER

The overwhelming majority of convictions in criminal cases (usually over 90 per cent) are not the product of a combative, trial-by-jury process at all, but instead merely involve the sentencing of the individual after a negotiated, bargained-for plea of guilty has been entered.[7] Although more recently the overzealous role of police and prosecutors in producing pretrial confessions and admissions has achieved a good deal of notoriety, scant attention has been paid to the organizational structure and personnel of the criminal court itself. Indeed, the extremely high conviction rate produced without the features of an adversary trial in our courts would tend to suggest that the "trial" becomes a perfunctory reiteration and validation of the pretrial interrogation and investigation.[8]

The institutional setting of the court defines a role for the defense counsel in a criminal case radically different from the one traditionally depicted.[9] Sociologists and others have focused their attention on the deprivations and social disabilities of such variables as race, ethnicity, and social class as being the source of an accused person's defeat in a criminal court. Largely overlooked is the variable of the court organization itself, which possesses a thrust, purpose, and direction of its own. It is grounded in pragmatic values, bureaucratic priorities, and administrative instruments. These exalt maximum production and the particularistic career designs of organizational incumbents, whose occupational and career commitments tend to generate a set of priorities. These priorities exert a higher claim than the stated ideological goals of "due process of law," and are often inconsistent with them.

Organizational goals and discipline impose a set of demands and conditions of practice on the respective professions in the criminal court, to which they respond by abandoning their ideological and professional commitments to the accused client, in the service of these higher claims of the court organization. All court personnel, including the accused's own lawyer, tend to be coopted to become agent-mediators[10] who help the accused redefine his situation and restructure his perceptions concomitant with a plea of guilty.

Of all the occupational roles in the court the only private individual who is officially recognized as having a special status and concomitant obligations is the lawyer. His legal status is that of "an officer of the court" and he is held to a standard of ethical performance and duty to his client as well as to the court. This obligation is thought to be far higher than that expected of ordinary individuals occupying the various occupational statuses in the court community. However, lawyers, whether privately retained or of the legal-aid, public defender variety, have close and continuing relations with the prosecuting office and the court itself through discreet relations with the judges via their law secretaries or "confidential" assistants. Indeed, lines of communication, influence and contact with those offices, as well as with the Office of the Clerk of the Court, Probation Division, and with the press, are essential to present and prospective requirements of criminal law practice. Similarly, the subtle involvement of the press and other mass media in the court's organizational network is not readily discernible to the casual observer. Accused persons come and go in the court system **schema,** but the structure and its occupational incumbents remain to carry on their respective career, occupational and organizational enterprises. The individual **stridencies,** tensions, and conflicts a given accused person's case may present to all the participants are overcome, because the formal and informal relations of all the groups in the court setting require it. The probability of continued future relations and interactions must be preserved at all costs.

This is particularly true of the "lawyer regulars," i.e., those defense lawyers, who by virtue of their continuous appearances on behalf of defendants, tend to represent the bulk of a criminal court's non-indigent case workload, and those lawyers who are not "regulars," who appear almost casually in behalf of an occasional client. Some of the "lawyer regulars" are highly visible as one moves about the major urban centers of the nation, their offices line the back streets of the courthouses, at times sharing space with bondsmen. Their political "visibility" in terms of local club house ties, reaching into the judge's chambers and prosecutor's office, are also deemed essential to successful practitioners. Previous research has indicated that the "lawyer regulars" make no effort to conceal their dependence upon police, bondsmen, and jail personnel. Nor do they conceal the necessity for maintaining intimate relations with all levels of personnel in the court setting as a means of obtaining, maintaining, and building their practice. These informal relations are the **sine qua non** not only of retaining a practice, but also in the negotiation of pleas and sentences.[11]

The client, then, is a secondary figure in the court system as in certain other bureaucratic settings.[12] He becomes a means to other ends of the organization's incumbents. He may present doubts, contingencies, and pressures which challenge existing informal arrangements or disrupt them; but these tend to be resolved in favor of the continuance of the organization and its relations as before. There is a greater community of interest among all the principal organizational structures and their incumbents than exists elsewhere in other settings. The accused's lawyer has far greater professional, economic, intellectual and other ties to the various elements of the court system than he does to his own client. In short, the court is a closed community.

This is more than just the case of the usual "secrets" of bureaucracy which are fanatically defended from an outside view. Even all elements of the press are zealously determined to report on that which will not offend the board of judges, the prosecutor, probation, legal-aid, or other officials, in return for privileges and courtesies granted in the past and to be granted in the future. Rather than any view of the matter in terms of some variation of a "conspiracy" hypothesis, the simple explanation is one of an ongoing system handling delicate tensions, managing the trauma produced by law enforcement and administration, and requiring almost pathological distrust of "outsiders" bordering on group **paranoia.**

The hostile attitude toward "outsiders" is in large measure engendered by a defensiveness itself produced by the inherent deficiencies of assembly line justice, so characteristic of our major criminal courts. Intolerably large caseloads of defendants which must be disposed of in an organizational context of limited resources and personnel, potentially subject the participants in the court community to harsh scrutiny from appellate courts, and other public and private sources of condemnation. As a consequence, an almost irreconcilable conflict is posed in terms of intense pressures to process large numbers of cases on the one hand, and the stringent ideological and legal requirements of "due process of law," on the other hand. A rather **tenuous** resolution of the dilemma has emerged in the shape of a large variety of bureaucratically ordained and controlled "work crimes," short cuts, deviations, and outright rule violations adopted as court practice in order to meet production norms. Fearfully anticipating criticism on ethical as well as legal grounds, all the significant participants in the court's social structure are bound into an organized system of complicity. This consists of a work arrangement in which the patterned, covert, informal breaches, and evasions of "due process" are institutionalized, but are nevertheless denied to exist.

These institutionalized evasions will be found to occur to some degree, in all criminal courts. Their nature, scope and complexity are largely determined by the size of the court, and the character of the community in which it is located, e.g., whether it is a large, urban institution, or a relatively small rural county court. In addition, idiosyncratic, local conditions may contribute to a unique flavor in the character and quality of the criminal law's administration in a particular community. However, in most instances a variety of **strategems** are employed—some subtle, some crude, in effectively disposing of what are often too large caseloads. A wide variety of coercive devices are employed against an accused-client, couched in a depersonalized, instrumental, bureaucratic version of due process of law, and which are in reality a perfunctory **obeisance** to the ideology of due process. These include some very explicit pressures which are exerted in some measure by all court personnel, including judges, to plead guilty and avoid trial. In many instances the sanction of a potentially harsh sentence is utilized as the visible alternative to pleading guilty, in the case of recalcitrants. Probation and psychiatric reports are "tailored" to organizational needs, or are at least responsive to the court organization's requirements for the refurbishment of a defendant's social biography, consonant with his new status. A resourceful judge can, through his subtle domination of the proceedings, impose his will on the final outcome of a trial. Stenographers and clerks, in their function as record keepers, are on occasion pressed into service in support of a judicial need to "rewrite" the record of a courtroom event. Bail practices are usually employed for purposes other than simply assuring a defendant's presence on the date of a hearing in connection with his case. Too often, the discretionary power as to bail is part of the arsenal of weapons available to collapse the resistance of an accused person. The foregoing is a most cursory examination of some of the more prominent "short cuts" available to any court organization. There are numerous other procedural strategies constituting due process deviations, which tend to become the work style artifacts of a court's personnel. Thus, only court "regulars" who are "bound in" are really accepted; others are treated routinely and in almost a coldly correct manner.

The defense attorneys, therefore, whether of the legal-aid, public defender variety, or privately retained, although operating in terms of pressures specific to their respective role and organizational obligations, ultimately are concerned with strategies which tend to lead to a plea. It is the rational, impersonal elements involving economies of time, labor, expense and a superior commitment of the defense counsel to these rationalistic values of maximum production[13] of court organization that prevail, in his relationship with a client. The lawyer "regulars" are frequently former staff members of the prosecutor's office and utilize the prestige, know-how and contacts of their former affiliation as part of their stock in trade. Close and continuing relations between the lawyer "regular" and his former colleagues in the prosecutor's office generally overshadow the relationship between the regular and his client. The continuing colleagueship of supposedly adversary counsel rests on real professional and organizational needs of a *quid pro quo*, which goes beyond the limits of an accommodation or *modus vivendi* one might ordinarily expect under the circumstances of an otherwise seemingly adversary relationship. Indeed, the adversary features which are manifest are for the most part muted and exist even in their attenuated form largely for external consumption. The principals, lawyer and assistant district attorney, rely upon one another's cooperation for their continued professional existence, and so the bargaining between them tends usually to be "reasonable" rather than fierce.

FEE COLLECTION AND FIXING

The real key to understanding the role of defense counsel in a criminal case is to be found in the area of the fixing of the fee to be charged and its collection. The problem of fixing and collecting the fee tends to influence to a significant degree the criminal court process itself, and not just the relationship of the lawyer and his client. In essence, a lawyer–client "confidence game" is played. A true confidence game is unlike the case of the emperor's new clothes wherein that monarch's nakedness was a result of inordinate gullibility and credulity. In a genuine confidence game, the perpetrator manipulates the basic dishonesty of his partner, the victim or mark, toward his own (the confidence operator's) ends. Thus, "the victim of a con scheme must have some larceny in his heart."[14]

Legal service lends itself particularly well to confidence games. Usually, a plumber will be able to demonstrate empirically that he has performed a service by clearing up the stuffed drain, repairing the leaky faucet or pipette and therefore merits his fee. He has rendered, when summoned, a visible, tangible boon for his client in return for the requested fee. A physician, who has not performed some visible surgery or otherwise engaged in some readily discernible procedure in connection with a patient, may be deemed by the patient to have "done nothing" for him. As a consequence, medical practitioners may simply prescribe or administer by injection a placebo to overcome a patient's potential reluctance or dissatisfaction in paying a requested fee, "for nothing."

In the practice of law there is a special problem in this regard, no matter what the level of the practitioner or his place in the hierarchy of prestige. Much legal work is intangible either because it is simply a few words of advice, some preventive action, a telephone call, negotiation of some kind, a form filled out and filed, a hurried conference with another attorney or an official of a government agency, a letter or opinion written, or a countless variety of seemingly innocuous, and even prosaic procedures and actions. These are the basic activities, apart from any possible court appearance, of almost all lawyers, at all levels of practice. Much of the activity is not in the nature of the exercise of the traditional, precise professional skills of attorney such as library research and oral argument in connection with appellate briefs, court motions, trial work, drafting of opinions, memoranda, contracts, and other complex documents and agreements. Instead, much legal activity, whether it is at the lowest or highest "white shoe" law firm levels, is of the brokerage, agent, sales representative, lobbyist type of activity, in which the lawyer acts for someone else in pursuing the latter's interests and designs. The service is intangible.[15]

The large scale law firm may not speak as openly of the "contacts," their "fixing" abilities, as does the lower level lawyer. They trade instead upon a facade of thick carpeting, walnut paneling, genteel low pressure, and superficialities of traditional legal professionalism. There are occasions when even the large firm is on the defensive in connection with the fees they charge because the services rendered or results obtained do not appear to merit the fee asked.[16] Therefore, there is a recurrent problem in the legal profession in fixing the amount of fee, and in justifying the basis for the requested fee.

Although the fee at times amounts to what the traffic and the conscience of the lawyer will bear, one further observation must be made with regard to the size of the fee and its collection. The defendant in a criminal case and the material gain he may have acquired during the course of his illicit activities are soon parted. Not infrequently the ill-gotten fruits of the various modes of larceny are sequestered by a defense lawyer in payment of his fee. Inexorably, the amount of the fee is a function of the dollar value of the crime committed, and is frequently set with meticulous precision at a sum which bears an uncanny relationship to that of the net proceeds of the particular offense involved. On occasion, defendants have been known to commit additional offenses while at liberty on bail, in order to secure the requisite funds with which to meet their obligations for payment of legal fees. Defense lawyers condition even the most obtuse clients to recognize that there is a firm interconnection between fee payment and the zealous exercise of professional expertise, secret knowledge, and organizational "connections" on their behalf. Lawyers, therefore, seek to keep their clients in a proper state of tension, and to arouse in them the precise edge of anxiety which is calculated to encourage prompt fee payment. Consequently, the client attitude in the relationship between defense counsel and an accused is in many instances a **precarious admixture** of hostility, mistrust, dependence, and sycophancy. By keeping his client's anxieties aroused to the proper pitch, and establishing a seemingly causal relationship between a requested fee and the accused's ultimate extrication from his onerous difficulties, the lawyer will have established the necessary preliminary groundwork to assure a minimum of haggling over the fee and its eventual payment.

In varying degrees, as a consequence, all law practice involves a manipulation of the client and a stage management of the lawyer–client relationship so that at least an *appearance* of help and service will be forthcoming. This is accomplished in a variety of ways, often exercised in combination with each other. At the outset, the lawyer-professional employs with suitable variation a measure of sales-puff which may range from an air of unbounding self-confidence, adequacy, and dominion over events, to that of complete arrogance. This will be supplemented by the affectation of a studied, faultless mode of personal attire. In the larger firms, the furnishings and office trappings will serve as the backdrop to help in impression management and client intimidation. In all firms, solo or large scale, an access to secret knowledge, and to the seats of power and influence is inferred, or presumed to a varying degree as the basic **vendible** commodity of the practitioners.

The lack of visible end product offers a special complication in the course of the professional life of the criminal court lawyer with respect to his fee and in his relations with his client. The plain fact is that an accused in a criminal case always "loses" even when he has been exonerated by an acquittal, discharge, or dismissal of his case. The hostility of an accused which follows as a consequence of his arrest, incarceration, possible loss of job, expense and other traumas connected with his case is directed, by means of displacement, toward his lawyer. It is in this sense that it may be said that a criminal lawyer never really "wins" a case. The really satisfied client is rare, since in the very nature of the situation even an accused's vindication leaves him with some degree of dissatisfaction and hostility. It is this state of affairs that makes for a lawyer–client relationship in the criminal court which tends to be a somewhat exaggerated version of the usual lawyer-client confidence game.

At the outset, because there are great risks of nonpayment of the fee, due to the **impecuniousness** of his clients, and the fact that a man who is sentenced to jail may be a singularly unappreciative client, the criminal lawyer collects his fee *in advance*. Often, because the lawyer and the accused both have questionable designs of their own upon each other, the confidence game can be played. The criminal lawyer must serve three major functions, or stated another way, he must solve three problems. First, he must arrange for his fee; second, he must prepare and then, if necessary, "cool out" his client in case of defeat[17] (a highly likely contingency); third, he must satisfy the court organization that he has performed adequately in the process of negotiating the plea, so as to preclude the possibility of any sort of embarrassing incident which may serve to invite "outside" scrutiny.

In assuring the attainment of one of his primary objectives, his fee, the criminal lawyer will very often enter into negotiations with the accused's kin, including collateral relatives. In many instances, the accused himself is unable to pay any sort of fee or anything more than a token fee. It then becomes important to involve as many of the accused's kin as possible in the situation. This is especially so if the attorney hopes to collect a significant part of a proposed substantial fee. It is not uncommon for several relatives to contribute toward the fee. The larger the group, the greater the possibility that the lawyer will collect a sizable fee by getting contributions from each.

A fee for a felony case which ultimately results in a plea, rather than a trail, may ordinarily range anywhere from $500 to $1,500. Should the case go to trial, the fee will be proportionately larger, depending upon the length of the trial. But the larger the fee the lawyer wishes to exact, the more impressive his performance must be, in terms of his stage managed image as a personage of great influence and power in the court organization. Court personnel are keenly aware of the extent to which a lawyer's stock in trade involves the precarious stage management of an image which goes beyond the usual professional flamboyance, and for this reason alone the lawyer is "bound in" to the authority system of the court's organizational discipline. Therefore, to some extent, court personnel will aid the lawyer in the creation and maintenance of that impression. There is a **tacit** commitment to the lawyer by the court organization, apart from formal etiquette, to aid him in this. Such augmentation of the lawyer's stage-managed image as this affords, is the partial basis for the *quid pro quo* which exists between the lawyer and the court organization. It tends to serve as the continuing basis for the higher loyalty of the lawyer to the organization; his relationship with his client, in contrast is transient, **ephemeral** and often superficial.

DEFENSE LAWYER AS DOUBLE AGENT

The lawyer has often been accused of stirring up unnecessary litigation, especially in the field of negligence. He is said to acquire a vested interest in a cause of action or claim which was initially his client's. The strong incentive of possible fee motivates the lawyer to promote litigation which would otherwise never have developed. However, the criminal lawyer develops a vested interest of an entirely different nature in his client's case: to limit its scope and duration rather than do battle. Only in this way can a case be "profitable." Thus, he enlists the aid of relatives not only to assure payment of his fee, but he will also rely on these persons to help him in his agent-mediator role of convincing the accused to plead guilty, and ultimately to help in "cooling out" the accused if necessary.

It is at this point that an accused-defendant may experience his first sense of "betrayal." While he had perhaps perceived the police and prosecutor to be adversaries, or possibly even the judge, the accused is wholly unprepared for his counsel's role performance as an agent-mediator. In the same vein, it is even less likely to occur to an accused that members of his own family or other kin may become agents, albeit at the behest and urging of other agents or mediators, acting on the principle that they are in reality helping an accused negotiate the best possible plea arrangement under the circumstances. Usually, it will be the lawyer who will activate next of kin in this role, his ostensible motive being to arrange for his fee. But soon latent and unstated motives will assert themselves, with entreaties by counsel to the accused's next of kin, to appeal to the accused to "help himself" by pleading. *Gemeinschaft* sentiments are to this extent exploited by a defense lawyer (or even at times by a district attorney) to achieve specific secular ends, that is, of concluding a particular matter with all possible dispatch.

The fee is often collected in stages, each installment usually payable prior to a necessary court appearance required during the course of an accused's career journey. At each stage, in his interviews and communications with the accused, or in addition, with members of his family, if they are helping with the fee payment, the lawyer employs an air of professional confidence and "inside-dopesterism" in order to **assuage** anxieties on all sides. He makes the necessary bland assurances, and in effect manipulates his client, who is usually willing to do and say the things, true or not, which will help his attorney extricate him. Since the dimensions of what he is essentially selling, organizational influence and expertise, are not technically and precisely measurable, the lawyer can make extravagant claims of influence and secret knowledge with impunity. Thus, lawyers frequently claim to have inside knowledge in connection with information in the hands of the D.A., police, probation officials or to have access to these functionaries. Factually, they often do, and need only to exaggerate the nature of their relationships with them to obtain the desired effective impression upon the client. But, as in the genuine confidence game, the victim who has participated is loath to do anything which will upset the lesser plea which his lawyer has "conned" him into accepting.[18]

In effect, in his role as double agent, the criminal lawyer performs an extremely vital and delicate mission for the court organization and the accused. Both principals are anxious to terminate the litigation with a minimum of expense and damage to each other. There is no other personage or role incumbent in the total court structure more strategically located, who by training and in terms of his own requirements, is more ideally suited to do so than the lawyer. In recognition of this, judges will cooperate with attorneys in many important ways. For example, they will adjourn the case of an accused in jail awaiting plea or sentence if the attorney requests such action. While explicitly this may be done for some **innocuous** and seemingly valid reason, the tacit purpose is that pressure is being applied by the attorney for the collection of his fee, which he knows will probably not be forthcoming if the case is concluded. Judges are aware of this tactic on the part of lawyers, who, by requesting an adjournment, keep an accused incarcerated awhile longer as a not too subtle method of

dunning a client for payment. However, the judges will go along with this, on the ground that important ends are being served. Often, the only end served is to protect a lawyer's fee.

The judge will help an accused's lawyer in still another way. He will lend the official **aura** of his office and courtroom so that a lawyer can stage-manage an impression of an "all out" performance for the accused in justification of his fee. The judge and other court personnel will serve as a backdrop for a scene charged with dramatic fire, in which the accused's lawyer makes a stirring appeal in his behalf. With a show of restrained passion, the lawyer will **intone** the virtues of the accused and recite the social deprivations which have reduced him to his present state. The speech varies somewhat, depending on whether the accused has been convicted after trial or has pleaded guilty. In the main, however, the incongruity, superficiality, and ritualistic character of the total performance is underscored by a visibly impassive, almost bored reaction on the part of the judge and other members of the court retinue.

Afterward, there is a hearty exchange of pleasantries between the lawyer and district attorney, wholly out of context in terms of the supposed adversary nature of the preceding events. The fiery passion in defense of his client is gone, and the lawyers for both sides resume their offstage relations, chatting amiably and perhaps including the judge in their restrained banter. No other aspect of their visible conduct so effectively serves to put even a casual observer on notice, that these individuals have claims upon each other. These seemingly innocuous actions are indicative of continuing organizational and informal relations, which, in their intricacy and depth, range far beyond any priorities or claims a particular defendant may have.[19]

Criminal law practice is a unique form of private law practice since it really only appears to be private practice.[20] Actually it is bureaucratic practice, because of the legal practitioner's enmeshment in the authority, discipline, and perspectives of the court organization. Private practice, supposedly, in a professional sense, involves the maintenance of an organized, disciplined body of knowledge and learning; the individual practitioners are imbued with a spirit of autonomy and service, the earning of a livelihood being incidental. In the sense that the lawyer in the criminal court serves as a double agent, serving higher organizational rather than professional ends, he may be deemed to be engaged in bureaucratic rather than private practice. To some extent the lawyer–client "confidence game," in addition to its other functions, serves to conceal this fact.

THE CLIENT'S PERCEPTION

The "cop-out" ceremony, in which the court process culminates, is not only invaluable for redefining the accused's perspectives of himself, but also in reiterating publicly in a formally structured ritual the accused person's guilt for the benefit of significant "others" who are observing. The accused not only is made to assert publicly his guilt of a specific crime, but also a complete recital of its details. He is further made to indicate that he is entering his plea of guilty freely, willingly, and voluntarily, and that he is not doing so because of any promises or in consideration of any commitments that may have been made to him by anyone. This last is intended as a blanket statement to shield the participants from any possible charges of "coercion" or undue influence that may have been exerted in violation of due process require-ments. Its function is to preclude any later review by an appellate court on these grounds, and also to obviate any second thoughts an accused may develop in connection with his plea.

However, for the accused, the conception of self as a guilty person is in large measure a temporary role adaptation. His career socialization as an accused, if it is successful, eventuates in his acceptance and redefinition of himself as a guilty person.[21] However, the transforma-tion is ephemeral, in that he will, in private, quickly reassert his innocence. Of importance is that he accept his defeat, publicly proclaim it, and find some measure of pacification in it.[22] Almost immediately after his plea, a defendant will generally be interviewed by a representa-tive of the probation division in connection with a presentence report which is to be prepared. The very first question to be asked of him by the probation officer is: "Are you guilty of the crime to which you pleaded?" This is by way of double affirmation of the defendant's guilt. Should the defendant now begin to make bold assertions of his innocence, despite his plea of guilty, he will be asked to withdraw his plea and stand trial on the original charges. Such a threatened possibility is, in most instances, sufficient to cause an accused to let the plea stand and to request the probation officer to overlook his exclamations of innocence. Table I that fol-lows is a breakdown of the categorized responses of a random sample of male defendants in Metropolitan Court[23] during 1962, 1963, and 1964 in connection with their statements dur-ing presentence probation interviews following their plea of guilty.

It would be well to observe at the outset, that of the 724 defendants who pleaded guilty before trial, only 43 (5.94 per cent) of the total group had confessed prior to their indictment. Thus, the ultimate judicial process was predicated upon evidence independent of any confession of the accused.[24]

As the data indicate, only a relatively small number (95) out of the total number of defendants actually will even admit their guilt, following the "cop-out" ceremony. However, even though they have affirmed their guilt, many of these defendants felt that they should have been able to negotiate a more favorable plea. The largest aggregate of defendants (373) were those who reasserted their "innocence" following their public pro-fession of guilt during the "cop-out" ceremony. These defendants employed differential degrees of fervor, **solemnity** and credibility, ranging from really mild, wavering assertions of innocence which were embroidered with a variety of stock explanations and rational-izations, to those of an adamant, "framed" nature. Thus, the "innocent" group, for the most part, were largely concerned with underscoring for their probation interviewer their essential "goodness" and "worthiness," despite their formal plea of guilty. Assertion of his innocence at the post-plea stage, resurrects a more respectable and acceptable self concept for the accused defendant who has pleaded guilty. A recital of the structural exigencies which precipitated his plea of guilt, serves to embellish a newly proffered claim of innocence, which many defendants mistakenly feel will stand them in good stead at the time of sentence, or ultimately with probation or parole authorities.

Relatively few (33) maintained their innocence in terms of having been "framed" by some person or agent-mediator, although a larger number (86) indicated that they had been manipulated or "conned" by an agent-mediator to plead guilty, but as indicated, their assertions of innocence were relatively mild.

A rather substantial group (147) preferred to stress the pragmatic aspects of their plea of guilty. They would only perfunctorily assert their innocence and would in general refer to some adverse aspect of their situation which they believed tended to negatively affect their bargaining leverage, including in some instances a prior criminal record.

One group of defendants (92), while maintaining their innocence, simply employed some variation of a theme of following "the advice of counsel" as a covering response, to explain their guilty plea in the light of their new affirmation of innocence.

The largest single group of defendants (248) were basically fatalistic. They often verbalized weak suggestions of their innocence in rather halting terms, wholly without conviction. By the same token, they would not admit guilt readily and were generally evasive as to guilt or innocence, preferring to stress aspects of their **stoic** submission in their decision to plead. This sizable group of defendants appeared to perceive the total court process as being caught up in a monstrous organizational apparatus, in which the defendant role expectancies were not clearly defined. Reluctant to offend anyone in authority, fearful that clear-cut statements on their part as to their guilt or innocence would be negatively construed, they adopted a stance of passivity, resignation and acceptance. Interestingly, they would in most instances invoke their lawyer as being the one who crystallized the available alternatives for them, and who was therefore the critical element in their decision-making process.

In order to determine which agent-mediator was most influential in altering the accused's perspectives as to his decision of plead or go to trial (regardless of the proposed basis of the plea), the same sample of defendants were asked to indicate the person who first suggested to them that they plead guilty. They were also asked to indicate which of the persons or officials who made such suggestion, was most influential in affecting their final decision to plead. Table 1 indicates the breakdown of the responses to the two questions.

It is popularly assumed that the police, through forced confessions, and the district attorney, employing still other pressures, are most instrumental in the inducement of an accused to plead guilty.[25] As Table 2 indicates, it is actually the defendant's own counsel who is most effective in this role. Further, this phenomenon tends to reinforce the extremely rational nature of criminal law administration, for an organization could not rely upon the sort of idosyncratic measures employed by the police to induce confessions and maintain its efficiency, high production and overall rational-legal character. The defense counsel becomes the ideal agent-mediator since, as "officer of the court" and confidant of the accused and his kin, he lives astride both worlds and can serve the ends of the two as well as his own.[26]

While an accused's wife, for example, may be influential in making him more amenable to a plea, her agent-mediator role has, nevertheless, usually been sparked and initiated by defense counsel. Further, although a number of first suggestions of a plea came from an accused's fellow jail inmates, he tended to rely largely on his counsel as an ultimate source of influence in his final decision. The defense counsel, being a crucial figure in the total organizational scheme in constituting a new set of perspectives for the accused, the same sample of defendants were asked to indicate at which stage of their contact with counsel was the suggestion of a plea made. There are three basic kinds of defense counsel available in Metropolitan Court: Legal-aid, privately retained counsel, and counsel assigned by the court (but may eventually be privately retained by the accused).

Table 1   DEFENDANT RESPONSES AS TO GUILT OR INNOCENCE AFTER PLEADING GUILTY, 1962, 1963, 1964

Nature of Response		Number of Defendants
Innocent (manipulated)	"The lawyer or judge, police or D.A. 'conned me'"	86
Innocent (pragmatic)	"Wanted to get it over with"	147
	"You can't beat the system"	
	"They have you over a barrel when you have a record"	
Innocent (advice of counsel)	"Followed my lawyer's advice"	92
Innocent (defiant)	"Framed"	33
	"Betrayed by 'Complainant,' 'Police,' 'Squealers,' 'Lawyer,' 'Friends,' 'Wife,' 'Girlfriend'"	
Innocent (Adverse social data)	Blames probation officer or psychiatrist for "Bad Report," in cases where there was pre-pleading investigation	15
Guilty	"But I should have gotten a better deal"	74
	Blames Lawyer, D.A., Police, Judge	
Guilty	Won't say anything further	21
Fatalistic	"I did it for convenience"	248
(doesn't press his "innocence," won't admit "guilt")	"My lawyer told me it was only thing I could do"	
	"I did it because it was the best way out"	
No response		8
Total		794

Table 2   ROLE OF AGENT-MEDIATORS IN DEFENDANT'S GUILTY PLEA

Person or Official	First Suggested Plea of Guilty	Influenced the Accused Most in His Final Decision to Plead
Judge	4	26
District attorney	67	116
Defense counsel	407	411
Probation officer	14	3
Psychiatrist	8	1
Wife	34	120
Friends and kin	21	14
Police	14	4
Fellow inmates	119	14
Others	28	5
No response	8	10
Total	724	724

The overwhelming majority of accused persons, regardless of type of counsel, related a specific incident which indicated an urging or suggestion, either during the course of the first or second contact, that they plead guilty to a lesser charge if this could be arranged. Of all the agent-mediators, it is the lawyer who is most effective in manipulating an accused's perspectives, notwithstanding pressures that may have been previously applied by police, district attorney, judge or any of the agent-mediators that may have been activated by them. Legal-aid and assigned counsel would apparently be more likely to suggest a possible plea at the point of initial interview as response to pressures of time. In the case of the assigned counsel, the strong possibility that there is no fee involved, may be an added impetus to such a suggestion at the first contact.

In addition, there is some further evidence in Table 3 of the perfunctory, ministerial character of the system in Metropolitan Court and similar criminal courts. There is little real effort to individualize, and the lawyer's role as agent-mediator may be seen as unique in that he is in effect a double agent. Although, as "officer of the court" he mediates between the court organization and the defendant, his roles with respect to each are rent by conflicts of interest. Too often these must be resolved in favor of the organization which provides him with the means for his professional existence. Consequently, in order to reduce the strains and conflicts imposed in what is ultimately an overdemanding role obligation for him, the lawyer engages in the lawyer–client "confidence game" so as to structure more favorably an otherwise onerous role system.[27]

CONCLUSION

Recent decisions of the Supreme Court, in the area of criminal law administration and defendant's rights, fail to take into account three crucial aspects of social structure which may tend to render the more libertarian rules as nugatory. The decisions overlook (1) the nature of courts as formal organization; (2) the relationship that the lawyer-regular *actually* has with the court organization; and (3) the character of the lawyer–client relationship in the

Table 3   STAGE AT WHICH COUNSEL SUGGESTED ACCUSED TO PLEAD

| | Counsel Type | | | | | | | |
| | Privately Retained | | Legal-Aid | | Assigned | | Total | |
Contact	N	%	N	%	N	%	N	%
First	66	35	237	49	28	60	331	46
Second	83	44	142	29	8	17	233	32
Third	29	15	63	13	4	9	96	13
Fourth or more	12	6	31	7	5	11	48	7
No response	0	0	14	3	2	4	16	2
Total	190	100	487	101 *	47	101 *	724	100

criminal court (the routine relationships, not those unusual ones that are described in "heroic" terms in novels, movies, and TV).

Courts, like many other modern large-scale organizations possess a monstrous appetite for the cooptation of entire professional groups as well as individuals.[28] Almost all those who come within the **ambit** of organizational authority, find that their definitions, perceptions and values have been refurbished, largely in terms favorable to the particular organization and its goals. As a result, recent Supreme Court decisions may have a long range effect which is radically different from that intended or anticipated. The more libertarian rules will tend to produce the rather ironic end result of augmenting the *existing* organizational arrangements, enriching court organizations with more personnel and elaborate structure, which in turn will maximize organizational goals of "efficiency" and production. Thus, many defendants will find that courts will possess an even more sophisticated apparatus for processing them toward a guilty plea!

NOTES

1. H. W. Jones, *A View from the Bridge,* Law and Society: Supplement to Summer, 1965 Issue of Social Problems 42 (1965). See G. Geis. *Sociology, Criminology, and Criminal Law,* 7 Social Problems 40–47 (1959); N. S. Timasheff, *Growth and Scope of Sociology of Law,* in *Modern Sociological Theory in Continuity and Change,* 424–49 (H. Becker & A. Boskoff, eds., 1957), for further evaluation of the strained relations between sociology and law.

2. This decision represented the climax of a line of cases which had begun to chip away at the notion that the Sixth Amendment of the Constitution (right to assistance of counsel) applied only to the federal government, and could not be held to run against the states through the Fourteenth Amendment. An exhaustive historical analysis of the Fourteenth Amendment and the Bill of Rights will be found in C. Fairman, *Does the Fourteenth Amendment Incorporate the Bill of Rights? The Original Understanding,* 2 Stan. L. Rev. 5-139 (1949). Since the *Gideon* decision, there is already evidence that its effect will ultimately extend to indigent persons charged with misdemeanors—and perhaps ultimately even traffic cases and other minor offenses. For a popular account of this important development in connection with the right to assistance of counsel, see A. Lewis, *Gideon's Trumpet* (1964). For a scholarly historical analysis of the right to counsel see W. M. Beaney, *The Right to Counsel in American Courts* (1955). For a more recent comprehensive review and discussion of the right to counsel and its development, see Note, *Counsel at Interrogation,* 73 Yale L. J. 1000-57 (1964).

   With the passage of the Criminal Justice Act of 1964, indigent accused persons in the federal courts will be defended by federally paid legal counsel. For a general discussion of the nature and extent of public and private legal aid in the United States prior to the Gideon case, see E. A. Brownell, *Legal Aid in the United States* (1961); also R. B. van Mehren et al., *Equal Justice for the Accused* (1959).

3. In the case of federal defendants the issue is clear. In *Mallory v. United States,* 354 U.S. 449 (1957), the Supreme Court unequivocally indicated that a person under federal arrest must be taken "without any unnecessary delay" before a U.S. commissioner where he will receive information as to his rights to remain silent and to assistance of counsel which will be furnished, in the event he is indigent, under the Criminal Justice Act of 1964. For a most interesting

and richly documented work in connection with the general area of the Bill of Rights, see C. R. Sowle, *Police Power and Individual Freedom* (1962).

4. See *N.Y. Times*, Nov. 20, 1965, p. 1, for Justice Nathan R. Sobel's statement to the effect that based on his study of 1,000 indictments in Brooklyn, N.Y. from February–April, 1965, fewer than 10% involved confessions. Sobel's detailed analysis will be found in six articles which appeared in the *New York Law Journal,* beginning November 15, 1965, through November 21, 1965, titled *The Exclusionary Rules in the Law of Confessions: A Legal Perspective—A Practical Perspective.* Most law enforcement officials believe that the majority of convictions in criminal cases are based upon confessions obtained by police. For example, the District Attorney of New York County (a jurisdiction which has the largest volume of cases in the United States), Frank S. Hogan, reports that confessions are crucial and indicates "if a suspect is entitled to have a lawyer during preliminary questioning…any lawyer worth his fee will tell him to keep his mouth shut," *N.Y. Times,* Dec. 2, 1965, p. 1. Concise discussions of the issue are to be found in D. Robinson, Jr. *Massiah, Escobedo and Rationales for the Exclusion of Confessions,* 56 J. Crim. L. C. & P.S. 412-31 (1965); D.C. Dowling, *Escobedo and Beyond: The Need for a Fourteenth Amendment Code of Criminal Procedure,* 56 J. Crim. L.C. & P.S. 143-57 (1965).

5. *Miranda v. Arizona,* 384 U.S. 436 (1966).

6. Even under optimal circumstances a criminal case is a very much one-sided affair, the parties to the "contest" being decidedly unequal in strength and resources. See A. S. Goldstein, *The State and the Accused: Balance of Advantage in Criminal Procedure,* 69 Yale L.J. 1149-99 (1960).

7. F. J. Davis et al., *Society and the Law: New Meanings for an Old Profession* 301 (1962); L. Orfield. *Criminal Procedure from Arrest to Appeal* 297 (1947).

    D. J. Newman, *Pleading Guilty for Considerations: A Study of Bargain Justice,* 46 J. Crim. L.C. & P.S. 780–90 (1954). Newman's data covered only one year, 1954, in a midwestern community, however, it is in general confirmed by my own data drawn from a far more populous area, and from what is one of the major criminal courts in the country, for a period of fifteen years from 1950 to 1964 inclusive. The English experience tends also to confirm American data, see N. Walker, *Crime and Punishment in Britain: An Analysis of the Penal System* (1965). See also D. J. Newman, *Conviction: The Determination of Guilt or Innocence without Trial* (1966), for a comprehensive legalistic study of the guilty plea sponsored by the American Bar Foundation. The criminal court as a social system, an analysis of "bargaining" and its functions in the criminal court's organizational structure, are examined in my forthcoming book, *The Criminal Court: A Sociological Perspective,* to be published by Quadrangle Books, Chicago.

8. G. Feifer, *Justice in Moscow* (1965). The Soviet trial has been termed "an appeal from the pretrial investigation" and Feifer notes that the Soviet "trial" is simply a recapitulation of the data collected by the pretrial investigator. The notions of a trial being a "tabula rasa" and presumptions of innocence are wholly alien to Soviet notions of justice. "…the closer the investigation resembles the finished script, the better.…" *Id.* at 86.

9. For a concise statement of the constitutional and economic aspects of the right to legal assistance, see M. G. Paulsen, *Equal Justice for the Poor Man* (1964); for a brief traditional description of the legal profession see P.A. Freund, *The Legal Profession,* Daedalus 689–700 (1963).

10. I use the concept in the general sense that Erving Goffman employed it in his *Asylums, Essays on the Social Situation of Mental Patients and Other Inmates* (1961).

11. A. L. Wood, *Informal Relations in the Practice of Criminal Law,* 62 Am. J. Sac. 48–55 (1956); J. E. Carlin, *Lawyers on Their Own* 105–109 (1962); R. Goldfarb, *Ransom—A Critique of the American Bail System* 114–15 (1965). Relatively recent data as to recruitment to the legal profession, and variables involved in the type of practice engaged in, will be found in J. Ladinsky,

Careers of Lawyers, Law Practice, and Legal Institutions, 28 Am. Soc. Rev. 47–54 (1963). See also S. Warkov & J. Zelan, *Lawyers in the Making* (1965).

12. There is a real question to be raised as to whether in certain organizational settings, a complete reversal of the bureaucratic-ideal has not occurred. That is, it would seem, in some instances the organization appears to exist to serve the needs of its various occupational incumbents, rather than its clients. A. Etzioni, *Modern Organizations,* 94–104 (1964).

13. Three relatively recent items reported in the *New York Times* tend to underscore this point as it has manifested itself in one of the major criminal courts. In one instance the Bronx County Bar Association condemned "mass assembly-line justice," which "was rushing defendants into pleas of guilty and into convictions, in violation of their legal rights." *N.Y. Times,* March 10, 1965, p. 51. Another item, appearing somewhat later that year reports a judge criticizing his own court system (the New York Criminal Court), that "pressure to set statistical records in disposing of cases had hurt the administration of justice." *N.Y. Times,* Nov. 4, 1965, p. 49. A third, and most unusual recent public discussion in the press was a statement by a leading New York appellate judge decrying "instant justice" which is employed to reduce court calendar congestion "converting our courthouses into counting houses…, as in most big cities where the volume of business tends to overpower court facilities." *N.Y. Times,* Feb. 5, 1966, p. 58.

14. R. L. Gasser, *The Confidence Game,* 27 Fed. Prob. 47 (1963).

15. C. W. Mills, *White Collar,* 121–29 (1951); J. E. Carlin, *supra,* note 11.

16. E. O. Smigel, *The Wall Street Lawyer* (New York: The Free Press of Glencoe, 1964), p. 309.

17. Talcott Parsons indicates that the social role and function of the lawyer can be therapeutic, helping his client psychologically in giving him necessary emotional support at critical times. The lawyer is also said to be acting as an agent of social control in the counseling of his client and in the influencing of his course of conduct. See T. Parsons, *Essays in Sociological Theory,* 382 et seq. (1954); E. Goffman, *On Cooling the Mark Out; Some Aspects of Adaptations to Failure,* in *Human Behavior and Social Processes,* 482–505 (A. Rose, ed., 1962). Goffman's "cooling out" analysis is especially relevant in the lawyer-accused client relationship.

18. The question has never been raised as to whether "bargain justice," "copping a plea," or justice by negotiations is a constitutional process. Although it has become the most central aspect of the process of criminal law administration, it has received virtually no close scrutiny by the appellate courts. As a consequence, it is relatively free of legal control and supervision. But, apart from any questions of the legality of bargaining, in terms of the pressures and devices that are employed which tend to violate due process of law, there remain ethical and practical questions. The system of bargain-counter justice is like the proverbial iceberg, much of its danger is concealed in secret negotiations and its least alarming feature, the final plea, is the one presented to public view. See A. S. Trebach, *The Rationing of Justice,* 74–94 (1964); Note, *Guilty Plea Bargaining: Compromises by Prosecutors to Secure Guilty Pleas,* 112 U. Pa. L. Rev. 865-95 (1964).

19. For a conventional summary statement of some of the inevitable conflicting loyalties encountered in the practice of law, see E. E. Cheatham, *Cases and Materials on the Legal Profession,* 70–79 (2d ed., 1955).

20. Some lawyers at either end of the continuum of law practice appear to have grave doubts as to whether it is indeed a profession at all. J. E. Carlin, *op. cit., supra,* note 11, at 192: E. O. Smigel, *supra,* note 16 at 304-305. Increasingly, it is perceived as a business with widespread evasion of the Canons of Ethics, duplicity and chicanery being practiced in an effort to get and keep business. The poet, Carl Sandburg, epitomized this notion in the following vignette: "Have you a criminal lawyer in this burg?" "We think so but we haven't been able to prove it on him." C. Sandburg. *The People, Yes,* 154 (1936).

Thus, while there is considerable amount of dishonesty present in law practice involving fee splitting, thefts from clients, influence peddling, fixing, questionable use of favors and gifts to obtain business or influence others, this sort of activity is most often attributed to the "solo," private practice lawyer. See A. L. Wood, *Professional Ethics Among Criminal Lawyers,* Social Problems (1959). However, to some degree, large scale "downtown" elite firms also engage in these dubious activities. The difference is that the latter firms enjoy a good deal of immunity from these harsh charges because of their institutional and organizational advantages, in terms of near monopoly over more desirable types of practice, as well as exerting great influence in the political, economic and professional realms of power.

21. This does not mean that most of those who plead guilty are innocent of any crime. Indeed, in many instances those who have been able to negotiate a lesser plea have done so willingly and eagerly. The system of justice-by-negotiation, without trial, probably tends to better serve the interests and requirements of guilty persons, who are thereby presented with formal alternatives of "half a loaf," in terms of, at worst, possibilities of a lesser plea and a concomitant shorter sentence as compensation for their acquiescence and participation. Having observed the prescriptive etiquette in compliance with the defendant role expectancies in this setting, he is rewarded. An innocent person, on the other hand, is confronted with the same set of role prescriptions, structures and legal alternatives, and in any event, for him this mode of justice is often an ineluctable bind.

22. Any communicative network between persons whereby the public identity of an actor is transformed into something looked on as lower in the local scheme of social types will be called a "status degradation ceremony." H. Garfinkel, *Conditions of Successful Degradation Ceremonies,* 61 Am. J. Soc. 420-24 (1956). But contrary to the conception of the "cop out" as a "status degradation ceremony," is the fact that it is in reality a charade, during the course of which an accused must project an appropriate and acceptable amount of guilt, penitence and remorse. Having adequately feigned the role of the "guilty person," his hearers will engage in the fantasy that he is contrite, and thereby merits a lesser plea. It is one of the essential functions of the criminal lawyer that he coach and direct his accused-client in that role performance. Thus, what is actually involved is not a "degradation" process at all, but is instead, a highly structured system of exchange cloaked in the rituals of legalism and public professions of guilt and repentance.

23. The name is of course fictitious. However, the actual court which served as the universe from which the data were drawn, is one of the largest criminal courts in the United States, dealing with felonies only. Female defendants in the years 1950 through 1964 constituted from 7–10% of the totals for each year.

24. My own data in this connection would appear to support Sobel's conclusion (see note 4 *supra),* and appears to be at variance with the prevalent view, which stresses the importance of confessions in law enforcement and prosecution. All the persons in my sample were originally charged with felonies ranging from homicide to forgery; in most instances the original felony charges were reduced to misdemeanors by way of a negotiated lesser plea. The vast range of crime categories which are available, facilitates the patterned court process of plea reduction to a lesser offense, which is also usually a socially less opprobrious crime. For an illustration of this feature of the bargaining process in a court utilizing a public defender office, see D. Sudnow, *Normal Crimes: Sociological Features of the Penal Code in a Public Defender Office,* 12 Social Problems 255–76 (1964).

25. Failures, shortcomings and oppressive features of our system of criminal justice have been attributed to a variety of sources including "lawless" police, overzealous district attorneys. "hanging" juries, corruption and political connivance, incompetent judges, inadequacy or

lack of counsel, and poverty or other social disabilities of the defendant. See A. Barth, *Law Enforcement versus the Law* (1963) for a journalist's account embodying this point of view; J. H. Skolnick, *Justice without Trial: Law Enforcement in Democratic Society* (1966) for a sociologist's study of the role of the police in criminal law administration. For a somewhat more detailed, albeit legalistic and somewhat technical discussion of American police procedures, see W. R. LaFave, *Arrest: The Decision to Take a Suspect into Custody* (1965).

26. Aspects of the lawyer's ambivalences with regard to the expectancies of the various groups who have claims upon him are discussed in H. J. O'Gorman, *The Ambivalence of Lawyers*, paper presented at the Eastern Sociological Association meetings, April 10, 1965.

27. W. J. Goode, *A Theory of Role Strain.* 25 Am. Soc. Rev. 483-96 (1960); J. D. Snok, *Role Strain in Diversified Role Sets,* 71 Am. J. Soc. 363-72 (1966).

28. Some of the resources which have become an integral part of our courts, e.g., psychiatry, social work and probation, were originally intended as part of an ameliorative, therapeutic effort to individualize offenders. However, there is some evidence that a quite different result obtains than the one originally intended. The ameliorative instruments have been coopted by the court in order to more "efficiently" deal with a court's caseload, often to the legal disadvantage of an accused person. See F. A. Allen, The *Borderland of Criminal Justice* (1964); T. S. Szasz, *Law, Liberty and Psychiatry* (1963) and also Szasz's most recent, *Psychiatric Justice* (1965); L. Diana, "The Rights of Juvenile Delinquents: An Appraisal of Juvenile Court Procedures," 47 *J. Crim. L. C. & P.S.* 561-69 (1957).

QUESTIONS FOR DISCUSSION

1. How does the court structure define the role of the defense attorney? Cite examples to support your answer.

2. List and discuss the three functions that, according to Blumberg, must be served by a criminal lawyer.

3. Explain why the author refers to defense attorneys as "double agents."

4. According to the author, the U. S. Supreme Court in recent decisions has not taken into account three crucial aspects of the social structure that render libertarian rules valueless. What do these decisions overlook, and why is this occurring?

APPLICATIONS

1. Contact a local defense attorney and inquire about courtroom politics. Is the practice of law a con game? Is the defendant a secondary figure in the politics and bureaucracy of the court environment? (You may want to have an attorney read this article and comment as to whether Blumberg is asserting a valid and fair appraisal of the legal profession.) Report your findings to the class.

2. Based on your reading of Blumberg's article, how might "the practice of law as a con game" be discouraged or abolished?

Guilty until Proved Innocent

Wrongful Conviction and Public Policy

C. Ronald Huff • Arye Rattner • Edward Sagarin

The prisons are filled with convicts who claim that they were "framed" or "railroaded." Others who have already "done time" claim that they were erroneously convicted and imprisoned. Still others have pleaded guilty only to go free on probation or with suspended sentences. Some of these men and women have firm adherents who believe in their denials of guilt: family, friends, counsel, the general publics—even victims—who uphold the contention that they, the convicted, are themselves the victims of a miscarriage of justice. If there is some reasonable doubt as to their guilt (that is, if they have been convicted although the evidence does not demonstrate guilt beyond a reasonable doubt), then the verdict of guilt was wrong, and it can be said to be a *wrongful conviction,* from a strictly legal point of view. However, so long as guiltlessness has itself not been established, one cannot categorize such individuals as convicted innocents.

Our definition of *wrongful conviction* includes only those cases in which a person is convicted of a felony but later is found to be innocent beyond a reasonable doubt, generally due to a confession by the actual offender, evidence that had been available but was not sufficiently used at the time of conviction, new evidence that was not previously available, and other factors.

We are, in short, focusing our attention on convicted innocents. Few of these cases become **causes célèbres**, for the convicted are generally unknown, often penniless, persons who are punished for crimes that they did not commit. In seeking to further our understanding of such miscarriages of justice, we shall address three major questions: (1) How frequent is wrongful conviction? (2) What are the major causes of error in such cases? and (3) What policy implications may be derived from this study?

C. Ronald Huff, Arye Rattner, and Edward Sagarin, *Crime & Delinquency*, "Guilty until Proved Innocent: Wrongful Conviction and Public Policy." Reprinted by permission of Sage Publications.

HOW BIG IS THE PROBLEM?

This is perhaps the most frequently asked question, and it is a query for which there is no definitive answer. Just as we have no precise method of measuring the universe of criminal behavior, we cannot quantify the universe of wrongful convictions because only the most highly publicized cases ever come to the public's attention.

Most of those who have addressed the problem of wrongful conviction have come away convinced that it is not a rare phenomenon. Radin (1964:9) cites an estimate by a highly respected judge (whom he does not name), who opined that there might be as many as 14,000 cases of false conviction in the United States in a given year. At the time this estimate was made, it would have represented a 5% error!

Reported estimates of the frequency of wrongful conviction range from very few cases each year up to 20% of all convictions. Given such a considerable variance in estimates, we decided to conduct a survey, using a "panel of judges" (some of whom really were judges!).

Our sample consisted of (1) the universe of attorneys general in the United States and its territories and (2) an Ohio sample, which included all presiding judges of common pleas courts; all county prosecutors; all county public defenders; all county sheriffs; and the chiefs of police of Ohio's seven major cities (Columbus, Cleveland, Cincinnati, Toledo, Akron, Dayton, and Youngstown).

Comments volunteered by our respondents suggested the controversial nature of research on wrongful conviction. One judge wrote that after having served as a visiting judge in all of Ohio's major cities, "I have a strong suspicion that each year in Ohio, at least one or two dozen persons are convicted of crimes of which they are innocent." On the other hand, another respondent, an Ohio State alumnus, was so upset by our study that he seemed ready to return his football tickets: "I am deeply disappointed that my old university is even remotely involved in this type of venture. Aren't there more pressing topics in this world that your efforts can be funneled to?"

Nearly three-fourths of those who provided estimates agreed that wrongful conviction comprises less than 1% of all felony convictions in the United States. Another 20% of our estimates were in the 1%–5% range.

Thus if these apparently conservative estimates are reasonable, we could be facing an interesting dilemma: A high-volume criminal justice system, even if 99.5% accurate, could still generate nearly 6,000 erroneous convictions (for index crimes alone) each year.

Therefore, although there is no known method of determining exactly how many wrongful convictions occur each year, our literature review, our survey, our own primary database of nearly 500 wrongful conviction cases, and our analysis of the dynamics of wrongful conviction cause us to feel relatively confident in this conservative estimate of less than 1%. In other words, for every 200 persons convicted of felonies in the United States, we (and the great majority of our survey respondents) believe that 1 or 2 of them may well be innocent. The frequency of error may well be much higher in cases involving less serious felonies and misdemeanors.

HOW DOES IT HAPPEN?

How can an innocent defendant be convicted? What would possibly induce an innocent person to plead guilty? What goes wrong with a criminal justice system that has created an elaborate system of safeguards to protect suspects' and defendants' rights?

In seeking to answer these questions, we have developed a large database, currently consisting of nearly 500 cases (and growing almost daily) of wrongful felony conviction, the great majority having occurred in the United States. This database is the product of our ongoing review of published literature, newspapers, and legal documents from around the country, as well as cases identified through our survey. Our analysis of these cases has enabled us to identify the major factors responsible for the conviction of innocent defendants. Our data suggest that, in general, more than one of these factors is involved in a case of wrongful conviction; in other words, it appears to us that the most likely scenario for wrongful conviction is when the system breaks down in more than one way.

Eyewitness Error

We believe that the single most important factor leading to wrongful conviction in the United States and England (Brandon and Davies, 1973) is eyewitness misidentification. Nearly 60% of the cases in our database involve such errors.

Sometimes these eyewitnesses have no doubt whatsoever about the accuracy of their testimony; in other cases, they had either slight or lingering questions in their own minds, but nevertheless felt sufficiently confident that they were willing to testify against a defendant.

Item: Lenell Geter, a young black engineer employed in the Dallas area, is at work one day when a fast food restaurant is robbed 50 miles away. A white woman tells of Geter's "suspicious" habit of reading and feeding ducks in the park near her home. Several witnesses to the crime identify Geter from photographs, even though their previous descriptions of the robber bore little resemblance to Geter. Geter's coworkers testify that he was at work when the robbery occurred. There is no physical evidence linking Geter to the crime. Nonetheless, Geter is convicted and sentenced to life in prison. Following intense national publicity, including a feature story on CBS's *60 Minutes*, Geter is finally released (*New York Times*, 1984, March 28).

Item: Steven Titus and his girlfriend have just left a restaurant, where they were celebrating her twenty-first birthday. While driving, they are stopped by police, who ask if Steven minds their taking his photograph. He agrees, joking that it is a good chance to be photographed with his girlfriend. The next day, a 17-year-old rape victim finds herself staring at Titus's picture in a "photo lineup." Saying, "This one is the closest; it has to be the one," she identifies Titus as the man who raped her on a secluded road near the Seattle–Tacoma airport. Titus is convicted and nearly goes to prison before his innocence is established—not through the efforts of the police or the prosecutor, but through his own efforts and the investigative reporting of Paul Henderson of the *Seattle Times*. Henderson wins a Pulitzer Prize; Titus is still trying to put his life back together (*Seattle Times, 1982; Los Angeles Times,* 1983, January 4:9).

Many of the cases we have identified involve errors by victims of robbery and rape, where the victim was close to the offender and was able to get a look at him—but under conditions of extreme stress. As Loftus (1979), Buckhout (1974), and Brigham and Barkowitz (1978) have shown in their published research, such stress can significantly affect perception and memory and should give us cause to question the reliability of such eyewitness testimony.

Although jurors attach great significance to eyewitness testimony, experts and judges increasingly share the view of Judge Lumbard of the Second Circuit, who observed:

> Centuries of experience in the administration of criminal justice have shown that convictions based solely on testimony that identifies a defendant previously unknown to the witness is highly suspect. Of the various kinds of evidence it is the least reliable, especially where unsupported by corroborating evidence [*Jackson v. Fogg, 1978*].

Despite the steps taken by the Supreme Court to establish safeguards against eyewitness misidentification, such errors continue to surface. In 1982, a Texas prisoner, Howard Mosley of Galveston, who had been convicted in a stabbing death and sentenced to a life term, was exonerated after new evidence indicated that the crime had been committed by a man who also admitted killing eleven others (*Houston Chronicle,* 1982). In a highly publicized Ohio case where great weight was placed on eyewitness identification by the victims of rape, William Jackson spent nearly five years in prison for two rapes he did not commit. He was released from prison after a grand jury indicted a Columbus physician (also named Jackson, but unrelated) on 36 counts of rape and 46 counts of aggravated burglary (*Columbus Citizen-Journal,* 1982, September 25; *New York Times,* 1982, September 24). These two cases also illustrate that the wrongly accused may or may not physically resemble the actual offender. Although fully a foot taller than Watts (the actual offender), Mosley was nevertheless identified and a jury was convinced of his guilt beyond a reasonable doubt. By contrast, in the Ohio case, both men bore the same last name; both were black; and both had trimmed Afro haircuts, similar facial shapes and mustaches, and were approximately the same height.

Accounts of eyewitness error are myriad, and sometimes bizarre. In one incredible case, Jeffrey Streeter was convicted without even having been arrested! Streeter had been sitting outside a courtroom and was asked by a defense attorney if he would sit next to him as a way of testing the credibility of the eyewitnesses. The defense attorney failed to inform the judge of the switch. Despite the fact that the real defendant was also in the courtroom at the time, three eyewitnesses pointed to the startled Streeter, who was seated next to the defense attorney. Streeter was convicted and sentenced to a year in jail for beating up an old man. He spent the night in jail before being released on his own recognizance. His conviction was subsequently reversed (*Atlanta Constitution,* 1980).

In another case, Robert Duncan, president of the Missouri Association of Criminal Defense Lawyers, was representing a Mexican-American defendant who had been arrested after being identified by a woman who was raped by "an Italian-looking man." When a second suspect was brought in, she identified him, too, as the guilty offender. She reportedly told authorities, "I'm getting tired of coming down here to identify this man." According to defense attorney Duncan, "The second guy didn't look anything at all like my client" (*U.S. News & World Report,* 1984:46).

Errors and/or Unprofessional Conduct by Police and Prosecutors

> Far too many cases come from the states to the Supreme Court presenting dismal pictures of official lawlessness, of illegal searches and seizures, illegal detentions attended by prolonged interrogation and coerced admissions of guilt, of the denial of counsel, and downright brutality [Brennan, 1961:20–21].

Our survey respondents ranked police and prosecutorial errors, respectively, as the second and third most frequent contributing causes, and this rank order is justified, based on the cases in our own database. A common scenario in this type of error is the overzealous officer and/or prosecutor. Convinced of the suspect's or defendant's guilt, there is a temptation to buttress the case by prompting witnesses, suggesting what may have occurred at the time of the crime, concealing or fabricating evidence, or even committing perjury in court to "get their man."

Such unprofessional behavior is often well-intentioned, motivated by a sincere desire to strengthen the case against a suspect or defendant they "just know" is guilty. Given the view that police and prosecutors are part of that "thin line" that is civilized society's last hope for protection against the forces of evil, it is tempting for a police officer to twist the facts just enough to ensure that the "twelve rocks in a box" (the jury) won't fail to convict the defendant. Likewise, crusading prosecutors who are bent on seeking convictions, rather than justice, often fail to advise defense attorneys of exculpatory evidence.

Item: A prosecutor brings as evidence a pair of men's undershorts found a mile from the crime scene. Alleging that these shorts belong to the accused and are heavily stained with blood that is the same type as the victim's, the prosecutor calls a chemist who verifies these "facts." The defense requests, and is denied, an opportunity to examine the shorts. Despite the defendant's denial that the shorts (the only link in a chain of circumstantial evidence) are his, the jury convicts him. The convicted prisoner subsequently petitions the Supreme Court for habeas corpus. A microanalyst appears for the petitioner and testifies that the shorts were indeed stained—with paint! The prosecutor later admits having known that the stains were paint—a fact that was unknown to the defense (*Miller v. Pate,* 1967).

Item: An innocent man, George Reissfelder, is convicted of first degree murder and armed robbery and is sentenced to life imprisonment with no possibility of parole. He spends 16 years in prison, despite the fact that his codefendant testified that Reissfelder was not his partner. Five policemen, an FBI agent, and a probation officer later submit statements indicating that authorities conducting the original investigation knew that Reissfelder was not Sullivan's partner in the robbery (*Atlanta Constitution,* 1983).

Item: In May, 1980, Juan Venegas, along with Lawrence Reyes, is convicted of murdering a 65 year-old man. Despite the fact that Reyes confesses to the murder, Venegas spends 2½ years in prison in California before being released and winning a civil award of $1 million (*San Francisco Chronicle,* 1980). Evidence presented at the civil trial shows that the police intimidated witnesses to perjure themselves and orchestrated a "frameup" of Mr. Venegas (Granelli, 1980).

Plea Bargaining

Many innocent defendants were convicted after "willingly" pleading guilty via the plea bargaining process. For most people, this may be the most puzzling of all such cases; after all, why would a perfectly innocent person plead guilty? This is one of the least publicized dynamics of wrongful conviction. Typically, the innocent defendant protests his innocence to counsel (and because many guilty defendants also claim innocence, counsel may regard such claims with cynicism) and to others, but not to the judge (at least not in open court), who must approve the plea bargain.

As for the question of why an innocent person would plead guilty, a social psychological experiment using role playing casts some light on the issue. Gregory (1978) found that innocent "defendants" were more likely to accept a plea bargain when they faced a number of charges or when the probable severity of punishment was great. For this reason, we are particularly concerned about the possible effect of resuming executions in the United States. With so much to lose, who among us would not plead guilty if he thought that by doing so, he could save his own life and, perhaps, eventually go free when the error is discovered?

Item: In Richmond, Virginia, Harry Siegler awaits the verdict of a jury who has heard the prosecution's case against him. Siegler, charged with first degree murder, fears that the jury will find him guilty and sentence him to death by electrocution. Minutes before the jury returns, Siegler desperately changes his plea to guilty. Meanwhile, the jury had already voted to find him not guilty (*Columbus Dispatch,* 1982, September 26).

In cases of less serious charges, a defendant who is unable to make bail and is offered, in exchange for a plea of guilt, immediate release with nothing more consequential than a minor criminal record (typically in a community where such records are not uncommon and not highly **stigmatizing**), cannot easily resist the lure of a guilty plea. That one will be found not guilty, although the defendant knows himself to be guiltless, is not at all certain. Alibis are difficult to establish; eyewitnesses can swear that they are confident in their identification of the defendant (even though they are often wrong); an assigned lawyer may not have the time or other resources for a good investigation; or an attorney unconvinced of his client's innocence may not proceed with enthusiasm, thus compromising the entire concept of the adversarial process.

In the subculture of the courts, the defense attorney, like the prosecutor, feels pressure to play the game of speedy disposal of cases (Rosett and Cressey, 1976; Heumann, 1978). Unwilling to bargain in one case, he is offered little opportunity to bargain in another where he desires to do so. If his client has a criminal record, he informs him of the difficulty in placing him on the stand.

Guilty pleas are usually accompanied by a ritualistic **colloquy** between the judge and the accused, in which the judge may subtly compel the defendant to confess to his guilt. Insofar as there has been a "bargain," the judge does not wish to clutter the record with the suspicion that an innocent person was compelled to plead guilty. Actually, it adds little to the record, in that the distinction between a plea of guilty and an admission of guilt is not one that is carefully drawn, although such a distinction becomes clear when the not guilty plea is contrasted with a denial of guilt.

COMMUNITY PRESSURE FOR A CONVICTION

In a period of high crime and great public outcry against criminals, and a period when group pressures are felt in the courtroom, conviction rates may be higher. Pressure by whites has sometimes resulted in verdicts against blacks where there was at least reasonable doubt; blacks and other minority groups have sometimes tried to exert pressure in cases where whites were being tried for crimes against minorities, particularly when the alleged crimes appeared to be racially motivated. Certainly there has been pressure by women's groups (feminist and other) in some rape cases.

Pressure from the public, sometimes intensified by newspaper coverage, can be an expression of democratic participation in the criminal justice process. It can sometimes make the system more responsive to the social needs, values, and feelings of large numbers of residents. It can serve as watchdog, lest corruption and malfeasance in the system go unmentioned. It may thus result in prosecution of a case that warrants pursuit, but that might otherwise be dropped because of the standing and influence of the accused and his family, or in an appropriate finding of not guilty when the spotlight is on the court.

Public pressure, then, is a two-edged sword. It may be democratic pressure for social and criminal justice, or it may simply reflect public vengeance and fears, easily manipulated by **demagogues** who are ready and willing to oblige.

Inadequacy of Counsel

Since at least 1932 (*Powell v. Alabama*), inadequacy of counsel has been a basis for appealing conviction in criminal cases. The basic rationale of such an appeal is that the original defense counsel, for whatever reasons, did not adequately represent his client's interests in the case. Such appeals are not easy to win, despite the fact that many attorneys are inadequately prepared for trial work. Collegial relationships within the legal profession, though pitting lawyer against lawyer as adversaries, stop short of promoting the idea of attacking colleagues for mishandling a case (just as doctors are not eager to testify against other doctors). Lawyers assigned anew, or on appeal, are not eager to pursue this line for a reversal, preferring to characterize as "new evidence" that which had formerly been overlooked, for example.

Such cases as appear in the literature and in our database do not generally show a defense attorney in league with prosecutors or working against the interests of a client. Rather, the counsel for the defense is more likely to have been inexperienced, **harried**, overworked, with few or no investigative resources. Sometimes the defense counsel is unreceptive to a client's wishes because of a belief in the defendant's guilt and in the futility, even self-destructiveness, of pursuing the line of defense suggested by the accused.

Defense attorney errors include failure to make discovery motions or to pursue them vigorously, using poor judgment in placing a defendant on the stand, allowing a defendant to take a polygraph exam (especially in the absence of the defense attorney), and failure to challenge vigorously contentions made by the prosecution in court (Finer, 1973).

False Accusations

Item: Nathaniel Carter is arrested for murder in the stabbing death of Clarice Herndon. Carter's chief accuser is his estranged wife, who says she watched helplessly as Carter attacked her foster mother with a knife, inflicting 23 stab wounds. Carter is sentenced to a prison term of 25 years to life. After he serves 2 years in prison, his former wife admits that she, in fact, killed her foster mother. The police state that the cuts on Mrs. Carter's hands at the time of the crime made them believe she had also been attacked by her former husband. She seemed to be the perfect witness (*New York Times,* 1984).

False accusations fall into two categories: those in which a crime did occur and someone is deliberately and falsely accused (sometimes, in fact, by the perpetrator, as in the Carter case above), and others in which no crime ever occurred. There are several cases of men who have served prison terms for "murders" that never took place, only to have the **putative** "victim" turn up, alive and well.

Knowledge of Criminal Record

The old adage, "where there's smoke, there's fire," seems alive and well in the minds of the public and some criminal justice personnel. Where the accused has a history of prior arrest (not necessarily even conviction), many would more readily believe current accusations. This becomes a factor in wrongful conviction insofar as the police and other criminal justice personnel are likely to believe the worst about such suspects and perhaps ignore other leads. Also, the accused's past criminal record may be made known when the defendant voluntarily takes the stand or may be brought out through the questioning of other defense witnesses. It is sometimes common knowledge in the community that the accused has "a record." Where any of these factors is present, it makes the task of confining the verdict to the current facts more difficult. If one is conceived of as evil, there is no loss, it is reasoned, and there may even be social good, in punishment.

Other Factors

Other factors that are either less prevalent or about which less is known include judicial errors, bias, or neglect of duty; errors (generally, though not always unintentional) made by criminalists, medical examiners, and forensic science experts; errors in criminal record-keeping and computerized information systems; voluntary and deliberate false confessions; and the mental incompetency of the accused.

IMPLICATIONS FOR PUBLIC POLICY

It is not within the realm of possibility to prevent all wrongful convictions. A system of law that never caught an innocent person in its web would probably be so narrow that it would catch few of the guilty, as well.

Moreover, our research has established the existence of an important systemic phenomenon that has significant implications for the production of false convictions. We call this phenomenon the *ratification of error.* That is, the criminal justice system, starting with the police investigation of an alleged crime and culminating in the appellate courts, tends to **ratify** errors made at lower levels in the system. The further a case progresses in the system, the less chance there is that an error will be discovered and corrected, unless it involves a basic issue of constitutional rights and due process.

Recall the case of Nathaniel Carter, who was falsely convicted of stabbing his ex-wife's foster mother. A *New York Times* (1984) analysis of police reports, court records, and more than 100 interviews reveals a succession of serious errors, neglect, and incompetence that collectively led to Mr. Carter's wrongful conviction:

1. An officer and another witness saw a man in bloody clothes running from the murder scene—a man whose description did not match Mr. Carter's. But in violation of prescribed practices, their accounts were never passed on to the prosecutors or the defense attorney, and the incident remains unexplained.

2. A prosecutor lied at the trial, leading the jury to believe that Mr. Carter had admitted he was at the crime scene on the day of the murder.

3. The District Attorney's staff never questioned Mrs. Carter's story, despite her background of violence. Instead, shortly after receiving the case, she was granted immunity from prosecution.

4. The defense attorney failed to contact many of the witnesses who saw Mr. Carter far from the scene of the murder. Of at least ten such witnesses, only two were called to testify.

As one observer commented, "This was a breakdown of major proportions in the justice system....It is a justice system so overworked that it has grown cynical to the possibility of a man's innocence." Mr. Carter characterized his experience more succinctly: "I was railroaded" (*New York Times,* 1984).

Compensation

Item: A 20-year-old man is wrongfully convicted of rape and robbery and spends nearly 2 years in prison before another man confesses to these crimes. While in prison, the innocent man is treated as a rapist by other prisoners. Following his release from prison, he is still unable to function sexually due to the psychological humiliation he experienced concerning his sexuality. The case is now in **civil litigation** (anonymous interview, 1983).

Item: 34-year-old Charles Daniels, though innocent, is convicted of sexually attacking a 2-year-old boy and attempting to murder him by hurling him from a rooftop. Despite alibi witnesses, Daniels is convicted and sentenced to 6–18 years in prison. While in prison, he is treated as any child sex molester might be treated: he is beaten, scalded with boiling water and, due to threats against his life, kept in virtual solitary confinement for 4 years before being exonerated. In an out-of-court settlement, he is awarded $600,000. Mr. Daniels says of his experience in prison, "Going through what I did is almost as bad as being executed for a crime you didn't commit. Because the other prisoners thought I had raped a child I knew I could be killed at any moment while I was in prison" (*New York Times*, 1985).

How much financial compensation are such experiences worth? Occasionally, one hears of a seemingly large award, such as that in the Daniels case (above); the $1 million award won by Isidore Zimmerman, who spent 24 years in prison, including 9 months on death row, and came within 2 hours of being executed for a murder he never committed (Wise, 1983), or the $1 million awarded to Juan Venegas, whose ordeal we discussed earlier (Granelli, 1980). However, our study reveals that in the great majority of cases where, as a result of wrongful conviction, innocent persons have lost their families, opportunities to pursue careers, and have been humiliated, little or no compensation has been provided for such suffering. As Rosen (1976) noted, "The United States has lagged far behind many nations in its failure to compensate the innocent victims of erroneous criminal accusations."

In most states, in order to compensate a citizen who was convicted but innocent, a special bill must be introduced and passed by the state legislature. Such bills generally empower the state claims court to set the amount of the award, and claims courts tend to apply very conservative criteria, such as "lost wages" and legal expenses. Given the economic status of most wrongfully convicted persons, the use of criteria such as "lost wages" cannot begin to approximate the "value" of time spent in prison as a result of false conviction.

Only a handful of states (California, Wisconsin, Illinois, New York, and Tennessee) have established special funds for compensating the victims of wrongful conviction. Even in these states, however, the awards are generally small and, in some cases, the statutorily prescribed ceilings on such awards amount to $5,000 or less per year of imprisonment (American Bar Association, 1984). The other option, of course, is through civil litigation. But one attorney, whose client was awarded only $5,800 by the Wisconsin Claims Board after serving 14 months in prison for an armed robbery he didn't commit, commented:

You're talking about an expensive proposition. My client certainly doesn't have the money to pursue a civil suit. Most of these cases aren't like Geter. They're not getting the publicity. These are small cases in comparison and these people have to take what they can get. Sometimes they don't get anything [American Bar Association, 1984].

States should acknowledge their responsibility to provide fair compensation for innocent citizens who are wrongfully convicted, or at least for those who are wrongfully incarcerated. As Ohio's Tenth District Court of Appeals recently proclaimed in reversing a "grossly inadequate" Court of Claims award that "shocked the conscience" of the appellate court:

> No society has developed a perfect system of criminal justice in which no person is ever treated unfairly. The American system of justice has developed a myriad of safeguards to prevent the type of miscarriage to which the claimant herein was subjected, but it, too, has its imperfections. Fortunately, cases in which courts have unlawfully or erroneously taken a person's freedom by finding him or her guilty of a crime which he or she did not commit are infrequent. But, when such a case is identified, the legislature and the legal system have a responsibility to admit the mistake and diligently attempt to make the person as whole as is possible where the person has been deprived of his freedom and forced to live with criminals. Indeed the legal system is capable of creating few errors that have a greater impact upon an individual than to incarcerate him when he has committed no crime [Leonard O'Neil v. State of Ohio, 1984].

We are aware that many people regard wrongful convictions as the inevitable errors of a criminal justice system that is our social defense against crime—that such errors are indications of the essential strength of the system (social defense) and that in a time of high crime rates, an effort to reduce the incidence of such errors would result in so few convictions that the system could not tolerate the large numbers of guilty going free. Contrary to this belief, we suggest that the opposite effect may be at work. That is, the knowledge of false convictions, through the rather frequent newspaper and media accounts of such cases, may instill in the minds of many jurors and other citizens doubts as to the guilt of large numbers of accused, as well as those found guilty. Thus these "false positives" may be (or could become) a force working to reduce the rate of conviction for those whose guilt seems to be apparent beyond a reasonable doubt. A reduction in the number of wrongful convictions, then, could have important positive effects by increasing public respect for the criminal justice system and, perhaps, increasing the rate of conviction for those who are truly guilty— not to mention the most positive outcome of all, protecting the innocent.

Finally, wrongful conviction is not really an issue that should separate "liberals" from "conservatives." It does not require a fervent devotion to due process rights to comprehend that for every case of wrongful conviction, the real criminal may still be at large, free to victimize others.

Acknowledgment

This article is dedicated to the memory of our coauthor, colleague, and close friend, Ed Sagarin, who passed away on June 10, 1986. Ed's scholarly contributions were enormous, and this article reflects two of the concerns for which he will best be remembered: human rights and disvalued people.

Ed was a constant source of intellectual stimulation and encouragement to many younger criminologists. We were fortunate to be among them, and we shall miss him greatly.

REFERENCES

AMERICAN BAR ASSOCIATION (1984) "Innocents in jail." Amer. Bar Assn. J. 70 (June): 34–35.

Atlanta Constitution (1980) "Court stand-in is convicted of crime he didn't commit." July 17: 12A.

Atlanta Constitution (1983) "16 years in jail, case dismissed." August 31: 1 A.

BRANDON, R., AND C. DAVIES (1973) Wrongful Imprisonment: Mistaken Convictions and their Consequences. London: Allen and Unwin.

BRENNAN, W. J. (1961) The Bill of Rights and the States. Santa Barbara, CA: Center for the Study of Democratic Institutions.

BRIGHAM, J.C., AND P. BARKOWITZ (1978) "Do they all look alike? The effects of race, sex, experience, and attitudes on the ability to recognize faces." J. App. Psychol. 8: 306–18.

BUCKHOUT, R. (1974) "Eyewitness testimony." Sci. Amer. 231: 23–33.

FINER, J. J. (1973) "Ineffective assistance of counsel." Cornell Law Rev. 58: 1077–1120.

GRANELLI, J. S. (1980) "Trials—and errors." Nat. Law J., December 15: 1.

GREGORY, W. L., ET AL. (1978) "Social psychology of plea bargaining—applications, methodology, and theory." J. Personality Social Psychol. 36: 1521–30.

HEUMANN, M. (1978) Plea Bargaining: The Experiences of Prosecutors, Judges, and Defense Attorneys. Chicago: Univ. of Chicago Press.

Houston Chronicle (1982) "Monday finally comes for weekend killer." August 15.

LOFTUS, E. F. (1979) Eyewitness Testimony. Cambridge, MA: Harvard Univ. Press.

New York Times (1984) "How errors convicted the wrong man." March 15: B1.

New York Times (1985) "Man wrongfully imprisoned by New York to get $600,000." March 18: 1.

RADIN, E. D. (1964) The Innocents. New York: William C. Morrow.

ROSEN, S. K. (1976) "Compensating the innocent accused." Ohio State Law J. 37: 705–28.

ROSETT, A., AND D. R. CRESSEY (1976) Justice by Consent: Plea Bargains in the American Courthouse. Philadelphia: Lippincott.

San Francisco Chronicle (1980) "Innocent prisoner gets $1 million." September 4: 38.

Seattle Times (1982) Special reprint of P. Henderson's Pulitzer Prize-winning reports.

U.S. News & World Report (1984) "When nightmare of false arrest comes true." December 17: 45–47.

QUESTIONS FOR DISCUSSION

1. How frequent are wrongful convictions in the criminal justice system?

2. What are the major causes of errors in the wrongful convictions that do occur? Provide examples of these errors.

3. The author states that "it is not possible to prevent all of the wrongful convictions" in the Criminal Justice system. Given that this is the case, what suggestions are presented, in terms of public policy, to rectify this problem?

APPLICATIONS

1. Contact a local criminal justice official. Ask the official to make a guess as to the number of wrongful convictions that he or she believes occur in the in the criminal justice system. Compare the response to the information presented in this article. Are there any similarities or differences in the response of the official and the information in the article? Discuss what you have discovered with other members of your class.

2. Estimates vary as to the percentage of wrongful convictions in the criminal justice system. Do you believe that the article exaggerated this problem? Why? Discuss with other members of your class.

Priority Prosecution of High-Rate Dangerous Offenders

Marcia R. Chaiken • *Jan M. Chaiken*

INTRODUCTION

Faced with high caseloads, long delays in the courts, and public demand for swifter and more effective justice, criminal justice practitioners must make hard choices in allocating resources. This *Research in Action* summarizes the results of a recent study conducted by the authors under the sponsorship of the National Institute of Justice.[1] It provides research findings about information district attorneys can use to focus attention on dangerous offenders who commit crimes at high rates.

The study examined official record data available to prosecutors in two jurisdictions to learn which items of information most accurately identified offenders as high-rate (committing crimes frequently) and dangerous (committing violent crimes). While much of the information usually available to prosecutors was found useful for identifying high-rate dangerous offenders, the study revealed that other commonly used information can be misleading or ineffective for purposes of identification. As with all studies based on data from a small number of jurisdictions, these findings require replication in other jurisdictions before they can be considered generally applicable.

PRIORITY PROSECUTION PROGRAMS

Almost all prosecutors deal with a wide variety of criminal offenders. They must regularly decide what kinds of offenders or offenses are to receive attention from the best or most experienced attorneys or from staff members with specialized training or knowledge. District attorneys around the country have established a variety of priority prosecution programs. Some focus on major narcotics dealers, organized crime figures, arsonists, or sex offenders; others concentrate on offenders whose victims are children, or on cases likely to entail lengthy or complex trials.

A popular form of priority prosecution program—and the type upon which our research focused—is commonly known as career criminal prosecution. The earliest career criminal programs were established over 10 years ago and were targeted primarily to habitual offenders who had extensive records of felony convictions.[2] Since then, more than a hundred U.S. jurisdictions have adopted some form of priority prosecution for career criminals.[3]

Most types of priority prosecution programs are intended to help prosecutors meet the following goals:[4]

- Conviction on the most serious applicable charge—for example, conviction for burglary rather than possession of stolen property
- Increased likelihood of incarceration of convicted offenders
- Increased length of sentence
- Increased pretrial detention
- Reduced time until the case is disposed

The specific practices used in prosecutors' priority prosecution programs vary among jurisdictions. However, the following procedures are commonly followed:[5]

- Close cooperation with police officers. Police alert prosecutors to arrestees who appear to warrant priority prosecution. In turn, to ensure the technical soundness of cases, attorneys advise police about practices such as obtaining warrants and collecting evidence.
- Screening of defendants. Records of defendants charged with or wanted for specific types of serious crimes are reviewed to determine if they meet specified criteria for priority prosecution.
- Assignment of experienced attorneys to prosecute cases selected for priority prosecution.
- Vertical prosecution. The same attorney is assigned to the case from the time it is first accepted for prosecution until the case is completed.
- **Coalescing** of cases. The same attorney is assigned to all pending cases involving the same defendant.
- Close supervision of selected cases by a senior prosecutor. Senior attorneys, typically program directors, frequently monitor the progress and procedures used in cases chosen for priority prosecution.
- Curtailment of plea negotiations. Attorneys seek prosecution for the most serious crime charged and do not allow "bargaining" for guilty pleas to lesser crimes and shorter sentences.
- Caseload reduction. Attorneys prosecuting priority cases are assigned relatively few other cases to prosecute.

DEFINING "CAREER CRIMINALS"

Although prosecutors in existing career criminal programs try to target certain types of defendants for priority prosecution, there is no uniform understanding across the country of what is meant by a "career criminal." In reality, three overlapping types of offender profiles could be called career criminals:

- Persistent offenders, also known as long-term offenders or habitual offenders, are those who commit crimes over a long period of time. This study included as persistent offenders all the offenders who had been committing crimes for at least one-third of their lifetimes.

- High-rate offenders are those who commit numerous crimes per year whenever free to do so (whether they have been doing so for many years or relatively recently). For example, an offender who commits 104 burglaries per year (an average of 2 burglaries per week) when not locked up is a high-rate offender.

- Dangerous offenders are those who commit crimes of violence, often injuring their victims. The study included in this category all those who were high-rate robbers or who had assaulted, threatened with a weapon, shot at, or tried to cut, beat, or strangle another person.

While some offenders fit into more than one category, others do not. For example, a 30-year-old who has committed occasional burglaries since age 17 would be categorized as a long-term persistent offender but not necessarily either high-rate or dangerous. A person who had committed three assaults, two robberies, and a burglary in the past month, however, would be both high-rate and dangerous.

In response to changing public concerns and growing research knowledge, many career criminal prosecution programs have gradually begun to focus on offenders who are both high-rate and dangerous. High-rate dangerous offenders—and how to identify them—are the topics of the remaining sections of this [article]. These offenders should receive career criminal prosecution whether or not they have been involved in crime for a long time. The high-rate dangerous offenders are a small proportion of all felony defendants.

Although some prosecutors still have programs for dealing with habitual offenders, some research evidence indicates that many criminals who persistently cycle in and out of the criminal justice system are not worth special attention from prosecutors: these offenders may commit relatively few crimes but get caught nearly every time they do.[6]

IDENTIFYING HIGH-RATE DANGEROUS OFFENDERS

The first step in priority prosecution of high-rate dangerous offenders is to select appropriate cases. Some cases are so obvious that little attention needs to be given to selection decisions. A defendant charged with 10 or 12 eye-witnessed robberies clearly qualifies as high-rate and dangerous. Most cases are not so clear cut. For example, should a defendant arrested for two separate robberies on the same day be classified as a high-rate dangerous offender? What of the defendant who held up five victims at gunpoint at a local convenience store at midnight? Selections often must depend on information obtained from several sources, such as rap sheets (records of past arrests and convictions), the police officer's arrest report, or the investigating police officer's report.

In some jurisdictions, selection decisions must follow strict guidelines established by State law or local regulations. (When the number of defendants who qualify under law exceeds program capacity, prosecutors may then use additional information to define a subset of defendants who will actually receive priority prosecution.)

In other programs the guidelines are less formal, and prosecutors have wider discretion in choosing candidates for priority prosecution. While some guidelines and discretionary information currently used to make priority prosecution decisions are in fact helpful in identifying high-rate dangerous offenders, this study found that other information is redundant or misleading.

Clearly, if prosecutors knew exactly how many and what types of crimes an offender had committed, classification would be simple. Instead, only limited data exist; a rap sheet, for example, will report only arrests and convictions—not crimes committed successfully and without detection. In a sense, then, the task in identifying high-rate dangerous offenders is one of using limited data to draw inferences about actual (but unreported) behavior. Simply stated, do the rap sheet and other available data create a profile of a person who—if all the unreported facts were known—would in fact be high-rate dangerous?

Which factors in the official sources commonly available to prosecutors most accurately identify those offenders who are in fact high-rate and dangerous? To answer this critical question, the research:

1. Analyzed information available to prosecutors for identifying arrested persons for priority prosecution.
2. Statistically compared it to data obtained from confidential self-reports from convicted offenders.

The accuracy of data from the self-reports was controlled to the maximum extent possible. Respondents were assured of confidentiality. Repetitive questions were used to check consistency of response. Analyses controlled for self-reports that did not contain consistent data.

INTERVIEWS WITH PROSECUTORS

In-depth research studies were carried out in Los Angeles County, California, and Middlesex County, Massachusetts. Selection procedures were also reviewed with prosecutors from a wide and diverse group of additional jurisdictions.

The Los Angeles Career Criminal Division exemplifies programs that operate under fairly rigid and restrictive selection rules and are carried out by a limited number of attorneys who follow cases from their initiation.

Priority prosecution cases in Middlesex County, by contrast, can be handled by a large number of designated senior assistant attorneys (not just those in a special unit). Broader selection guidelines are used to target high-rate dangerous offenders, and cases can be selected for priority prosecution at any stage of their processing.

The two study sites also differ in size, resulting in differing levels of selectivity. The Los Angeles County District Attorney's Office is the largest in the United States, processing more than 100,000 criminal cases a year. Its Central Branch office, the locus of this study, handles the bulk of the county's most serious offenses. The Middlesex County office serves 54 cities and towns near Boston. It ranks number 42 in size among district attorneys' offices (in terms of the volume of cases handled) and processes 35,000 criminal cases a year.

In Los Angeles, the Career Criminal Division concentrates on a relatively small number of robbery and burglary defendants. In Middlesex County, a subset of defendants charged with robbery, burglary, rape, aggravated assault, homicide/murder, and drug sales receive priority prosecution.

In both sites, interviews and observation of attorneys who select cases for priority prosecution revealed the criteria they use in making their judgments and the procedures they follow. Attorneys then examined anonymous versions of cases that had previously been eligible for possible priority prosecution in either their own county or the other study site. Their responses were analyzed to determine the extent to which judgments were consistent between the two sites. This procedure also verified that the information about defendants and their offenses claimed to be taken into account actually had been taken into account.

The criteria used in the two study sites were also presented to career criminal program directors from many other counties in California for comments or additions. During the course of the study, researchers met informally with prosecutors from other States and discussed the information they used to select career criminals.

DEFENDANTS' REPORTS OF OFFENSES AND RECORDED DATA

The study collected data from and on 500 male defendants who were ultimately convicted. The sample included nearly all defendants selected for priority prosecution during the study period; they made up 17 percent of the sample. The remaining defendants selected for the study did not receive priority prosecution, but their charged offense—for example, robbery or burglary—was one of those targeted by the priority prosecution attorneys.

By examining records in these defendants' case folders, the study was able to code hundreds of items of data about them, their criminal history, and the instant offense. Since the researchers found the data in criminal justice agency records, obviously prosecuting attorneys had access to the same information. The wording of California State career criminal legislation, observations and interviews with prosecuting attorneys, and the results of prior research determined which items of data were coded.

Immediately after their cases were disposed, all defendants who had been selected for the study completed self-report questionnaires. The questionnaires asked about 10 types of crimes (e.g., robbery, burglary, assault)[7] that they might have committed in the period preceding their arrest, and their frequency of committing each of them.

Because the **veracity** of self-reports on these sensitive topics is questionable, analytical techniques have been developed to permit drawing valid conclusions from such data. Although some of the respondents were untruthful in their survey responses, the quality of the defendants' data was the same or slightly better than that of data previously collected in similar surveys of jail and prison inmates who had several months to adjust to incarceration before completing the questionnaire.[8]

Although 500 defendants were interviewed, 12 were excluded from the study because they did not provide any usable self-report information about the numbers or types of crimes they had committed. Official record data were obtained for 452 of the remaining respondents; these 452 constitute the sample used in the analyses that compare official record data with self-reports.

WHAT THE STUDY FOUND

The study resulted in 10 major findings:

Finding 1.   Prosecutors evaluate separately the three dimensions of a defendant's criminality: rates of committing crimes, dangerousness, and persistence. They also consider other aspects of seriousness.

The prosecutors interviewed did not think of serious offenders as a **homogeneous** category. Instead, they often judged separately whether a particular defendant committed crimes at high rates, whether he was dangerous, and then whether he was a persistent offender.

Additional categories of seriousness, not specifically addressed by the study, were also considered in some cases. For example, defendants were considered serious offenders worthy of priority prosecution if their crimes reflected "professionalism," such as careful planning involving several defendants for extremely high criminal gain. Other defendants considered serious enough for priority prosecution were involved in crimes receiving intense coverage by the media.

Finding 2.   Defendants who were identified as high-rate and dangerous by prosecutors in one site were also identified as high-rate and dangerous by prosecutors in the second site.

Despite wide differences in the selection criteria and procedures in the two study sites, the defendants actually selected for priority prosecution were remarkably similar across the two sites. However, the Los Angeles County prosecutors had a more restrictive view of the type of offender that is high-rate and dangerous. After the attorneys had reviewed the same group of anonymously presented cases, every defendant designated as high-rate and dangerous by the Los Angeles attorneys was also so characterized by the Middlesex County attorneys. But the Middlesex County attorneys also evaluated as high-rate and dangerous some defendants who were considered less serious by the Los Angeles attorneys.

Finding 3.   Written office guidelines concerning selection criteria for "career criminals" promote consistency in deputy district attorneys' judgements about the kinds of defendants who are high-rate dangerous offenders.

The evaluations of the prosecutors are clearly shaped by their department policies. The more inclusive evaluations of the Middlesex County attorneys reflect the district attorney's policy of casting a wide net to prevent serious offenders from escaping punishment. The more restrictive evaluations of the attorneys in Los Angeles reflect their concentration on the most serious offenders among the many offenders who have committed serious crimes.

The study found that in offices where selection of "career criminals" must be justified using established criteria, attorneys have developed a consistent mental model of the information that is relevant for judging a defendant to be high-rate or dangerous. The career criminal selection criteria they work with daily enter into these judgments and into their general understanding of criminal behavior. The Middlesex County attorneys, who did not use mandated selection rules, were found to have varied views about what information indicates a defendant is high-rate or dangerous.

Finding 4.   Long-term persistent offenders may or may not be high-rate dangerous offenders. Habitual criminality should not be confused with high-rate dangerous criminality.

The study found that thinking about offenders in terms of persistent or habitual criminal behavior is probably more confusing than productive. Many different measures of "a rap sheet as long as your arm" are valid **indicators** of persistence, but they bear little relationship to the type of offender the priority prosecution units would like to target.

Some indicators of persistence are also indicators of high-rate or dangerous behavior, but if they are not listed in the findings below, they are not as strong as the listed factors. Other indicators of persistence, such as a large number of adult arrests for burglary, actually were found to be **counterindicators** of high-rate dangerous behavior.

Finding 5.   While some existing guidelines for identifying high-rate dangerous offenders are valid and useful, greater accuracy may be obtained through a two-stage screening process.

The study found that information used because of formal rules or State laws does help focus resources on high-rate, dangerous, and persistent offenders. Moreover, some of the discretionary criteria applied by prosecutors increase the accuracy of these selections. Additionally, other information available but not generally used by prosecutors can be used to hone even finer selections. In all, 31 indicators of high-rate dangerous offenders were found.

The research indicated that the best way to use this information in identifying high-rate dangerous offenders is to ask questions in two stages: First, who is high-rate? Then, of those, who is high-rate dangerous? The first stage is less accurate than the second, but the two stages together result in a practical and useful selection method.

Finding 6.   The strongest official-record indicators of high-rate offending in the two study sites were found if a defendant:

- Had a prior adult conviction for robbery, burglary, arson, forcible rape, sex crime involving a child, kidnapping, or murder.
- Was currently charged for three separate criminal transactions of burglary.

- Was wanted by the authorities for failure to complete a previous sentence (probation, parole, prison, or jail).
- Was on parole when arrested.
- Had one or more adult arrests for receiving stolen property.
- Was on pretrial release (bail or own recognizance) when arrested.
- Was known to have a drug problem.

The above indicators are listed generally in order of the accessibility and acceptability of the information to prosecutors for decisionmaking purposes.

Despite this, all the indicators, taken together, were not strongly associated with high-rate offending. The study sample, which included many defendants who had already been chosen for priority prosecution, contained a larger proportion (43 percent) of offenders classified as high-rate than is commonly found in offender populations. Yet, in common with earlier research,[9] this study did not find many items of information that are available to prosecutors and that validly and decisively distinguish high-rate offenders from others. One of the strongest of these indicators was the California legislatively mandated criterion listed first above (prior conviction for robbery, burglary, arson, etc.).

Several factors in the list are used as bases for enhancing sentences in some jurisdictions. Judges may impose longer sentences on convicted offenders who have failed to complete a previous sentence or who have violated their terms of parole or pretrial release. These factors may be particularly **pertinent** for triggering priority prosecution in those jurisdictions.

These seven indicators can be used to divide defendants into subgroups having widely divergent probabilities of being high-rate. In fact, defendants in the study sample who had any three or more of these characteristics had a greater than 90-percent chance of being high-rate. The selection rule based on this method was found to have very few false positives. Less than 2 percent of low-rate offenders in the sample would be classified as high-rate by this rule. But the selection rule would have many false negatives. It would not identify most defendants who are actually high-rate. For this reason, prosecutors who use these seven listed factors as a rough "first stage" screen for high-rate offenders should require no more than two of the seven factors to be positive.

Although in the study information about a defendant's drug problem could have been entered in the official records from various sources—such as probation reports or pretrial release investigation reports—more accurate information can be obtained from urine test results. However, a single positive drug test at the time of arrest may provide misleading information. The majority of arrestees test positive in many jurisdictions,[10] but only a small percentage of arrestees are high-rate offenders. Rather, the results of drug tests might be assembled over a period of time, covering multiple arrests. Defendants who have a persistent history of positive drug tests could then be considered to have a drug problem in the sense intended here—relatively long-term use of opiates or other addictive drugs.

Finding 7.   Once a group of high-rate offenders was identified, the subset of high-rate dangerous offenders could be identified using a small number of criteria that include elements of the instant crime. The criteria for such determination are the following:

- The defendant was wanted by the authorities for failure to complete a previous sentence.
- A knife was **brandished** or used to injure someone in the instant offense.
- A victim in the instant offense was female.
- The offense was committed in an outside public location (e.g., street, alley, parking lot).
- The defendant had one or more juvenile convictions for robbery (armed or unarmed).

These criteria are strongly related to high-rate dangerous offending, in contrast with the situation for high-rate offending (Finding 6). Further, they are much more powerful than personal characteristics (e.g., age at first arrest, race, employment) over which the defendant has little control at the time of arrest.

Although prosecutors have available to them numerous valid indicators of dangerousness, the five official-record items listed above are statistically nearly equal in value to using all valid indicators of high-rate dangerous offending found in the study. It may therefore be **superfluous** to collect information about all the possibly relevant data items and evaluate them as a means of screening defendants for priority prosecution.

Other factors—strong in themselves but not adding any significant information after taking the above five indicators into account—included victim injury and multiple current charges for robbery.

Purse-snatches or strong-arm street robberies are often considered by police and prosecutors to be less serious than inside robberies with the use of a gun. However, neither commission of crimes inside buildings nor gun use was found to distinguish high-rate offenders from others, or dangerous from less dangerous offenders.

All indicators of high-rate dangerous behavior identified in the study were drawn from criminal justice agency records. The defendants' self-reports were used only to classify them as high-rate, dangerous, persistent, or not.

Finding 8.   Several factors that are commonly perceived as indicative of high-rate dangerousness in fact proved not to be, and in some cases were counterindicators.

Our study found 23 factors not to be associated with high-rate dangerous offending. Examples include:

- Display or use of a gun to threaten a victim
- Alcoholism
- Number of prior arrests for drug distribution or possession
- Number of adult convictions for assault, burglary, auto theft, robbery, or receipt of stolen property

- Record of previous probation or parole **revocations**
- Record of previous incarceration

While prosecutors may wish to assign such cases for priority prosecution on other grounds, these findings suggest that such factors are not in themselves dependable indicators of high rate dangerousness or of persistence.

Finding 9.   Some factors may preclude the selection and priority prosecution of defendants who are in fact dangerous offenders:

- An instant charge for a crime that can carry only light penalties. Even if the defendant is recognized as a high-rate dangerous offender due to past violent offenses, prosecutors would be legally unable to obtain a severe sentence for a minor new offense. For example, the study found a defendant with a long juvenile and adult record for robberies and assaults who was not recommended for priority prosecution because the current charge involved a single breaking and entering in an unoccupied business establishment. The case was satisfactorily handled by the assistant district attorney who originally received it, and priority prosecution resources could not have yielded a more severe sentence.
- Constraints on resources for prosecution. In Los Angeles, because Career Criminal Division attorneys had high caseloads, they could not prosecute some defendants evaluated as high-rate and dangerous. This constraint was not present in Middlesex County, where a large number of senior prosecutors handled priority cases.
- Constraints on resources leading to inadequate identification of priority prosecution candidates. In both sites, because records for screening defendants were inadequate, some high-rate dangerous offenders "slipped through the cracks." Later, when presented with **anonymous** profiles corresponding to these overlooked offenders, prosecutors accurately identified them as high-rate and dangerous. The study showed that in most cases the original oversight occurred because official record information was not available at the time of screening or was **fragmentary**. In some cases the necessary information was located in another office in the same building as the district attorney's office.

Timely availability of critical official-record information is a problem to prosecutors throughout the country. In a recent survey sponsored by the National Institute of Justice,[11] 58 percent of district attorneys noted difficulty in obtaining early information on defendants' backgrounds.

Since the study indicated that a small number of official-record items can help distinguish high-rate dangerous defendants, prosecutors who lack rapid access to official records should develop systematic date retrieval systems focusing on these few specific items.

Finding 10.   The most criminally active defendants in Middlesex County, Massachusetts, and the most criminally active defendants in Los Angeles County commit crimes at essentially the same rates.

Although fewer people in Middlesex County than in Los Angeles are prosecuted for robbery each year, the most active 30 percent of robbers in Middlesex County commit essentially the same number of robberies as the most active 30 percent of robbers in Los Angeles County. Similarly, the 30 percent most active defendants in both jurisdictions who committed burglary, forgery, fraud, and drug dealing also committed these crimes at essentially the same rates. Car theft proved an exception. The most active car thieves in Los Angeles committed four times as many thefts as their counterparts in Massachusetts.

RECOMMENDATIONS

The study was limited to two jurisdictions; **replication** of the findings in other jurisdictions should precede any limitation of a jurisdiction's selection criteria to the factors found in this research alone. However, the broad implications of the findings fit the results of other research, and so several recommendations can be drawn from them.

Prosecutors planning priority prosecution programs should target dangerous offenders who commit crimes at high rates. The offenders can be identified more accurately than high-rate offenders who are not dangerous, and the crimes they commit are more serious. The high-rate dangerous offenders are also more serious than some of the habitual offenders who are continually cycling through the criminal justice system.

Selection for priority prosecution can be enhanced by systematic searches of record information, including rap sheets and other records of prior arrests and convictions, offense reports, arrest reports, and—whenever relevant—reports of other criminal justice agencies with whom the defendant had prior contact (probation, parole, police, pretrial release, courts). To promote consistency in selection, jurisdictions can develop standard office selection guidelines that include factors associated with high-rate dangerous criminality, like those described above in findings 6 and 7, along with any other criteria that are considered important locally.

Prosecutors can prepare a checklist of factors that should be taken into account when selecting offenders for priority prosecution. Such a checklist assists in defining office policy and helps screening attorneys identify the small percentage of defendants likely to be high-rate dangerous. This eliminates unnecessary effort looking for official-record items that apparently do not contribute to the screening process. The checklist also flags cases that at the time of screening lack a key piece of information for selection purposes.

Prosecutors who have adopted such a checklist should review the list with both police and judges. If they do not, the criminal justice system risks operating at cross-purposes by having prosecutors target offenders having certain characteristics (for example, being addicted to drugs at the time of the crime) while police or sentencing judges consider the same characteristics to be mitigating factors.

In addition to a checklist, jurisdictional policies should allow screening prosecutors discretion in recommending priority prosecution based on other information. The study found that while defendants who have many of the characteristics listed in findings 6 and 7 were very likely to be high-rate and dangerous, other defendants also were high-rate dangerous. Some kinds of circumstances, not readily captured in a checklist, indicate to the screening attorney that the case involves a high-rate or dangerous offender. Cases selected for exceptional reasons could be subjected to higher level review within the district attorney's office.

NOTES

1. Chaiken, Marcia, and Jan Chaiken, "Selecting 'Career Criminals' for Priority Prosecution," report to the National Institute of Justice. 1987, NCJ 106310. This research report is summarized in an *Issues and Practices* publication intended for prosecutors: Chaiken, Marcia, and Jan Chaiken. *Redefining the Career Criminal: Priority Prosecution of High-Rate Dangerous Offenders*. National Institute of Justice. 1990, NCJ 124136. (Contact National Institute of Justice/NCJRS, Box 6000, Rockville, MD 20850, telephone 800-851-3420 or 301-251-5500, to obtain a copy.)

2. A felony is a more serious crime than a misdemeanor. Generally, conviction of a felony can result in imprisonment for 1 year or more.

3. Phillips, Joel L., and Lynne P. Cannady, *The Effectiveness of Selective Prosecution by Career Criminal Programs*. EMT Associates, Inc., Sacramento, California, 1985.

4. Ibid.

5. Ibid.; Bureau of Justice Assistance, *Career Criminal Prosecution Program*. Program brief, Washington, D.C., March 1985; Chaiken and Chaiken (see note 1).

6. The proportions shown in the figure are based on defendant survey data from the two study sites.

7. Chaiken, Marcia, and Jan Chaiken. "Who Gets Caught Doing Crime?" Bureau of Justice Statistics Discussion Paper, U.S. Department of Justice, Washington, D.C., 1985: Williams, Terry M., and William Kornblum, *Growing Up Poor*, Lexington Books, Lexington, Massachusetts, 1985.

8. Specifically, defendants were asked to report about incidents within the past 2 calendar years (excluding incarcerated periods) in which they had committed burglary; committed business robbery or other robberies or muggings; hurt or killed someone during a burglary or robbery; assaulted someone not during a burglary or robbery; committed motor vehicle theft or other theft; committed forgery, fraud, or credit card offenses; or dealt drugs (made, sold, smuggled, or moved drugs).

9. For details of these comparisons, see appendix B of the *Issues and Practices* report cited in note 1.

10. Chaiken, Jan, and Marcia Chaiken. *Varieties of Criminal Behavior*, the RAND Corporation, Santa Monica, California, R-2814-NIJ, August 1982; Rolph, John, and Jan Chaiken, *Identifying High-Rate Serious Criminals from Official Records*, the RAND Corporation, R-3433-NIJ, 1987; Blumstein, Alfred, et al., *Criminal Careers and "Career Criminals,"* National Academy Press, Washington, D.C., 1986.

11. Wish, Eric D., Mary A. Toborg, and John Bellassai, *Identifying Drug Users and Monitoring Them During Conditional Release*, National Institute of Justice, U.S. Department of Justice, 1988, NCJ 114730. (Contact National Institute of Justice/NCJRS, Box 6000, Rockville, MD 20850, telephone 800-851-3420 or 301-251-5500, to obtain a copy.)

QUESTIONS FOR DISCUSSION

1. What are the three types of offender profiles utilized to identify career criminals? Why do the authors suggest that prosecutors need to identify high-rate dangerous offenders? Explain.
2. Summarize the ten major findings of the study conducted by Chaiken and Chaiken.
3. What are the recommendations made by the Chaikens, based on the results of their study?

APPLICATIONS

1. Consider the seven indicators of high-rate offending presented in the article. Other than the recommendations presented by the authors, can you think of any additional recommendations that could be made to address the problem of high-rate dangerous offenders? Discuss with other members of your class.
2. Contact the prosecutor or an assistant prosecutor in your community. Share the information in the article from Findings 6, 7, and 8. Ask the prosecutor if, based on his or her experience, he or she agrees or disagrees with these findings. Why? What special provisions are made in your community to directly address the high-rate dangerous offender?

Corrections

The prison population in the United States has never been greater. Incarcerating a person for long periods for corrective purposes is a relatively new idea in the history of punishment. In ancient times, for example, the death penalty was a universal form of punishment used for retribution and deterrence. Corporal punishments were also common until long-term incarceration became the acceptable alternative with the rise of modern prison building. With long-term incarceration came the rehabilitative models and the advocacy that while incarcerated, a person could be transformed into a law-abiding citizen deserving of a second chance. The vacillation between retribution, deterrence, incapacitation, and rehabilitation still creates most of the confusion and controversy that surround the corrective process.

Although corrections is often blamed for the larger and more serious problems in the criminal justice system, it is but a component inevitably interdependent with the police, courts, and larger society. As is so often the case, the question of what we expect from incarceration, probation, parole, rehabilitation programs, boot camps, and even the death penalty has grown increasingly nebulous. Remember, expectations of what we want our system of justice to accomplish permeate everything in the system but refer to the whole and not simply to the parts. The nonsynergistic approach in the criminal justice system has lead to the more serious challenges that each of the respected components must often face alone. Corrections cannot be the redeemers of all social ills, a final resting place for the socially dead and unwanted; it must be a dynamic, multifaceted approach to producing ex-convicts who accept responsibility and are subsequently reintegrated as taxpaying citizens. In reality, some cannot and frankly should not, be salvaged. These are the violent, habitual recidivists that account for as much as half of the crimes committed. We must incapacitate these people early in their criminal careers and simply neutralize their dangerousness. All others who come to the various departments of corrections have the potential to get their lives on track, given the right training and opportunity.

Most modern correctional systems in the United States have a combination of approaches when dealing with those convicted of crimes. Institutions include maximum, medium, minimum, and open security levels usually based on type of crime, background, and administrative protocol in relation to each inmate. Other correctional methods include probation, parole, work-release, study-release, restitution, and training programs. In a general sense, one inmate's needs may be very simple, whereas another inmate requires substantially more to achieve the true end of crime cessation.

As you begin to read the collection of articles dealing with correctional issues, you will discover that few concentrate on the many successes of correctional programs. Most dwell on the problems of the system and by so doing increase the failure potential of those who are self correcting or are sincere in their desire to overcome past failures. Success after incarceration lies solely with the individual. Without the desire to overcome failure on the part of the individual, no correctional program will ever succeed in halting criminal behavior. Our society must be willing to accept those who want to reform themselves, and be extremely strict on those who will not stop their own failure cycle.

We open our section on corrections with a look at the subcultural world of prisons examined in a classic article, "The Pains of Imprisonment," by Gresham Sykes. The major pains for anyone incarcerated is deprivation of contact with others, the lack of liberty, and in many respects, the lack of normal interaction. Perhaps nothing is more painful than isolation from other human beings. This is not to suggest that prisons have no place but to provide some insight into what we have created in the American prison experience. The subcultural studies by Sykes and others point out that almost everyone incarcerated will eventually be released and that the unnatural structure of our current prison system often contributes to maladjustments after release.

In a superb article, Richard A. Wright examines some interesting information concerning deterrence and incapacitation. Wright suggests "In Support of Prisons" that prisons have been successful agents of social control. Prisons have not been disastrous failures as many have contended and the positive support of prisons has the most reliable evidence of support. Especially intriguing here is the recommendation that prisons be used to achieve general and specific deterrence, and selective incapacitation. If the United States is to reduce the total crime rate, especially violent crime, it would be wise to consider following the recommendations presented by Wright.

Harold E. Pepinsky is a prison abolitionist who lays down the foundational framework of this line of thinking in his article "Abolishing Prisons." Pepinsky argues that punishment fails and that any system that uses routinized punishment for social control is also destined to fail. Alternatives to punishment are offered and the economics of our current incarceration binge exposed. Although many have rejected Pepinsky's ideas, others argue that rejecting punishment is the first step in creating justice.

Focusing on the issues of costs, the loss of humanitarian values, and societal divisiveness, John Irwin and James Austin point out the possible negative consequences of overusing incarceration in their article "It's About Time: Solving America's Prison Crowding Crisis." Irwin and Austin maintain that increased fear of crime and other factors have lead to the overuse of incarceration and further, that these processes make our society more dangerous rather than safer. There are no easy solutions to be found regarding prison overcrowding. It is easy and politically safe to present a "get tough" attitude on crime, but the long-term effects are staggering. Economic considerations alone should be enough to search for alternatives, but these data are often obscured by protective bureaucrats or under political agendas. On average, the United States spends around $30,000 per inmate for incarceration per year. At what point will we decide that the costs are too high and begin to search for real solutions to prison overcrowding and the resulting problems of this process?

If the costs, both financial and social, are too high, how will we as a nation deal with crime violators? Many people have advocated incarcerating more people for longer periods to lower crime rates. In "The Greatest Correctional Myth: Winning the War on Crime through Incarceration," Joseph W. Rogers suggests that the incarceration boom has drawn correctional systems throughout the country into crisis and continues to do more harm than good. He claims there are eight major prison issues that must be considered if we are to start thinking clearly about societal reactions to crimes: (1) overcrowding; (2) cost; (3) litigation; (4) race/ethnicity; (5) long-term stays; (6) AIDS; (7) officer stress; and (8) the war on drugs. The nation is not succeeding with more prisons or more police, and the basic failure is lack of a clear, comprehensive set of goals for the system of justice as a whole.

The Pains of Imprisonment

Gresham Sykes

THE DEPRIVATION OF LIBERTY

Of all the painful conditions imposed on the inmates of the New Jersey State Prison, none is more immediately obvious than the loss of liberty. The prisoner must live in a world shrunk to thirteen and a half acres and within this restricted area his freedom of movement is further confined by a strict system of passes, the military formations in moving from one point within the institution to another, and the demand that he remain in his cell until given permission to do otherwise. In short, the prisoner's loss of liberty is a double one—first, by confinement to the institution and second, by confinement within the institution.

The mere fact that the individual's movements are restricted, however, is far less serious than the fact that imprisonment means that the inmate is cut off from family, relatives, and friends, not in the self-isolation of the hermit or the **misanthrope**, but in the involuntary seclusion of the outlaw. It is true that visiting and mailing privileges partially relieve the prisoner's isolation—if he can find someone to visit him or write to him and who will be approved as a visitor or correspondent by the prison officials. Many inmates, however, have found their links with persons in the free community weakening as the months and years pass by. This may explain in part the fact that an examination of the visiting records of a random sample of the inmate population, covering approximately a one-year period, indicated that 41 percent of the prisoners in the New Jersey State Prison have received no visits from the outside world.

It is not difficult to see this isolation as painfully depriving or frustrating in terms of lost emotional relationships, of loneliness and boredom. But what makes this pain of imprisonment bite most deeply is the fact that the confinement of the criminal represents a deliberate, moral rejection of the criminal by the free community. Indeed, as Reckless has pointed out, it is the moral condemnation of the criminal—however it may be symbolized—that converts hurt into punishment, i.e., the just consequence of committing an offense, and it is this condemnation that confronts the inmate by the fact of his seclusion.

Now it is sometimes claimed that many criminals are so **alienated** from conforming society and so identified with a criminal **subculture** that the moral condemnation, rejection, or disapproval of legitimate society does not touch them; they are, it is said, indifferent to the penal sanctions of the free community, at least as far as the moral stigma of being defined as a criminal is concerned. Possibly this is true for a small number of offenders such as the professional thief described by Sutherland[1] or the psychopathic personality delineated by William and Joan McCord.[2] For the great majority of criminals in prison, however, the evidence suggests that neither alienation from the ranks of the law-abiding nor involvement in a system of criminal value is sufficient to eliminate the threat to the prisoner's ego posed by society's rejection.[3] The signs pointing to the prisoner's degradation are many—the anonymity of a uniform and a number rather than a name, the shaven head,[4] the insistence on gestures of respect and subordination when addressing officials, and so on. The prisoner is never allowed to forget that, by committing a crime, he has foregone his claim to the status of a full-fledged, *trusted* member of society. The status lost by the prisoner is, in fact, similar to what Marshall has called the status of citizenship—that basic acceptance of the individual as a functioning member of the society in which he lives.[5] It is true that in the past the imprisoned criminal literally suffered civil death and that although the **doctrines of attainder** and **corruption of blood** were largely abandoned in the 18th and 19th centuries, the inmate is still stripped of many of his civil rights such as the right to vote, to hold office, to sue in court, and so on.[6] But as important as the loss of these civil rights may be, the loss of that more diffuse status which defines the individual as someone to be trusted or as morally acceptable is the loss which hurts most.

In short, the wall which seals off the criminal, the contaminated man, is a constant threat to the prisoner's self-conception and the threat is continually repeated in the many daily reminders that he must be kept apart from "decent" men. Somehow this rejection or degradation by the free community must be warded off, turned aside, rendered harmless. Somehow the imprisoned criminal must find a device for rejecting his rejectors, if he is to endure psychologically.[7]

THE DEPRIVATION OF GOODS AND SERVICES

There are admittedly many problems in attempting to compare the standard of living existing in the free community and the standard of living which is supposed to be the lot of the inmate in prison. How, for example, do we interpret the fact that a covering for the floor of a cell usually consists of a scrap from a discarded blanket and that even this possession is forbidden by the prison authorities? What meaning do we attach to the fact that no inmate owns a common piece of furniture, such as a chair, but only a homemade stool? What is the value of a suit of clothing which is also a convict's uniform with a stripe and a stencilled number? The answers are far from simple although there are a number of prison officials who will argue that some inmates are better off in prison, in strictly material terms, than they could ever hope to be in the rough-and-tumble economic life of the free community. Possibly this is so, but at least it has never been claimed by the inmates that the goods and services provided the prisoner are equal to or better than the goods and services which the prisoner could obtain if he were left to his own devices outside the walls. The average inmate finds himself in a harshly Spartan environment which he defines as painfully depriving.

Now it is true that the prisoner's basic material needs are met—in the sense that he does not go hungry, cold, or wet. He receives adequate medical care and he has the opportunity for exercise. But a standard of living constructed in terms of so many calories per day, so many hours of recreation, so many cubic yards of space per individual, and so on, misses the central point when we are discussing the individual's feeling of deprivation, however useful it may be in setting minimum levels of consumption for the maintenance of health. A standard of living can be hopelessly inadequate, from the individual's viewpoint, because it bores him to death or fails to provide those subtle symbolic overtones which we invest in the world of possessions. And this is the core of the prisoner's problem in the area of goods and services. He wants—or needs, if you will—not just the so-called necessities of life but also the amenities: cigarettes and liquor as well as calories, interesting foods as well as sheer bulk, individual clothing as well as adequate clothing, individual furnishings for his living quarters as well as shelter, privacy as well as space. The "rightfulness" of the prisoner's feeling of deprivation can be questioned. And the objective reality of the prisoner's deprivation—in the sense that he has actually suffered a fall from his economic position in the free community—can be viewed with skepticism, as we have indicated above. But these criticisms are irrelevant to the significant issue, namely that legitimately or illegitimately, rationally or irrationally, the inmate population defines its present material impoverishment as a painful loss.

Now in modern Western culture, material possessions are so large a part of the individual's conception of himself that to be stripped of them is to be attacked at the deepest layers of personality. This is particularly true when poverty cannot be excused as a blind stroke of fate or a universal calamity. Poverty due to one's own mistakes or misdeeds represents an indictment against one's basic value or personal worth and there are few men who can philosophically bear the want caused by their own actions. It is true some prisoners in the New Jersey State Prison attempt to interpret their low position in the scale of goods and services as an effort by the State to exploit them economically. Thus, in the eyes of some inmates, the prisoner is poor not because of an offense which he has committed in the past but because the State is a tyrant which uses its captive criminals as slave labor under the hypocritical guise of reformation. Penology, it is said, is a racket. Their poverty, then, is not punishment as we have used the word before, i.e., it is just consequence of criminal behavior; rather, it is an unjust hurt or pain inflicted without legitimate cause. This attitude, however, does not appear to be particularly widespread in the inmate population and the great majority of prisoners must face their privation without the aid of the wronged man's sense of injustice. Furthermore, more prisoners are unable to fortify themselves in their low level of material existence by seeing it as a means to some high or worthy end. They are unable to attach any significant meaning to their need to make it more bearable, such as present pleasures foregone for pleasures in the future, self-sacrifice in the interests of the community, or material **asceticism** for the purpose of spiritual salvation.

The inmate, then, sees himself as having been made poor by reason of his own acts and without the rationale of compensating benefits. The failure is his failure in a world where control and possession of the material environment are commonly taken as sure indicators of a man's worth. It is true that our society, as materialistic as it may be, does not rely exclusively on goods and services as a criterion of an individual's value; and, as we shall see shortly, the inmate population defends itself by stressing alternative or supplementary measures of merit. But impoverishment remains as one of the most bitter attacks on the individual's self-image that our society has to offer and the prisoner cannot ignore the implications of his straitened circumstances.[8] Whatever the discomforts and irritations of the prisoner's Spartan existence may be, he must carry the additional burden of social definitions which equate his material deprivation with personal inadequacy.

THE DEPRIVATION OF HETEROSEXUAL RELATIONSHIPS

Unlike the prisoner in many Latin American countries, the inmate of the maximum security prison in New Jersey does not enjoy the privilege of so-called conjugal visits. And in those brief times when the prisoner is allowed to see his wife, mistress, or "female friend," the woman must sit on one side of a plate glass window and the prisoner on the other, communicating by means of a phone under the scrutiny of a guard. If the inmate, then, is rejected and impoverished by the facts of his imprisonment, he is also figuratively castrated by his involuntary celibacy.

Now a number of writers have suggested that men in prison undergo a reduction of the sexual drive and that the sexual frustrations of prisoners are therefore less than they might appear to be at first glance. The reports of reduced sexual interest have, however, been largely confined to accounts of men imprisoned in concentration camps or similar extreme situations where starvation, torture, and physical exhaustion have reduced life to a simple struggle for survival or left the captive sunk in apathy. But in the American prison these factors are not at work to any significant extent and Lindner has noted that the prisoner's access to mass media, pornography circulated among inmates, and similar stimuli serve to keep alive the prisoner's sexual impulses.[9] The same thought is expressed more crudely by the inmates of the New Jersey State Prison in a variety of obscene expressions and it is clear that the lack of heterosexual intercourse is a frustrating experience for the imprisoned criminal and that it is a frustration which weighs heavily and painfully on his mind during his prolonged confinement. There are, of course, some "habitual" homosexuals in the prison—men who were homosexuals before their arrival and who continue their particular form of deviant behavior within the all-male society of the custodial institution. For these inmates, perhaps, the deprivation of heterosexual intercourse cannot be counted as one of the pains of imprisonment. They are few in number, however, and are only too apt to be victimized or raped by aggressive prisoners who have turned to homosexuality as a temporary means of relieving their frustration.

Yet as important as frustration in the sexual sphere may be in physiological terms, the psychological problems created by the lack of heterosexual relationships can be even more serious. A society composed exclusively of men tends to generate anxieties in its members concerning their masculinity regardless of whether or not they are coerced, bribed, or seduced into an overt homosexual **liaison.** Latent homosexual tendencies may be activated in the individual without being translated into open behavior and yet still arouse strong guilt feelings at either the conscious or unconscious level. In the tense atmosphere of the prison with its known perversions, its importunities of admitted homosexuals, and its constant references to the problems of sexual frustration by guards and inmates alike, there are few prisoners who can escape the fact that an essential component of a man's self conception—his status of male—is called into question. And if an inmate has in fact engaged in homosexual behavior within the walls, not as a continuation of an habitual pattern but as a rare act of sexual deviance under the intolerable pressure of mounting physical desire, the psychological onslaughts on his ego image will be particularly acute.[10]

In addition to these problems stemming from sexual frustration per se, the deprivation of heterosexual relationships carries with it another threat to the prisoner's image of himself— more diffuse, perhaps, and more difficult to state precisely and yet no less disturbing. The inmate is shut off from the world of women which by its very polarity gives the male world much of its meaning. Like most men, the inmate must search for his identity not simply within himself but also in the picture of himself which he finds reflected in the eyes of others; and since a significant half of his audience is denied him, the inmate's self image is in danger of becoming half complete, fractured, a monochrome without the hues of reality. The prisoner's looking-glass self, in short—to use Cooley's fine phrase—is only that portion of the prisoner's personality which is recognized or appreciated by men and this partial identity is made hazy by the lack of contrast.

THE DEPRIVATION OF AUTONOMY

We have noted before that the inmate suffers from what we have called a loss of autonomy in that he is subjected to a vast body of rules and commands which are designed to control his behavior in minute detail. To the casual observer, however, it might seem that the many areas of life in which self-determination is withheld, such as the language used in a letter, the hours of sleeping and eating, or the route to work, are relatively unimportant. Perhaps, it might be argued, as in the case of material deprivation, that the inmate in prison is not much worse off than the individual in the free community who is regulated in a great many aspects of his life by the iron fist of custom. It could even be argued, as some writers have done, that for a number of imprisoned criminals, the extensive control of the custodians provides a welcome escape from freedom and that the prison officials thus supply an external Super-Ego which serves to reduce the anxieties arising from an awareness of deviant impulses. But from the viewpoint of the inmate population, it is precisely the triviality of much of the officials' control which often proves to be most galling. Regulation by a bureaucratic staff is felt far differently than regulation by custom. And even though a few prisoners do welcome the strict regime of the custodians as a means of checking their own **aberrant** behavior which they would like to curb but cannot, most prisoners look on the matter in a different light. Most prisoners, in fact, express an intense hostility against their far-reaching dependence on the decisions of their captors and the restricted ability to make choices must be included among the pains of imprisonment along with restrictions of physical liberty, the possession of goods and services, and heterosexual relationships.

Now the loss of autonomy experienced by the inmates of the prison does not represent a grant of power freely given by the ruled to the rulers for a limited and specific end. Rather, it is total and it is imposed—and for these reasons it is less endurable. The nominal objectives of the custodians are not, in general, the objectives of the prisoners.[11] Yet regardless of whether or not the inmate population shares some aims with the custodial bureaucracy, the many regulations and orders of the New Jersey State Prison's official regime often arouse the prisoner's hostility because they don't "make sense" from the prisoner's point of view. Indeed, the incomprehensible order or rule is a basic feature of life in prison. Inmates, for example, are forbidden to take food from the messhall to their cells. Some prisoners see this as a move designed to promote cleanliness; others are convinced that the regulation is for the purpose of preventing inmates from obtaining anything that might be used in the *sub rosa* system of barter. Most, however, simply see the measure as another irritating, pointless gesture of authoritarianism. Similarly, prisoners are denied parole but are left in ignorance of the reasons for the decision. Prisoners are informed that the delivery of mail will be delayed—but they are not told why.

Now some of the inmate population's ignorance might be described as "accidental"; it arises from what we can call the principle of bureaucratic indifference, i.e., events which seem important or vital to those at the bottom of the heap are viewed with an increasing lack of concern with each step upward. The rules, the commands, the decisions which flow down to those who are controlled are not accompanied by explanations on the grounds that it is "impractical" or "too much trouble." Some of the inmate population's ignorance, however, is deliberately fostered by the prison officials in that explanations are often withheld as a matter of calculated policy. Providing explanations carries an implication that those who are ruled have a right to know—and this in turn suggests that if the explanations are not satisfactory, the rule or order will be changed. But this is in direct contradiction to the theoretical power relationship of the inmates and the prison officials. Imprisoned criminals are individuals who are being punished by society and they must be brought to their knees. If the inmate population maintains the right to argue with its captors, it takes on the appearance of an enemy nation with its own **sovereignty;** and in so doing it raises disturbing questions about the nature of the offender's deviance. The criminal is no longer simply a man who has broken the law; he has become a part of a group with an alternative viewpoint and thus attacks the validity of the law itself. The custodians' refusal to give reasons for many aspects of their regime can be seen in part as an attempt to avoid such an intolerable situation.

The indignation aroused by the "bargaining inmate" or the necessity of justifying the custodial regime is particularly evident during a riot when prisoners have the "impudence" to present a list of demands. In discussing the disturbances at the New Jersey State Prison in the Spring of 1952, for example, a newspaper editorial angrily noted that "the storm, like a nightmarish April Fool's dream, has passed, leaving in its wake a partially wrecked State Prison as a debasing monument to the ignominious rage of desperate men."

The important point, however, is that the frustration of the prisoner's ability to make choices and the frequent refusals to provide an explanation for the regulations and commands descending from the bureaucratic staff involve a profound threat to the prisoner's self image because they reduce the prisoner to the weak, helpless, dependent status of childhood. As Bettelheim has tellingly noted in his comments on the concentration camp, men under guard stand in constant danger of losing their identification with the normal definition of an adult and the imprisoned criminal finds his picture of himself as a self-determining individual being destroyed by the regime of the custodians.[12] It is possible that this psychological attack is particularly painful in American culture because of the deep-lying insecurities produced by the delays, the conditionality and the uneven progress so often observed in the granting of adulthood. It is also possible that the criminal is frequently an individual who has experienced great difficulty in adjusting himself to figures of authority and who finds the many restraints of prison life particularly threatening in so far as earlier struggles over the establishment of self are reactivated in a more virulent form. But without asserting that Americans in general or criminals in particular are notably ill equipped to deal with the problems posed by the deprivation of autonomy, the helpless or dependent status of the prisoner clearly represents a serious threat to the prisoner's self image as a fully accredited member of adult society. And of the many threats which may confront the individual, either in or out of prison, there are few better calculated to arouse acute anxieties than the attempt to reimpose the subservience of youth. Public humiliation, enforced respect and deference, the finality of authoritarian decisions, the demands for a specified course of conduct because, in the judgment of another, it is in the individual's best interest—all are features of childhood's helplessness in the face of a superior adult world. Such things may be both irksome and disturbing for a child, especially if the child envisions himself as having outgrown such servitude. But for the adult who has escaped such helplessness with the passage of years, to be thrust back into childhood's helplessness is even more painful, and the inmate of the prison must somehow find a means of coping with the issue.

THE DEPRIVATION OF SECURITY

However strange it may appear that society has chosen to reduce the criminality of the offender by forcing him to associate with more than a thousand other criminals for years on end, there is one meaning of this involuntary union which is obvious—the individual prisoner is thrown into prolonged intimacy with other men who in many cases have a long history of violent, aggressive behavior. It is a situation which can prove to be anxiety-provoking even for the hardened recidivist and it is in this light that we can understand the comment of an inmate of the New Jersey State Prison who said, "The worst thing about prison is you have to live with other prisoners."

The fact that the imprisoned criminal sometimes views his fellow prisoners as "vicious" or "dangerous" may seem a trifle unreasonable. Other inmates, after all, are men like himself, bearing the legal stigma of conviction. But even if the individual prisoner believes that he himself is not the sort of person who is likely to attack or exploit weaker and less resourceful fellow captives, he is apt to view others with more suspicion. And if he himself is prepared to commit crimes while in prison, he is likely to feel that many others will be at least equally ready....Regardless of the patterns of mutual aid and support which may flourish in the inmate population, there are a sufficient number of outlaws within this group of outlaws to deprive the average prisoner of that sense of security which comes from living among men who can be reasonably expected to abide by the rules of society. While it is true that every prisoner does not live in constant fear of being robbed or beaten, the constant companionship of thieves, rapists, murderers, and aggressive homosexuals is far from reassuring.

An important aspect of this disturbingly problematical world is the fact that the inmate is acutely aware that sooner or later he will be "tested"—that someone will "push" him to see how far they can go and that he must be prepared to fight for the safety of his person and his possessions. If he should fail, he will thereafter be an object of contempt, constantly in danger of being attacked by other inmates who view him as an obvious victim, as a man who cannot or will not defend his rights. And yet if he succeeds, he may well become a target for the prisoner who wishes to prove himself, who seeks to enhance his own prestige by defeating the man with a reputation for toughness. Thus both success and failure in defending one's self against the aggressions of fellow captives may serve to provoke fresh attacks and no man stands assured of the future.[13]

The prisoner's loss of security arouses acute anxiety, in short, not just because violent acts of aggression and exploitation occur but also because behavior constantly calls into question the individual's ability to cope with it, in terms of his own inner resources, his courage, his "nerve." Can he stand up and take it? Will he prove to be tough enough? These uncertainties constitute an ego threat for the individual forced to live in prolonged intimacy with criminals, regardless of the nature or extent of his own criminality; and we can catch a glimpse of this tense and fearful existence in the comment of one prisoner who said, "It takes a pretty good man to be able to stand on an equal plane with a guy that's in for rape, with a guy that's in for murder, with a man who's well respected in the institution because he's a real tough cookie...." His expectations concerning the conforming behavior of others destroyed, unable and unwilling to rely on the officials for protection, uncertain of whether or not today's joke will be tomorrow's bitter insult, the prison inmate can never feel safe. And at a deeper level lies the anxiety about his reactions to this unstable world, for then his manhood will be evaluated in the public view.

NOTES

1. Cf. Edwin H. Sutherland, *The Professional Thief*. Chicago: The University of Chicago Press, 1937.
2. Cf. William and Joan McCord, *Psychopathy and Delinquency*. New York: Grune and Stratton, 1956.
3. For an excellent discussion of the symbolic overtones of imprisonment, see Walter C. Reckless, *The Crime Problem*. New York: Appleton-Century-Crofts, Inc., 1955, pp. 428–429.

4. Western culture has long placed a peculiar emphasis on shaving the head as a symbol of degradation, ranging from the enraged treatment of collaborators in occupied Europe to the more measured barbering of recruits in the Armed Forces. In the latter case, as in the prison, the nominal purpose has been cleanliness and neatness, but for the person who is shaved the meaning is somewhat different. In the New Jersey State Prison, the prisoner is clipped to the skull on arrival but not thereafter.

5. See T. H. Marshall. *Citizenship and Social Class.* Cambridge, England: The Cambridge University Press, 1950.

6. Paul W. Tappan, "The Legal Rights of Prisoners," *The Annals of the American Academy of Political and Social Science,* Vol. 293, May 1954, pp. 99–111.

7. See Lloyd W. McCorkle and Richard R. Korn, "Resocialization within Walls." *Ibid.,* pp. 88–98.

8. Komarovsky's discussion of the psychological implications of unemployment is particularly apposite here, despite the markedly different context, for she notes that economic failure provokes acute anxiety as humiliation cuts away at the individual's conception of his man-hood. He feels useless, undeserving of respect, disorganized, adrift in a society where economic status is a major anchoring point. Cf. Mirra Komarovsky's, *The Unemployed Man and His Family,* New York: The Dryden Press, 1940, pp. 74–77.

9. See Robert M. Lindner, "Sex in Prison," *Complex.* Vol. 6, Fall 1951, pp. 5–20.

10. Estimates of the proportion of inmates who engage in homosexuality during their confinement in the prison are apt to vary. In the New Jersey State Prison, however, Wing Guards and Shop Guards examined a random sample of inmates who were well known to them from prolonged observation and identified 35 per cent of the men as individuals believed to have engaged in homosexual acts. The judgments of these officials were substantially in agreement with the judgments of a prisoner who possessed an apparently well-founded reputation as an aggressive homosexual deeply involved in patterns of sexual deviance within the institution and who had been convicted of sodomy. But the validity of these judgments remains largely unknown and we present the following conclusions, based on a variety of sources, as provisional at best: First, a fairly large proportion of prisoners engage in homosexual behavior during their period of confinement. Second, for many of those prisoners who do engage in homosexual behavior, their sexual deviance is rare or sporadic rather than chronic. And third, as we have indicated before, much of the homosexuality which does occur in prison is not part of a life pattern existing before and after confinement; rather, it is a response to the peculiar rigors of imprisonment.

11. The nominal objectives of the officials tend to be compromised as they are translated into the actual routines of day-to-day life. The modus vivendi reached by guards and their prisoners is oriented toward certain goals which are in fact shared by captors and captives. In this limited sense, the control of the prison officials is partly concurred in by the inmates as well as imposed on them from above. In discussing the pains of imprisonment our attention is focused on the frustrations or threats posed by confinement rather than the devices which meet these frustrations or threats and render them tolerable. Our interest here is in the vectors of the person's social system—if we may use an analogy from the physical sciences—rather than the resultant.

12. Cf. Bruno Bettelheim, "Individual and Mass Behavior in Extreme Situations," in *Readings in Social Psychology,* edited by T. M. Newcomb and E. L. Hartley. New York: Henry Holt and Company, 1947.

13. As the Warden of the New Jersey State Prison has pointed out, the arrival of an obviously tough professional hoodlum creates a serious problem for the recognized "bad man" in a cellblock who is expected to challenge the newcomer immediately.

QUESTIONS FOR DISCUSSION_____

1. Sykes describes the society of prison as one that causes "pain" by the mere conditions inherent with incarceration. Describe, in your own words, the following types of deprivation that are inherent to the prison experience:

   (a) The deprivation of liberty

   (b) The deprivation of goods and services

   (c) The deprivation of heterosexual relationships

   (d) The deprivation of autonomy

   (e) The deprivation of security

2. What role does the prison bureaucracy play in the deprivation of autonomy for inmates? Provide an example to support your answer.

3. One would expect a prison to have a great deal of security. Why is there, in fact, a deprivation of security in prisons?

APPLICATIONS _____

1. Much of the public would say that prisons are not "tough " enough and that greater deprivation and punishment are needed to "teach offenders a lesson." Based on your opinion and the Sykes article, what is your position on how offenders are handled? Are prisons too lax or too tough in handling offenders? Explain your response.

2. Contact a local official from the county jail or a correctional facility. Ask him or her to describe the conditions at the facility where he or she works. Ask if the person thinks that the conditions in the institution are good or poor for offenders. Compare the responses with those of members of your class.

In Support of Prisons

Richard A. Wright

INTRODUCTION

The critics of prisons come in all shapes, sizes, political persuasions, and walks of life. Criticisms of various degrees of ferocity and **vociferousness** have been raised by political radicals (Wright, 1973), liberals (Currie, 1985), and conservatives (von Hirsch, 1976), and by attorneys (Stender, 1973), journalists (Bagdikian, 1972), psychologists (Sommer, 1976), religious groups (American Friends Service Committee, 1971), ex-corrections officials (Nagel, 1973; Murton, 1976), ex-convicts (Irwin, 1980), and (not surprisingly) current convicts (Abbott, 1982). Prison critics vary from unbridled **hyperbole** (e.g., Sommer's—1976, p. 171—bold assertion that "imprisoning offenders for long periods [sic] has failed as a social policy") to studied reservation (e.g., Currie's—1985, p. 52—more measured claim that "although imprisonment is all too often an unavoidable necessity, it is not an effective way to prevent crime"). In summarizing the history of the failure of punishment, Rennie (1978, p. 273) concludes:

> [T]here is nothing more disconcerting than the realization that what is being proposed now for the better management of crime and criminals—to get tough, to increase sentences and make them mandatory, and to kill more killers—has been tried over and over again and abandoned as unworkable. [Thus] we are left to contemplate the evidence that we have for centuries been going in circles.

I contend that the critics are wrong when they claim that prisons are ineffective agents of social control. Current empirical research suggests that punishment works and that prisons are at least modestly successful in controlling crime. This evidence is referred to as the *positive support* for prisons. Furthermore, I argue that the alternatives typically offered for imprisonment—including nonintervention, a return to corporal punishment, and the radical transformation of capitalism—are either unworkable, inhumane, or unfeasible. This is referred to as the *negative support* for prisons. I begin, though, with an analogy to the police and a discussion of the objectives of punishment.

THE ABOLITION OF LAW ENFORCEMENT

Some of the harshest twentieth-century prison critics advocate either the outright abolition of imprisonment or its drastic curtailment (Irwin, 1980). Robert Sommer's *The End of Imprisonment* (1976) typifies this position. After discussing what he perceives are the major failures of prisons—most importantly, the inability of correctional officials and policy-makers to agree about which rationales for punishment (i.e., deterrence, incapacitation, or rehabilitation) should be implemented, Sommer concludes that the cost of imprisonment outweighs its benefits. His policy recommendations include the reduction of current prison populations by *90 percent* and amnesty for many types of criminals (where the states chooses to "forget the specific acts" of nonviolent property and public morality offenders—Sommer, 1976, p. 189).

Interestingly, by exaggerating the importance of a few perceived failures, one also could make a "case" for the end of law enforcement, the courts, and perhaps every other modern social institution. Much evidence, for example, can be compiled to demonstrate the "failure" of the police. Research shows that:

- Increasing the size and budgets of police departments has little effect on the proportion of crimes solved (Skolnick & Bayley, 1986).

- The speed with which police respond to citizens' calls has little effect on their chances for solving particular crimes (Wilson, 1985).

- Modest increases in the size of motorized patrols have little effect on the amount of criminal activity in a neighborhood (Kelling et al., 1974).

- Crimes are typically solved only when actual witnesses are located or when suspects are apprehended at the crime scene, and not through other forms of police investigation (Skolnick & Bayley, 1986).

Why not abolish the police (or following Sommer's logic, cut their strength by 90 percent)? The answer seems obvious: While the crime problem probably may not improve dramatically by increasing the number of police officers (or by altering their duties), crime rates certainly would worsen if police strength were cut (and if the few remaining officers were ordered to ignore "harmless" nonviolent property and public morality offenders). Much the same reasoning can be used to justify maintaining current incarceration levels.

THE OBJECTIVES OF PUNISHMENT

The two most general objectives of punishment are retributive and utilitarian (Meier, 1989). Retributive justice requires that wrongs must be repaid "in a manner that is proportionate to the wrongfulness of the act" (Bartollas & Dinitz, 1989, p. 109). Retribution does not weigh the costs and benefits of punishment to the offender or to the community. Consequently, there is no empirical way to measure the success of prisons in achieving retribution, beyond the somewhat subjective admonition that the length and conditions of incarceration should be commensurate with the nature of the offense (von Hirsch, 1976, 1987).

In contrast, utilitarianism assumes that humans are rational and hedonistic actors who calculate pleasures and pains (Bentham [1823], 1948). Unitarian philosophy recognizes that punishment strategies can be evaluated by their benefits to society (Wilson, 1985; Bartollas & Dinitz, 1989). The most sophisticated version of utilitarianism in contemporary criminology is "rational choice theory" (Cornish & Clarke, 1986, 1987). This perspective assumes that offenders are "decisionmakers" who seek benefits through their criminal activity, but also acknowledges that criminal rationality is limited by the constraints of time, offender cognitive ability, and the availability of relevant information (Cornish & Clarke, 1987). Rational choice proponents argue that specific crimes are chosen and committed for specific reasons, so that different clusters of motives, opportunities, rewards, and costs exists for different types of offenses and offenders (Cornish & Clarke, 1987).

Four imprisonment strategies are consistent with utilitarian/rational choice principles— rehabilitation, general deterrence, specific deterrence, and incapacitation. Rehabilitation refers to the reform of inmates through various prison therapeutic, educational, and industrial programs. General deterrence is the use of the threat of imprisonment to convince those who are not being punished not to commit crimes. Specific deterrence is the use of imprisonment to convince those who are being punished not to commit future crimes. Incapacitation refers to the prevention of crimes in free society by using imprisonment to take known criminals out of circulation.

The best available research shows that prisons are ineffective as agents of rehabilitation (Lipton, Martinson, & Wilks, 1975; Greenberg, 1977). In a famous meta-evaluation of 231 previous studies of rehabilitation programs, Lipton, Martinson, and Wilks (1975) found no clear and consistent evidence that rehabilitation programs work. Examining more recent studies, Greenberg's (1977) replication of the Lipton, Martinson, and Wilks meta-evaluation reached essentially the same conclusion.

POSITIVE SUPPORT: THE SUCCESSES OF PRISONS IN DETERRENCE AND INCAPACITATION

In his summary of recent research on deterrence and incapacitation, Currie (1985, p. 52) argues that only "the more extreme proponents of an 'economic' view of crime" believe that crime can be prevented by incarceration. Gibbs (1981, p. 143) adds that "only incorrigible

partisans regard the evidence [relating to deterrence] as compelling one way or the other."
At the risk of being called an extremist or an incorrigible partisan, I think that clear and
compelling evidence exists to suggest that prisons are effective agents of general deterrence,
specific deterrence, and incapacitation.

General Deterrence

Some criminologists still dispute the idea that prisons can achieve the objective of general
deterrence (see Biles, 1979; Currie, 1985; Brodt & Smith, 1988). These critics note that
historical research shows that incarceration rates and crime rates often rise simultaneously.
For example, Biles' (1979) historical study of the levels of imprisonment and crime rates
in the United States, Canada, and Australia actually shows a *positive* relationship between
the variables.

Interestingly, these same critics conveniently ignore other bivariate evidence which
shows that punishment sometimes achieves general deterrence. For example, the United
States faced a dramatically escalating rate of bank robbery in the 1930s (MacDonald,
1975). The FBI chose to attack this problem by pursuing a well-publicized get-tough policy
where particularly notorious bank robbers (e.g., John Dillinger, Bonnie & Clyde Barrow)
summarily were ambushed and shot to death. The result was a *drop* in bank robbery rates
from a high of 609 in 1932 to 129 in 1937 (MacDonald, 1975).

More important are two methodological shortcomings that render suspect any criticism
of general deterrence that merely associates incarceration rates and crime rates. First, the
causal ordering of the relationship is difficult to establish: Are higher incarceration rates
causing higher crime rates, or vice versa? Only the former relationship suggests the failure
of general deterrence. Further, bivariate studies which simply relate incarceration rates to
crime rates ignore many potential rival causal factors (e.g., the percent of the population
unemployed and the percent of the population in a crime-prone age group) which probably
confound the relationship.

More sophisticated **multivariate regression** research shows that punishment is an
effective general deterrent when crime control polices are well-publicized. For example,
recent regression studies indicate that the execution of murderers has a negative effect on
homicide rates (Layson, 1985; Stack, 1987). By examining newspaper articles published
between 1950 to 1980, Stack (1987) found that well-publicized executions resulted in a
drop of thirty homicides during the month in which the news stories appeared (little-
publicized executions had no general deterrent effect).

Other multivariate research shows that the specific threat of arrest and incarceration
has a general deterrent effect on draft evaders (Blumstein & Nagin, 1977) and drunk drivers
(Ross, 1984). Controlling for other variables (e.g., the socioeconomic characteristics of
various states), Blumstein and Nagin (1977) found that states with higher conviction rates
of draft evaders have lower evasion rates. Ross's (1984) summary of sophisticated studies of
drunk driving penalties shows that tougher enforcement efforts and more certain punishments generally reduce drunk driving rates.

Specific Deterrence

Critics who contend that prisons are ineffective agents of specific deterrence usually rely on recidivism rates (or the percent of ex-convicts who are rearrested and/or re-incarcerated) to make their arguments. For example, Currie (1985, p. 70) cites what he claims is "astonishing" evidence which shows that between one-third to two-thirds of all inmates eventually return to prison. He (1985, p. 70) concludes: "High recidivism rates are a troubling, stubborn **prima facie** case that if imprisonment deters individual criminals at all, it clearly doesn't do so reliably or consistently."

However, simple recidivism rates are invalid measures of the specific deterrent effect of prisons for three reasons. First, simple recidivism rates offer no comparisons of offenders who are arrested and incarcerated with those who avoid apprehension. While it is clear that a large percent of those arrested and incarcerated persist in their criminality, it is also likely that a far *larger* percent of offenders who avoid arrest persist in crime (Packer, 1968).

In addition, for recidivism rates to be valid measures of the effectiveness of specific deterrence, criminal justice personnel need to randomize the assignment of punishments to those apprehended (Sherman & Berk, 1984; Wilson, 1985). Otherwise, studies which compare various forms of intervention—e.g., arrest and detention versus nonarrest and informal mediation—may mistakenly conclude that the former fails because only higher risk offenders (who are more likely to be recidivists) are arrested and detained.

Finally, simple recidivism rates ignore the "suppression effects" of various forms of punishment (Murray & Cox, 1979; Farrington, 1987). Using only *one* arrest following incarceration as an indicator of recidivism ignores the fact that the "recidivist" still may be committing *fewer* crimes after incarceration. To measure suppression effects, researchers must have indicators of the *rate* of an offender's criminality both after *and before* incarceration.

More sophisticated studies which use comparison groups, randomly assign punishments, and/or include before and after indicators of offender criminality largely support the argument that arrest and detention are effective agents of specific deterrence (Murray & Cox, 1979; Sherman & Berk, 1984; Smith & Gartin, 1989). In their cohort analysis of 325 young males with a history of at least one police contact for a felony or misdemeanor, Smith and Gartin (1989) found that: (1) arrested and detained novice offenders are significantly *less likely* to have future police contacts than nonarrested novice offenders; and (2) although the specific deterrent effects of arrest/detention versus nonarrest diminish the longer the offender persists in his criminal career, the *effects remain significant*. These findings persist even when offender age and offense seriousness are controlled.

Sherman and Berk (1984) provide evidence that arrest and brief incarceration have a significant specific deterrent effect on male offenders in domestic assault cases. For eighteen months, a special unit of the Minneapolis police force randomly assigned one of three "strategies"—arrest and detention, ordering offenders to leave the premises for eight hours, or advice and mediation—to male offenders in misdemeanor domestic assault cases. The 314 processed cases were then followed for six months to determine if: (1) male offenders experienced a subsequent police contact for domestic assault; and (2) interviewed female victims reported subsequent assaults. Both police and victim data show that arrested and detained offenders were significantly less likely to become recidivists than informally processed offenders.

Support for the argument that incarceration exerts a suppression effect on criminal careers is found in Murray and Cox's (1979) study of 317 young male offenders from Chicago. The researchers examined offender arrest records for one year before and seventeen months after each received his first prison sentence (the average age of offenders was 16 and the average time spent in prison was ten months). The offenders studied were hard-core delinquents, averaging 13 arrests prior to incarceration. Murray and Cox (1979) found that on average, the offenders were arrested 6.3 times each in the year before imprisonment, but only 2.9 times each during the seventeen months following release. Note that an analysis of the simple recidivism rates in this study would reach the erroneous conclusion that incarceration *failed* as a specific deterrent (because most offenders were subsequently arrested following imprisonment). The much more important conclusion supporting specific deterrence is that offenders had *far fewer* arrests *after* imprisonment.

Deterrence: Some Concluding Remarks

While punishment generally and imprisonment specifically appear to exert both a general deterrent effect on society-at-large and a specific deterrent effect on the offender, three additional important research questions remain: (1) Does deterrence work better for some types of offenders than others? (2) Do celerity (swiftness), certainty, and severity of punishments affect the success of deterrence? (3) Are punishments more effective as general deterrents or specific deterrents?

With respect to the first question, research suggests that arrest and detention may be more effective in reducing the criminality of novice offenders rather than more seasoned criminals (Cameron, 1964; Packer, 1968; Smith & Gartin, 1989). Also, Witte's (1980) study of 641 convicts released from North Carolina prisons shows that while imprisonment works as a specific deterrent for most types of offenders, drug traffickers and drug-addicted robbers and burglars may be less susceptible to deterrence.

Much additional debate surrounds the **celerity**, certainty, and severity of punishments and deterrence. Most utilitarian theorists since Bentham ([1823] 1948) concur that celeritious punishment is a superior deterrent compared to delayed punishment (Van den Haag, 1975). However, the criminal justice system poses numerous obstacles to swift punishment—including problems in detecting and apprehending offenders, court delays, and excessive caseloads. Regrettably, some of these obstacles cannot be solved merely by adopting more efficient criminal justice practices (Bartollas & Dinitz, 1989).

Researchers disagree about the relationship between certainty and severity of punishments and crime deterrence. In their analysis of national prisoner statistics and *Uniform Crime Reports* data, Chiricos and Waldo (1970) found that certainty and severity of punishments has little effect on crime rates. In contrast, Ehrlich (1973), Tittle and Rowe (1973), Ross (1984), and Gray, Ward, Stafford, and Menke (1985) argue that punishments with higher levels of certainty are more likely to deter than less certain punishments. Even more debate surrounds the severity of punishments: Witte (1980) found that harsher punishments have greater deterrent effect than less severe punishments for both violent offenders and drug addicts, while other research shows that longer sentences have no superior deterrent effect on robbers (Ehrlich, 1973), hardcore delinquents (Murray & Cox, 1979), and drunk drivers (Ross, 1984).

Finally, Gray, Ward, Stafford, and Menke (1985) cite important evidence *comparing* the relative effectiveness of punishments as general *versus* specific deterrents. The authors designed a computer-assisted small groups experiment that compared the relative effects of *vicarious reinforcement/punishment* (social psychological parlance for general deterrence) versus *direct/experiential reinforcement/punishment* (social psychological parlance for specific deterrence) on the subsequent behavior of subjects. They found that *both* forms of punishment have a statistically significant effect on subsequent behavior, but that direct punishment is *three times more effective* than vicarious punishment. (Gray et al., 1985). This study is further evidence that deterrence works, but also suggests that specific deterrence may be more effective than general deterrence.

Incapacitation

Although there is fairly compelling evidence that arrest and incarceration can deter many potential and actual offenders, a few criminals may be beyond the pale of appeals to conventional rationality. The existence of "habitual offenders"—or a small number of criminals who commit a great number of crimes—shows that deterrence certainly is no panacea for the problem of crime in America. Researchers have for some time noted the problem of the habitual, career offender—for example, in their study of arrest records of 9,945 Philadelphia boys born in 1945, Wolfgang, Figlio, and Sellin (1972) found that six percent of this cohort were responsible for 52 percent of all the arrests. A replication of this study examining Philadelphia boys and girls born in 1958 found that 7.5 percent of the cohort was responsible for 61 percent of the arrests (Tracy, Wolfgang, & Figlio, 1985). A RAND Corporation study of 2,200 prison inmates in California, Michigan, and Texas revealed that the most active robbers and burglars averaged committing respectively 87 and 232 offenses annually (Greenwood, 1982). In addition, a review of the literature on habitual offenders estimates that the most active ten percent of offenders commits up to 100 crimes annually (Blumstein et al., 1986).

The habitual criminal problem suggests that the use of prisons for incapacitation is an important crime prevention strategy. There are two types of incapacitation: collective incapacitation (where long prison sentences are given indiscriminately to all felons) and selective incapacitation (where long prison sentences are specifically targeted only to those offenders who commit the most crimes—see Forst, 1984; Wilson, 1985). A policy of selective incapacitation targeted toward habitual offenders holds some promise for preventing crime in society at large.

The effectiveness of selective incapacitation on crime prevention depends on the success of risk assessment instruments (or the formulation of factors which can predict an offender's future criminality). Greenwood (1982) and Forst (1984) recently have devised two important risk assessment instruments for selective incapacitation purposes. Based on the previously mentioned RAND Corporation study of prison inmates in three states, Greenwood (1982) discovered seven factors that could be used to predict high-rate, habitual offenders: (1) conviction for juvenile offenses (before age 16); (2) the use of illegal drugs as a juvenile; (3) the use of illegal drugs during the past two years; (4) unemployment for more than 50 percent of the past two years; (5) time served in a juvenile facility; (6) incarceration for more than 50 percent of the past two years; and (7) a previous conviction for the current offense. Using these factors, Greenwood (1982) was able to separate low-rate from medium- and high-rate offenders with 82 percent accuracy. Greenwood (1982) originally estimated that California could reduce its burglary rate by 20 percent by pursuing selective incapacitation sentencing strategy, but reanalyses of Greenwood's data have cut these burglary reduction estimates by approximately 50 percent (Blumstein et al., 1986).

In his study of habitual offenders in the federal prison system, Forst (1984) reached similar conclusions to Greenwood. Using essentially the same predictive factors as Greenwood, Forst (1984) estimates that habitual offenders could be isolated and selectively incarcerated with sufficient success to prevent five to ten percent of all federal offenses (or as many as 45,000 serious crimes each year).

Despite evidence which suggests that prisons can be effective agents of selective incapacitation for habitual offenders, incapacitation strategies are not without their critics (see Currie, 1985; von Hirsch, 1987, 1988). Currie, for example, contends that a serious policy of incapacitation would dramatically increase the number of incarcerated offenders, resulting in $70 billion in additional prison construction expenses while escalating the national annual operating costs of prisons by $14 billion. While these costs certainly sound prohibitive, what Currie does not emphasize is that his estimates are based on pursuing a policy of *collective* incapacitation, where all imprisoned felons indiscriminately receive longer sentences. Built into the logic of selective incapacitation, however, is the crucial **proviso** that prison populations *not* be increased—the goal is to achieve incapacitation and reduce crime by allocating *existing* prison space more rationally (Greenwood, 1982; Forst, 1984).

Currie (1985) also raises the standard criticism that the risk assessment predictive instruments used for selective incapacitation produce an unacceptably high percent of false positives (or persons who are predicted as high-rate offenders who do not become habitual criminals). False positives are undoubtedly a problem in current predictive instruments—for example, Greenwood's (1982) instrument misdiagnosed 18 percent of the low-rate offenders as medium- or high-rate offenders. In his review of the previous research, however, Forst (1984) found that traditional nonstatistical prediction strategies for bail and sentencing annually result in a *higher* rate of false positives than strategies using selective incapacitation predictive instruments. Forst (1984, pp. 157–158—emphasis in the original) concludes that selective incapacitation instruments "not only do not 'cause' false positives where none existed before," but more importantly "generally *reduce* the rate of false positives." In addition, Wilson and Hernnstein (1985) note that more sophisticated longitudinal research on habitual offenders soon promises improved selective incapacitation instruments which will further reduce false positives.

Finally, retribution proponents argue that selective incapacitation sentencing is unjust because the sentences are not proportional to the crime—i.e., sentences based on predictive instruments may not "fit" the gravity of the offense (von Hirsch, 1987, 1988). Here, von Hirsch (1988) raises the disturbing specter of the trivial offender who receives a long prison sentence merely because of the diagnostic label of some predictive instrument. One can cynically note, however, that the proportionality debate already has been decided by the enactment of habitual offender statutes in numerous states (these statutes permit judges to impose Draconian sentences of up to life imprisonment on offenders with multiple felony convictions). Certainly selective incapacitation predictive instruments offer a more rational and scientific sentencing alternative to most current habitual offender statutes.

NEGATIVE SUPPORT: THE ABSENCE OF ALTERNATIVES TO PRISONS

While there are an abundance of contemporary prison critics, Irwin (1980) and Wilson (1985) observe that few have suggested any reasonable alternatives to imprisonment. Asylum historian David Rothman (1980) notes that the first prison critics in the 1870s—including Enoch Wines, Franklin Sanborn, and Zebulon Brockway—believed that although prisons were often overcrowded, understaffed, and brutal, the alternatives to prisons were far worse. Rothman (1980, p. 29) argues that 1870s reformers "looked back to the period before the penitentiary—with its gallows, whipping posts, and edicts of banishment—and reasoned that the abolition of the prison would inevitably restore such horrid practices." It also is quite likely that the few alternatives to prisons which have been proposed by contemporary critics—including nonintervention, a return to corporal punishment, and the radical transformation of capitalism—are less workable, humane, and feasible than current imprisonment strategies.

Nonintervention

Because many social scientists in the 1960s and 1970s believed that a wide variety of institutions had failed in their objectives to heal the sick and reform the **perfidious,** some endorsed a policy of nonintervention (Szasz, 1961; Schur, 1973; Sommer, 1976). Nonintervention is based on the labeling theory argument that judicial intrusion and institutionalization stigmatize deviants, driving them into deviant subcultures which reinforce and **exacerbate** their deviant identities and behavior (Lemert, 1951; Schur, 1973). Implication of nonintervention is that less is better when it comes to governmental intrusions into the lives of deviants (Currie, 1985).

Although recent empirical research offers little support for labeling theory (Sherman & Berk, 1984; Smith & Gartin, 1989), nonintervention sentiments nevertheless resulted in an influential deinstitutionalization movement which curtailed the placement of juvenile offenders (Vinter, Downs & Hall, 1975) and the mentally ill (Torrey, 1988) in state-funded institutions. The number of juvenile offenders housed in state reformatories fell from

43,447 in 1969 to 28,001 in 1974 (Vinter, Downs & Hall, 1975) while placement in state mental hospitals declined from 552,150 in 1955 to 118,647 in 1984 (Torrey, 1988).

Recent research shows that the deinstitutionalization movement among juvenile offenders was **illusory**—while fewer youths were being housed in state reformatories, more were being detained in privately operated youth centers, mental health facilities, and chemical dependency clinics (Sarri, 1981; Schwartz, Jackson-Beck & Anderson, 1984). Sarri (1981, p. 35) flatly concludes that juvenile offenders in the 1970s were merely "recycled from public facilities to those under private auspice[s]." In contrast, the decreases in the number of patients in state mental hospitals were real—patients were typically released outright into the community only with the admonition to seek periodic outpatient treatment at community mental health centers (Torrey, 1988).

Torrey's (1988) analysis of the deinstitutionalization movement among mental patients shows that the policy was an unprecedented disaster. Expatients usually were dumped out into the streets and boarding houses where living conditions were generally far inferior to state hospitals. Community mental health centers largely **abdicated** their responsibility to treat ex-patients—Torrey (1988) argues that the staff in these centers prefers counseling the "worried well" (middle-class patients with relatively minor mental problems) over treating the indigent and truly sick. The result has been the "criminalization of psychosis," where many ex-patients are constantly shuffled from the streets (where they commit various trivial offenses such as defecating in public), to jails, to the psychiatric units of general hospitals, and then back out onto the streets (Torrey, 1988). Of the more than 400,000 mental patients released from state hospitals in recent years, Torrey (1988) estimates that over *half* are caught in this demeaning street-to-jail-to-psychiatric unit-to-street cycle. Torrey (1988) also estimates that fully one-third of the nation's homeless is seriously mentally ill and would have received more humane treatment in state mental hospitals prior to the deinstitutionalization movement.

Without an immense and improbable governmental commitment to community substance-abuse treatment, family counseling, job training, and full-employment programs, it is likely that nonintervention among offenders and the deinstitutionalization of prisoners would suffer a similar dismal fate. Specifically, a substantial decrease in the number of imprisoned offenders almost certainly would result in dramatic increases in street crime and the number of persons jailed. Given the current conservative political mood of the nation (where the public is demanding *more* rather than less punishment) and the failed precedent of the release of mental patients from state hospitals, nonintervention/deinstitutionalization is an unworkable policy for criminal offenders.

A Return to Corporal Punishment

A few scholars have proposed a return to the use of corporal punishment as an alternative to imprisonment (Hooton, 1939; Mark & Ervin, 1970; Newman, 1983). Hooton (1939) and Mark and Ervin (1970) advocate critical organ surgery as a superior form of treatment to incarceration, while Newman (1983) endorses the use of electric shock punishment rather than imprisonment for less serious offenders.

Both critical organ surgery and electric shock punishment often have been practiced on offenders in twentieth-century America. Bartollas and Dinitz (1989) note that involuntary castrations frequently were performed on violent rapists until the U.S. Supreme Court abolished the practice in 1921. In addition, electric shock therapy was a common treatment for homosexuals, rapists, voyeurs, and alcoholics during the 1930s while prison officials as recently as the 1960s occasionally disciplined wayward inmates with electric shocks to the testes (Bartollas & Dinitz, 1989).

Proponents of critical organ surgery believe that the causes of crime are largely biological (Hooton, 1939; Mark & Ervin, 1970). Hooton (1939) advocates the compulsory sterilization of habitual criminals as a form of "biological housecleaning" to eliminate inferior criminal types. Mark and Ervin (1970) contend that violent offenders often suffer from a "dyscontrol **syndrome**" in their brains, which in its more severe manifestations requires a lobotomy of the temporal lobe.

In contrast, electric shock punishment has been proposed as a superior deterrent to imprisonment (Newman, 1983). To achieve the celerity and certainty of punishment, Newman (1983) argues that electric shocks should be administered to offenders immediately following conviction. The severity of the punishment can be made to "fit" the seriousness of the offense by varying the imposed voltage (Newman, 1983).

Whatever failures the harshest critics attribute to prisons, these proposals hardly can be expected to improve matters. As early prison reformers realized, a return to corporal punishment undoubtedly would be a far less humane alternative to imprisonment (Rothman, 1980).

The Radical Transformation of Capitalism

Radical criminologists view prisons as the ultimate mechanisms of social control in capitalism (Wright, 1973; Quinney, 1977). Wright (1973) argues that prisons regulate criminal activity and protect capitalistic power relationships by clearly delimiting low-risk and high-risk crimes. Prisons are seldom used to punish the low-risk crimes committed by the privileged (e.g., tax evasion and price fixing) and instead are used to deter the high-risk street crimes of the poor (Wright, 1973). In this way, prisons help to perpetuate capitalist exploitation by protecting the rich from the crimes of the poor without protecting the poor from the crimes of the rich. Quinney (1977) additionally argues that imprisonment is the capitalist's response to crises in capitalism—higher incarceration rates "solve" the periodic threats created by high unemployment rates and the demands of the poor and the powerless.

The radical solution to the problems of prisons is the abolition of capitalism and its replacement with a radically egalitarian and democratic socialism (Wright, 1973; Quinney, 1977). Both Wright (1973) and Quinney (1977) reject prison reforms which they contend merely reinforce capitalism by strengthening the effectiveness of prisons as social control mechanisms. Because prisons are inevitably as exploitative as the societies which they protect, prisons cannot be fundamentally transformed without the radical transformation of capitalism. It is important to note, however, that most radicals are *not* opposed to the use of prisons *per se*—Wright (1973; 343–344) **cryptically** remarks that prisons would continue to be used in socialist societies to punish "class enemies" who "pose a serious threat to the social order."

Regardless of one's opinions about the merits of these arguments, there is no suitable blueprint for an immediate alternative to imprisonment in the radical agenda. It simply is unfeasible to wait for an elusive socialist millenium to usher in more humane forms of punishment.

SUMMARY AND SOME FINAL THOUGHTS

On balance, the evidence presented here suggests that prison critics are wrong in their assessment that prisons have failed as a form of punishment. Sophisticated multivariate, quasi-experimental, and experimental research suggests that prisons are at least modestly successful in achieving the objectives of general deterrence, specific deterrence, and incapacitation. Furthermore, imprisonment is more workable, humane, and feasible than the few alternatives offered by critics.

In addition, punishment research grounded in the assumptions of rational choice theory seems to hold much future promise. Rational choice theorists argue that different clusters of costs, rewards, motives, and opportunities exist for different types of offenses and offenders (Cornish & Clarke, 1986, 1987). This suggests the importance of additional research which situationally analyzes different types of criminal activity to determine: (1) those types of offenses and offenders most susceptible to deterrence; and (2) the relative importance of celerity, certainty, and severity of punishments for different types of offenses and offenders. Some preliminary research already shows that prison sentences have relatively little deterrent effect on drug traffickers and drug-addicted robbers and burglars (Witte, 1980) but relatively great deterrent effect on white-collar criminals (Conklin, 1977). This research is crucial in determining the *relative effectiveness of deterrence versus incapacitation*—shorter prison terms may be more appropriate for those types of offenses and offenders more susceptible to deterrence while longer prison terms (emphasizing incapacitation) may be more appropriate for those types of offenses and offenders less susceptible to deterrence.

Importantly, this suggests that deterrence and incapacitation ultimately are *complementary* imprisonment objectives—a policy of selective *incapacitation* directed toward those who cannot be deterred also assumes a policy of selective *deterrence* directed toward those who can be deterred. Perhaps the most rational punishment policy is to use prisons to achieve the complementary objectives of general deterrence, specific deterrence, and selective incapacitation.

REFERENCES

Abbot, J. H. (1982) *In the Belly of the Beast. Letters from Prison.* New York: Vintage.

American Friends Service Committee (1971) *Struggle for Justice.* New York: Hill and Wang.

Bagdikian, B. H. (1972) *The Shame of the Prisons.* Washington, DC: *The Washington Post* National Reports.

BARTOLLAS, C. & S. DINITZ (1989) *Introduction to Criminology: Order and Disorder.* New York: Harper and Row.

BENTHAM, J. (1823) 1948. *An Introduction to the Principles of Morals and Legislation.* New York: Hafner.

BILES, D. (1979) "Crime and the Use of Prisons." *Federal Probation* 43 (2):39–43.

BLUMSTEIN, A., J. COHEN, J. A. ROTH & C. A. VISHER (eds.) (1986) *Criminal Careers and "Career Criminals,"* Vol. 1. Washington, DC: National Academy Press.

BLUMSTEIN, A. & D. NAGIN (1977) "The Deterrent Effect of Legal Solutions on Draft Evasion." *Stanford Law Review* 28(2): 241–275.

BRODT, S. J. & J. S. SMITH (1988) "Part I: Public Policy and the Serious Juvenile Offender." *Criminal Justice Policy Review* 2(1):70–85.

CAMERON, M. O. (1964) *The Booster and the Snitch.* Glencoe, IL: Free Press.

CHIRICOS, T. & G. WALDO (1970) "Punishment and Crime: An Examination of Some Empirical Evidence." *Social Problems* 18(2):200–217.

CONKLIN, J. E. (1977) *"Illegal But Not Criminal": Business Crime in America.* Englewood Cliffs, NJ: Prentice-Hall.

CORNISH, D. B. & R. V. CLARKE (eds.) (1986) *The Reasoning Criminal.* New York: Springer-Verlag.

——. (1987) "Understanding Crime Displacement: An Application of Rational Choice Theory." *Criminology* 25(4):933–947.

CURRIE, E. (1985) *Confronting Crime: An American Challenge.* New York: Pantheon.

EHRLICH, I. (1973) "Participation in Illegitimate Activities: A Theoretical and Empirical Investigation." *Journal of Political Economy* 81 (3):521–565.

FARRINGTON, D. (1987) "Predicting Individual Crime Rates." In D. M. Gottfredson & M. Tonry (eds.), *Crime and Justice: An Annual Review of Research,* vol. 9, pp. 53–101. Chicago: University of Chicago Press.

FORST, B. (1984) "Selective Incapacitation: A Sheep in Wolf's Clothing?" *Judicature* 68(4 and 5):153–160.

GIBBS, J. P. (1981) *Norms, Deviance, and Social Control.* New York: Elsevier.

GRAY, L. N., D A. WARD, M. C. STAFFORD & B. A. MENKE (1985) "Observational and Experiential Effects in Probability Learning: The Case of a Deviant Behavior." *Social Psychology Quarterly* 48(1):78–85.

GREENBERG, D. F. (1977) "The Correctional Effects of Corrections: A Survey of Evaluations." In D. R Greenberg (ed.), *Corrections and Punishment,* pp. 111–148. Beverly Hills, CA: Sage Publications.

GREENWOOD, P. W. (1982) *Selective Incapacitation.* Santa Monica, CA: RAND Corporation.

HOOTON, E A. (1939) *Crime and the Man.* Cambridge, MA: Harvard University Press.

IRWIN, J. (1980) *Prisons in Turmoil.* Boston: Little, Brown.

KELLING, G. L., T. PATE, D. DIECKMAN & C. E. BROWN (1974) *The Kansas City Preventive Patrol Experiment: A Summary Report.* Washington, DC: Police Foundation.

LAYSON, S. K. (1985) "Homicide and Deterrence: A Reexamination of the U.S. Time-Series Evidence." *Southern Economic Journal* 52(1):68–69.

LEMERT, E. M. (1951) *Social Pathology.* New York: McGraw-Hill.

LIPTON, D., R. MARTINSON & J. WINKS (1975) *The Effectiveness of Correctional Treatment: A Survey of Treatment Evaluation Studies.* New York: Praeger.

MACDONALD, J. M. (1975) *Armed Robbery: Offenders and Their Victims.* Springfield, IL: Charles C Thomas.

MARK, V. H. & F. R. ERVIN (1970) *Violence and the Brain.* New York: Harper and Row.

MEIER, R. F. (1989) *Crime and Society.* Boston: Allyn and Bacon.

MURRAY, C.A. & L. A. COX, JR. (1979) *Beyond Probation. Juvenile Corrections and the Chronic Delinquent.* Beverly Hills, CA: Sage Publications.

MURTON, T. O. (1976) *The Dilemma of Prison Reform.* New York: Holt, Rinehart, and Winston.

NAGEL, W. G. (1973) *The New Red Barn: A Critical Look at the Modern American Prison.* New York: Walker.

NEWMAN, G. (1983) *Just and Painful: A Case for the Corporal Punishment of Criminals.* New York: Macmillan.

PACKER, H. L. (1968) *The Limits of the Criminal Sanction.* Stanford, CA: Stanford University Press.

QUINNEY, R. (1977) *Class, State, and Crime: On the Theory and Practice of Criminal Justice.* New York: David McKay.

RENNIE, Y. (1978) *The Search for Criminal Man: A Conceptual History of the Dangerous Offender.* Lexington, MA: Heath.

ROSS, H. L. (1984) "Social Control through Deterrence: Drinking-and-Driving Laws." *Annual Review of Sociology* 10:21–35.

ROTHMAN, D. J. (1980) *Conscience and Convenience: The Asylum and Its Alternatives in Progressive America.* Boston: Little, Brown.

SARRI, R. (1981) "The Effectiveness Paradox: Institutional Versus Community Placement of Offenders." *Journal of Social Issues* 37(3):34–50.

SCHUR, E. (1973) *Radical Nonintervention: Rethinking the Delinquency Problem.* Englewood Cliffs, NJ: Prentice-Hall.

SCHWARTZ, I. M., M. JACKSON-BECK & R. ANDERSON (1984) "The 'Hidden System' of Juvenile Control." *Crime and Delinquency* 30(3):371–385.

SHERMAN, L. W. & R. A. BERK (1984) "The Specific Deterrent Effects of Arrest for Domestic Assault." *American Sociological Review* 49(2):261–272.

SKOLNICK, J. H. & D. BAYLEY (1986) *The New Blue Line: Police Innovations in Six American Cities.* New York: Free Press.

SMITH, D. A. & P. R. GARTIN (1989) "Specifying Specific Deterrence: The Influence of Arrest on Future Criminal Activity." *American Sociological Review* 54(1):94–105.

SOMMER, R. (1976) *The End of Imprisonment.* New York: Oxford University Press.

STACK, S. (1987) "Publicized Executions and Homicide, 1950–1980." *American Sociological Review* 52(4): 532–540.

STENDER, F. (1973) "Violence and Lawlessness at Soledad Prison." In E. O. Wright (ed.), *The Politics of Punishment: A Critical Analysis of Prisons in America,* pp. 222–223. New York: Harper Torchbooks.

SZASZ, T. (1961). *The Myth of Mental Illness.* New York: Harper and Row.

TITTLE, C. & A. ROWE (1973) "Moral Appeal, Sanction Threat, and Deviance: An Experimental Test." *Social Problems* 20(4):488–498.

TORREY, F. (1988) *Nowhere to Go: The Tragic Odyssey of the Homeless Mentally Ill.* New York: Harper and Row.

TRACY, P. E., M. E. WOLFGANG & R. M. FIGLIO (1985) *Delinquency in Two Birth Cohorts: Executive Summary.* Washington, DC: U.S. Department of Justice (Government Printing Office).

VAN DEN HAAG, E. (1975) *Punishing Criminals: Concerning a Very Old and Painful Question.* New York: Basic Books.

VINTER, R. D., G. DOWNS & J. HALL (1975) *Juvenile Corrections in the States: Residential Programs and Deinstitutionalization: A Preliminary Report.* Ann Arbor, Ml: University of Michigan School of Social Work.

VON HIRSCH, A. (1976) *Doing Justice: The Choice of Punishments.* New York: Hill and Wang.

—— (1987) *Past or Future Crimes: Deservedness and Dangerousness in the Sentencing of Criminals.* New Brunswick, NJ: Rutgers University Press.

—— (1988) "Selective Incapacitation Reexamined: The National Academy of Sciences' Report on Criminal Careers and 'Career Criminals.'" *Criminal Justice Ethics* 7(1):19–35.

WILSON, J. Q. (1985) *Thinking about Crime,* Rev. Ed. New York: Vintage.

WILSON, J. Q. & R. J. HERRNSTEIN (1985) *Crime and Human Nature.* New York: Simon and Schuster.

WITTE, A. DRYDEN (1980) "Estimating the Economic Model of Crime with Individual Data." *Quarterly Journal of Economics* 94(1):57–84.

WOLFGANG, M. E., R. M. FIGLIO & T. SELLIN (1972) *Delinquency in a Birth Cohort.* Chicago: University of Chicago Press.

WRIGHT, E. O. (ed.) (1973) *The Politics of Punishment: A Critical Analysis of Prisons in America.* New York: Harper Torchbooks.

QUESTIONS FOR DISCUSSION

1. List and discuss the two most general objectives of punishment, according to the author.

2. According to the author, how have prisons succeeded in deterrence and incapacitation? Cite examples to support your answer.

3. Discuss three major criticisms of imprisonment.

4. Explain rational-choice theory. Cite examples of how this theory is purported to work.

APPLICATIONS

1. The author states that it is "…quite likely that the few alternatives to prisons which have been proposed by contemporary critics"…are not workable. He names non-intervention, corporal punishment, and the radical transformation of capitalism as the apparent proposed strategies. No mention is made of probation, work camps, restitution, decriminalization of adult consensual crime, or substance abuse treatment as feasible alternatives to imprisonment. Why is this the case? Discuss your views about alternatives to prison with your classmates.

2. Assuming that imprisonment is the best method of effectively dealing with crime, how many additional prisons should we construct to obtain a major decrease in crime? With the help of your instructor, design a cost-benefit analysis of how much money we must spend and what we can expect to be the rate of crime reduction as a result of increases in imprisonment.

chapter 18

Abolishing Prisons

Harold E. Pepinsky

INTRODUCTION

I belong to a group which holds meetings every other year on alternate sides of the Atlantic, called the International Conference on Penal Abolition (ICOPA). ICOPA IV met in Kazimierz Dolny, Poland, in May 1989, and ICOPA V met in Bloomington, Indiana in May 1991. I see us as a part of the pacifist movement in criminal justice. Many other people are criminal justice pacifists too, often in permanent organizations. Pacifist traditions in criminal justice are millenia old. Among the more active pacifist groups with long traditions of work in criminal justice are traditional Native Peoples, and peace churches of European origin like the Mennonites and the Quakers.

ICOPA used to be the International Conference on *Prison* Abolition. The name was changed from "prison abolition" to "penal abolition" because activists and scholars began to see that prisons merely reflected the violence in our daily lives. For instance, Scandinavian countries have a fraction of the proportion of their population imprisoned in comparison to the United States. Spanking children is also a finable infraction throughout Scandinavia, while child spanking is widely endorsed in the United States. Spanking and prison happen in Scandinavia, but overall, Scandinavians are less punitive than people in the United States. It is that punitiveness that needs to be addressed before the body politic allows United States prison populations to fall.

Prison abolitionists are like oncologists who oppose cancer and yet scarcely imagine eliminating it. We see no redeeming features in imprisonment, although we fully expect the struggle to find other ways to confront conflict to last far beyond our short lifetimes. Every effort, every struggle, every criticism helps, that's all. Political revolution is no solution.

One set of rulers is no better than any other. Violence breeds violence. Making peace, as by reconciling victims and offenders rather than sending offenders to prison, progresses ever so slowly. But as the popular saying among pacifists goes, the only path to peace is peace itself.

By far the most common, immediate, heated reaction to us penal abolitionists is that we are willing to let offenders go and get away with whatever they want. Actually, we oppose punishment because we believe in confrontation, and punishment gets in the way.

Believing as I do in confrontation, I would want my child to grab me and try her best to stop me if I start out into the street in front of a car. I don't expect to be grounded, let alone spanked, afterward. I would do the same for my daughter.

Believing as I do in confrontation, I would want my child to let me know in no uncertain terms if I hurt her or if she feels I have done an injustice. I feel obliged to listen, argue if I disagree, apologize for any harm done, try to make up and go on. That is, I welcome conflict when it happens, as it often must. I don't expect my child to ground me or spank me after the confrontation. I think my daughter has deserved the same since she let out her first post-natal cry (I did, wrongly in retrospect, spank her or send her into her room a few times, until as I recall, she turned five. Pacifists are violent too. We just don't feel we can justify any punishment, including our own, and try to grow out of it.)

WHAT MAKES PEOPLE BEHAVE

In what criminologist Leslie T. Wilkins calls a "law'n'order" society, children are heavily propagandized to believe that only the threat of punishment keeps them from hurting people. I bought the idea. I can recall picking up a sharp knife and thinking if it weren't for punishment of murderers, nothing would stop me from casually plunging the knife into the nearest available human being. Some people who have been punished severely and often enough have no lingering doubts; they are convinced that they are savage beasts who have to be closely confined. One friend of mine who has killed five people will tell you up front that he is too dangerous to be free. The irony is that he has a strong code of personal ethics in which friendship is sacred, and he poses a danger only to "bullies" who unfortunately abound in daily life in and out of United States prisons.

Violence is like a powerful sound system which drowns out our awareness of the love and compassion which sustain our lives. Cockroaches do not have to give each other something for nothing. They do not have to teach one another how to adapt or die. They do not have to feed one another. Cockroaches multiply so fast that almost all of them can die, while the species thrives on the survival of a lucky few. Human beings are not like cockroaches. Each mating pair of humans produces a handful of offspring at most. To survive, newborns depend heavily on adult charity for an extended period. A high percentage of offspring must at least survive some twenty years to sustain the population into the next generation. All it takes is an average of a few brief lapses of adult charity to children over a thirty-year period, and humans have wiped themselves out as surely as they would by launching all-out nuclear war. The miracle is that humans have held but not exercised the simple power of species self-destruction for every one of hundreds of thousands of generations. The irony is that while our very survival proves that compassion is the overriding force in our lives, our alarm over and preoccupation with violence drowns out our awareness that compassion exists, is real, or is practical at all.

We take the human will to live for granted. We understand full well it is in our nature to fight to get enough to eat, or clean water to drink. How, then, can it not be in our nature to fight to enjoy social relations which provide us with a better diet and clean water? People do want to get along, including my murderous friend. People do want to be respected and accepted, and understand that the only secure respect and acceptance is mutual, again including my friend.

Let me illustrate with a seminar I am teaching on feminist justice. This seminar is offered for what our campus calls "required intensive writing." To get approval to offer intensive writing credit, the instructor must promise close monitoring of the writing of at least 5,000 words in at least four progressive essays over the semester.

Students dread these courses. They are usually asked to write about topics that may only interest the instructor, and expect to be told relentlessly how poorly they write. Good style is some kind of recipe to be memorized and rigidly followed. Good writing hurts, and so it is a relief to get intensive writing out of the way.

I see no harm in carefully correcting misspelling, bad grammar and cumbersome prose. After all, the purpose of writing is to communicate, and good clear English facilitates communication. But it must be remembered that good English is a means to good communication, not an end in itself. First and foremost, dedicated writers are seeking a response to *what* they say above and beyond how they say it. Otherwise writing loses its point. To paraphrase sociologist Peter Berger, in writing, as in lovemaking, too much concentration on technique breeds impotence.

I encourage students to write me a series of ten 500-word essays over the semester. Initially, I ask them to respond to readings, then encourage them to respond to anything else relevant to the course material. They may respond to my response to their previous writing, or to something said in class. They may reflect on their own past and present. I discourage reports on readings or discussion, which bore me since I know them already. I encourage writers to write about what *they* want me or another reader to know.

The trick is to confront what is written in the essays without punishing it. Grades are out. The only essays I have not given credit for have been blatantly plagiarized. Ten satisfactory essays earn intensive writing credit and an A.

There is a simple test of whether an action is punitive or confrontive. Punishment violates the Golden Rule. The punished is not entitled to retaliate in kind against the punisher. While it could be argued that students' course evaluations can have an infinitesimal impact on my salary as a tenured full professor, students have nowhere near the legitimate opportunity to do to me what a bad grade would do to them. Nor if I have worked hard to teach well am I inclined to accept without **recrimination** a bad grade on my teaching evaluations. If I were to grade each essay and give "honest" low grades, I would do so with the conviction that I am entitled to do unto students as they are not entitled to do unto me. Grading would be an act of subordination. Grading would stand for the proposition that in any conflict of standards, I am somehow divinely ordained to be right and hurt the student for being different.

As I edit I try to be constructive, as by rewriting sentences and saying "Isn't this what you meant?" I find that most students are quite natural and good at speaking, and so when they are writing clumsily, I advise them to read their sentences out loud, say what they mean, and write what they have said. Good writing, I suggest, comes of talking to yourself as you work.

To give substance its rightful priority over technique, I spend more time and space writing substantive reactions than editing. Sometimes my comments are longer than the essay itself. I try to begin and end closing comments with honest positive reactions to something in the essay, and in marginal comments to note points of agreement and pleasure as easily as I criticize. I often invite a response to my response. And when the reading is done, I sit down and write an essay of my own, in the form of a letter to the seminar, putting down my own reactions to readings, discussion and essays. In them I try to write my best, and to show I enjoy writing myself.

Within two or three weeks the great majority of the essays flow beautifully. I find dread of reading them turning to anticipation and enjoyment. I eventually invite students to join in editing and commenting on each other's work. We come to know where we stand and what we are getting out of the course more fully, and class discussions grow more sophisticated and meaningful. I am repeatedly surprised at how seriously many of the students take the readings.

The joke is on people who write claiming that grades, competition, punishment and other systems of domination are the only things that make them work. I find them doing so in an enthusiastically written, polished piece of prose. And I wonder with them what really makes them write their best.

It helps that the seminar meets in the high school classroom of a remarkable alternative school, Harmony School, just off the college campus. Here, high school students and their teachers and parents may participate as actively as college undergraduates and graduate students. The Harmony students become role models of people who are confident that they can learn as well as any teacher. We sit on bean bags in a circle in a setting where confrontation rather than punishment is normal.

What works for students of all ages works equally for all people, including those doing time in maximum security prisons. Most repeat felons do stop being arrested by the time they get into their thirties or forties. How do they do it? I have many friends whose imprisonment is long behind them. What they invariably have is the love and support of legitimate friends and "family" who have helped them find a respectable life to lead. I put "family" in quotes because many inmates have been intolerably abused by their biological or adoptive families, and obtain a functional substitute by building a new and compassionate set of close relations often with newfound friends.

In a book on *Maternal Thinking,* Sara Ruddick calls the magic of what makes people behave "attentive love." It is a good bet that a child who acts out needs more attentive love rather than a spanking. That is, if the child can get more attention and respect for creative non-violence than for violence, the child has no reason to act out.

I don't mean to lay a guilt trip on parents. In the feminist justice seminar, mothers among us have made us acutely aware that attentive love is a luxury many parents cannot afford. If I'm working full-time, have just picked up my child at the end of the day, am starving and have a headache, and am scrambling to pick up dinner at the supermarket to get it ready for my husband before he gets angry, I won't have much patience for my toddler when she starts pulling candy off the rack. We need attentive love to behave, but if we are not getting much attentive love ourselves, we may not have much to offer, and life is bound to be a constant struggle for control.

The challenge, then, in getting people to behave is to rearrange our lives to offer one another more attentive love. For instance, it is well established that even trained athletes can't keep up with the creative physical activity of children. It is much more difficult for a single adult to meet the responsibility of giving a child attentive love. That's why quality daycare centers have several adults per small group of children to spell and support one another. If we care about children, if we care whether they grow up to be violent, disrespectful felons, we owe ourselves time out from other paid work to provide shared, leisurely attentive love to take care of all our children, whether we happen to "own" them or not. And we cannot do so unless we take care of ourselves, and place a higher value on spiritual nourishment than material efficiency and expediency.

WHAT PUNISHMENT DOES

Criminologist Doug Osborne visited the feminist justice seminar, and asked us to consider Graeme Newman's argument (in *Just and Painful*) that electric shock is a cleaner, fairer, more humane punishment than imprisonment. We had been discussing child-rearing. It suddenly occurred to me: Graeme is right, and by extension, the purest, best discipline we could offer our children is to shock them with a cattle prod with a rheostat. Ideally, if we believe in just deserts, the people through their government ought to be able to determine how many volts the child should get for each kind of infraction. The parent would then be legally obliged to do nothing but administer the prod when misbehavior occurred.

It requires absolute parent compliance to make pure punishment work (and of course if pure punishment doesn't work, impure, sloppy, sentimental punishment is going to work worse). Let's be realistic. We know how common child abuse is, and suspect many other parents of overindulgence. Parents need punishment just as much as children. It would be unrealistic to expect children to punish their own parents, who after all are much bigger. Therefore, each child needs to be able to run away and dial 911, so that the police can come with cattle prods, hear the situation out, and give the parents whatever shock is called for. Punishment, you see, has to be swift to be effective. In the vagaries of our plea bargaining process, prosecution and trial obscure more than enlighten. The police are best qualified to make and execute judgment.

We also know that police abuse power. Therefore, sergeants and so forth on up through the courts have to be available to come with cattle prods at a moment's notice to hear and act on charges of abuse of power. Of course if any complaint is found false, the complainant gets the prod.

Believe it or not this was penal law as written in later dynastic codes in China. A magistrate's disposition, including the sentence, was subject to review. If the Board of Punishments found the magistrate in error, the magistrate was subject to the sentence he had imposed, or one degree less if the sentence had not yet been executed. Once the magistrate had taken a complaint, he had to dispose of it properly within a specified period or face punishment as well.

Of course this system was thoroughly corrupt, and magistrates generally managed either to hide cases or buy their way out of trouble. But if you believe in punishment, this system ought to be just the right stuff to make people learn to behave.

We often presume that violent prison inmates are different from us. That is a mistake. The most violent inmate I have known has a rigid moral code of honor which is a **parody** of conventional values. Whether it is honor, a woman or one's hard-earned stash, if you own it, it is yours to protect and defend, and you have to punish people who violate your rights. Inmates are no dummies. They know that an Oliver North can get away with more murders than all the deathrow inmates put together. They know they don't have much of an edge in life. They learn that other cons are the only ones who may give them genuine respect. This makes discipline all the more imperative, to hang onto the little that one has. It makes it all the more imperative to give swift, sure punishment when punishment is due. The violent prisoner is a highly moral person who believes in punishment as strongly as you do, probably more.

The tragedy is that the swifter and surer we try to punish, the more we lose control of ourselves and of others. In a society where full enforcement of the law would mean almost all of us were in prison a good deal of the time, punishment cannot work. Instead, we cloak ourselves in "authority" and ownership to insulate ourselves from the punishment we feel we have to mete out to others. There is no way that the punitive parent will accept like punishment for like transgressions from the child. There is no way that police officers will turn each other in for crimes as readily as they arrest street people. There is no way that an authoritarian teacher will accept being sent to the principal for talking back to a student. The harder we try to give our subordinates their just deserts, the more we live a simple truth: might makes right.

Children who take punishment to heart learn it is their rightful place to abuse their own children. The lesson is simple: big people are entitled to hurt little people in the confines of the home they own. Little people have to learn to bide their time until they grow mightier. This is what we call learning to delay gratification, becoming disciplined, planning ahead, or learning to accept consequences for one's actions.

Punishment is a game of power over others. Such a game follows a very simple rule: those who have more power to begin with are favored to win. To rely on punishment is to give more powerful people greater opportunity to hurt others with **impunity**. The most common, most serious crimes will be concentrated among those who have the greatest authority to punish, who can order murders by the thousands under color of law, and see to it that the least powerful bear the brunt of punishment: underclass young men of color in prison, women and children trapped in abusive homes and schools—criminals perhaps, but whose crimes **pale** beside the crimes emanating from the ranks of the punishers. In sum, punishment promotes and hardens injustice. Crime moves up while punishment gets passed down.

Opponents of punishment are often labeled naive romantics. I ask you, what could be more naive and romantic than believing that punishment works?

ALTERNATIVES TO PUNISHMENT

It may because they have been abused themselves, but some people are **unrecalcitrant** jerks who need to be kept at bay. I would have trouble myself trusting a repeat rapist free among women in my community. Consider, though, that for the price of being kept in prison, we could hire two or three people to stick with an offender around the clock, with help on call, to keep the offender safe. They could, for example, see that a rapist was never left alone with a woman who did not know his past and volunteer to be alone with him. They could see that an alcoholic did not get behind the wheel of a car unless sober. Meanwhile, under supervision, the offender would be free to make his or her way in the world, and amount to more than a drain on society. That is confrontation without punishment. Confrontation means standing in the way of those who are hurting themselves or others. Punishment means bringing them to their knees for good measure. Incapacitation without punishment is simple to conceive. Those who still require punishment can add an electric shock quickly and cheaply, but the pain is not necessary to the incapacitation, and may even get in the way.

Of course penal abolitionists aspire to more than incapacitation, and believe incapacitation is seldom necessary. We aim, if possible, to heal social wounds and provide more attentive love where violence breaks out. Victim Offender Reconciliation Programs (VORPs), sponsored by the Mennonite Central Committee of Elkhart, Indiana, are a nationwide case in point. The Mennonites are known as one of the "peace churches." People are free to leave the church, but believers are pacifists—at home, at work, everywhere. Even in cases of rape and drunken vehicular manslaughter, VORPs have sometimes gotten victims (or their families) and offenders to volunteer to meet. Victims, are given an opportunity to let out their anger and fear. Offenders are given a chance to explain themselves. Remarkably often, the parties got past anger and fear, and work out terms of accommodation, where the offender is allowed in some measure to make amends.

Many victims are loath to face offenders. In such cases, we could easily allow victims (and for that matter offenders) a chance at least to begin by having a personal representative appear for them (never for a fee, only out of personal concern). I can almost see requiring victims and offenders to try confrontation and mediation as a condition for taking cases to criminal prosecution. This is not just placing a burden on victims. Victims, whose anger toward offenders is unexpressed, victims who fear that the strange thief or assailant will return to victimize them again, have no chance to be healed themselves by taking a chance on confrontation. As a society we owe it to ourselves not to let these wounds fester without trying to heal them.

In a larger sense prisoners need attentive love to behave as much as the rest of us, probably more. The typical prisoner, like others trapped in the underclass, needs to own something legitimate and honest. There is a wealth of experience and literature on how to organize businesses to be democratically, fairly owned and operated jointly by workers and customers, on how to organize housing cooperatives to be open and safe, on how to provide free, nurturant and open education and care for children and adults alike. I refer to these efforts as investments in friendship and democracy, rather than investments in Wall Street and "success." Much of the money we now spend on prisons could be used to get such enterprises under way for displaced offenders. A portion of any profits of such enterprises would go to the owners, and other portions could be dedicated to paying off start-up loans, contributing to victim compensation funds and the like.

It would be unjust and foolish to reserve any such initiatives for offenders. Rather, investing in democracy—and the attendant opportunities for attentive love—ought to be a priority for all of us who want to live safe, secure lives in our communities. Crime control means more than doing things to offenders who get caught and convicted. We need to confront crime in its entirety—as it permeates and infects the lives of all of us in a violent society. Fifty thousand dollars spent constructing a prison cell will prevent a lot more crime if invested in democracy first and foremost for those among us who own least.

You don't have to wait for society to change to engage in penal abolition. As we have discovered time and again in the feminist justice seminar, each of us has the opportunity in the most violent world to gain greater personal security by investing in friendship rather than in Wall Street and in advocacy of prison construction. Penal abolition pays. It is a way to get respect from your own children, and to gain self-respect on the job. And there is no greater economic security than commitment among friends when the bottom drops out of the market.

Now you see why I have made a personal choice to commit myself to penal abolition. It feels good. It works. I have no illusions that prisons are about to close; the trend in my country now is quite the reverse. It doesn't matter. It doesn't change the truth. Punishment fails, and I'd rather not just go along and fail with it.

QUESTIONS FOR DISCUSSION

1. According to Pepinsky, confrontation is a better alternative than punishment when dealing with offenders. Why? Cite examples to support your answer.
2. As children in U.S. society, we are "propagandized to believe that only the threat of punishment" keeps people from hurting one another. Explain.
3. What proposals does the author make as alternatives to punishment?

APPLICATIONS

1. Is it possible to abolish many of the prisons that now exist? What would you suggest as a feasible alternative to incarceration? Should violent and nonviolent offenders be handled differently? Discuss your views with other members of your class.

2. Some would argue that victims of crime should play a greater role in the decision-making process about what happens to the offender that has committed a crime against them. Do you agree or disagree? Why?

c h a p t e r   1 9

It's About Time

Solving America's Prison Crowding Crisis

John Irwin • James Austin

AMERICA'S IMPRISONMENT BINGE

Since 1880, the year criminologists began keeping track of prison populations, the number of people locked up in America's jails and prisons has steadily increased. A century ago, the daily imprisonment rate (i.e., the number of persons imprisoned on any given day) was about 120 per 100,000 citizens. Today it is more than 300 per 100,000—*almost a threefold increase.*

In absolute numbers, there are almost 530,000 people in state and federal prisons, 235,000 people in jail, and another 85,000 children in juvenile facilities. The total number of people confined, 850,000, would comprise a city larger than most of the nation's major cities including San Francisco, Cleveland, Denver, San Diego, and St. Louis. There are another 2.5 million adults and juveniles on probation or parole. On any given day, therefore, the criminal justice system supervises 3.2 million people.

But such large figures fail to reflect the tremendous scope of imprisonment and correctional supervision. The U.S. Justice Department reports that more than 8 million people, most of them arrested but not convicted of misdemeanor crimes, are booked into jails each year. The number of people admitted to jails plus the large numbers of adults and children admitted to prison and juvenile facilities, makes a total of close to 9 million people put in jail or prison each year.

What is particularly disturbing, however, is the recent rapid expansion of state prison populations. In 1970, there were less than 200,000 people in state and federal prisons. Now, more than 500,000 inmates are jammed into the nation's bulging prisons.

According to the U.S. Department of Justice, an additional 750 prisoners are being added to prison populations *each week.*[1] Some states are experiencing explosive increases.

California's prison population, which is the largest in the country, rose 33 percent in one year (1986). By 1995, California officials project that the adult prison population will surpass 110,000.[2] Another 100,000 will be held in California's jails and juvenile facilities. Nevada, which has the highest incarceration rate in the nation (420 per 100,000 citizens) is expected to double its prison population by 1995, at which time Nevada's imprisonment rate will approach 700 per 100,000.[3]

While most states will not experience the astronomic increases of California and Nevada, they will continue to grow at rates that far exceed population increases. The National Council on Crime and Delinquency (NCCD), which provides forecasts for seven states that incarcerate almost one-third of the nation's prison population, projects that inmate populations will increase by 50 percent in the next 10 years.[4]

What is causing these recent phenomenal increases? It is not increases in the nation's population, which has grown by about 10 percent since 1975, nor crime rates, which have been fairly constant for the last 10 years. Prison populations have more than doubled in the same period.

The evidence suggests that *sentencing legislation,* approved by elected officials, has resulted in courts sending a higher percentage of persons convicted of felonies to prison and for longer terms of imprisonment. For example, 18 percent of California's felony convictions in 1976 resulted in imprisonment. In 1986, the proportion of felons convicted and sentenced to prison approached 35 percent.[5] In addition, prison terms are much longer, especially for those convicted of burglary, drug dealing, and crimes of violence. Federal courts have increased prison sentences by almost 33 percent according to a recent study by the U.S. Department of Justice. In Illinois, prison terms for many crimes of violence are several years longer than sentences given out for similar crimes less than a decade ago.[6]

THE MILLION-DOLLAR CELL

Most people are aware that prisons are expensive to build and operate, but few understand just how expensive. Indeed, previous estimates routinely cited by public officials have dramatically underestimated the amounts of money spent on housing prisoners and building new prisons.

Prison and jail administrators typically calculate operating costs by dividing their annual budget by the average daily prison population. However, this accounting practice is quite misleading and produces patently low estimates of the true costs of imprisonment. For example, agency budgets often exclude contracted services for food, medical care, legal services, and transportation provided by other government agencies. According to two studies conducted in New York, these additional expenses increased the official **per diem** operating costs by 20 to 25 percent.[7] An independent audit of the Indiana prison system found that actual expenditures were one-third higher than those reported by the agency.[8] Besides these "hidden" direct expenditures, there are other costs which are rarely included in calculations of imprisonment costs. For instance, the state loses taxes that would be paid by many of the imprisoned, pays more welfare to their families, and maintains spacious prison grounds that are exempt from state and local real estate taxation. In the New York study conducted by Coopers and Lybrand in 1977, these costs amounted to over $21,000 per inmate.[9]

While there is considerable variation among the states, on the average, prison officials claim that it costs about $20,000 per year to house, feed, clothe, and supervise a prisoner.[10] Because this estimate does not include indirect costs, the true annual expenditure probably exceeds $30,000 per prisoner.

The other enormous cost is prison construction. Prisons are enclosed, "total" institutions in which prisoners are not only housed, but guarded, fed, clothed and worked. They also receive schooling and medical and psychological treatment. These needs require—in addition to cellblocks or dormitories—infirmaries, classrooms, laundries, offices, and kitchens. Dividing the total construction costs of one of these institutions by the number of prisoners it houses, produces a cost per "bed" as low as $7,000 for a minimum security prison, to $155,000 for a maximum security prison.

However, instead of using current tax revenues to pay directly for this construction, the state does what most citizens do when buying a house—they borrow the money, which must be paid back over several decades. The borrowing is done by selling bonds or using other financing instruments that may triple the original figure. The costs of prison construction are further increased by "errors" in original bids by contractors and cost overruns due to delays in construction, which seem to be the rule rather than the exception. A recent survey of 15 states with construction projects revealed that cost overruns averaged *40 percent* of the original budget projections.[11]

Consequently, when a state builds and finances a typical medium security prison it will spend approximately $268,000 per bed for construction alone. However, operating costs will greatly surpass construction costs in a little more than 10 years. Assuming a *conservative* $25,000 yearly operating cost per inmate with a two percent inflation factor, taxpayers will spend over *one million dollars* for each prisoner they incarcerate over a 30-year period.[12]

The enormous increases in the cost of imprisonment are just beginning to be felt by the states. For example, in California, a $300 million state expenditure deficit, caused, in part, by the uncontrolled rising costs of the prison system, resulted in a cutback in funds for public education and medical services for the poor. Budgetary battles have begun in which important state services for children, the elderly, the sick, and the poor are gutted to pay for prisons.

PRISONS FOR PROFIT

Some private businessmen, such as the prime mover of Kentucky Fried Chicken and the Hospital Corporation of America, are offering private prisons as a solution to the enormous costs of incarceration. They argue that "lean and mean" private entrepreneurs can avoid creating cumbersome bureaucracies and employ all the cost-cutting and efficiency-promoting procedures of private businesses. However, private prisons want minor- or minimum-security inmates, not maximum-security prisoners, who are the most expensive to lock up. Also, private prisons will be operated primarily to make a profit. As the director of one of the private companies bidding for state money said: "We'll hopefully make a buck at it. I'm not going to kid any of you and say we are in this for humanitarian reasons."[13]

The profit comes from the state paying the private corporation a fee for housing and caring for prisoners. At the start of the arrangement, the fee may be less than the state has been spending. But owners or shareholders of the corporation will persistently pressure the corporation to increase profits, which can only be done by increasing the fee or reducing the unit cost of caring for prisoners.

Such abuses are already occurring. In Tennessee, the Corrections Corporation of America's Tennessee facility had an early cost overrun of $200,000. In a court action in Texas (*Medina v. O'Neill*, 589 F. Supp. 1028, S.D. Tex, 1984), a private corporation was charged with holding 16 prisoners in a single, windowless, 12-foot by 20-foot cell. Privately operated prisons will probably end up being more expensive than state facilities and will cut services to the bone. Moreover, continued expansion of prison populations will be to the private corporations' interests and they will be another force encouraging more use of imprisonment.

CRIME RATES AND IMPRISONMENT

Just what kind of protection does imprisonment offer? The public is told that the unprecedented increase in the use of imprisonment is necessary to deter crime and to remove a growing number of dangerous criminals from the streets. But neither of these objectives has been or can be accomplished by expansion of prison populations.[14] The phenomenal growth in imprisonment has not reduced crime in our society.

The U.S. crime rate, as measured by crimes reported to the police, increased significantly between 1960 and 1974—the same time the baby-boom generation hit its high crime years—ages 16 to 25. Official crime rates did not change between 1975 and 1980, but a moderate decline began after 1980.[15] However, since 1984, there has been an upturn in most categories of crime—just when the supporters of imprisonment had begun to take credit for the 1980–84 declines. More significantly, violent crime rates have *increased* by almost 20 percent since 1976, despite well-publicized efforts to imprison the dangerous or career criminal.[16]

JUST HOW DANGEROUS ARE THEY?

Politicians have attempted to justify the increased use of imprisonment claiming there is a growing number of dangerous criminals who must be incarcerated. But their argument is not supported by the facts. Only 30 percent of those now sent to prison have been convicted of crimes of violence—a rate that has actually declined since 1926.[17]

Of those convicted of violent crimes, many are accused of assaults and homicides involving family members, neighbors, and other persons they have known for many years.

These are reprehensible acts, but are not the kind of "stranger-on-stranger" crimes that frighten the public. Most of the other violent criminals commit "strong-arm robberies" or "muggings." Again, reprehensible acts, but these crimes, the motivations behind them, and the people committing them, are usually quite different than the image of the "uncontrollable predator" that has been sold to the public.

The majority of prisoners have never been to prison before. In California, 33 percent of those sent to prison have served a prior prison term. And only 3 percent have served prior terms for violent crimes.[18] Seventy-five percent of those admitted to prison in Nevada are serving their first prison sentence. Forty-five percent have no prior felony conviction and 65 percent have never been sentenced to jail before.[19]

While imprisoned, most inmates do not commit crimes or become management problems. More than 80 percent of inmates released from prison have no serious disciplinary record while imprisoned.[20] Most inmates are assigned to minimum- or medium-security prisons. Only a small percentage (usually 10 to 15 percent) require maximum security in those notorious prisons the public reads about and sees on television—San Quentin, Stateville, Folsom and Marion. And, most inmates do not return to prison once released. For many decades, the average return rate to prison after three years, the time when most ex-convicts are likely to return, has consistently been about 30 to 35 percent.[21]

Despite these facts, the media and aspiring politicians portray most street criminals as men who, in spite of many brushes with the law, numerous "breaks" by lenient judges resulting in probation instead of jail, and even repeated prison and jail terms, refuse to live a law-abiding life. According to this stereotype, the greed, maliciousness, unwillingness to work, and perverted desires of criminals cause them repeatedly to commit vicious crimes against the innocent.

A more factual portrayal of prisoners presents a different reality—most prisoners are poorly educated young men raised in slum neighborhoods by low income parents, often a single mother who is underemployed or unemployed. These young men have virtually no job skills or job experience, and no hope of ever getting a stable and adequate job. Most of them grow up in the streets where they live from day-to-day, engaging in ill-planned and unskilled crimes in order to obtain money for their daily needs. The case of Eddie Turner exemplifies this type of offender.

Turner, shiftless and muscular, his body tattooed and scarred, joined the group after returning from a unsuccessful morning's search for work. "They say, 'Sorry there are no openings, but if you take a seat and fill out an application, we will get back to you when there is.' They never do," he said. Because there are so few businesses in Watts—most fled after the riot 17 years ago and never returned—job hunting usually involves going outside the community. Turner's journeys have taken him from Redondo Beach to the Los Angeles factories, fast food restaurants, and hotels. At least three times a week, he said, he was making a journey in search of work. "I go by bus, my mother's car, sometimes a friend drops me off," he said. "Sometimes it gets frustrating, I feel bad about being rejected. I feel like I'm not accepted; they don't want me. But I can't let one job stop me. If they don't call me back, I can't sweat it. There are jobs out there—I know it. You got to get out and get them. So every day I think about getting a job…I need one real bad." There is another dilemma, a hidden penalty. Because Turner and his two brothers are over 18 and out of school, their mother's welfare check has been cut, even though they continue to rely on her for support. Lucita Turner winds up struggling to raise her four children with money meant for her and her 17 year-old daughter. So Turner's mother pressures him to move out and his need for a job, money and independence grow (but he is) **stymied** by meager qualifications—high school dropout and former street gang member. It was not supposed to be this way. He used to dream of becoming a plumber, carpenter, or mechanic. He wanted to move to the mountains where a teacher once took him to spend a few weeks away from the inner city, and where he vowed to return. For a brief while, his ambitions seemed to have a chance. Turner worked as a plumber's assistant. But he was injured on the job and replaced. Now ambition labors against the lure of "the streets"—alcoholism, welfare, broken homes—and the pull of an underground economy in which a career can be had selling drugs.

It was eight days ago that Eddie Turner talked about the pain of trying to find a job. It was three days later that Lucita Turner talked about her worst fears that "the streets" would capture her son. And it was a day later that the streets did just that. Eddie Turner was arrested on suspicion of robbing a man at gunpoint not far from his Jordan Downs apartment. He was jailed in the county's Wayside Honor Rancho in Saugus in lieu of $5,000 bail. He faces at least two years in prison if convicted.[22]

Turner, a typical first-termer, is very different from the popular image of a vicious criminal. As a matter of fact, so are the vast majority of those sent to prison.

In the last ten years there has been an intensive, but futile, scientific search for the "career criminal," an individual permanently oriented to a lifestyle of serious, predatory crime.[23] This research effort has discovered that most of those arrested for felonies are guilty of very petty property or drug crimes. Some of these people commit a lot of petty crimes, particularly between the ages of 16 and 21. But to see all prisoners as deeply and permanently committed to crime is to greatly distort the accumulated evidence.[24] Most offenders tend to be persons like Eddie Turner, who carry on a life of petty crime and offensive deviance—such as using drugs and alcohol in a very open fashion—until they reach their mid-30s. Then, most of them retire to menial work, less serious crimes, or **dereliction.** And by the time the Eddie Turners of America "burn out" a new generation of young men just like him will have taken their place in America's growing slums, jails and prisons.

THE FEAR OF CRIME

Though increases in crime rates have generally slowed since 1974, the public still fears crime and demands more and more punitive measures to control it, even at the extreme costs described above. Paradoxically, the public's concern over crime is not closely tied to actual levels of crime. Nor is the fear of crime related to the probability of being a victim.

Fear of crime is primarily fueled by attention from politicians and the media. Politicians **harangue** the *street* crime problem because it is a safe issue. It is easy to cast in simple terms of good versus evil and no powerful constituency is directly offended by a campaign against street crime. Some politicians also use street crime to divert attention away from other pressing social problems—such as the threat of nuclear war, unemployment, high living costs and the economy—all of which persistently top the list of public concerns. Measures to solve these problems would require changes that would offend powerful interest groups.

The impact of political and media attention focusing on a problem is dramatically demonstrated by the public's widely shifting concern about drug abuse. National studies conducted by the federal government indicate that the use of marijuana, opiates, cocaine and other illegal drugs, both by the general public and by high school students, increased through the 1970s leveled off after 1979, and since then has declined slightly.[25]

However, there have been radical changes in the public's concern about drugs which, as reflected in Gallup Poll surveys, bear little resemblance to actual drug use patterns. Political and media attention obviously does have an effect on public opinion. During the two short intervals in which the public concern rose sharply, Presidents Nixon and Reagan (and, in the second instance, his wife) had declared well-publicized wars on drugs.

The United States does have a crime (and drug) problem, and there are legitimate reasons for public figures to alert people to serious social problems. However, politicians, in their **fulminating** against "street crime," have argued fallaciously that it is mostly perpetrated by vicious career criminals, and have greatly exaggerated its extent and cost.

The average loss of a burglary, robbery, or larceny—the major property crimes—is $40. The total loss for all street crimes in a year is estimated to be $11 billion. Significantly, the United States spends more than four times that amount ($45.6 billion) on the criminal justice system to fight property crimes.[26] On the other hand, white collar crime, which is rarely included in political campaigns against crime or in criminal justice appropriation, has been estimated by the U.S. Senate Judiciary Subcommittee to cost between $175 billion and $231 billion annually.[27] By way of contrast with other "social" costs, Americans spend more than $50 billion per year on medical costs related to smoking, and are charged an additional $65 billion each year for import tariffs.[28]

Political and media harangues about street crime have resulted in irrational fear and an excessive, ineffective, punitive response to crime.

SOCIAL COSTS OF IMPRISONMENT

As demonstrated in this paper, the best evidence indicates that our drastically increased use of imprisonment has not made society safer. Even worse, there is increasing evidence that it is making society more dangerous.

In our careless extension of the use of imprisonment, thousands of people, who have no prior prison records and are guilty of relatively minor felonies—petty burglaries, forgeries, minor drug offenses—have been packed into dangerous, crowded prisons. A growing number of prisoners are being subjected to extremely long sentences. These long-termers are not only stacking up in prisons and filling all available space, but their long terms make return to a productive, conventional life extremely difficult, if not impossible. Many marginally involved petty criminals are converted into hard core "outlaws"; mean, violence-prone convicts who dominate crowded prison wards.[29]

The social cost of imprisonment, that is its tendency to increase ex-prisoners' criminal activity, continues to be confirmed by research. The RAND Corporation[30] compared carefully matched groups of convicted felons sent to prison or granted probation and found those sentenced to prison had significantly higher rates of rearrest after release than those on probation. In the last five years, the recidivism rate (the rate of re-imprisonment of inmates released on parole) in California, by far the nation's most overcrowded prison system, has doubled.

Even more tragically, imprisonment is increasingly falling upon blacks, Hispanics and other people of color. Sixty years ago, almost one-fourth of all prison admissions were non-white. Today, nearly half of all prison admissions are non-white. in many states like Florida and California, the imprisonment rate of blacks is at least 10 times higher than for whites. Hispanics are incarcerated at a rate three times higher than whites. Studies show that if one is born black and male, there is a 50 percent chance of being arrested once by age 29.[31] These tragic figures show that if blacks and Hispanics were imprisoned at the same rate as whites, there would be no national prison crowding crisis.

IT'S ABOUT TIME

Many methods of reducing prison populations have been advanced. Some argue that certain classes of felony crimes should be reclassified as misdemeanors or decriminalized completely. In the late 1960s there was a great deal of support to do this for many minor drug offenses. Others claim that a significant number of those convicted of felonies could be diverted from prison to probation and new forms of alternatives to prison including intensive probation, house arrest, electronic surveillance, and greater use of fines and restitution.

However, we are not persuaded that these "front-end" reforms would substantially reduce prison crowding. Historically, well-intentioned alternatives have had marginal impact on reducing prison populations. Rather, they have had the unintended consequence of widening the net of criminal justice by imposing more severe sanctions on people who otherwise would not be sentenced to prison.[32] Moreover, they have little support with public officials who, like the public, are increasingly disenchanted with probation and other forms of community sanctions.

For alternatives to work, legislators, prosecutors, police, judges and correctional agencies would all have to agree on new laws and policies to implement them. Such a consensus is unlikely to occur in the near future, since these measures are replete with controversy and disagreement. Even if the forces that are presently driving the punitive response to crime abated considerably, it would take several years to work through these disagreements and effect changes in the laws and policies which would slowly produce an easing of prison population growth. Such a slow pace of reform would not allow states to avoid the catastrophe that is rapidly developing in our prisons.

Even diversion of a substantial number of offenders from prison would not have a major impact on prison population growth. "Front end" diversion reforms are targeted for those few offenders who are already serving the shortest prison terms (usually less than a year). The recent flood of tougher sentencing laws have greatly lengthened prison terms for offenders charged with more serious crimes and repeat property or drug offenders. Consequently, it is this segment of the prison population which is piling up in the prisons. The problem is too much time for those offenders unlikely to be candidates for diversion from prison.[33]

There is only one viable solution that would have an immediate and dramatic impact on prison crowding: *shorter prison terms.* This could be done swiftly and fairly through a number of existing mechanisms such as greater use of existing good-time credit statutes and/or accelerating parole eligibility. And, as demonstrated in several states, there would be no significant impact on crime rates.

In Illinois between 1980 and 1983, the Director of Corrections released more than 21,000 prisoners an average of 90 days early because of severe prison crowding. The impact on the state's crime rate was insignificant, yet the program saved almost $50 million in tax dollars. A study of the program found that the amount of crime that could be attributed to early release was less than 1 percent of the total crime of the state. In fact, the state's crime rate actually *declined* while the early release program was in effect.[34]

Another demonstration of how swiftly and easily prison populations can be reduced occurred in California from 1967 to 1970. When Ronald Reagan became governor, he instructed the parole board to reduce the prison population. The board began shortening sentences, which it had the power to do within the indeterminate sentence system, and in two years, lowered the prison population from 28,000 to less than 18,000. Many other states are following these examples. Texas, Oklahoma, Oregon, Tennessee and Florida are just a few states which have been required by the federal courts to reduce overcrowded prison systems by shortening prison terms.

For such a policy to work, prison terms would have to be shortened across the board. Any attempt by legislators, judges, or parole boards to select certain categories of prisoners for shorter sentences would compound the already discriminatory sentencing patterns and not produce population reductions.[35] The average prison stay in the U.S. now ranges from two to four years, meaning that even marginal reductions in the length of stay for large categories of inmates would have substantial effects on population size. For example, in 1984, 167,000 people were sentenced to prison. If 80 percent of those people had their sentences reduced by 30 days, the nation's prison population would have declined by 11,000 inmates. A 90-day reduction would have resulted in 33,000 fewer inmates and a 6-month reduction, 66,000 fewer inmates.

A maximum prison population should be determined by officials of each state and policies adopted that marginally reduce prison terms to avoid surpassing the maximum population. Unless such reform is adopted, prison populations will continue to rise indefinitely into the twenty-first century. Reducing prison terms by the amounts advocated may only slow the rate of expansion. But it can be done with no cost to public safety, no changes in crime rates and with enormous dollar savings. It has been done before.[36]

We *must* turn away from the excessive use of prisons. The current incarceration binge will eventually consume large amounts of tax money, which will be diverted from essential public services such as education, child care, mental health and medical services. We will continue to imprison millions of people under intolerably cruel and dangerous conditions. We will accumulate a growing number of ex-convicts who are more or less psychologically and socially crippled, excluded from conventional society—posing a continuing threat to others. We will severely damage some of our more cherished humanitarian values, which are corroded by our excessive focus on **vindictiveness.** And we will further divide our society into the white affluent classes and a poor non-white underclass, many of them convicts and ex-convicts. In effect, we are putting our own **apartheid** into place.

NOTES

1. *Prisoners in 1985,* Bureau of Justice Statistics, 1986.
2. See *The Growing Imprisonment of California,* Austin and Pannell, 1986.
3. See "Review of the Nevada Department of Prisons Prison Population Projections," Austin and McVey, 1987.
4. See *The NCCD Prison and Parole Populations Forecast,* Austin and McVey, 1987.
5. See *Crime and Delinquency, 1985,* California Department of Justice, 1986.
6. See "Using Early Release to Relieve Prison Crowding," Austin, 1986.
7. See *The Price of Punishment,* McDonald, 1980, and "The Cost of Jailing," Loeb, 1975.
8. See *Time to Build?* Cory and Gettinger, 1984.
9. See Loeb, 1975.
10. Identifying the true operating costs of a prison can be a very difficult task. The Criminal Justice Institute (1986) survey reported ranges from $7,023 to $30,909 from the various states with an average cost of $14,591. However, this "average" cost figure underestimates the true "average" cost due to overcrowding which now plagues a majority of the state prison systems. As prisons become more crowded, the average cost per inmate is lowered as the prisons handle more inmates at about the same cost. If prisons were not overcrowded and were meeting constitutional standards, the costs per inmate would be significantly higher.
11. See Cory and Gettinger, 1984.
12. This method for estimating the costs of incarceration ignores what economists refer to as the time value of money. Assuming a state had sufficient funds to invest in interest bearing accounts, as little as $400,000 would be needed to cover the construction and operational costs of the prison cell over the 30-year-period.
13. See *Desert News,* June 20–21, 1985, B7.
14. A number of studies, as summarized by the National Research Council (NRC) (1986) have concluded that the amount of crime that can be prevented by increasing the use of imprisonment is considerably less than advertised by proponents of such a policy and thus at enormous cost to taxpayers. Specifically, NRC states that to reduce the crime rate by as little as 10 percent would require a doubling of the half million people now in prison. See also Visher, 1986, and Gottfredson and Hirschi, 1986.
15. The measurement of crime comes from two sources: the Uniform Crime Reports and the National Crime Survey (NCS). The former reflects crimes reported to the police while the latter reflects crimes reported by citizens from a national survey conducted by the U.S.

Census. NCS began in 1973 and showed a steady rate of crime until 1980 when it, too, showed a decline in crimes, especially for property related crime. However, the 1986 survey showed a leveling off in the 1980–1985 declines and increases for the crimes of burglary, rape, and robbery. Regardless of which crime measure one employs there has been no direct relationship established between crime and use of imprisonment.

16. See *Crime in the United States, 1985,* Federal Bureau of Investigation, 1986. Moreover, there is no consistent pattern among the states with respect to crime rates and use of imprisonment. For example, Illinois, Michigan, Washington, Tennessee, Pennsylvania and Minnesota, at various times during the past decade, enacted reforms that limited prison population growth. While these reforms were in effect, their crime rates followed essentially the same pattern of the nation. In fact, some of these states actually showed *reductions* in crime rates while restricting prison population growth (Austin, 1986, *The Use*).

17. Based on information provided by the Bureau of Justice Statistics at the National Research Council's Panel on Prison and Jail Overcrowding, Chicago, Illinois.

18. See *Report on Sentencing Practices,* California Board of Prison Terms, 1985.

19. See *Prison Master Plan* and *The Function of Parole in the Criminal Justice System,* State of Nevada, 1982, 1984.

20. See *An Evaluation of Objective Prison Classification Systems,* Correctional Services Group, 1986, and *Inmate Classification System Study,* California Department of Corrections, 1986.

21. See *Returning to Prison,* Bureau of Justice Statistics, 1984. It should also be noted that many states are now reporting higher rates of failure on parole. For example, California's two-year failure rate has grown from 25 percent to well over 50 percent. It may be no accident that California has the nation's most overcrowded system and has purposely moved away from an emphasis on prison programs to an emphasis on punishment. If this rate of failure continues there will be more people entering prison as parole violators than as new court commitments.

22. *Los Angeles Times,* Aug. 21, 1982, pp. 1, 6.

23. See Gottfredson and Hirschi, 1986 for an excellent critique of the illusive search for career criminals. Furthermore, one of the original advocates for selective incapacitation of "career criminals" has now recanted his previous claims that (1) career criminals can be identified and (2) that such a policy would have a major impact on crime rates (Greenwood and Turner, 1987).

24. The RAND Corporation in a major study of career criminals found that over 50 percent of inmates sentenced to prison were "low rate" offenders while only 25 percent were "high rate" criminals (Greenwood and Abrahamse, 1982; Visher, 1986). More significantly, even when these inmates are released from prison their rate of offending declines substantially principally due to maturation (Austin, 1986, *Using*; Gottfredson and Hirschi, 1986).

25. See *Use of Licit and Illicit Drugs by America's High School Students 1975–1984,* Johnson et al., 1985.

26. See *The Economic Cost of Crime* and *Crime and Justice Facts,* Bureau of Justice Statistics, 1984, 1986.

27. See *Corporate Crime,* Clinard and Yeager, 1980, p. 8.

28. See *San Francisco Chronicle,* March 20, 1987, p. 27, and *Harper's Index,* Harper's, March 1987.

29. See *Prisons in Turmoil* and *The Jail,* Irwin, 1980, 1986.

30. *Prison versus Probation,* Petersilia and Turner, 1986.

31. See *The Growing Imprisonment of California,* Austin and Pannell, 1986, and *The Prevalance and Incidence of Arrest among Adult Males in California,* Tillman, 1987.

32. "The Unmet Promise of Alternatives to Incarceration," Austin and Krisberg, 1982.

33. For example, in Ohio, which sentences almost half of its inmates to prison terms of less than one year, if the state diverted them from prison to probation or jail, it would reduce the

prison population by only 10 percent. Similarly, in many states, there will continue to be substantial increases in prison populations even if prison admissions do not increase over the next decade.

34. Many will ask how such seemingly contradictory results of shorter prison terms, reduced prison populations and decreases in crime rates are possible. Again, one must remember that most inmates in prison are not career criminals, are unlikely to return to prison after release, and are slowing down in their episodic tendencies to commit street crimes. Most crimes in our society are not committed by aging ex-convicts but by the next generation of adolescent youth. All of the accumulated research to date consistently shows that prison terms can be reduced without (1) increasing the probability that an inmate will commit street crimes and (2) without adversely impacting the overall crime rate. See Austin (1986, *Using*) for a review of this literature and the detailed data on measuring the impact of early release in Illinois and elsewhere.

35. At every decision-making level—arrest, prosecution, sentencing, and parole—discriminatory practices can and have been found to exist. Most recently, Petersilia (1983) found that black and Hispanic offenders receive harsher sentences and serve longer prison terms than white offenders. These differences are especially alarming given that little difference exists among offenders with respect to social class. In the juvenile area, Elliott et al., have found that the level of crime reported by minority versus white youth do not explain the sharply higher arrest rates for minority youth.

36. Many states are now successfully using a variety of informal methods to reduce prison terms (see Austin, 1986, *The Use*). These generally include increasing the amount of credits an inmate can earn for good behavior which in turn reduces length of stay. Other influential scholars are also in support of this strategy. For example, James Q. Wilson has recently advocated a policy of shorter sentences. In some ways the policy has greater political merit than front end reforms which seek to divert offenders from prison. No debate is required on who should go to prison, ensuring that same use of imprisonment sanction is maintained. Instead, the questions become how long, and at what cost to taxpayers.

REFERENCES

AUSTIN, J. (1986) *The Use of Early Release and Sentencing Guidelines to Ease Prison Crowding*. Paper prepared for the National Academy of Sciences Conference on Prison and Jail Crowding, Chicago, IL.

AUSTIN, J. (1986) "Using Early Release to Relieve Prison Crowding: A Dilemma in Public Policy." *Crime and Delinquency*, Vol. 32, No. 4:404–501.

AUSTIN, J. & B. KRISBERG (1982) "The Unmet Promise of Alternatives to Incarceration." *Crime and Delinquency*, Vol. 28, No. 3:374–409.

AUSTIN, J. & A. MCVEY (1987) *Review of the Nevada Department of Prisons Forecast*. (NIC Technical Assistance Report 87-N042). San Francisco, CA: NCCD.

AUSTIN, J. & A. MCVEY (1987) *The NCCD Prison and Parole Populations Forecast*. San Francisco, CA: NCCD.

AUSTIN, J. & W. PANNELL (1986) *The Growing Imprisonment of California*. San Francisco, CA: NCCD.

BUREAU OF CRIMINAL STATISTICS (1986) *Crime and Delinquency in California, 1985*. Sacramento, CA: California State Attorney General.

BUREAU OF JUSTICE STATISTICS (1984) *Returning to Prison.* Bulletin NCJ-957000. Washington, DC: Department of Justice.

BUREAU OF JUSTICE STATISTICS (1984) *The Economic Cost of Crime to Victims.* Special Report. Washington, DC: Department of Justice.

BUREAU OF JUSTICE STATISTICS (1986) *Crime and Justice Facts, 1985.* Washington, DC: Department of Justice.

BUREAU OF JUSTICE STATISTICS (1986) *National Crime Survey.* Washington, DC: Department of Justice.

BUREAU OF JUSTICE STATISTICS (1986) *Prisoners in 1985.* Washington, DC: Department of Justice.

CALIFORNIA BOARD OF PRISON TERMS (1985) *Report on Sentencing Practices Determinate Sentencing Law. (July 1, 1982 through June 80, 1983).* Sacramento, CA:

CALIFORNIA DEPARTMENT OF CORRECTIONS (1986) *Inmate Classification Study: Final Report.* Sacramento, CA: CDC.

CALIFORNIA DEPARTMENT OF JUSTICE (1986) *Crime and Delinquency, 1985.* Sacramento, CA: Bureau of Criminal Statistics.

CLINARD, M. B. & P. C. YEAGER (1980) *Corporate Crime.* New York: Free Press.

CORRECTIONAL SERVICES GROUP (1986) *An Evaluation of Objective Classification Systems.* Kansas City, MO: CSG.

CORY, B. & S. GETTINGER (1984) *Time to Build? The Realities of Prison Construction.* New York: Edna McConnell Clark Foundation.

CRIMINAL JUSTICE INSTITUTE, INC. (1986) *The Corrections Yearbook.* South Salem, NY: CJI.

ELLIOTT, D. S. AND S. S. AGETON (1980) "Reconciling Race and Class Differences in Self-Reported and Official Estimates of Delinquency." *American Sociological Review,* Vol. 45, No. 1.

FEDERAL BUREAU OF INVESTIGATION (1986) *Crime in the United States, 1985.* Washington, DC: Department of Justice.

GOTTFREDSON, M. & T. HIRSCHI (1986) "The True Value of Lambda Would Appear to Be Zero: An Essay on Career Criminals, Criminal Careers, Selective Incapacitation, Cohort Studies, and Related Topics." Criminology, Vol. 24, No. 2: 213–234.

GREENWOOD, P. W. & A. ABRAHAMSE (1982) *Selective Incapacitation.* Santa Monica, CA: RAND Corporation.

GREENWOOD, P. W. & S. TURNER (1987) *Selective Incapacitation Revisited. Why the High-Rate Offenders Are Hard to Predict.* Santa Monica, CA: RAND Corporation.

IRWIN, J. (1980) *Prisons in Turmoil.* Boston: Little, Brown, Inc.

IRWIN, J. (1985) *The Jail: Managing the Underclass in American Society.* Berkeley, CA: University of California Press.

JOHNSON, L., ET AL. (1985) *Use of Licit and Illicit Drugs by America's High School Students, 1974–1984.* National Institute of Drug Abuse. Washington, DC: U.S. Government Printing Office.

LOEB, C. M., JR. (1978) "The Cost of Jailing in New York City." *Crime and Delinquency* (October): 446–452.

MCDONALD, D. (1980) *The Price of Punishment: Public Spending for Corrections in New York.* Boulder, CO: Westview Press.

NATIONAL RESEARCH COUNCIL (1986) *Criminal Careers and "Career Criminals," Vol. I and II.* Washington, DC: National Academy Press.

PETERSILIA, J. & S. TURNER, WITH J. PETERSON (1983) *Racial Disparities in the Criminal Justice System.* Santa Monica, CA: RAND Corporation.

PETERSILIA, J. & S. TURNER, WITH J. PETERSON (1986) *Prison versus Probation in California: Implications for Crime and Offender Recidivism.* Santa Monica, CA: RAND Corporation.

STATE OF NEVADA (1982) *Prison Master Plan.* Bulletin 83-3, Legislative Counsel Bureau.

TILLMAN, R. (1987) *The Prevalence and Incidence of Arrest Among Adult Males in California.* Sacramento, CA: California State Attorney General.

VISHER, C. A. (1986) "The RAND Inmate Survey: A Reanalysis," in *Criminal Careers and "Career Criminals."* Washington, DC: National Academy Press.

QUESTIONS FOR DISCUSSION

1. Consider the expense of building and operating prisons. According to the authors, why are the cost estimates much lower than the actual cost of the prison? Why might someone in a political office present an artificially low figure to the public?

2. A large segment of the public believes that the vast majority of inmates are dangerous criminals. What evidence is presented by the authors that is contrary to this belief?

3. What recommendations are made by the authors that would decrease prison populations? Why is it desirable to decrease prison populations? Provide examples to support your answer.

APPLICATIONS

1. The public's fear of crime has a great deal to do with how aspiring politicians arrange their agendas and campaign issues. The media also play a significant role in exacerbating the public's fear of crime. Evidence in this article suggests that the fear of certain crimes is exponentially higher than the reality of crime, whereas very costly crimes, such as white-collar crime, receive relatively little attention. Discuss with other members of your class why this is happening and how we might change this phenomenon.

2. Crime has moved to the top of the national agenda. Politicians have responded by passing yet another crime bill, which appropriates large sums of tax dollars for hiring more police and building more prisons. What impact will these measures have on crime?

The Greatest Correctional Myth

Winning the War on Crime through Incarceration

Joseph W. Rogers

When the time comes, will there be room enough for your child?

Quarterly Journal of Corrections, Summer 1977: front cover

Since this **poignant** inquiry appeared in 1977, this country's prison population has more than doubled from 265,000 to a historic high exceeding 600,000. By the end of 1989 (with turnover), over one million persons will have been incarcerated during the year—1 in 240 Americans, triple the total just two decades ago ("The Far Shore," 1988:11; see also Walker, 1989:3–5). To gain some idea of pace, we need go no further than a recent governmental report which shows a 1985 imprisonment growth rate of 8.7 percent (Bureau of Justice Statistics, December 1987:52). Were we to continue at this annual growth, the prison population would double in less than 9 years! The implications of such acceleration simply cannot be ignored.

Unfortunately, the recent presidential campaign provided little relief from either party or candidate. So many volleys were fired, we can hardly expect any serious attempt to win the "war on crime" by means other than through more concrete, mortar, and metal of additional penal institutions. Indeed, our political leadership seems second to none in seeking "room at the inn" of imprisonment for the Nation's criminal offenders. On the one hand, we have long-standing belief in the powers of imprisonment, no matter how futile; on the other, we have the public's escalating fear of victimization, which seems to turn alternative approaches into perceptions of unforgivable "softness" on offenders. While we could hope this approach will succeed, honesty requires expression of doubt.

The contemporary *wave* of punitiveness is traceable to the mid-sixties. When Garrett Heyns (1967) wrote that "the 'treat-em-rough' boys are here again," little did he realize they would continue to dominate our justice system for more than two decades. What this

Reprinted by permission of the publisher.

former Michigan warden and Washington State director of corrections saw was only the tip of an iceberg. It has since merged as a punishment glacier, composed of the hard ice of fear, hardened further in the cold atmosphere of deterrence and vengeance.

We must not make light of such fear, or the public's motives, for that matter. We have every right to want and seek security in our person and our property. Nor is it useful to advocate "tearing down the walls" or the abolition of maximum-security institutions. The position here concerns the narrowing focus and dependency on imprisonment to the neglect of a larger front in our battle against criminal victimization. Frankly, I am concerned lest the overwhelming success of the Willie Horton campaign waged against presidential candidate, Massachusetts Governor Michael Dukakis, makes cowards of us all. Differences in viewpoint notwithstanding, be assured that all of us are in this together.

THE MYTH OF THE IMPRISONMENT SOLUTION

From the outset we must realize the fundamental weaknesses in an extreme incarceration approach, which must take into account at least several basic factors.

First, 99 percent of those entering prison eventually return to society to become our neighbors in the communities where we live and work. Among the half-million inmates housed in state and federal prisons in 1985 (not including another quarter million in jails), there were only 1,175 recorded deaths (1,148 males, 27 females). Of these, 731 were attributed to natural causes; 112 to suicides; 33 to accidents; 18 to executions; 105 to another person; and 176 to unspecified reasons. These deaths represented less than three-tenths of one percent of the population, not taking into account either turnover or length of stay (Bureau of Justice Statistics, December 1987:71). With few exceptions we can count on those persons entering prison to come out again better or worse for their experience.

Second, the median stay in prison varies from state to state within a range of 15 to 30 months (Bureau of Justice Statistics, June 1984:3). Actual time served (including jail and prison time) is generally much less than the maximum sentence length. For example, while the 1983 admissions reveal a median sentence length of 36 months, the median time served by releases that year was 19 months (Bureau of Justice Statistics, September 1987:7).

Third, there is a yearly turnover involving approximately a half-million prisoners. While 234,496 individuals were exiting state or federal jurisdictions in 1985, even more, 275,366 were taking their places (Bureau of Justice Statistics, December 1987:61–62).

Fourth, as striking as these data are, a crime-prevention policy based primarily on increased imprisonment is at best inadequate; at worst, a clogged pipe of human beings. The problems for criminal justice personnel exist at several junctures in the system, of course; but here our "trouble shooting" must be directed back to the community where the flow begins. Upon so doing, we discover an estimated 40 million victimizations for 1983 alone. In 1982, an estimated 3.2 percent of the Nation's population were victims of rape, robbery, or assault—the equivalent of about 6 million persons (Finn, n.d.:1). Viewed somewhat differently, according to the respected National Crime Survey (NCS), more than 22 million *households* were victimized during 1985 by *at least* one crime of violence or theft. Their estimated total of 35 million individual victimizations is staggering when one considers the possibility of underreporting (Bureau of Justice Statistics, March 1988:11–12).

Fifth, the bulk of offenders are never caught, much less convicted or imprisoned (Ennis, 1967; Clark, 1970; Van den Haag, 1975). During the period 1973–1985 only about one-third of all crimes were reported to the police (Bureau of Justice Statistics, March 1988:34). Further, a review of *Uniform Crime Reports* covering the same time period will reveal an index crime clearance rate approximating 21 percent. In a compelling reanalysis of the President's Crime Commission Task Force Data, Charles Silberman (1978: 257–261) provides a reasonable guide beyond this point. Of some 467,000 adults arrested (using rounded figures) 322,000 were punished in some way, with 63,000—about 14 percent—going to prison (Walker, 1989:36–39).

Sixth, prisons can hardly claim any great success when it comes to restoring criminals to law-abiding citizens. Assessments vary from about one-third to two-thirds for recidivism rates of released inmates. In his classic study, Daniel Glaser (1964:13–35) considers the latter figure as mythical, the former as more on target. While I agree with Glaser's **cogent** analysis, there can be little joy over even this positive claim. For example, Steven Schlesinger (1987:3), Director of the Bureau of Justice Statistics, recently asserted that their studies indicate about half of those released from prisons will return. He also points out that more than two-thirds of the burglars, auto thieves, forgers, defrauders, and embezzlers going to prison have been there before. Half of all the recidivists studied have been out of prison less than 23 months (Schlesinger, 1987:2).

Consider, then, the implications of these six propositions which show that while we keep 600,000 adults locked up, some 35 to 40 million crimes are being committed annually. While all those incarcerated men and women were unable to engage in crime, who were these other people preying upon the public? Many were repeaters, and the Uniform Crime Report Program has been trying to learn more about them and about careers in crime. Doubtless, some were under some alternative form of correctional supervision. For example, in 1985, 254,000 were in jail; 1,870,000 were on probation; and 277,438 were on parole (Bureau of Justice Statistics, December 1987: front cover). Some were juveniles, of whom almost 50,000 were in some sort of custodial facility on February 1, 1985 (Bureau of Justice Statistics, September 1987:43).

The above statistics, fragile though they are, underscore the importance of the "war on crime" being waged outside of institutions, not in them. But to the extent we believe in prisons as our justice centerpiece, we must recognize the crucial importance of what we do with (or to) persons during whatever time period they are in custody. Simply put, post-release failure rates are not acceptable.

BYPRODUCTS OF CONTEMPORARY PRISON POLICY

The current emphasis on incarceration should take into account at least eight major prison issues: (1) overcrowding; (2) cost; (3) litigation; (4) race/ethnicity; (5) long-term stays; (6) AIDS; (7) officer stress; and (8) the war on drugs.

Institutional Overcrowding

American prisons have come to resemble bloated sponges. As extra sponges are added, they too become glutted. There are over 700 state and Federal prisons (Innes, 1986:3; see also Gottfredson & McConville, 1987). The federal government, almost all of the states, and many countries have embarked upon prison and jail construction programs that will remain a legacy of dubious merit from the 1980s. As one observer sees it, "While this expansion will permit incarceration of more people, it is unclear whether the additional facilities will succeed in relieving crowding; there seems to be almost limitless demand for prison beds" (Jacobs; n.d.:l).

One clear indicator is the population density of state prisons which are struggling to keep abreast of national standards. Both the American Correctional Association and the U.S. Department of Justice call for 60 square feet per single cell, provided inmates spend no more than 10 hours per day there; at least 80 square feet when cell confinement exceeds 10 hours daily (Innes, 1986:4). As of June 30, 1984, an assessment of 694 prisons revealed an average of 57.3 square feet per inmate: an average of 11.3 hours per day in unit confinement; and 66.5 percent of the inmates in multiple occupancy. This census also disclosed that 33.4 percent were in maximum security; that 11.8 percent of the facilities were over 100 years old, another 22.7 percent 50 to 99 years old; and that 50.8 percent of the institutions held more than 1,000 prisoners (Innes, 1986:2).

Some jurisdictions are desperate. New York City, for example, is now housing 400 inmates on a five-story barge anchored in the Hudson River. Reminiscent of eighteenth century England, authorities are planning to add two more barges, one with berths for 800 convicts. Their sense of urgency is conveyed by one official, who says bluntly: "We don't have the luxury of waiting five years to build from the ground up" ("The Far Shore," 1988:11).

Newspaper releases from the State of Texas have reached near-ludicrous proportions with a cycle of prison "openings" and "closings," as their facilities exceed the allowable 95 percent capacity. Texas prison capacity expanded by 50 percent from 1980 to 1987, while the number of new prisoners increased by 113 percent. During the same period a federal court ordered the State to ease overcrowding through reducing its prison population by 6,500 inmates! Texas is constructing prisons at a pace to increase their capacity by more than 65 percent in just 4 years—a stopgap measure at best. According to their criminal justice director, Rider Scott, the addition of some 26,500 beds will be overly filled by the end of 1990 to the point of again shutting down the institutions, and backing up the overflow in county jails. Even as this was being written, Texas held 38,500 persons in 28 institutions, while another 4,000 state prisoners were serving time in county jails awaiting a prison bed (1988:4B).

A third illustration comes from the District of Columbia where prison overcrowding reached a state of crisis in responding to court-imposed population caps by closing the District's prisons to newly sentenced inmates. Imagine a situation (after October 5, 1988) in which some arrivals were distributed to police precinct holding cells: some to the District of Columbia Superior Court cell block which was never designed for feeding people or for overnight incarceration; some to federal prisons outside the District; and some to institutions across the country, e.g., already crowded facilities in Washington State ("Court Orders," 1987:7 see also, J. Mullen, 1987).

Cost of Imprisonment

Criminal justice is big business, as indicated by its "top 10" status among all government expenditures. Federal, state, and local spending for all such activities in fiscal year 1983 was $39.7 billion—almost 3 percent of all government spending in this country. Approximately $23 billion was spent at the local level, $12 billion by the states, and $5 billion by the federal government. Police protection accounted for the highest amount spent, 52 percent, followed by corrections with 26 percent, and judicial/legal services with 22 percent (Bureau of Justice Statistics, June 1988: front cover).

Among types of justice spending, corrections increased the most—by 15.1 percent from 1982 to 1983; by 50.9 percent from 1980 to 1983 (Bureau of Justice Statistics, September 1987:23). And although estimates vary widely, prison construction costs typically range from $50,000 to $100,000 per cell. The "capital investments" are supplemented by a yearly operating/maintenance expenditure ranging from $10,000 to $25,000 per inmate (Blumstein, n.d.:3; Jacobs, n.d.:l). The Criminal Justice Institute counts 130 prisons for some 53,000 inmates now being constructed at a cost of $2.5 billion, with still another 75,000 convict beds in the planning stage. Moreover, President George Bush is said to favor doubling the current federal prison budget to a new high of $2 billion, about three and one-half times the 1983 figures ("The Far Shore," 1988:11).

In short, we are talking big bucks here in an era of budget deficits, and fears of tax increases and, as Clear and Harris (1987:51) point out, proposals often seriously underestimate eventual correctional expenditures. The money being poured into incarceration makes probation, parole, and college education look like great buys, at least on a cost-per-person basis. You can send your son or daughter to your choice of some of the finest private universities in the land—Cornell, Harvard, Stanford—for less! And if you are not too choosy, their entire 4 years of college tuition will cost less at a good state university than will housing a single inmate for 1 year in a typical state prison! And make no mistake, public education must compete for these dollars, just as do public welfare, housing, environment, hospitals, health, highways, and others (Bureau of Justice Statistics, September 1987:22). Given the recent concern with the quality of our public school system, where do you think an extra one billion dollars a year might be well spent to fight crime?

Litigating Prison Conditions

Litigation has become such an American prison way of life that by the end of 1983, eight states had their prison systems declared unconstitutional; 22 had facilities operating under either a court order or consent decree; and nine more were engaged in litigation. By December 1985, only eight states (Alaska, Minnesota, Montana, Nebraska, New York, New Jersey, North Dakota, and Vermont) had remained **unencumbered** by judicial intervention (Taggart, 1989).

Prison litigation is both intriguing and complex, but prior to the 1960s had been subject to a "hands-off" policy by the federal courts (Bronstein, 1985; see also Conrad 1985. However, with the advent of the Warren court, this posture was abandoned through a series of decisions enlarging the federal court's role in prison administration. The stage was set with two key cases: (1) *Jones v. Cunningham* (1963) in which the Supreme Court ruled that the state prison could employ a **writ of habeas corpus** to challenge not only the legality of their imprisonment, but also to contest the conditions of incarceration; and (2) *Cooper v. Pate* (1964) in which the Court held that prisoners possessed standing to sue in federal court under the Civil Rights Acts of 1871 (see Taggart, 1989).

These were quickly followed by several other cases expanding inmate legal rights, with filings by state prisoners increasing in the federal courts over 120 percent between 1970 and 1983. Arkansas became the initial state affected by this new "hands-on" stance when its entire prison system was found in violation of the cruel and unusual punishment prohibition of the Eighth Amendment (*Holt v. Sarver,* 1969). The district court found constitutional deficiencies in such major areas as facilities, safety, medical services, staff practices, and security. Within the next five years Mississippi and Oklahoma were to be found similarly deficient and under court orders (Taggart, 1989). For two instructive state histories, see Hopper (1985) on Mississippi; Mays and Taggart (1985) on New Mexico. For a focused discussion of Eighth Amendment litigation, see Ingraham and Welford (1987).

In a very carefully constructed study of the first 10 states subject to federal court intervention, Taggart (1989) employed a longitudinal model to examine the impact of court-ordered prison reform on state expenditures for corrections. Controlling for the state's prison population, previous expenditures for corrections, and total state expenditures, he found the greater impact on the capital side of the budget than on the operating side. This has significant implications according to Taggart (1989):

> Although the construction of new facilities may function to redress certain problems iden-
> tified by the courts (e.g., inadequate cell sizes or dormitory living conditions), it is by no
> means a panacea for compliance. It does not ensure changes in administrative practices or
> employee behaviors which many times are of equal importance to the bench. Moreover, if
> capital expenditures are made in response to overcrowded prisons, the lack of concurrent
> expansion in operating budgets may suggest that some other problem areas are only growing
> substantially worse (e.g., inmate/staff ratios). It is entirely possible that a capital intensive
> reform program has helped to make some inmates worse off (Horowitz, 1983).

Certainly, some of these capital outlays would have been spent just as wisely for improving the everyday conditions and programs of existing prisons as for building still more institutions.

Race and Ethnicity

Prisons have long been known for their disproportionate housing of blacks and Hispanics. In 1986 the proportion of blacks in state prisons was 47 percent, almost four times the 1980 proportion of 12 percent in the general United States population; the proportion of Hispanics in these facilities was 13 percent, over twice the 6 percent of the 1980 census (Bureau of Justice Statistics, March 1988:41; Innes, 1988:3). The *lifetime* estimates of incarceration is six times higher for blacks (18%) than for whites (3%). After the initial confinement, probability of further commitments is similar for both races: about one-third of each group who have ever been incarcerated will have been confined four times by age 64 (Bureau of Justice Statistics, 1988:47).

Causes are multiple and controversial (e.g., see Hawkins, 1986; Bridges, Crutchfield & Simpson, 1987; Palley & Robinson, 1988). Nevertheless, genuine concern must be expressed about minority youth being incarcerated in juvenile correctional facilities at rates three to four times that of whites. Their numbers are growing even though overall rates of serious youth crime are declining, with minority youth more likely to be arrested and charged than comparably delinquent white juveniles. As Barry Krisberg and his associates (1987:173) see it, "Although further research on these issues is imperative, it is also crucial that public officials begin testing out new strategies to reduce the tragic trend of ever more minority children growing up behind bars."

Long-Term Incarceration

Deborah Wilson and Gennaro Vito (1988) observe that society's response to crime has contributed to several trends resulting in longer prison terms for convicted felons. Determinate and mandatory sentencing, modifications in parole eligibility criteria, enhanced sentences for recidivists, and longer terms for violent offenders have resulted in increased time served plus a subsequent increase in the proportion of long-term inmates in state facilities. These changes result in programmatic and management concerns to correctional administrators which must be addressed.

These authors define a long-term inmate as "one who has or will be continuously confined for a period of seven years" (Unger & Buchanan, 1985), given a 1986 average time served of 24.8 months. Survey data from 23 correctional agencies reported the percentage of men serving sentences of 7 years or more in state correctional facilities increased from 20.4 percent in 1979 to 24.8 percent in 1984. Some states reported proportions of long-term prisoners as high as 68 percent for males and 55 percent for females (Unger & Buchanan, 1985, cited in Wilson & Vito, 1988:21). Moreover, the percentage of inmates serving sentences of 20 years or more increased from 13.4 percent of all state inmates in 1983 to 15.7 percent in 1987 (Camp & Camp, 1987, cited in Wilson & Vito, 1988:22).

Wilson and Vito (1985:23–24) invoke a vast literature (e.g., Sykes, 1958; Clemmer, 1958; Fox, 1985; Jacobs, 1977) to demonstrate the negative effects of long-term incarceration. They then identify at least eight "demands" which will be created by growing numbers of long-term inmates (Wilson & Vito, 1988:24–25): (1) the need for more bed space; (2) increased financial cost for extended duration of confinement; (3) higher, more costly levels of security; (4) structured activities to fill time voids; (5) specialized mental health services to promote personal adjustment and reduce disciplinary problems; (6) institutional financial assistance to replace diminished outside help; (7) specialized housing and medical services for those becoming elderly; and (8) enhanced pre-release and post-release programs to facilitate readjustment into a changed community after extended absence.

AIDS in Correctional Facilities

Perhaps no one has made a more forceful statement on this issue than National Institute of Justice Director, James K. Stewart (Hammett, April 1987:iii):

For correctional agencies, the problem of AIDS is a formidable challenge. A substantial percentage of inmates fall within identified high-risk groups for AIDS. The presence—or potential presence—of AIDS within the prison is more than a simple health problem; correctional administrators are faced with tough decisions about prevention, institutional management, the best and most equitable means of identifying and treating inmates with AIDS, potential legal issues, and the costs of medical care.

Although data are still lacking, Stewart's concerns are real. As of October 1, 1986, there had been 784 confirmed AIDS cases in 31 state and federal correctional systems—up 72 percent from 455 cases reported as of November 1, 1985, the time of the original survey. This is a large increase in cases, but is actually smaller than the 79 percent national increase from 14,519 cases to 26,002 cases during the same relative time period (Hammett, 1987:4).

The foregoing figures are *cumulative* totals covering the record-keeping period. Twenty-three state and federal systems reported 174 *current* cases of AIDS. Further, they reported a cumulative total of 463 prisoners have died from AIDS while in custody. One study of 177 inmate deaths from AIDS in the New York correctional system revealed the following: 97 percent were males; 76 percent were between 25 and 39 years old; 40 percent were Hispanic; 39 percent were black; 86 percent came from New York City; and 92 percent *admitted* to intravenous drug abuse (Hammett, 1987:4–5).

On the good news side, neither the 1985 nor the 1986 survey identified any AIDS cases among correctional staff attributable to contact with inmates. Ninety-six percent of the federal and state systems have instituted some type of education or training for staff; 86 percent for inmates (Hammett, 1987:6). This is especially important in view of fears (some false) of contamination through biting, spitting, knives, inmate wounds, body searches, disposition of deceased persons, etc.

In sum, AIDS has added still another negative factor to diminish the quality of prison life for both inmates and staff through fear, HIV antibody testing, and a host of lawsuits, some of which are already pending.

Correctional Officer Stress

In summarizing the lot of correctional officers, Peter Kratcoski (1988:27) recently asserted:

> The fear of experiencing assaults from prisoners is part of the daily mindset of a prison guard. Morris and Morris (1980:51) state that the prison officer knows only too well that violence is seldom far below the surface of prison life, and Jacobs and Retsky (1977:61) characterize the guard's world as increasingly pervaded by fear and uncertainty. Fogel (1975:70) stated that a guard performs in a world of fear of the unanticipated.

In his study of one federal institution, Kratcoski (1988) found four particular factors related to assaults against staff: (1) more than 70 percent of the assaults occurred in the detention/high security areas; (2) the majority of all assaults occurred during the day shift (8 A.M. to 4 P.M.); (3) staff with less than 1 year received a disproportionate number of assaults (15% of the staff, yet 35% of assaults); and (4) the majority of assaults were committed by inmates age 25 and younger. These, observes Kratcoski, suggest problems of high staff turnover, inadequate training, and questionable staff support.

Gerald Gaes and William McGuire (1986:41–51), in their comprehensive examination of 19 federal prisons over a 33-month period, found crowding by far to be the most influential variable for predicting both inmate-inmate and inmate-staff assaults (without a weapon).

Cullen, Link, Wolfe, and Frank (1985) advocate separate measurement of work and life stress among correctional officers. In their study of a southern correctional system, they found that role problems and perceived danger were related to life stress among the officers. These variables plus six others (being female, location in maximum security prison; more experience as a C.O.; and lack of peer, family, or supervisory support) were related significantly to work stress.

Such studies and the excellent literature review by Susan Philliber (1987) underscore the importance of stress factors to both staff and inmate welfare. Other than their peers, the guard is said to be the most important person in the inmate's world. If true, their safety, morale, and even their careers are intimately linked with a society of captives and keepers (Sykes, 1958).

The Escalating War on Drugs

It was recently announced that William J. Bennett, the former Secretary of Education, has been selected as the new administration's first "Drug Czar." It seems quite certain that drug use, abuse, and distribution will loom larger as incarceration factors as we step up the war of those fronts.* A recent signal to this effect was given by the first charges filed under a new federal antidrug law which requires federal judges to impose life sentences without parole on defendants convicted of drug trafficking under certain circumstances ("California 1st," 1989:6A; see also Inciardi, 1986).

Drug use is far greater among prison inmates (78%) than in the general population (37%). Moreover, two out of five prison inmates reported they were under the influence of drugs or were very drunk around the time of their incarceration offense (Bureau of Justice Statistics, March 1988:50–51). Yet we have to wonder to what degree drug abuse receives adequate attention in prison. The recent news from Texas is not encouraging when it is reported 67 percent of their drug-abusing inmates are released from prison without receiving any treatment. Reportedly, in 1988 Texas provided only one drug-abuse counselor for 1,667 addicted prisoners; those receiving help averaged only 10 hours of treatment during their confinement. Only 75 inmates received "intensive treatment" during the year ("67% of Drug-Abuse Inmates," 1988:4B). The Governor of Texas is asking the 1989 legislature to authorize drug testing of inmates in prison and before they are released on parole (*El Paso Times,* 1989:4B). Governor Clements is also seeking an additional $343 million for new prison construction to provide 11,000 more prison beds ("Clements: Prisons Need," 1989:4B). The pressure for space continues.

CONCLUSIONS

Stephen D. Gottfredson and Sean McConville (1988:9) have recently described this state of affairs as "America's Correctional Crisis," where far-reaching decisions are made with uncertainty and compromise. Instead, they hope, "for more informed and balanced debate and for the encouragement of productive and acceptable solutions to problems that can be neglected only at some considerable risk to our nation's future (1988:10)." We should be listening to such counsel which, if anything, seems understated, requiring added emphasis and urgency.

Accordingly, two broad proposals are offered.

First, it is time to convene another President's Commission on Law Enforcement and Administration of Justice (1967). President Lyndon B. Johnson established his Commission on July 23, 1965, almost a quarter century ago. President Bush could initiate the largest scale "brain trust" this Nation has ever known to plan the most comprehensive strategy for crime prevention, treatment, and control in history. So doing is panacea, of course, for many difficulties are attached to such task forces (e.g., see Allen, 1973). But somehow, a concerted collective effort must be made to bring together the vast reservoir of knowledge and ideas accumulating in various disparate forms and places, both here and abroad, during the past three decades.

It would be presumptuous to suggest an agenda here, but no issue should be **sacrosanct** or beyond debate. From the start it must be recognized that corrections is a component of an interdependent but uncoordinated system of justice which must be understood in relation to the wider structures of social control in American society. This means we must examine criminality in a multilayered fashion—from inception and process to change; from societal ills and malfunctioning to social reform; from community roots to community return. Criminality and delinquency are not unrelated to conditions and problems of other social institutions—family (e.g., domestic violence, runaways); economy (e.g., poverty, unemployment, homelessness); education (e.g., dropouts, drugs); and government (e.g., mismanagement, inadequate funding).

Each of us probably possesses favored issues. For instance, one central probe could (should) be directed at what Shover and Einstadter (1988:204–206) call the "ironies of correctional reform," wherein promising proposals and programs such as diversion or halfway houses become perverted into the much criticized widening effect (Lemert, 1981). Is it possible to prevent a similar fate and abuse of, say a technologically feasible notion such as home incarceration through electronic monitoring (Ball, Huff & Lilly, 1988)? This would also be an excellent forum to sweep aside numerous myths about crime, delinquency, and corrections (for example, see Bohm, 1987; Pepinsky & Jesilow, 1984, 1985; Walker, 1989; Walters & White, 1988; and Wright, 1987). The crime crisis is bad enough without being haunted by widespread misconceptions held by the public, criminal justice practitioners, and professional criminologists.

Second, it would be appropriate to seriously consider William G. Nagel's (1977) advocacy of a moratorium on prison construction. Imagine such a joint state and federal policy effective from, say, 1991 through 1995. The 5-year "savings" could be well invested in the Commission's work; to improving existing prisons; to upgrading community-based corrections; and to fundamental programs involving the health, education, and welfare of the nation's youth.

This last point is particularly important in light of Lamar Empey's (1974:1096) fear that a war on crime could be waged against our country's youth, with a severe loss to basic humanitarian values. Indeed, we must take exception to a social control policy based primarily on measures of exclusion (e.g., isolation, segregation) rather than inclusion (e.g., resocialization, integration) (Cohen, 1985). Shover and Einstadter (1988:208), have stated well the implications.

> ...precisely those conditions which prevent persons from becoming productive, socially conscious members of society, conditions which exclude and cast them out, are the conditions which create the dangerous crime potential we wish to prevent.
>
> The current direction corrections is taking is exclusionary. Whether the cycle will change in the near future remains an open question, but our ultimate well-being as a democratic society depends on the answer.

There are no easy answers to complex problems (Conrad, 1985). But perhaps we could discover some profound responses through starting the final decade of this millenium with a high-level Commission with the authority, organization, talent, time, and incentives to develop imaginative, innovative, comprehensive policies on behalf of the Nation's citizenry.

REFERENCES

ALLEN, H. E. "The Task Force Model: As a Vehicle for Correctional Change." *Georgia Journal of Corrections,* July 1973, pp. 35–39.

BALL, R. A., G. R. HUFF & J. R. LILLY. *House Arrest and Correctional Policy: Doing Time at Home,* Newbury Park, CA: Sage Publications, 1988.

BLUMSTEIN, A. "Prison Crowding" (Crime File Study Guide). Washington, DC: National Institute of Justice, no date.

BOHM, R. M. "Myths about Criminology and Criminal Justice: A Review Essay." *Justice Quarterly,* 4(4), December 1987, pp. 631–642.

BRIDGES, G. S., R. D. CRUTCHFIELD & E. E. SIMPSON. "Crime, Social Structure and Criminal Punishment: White and Nonwhite Rates of Imprisonment." *Social Problems,* 34(4), October 1987, pp. 345–361.

BRONSTEIN, A. J. "Prisoners and Their Endangered Rights." *The Prison Journal,* 65(1). Spring–Summer 1985, pp. 3–17.

BUREAU OF JUSTICE STATISTICS. *Time Served in Prison.* Washington, DC: U.S. Department of Justice, June 1984.

BUREAU OF JUSTICE STATISTICS. *BJS Data Report, 1986.* Washington DC: U.S. Department of Justice, September 1987.

BUREAU OF JUSTICE STATISTICS. *Correctional Populations in the United States, 1985.* Washington, DC: U.S. Department of Justice, December 1987.

BUREAU OF JUSTICE STATISTICS. *Report to the Nation on Crime and Justice,* 2nd ed. Washington, DC: U.S. Department of Justice, March 1988.

BUREAU OF JUSTICE STATISTICS. *Justice Expenditure and Employment Extracts: 1982 and 1983.* Washington, DC: U.S. Department of Justice, June 1988.

"California 1st to Try No-Parole Drug Law." *El Paso Times*, January 5, 1989, p. 6A.

CAMP, G. M. & C. G. CAMP. *The Corrections Yearbook.* South Salem, NY: Criminal Justice Institute, 1983.

CLARK R. *Crime in America: Observations on Its Nature, Causes, Prevention, and Control.* New York: Simon and Schuster, 1970.

CLEAR, T. R. & P. M. HARRIS. "The Costs of Incarceration." In S. D. Gottfredson & S. McConville (eds.), *America's Correctional Crisis.* New York: Greenwood Press, 1987, pp. 37–55.

"Clements: Prisons Need 11,000 Beds." *El Paso Times,* January 13, 1989, p. 4b.

"Clements Urges Inmate Drug Testing." *El Paso Times,* January 11, l989, p. 4b.

CLEMMER, D. *The Prison Community* New York: Holt, Rinehart & Winston, 1958.

COHEN, S. *Visions of Social Control.* Cambridge, U.K.: Polity Press, 1985.

CONRAD, J. R. "The View from the Witness Chair." *The Prison Journal,* 65(1), Spring–Summer 1985, pp. 18–25.

"Court Orders Trigger Closing of D.C. Prisons to New inmates." *Criminal Justice Newsletter,* 19(21), November 1, 1988 p. 7.

CULLEN, F. T., B. G. LINK, N. T. WOLFE & J. FRANK. "The Social Dimensions of Officer Stress." *Justice Quarterly,* 2(4), December 1985, pp. 505–533.

EMPEY, L. T. "Crime Prevention: The Fugitive Utopia." In D. Glaser (ed.), *Handbook of Criminology.* Chicago: Rand McNally, 1974.

ENNIS, P. H. "Crime, Victims, and the Police." *Transaction,* 4, June 1967, pp. 36–44.

"The Far Shore of America's Bulging Prisons." *U.S. News and World Report,* 105(19), November 14, 1988, pp. 11–12.

FINN, P. "Victims" (Crime File Study Guide). Washington, DC: National Institute of Justice, no date.

FOGEL, D. *We Are Living Proof.* Cincinnati, OH: Anderson Publishing Co., 1975.

FOX, V. *Introduction to Corrections,* 3rd ed. Englewood Cliffs, NJ: Prentice-Hall, 1985.

GAES, G. G. & N. J. MCGUIRE. "Prison Violence: The Contribution of Crowding versus Other Determinants of Prison Assault Rates." *Journal of Research in Crime and Delinquency,* 22(1). February 1985, pp. 41–65.

GLASER, D. *The Effectiveness of a Prison and Parole System.* Indianapolis, IN: Bobbs-Merrill, 1964.

GOTTFREDSON, S. D. & S. MCCONVILLE (eds.). *America's Correctional Crisis: Prison Populations and Public Policy.* New York: Greenwood Press, 1987.

HAMMET, T. M. *1986 Update: AIDS in Correctional Facilities,* Washington, DC: National Institute of Justice, April 1987.

HAWKINS, D. R. "Race, Crime Type, and Imprisonment." *Justice Quarterly,* 3(3), September 1986, pp. 251–269.

HEYNS, G. "The 'Treat-'em-Rough' Boys Are Here Again." *Federal Probation,* 31(2), June 1967, pp. 6–10.

HOPPER, C. B. "The Impact of Litigation on Mississippi's Prison System." *The Prison Journal,* 65(1), Spring–Summer 1985, pp. 54–63.

HOROWITZ, D. L. "Decreeing Organizational Change: Judicial Supervision of Public Institutions." *Duke Law Journal,* 1983, pp. 1265–1307.

INCIARDI, J. A. *The War on Drugs: Heroin, Cocaine, Crime and Public Policy.* Palo Alto, CA: Mayfield Publishing Company, 1986.

INGRAHAM, B. L. & C. R WELLFORD. "The Totality of Conditions Test in Eighth-Amendment Litigation." In S.D. Gottfredson & S. McConville (eds.), *America's Correctional Crisis.* New York: Greenwood Press, 1987, pp. 13–36.

INNES, C. A. *Population Density in State Prisons.* Bureau of Justice Statistics Special Report. Washington, DC: National Institute of Justice, December 1986.

INNES, C. A. *Profile of State Prison Inmates, 1986.* Bureau of Justice Statistics Special Report. Washington, DC: National Institute of Justice, January 1988.

JACOBS, J. B. "Inside Prisons" (Crime File Study Guide). National Institute of Justice, no date.

JACOBS, J. B. *Statesville: The Penitentiary in Mass Society.* Chicago: University of Chicago Press, 1977.

JACOBS, J. B. & H. G. RETSKY. "Prison Guard." In R. G. Leger & J. R. Stratton (eds.), *The Sociology of Corrections: A Book of Readings.* New York: John Wiley and Sons, 1977.

KRATCOSKI, P. C. "The Implications of Research Explaining Prison Violence and Disruption." *Federal Probation,* 52(1), March 1988, pp. 27–32.

KRISBERG, B. I., I. SCHWARTZ, G. FISHMAN, Z. EISIKOVITS, E. GUTTMAN & K. JOE. "The Incarceration of Minority Youth." *Crime and Delinquency,* 33(2), April 1987, pp. 173–205.

LEMERT, E. M. "Diversion in Juvenile Justice: What Hath Been Wrought?" *Journal of Research in Crime and Delinquency,* 18(1), January 1981, pp. 34–46.

MAYS, G. L. & W. A. TAGGART. "The Impact of Litigation on Changing New Mexico Prison Conditions." *The Prison Journal, 65*(1), Spring–Summer 1985, pp. 38–53.

MORRIS, T. P. & P. J. MORRIS. "Where Staff and Prisoners Meet," in B. M. Crouch (ed.), *The Keepers— Prison Guards and Contemporary Corrections.* Springfield, IL: Charles C Thomas, 1980.

MULLEN, J. "State Responses to Prison Crowding: The Politics of Change." In S. D. Gottfredson & S. McConville (eds.), *America's Correctional Crisis,* New York: Greenwood Press, 1987, pp. 79–109.

NAGEL, W. G. "On Behalf of a Moratorium on Prison Construction." *Crime and Delinquency.* 23(2), April 1977, pp. 154–172.

PALLEY, H. A. & D. A. ROBINSON, "Black on Black Crime." *Society,* 25(5), July–August 1988, pp. 59–62.

PEPINSKY, H. E. & P. JESILOW. *Myths That Cause Crime.* Cabin John, MD: Seven Locks Press, 1984, 1985.

PHILLIBER, S. "Thy Brother's Keeper: A Review of the Literature on Correctional Officers." *Justice Quarterly, 4*(1), March 1987, pp. 9–37.

PRESIDENT'S COMMISSION ON LAW ENFORCEMENT AND ADMINISTRATION OF JUSTICE. *The Challenge of Crime in a Free Society.* Washington, DC: U.S. Government Printing Office, 1967.

SCHLESINGER, S. "Prison Crowding in the United States: The Data." *Criminal Justice Research Bulletin,* 3(1),1987, pp. 1–3.

SHOVER, N. & W. J. EINSTADTER. *Analyzing American Corrections.* Belmont, CA: Wadsworth Publishing Company, 1988.

SILBERMAN, C. *Criminal Violence, Criminal Justice.* New York: Random House, 1978.

"67% of Drug-Abuse Inmates Go Untreated in Prison." *El Paso Times.* December 19, 1988, p. 4B.

SYKES, G. *The Society of Captives.* Princeton, NJ: Princeton University Press, 1958.

TAGGART, W. A. "Redefining the Power of the Federal Judiciary: The Impact of Court-Ordered Prison Reform on State Expenditures for Corrections." *Law and Society Review,* 23(2), 1989, pp. 501–531.

UNGER, C. A. & R. A. BUCHANAN. *Managing Long-Term Inmates.* Washington, DC: National Institute of Corrections, 1985.

VAN DEN HAAG, E. *Punishing Criminals: Concerning a Very Old and Painful Question.* New York: Basic Books, 1975.

WALKER, S. *Sense and Nonsense about Crime: A Policy Guide,* 2nd ed. Pacific Grove, CA: Brooks/Cole, 1989.

WALTERS, G. D. & T. W. WHITE. "Crime, Popular Mythology, and Personal Responsibility." *Federal Probation,* 52(1), March 1988, pp. 18–26.

WILSON, D. G. & G. R VITO. "Long-Term Inmates: Special Needs and Management Considerations." *Federal Probation,* 52(3), September 1988, pp. 21–26.

WRIGHT, K. N. *The Great American Crime Myth.* Westport, CT: Greenwood Press, 1987.

CASES CITED

Cooper v. Pate, 378 U.S. 546 (1964).
Holt v. Sarver, 300 F. Supp. 825 (E. D. Ark. 1969).
Jones v. Cunningham, 371 U.S. 236 (1963).

QUESTIONS FOR DISCUSSION

1. List and discuss the evidence presented that imprisonment, as a solution to crime, is a myth.
2. The author presents eight issues about prisons that he considers to be particularly important. List and discuss any five of these issues.
3. This article states that "we must take exception to a social control policy based primarily on measures of exclusion rather than inclusion." What is meant by this statement?

APPLICATIONS

1. Let us assume that you are an expert in the area of criminology and corrections. You have been asked to provide recommendations that address the issue of crime, prison overcrowding, and alternatives to imprisonment. List and discuss five recommendations for each issue based on what you have read as well as your own experiences.
2. From application 1, compare your recommendations with those of other members of your class. Are there any similarities or differences? In your discussions, listen carefully to how other class members justify their recommendations and compare to your own justifications. What happens?

Juvenile Justice

The system of juvenile justice, which emerged and formed over the last century and a half, is perhaps the most enigmatic feature of the entire criminal justice system. Issues such as age of culpability, jurisdiction, philosophy behind a separate system, and status offenses serve as fuel in the evolution of this enigma. The child-saving movements and the age of culpability are two of the major forces that have shaped this system. Those under a certain age were and are seen as less capable of knowing how to act responsibly or to distinguish between right and wrong. In addition, those under a certain age were and are seen as salvageable. They deserve another chance and need help to correct and go on to lead productive lives. After a certain age, usually 18, a person is considered totally responsible for his or her behavior. However, any person under this magic age of responsibility is generally viewed as somehow less than responsible for his or her actions. The statuses related to age alone have caused more confusion than any other single variable related to the juvenile justice system.

There are no simple explanations regarding the development of the juvenile justice system in the United States. There are, however, several issues and developments that provide some historical relevance in these matters. Processes such as industrialization, urbanization, economic development, political liberalism, and secularization produced social and cultural changes for the entire world. These processes, especially over the last 200 years, significantly changed societal reactions to youth. Youth statuses and roles have changed so dramatically that the individual rights of teens and children are essentially equal to those of adults. In a broad sense, it is more important to understand the changing societal reactions to youths rather than the behavior of youths. As the family changed, the authority of the state began to intercede as a superparent charged with relieving the ills of children and youths. The result has been less parental authority and more intervention by government into the lives of young people who are neglected, abused, or delinquent. In addition, youth culture has grown tremendously, so that teens have vast economic, social, and even political power and influence. The affluence of children and teens today is remarkable compared to that of their parents and especially, their grandparents. As the statuses and roles of modern youth have increased, so have the problems they face. The social world has become extremely complicated, and teens especially have problems adjusting to these changes. In a concomitant sense, the social milieu of families, schools, peer groups, and many others have transformed many youths into the worst of possibilities. At-risk groups of youths and children include, but are not restricted to, dysfunctional families, victims of child sexual and physical abuse, neglect, and family disorganization; and unprecedented substance abuse by adults and teens—in addition to levels of violence that are unacceptable. Experts and other citizens share the sense that the problems are getting worse, not better. The rate of social and cultural change has transformed the United States, and juvenile delinquency has become a top concern for the country. Issues such as violent youth gangs, school violence, drug addiction, and other teen-related criminality cry out for solutions.

In reality, solutions have often been directed toward treating the symptoms rather than treating the causes of delinquency. Essentially, all youths misbehave and deviate, but the most serious forms of delinquency are produced and perpetuated by particular social environments and influences. Solutions must be directed at processes that produce greater individual responsibilities and not just greater individual freedom for youths. As you study the articles contained in this part of the anthology, bear in mind that the majority of the most serious career criminals in our maximum security prisons come from environments of violence, neglect, and abuse. These people care little for themselves and even less for others because of the ways they were responded to beginning early in their lives. Just as the physical body would not grow and mature properly if deprived of vitamins and nourishment, the normal psychology cannot develop without continuous nurturing and love. After only a few short years of abuse and/or neglect, with the resulting poor self-concept, the person may never accept total responsibility for his or her actions and may spend the remainder of his or her life blaming others for failure. Without efforts and resources directed at making the very early years of a child's life the most positive and loving, we will only continue to react to the worst rather than creating the best in our nation's youths.

The United States inherited the doctrine of *parens patriae* from England and it became the cornerstone of our juvenile justice system. The doctrine advocates that the state serve as a substitute parent for children of neglect and abuse. Ralph A. Weisheit and Diane M. Alexander examine this important doctrine in "Juvenile Justice Philosophy and the Demise of *Parens Patriae*." The doctrine tends to have significant support among judges due to the tremendous number of concerns that come before the court. The court's authority has greatly increased and the main concern is still the welfare of the juveniles that come within the purview of the court.

Ilene R. Bergsmann further champions the concerns of females in the juvenile justice system in "The Forgotten Few: Juvenile Female Offenders " Important here are the processes of gender bias and stereotyping that permeate social institutions besides the major components of the Juvenile Justice system.

When reading "The Saints and the Roughnecks," keep clearly in mind that societal reactions are often the keys to understanding delinquency. As Bergsmann points out in the preceding article, much of the delinquency is a result of ascription rather than behavior.

Most of us can immediately relate this article to our own teenaged school days. The societal reaction perspective is eloquently explained by William Chambliss in this fine piece of research

   We close our section on juvenile justice with Martha-Elin Blomquist and Martin L. Forst's article "Punishment, Accountability, and the New Juvenile Justice." These authors suggest, as do many others, that the new system of juvenile justice is emerging due more to political expediency than to clearly specified goals regarding the system. This does not necessarily suggest that the rehabilitation model is dead, but that the transformations currently under way show up weaknesses in the old system in light of new knowledge and facts regarding juveniles and their care.

Juvenile Justice Philosophy and the Demise of *Parens Patriae*

Ralph A. Weisheit • Diane M. Alexander

INTRODUCTION

The cornerstone of juvenile justice philosophy in America has been the principle of *parens patriae*. Under this principle, the state was to act in *loco parentis* or as a substitute parent to the child. The concept is English in origin and was developed specifically to allow the state to intervene in behalf of dependent children, usually those with money. It was *not* originally applied to delinquent children, and thus the concept of rehabilitation was not regarded as relevant (Curtis, 1976:899):

> The motivating reason to apply the *parens patriae* theory was the need to support and to care for children, not to reform or rehabilitate them. The chancery courts, in applying and developing the theory, did not have to grapple with the problems of deviant conduct. The theory was conceived to aid the children who stood as a source of hope for the kingdom, not as a threat to its stability.

Although the principle of *parens patriae* has been traced to English law, the legal justification for applying this principle to delinquents in the United States was first spelled out in the 1838 case of *Exparte Crouse* (Curtis, 1976; *Rendleman, 1971; Schlossman, 1977*). In this case, Mary Ann Crouse was committed to the Philadelphia House of Refuge by her mother for being incorrigible. Her father opposed the incarceration and argued that since she had been incarcerated without a jury trial the state's actions were unconstitutional. The court denied the father's petition, noting that: "The House of Refuge is not a prison, but a school where reformation and not punishment is the end" (cited in Pisciotta, 1982:411).

While the idea of *parens patriae* is familiar to most, the kinds of responses which constitute *parens patriae* are more ambiguous. For some, the term has been treated as synonymous with rehabilitation and has been contrasted with a desire for punishment (Cullen, Golden, and Cullen, 1983). There is nothing inherent in the idea of *parens patriae,* however, which requires that it be tied directly to rehabilitation or which precludes punishment. There are several ways in which punishment is consistent with *parens patriae.* First, it is possible to believe that punishment is the best way to rehabilitate and reform youth, as can be seen in such approaches as "reality therapy" (Glasser, 1965). Second, punishment may be administered "for the child's own good" without any necessary direct link to rehabilitation. In the case of *Schall v. Martin* (1984), for example, the Supreme Court held that preventive detention of juveniles was consistent with the principle of *parens patriae* even though there was no intention to provide treatment or rehabilitation. Protecting the community and protecting the child from his or her own misbehavior were deemed legitimate objectives of *parens patriae* (1984:2410):

> Children, by definition, are not assumed to have the capacity to take care of themselves. They are assumed to be subject to the control of their parents, and if parental control falters, the State must play its part as *parens patriae*…In this respect, the juvenile's liberty interest may, in appropriate circumstances, be subordinated to the State's "*parens patriae* interest in preserving and promoting the welfare of the child."

Understanding of *parens patriae* can be clouded by equating it with rehabilitation since the "fit" of these two ideas is imperfect at best. Thus, it has led liberals to be shocked and dismayed at the harsh treatment some juveniles have received in the hands of the court (e.g., Kittrie, 1971; Platt, 1969; Schur, 1973). At the same time, conservatives and the public have been equally dismayed at the lenient treatment afforded some juveniles (see Cullen and Gilbert, 1982; Cullen, Golden, and Cullen, 1983). Some have argued that although the language used in the handling of juveniles periodically shifts between treatment and punishment, the actual manner in which juveniles are handled has changed little since the origins of the juvenile court (Miller, 1979). Further, what changes have been introduced have not been the result of changing philosophies of those responsible for juvenile offenders, but in the Supreme Court's changing applications of the Constitution to juvenile cases.

These apparent contradictions in the treatment of juveniles in the justice system make sense when the term *parens patriae* is equated with the idea of *paternalism* rather than rehabilitation. Paternalism implies no firm commitment to rehabilitation but suggests a general attitude of protectiveness from which either gentle or harsh treatment might be justified. At a policy level, paternalism implies broad discretion for the courts to deal with juvenile offenders as the court deems best, with kindness being shown to the deserving (i.e., compliant) and harsh treatment for the recalcitrant. It also implies a willingness to intervene in the lives of juveniles to prevent more serious misbehaviors in the future.

The manner in which paternalism operates, and the distinction between paternalism and rehabilitation, can be shown with examples from outside of the juvenile justice system. For example, under early paternalistic laws, female offenders were "protected" by giving them indeterminate prison sentences which were frequently longer than the fixed sentences given men for the same offense (Rafter, 1985; Moulds, 1978; Temin, 1973). Further, this discrepancy is particularly marked for status offenses in which the court has had the greatest discretion (Anderson, 1976; Chesney-Lind, 1977, 1979, 1988). It has also been argued that under paternalism, the ultimate result of state intervention has not been independence, as rehabilitation implies, but forced dependence (Liazos, 1974). Thus, the relationship between rehabilitation and *parens patriae* has not been clear.

These apparent contradictions in the treatment of juveniles in the justice system make it difficult to talk about the "philosophy of the juvenile" court as a single widely agreed upon idea. Understanding how *parens patriae* works is further complicated by the fact that in the 1980's there have been a number of changes in the formal response to juvenile offenders. Some argue that these changes are so sweeping that they may threaten the very existence of the juvenile court (McNally, 1983, 1984; Sanborn, 1982).

THE CHANGING NATURE OF *PARENS PATRIAE*

In recent years, concern about the problem of crime and frustration over the seeming ineffectiveness of efforts to treat offenders has led to a tougher stance toward criminals. Longer prison sentences are being imposed, the death penalty has been resurrected, and more restrictive community-based sentencing has been implemented. Further, the rationale for sentencing has shifted from rehabilitation to just deserts. This changing sentiment regarding adult offenders has also influenced the response to juveniles. The execution of juveniles is now a real possibility, many states have increased the number of offenses for which juveniles may be waived to adult courts, the age at which juveniles could be tried as adults has been lowered in several states, and incarceration has become a frequent response to juvenile crime (Hufstedler, 1984; Krisberg et al., 1986; Ohlin, 1983; Skibinski and Koszuth, 1986; Streib, 1987). Further, the goal of removing juveniles from adult jails is little closer to realization than when it was first advocated as a national priority in 1974 (Schwartz, 1988).

The purpose of this study is to examine the principle of *parens patriae* during a period in which the rehabilitative ideal had come under attack and to describe current judicial philosophy regarding juveniles. It does this by treating *parens patriae* as having several dimensions, including discretion, intervention, and treatment.

THE DATA

The data for this story were gathered using a self-report mail survey. The sampling frame was a list of all 738 circuit court judges in the state of Illinois as of April 1987. This list was provided by the Administrative Office of the Illinois Courts, the agency responsible for court administration throughout the state. There is no single list of juvenile court judges in Illinois, as judges rotate in this position and in many rural and suburban areas split their caseloads between juvenile and adult cases. Thus, even judges who do not routinely handle juvenile cases now may have done so in the past or might in the future. Further, it was deemed important to include all circuit court judges because in cases involving serious offenses juveniles are sometimes transferred to adult court. Systematic sampling was used to select one-half (368) of these judges for the survey sample. Of the 368 surveyed judges, responses were obtained from 220 (60 percent). Of these, 199 provided usable surveys; the remaining indicated they felt they knew too little about juvenile cases to provide informed responses.[1]

As Table 1 shows, the responding judges were relatively homogenous on several demographic characteristics. Only 10 (5 percent) were female and only 8 (4 percent) were nonwhite. Their ages ranged from 33 to 74, with an average of 51 years. On the average these judges had been on the bench for 8.6 years, and 30 percent routinely had juveniles make up more than 10 percent of their caseload.

Illinois is a good state in which to study *parens patriae* in a changing political climate. In the last decade Illinois has instituted several changes in the legal response to juveniles which mirror those occurring nationally. First, it has sharpened the distinction between criminal and noncriminal juvenile offenders by shifting primary responsibility for status offenses away from the juvenile court and to social service agencies. Second, the law now allows juveniles to be sentenced directly to detention for up to 30 days. Before this the only option for incarceration was commitment to the state Department of Corrections, which itself placed restrictions on which youth could be incarcerated. Third, juveniles found to be "habitual offenders" are given a mandatory determinate sentence to the Department of Corrections until they turn 21. Further, this is the only circumstance under which a juvenile has a right to a jury trial, aside from being waived to an adult court. Finally, the Illinois

Table 1   CHARACTERISTICS OF JUDGES IN THE SAMPLE (199 CASES)

Mean age (years)	51.2
Percent male	95.0
Percent white	96.5
Percent of caseload which involves juveniles	
Less than 10 percent	70.5
10 to 25 percent	16.8
26 percent or more	6.6
Only juvenile cases	6.1
Political position (%)	
Extremely liberal	1.5
Somewhat liberal	14.1
Moderate	45.5
Somewhat conservative	36.4
Extremely conservative	2.5
Years as a judge (%)	
Less than 1 year	8.5
1 to 5 years	30.2
5 to 10 years	28.1
10 to 15 years	16.1
More than 15 years	17.1

statutes were changed to provide for the mandatory waiver to adult court for a variety of offenses committed by those 15 years old or older. Offenses which result in a mandatory waiver include first degree murder, aggravated criminal sexual assault, armed robbery with a firearm, possession of weapons on school grounds, and the possession of controlled substances on school grounds. Thus, in a number of respects changes in Illinois reflect those in other states. The issue addressed in this article is whether these administrative changes reflect a basic rejection of *parens patriae*.

DISCRETION

While *parens patriae* is an elusive concept, one of its key elements is discretion by criminal justice authorities. In principle, discretion allows authorities to tailor their responses to the unique characteristics of each offender. Several questions in the study focused on the legal rights which should be afforded juveniles, an issue which directly corresponds to the discretion available to the court. The responses to these items are shown in Table 2 and indicate a reluctance to undermine judicial discretion. For example, when asked if juveniles had too few or too many legal rights when appearing in juvenile court, only 16 percent thought that juveniles currently had too many legal rights. Most judges (76 percent) thought that juveniles had about the proper number of legal rights. Only 15 percent favored abolishing the juvenile court and handling all juvenile cases under adult rules of law. It was clear from their responses that judges favored formal procedures for handling juveniles but wanted to keep these procedures separate from those for adults. Only 8 percent of respondents would support giving judges the power to waive juveniles to adult court for misdemeanors and only 12 percent believed that the legal age at which juveniles should be treated as adults in court should be lowered. (In Illinois the minimum age for waiver to adult court is 13 years.)

Though opinions were divided, there was limited support for a more formalized procedure for the handling of juveniles. Forty-four percent, for example, thought that

Table 2   PERCENT OF JUDGES AGREEING WITH STATEMENTS REGARDING DISCRETION AND PUNISHMENT BY THE COURT (199 CASES)

Juveniles who appear in juvenile court currently have too many legal rights	16.8
Juvenile court should be abolished and juvenile cases should be decided using the same rules of law that apply to adults	15.1
Juvenile court procedures should be more similar to those in adult court	43.9
Juvenile court hearings should be open to the public in the same way that adult hearings are open	43.9
In 1986 the Illinois Supreme Court ruled that determinate or fixed sentences for juveniles were allowable. Do you approve or disapprove of allowing determinate sentences in juvenile court?	80.2

juvenile courts should more closely model themselves after adult courts. Given this, it should not be surprising that many (44 percent) favor making juvenile court proceedings public and most (80 percent) agree with a 1986 Illinois Supreme Court ruling which allowed fixed or determinate sentencing in the juvenile court.

Overall, these judges prefer a more formal processing of juvenile offenders. This did not mean they favored abandoning the juvenile court or dramatically altering the number of legal rights available to juveniles. They did favor having more options in handling juvenile cases, such as the authority to give determinate sentences.

INTERVENTION BY THE COURT

The discussion of judicial discretion focused on one aspect of *parens patriae*—procedural formality in handling of juvenile offenders. Another important issue raised by the application of *parens patriae* is the nature and extent to which the legal system intrudes into the lives of juveniles. Judges were asked whether they believed that the courts generally intervene too early, too late, or at about the right time in the lives of juvenile offenders. Sixty percent thought that the courts intervened too late and only 4 percent thought they intervened too early, thus suggesting that using the court as a tool for early intervention is still a popular idea.

The court is not the only agency which serves as a **surrogate** parent. The school is also an important agency of social control. One way to assess the extent to which judges support court intervention is to determine where they would prefer to draw the boundary between the authority of the school and of the court. One way to determine this is to find out if judges support intervention for *noncriminal* misbehavior in the school. Over two-thirds of the judges in this sample (67 percent) favored sending **truants** to the juvenile court.

Events in Illinois demonstrate the extent to which judges view this kind of intervention for truancy as important. Prior to 1982, judges in Illinois took a firm stance regarding truancy. Truancy was not a separate criminal offense, but being truant could lead a youngster to be defined as a Minor in Need of Supervision (MINS), for which legal punishment was not an option for the court. A number of judges circumvented this by first ordering the minor to attend school and if the truancy persisted, then charging them with indirect contempt of court. This gave the judge the option of sentencing the truant to up to 6 months in detention, a fine, and probation. In 1982 the statutes were changed and social service agencies were given primary jurisdiction over status offenders, undercutting the power of judges to impose legal penalties for truancy. Many judges opposed these revisions, preferring to keep truancy under judicial authority.

To place their views on truancy in some perspective, judges were also asked about *criminal* misbehavior in the school. Judges were given a list of 11 crimes in the school and asked whether school officials should always, sometimes, or never report these to the police for formal legal actions. Table 3 shows that in general, these judges favored active legal intrusion into criminal behavior which occurs in the school. What is surprising is that they favor a legal response to truancy *more often* than they favor a legal response to the use of alcohol, theft, threatening other students, threatening teachers, fighting, or altering driver's licenses. In fact, they give the same support to legal intervention for truancy as they show for intervention for marijuana use in school. It appears that these judges support the idea that the court should be used not only as a formal response to juvenile crime but as a tool for crime prevention. This interpretation is supported by the responses of judges to our survey, 85 percent of whom agreed that "Preventing truancy is a good way to prevent delinquency." This emphasis on prevention, of course, is a key element of *parens patriae* and a justification for court intervention.

REHABILITATION

The general concept of rehabilitation, like such ideas as justice, honesty, or patriotism, is difficult to oppose. In the abstract, such ideas are vague and are likely to elicit responses which are strongly colored by social desirability. Consequently, asking whether judges (or anyone else) support or oppose rehabilitation as an abstract principle is not a fruitful approach. Instead, other measures were utilized. One group of measures forced judges to prioritize treatment among other criminal justice objectives (such as punishment or restitution). A second set of measures tapped perceived treatment effectiveness.

Support for Rehabilitation

The most direct measures of support for rehabilitation were two questions in which judges were asked the most important considerations when (1) deciding whether to waive a juvenile

Table 3   SUPPORT FOR FORMAL LEGAL ACTION AGAINST MISBEHAVIOR IN THE SCHOOL (199 CASES)

Misbehavior	Percent Believing the Act Should Always Be Referred for Formal Legal Action
Use of alcohol in school	37.1%
Use of marijuana in school	68.0
Use of hard drugs in school	93.9
Stealing something of value from a student	38.8
Evidence of gang recruitment in school	84.2
A student threatens to physically harm another student	32.3
A student threatens to physically harm a teacher	57.4
An in-school fight between two students	4.1
A student strikes a teacher with his fist	75.0
A student is forced to pay money to another student to be left alone	79.8
A teacher finds a driver's license which was altered to make the student appear 21	50.0

to an adult court and (2) deciding a case involving an adult offender. For each of these situations judges were asked to rank the following five considerations: "Treatment of the Offender," "Punishment of the Offender," "Protection of Society by Removal of the Offender," "Set an Example for Others," and "Restitution to Victims." The relative ranking of treatment in each of these situations is an indication of support for rehabilitation.

Regarding both juveniles who might be waived to adult court and the trying of adult cases, judges differed widely in the priority they assigned treatment. For transfers to adult court, about one-fifth ranked treatment first among their considerations, but 30 percent ranked it fourth or fifth. As Table 4 shows, there was less emphasis on rehabilitation for adult cases, but it was by no means discounted. Nearly one-third of the judges ranked treatment first or second among considerations for adult offenders.

These two indicators suggest that the principle of rehabilitation is very much alive for both serious juvenile offenders and for adults but that it is by no means universally embraced and that some judges give it little weight at all. In fact, the consideration most often ranked first for both juvenile transfers (63.4 percent) and adult cases (62.7 percent) was the protection of society. In light of the discussion above regarding paternalism this is an interesting response, for it has little to do with either reforming or protecting the offender (and hence with paternalism). It is also interesting because larger differences might have been expected between the rankings for juvenile and adult cases. It is possible that judges make no distinctions between the two groups or that they view juveniles transferred to adult court (the example used here) as not "really" juveniles and not deserving of paternalistic handling.[2]

Effectiveness of Rehabilitation

It might be expected that support for rehabilitation is strongly associated with a perception of its effectiveness. Even those who support the principle of rehabilitation may have reservations about using it as a criteria for decisionmaking if rehabilitation is ineffective or an unreachable objective. To address this issue judges were asked the following two questions:

Table 4   RELATIVE RANKING OF REHABILITATION AMONG FIVE FACTORS JUDGES CONSIDER WHEN DECIDING JUVENILE TRANSFER TO ADULT COURT OR ADULT CASES

Rank of Rehabilitation	Transfer to Adult Court (%)	Adult Offenders (%)
1	20.5	12.0
2	27.4	20.4
3	21.6	22.6
4	18.9	23.0
5	11.6	22.0
	100.0	100.0
Number of cases	190	191

1. In your opinion, if adequately staffed and funded treatment programs were available, what percent of juveniles who are arrested for *misdemeanors* would be changed or rehabilitated by these programs?

2. In your opinion, if adequately staffed and funded treatment programs were available, what percent of juveniles who are arrested for *felonies* would be changed or rehabilitated by these programs?

Judges in the sample represented the full range of opinions regarding the viability of treatment. Their responses ranged from 0 percent to 100 percent success for misdemeanor offenders (Mean = 54 percent). For felony offenders responses ranged from 0 percent to 90 percent success (Mean = 41 percent).

As expected, these two measures of the perceived effectiveness of rehabilitation had a moderately strong correlation ($r = .74$). What was surprising was that neither was significantly correlated with the priority judges attached to treatment for either juvenile waivers to adult court or for adult offenders. In other words, a belief in treatment as a guiding principle for the handling of offenders is independent of a belief that treatment is, or can be, effective.

The nature of the link between support for the principle of treatment and a belief in its effectiveness can be further clarified by considering: (1) the extent to which judges believe they can accurately assess which juveniles are in need of treatment and (2) the reasons why judges believe treatment might fail.

Assessing the Need for Treatment

In deciding the disposition of juvenile offenders, judges must make predictions of which youth will stay out of trouble and which will eventually be returned to court. It is this latter group for which treatment programs are generally aimed, and the very idea of "successful treatment" is premised on accurately identifying this group. Judges were asked, "In about what percent of the cases involving juveniles would you say that judges can accurately predict which offenders will get into trouble with the law again?" Their responses ranged from 0 to 95 percent, but on average judges believed that they could make successful predictions in about 60 percent of the cases. For these judges, the belief that they could accurately predict recidivism was weakly correlated with their belief that adequately staffed and funded treatment programs for both misdemeanants ($r = .18$; $p = .02$) and felons ($r = .16$; $r = .02$) could successfully reform juveniles. That is, those judges who were most optimistic about their ability to predict recidivism were also most optimistic about the possibility of treatment success. What is interesting is that the perceived ability to predict recidivism was unrelated to the priority they attached to treatment for juvenile waivers or to adult offenders. This again highlights the fact that for judges support for the idea of treatment is distinct from their belief in the effectiveness of treatment.

Why Treatment Might Fail

To determine why judges thought treatment might be ineffective, they were given four reasons and were asked to rank these from the most to the least frequent reason for program failure. These reasons were "Inadequate Financial Resources for the Program,"

"Poorly Designed Programs," "Poorly Trained or Unmotivated Staff," and "Many Juveniles are Simply Not Amenable to Treatment." The first three reflect problems which derive from the design or implementation of the program itself, i.e., technical problems related to program implementation. The last problem identifies the juvenile offender as the source of failure in rehabilitation.

Believing that many juveniles will simply not be **amenable** to treatment reflects a fundamental lack of faith in the effectiveness of current rehabilitation programs. The analysis of this question focused on the rank assigned to the reason "Many Juveniles Are Simply Not Amenable to Treatment." Just under half of the judges (43 percent) saw the individual juvenile offender as the number one reason for the failure of treatment. As might be expected, the importance judges gave to the juveniles themselves as the source of the problem (and conversely the more weight they gave technical factors) was related to their view of treatment. The more they saw the juveniles themselves as the problem, the lower the priority they gave treatment in cases of juveniles waived to adult courts ($r = -.16$; $p = .03$) or in cases of adults ($r = -.17$; $p = .02$). Similarly, the more weight they gave to technical reasons for program failure, the more likely they were to believe that juveniles who committed misdemeanors ($r = .31$; $p = .00$) or felonies ($r = .30$; $p = .00$) could be successfully reformed. In other words, those judges who see the failure of treatment as primarily a problem with the youth themselves are also those least supportive of the principle of treatment and most pessimistic about the effectiveness of adequately funded and staffed treatment programs.

THE ROLE OF CONSERVATIVE POLITICS

It might be expected that a conservative political climate accounts for the trend toward a more legalistic handling of juvenile offenders and the apparent decline of *parens patriae*. As a cross-sectional study this survey cannot be used to directly measure changes in the views of these judges. It is possible, however, to determine whether judges differ on these dimensions of *parens patriae* depending ipon their self-described political philosophy. As Table 1 shows, judges fell across the entire range of the political spectrum, though most described themselves as moderate. What is interesting is that their self-described political philosophy was unrelated to *any* of the indicators of *parens patriae* discussed above. Knowing that the judge was either liberal or conservative did nothing to help predict his views on court intervention, discretion for the court, the importance of rehabilitation, the likely success of treatment, or the judge's own ability to predict which juveniles would recidivate. This suggests that the issues addressed here transcend any single political philosophy and that politically conservative outcomes are not always the product of a politically conservative climate.

Similarly, the views of these judges cannot be explained by looking at the generation in which they grew up, the time during which they received their legal training, or their actual exposure to juvenile offenders. Their views showed little statistical association with their age, years of experience as a judge, or the percent of their caseload which is typically made up of juveniles.

Thus, just as the idea of *parens patriae* defies any simple description, the factors which shape the philosophy of how juveniles should be handled in court cannot be simply explained away by such things as political conservatism or a new generation of judicial officers.

DISCUSSION

The concept of *parens patriae* is deeply rooted in the American system of juvenile justice. This study suggests that it is an idea with several interrelated dimensions. Regarding *discretion,* these judges favored retaining the juvenile court as a separate administrative unit but at the same time did not believe that juveniles currently have too many legal rights. Further, they did not favor expanding the jurisdiction of adult courts over juvenile cases by either increasing the use of waivers to adult courts or by lowering the age at which juveniles can be waived.

Judges also favored early *intervention* by the court, with most believing that the court typically becomes involved too late in the lives of most juvenile offenders. Their support for active intervention by the court is most apparent in regards to truancy. Judges believed that preventing truancy would also prevent delinquency and that the court should handle truants. Similarly, they also thought that the legal system should be used to deal with a variety of misbehaviors in the school.

These judges also supported the idea of *treatment* for juvenile offenders. Many believed they could recognize which youth were headed for further trouble and hence in need of treatment. Interestingly, the support they showed for treatment and their faith in their own ability to identify juveniles in need of treatment was unrelated to whether they thought even the best treatment programs could succeed. Finally, there were many judges who saw the juveniles themselves as the reason for program failure, and these judges were most pessimistic about the effectiveness of adequately funded and staffed treatment programs.

Overall, the responses of these judges provides little support for the belief that the principles underlying *parens patriae* have been abandoned. While judges vary in their opinions, there is a persistent level of support for continued court discretion, intervention by the count, and treatment as a guiding principle in the processing of juvenile cases. These responses suggest that Miller (1979) may be right when he argues that in juvenile justice the rhetoric changes more rapidly than the reality. While the rhetoric in Illinois, and a number of other states, has been to treat juvenile offenders more like adults, this has not led judges to abandon many of their paternalistic views. The truth of Miller's statement is also supported by the finding that how judges stand on these issues has little to do with whether they define themselves as politically liberal or conservative. Similarly, their views have little to do with such personal characteristics as their age or years of experience as a judge. It is likely that *parens patriae* has survived and will continue to survive precisely *because* its appeal transcends political philosophies. Those who lament the demise of the juvenile court may be reaching hasty conclusions. While many of the legal-technical procedures governing the juvenile court have changed in the past two decades, changing procedures do not always mean changing philosophies.

NOTES

1. There was a pattern of response which was initially a cause for concern. In the original sample, 168 of the 368 judges (46 percent) were from Cook County, which includes the city of Chicago and is the most populous county in Illinois. The response rate for Cook County was considerably lower than that in the rest of the state (46 percent vs. 71 percent). The size of this difference suggested the importance of treating Cook County separately from downstate counties. In the analyses which follow, each relationship or pattern of responses was also examined for Cook County and downstate separately. The results of these separate analyses indicated there were no statistically significant differences between the responses provided by judges from these two general areas of the state.

2. Unfortunately the survey did not ask judges to rank the importance of treatment for juvenile misdemeanants or for juvenile felons.

REFERENCES

ANDERSON, E. A. "The 'Chivalrous' Treatment of the Female Offender in the Arms of the Criminal Justice System: A Review of the Literature." *Social Problems, 23*(3), 1976, pp. 350–57.

CHESNEY-LIND, M. "Judicial Paternalism and the Female Status Offender: Training Women to Know Their Place," *Crime and Delinquency 23*(2), 1977, pp. 121–30.

CHESNEY-LIND, M. "Young Women in the Arms of the Law: An Inquiry into the Treatment of Female Delinquents in the Juvenile Justice System." In R. Crow and G. McCarthy (eds.), *Teenage Women in the Juvenile Justice System.* Tucson, AZ: New Directions, 1979, pp. 53–83.

CHESNEY-LIND, M. "Girls in Jail." *Crime and Delinquency 34*(2), 1988, pp. 150–168.

CULLEN, F. T. AND K. E. GILBERT. *Reaffirming Rehabilitation.* Cincinnati, OH: Anderson, 1982.

CULLEN, F. T., K. M. GOLDEN, AND J. B. CULLEN. "Is Child Saving Dead? Attitudes toward Juvenile Rehabilitation in Illinois." *Journal of Criminal Justice 11*(1), 1983, pp. 1–13.

CURTIS, G. B. "The Checkered Career of *Parens Patriae:* The State as Parent or Tyrant?" *Depaul Law Review 25,* 1976, pp. 895–915.

GLASSER, W. *Reality Therapy: A New Approach to Psychiatry.* New York: Harper & Row, 1965.

HUFSTEDLER, S. M. "Should We Give Up Reform?" *Crime and Delinquency 30*(3), 1984, 415–422.

KITTRIE, N. N. *The Right to Be Different: Deviance and Enforced Therapy.* Baltimore, MD: The Johns Hopkins Press, 1971.

KRISBERG, B., I. M. SCHWARTZ, P. LISTKY AND J. AUSTIN. "The Watershed of Juvenile Justice Reform." *Crime and Delinquency 32*(1), 1986, pp. 5–38.

LIAZOS, A. "Class Oppression: The Functions of Juvenile Justice." *The Insurgent Sociologist 5*(1), 1974, pp. 2–24.

McNALLY, R. B. "Juvenile Court: An Endangered Species." *Federal Probation 47*(1), 1983, pp. 32–37.

McNALLY, R. B. "The Juvenile Justice System: A Legacy of Failure?" *Federal Probation 47*(4), 1984, pp. 29–33.

MILLER, J. G. "The Revolution in Juvenile Justice: From Rhetoric to Rhetoric." In L. Empey (ed.), *The Future of Childhood and Juvenile Justice.* Charlottesville, VA: University of Virginia Press, 1979, pp. 66–111.

MOULDS, E. F. "Chivalry and Paternalism: Disparities of Treatments in the Criminal Justice System." *The Western Political Quarterly 31*(3), 1978, pp. 416–30.

OHLIN, L. E. "The Future of Juvenile Justice Policy and Research." *Crime and Delinquency* 29(3), 1983, pp. 463–472.

PISCIOTTA, A. W. "Saving the Children: The Promise and Practice of *Parens Patriae*, 1838–98." *Crime and Delinquency* 28(3), 1982, pp. 410–25.

PLATT, A. M. *The Child Savers: The Invention of Delinquency.* Chicago: University of Chicago Press, 1969.

RAFTER, N. H. *Partial Justice: Women in State Prisons, 1800–1935.* Boston: Northeastern University Press, 1985.

RENDLEMAN, D. R. "*Parens Patriae*: From Chancery to the Juvenile Court." *South Carolina Law Review,* 23, 1971, pp. 205–59.

Schall v. Martin, 104 S.Ct. 2403 (1984).

SANBORN, J. B. "The Rise and Fall of Juvenile Court: The Separation and Reunion of Constitution and Juvenile Defendant." In G. Stephens (ed.), *The Future of Criminal Justice.* Cincinnati, OH: Anderson Publishing, 1982, pp. 122–57.

SCHLOSSMAN, S. L. *Love and the American Delinquent.* Chicago: University of Chicago Press, 1977.

SCHUR, E. M. *Radical Non-intervention: Rethinking the Delinquency Problem.* Englewood Cliffs, NJ: Prentice-Hall, 1973.

SCHWARTZ, I. M. "Editors Introduction." *Crime and Delinquency* 34(2), 1988, pp. 131–32.

SKIBINSKI, G. J., AND A. M. KOSZUTH. "Getting Tough with Juvenile Offenders: Ignoring the Best Interests of the Child." *Juvenile and Family Court Journal* 37(5), 1986, pp. 43–50.

STRIEB, V. L. *Death Penalty for Juveniles.* Bloomington, IN: Indiana University Press, 1987.

TEMIN, C. E. "Discriminatory Sentencing of Women Offenders: the Argument for ERA in a Nutshell." *The American Criminal Law Review* 11(2), 1973, pp. 355–72.

QUESTIONS FOR DISCUSSION

1. Discuss how the principle of *parens patriae* has changed over time. Why do the authors contend that the apparent contradictions in the treatment of juveniles in the justice system make sense when the term *parens patriae* is equated with the idea of paternalism rather than rehabilitation?

2. Discuss the major findings of this study concerning the discretion of judges, intervention by the court, and rehabilitation.

3. In what way did the political philosophy of the judges who were studied affect their decisions in juvenile cases?

APPLICATIONS

1. In recent years there has been a tremendous increase in the number of juveniles who are being remanded to adult courts for their trials. In such cases the juvenile has been accused of a crime that is felt to be so serious that intervention or rehabilitation programs, typically afforded to juveniles, are not deemed to be appropriate by the juvenile court. This poses a difficult problem in deciding who should

or should not be remanded to adult court. Should there be a set age at which a juvenile is considered an adult by law? Should there be exceptions to the law? If we remand a 14-year-old youth to adult court, then why not a 10-year-old? Discuss.

2. In view of application 1, consider that it is against the law in most states for anyone to operate an automobile before 16 years of age. Similarly, you may not vote, nor can you be drafted before the age of 18, but you can join certain branches of the military when you are 17. The drinking age is 21. Are we sending mixed signals to our youth about adulthood and responsibility? Discuss.

chapter 22

The Forgotten Few
Juvenile Female Offenders

Ilene R. Bergsmann

INTRODUCTION

Adolescent female offenders have been described as a "specialty item in a mass market" (Grimes, 1983). Generally overlooked and frequently ignored, relegated to a footnote, and perceived as sexually deviant and in need of protection, these young women have received scant attention from members of the juvenile and criminal justice communities.

What about the juvenile female offender? Who pays attention to her special needs? Unfortunately, the courts and law enforcement pay too much attention for the wrong reasons, while litigators, legislators, and juvenile correctional administrators pay too little attention, also for the wrong reasons. During the past 25 years, few research studies, congressional inquiries, or litigation have focused on juvenile female offenders. Even when research is conducted on juvenile offenders, the data are not disaggregated by sex. When the Bureau of Justice Statistics provides valuable and much-needed data on juveniles in the justice system, one or two tables at most provide information by gender. *Uniform Crime Reports* data published by the Federal Bureau of Investigation also provide little information by gender.

Class action suits based on **parity** of programs, proven effective for adult women to increase their educational and vocational training opportunities while in prison, have not been filed on behalf of young women. Questionable correctional policies and practices are all too frequently the subject of policy debates within departments of youth services while in adult departments of corrections these same procedures have become the subject for litigation (Collins, 1987).

This article addresses the problems of young women in the juvenile justice system, including a description of who the female adolescent offender is, gender bias and stereotyping by correctional educators and administrators, and much-needed policy changes to ensure equitable programs.

PROFILE OF A JUVENILE FEMALE OFFENDER

Young women in trouble with the law are typically 16 years old, live in urban ghettos, are high school dropouts, and are victims of sexual and/or physical abuse or exploitation. Most come from single parent families, have experienced foster care placement, lack adequate work and social skills, and are substance abusers. Over half of these adolescent females are black or Hispanic (Bergsmann, 1988; Crawford, 1988; Sarri, 1988).

For youths in secure confinement, property crimes account for nearly 41 percent of all offenses, possession of drugs accounts for nearly 7 percent, status offenses 9 percent, and violent crime 32 percent (Beck, Kline, and Greenfield, 1988). Although the number of females in correctional facilities has remained about the same between 1975 and 1985 (17,192 and 17,009, respectively), a shift has occurred between placement in public and private facilities. In 1975, 53 percent of the female youthful offenders were in public institutions; in 1985, only 40 percent were in such institutions (Kline, 1989).

In a self-report study conducted by the American Correctional Association Task Force on the Female Offender (Crawford, 1988), 62 percent of the juveniles indicated that they were physically abused, 47 percent with 11 or more incidents of abuse. Thirty percent said the abuse began between ages five and nine, another 45 percent said onset occurred between 10 and 14 years of age. In most instances, parents were the primary abusers.

Sexual abuses follow similar but slightly less harsh patterns. Fifty-four percent of the juvenile females were victims of sexual abuse, 40 percent with abuse occurring once or twice, 33 percent with 3 to 10 occurrences. The age of onset of abuse occurred before age 5 in about 16 percent of the youths, from ages 5 to 9 for nearly 33 percent, and from ages 10 to 14 for nearly 40 percent. Fathers, stepfathers, and uncles accounted for nearly 40 percent of the attackers. Other research conducted on the national, state, and local levels show both higher and lower figures than those cited by Crawford. All, however, document the close connection between physical/sexual abuse and running away from home (Geller and Ford-Somma, 1979; Chesney-Lind, 1987).

Although most of the females were not convicted of drug abuse, self-report data indicate that they are frequent users of controlled substances, with alcohol, marijuana, speed, and cocaine the most frequent drugs used (Crawford, 1988).

Sarri predicts that 90 percent of all youthful female offenders will be single heads of households who will spend 80 percent of their income on housing and child care (1988). Yet, a majority of these youths, who have failed to obtain a high school diploma or a GED and are educationally disadvantaged, also suffer from societal biases against women and minorities.

A majority (64 percent) of female juvenile offenders in secure facilities indicate that a member(s) of their family has been incarcerated. Most (80 percent) also report being runaways. Contrary to staff perceptions, over half report growing up with love and acceptance. Typical of most teenagers, over 80 percent say that peers and friends influence them (Crawford, 1988).

Many teenage female offenders suffer from low self-esteem. Self-report data show that over half have attempted suicide, 64 percent of whom have tried more than once. They express reasons such as being depressed, life is too painful to continue, and no one cares (Crawford, 1988). While offenders are not a precise mirror of young women in society in the depths of their feelings of poor self-worth, studies demonstrate that lack of self-esteem is generally a common problem among young women. In a study begun in 1981 to measure the self-confidence of high school valedictorians, salutatorians, and honor students, males and females in roughly the same percentages believed that they had "far above average" intelligence at graduation. Four years later as college seniors, 25 percent of the males continued to share this opinion while none of the females did (Epperson, 1988). If women with above average intelligence, leadership ability, and the opportunity to achieve higher education experienced feelings of low self-esteem, it is not too difficult to understand how young women from broken homes, urban ghettos, poor schools, and abusive families develop feelings of despair and hopelessness about themselves and their chances for success.

GENDER BIAS AND STEREOTYPING IN THE JUVENILE JUSTICE SYSTEM

Differential treatment of females and males prevails in the juvenile justice system. Sexual promiscuity, including immoral conduct, has prevailed for much of the last 100 years as one basis for locking up juvenile females. Girls are expected to conform to traditional roles within the family and society. They should be inconspicuous; passive in their dealings with others and take few, if any, risks; and obedient to their parents, teachers, and elders. Boys, on the other hand, are expected to be rowdy, boisterous, and get into trouble now and then. They should be aggressive, independent, and strive for great achievements. As Chesney-Lind explains, "From sons, defiance of authority is almost normative whereas from daughters it may be seen as an extremely serious offense. And because so much of the adolescent female sex role evolved to control female sexual experimentation so as to guarantee virginity upon marriage, such defiance is virtually always cast in sexual terms" (Chesney-Lind, 1978).

The courts view female adolescents as "more vulnerable and in need of protection than boys" (Grimes, 1983) and thus have used their "discretionary power in the service of traditional sex roles...(while they) appear to be less concerned with the protection of female offenders than the protection of the sexual status quo" (Datesman, Scarpitti and Stephenson in Sarri, 1983). Of all the juveniles who appeared in court in 1984, females represented 45 percent of all status offender cases compared with only 19 percent of all delinquency cases. Of this 45 percent, 62 percent were runaways (Snyder et al., 1987.)

While young women comprised 14 percent of all juveniles in custody in 1985, they represented 52 percent of all status offenders (U. S. Department of Justice, 1986). *Uniform Crime Reports* data show that 18 percent of all female juvenile arrests are for curfew and loitering violations and running away, yet only 6.4 percent of male juvenile arrests are for these offenses (U.S. Department of Justice, 1987). The 1987 Children in Custody survey has increased since 1985 while the number of male status offenders has declined (Allen-Hagen, 1988). Today, less than 2 percent (1.6 percent) of males are held in training schools for the commission of status offenses compared to 9.3 percent of all females (Beck, Kline, and Greenfield, 1988).

Parents, law enforcement officers, and school administrators are **inextricably** linked to young women's contacts with the law. Often parents use the courts as a route to mending family feuds or as a last resort for addressing problems with promiscuous and sexually active daughters. Because judges have similar parental concerns, they tend to react sympathetically. Rarely are the courts employed as a quick fix for sons who exhibit similar sexual behaviors.

Female sexual activity also frequently becomes part of the record that judges and other court officers review, including levels and types of sexual activity and numbers of children, regardless of the offense for which they are being tried. According to several judges in Missouri, such information is almost never found in delinquent male records (Grimes, 1983).

Police contribute to the differential treatment of these adolescent females as well. Not only do they tend to arrest more females for sexual and relational activities than for criminal conduct, they also promote a different set of sanctions for them. Dating back to the 1950's, research has shown that girls were more likely than boys to be: (1) referred to social or welfare agencies rather than being released from custody; (2) placed on informal probation supervision; and (3) placed in secure treatment facilities for the commission of status offenses (Chesney-Lind, 1982). Females arrested for status offenses often remain in detention longer than males, according to a Minnesota study in which 82.9 percent of all status offenders held beyond the statutory limit were females (Osbun and Rode, 1982). And, 12 percent of all status offenders placed in secure detention were females contrasted with 9 percent for males (Snyder et al., 1987).

Self-report data, on the other hand, indicate that males engage in at least the same amount of sexual activity as females but rarely are arrested for such behavior. Adolescent females in self-report studies indicate that their engagement in criminal activity is greater than what court intake records show. If these studies are accurate, the number of females involved in criminal activity would remain below that of males, but the types of offenses for which they would be arrested would be much the same (Geller and Ford-Somma, 1979; Sarri, 1983; Chesney-Lind, 1987). As Chesney-Lind maintains, "…it is reasonable to assume that some bias (either unofficial or official) is present within the juvenile justice system and functions to filter out those young women guilty of criminal offenses while retaining those women suspected of sexual misconduct" (1982).

A third source of referral to juvenile courts is through the school system. In a study conducted in nine public and parochial high schools in the Midwest, 11 percent of all court referrals come from the schools (Sarri, 1983). These youths have become so disruptive that the teaching and administrative staff are no longer able to contain them.

ADMINISTRATIVE DISINTEREST

Like their adult counterparts, adjudicated juvenile females find themselves with few programs and services to meet their needs for developing socialization and life skills and an awareness of the world of work and their role in it. In the community, services are geared to preventing further physical or sexual harm but not to developing vocational and life skills (National Council of Jewish Women, 1984).

In secure confinement, the amount of staff time to work with these adolescents is limited to the average length of stay of 8 months (Bergsmann, 1988). Yet, it is during incarceration that these young women should be acquiring some of the tools they will need for economic independence and personal growth. The barriers to providing equitable treatment of these females come from several sources: (1) the traditional view of young women held by many female and male correctional administrators and staff; (2) the small number of females who, because of their limited population, are housed in co-correctional (co-educational) facilities; (3) limited resources that are mostly channeled to the males who constitute 93 percent of the incarcerated juvenile population; and 4) lack of program and service integration among state and local education, health, labor, and youth services agencies.

When educationally disadvantaged delinquent females enter the juvenile justice system, they also encounter administrative resistance in the provision of appropriate resources and programs to meet their unique needs. Departments of corrections and youth services rarely, if ever, designate a central office position to coordinate female programs and services (Ryan, 1984). Co-educational institutions are often the result of financial/administrative decisions based on the small number of females and the large number of male offenders. Often, the young women are imposed on all-male facilities in which policy and procedure frequently are not written from an equity perspective and where programs and services are more appropriate for males than females.

WORKFORCE CHANGES IN THE 1990'S

The traditional or stereotypical orientation of many youth services managers towards delinquent women is a great disservice not only to these young women but also to society. Major economic and workforce changes are anticipated during the 1990's, changes that will most certainly impact women and minorities. Consider the major trends for our economic future that the Hudson Institute forecasts for the year 2000: a growing economy, fueled by an increase in service-related jobs over manufacturing; a workforce that is "growing slowly, becoming older, more female and more disadvantaged," as well as minority; and jobs that require higher skill levels than those of today (Johnston, 1987). In other words, highly skilled employees will have greater employment options while the least skilled will face greater joblessness.

The 1990's will see more women and minorities entering the labor pool. Nearly 66 percent of all new workers will be women, many of whom will be poor single heads of households; non-whites will constitute 29 percent of the new work force. Although women will continue to work in jobs that pay less than those for men, they also will have greater opportunities for high-paying professional and technical positions. And, even with entry-level positions, employers who are facing a shrinking labor pool are beginning to invest time and money in finding and training new workers. Unless women offenders, who are disproportionately minority, receive sufficient education and training to perform the more complex jobs projected for the coming years, our economy will suffer and their poverty, dependence, and criminal activity will escalate (Johnston, 1987; Packer, 1988).

As jobs become more sophisticated, young women offenders, who have minimal occupational skills, will find it increasingly difficult, if not impossible, to become employed in an occupation with more than poverty-level wages. Many are high school dropouts, and nearly 26 percent suffer educational disadvantages, including learning disabilities and emotional problems (Bergsmann, 1988). Their exposure to vocational education is often limited to traditional programs of cosmetology, office skills, and food services. The Department of Labor's statistics on women, especially women and girls who are minorities, are not encouraging. In 1984, the unemployment rate for black female teenagers was almost three times as great as for white female teens, and for Hispanic women unemployment rates were almost 4 percent above the rates of all women (Council of Chief State School Officers, 1986).

POLICY CONSIDERATIONS

The inequitable treatment of juvenile female offenders is often exacerbated by the lack of adequate social and life skills programs and pre-vocational and vocational training programs that are critical for these youths in order to achieve economic and emotional self-sufficiency. Recognizing this problem, the American Correctional Association (ACA) has called for both juvenile and adult women offenders to receive programs comparable with those provided to males, as well as services that meet the unique needs of females. Integral to its policy on "Female Offender Services" is the provision for "access to a full range of work and programs designed to expand economic and social roles of women, with emphasis on education; career counseling and exploration of non-traditional as well as traditional vocational training; relevant life skills, including parenting and social and economic assertiveness; and pre-release and work/education release programs" (1986).

The Correctional Education Association (CEA) concurs with the need for appropriate education for women offenders. Its standards, promulgated in 1988, include a mandatory standard on educational equity which states that, "Institutions housing females provide educational programs, services and access to community programs and resources equitable with those provided for males within the system." This means that small numbers and thus high per capita costs of program delivery cannot be used to justify a lack of equitable programs that are defined "in terms of range and relevance of options, quality of offerings, staff qualifications, instructional materials and equipment, and curriculum design." Pennsylvania is the first state to use the standards to assess the status of its educational programs. A program to enforce the standards is being developed to ensure that all participating jurisdictions would be required to provide equitable educational programs for juvenile female offenders.

Troubled and delinquent offenders have often been the stepchildren of the educational system. Today, these offenders fall within the "at-risk" category of youths whose multiple problems have made their odds of educational success difficult at best. Many of these teenagers have failed academically, been chronic truants, and when they do go to school, frequently act out. Unfortunately, when they enter the juvenile justice system, education, one of their greatest needs and surest routes for entering the economic and social mainstream, becomes second to security, which takes preference above all else.

A Bill of Educational Rights for incarcerated youth has been called for (Price and Vitolo, 1988) which seeks "to establish minimum standards for protecting their rights and assuring them of an education program designed to meet their needs." Included in this Bill of Educational Rights are the rights to: (1) "...a public education fostering (youth) development as productive members of society" guaranteed by Federal policy that mandates education for all juvenile offenders; (2) a curriculum that "emphasize(s) the core subjects and skills" including basic academics and independent living skills that use a competency-based system for awarding credits; (3) "a thorough educational assessment" that appropriately identifies and addresses different learning styles and needs; (4) education on "affective development" to focus on positive self-esteem and interpersonal relationships; (5) special educational services; (6) state-certified instructors to design a curriculum consistent with the community's educational standards; (7) an educational program that meets "recognized community standards leading to a diploma" in order that youths can continue their education on release; and (8) transition services on release to assist with reintegration back to school, entry into a vocational education program, or job placement.

Inherent in this Bill of Educational Rights are many important elements for delinquent female offenders. These youths need academic encouragement, counseling to improve their self-esteem, introduction to the world of work to encourage them to consider high paying careers, vocational education courses, independent living skills, and transition planning and assistance.

Institutions interested in implementing the provisions of the ACA's policy on female offenders, the CEA standards, including the standard on equity, and the provisions of the Bill of Educational Rights could do so by: (1) developing equitable educational opportunities for adolescent females delivered through a continuum of interrelated programs and (2) establishing a collaborative educational program that links youth services staff with employees in the state departments of education, labor, and employment and training both inside and outside the training school.

To achieve pro-vocational, vocational, health, and life skills, a comprehensive, coordinated service delivery system must be in place within the institution and continue through transition back into the community. Such services include testing and evaluation; pre-vocational and vocational training; independent living and social skills; health education, including human sexuality; individual and group counseling; substance abuse programs and pre-release planning, including a network of support in the community.

Underlying any fundamental change in the way these youths perceive themselves is the need to raise their self-esteem. Contributing to many of these girls' involvement in the juvenile justice system is their poor self-esteem, brought on by abuse and/or exploitation at home, poor academic achievement, little assistance from teachers and administrators and minimal school involvement (Finn, Potts and Zarichny, 1988) and the **myriad** of social and economic problems in which they grown up. They tend to under-estimate their abilities; fail to consider a full range of career opportunities; become pregnant and then a single parent; perform poorly in school; be overly dependent on young men; fear success and assertiveness; and have an excessive need for external approval (Agonito and Moon, no date). Training school staff, not just educators, must work with these young women to enhance self-esteem through academic and vocational education programs that instill self-confidence and staff-offender interactions based on acceptance and approval.

More subtle, but equally compelling, is the need for staff members to be gender neutral in their interactions with all youthful offenders. For example, teachers need to design curricular materials that incorporate women and minorities. They should employ classroom strategies that encourage female participation, e.g., females, especially minority females, need more "wait time" than other students during classroom interactions. In co-correctional facilities, females should be included fairly in all classroom interactions. Finally, testing and counseling programs should avoid career segregation and stereotyping (Sadker and Sadker, 1988).

CONCLUSION

Little time, and even less effort, has been devoted to the juvenile female offender in the last century. Criminal and juvenile justice administrators pursue problems that are seemingly more pressing, such as crowding, or those that are more vocal, such as **litigation.** Researchers study juvenile offenders, generalizing their theories of male juveniles to females. Unfortunately, the adolescent female offender has been silent for so long that the few administrators and researchers who do champion her special needs are often unheard and even when heard go unheeded.

The differential treatment of females and males in the juvenile justice system begins with the schools, continues with law enforcement and the courts, and is perpetrated by the correctional system. Many delinquent females are locked up for running away from home as a result of physical and/or sexual abuse or exploitation. Many others suffer from low self-esteem, inequitable treatment in school from teachers and administrators, and inequitable programs during incarceration.

The need for educational equity for these offenders is paramount. Teachers must begin to design curricula with females in mind and interact in a gender-free environment. Law enforcement officers must stop arresting females for running away and for other status offenses. Judges and magistrates must stop treating girls differently from boys in the length of confinement in detention and the length and types of sentences imposed. Correctional educators and other staff must begin to provide equitable programs and services for this adolescent female population. Only then will female juvenile offenders have the opportunity to develop the social and educational/vocational skills to compete in the ever-changing technological world in which we live.

REFERENCES

AGONITO, R. AND MOON, M. *Promoting Self-Esteem in Young Women*. Albany, New York: The State Department of Education, Division of Community Relations and Intercultural Relations, no date

ALLEN-HAGEN, B. *Children in Custody, Public Juvenile Facilities, 1987*. Washington, DC: Department of Justice, Office of Juvenile Justice and Delinquency Prevention, 1988.

AMERICAN CORRECTIONAL ASSOCIATION. *Public Policy for Corrections: A Handbook for Decision Makers*. Laurel, Maryland: American Correctional Association, 1986, pp. 28–31.

BECK, A., KLINE, S., AND GREENFIELD, L. *Survey of Youth in Custody, 1987*. Washington. DC: Department of Justice, Bureau of Justice Statistics, 1988

BERGSMANN, I. R. *State Juvenile Justice Education Survey*. Washington DC: Council of Chief State School Officers, 1988.

CHESNEY-LIND, M. "Young Women in the Arms of the Law." In L. H. Bowker (ed.), *Women, Crime and the Criminal Justice System*. Lexington, Massachusetts: Lexington Books, 1978. pp. 171–196.

———. "Guilt by Reason of Sex: Young Women and the Juvenile Justice System." In B P. Price and N. J. Sokoloff (eds.), *Criminal Justice System and the Law*. New York: Clark Boardman Co., Ltd., 1982, pp. 77–103.

———. "Girls' Crime and Women's Place: Toward a Feminist Model of Female Delinquency." Paper presented at the American Society of Criminology, Montreal, Canada, 1987.

COLLINS, W. *Collins: Correctional Law, 1987*. Olympia, Washington. 1987, pp. 125–133.

CORRECTIONAL EDUCATION ASSOCIATION. *Standards for Adult Juvenile Correctional Education Programs*. College Park, Maryland: Correctional Education Association, 1988.

COUNCIL OF CHIEF STATE SCHOOL OFFICERS. *Equity Training for State Education Agency Staff*. Washington, DC: Resource Center on Educational Equity, 1986.

CRAWFORD, J. *Tabulation of a Nationwide Survey of Female Inmates*. Phoenix, Arizona: Research Advisory Services, 1988.

EPPERSON, S. E. "Studies Link Subtle Sex Bias in Schools with Women's Behavior in the Workplace." *Wall Street Journal*. September 16, 1988, p. 27.

FINN, J. D., STOTT, M. W. R., ZARICHNY, K. T. "School Performance of Adolescents in Juvenile Court." *Urban Education, 23*, 1988, pp. 150–161.

GELLER, M. AND FORD-SOMMA, L. *Caring for Delinquent Girls: An Examination of New Jersey's Correctional System*. Trenton, New Jersey: New Jersey Law Enforcement Planning Agency, 1979.

GRIMES, C. *Girls and the Law*. Washington, DC: Institute for Educational Leadership, 1983.

JOHNSTON W. B. *Workforce 2000*. Indianapolis, Indiana: Hudson Institute, 1987, pp. 75–104.

KLINE. S. *Children in Custody 1975–1985: Census of Public and Private Juvenile Detention, Correctional, and Shelter Facilities, 1975, 1977, 1979, 1983, 1985*. Washington, DC: Department of Justice, Bureau of Justice Statistics, 1989.

NATIONAL COUNCIL OF JEWISH WOMEN. *Adolescent Girls in the Juvenile Justice System*. New York: National Council of Jewish Women, 1984.

OSBUN, L. A. AND RODE, P. A. *Changing Boundaries of the Juvenile Court: Practice and Policy in Minnesota*. Minneapolis, Minnesota: University of Minnesota, 1982, pp. 33–49.

PACKER, A. "Retooling the American Worker." *The Washington Post,* July 10, 1988, p. C8.

PRICE, T. AND VITOLO, R. "The Schooling of Incarcerated Young People." Education Week, 27, June 15, 1988, pp. 36 and 27.

RYAN, T. A. *State of the Art Analysis of Adult Female Offenders and Institutional Programs*. Columbia, South Carolina: University of South Carolina, 1984, p. 22.

Sadker, M. and Sadker, D. *Equity and Excellence in Educational Reform*. Washington, DC: The American University. 1988, pp. 25–26.

Sarri, R. C. Keynote remarks, Conference on Increasing Educational Equity for Juvenile Female Offenders. Washington, DC: Council of Chief State School Officers, 1988.

———. "Gender Issues in Juvenile Justice." *Crime and Delinquency,* 29, 1983, pp. 381–397.

Snyer, H. N., Finnegan, T. A., Nimick. E. H., Sickmund, M. H., Sullivan, D. F. and Tierney, N. J. *Juvenile Court Statistics, 1984.* Pittsburgh, Pennsylvania: National Center for Juvenile Justice, 1987.

U.S. Department of Justice, Federal Bureau of Investigation. *Crime in the United States, 1987.* Washington, DC: U.S. Government Printing Office, 1987.

———. *Children in Custody, 1985.* Washington, DC: Bureau of Justice Statistics, 1986.

QUESTIONS FOR DISCUSSION

1. Describe the profile of the juvenile female offender presented in this article. Provide specific examples of data in the article that support the profile.

2. Discuss gender bias and stereotyping in the juvenile justice system. Cite specific examples of how this occurs.

3. List and discuss the policy recommendations made by the author to remedy the disparities in treatment between females and males in the juvenile justice system. Do you believe that these recommendations will work? Why?

APPLICATIONS

1. The author profiles typical young women in trouble as 16 years old, from urban ghettos, high school dropouts, victims of sexual and/or physical abuse, from single-parent families, and substance abusers. Are we, conversely, to believe that young women who are not 16, from middle-class neighborhoods, attend high school, have never been abused, are from two-parent families, and are drug free do not get in to trouble or commit delinquent acts? Discuss. What is the inherent danger of being overly dependent on profiles to understand variations in delinquency? Do youths of different social class levels receive different treatment by authorities? Discuss.

2. Some would argue that the only way for disparities in the justice system to be resolved is for the society as a whole to change its values and attitudes regarding gender bias. Do you agree or disagree? Why?

chapter 23

The Saints and the Roughnecks

William J. Chambliss

INTRODUCTION

Eight promising young men—children of good, stable, white upper-middle-class families, active in school affairs, good pre-college students—were some of the most delinquent boys at Hanibal High School. While community residents and parents knew that these boys occasionally sowed a few wild oats, they were totally unaware that sowing wild oats completely occupied the daily routine of these young men. The Saints were constantly occupied with truancy, drinking, wild driving, petty theft and vandalism. Yet not one was officially arrested for any misdeed during the two years I observed them.

This record was particularly surprising in light of my observations during the same two years of another gang of Hanibal High School students, six lower-class white boys known as the Roughnecks. The Roughnecks were constantly in trouble with police and community even though their rate of delinquency was about equal with that of the Saints. What was the cause of this disparity? The result? The following consideration of the activities, social class and community perceptions of both gangs may provide some answers.

THE SAINTS FROM MONDAY TO FRIDAY

The Saints' principal daily concern was with getting out of school as early as possible. The boys managed to get out of school with minimum danger that they would be accused of playing hooky through an elaborate procedure for obtaining "legitimate" release from class. The most common procedure was for one boy to obtain the release of another by fabricating a meeting of some committee, program or recognized club. Charles might raise his hand in his 9:00 chemistry class and asked to be excused—a euphemism for going to the bathroom. Charles would go to Ed's math class and inform the teacher that Ed was needed for a 9:30 rehearsal of the drama club play. The math teacher would recognize Ed and Charles as "good students" involved in numerous school activities and would permit Ed to leave at 9:30. Charles would return to his class, and Ed would go to Tom's English class to obtain his release. Tom would engineer Charles' escape. The strategy would continue until as many of the Saints as possible were freed. After a stealthy trip to the car (which had been parked in a strategic spot), the boys were off for a day of fun.

Over the two years I observed the Saints, this pattern was repeated nearly every day. There were variations on the theme, but in one form or another, the boys used this procedure for getting out of class and then off the school grounds. Rarely did all eight of the Saints manage to leave school at the same time. The average number avoiding school on the days I observed them was five.

Having escaped from the concrete corridors the boys usually went either to a pool hall on the other (lower-class) side of town or to a cafe in the suburbs. Both places were out of the way of people the boys were likely to know (family or school officials), and both provided a source of entertainment. The pool hall entertainment was the generally rough atmosphere, the occasional hustler, the sometimes drunk proprietor and, of course, the game of pool. The cafe's entertainment was provided by the owner. The boys would "accidentally" knock a glass on the floor or spill cola on the counter—not all the time, but enough to be sporting. They would also bend spoons, put salt in sugar bowls and generally tease whoever was working in the cafe. The owner had opened the cafe recently and was dependent on the boys' business which was, in fact, substantial since between the horsing around and the teasing they bought food and drinks.

THE SAINTS ON WEEKENDS

On weekends the automobile was even more critical than during the week, for on weekends the Saints went to Big Town—a large city with a population of over a million 25 miles from Hanibal. Every Friday and Saturday night most of the Saints would meet between 8:00 and 8:30 and would go into Big Town. Big Town activities included drinking heavily in taverns or nightclubs, driving drunkenly through the streets, and committing acts of vandalism and playing pranks.

By midnight on Fridays and Saturdays the Saints were usually thoroughly high, and one or two of them were often so drunk they had to be carried to the cars. Then the boys drove around town, calling obscenities to women and girls; occasionally trying (unsuccessfully so far as I could tell) to pick girls up; and driving recklessly through red lights and at high speeds with their lights out. Occasionally they played "chicken." One boy would climb out the back window of the car and across the roof to the driver's side of the car while the car was moving at high speed (between 40 and 50 miles an hour); then the driver would move over and the boy who had just crawled across the car roof would take the driver's seat.

Searching for "fair game" for a prank was the boys' principal activity after they left the tavern. The boys would drive alongside a foot patrolman and ask directions to some street. If the policeman leaned on the car in the course of answering the question, the driver would speed away, causing him to lose his balance. The Saints were careful to play this prank only in an area where they were not going to spend much time and where they could quickly disappear around a comer to avoid having their license plate number taken.

Construction sites and road repair areas were the special province of the Saints' mischief. A soon-to-be repaired hole in the road inevitably invited the Saints to remove lanterns and wooden barricades and put them in the car, leaving the hole unprotected. The boys would find a safe vantage point and wait for an unsuspecting motorist to drive into the hole. Often, though not always, the boys would go up to the motorist and commiserate with him about the dreadful way the city protected its citizenry.

Leaving the scene of the open hole and the motorist, the boys would then go searching for an appropriate place to erect the stolen barricade. An "appropriate place" was often a spot on the highway near a curve in the road where the barricade would not be seen by an oncoming motorist. The boys would wait to watch an unsuspecting motorist attempt to stop and (usually) crash into the wooden barricade. With saintly bearing the boys might offer help and understanding.

A stolen lantern might well find its way onto the back of a police car or hang from a street lamp. Once a lantern served as a prop for a reenactment of the "midnight ride of Paul Revere" until the "play," which was taking place at 2:00 A.M. in the center of a main street of Big Town, was interrupted by a police car several blocks away. The boys ran, leaving the lanterns on the street, and managed to avoid being apprehended.

Abandoned houses, especially if they were located in out-of-the-way places, were fair game for destruction and spontaneous vandalism. The boys would break windows, remove furniture to the yard and tear it apart, urinate on the walls and scrawl obscenities inside.

Through all the pranks, drinking and reckless driving the boys managed miraculously to avoid being stopped by police. Only twice in two years was I aware that they had been stopped by a Big City policeman. Once was for speeding (which they did every time they drove whether they were drunk or sober), and the driver managed to convince the policeman that it was simply an error. The second time they were stopped they had just left a nightclub and were walking through an alley. Aaron stopped to urinate and the boys began making obscene remarks. A foot patrolman came into the alley, lectured the boys and sent them home. Before the boys got to the car one began talking in a loud voice again. The policeman, who had followed them down the alley, arrested this boy for disturbing the peace and took him to the police station where the other Saints gathered. After paying a $5.00 fine, and with the assurance that there would be no permanent record of the arrest, the boy was released.

The boys had a spirit of frivolity and fun about their **escapades.** They did not view what they were engaged in as "delinquency," though it surely was by any reasonable definition of that word. They simply viewed themselves as having a little fun and who, they would ask, was really hurt by it? The answer had to be no one, although this fact remains one of the most difficult things to explain about the gang's behavior. Unlikely though it seems, in two years of drinking, driving, carousing and vandalism no one was seriously injured as a result of the Saints' activities.

THE SAINTS IN SCHOOL

The Saints were highly successful in school. The average grade for the group was "B," with two of the boys having close to a straight "A" average. Almost all of the boys were popular and many of them held offices in the school. One of the boys was vice-president of the student body one year. Six of the boys played on athletic teams.

At the end of their senior year, the student body selected ten seniors for special recognition as the "school wheels"; four of the ten were Saints. Teachers and school officials saw no problem with any of these boys and anticipated that they would all "make something of themselves."

How the boys managed to maintain this impression is surprising in view of their actual behavior while in school. Their technique for covering truancy was so successful that teachers did not even realize that the boys were absent from school much of the time. Occasionally, of course, the system would backfire and then the boy was on his own. A boy who was caught would be most contrite, would plead guilty and ask for mercy. He inevitably got the mercy he sought.

Cheating on examinations was rampant, even to the point of orally communicating answers to exams as well as looking at one another's papers. Since none of the group studied, and since they were primarily dependent on one another for help, it is surprising that grades were so high. Teachers contributed to the deception in their admitted inclination to give these boys (and presumably others like them) the benefit of the doubt. When asked how the boys did in school, and when pressed on specific examinations, teachers might admit that they were disappointed in John's performance, but would quickly add that they "knew that he was capable of doing better," so John was given a higher grade than he had actually earned. How often this happened is impossible to know. During the time that I observed the group, I never saw any of the boys take homework home. Teachers may have been "understanding" very regularly.

One exception to the gang's generally good performance was Jerry, who had a "C" average in his junior year, experienced disaster the next year and failed to graduate. Jerry had always been a little more nonchalant than the others about the liberties he took in school. Rather than wait for someone to come get him from class, he would offer his own excuse and leave. Although he probably did not miss any more classes than most of the others in the group, he did not take the requisite pains to cover his absences. Jerry was the only Saint whom I ever heard talk back to a teacher. Although teachers often called him a "cut up" or a "smart kid," they never referred to him as a troublemaker or as a kid headed for trouble. It seems likely, then, that Jerry's failure his senior year and his mediocre performance his junior year were consequences of his not playing the game the proper way (possibly because he was disturbed by his parents' divorce). His teachers regarded him as "immature" and not quite ready to get out of high school.

THE POLICE AND THE SAINTS

The local police saw the Saints as good boys who were among the leaders of the youth in the community. Rarely, the boys might be stopped in town for speeding or for running a stop sign. When this happened the boys were always polite, contrite and pled for mercy. As in school, they received the mercy they asked for. None ever received a ticket or was taken into the precinct by the local police.

The situation in Big City, where the boys engaged in most of their delinquency, was only slightly different. The police there did not know the boys at all, although occasionally the boys were stopped by a patrolman. Once they were caught taking a lantern from a construction site. Another time they were stopped for running a stop sign, and on several occasions they were stopped for speeding. Their behavior was as before: contrite, polite and penitent. The urban police, like the local police, accepted their demeanor as sincere. More important, the urban police were convinced that these were good boys just out for a lark.

THE ROUGHNECKS

Hanibal townspeople never perceived the Saints' high level of delinquency. The Saints were good boys who just went in for an occasional prank. After all, they were well dressed, well mannered and had nice cars. The Roughnecks were a different story. Although the two gangs of boys were the same age, and both groups engaged in an equal amount of wild-oat sowing, everyone agreed that the not-so-well-dressed, not-so-well-mannered, not-so-rich boys were heading for trouble. Townspeople would say, "You can see the gang members at the drugstore, night after night, leaning against the storefront (sometimes drunk) or slouching around inside buying cokes, reading magazines, and probably stealing old Mr. Wall blind. When they are outside and girls walk by, even respectable girls, these boys make suggestive remarks. Sometimes their remarks are downright lewd."

From the community's viewpoint, the real indication that these kids were in for trouble was that they were constantly involved with the police. Some of them had been picked up for stealing, mostly small stuff, of course, "but still it's stealing small stuff that leads to big time crimes." "Too bad," people said. "Too bad that these boys couldn't behave like the other kids in town; stay out of trouble, be polite to adults, and look to their future."

The community's impression of the degree to which this group of six boys (ranging in age from 16 to 19) engaged in delinquency was somewhat distorted. In some ways the gang was more delinquent than the community thought; in other ways they were less.

The fighting activities of the group were fairly readily and accurately perceived by almost everyone. At least once a month, the boys would get into some sort of fight, although most fights were scraps between members of the group or involved only one member of the group and some peripheral hanger-on. Only three times in the period of observation did the group fight together: once against a gang from across town, once against two blacks and once against a group of boys from another school. For the first two fights the group went out "looking for trouble"—and they found it both times. The third fight followed a football game and began spontaneously with an argument on the football field between one of the Roughnecks and a member of the opposition's football team.

Jack had a particular propensity for fighting and was involved in most of the brawls. He was a prime mover of the escalation of arguments into fights.

More serious than fighting, had the community been aware of it, was theft. Although almost everyone was aware that the boys occasionally stole things, they did not realize the extent of the activity. Petty stealing was a frequent event for the Roughnecks. Sometimes they stole as a group, and coordinated their efforts; other times they stole in pairs. Rarely did they steal alone.

The thefts ranged from very small things like paperback books, comics and ballpoint pens to expensive items like watches. The nature of the thefts varied from time to time. The gang would go through a period of systematically shoplifting items from automobiles or school lockers. Types of thievery varied with the whim of the gang. Some forms of thievery were more profitable than others, but all thefts were for profit, not just thrills.

Roughnecks siphoned gasoline from cars as often as they had access to an automobile, which was not very often. Unlike the Saints who owned their own cars, the Roughnecks would have to borrow their parents' cars, an event which occurred only eight or nine times a year. The boys claimed to have stolen cars for joy rides from time to time.

Ron committed the most serious of the group's offenses. With an unidentified associate the boy attempted to burglarize a gasoline station. Although this station had been robbed twice previously in the same month, Ron denied any involvement in either of the other thefts. When Ron and his **accomplice** approached the station, the owner was hiding in the bushes beside the station. He fired both barrels of a double-barreled shotgun at thee boys. Ron was severely injured; the other boy ran away and was never caught. Though he remained in critical condition for several months, Ron finally recovered and served six months of the following year in reform school. Upon release from reform school, Ron was put back a grade in school, and began running around with a different gang of boys. The Roughnecks considered the new gang less delinquent than themselves, and during the following year Ron had no more trouble with the police.

The Roughnecks, then, engaged mainly in three types of delinquency: theft, drinking and fighting. Although community members perceived that this gang of kids was delinquent, they mistakenly believed that their illegal activities were primarily drinking, fighting and being a nuisance to passersby.

Drinking would doubtless have been more prevalent had the boys had ready access to liquor. Since they rarely had automobiles at their disposal, they could not travel very far, and the bars in town would not serve them. Most of the boys had little money, and this, too, inhibited their purchase of alcohol. Their major source of liquor was a local drunk who would buy them a fifth if they would give him enough extra to buy himself a pint of whiskey or a bottle of wine.

The community's perception of drinking as prevalent stemmed from the fact that it was the most obvious delinquency the boys engaged in. When one of the boys had been drinking, even a casual observer seeing him on the corner would suspect that he was high.

There was a high level of mutual distrust and dislike between the Roughnecks and the police. The boys felt very strongly that the police were unfair and corrupt. Some evidence existed that the boys were correct in their perception.

The main source of the boys' dislike for the police undoubtedly stemmed from the fact that the police would sporadically harass the group. From the standpoint of the boys, these acts of occasional enforcement of the law were whimsical and uncalled for. It made no sense to them, for example, that the police would come to the comer occasionally and threaten them with arrest for loitering when the night before the boys had been out siphoning gasoline from cars and the police had been nowhere in sight. To the boys, the police were stupid on the one hand, for not being where they should have been and catching the boys in a serious offense, and unfair on the other hand, for trumping up "loitering" charges against them.

From the viewpoint of the police, the situation was quite different. They knew, with all the confidence necessary to be a policeman, that these boys were engaged in criminal activities. They knew this partly from occasionally catching them, mostly from circumstantial evidence ("the boys were around when those tires were slashed"), and partly because the police shared the view of the community in general that this was a bad bunch of boys. The best the police could hope to do was to be sensitive to the fact that those boys were engaged in illegal acts and arrest them whenever there was some evidence that they had been involved. Whether or not the boys had in fact committed a particular act in a particular way was not especially important. The police had a broader view: their job was to stamp out those kids' crimes; the tactics were not as important as the end result.

Over the period that the group was under observation, each member was arrested at least once. Several of the boys were arrested a number of times and spent at least one night in jail. While most were never taken to court, two of the boys were sentenced to six months' incarceration in boys' schools.

THE ROUGHNECKS IN SCHOOL

The Roughnecks' behavior in school was not particularly disruptive. During school hours they did not all hang around together, but tended instead to spend most of their time with one or two other members of the gang who were their special buddies. Although every member of the gang attempted to avoid school as much as possible, they were not particularly successful and most of them attended school with surprising regularity. They considered school a burden—something to be gotten through with a minimum of conflict. If they were "bugged" by a particular teacher, it could lead to trouble. One of the boys, Al, once threatened to beat up a teacher and, according to the other boys, the teacher hid under a desk to escape him.

Teachers saw the boys the way the general community did, as heading for trouble, as being uninterested in making something of themselves. Some were also seen as being incapable of meeting the academic standards of the school. Most of the teachers expressed concern for this group of boys and were willing to pass them despite poor performance, in the belief that failing them would only aggravate the problem.

The group of boys had a grade point average just slightly above "C." No one in the group failed either grade, and no one had better than a "C" average. They were very consistent in their achievement or, at least, the teachers were consistent in their perception of the boys' achievement.

Two of the boys were good football players. Herb was acknowledged to be the best player in the school and Jack was almost as good. Both boys were criticized for their failure to abide by training rules, for refusing to come to practice as often as they should, and for not playing their best during practice. What they lacked in sportsmanship they made up for in skill, apparently, and played every game no matter how poorly they had performed in practice or how many practice sessions they had missed.

TWO QUESTIONS

Why did the community, the school and the police react to the Saints as though they were good, upstanding, nondelinquent youths with bright futures but to the Roughnecks as though they were tough, young criminals who were headed for trouble? Why did the Roughnecks and the Saints in fact have quite different careers after high school—careers which, by and large, lived up to the expectations of the community?

The most obvious explanation for the differences in the community's and law enforcement agencies' reactions to the two gangs is that one group of boys was "more delinquent" than the other. Which group *was* more delinquent? The answer to this question will determine in part how we explain the differential responses to these groups by the members of the community and, particularly, by law enforcement and school officials.

In sheer number of illegal acts, the Saints were the more delinquent They were truant from school for at least part of the day almost every day of the week. In addition, their drinking and vandalism occurred with surprising regularity. The Roughnecks, in contrast, engaged sporadically in delinquent episodes. While these episodes were frequent, they certainly did not occur on a daily or even a weekly basis.

The difference in frequency of offenses was probably caused by the Roughnecks' inability to obtain liquor and to manipulate legitimate excuses from school. Since the Roughnecks had less money than the Saints, and teachers carefully supervised their school activities, the Roughnecks' hearts may have been as black as the Saints', but their misdeeds were not nearly as frequent.

There are really no clear-cut criteria by which to measure qualitative differences in antisocial behavior. The most important dimension of the difference is generally referred to as the "seriousness" of the offenses.

If seriousness encompasses the relative economic costs of delinquent acts, then some assessment can be made. The Roughnecks, probably stole an average of about $5.00 worth of goods a week. Some weeks the figure was considerably higher, but these times must be balanced against long periods when almost nothing was stolen.

The Saints were more continuously engaged in delinquency but their acts were not for the most part costly to property. Only their vandalism and occasional theft of gasoline would so qualify. Perhaps once or twice a month they would siphon a tankful of gas. The other costly items were street signs, construction lanterns and the like. All of these acts combined probably did not quite average $5.00 a week, partly because much of the stolen equipment was abandoned and presumably could be recovered. The difference in cost of stolen property between the two groups was trivial, but the Roughnecks probably had a slightly more expensive set of activities than did the Saints.

Another meaning of seriousness is the potential threat of physical harm to members of the community and to the boys themselves. The Roughnecks were more prone to physical violence; they not only welcomed an opportunity to fight, they went seeking it. In addition, they fought among themselves frequently. Although the fighting never included deadly weapons, it was still a menace, however minor, to the physical safety of those involved.

The Saints never fought. They avoided physical conflict both inside and outside the group. At the same time, though, the Saints frequently endangered their own and other people's lives. They did so almost every time they drove a car, especially if they had been drinking. Sober, their driving was risky; under the influence of alcohol it was horrendous. In addition, the Saints endangered the lives of others with their pranks. Street excavations left unmarked were a very serious hazard.

Evaluating the relative seriousness of the two gangs' activities is difficult. The community reacted as though the behavior of the Roughnecks was a problem, and they reacted as though the behavior of the Saints was not. But the members of the community were ignorant of the array of delinquent acts that characterized the Saints' behavior. Although concerned citizens were unaware of much of the Roughnecks' behavior as well, they were much better informed about the Roughnecks' involvement in delinquency than they were about the Saints'.

VISIBILITY

Differential treatment of the two gangs resulted in part because one gang was infinitely more visible than the other. This differential visibility was a direct function of the economic standing of the families. The Saints had access to automobiles and were able to remove themselves from the sight of the community. In as routine a decision as to where to go to have a milkshake after school, the Saints stayed away from the mainstream of community life. Lacking transportation, the Roughnecks could not make it to the edge of town. The center of town was the only practical place for them to meet since their homes were scattered throughout the town and any noncentral meeting place put an undue hardship on some members. Through necessity the Roughnecks congregated in a crowded area where everyone in the community passed frequently, including teachers and law enforcement officers. They could easily see the Roughnecks hanging around the drugstore.

The Roughnecks, of course, made themselves even more visible by making remarks to passersby and by occasionally getting into fights on the corner. Meanwhile, just as regularly, the Saints were either at the cafe on one edge of town or in the pool hall at the other edge of town. Without any particular realization that they were making themselves inconspicuous, the Saints were able to hide their time-wasting. Not only were they removed from the mainstream of traffic, but they were almost always inside a building.

On their escapades the Saints were also relatively invisible, since they left Hanibal and traveled to Big City. Here, too, they were mobile, roaming the city, rarely going to the same area twice.

DEMEANOR

To the notion of visibility must be added the difference in the responses of group members to outside intervention with their activities. If one of the Saints was confronted with an accusing policeman, even if he felt he was truly innocent of a wrongdoing, his demeanor was apologetic and penitent. A Roughneck's attitude was almost the polar opposite. When confronted with a threatening adult authority, even one who tried to be pleasant, the Roughneck's hostility and disdain were clearly observable. Sometimes he might attempt to put up a veneer of respect, but it was thin and was not accepted as sincere by the authority.

School was no different from the community at large. The Saints could manipulate the system by feigning compliance with the school norms. The availability of cars at school meant that once free from the immediate sight of the teacher, the boys could disappear rapidly. And this escape was well enough planned that no administrator or teacher was nearby when the boys left. A Roughneck who wished to escape for a few hours was in a bind. If it were possible to get free from class, downtown was still a mile away, and even if he arrived there, he was still very visible. Truancy for the Roughnecks meant almost certain detection, while the Saints enjoyed almost complete immunity from sanctions.

BIAS

Community members were not aware of the transgressions of the Saints. Even if the Saints had been less discreet, their favorite delinquencies would have been perceived as less serious than those of the Roughnecks.

In the eyes of the police and school officials, a boy who drinks in an alley and stands intoxicated on the street corner is committing a more serious offense than is a boy who drinks to inebriation in a nightclub or a tavern and drives around afterwards in a car. Similarly, a boy who steals a wallet from a store will be viewed as having committed a more serious offense than a boy who steals a lantern from a construction site.

Perceptual **bias** also operates with respect to the demeanor of the boys in the two groups when they are confronted by adults. It is not simply that adults dislike the posture affected by boys of the Roughneck ilk; more important is the conviction that the posture adopted by the Roughnecks is an indication of their devotion and commitment to deviance as a way of life. The posture becomes a cue, just as the type of the offense is a cue, to the degree to which the known transgressions are indicators of the youths' potential for other problems.

Visibility, demeanor and bias are surface variables which explain the day-to-day operations of the police. Why do these surface variables operate as they do? Why did the police choose to disregard the Saints' delinquencies while breathing down the backs of the Roughnecks?

The answer lies in the **class structure** of American society and the control of legal institutions by those at the top of the class structure. Obviously, no representative of the upper class drew up the operational chart for the police which led them to look in the ghettoes and on streetcorners—which led them to see the demeanor of lower-class youth as troublesome and that of upper-middle-class youth as tolerable. Rather, the procedures simply developed from experience—experience with irate and influential upper-middle-class parents insisting that their son's vandalism was simply a prank and his drunkenness only a momentary "sowing of wild oats"—experience with cooperative or indifferent, powerless, lower-class parents who acquiesced to the laws' definition of their son's behavior.

ADULT CAREERS OF THE SAINTS AND THE ROUGHNECKS

The community's confidence in the potential of the Saints and the Roughnecks apparently was justified. If anything, the community members underestimated the degree to which these youngsters would turn out "good" or "bad."

Seven of the eight members of the Saints went on to college immediately after high school. Five of the boys graduated from college in four years. The sixth one finished college after two years in the army, and the seventh spent four years in the air force before returning to college and receiving a B. A. degree. Of these seven college graduates, three went on for advanced degrees. One finished law school and is now active in state politics, one finished medical school and is practicing near Hanibal, and one boy is now working for a Ph.D. The other four college graduates entered submanagerial, managerial or executive training positions with larger firms.

The only Saint who did not complete college was Jerry. Jerry had failed to graduate from high school with the other Saints. During his second senior year, after the other Saints had gone on to college, Jerry began to hang around with what several teachers described as a "rough crowd"—the gang that was heir apparent to the Roughnecks. At the end of his second senior year, when he did graduate from high school, Jerry took a job as a used-car salesman, got married and quickly had a child. Although he made several abortive attempts to go to college by attending night school, when I last saw him (ten years after high school) Jerry was unemployed and had been living on unemployment for almost a year. His wife worked as a waitress.

Some of the Roughnecks have lived up to community expectations. A number of then were headed for trouble. A few were not.

Jack and Herb were the athletes among the Roughnecks and their athletic prowess paid off handsomely. Both boys received unsolicited athletic scholarships to college. After Herb received his scholarship (near the end of his senior year), he apparently did an about-face. His demeanor became very similar to that of the Saints. Although he remained a member in good standing of the Roughnecks, he stopped participating in most activities and did not hang around the comer as often.

Jack did not change. If anything, he became more prone to fighting. He even made excuses for accepting the scholarship. He told the other gang members that the school had guaranteed him a "C" average if he would come to play football—an idea that seems far-fetched, even in this day of highly competitive recruiting.

During the summer after graduation from high school, Jack attempted suicide by jumping from a tall building. The jump would certainly have killed most people trying it, but Jack survived. He entered college in the fall and played four years of football. He and Herb graduated in four years, and both are teaching and coaching in high schools. They are married and have stable families. If anything, Jack appears to have a more prestigious position in the community than does Herb, though both are well respected and secure in their positions.

Two of the boys never finished high school. Tommy left at the end of his junior year and went to another state. That summer he was arrested and placed on probation on a manslaughter charge. Three years later he was arrested for murder; he pleaded guilty to second degree murder and is serving a 30-year sentence in the state penitentiary.

Al, the other boy who did not finish high school, also left the state in his senior year. He is serving a life sentence in a state penitentiary for first degree murder.

Wes is a small-time gambler. He finished high school and "bummed around." After several years he made contact with a bookmaker who employed him as a runner. Later he acquired his own area and has been working it ever since. His position among the bookmakers is almost identical to the position he had in the gang; he is always around but no one is really aware of him. He makes no trouble and he does not get into any. Steady, reliable, capable of keeping his mouth closed, he plays the game by the rules, even though the game is an illegal one.

That leaves only Ron. Some of his former friends reported that they had heard he was "driving a truck up north," but no one could provide any concrete information.

REINFORCEMENT

The community responded to the Roughnecks as boys in trouble, and the boys agreed with that perception. Their pattern of deviancy was **reinforced**, and breaking away from it became increasingly unlikely. Once the boys acquired an image of themselves as deviants, they selected new friends who affirmed that self-image. As that self-conception became more firmly entrenched, they also became willing to try new and more extreme deviances. With their growing alienation came freer expression of disrespect and hostility for representatives of the legitimate society. This disrespect increased the community's negativism, perpetuating the entire process of commitment to deviance. Lack of a commitment to deviance works the same way. In either case, the process will perpetuate itself unless some event (like a scholarship to college or a sudden failure) external to the established relationship intervenes. For two of the Roughnecks (Herb and Jack), receiving college athletic scholarships created new relations and culminated in a break with the established pattern of deviance. In the case of one of the Saints (Jerry), his parents' divorce and his failing to graduate from high school changed some of his other relations. Being held back in school for a year and losing his place among the Saints had sufficient impact on Jerry to alter his self-image and virtually to assure that he would not go on to college as his peers did. Although the experiment of life can rarely be reversed, it seems likely in view of the behavior of the other boys who did not enjoy this special treatment by the school that Jerry, too, would have "become something" had he graduated as anticipated. For Herb and Jack outside intervention worked to their advantage; for Jerry it was his undoing.

Selective perception and **labelling**—finding, processing and punishing some kinds of criminality and not others—means that visible, poor, nonmobile, outspoken, undiplomatic "tough" kids will be noticed, whether their actions are seriously delinquent or not. Other kids, who have established a reputation for being bright (even though underachieving), disciplined and involved in respectable activities, who are mobile and monied, will be invisible when they deviate from sanctioned activities. They'll sow their wild oats—perhaps even wider and thicker than their lower class cohorts—but they won't be noticed. When it's time to leave adolescence most will follow the expected path, settling into the ways of the middle class, remembering fondly the delinquent but unnoticed fling of their youth. The Roughnecks and others like them may turn around, too. It is more likely that their noticeable deviance will have been so reinforced by police and community that their lives will be effectively channelled into careers consistent with their adolescent background.

QUESTIONS FOR DISCUSSION

1. In what ways are the Saints and the Roughnecks similar? How are they dissimilar?
2. How does "visibility" affect the delinquent definitions that are applied to the two groups of adolescents?
3. Discuss how money, success in school, and demeanor can influence and insulate being labeled "delinquent" by the community and the police.

APPLICATIONS

1. Draw upon your own experience and try to recall a positive or negative label that was applied to you.
   (a) Who assigned the label to you (friends, parents, a teacher, the police)?
   (b) Did the label affect the way you felt about yourself?
   (c) Was the label, (good or bad) reinforced by others around you?
   (d) Do you feel today that your life is a product of the labels that were applied to you and reinforced repeatedly?
2. Try to remember the various groups of students in your high school. Can you think of any groups that were considered to be "saints" or "roughnecks"? Write a short summary of your school, describing the characteristics of a saint group and a roughneck group.

chapter 24

Punishment, Accountability, and the New Juvenile Justice

Martha-Elin Blomquist • Martin L. Forst

INTRODUCTION

The juvenile justice system has undergone radical change in the past three decades. The procedural revolution that began at the end of the l 960s with the Gault decision has more recently evolved into a substantive evolution. The changes in juvenile justice have been many and in some instances drastic, particularly in the apparent demise of the rehabilitative ideal. New theories or models have emerged, incorporating terminology such as punishment, justice, and accountability into the vocabulary of juvenile justice practitioners and the lexicon of state juvenile codes.

The transformation in the philosophy and underlying goals of the system has been well-documented over the past decade or so.[1] It is now time to ask critical questions about the significance and meaning of this transformation and to bring attention to unresolved issues. This article suggests the issues that need to be addressed in order to make both practical and philosophical sense out of the changes in the mission of "juvenile justice."

BACKGROUND

Based on a variety of criticisms,[2] a movement arose within the last decade to make substantive changes in the philosophy of juvenile court and juvenile corrections law, including dispositional decision-making policy. This movement has rejected the rehabilitative ideal as traditionally conceived and has renewed interest in public protection, punishment, justice and accountability. As Gardner summarizes: "...[a] revolution in substantive theory is presently taking place as one jurisdiction after another expresses disenchantment with the rehabilitative ideal and embraces explicitly punitive sanctions as appropriate for youthful offenders."[3]

Notwithstanding their incongruities and unknown consequences, proposals to orient the philosophy and administration of the juvenile justice system around punishment and public protection have been supported by a diverse set of scholars, lawmakers, and practitioners. For example, the prestigious Joint Commission on Juvenile Justice Standards of the Institute of Judicial Administration and the American Bar Association (IJA/ABA) proposed in 1980 that the principles of criminal law and procedure replace the rehabilitative model of juvenile justice.[4] The Joint Commission advocated that juvenile justice sanctions be offense-based rather than based on the needs of the offender and that determinate sentencing should replace the traditional indeterminate sentencing system.

Moreover, these ideas have been supported by a variety of children's rights advocates who believe that a youth has a right to be punished for the offense committed rather than a need to be treated for what others perceive to be wrong with him or her. Other commentators have been concerned with the inequities and injustices resulting from the traditional offender-based system. Offense-based dispositions, by contrast, presumably prevent unjust and disproportionate periods of incarceration often found under a rehabilitation-oriented system. As Fox notes, "punishment clearly implies limits, whereas treatment does not."[5] Under this theory, a youth would not be incarcerated longer than is justified by the nature of the delinquent conduct, and certainly no longer than an adult convicted of the same offense.

Much of the philosophical and structural transformation, despite its lofty theory, is a direct result of public pressure to crack down on juveniles—to get tough with kids. Drs. Norman and Gillespie conclude, "The mood of the nation continues to move toward punishment and incapacitation of offenders."[6] Many statutory revisions are clearly designed to mollify the public's sense of fear and anger over juvenile crime.[7] Cracking down on juveniles has been accomplished in a variety of ways. Revising transfer laws to allow more juveniles to be tried as adults in criminal courts is but one example.[8] Moreover, numerous statutory changes have made sanctions meted out *within* the juvenile justice system more punitive. For example, the new Texas determinate sentencing law for juveniles, passed in 1987, provides that juveniles who have been adjudicated delinquent for one of six serious, violent offenses may receive a determinate sentence of as long as 30 years' confinement.[9]

Law and order groups have continued to propose more restrictive policies for controlling and sanctioning juvenile crime. The goal of these proposals is to make the juvenile justice system more like the criminal justice system. These proposals have resulted in "criminalizing" the juvenile justice system.

MOVING TO NEW MODELS

To institute these substantive reforms, many state legislatures have modified—sometimes extensively—the purpose clauses of their juvenile court or juvenile corrections statutes.[10] In some states, policy-makers simply added new phrases to the traditional language of *parens patriae* and "the best interests of the child"; in other states they replaced these time-honored goals all together. The new phraseology more closely approximates the underlying purposes of the criminal justice system, e.g., public protection, accountability, justice, punishment, deterrence, and incapacitation. Although these theoretical concepts are familiar to the criminal process, they remain confused and ill-defined in the juvenile justice system, particularly to the extent that they are merely grafted onto existing child welfare-based philosophies of traditional juvenile court law.

Examples of the new philosophies in juvenile justice abound. In passing the Juvenile Justice Act of 1977, Washington became the first state drastically to revamp its juvenile justice philosophy and enact a determinate sentencing statute for juvenile offenders. Mary Kay Becker, principal sponsor of the bill, said of the new statute:

> [T]he broad purpose of [the bill] should be fairly clear. In terms of the philosophical polarities that have characterized the juvenile court debate for more than a century, the new law moves away from the *parens patriae* doctrine of benevolent coercion, and closer to a more classical emphasis on justice. The law requires the court to deal more consistently with youngsters who commit offenses. The responsibility of providing services to youngsters whose behavior, while troublesome, is noncriminal, is assigned to the Department of Social and Health Services and the agencies with whom it may contract. The juvenile court is to view itself primarily as an instrument of justice rather than as a provider of services.[11]

This dramatic philosophical change is also demonstrated in the specific objectives of the legislation: (1) "Make the juvenile offender accountable for his or her criminal behavior," and (2) "Provide punishment commensurate with the age, crime, and criminal history of the juvenile offender."[12] This requirement of commensurate punishment creates the foundation for Washington's determinate sentencing system for juveniles.

Maine's statutes also permit the juvenile court to punish a child. Specifically, juvenile court law authorizes judges to remove a juvenile from parental custody for the minor's welfare or safety, or when "the protection of the public would otherwise be endangered, or where necessary *to punish* a child adjudicated…as having committed a…crime (emphasis added)."[13]

The California legislature has made a number of significant changes in the codes pertaining to the philosophy and operation of the juvenile court as well. Statutory revisions enacted in the past ten years have made accountability, victims' rights, and public safety high priorities in the juvenile justice system. The current statement of purpose of the juvenile court law reads, in relevant part:

> The purpose of the [Arnold–Kennick Juvenile Court Law] is to provide for the protection and safety of the public and each minor under the jurisdiction of the juvenile court.…Minors under the jurisdiction of the juvenile court as a consequence of delinquent conduct, shall in conformity with the interests of public safety and protection, receive care, treatment and guidance which is consistent with their best interest, which holds them accountable for their behavior, and which is appropriate for their circumstances. *Such guidance may include punishment.*…(emphasis added)[14]

But unlike Maine's statute, California law places a restriction on the punishment to be imposed: "Punishment for the purposes of this chapter does not include retribution."[15]

Minnesota's juvenile law incorporates slightly different terminology, requiring the juvenile court and system "promote public safety and reduce juvenile delinquency by maintaining the integrity of the substantive law by prohibiting certain behavior and by developing individual responsibility for lawful behavior."[16] The use of the phrase "promote the public safety" in the Minnesota statute suggests a social defense or public protection rationale, rather than a "justice" model. But the combined usage of "public safety" and "individual responsibility" is confusing. While these terms have some commonsensical appeal, their meaning or relationship to one another is unclear. Is public safety promoted by enhancing individual responsibility? If protecting the public conflicts with the promotion of individual responsibility, how would Minnesota law resolve the conflict?

Experts have used different terms to describe this shift in juvenile justice philosophy and structure. Scholars speak of new "models" of the juvenile justice system. Among others, these include the "criminal" model,[17] "punitive" model,[18] "penal" model,[19] "justice" model,[20] "accountability" model,[21] and "determinate sentencing" model.[22] Often these new terms or concepts are used interchangeably; insufficient thought has been given to the differences, sometimes subtle, among these models. In addition, the logical **corollaries** of the models have not been adequately explored. A number of issues need further clarification and analysis.

ADDRESSING UNRESOLVED ISSUES

Exploring the Nature of Punishment

Punishment is what the founders of the juvenile justice system presumably wanted to avoid. The idea was to extricate juveniles from the punitive adult system and to treat their underlying problems. As Melton explains, "At its deepest roots, [the] paternalistic vision of the juvenile court was based on the moral premise that youth do not deserve punishment for their violations of the law."[23]

But times changed—and so have statutes. The juvenile justice statutes in Washington, Maine, and California, as noted above, specifically mention the goal of punishment. And in Judge McGee's opinion, "There should be some form of punishment involved in every delinquency disposition, clearly identified to the perpetrator as being his just deserts."[24]

But what is punishment, particularly within the context of the juvenile justice system? There appear to be two substantially different conceptions. Punishment is viewed as **retributive** by some and **utilitarian** by others.

Gardner clearly summarizes the retributivist position. In his view, "...punishment entails the purposeful infliction of suffering upon an offender for his offense...."[25] Moreover, "...the primary thrust of punishment, rather than seeking to benefit the offender, is to exact from the recipient his debt to society, a payment of which nullifies his guilt."[26] This is a common theme. The retributivist position is thus "backward looking." That is, the key factor in disposition is the offense that took place in the past; the sanctioning system is based on the *offense*. The treatment needs of the offender are of little or no importance to the retributivist.[27]

By contrast, some commentators, particularly practitioners within the system, conceive of punishment in utilitarian, even humanitarian terms. They view punishment as an instrument of change for misbehaving youths. Some contend, for example, that punishment can be useful in helping foster a sense of responsibility in juveniles.[28] For this reason, according to Judge McGee, the juvenile court should punish juvenile offenders. "By doing so, the juvenile court is not **repudiating** its mission, it is helping to fulfill it."[29] Thus, punishment is miraculously transformed into rehabilitation.

California's statute is unique and raises profound issues. As noted above, the juvenile court in California is authorized to punish a juvenile offender; but the statute also provides that the punishment cannot be *retributive*. What does this mean? What is the difference between "retributive" punishment and "regular" or non-retributive punishment? Are the goals of these two types of punishment the same or different?

Presumably if the juvenile court is allowed to dispense punishment, the child must be protected from disproportionate punishment. As Fox asserts, "punishment implies limits."[30] If the idea is to punish the child and punishment implies limits, then the limits should be based on the seriousness of the offense. How is this reflected in California law? Does non-retributive punishment also imply limits? Or can non-retributive punishment be disproportionate to the seriousness of the offense? Is non-retributive punishment meant to right a wrong that has taken place in the past or is it intended to change a juvenile's personality or attitude?

To the extent that there is a move to punishment in juvenile justice, the logical corollaries must be more fully explored and articulated. Changing to a punishment-based system, particularly with a retributivist basis, has profound implications for sentencing structure, dispositional alternatives, and the internal logic of the entire juvenile justice system.

What Is "Justice" in Juvenile Justice?

The meaning of "justice" in juvenile justice has long been confused and the subject of debate. It might be argued that the concept does not belong in the juvenile system to the extent that the system's focus is on the best interests of the child and his or her rehabilitation. Thus under the rehabilitative model, with its indeterminate sentencing scheme, there is no necessary relationship between the offense committed and the disposition—that is, between the harm done and, for example, the length of stay in an institution.

Conversely, it could be argued that justice is what has long been missing from the juvenile justice system. But this begs the question: what is, or should be, "justice" within the context of the juvenile justice system? Moreover, what is the relationship between justice and punishment?

Justice and punishment seem somehow to be related. To be just, punishment must be proportionate to the seriousness of the offense committed. Seriousness is generally determined by the harmfulness of the act and the degree of culpability of the offender.[31] This notion is summarized in the simple phrase: "let the punishment fit the crime." This, in turn, implies a gradation of offenses by seriousness. It also implies some corresponding ranking of severity of punishment. Based on this internal logic, Washington state has adopted a determinate sentencing scheme for juvenile offenders.

California has at least partially adopted a just deserts schema. Prompted by the State Supreme Court's ruling in *People v. Olivas* to extend equal protection of the law to the term of confinement served by youthful offenders committed to the California Youth Authority,[32] the legislature modified the indeterminate sentencing law applicable to juveniles. As part of a major reform package adopted in 1976 which affected several aspects of the juvenile justice system, legislators enacted the provision that:

> ...in any case in which the minor is removed from the physical custody of his...guardian as a result of an order of wardship, the order shall specify that the minor may not be held in physical confinement for a period in excess of the maximum term of confinement which would be imposed upon an adult convicted of the offense...which brought the minor under the jurisdiction of the juvenile court.[33]

With a justice or just deserts philosophy, it follows that limits must be placed on dispositional alternatives, and specifically on the degree of punishment meted out to juvenile offenders. These limits can be, and often are, in direct conflict with the traditional goals and structure of the juvenile justice system.

Accountability

Some authorities use the term "accountability" to describe the new models of juvenile justice. Maloney, Romig, and Armstrong, for example, claim that accountability is one of the core values in the recent juvenile court and probation movement. According to them, "Accountability is firmly grounded in the justice theme that the system must respond to illegal behavior in such a way that the offender is made aware of and responsible for the loss, damage, or injury perpetrated upon the victim."[34]

But even this simple assertion raises questions. What is the relationship between accountability and justice or punishment? What is the relationship of accountability to individual responsibility? Does holding a youth accountable mean that the youth will be made to understand and appreciate the wrongfulness of his or her acts? Or does it mean the youth will be held personally responsible for the harm done and punished in direct proportion (no more and no less) to the offense?

Maloney, Romig, and Armstrong seem to use the term in the former way. That is, accountability appears to mean making the juvenile aware of and accept responsibility for his or her wrongful acts. Through the juvenile justice experience, accountability is something to be instilled into the misbehaving youth. For example, Maloney, Romig, and Armstrong suggest that restitution is one of the more promising approaches available to the court "for imposing a tangible and enforceable form of accountability on juvenile offenders."[35] Moreover, "Accountability has taken the form of imparting some sense of individual responsibility and social awareness to the youthful offender."[36] But is accountability something that one *instills* in a juvenile? Or is it something that one inflicts, like punishment, proportionate to the offense?

It is easy to envision the conflicts that could arise with differing notions of accountability—that is, instilling a sense of responsibility or inflicting punishment for wrongdoing. Take, for example, a 16-year-old armed robber with one prior adjudication for the same offense. Suppose that "justice" (i.e., proportionate punishment as defined by the legislature or a sentencing commission) dictates that a youth spend two years in confinement at a training school. Suppose further that at the end of the two year period the youth does not appreciate or acknowledge the wrongfulness of his or her acts? Should the youth be released at the end of the two year period? If accountability is related to instilling values and fostering responsibility, the answer is no. If accountability is related to just and proportionate punishment, the answer is yes.

Individual Responsibility

Punishment and accountability are related, in some manner, to responsibility. Generally, the infliction of punishment on a person for his or her acts presumes that a person is responsible for those acts. The law does not allow the punishment of the mentally ill or idiots, because they do not possess the requisite mental intent (*mens rea*) to be morally **culpable.** For the state to punish, the person receiving punishment must be viewed as a responsible actor. One of the emerging issues in juvenile justice is whether juveniles—or which juveniles under what circumstances—are responsible moral actors.

The traditional view is that juveniles are not fully responsible, especially for criminal activity. Even the IJA/ABA Standards provide, "Juveniles may be viewed as incomplete adults, lacking in full moral and experiential development."[37] This leads some authorities, like Zimring, to conclude that juvenile offenders must be protected from the full burden of adult responsibility while being "pushed along by degrees toward moral and legal accountability, that we consider appropriate to adulthood."[38]

But the current trend is to hold juveniles responsible (and accountable) for their actions. Melton observes, "As the rehabilitative underpinnings of the juvenile court have withered away, courts have increasingly been faced with the problem of determining individual juveniles' responsibility, especially in those jurisdictions in which punitive purposes have been expressly recognized in juvenile codes."[39] Gardner, moreover, concludes, "Because punishment is justifiable only if its recipient is a 'person' capable of moral agency, the movement toward a punitive model seriously questions the existing view that juveniles lack capacity for rational decision-making."[40]

Some states have officially adopted the view that juveniles are, at least in some instances, responsible moral actors. For example, in California, the administrative policies instituted by correctional officials in the California Youth Authority (CYA) system have begun to focus on the goals of accountability and public protection. In the comprehensive statement of mission and directions used by the Department of the Youth Authority in 1983, the Director stated that, "the most effective way to protect the public is to ensure that offenders are held accountable for their antisocial behavior."[41] According to this policy document, accountability "refers to the ward accepting *full responsibility* for his or her own behavior, including the commitment offense and behavior while in the institution and on parole" (emphasis added).[42]

As noted, this view of the individual responsibility of juveniles conflicts with traditional conceptions of juvenile responsibility and compelling legal precedent. In *Eddings v. Oklahoma,* the United States Supreme Court mentioned that children have a "special place" in the law, and this is evidenced by the fact that every state in the country has a separate juvenile court system.[43] The Court also expressed in *Eddings* that juveniles possess a lower level of maturity than adults: "Our [American] history is replete with laws and judicial recognitions that minors, especially in their earlier years, generally are less mature and responsible than adults."[44] The Court also stated, "...Even the normal 16-year-old customarily lacks the maturity of an adult."[45]

The issue of maturity—and responsibility—of juveniles surfaced again in *Thompson v. Oklahoma.* The Supreme Court stated:

> There is also broad agreement on the proposition that adolescents as a class are less mature and responsible than adults. We stressed this difference in explaining the importance of treating the defendant's youth as a mitigating factor in capital cases....[Moreover]...[i]nexperience, less education, and less intelligence make a teenager less able to evaluate the consequences of his or her conduct while at the same time he or she is much more apt to be motivated by mere emotion or peer pressure than is an adult. The reasons why juveniles are not trusted with the privileges and responsibilities of an adult also explain why their irresponsible conduct is not as morally responsible as that of an adult.[46]

This logic led the Court to conclude that "...less culpability should attach to a crime committed by a juvenile than to a comparable crime by an adult."[47]

A conflict—or Catch 22—is becoming apparent. On the one hand, juvenile law traditionally holds that juveniles should not be punished because they are *not* responsible actors. On the other hand, some authorities now hold that juveniles should be punished in order to *make* them more responsible. But issues remain unresolved: are juveniles fully responsible for their criminal actions? Under what conditions, if any, are they as responsible as adults? And how is punishment related to levels of responsibility?

The Infancy Defense

To the extent that the juvenile court has historically not been concerned with culpability, responsibility and punishment, the infancy defense was deemed to be irrelevant. Some states have continued to maintain this traditional view. As recently as a 1981, for example, the Rhode Island Supreme Court held,

> Once one accepts the principle that a finding of delinquency or waywardness in a juvenile proceeding is not the equivalent of a finding that the juvenile has committed a crime, there is no necessity of a finding that the juvenile has such maturity that he or she knew what he or she was doing was wrong.[48]

In the trend toward punishment, an opposing position is set forth: "Juvenile proceedings are 'criminal' in nature when punishment is the sanction imposed."[49] If juvenile court proceedings are now deemed criminal in nature, should not the infancy defense be relevant? Some jurisdictions are coming to that conclusion. For example, in *State v. Q.D.,* the Washington Supreme Court held, "The principles of construction of criminal statutes, made necessary by our recognition of the criminal nature of juvenile court proceedings, also compel us to conclude that [the infancy defense] applies to proceedings in juvenile courts."[50]

Thus, to the extent that juvenile codes now authorize punishment for juveniles, it follows that juveniles should be allowed to use the traditional criminal defenses. As Melton contends, "If juveniles are to be subjected to *any* punishment, then they should be provided the protections embedded within criminal procedure, modified as necessary to ensure that such proceedings meet the special demands of fundamental fairness as applied to youth."[51]

MIXED GOALS AND CONTINUING CONFUSION

Some states, as well as some scholars, have tried to blend the new goals of the juvenile justice system with the traditional goals. This mixed bag is evident in the statutory provisions of a few states. For example, the purpose of Florida's revised juvenile code is:

> *to protect society* more effectively by *substituting for retributive punishment,* whenever possible, methods of offender *rehabilitation and rehabilitative restitution,* recognizing that the application of *sanctions* which are consistent with the *seriousness of the offense* is appropriate *in all cases.* (emphasis added).[52]

The language of the Florida law is particularly confusing. On the one hand, the law appears to retain the traditional goal of rehabilitation, which implies variable lengths of confinement based on the ability of each youth to meet his or her treatment goals. On the other hand, the law implies a just deserts orientation, stressing that sanctions be proportionate to the seriousness of the criminal conduct in all cases. These two principles appear to be diametrically opposed. Which one is it going to be?

In a similar vein, Maloney, Romig, and Armstrong advocate a "balanced approach" to juvenile probation—and presumably to the rest of the juvenile court and correctional process. They claim that there are four "core values" that shape the juvenile court and probation movement: community protection, accountability, competency development, and individualized assessment and treatment.[53]

But these values can—and often do—conflict. Accountability, to the extent that it is associated with justice and punishment, may dictate that a youth stay in an institution for a specified period of time, based on the seriousness of the offense. However, community protection may demand that the youth remain incarcerated for a longer period; conversely, a youth's progress in treatment and rehabilitation may suggest a shorter period of confinement. Which core value is to be followed? How are conflicts to be resolved? Who is to resolve these conflicting principles? It may be difficult, but it may be necessary to acknowledge that some principles do not fit well with other principles. It simply will not work to say that the juvenile court should punish a juvenile offender in direct proportion to his or her offense (just deserts) and at the same time individualize the youth's sentence depending on his or her treatment needs.

The new "balanced" approach is probably not much different than in the "good old days" when statutes provided little, if any, guidance to juvenile court judges or officials (parole board or correctional personnel) who were responsible for deciding when juveniles were to be released from institutional placement. In reality, the balanced approach used to mean a lack of standards or guidelines for decision-making. In practice, some judges and correctional officials would emphasize public protection, others rehabilitation, and still others accountability for misdeeds. The same situation appears true today. The modern balanced approach perpetuates a muddled **jurisprudence** for responding to different types of juvenile offenders under different fact situations. It does not clearly delineate how much weight is to be given to each of the core values under different circumstances. Without such guidance, judges and correctional officials are likely to rely on their own values, and the "balance" may become skewed by personal bias or community pressures.

CONCLUSIONS

The juvenile justice system is wrestling with a changing philosophy. Disenchantment with the old system has demanded revision. But because of the lack of clarity of the emerging concepts, there is no consensus about the nature and purpose of the new vision of juvenile justice. Enormous confusion remains over the meaning of the new models and how they should be operationalized.

In responding to demands from the public to "crack down on crime" and give public protection a higher priority in crime control policies, lawmakers have used various terms to describe the juvenile justice system's new mission. Some of the new terms conflict with the traditional juvenile justice language that continues to govern the legal framework of many state juvenile justice systems.

Ambiguity over the new terms or models gives juvenile court judges, as well as correctional officials and staff, confused messages as to the purpose or purposes of the system and the relative priority of the system's various goals. "Accountability," for example, is currently an ill-defined concept that means substantially different things to different people. The accountability model is broad enough to encompass all of the ideas of justice, just deserts, punishment, nonretributive punishment, public safety, preventive detention, responsibility, and culpability. Accountability has also given rebirth to the tarnished concepts of treatment and rehabilitation to the extent that it has been associated with the moral improvement of the youthful offender.

Perhaps all of the philosophical debate is simply a guise or smokescreen, used to gloss over an underlying political and social agenda: crack down on kids and put them away for longer periods of time to satisfy the public's thirst for vengeance and demand for public protection. The new models in juvenile justice may not have grown out of an evolving jurisprudence of juvenile justice, but rather out of a political expediency to give juveniles longer and harsher sentences. Whatever the motivations for moving to new models, policy-makers must begin to clarify the goals and mission of the juvenile justice system, and must specify exactly how the system should respond to different types of offenders and offenses.

Notes

1. For example, see: P. Tamilia, "The Recriminalization of the Juvenile Justice System—The Demise of the Socialized Court," 31(2) *Juvenile and Family Court Journal* 15–22 (1980); B. Feld, "Criminalizing Juvenile Justice: Rules of Procedure for the Juvenile Court," 69 *Minnesota Law Review* 141–276 (1984); J. Glen, "Juvenile Court Reform: Procedural Process and Substantive Stasis," 1970 *Wisconsin Law Review* 431–449; B. Feld, "The Juvenile Court Meets the Principle of Offense: Punishment, Treatment and the Difference It Makes," 68 *Boston University Law Review* 821–915 (1988); M. Forst and M. Blomquist, "Cracking Down on Juveniles: The Changing Ideology of Youth Corrections," 5 *Notre Dame Journal of Law, Ethics and Public Policy* 323–375 (1991).

2. For example, see: F. A. Allen, "The Juvenile Court and the Limits of Juvenile Justice," 11 *Wayne Law Review* 676–687 (1965); M. Wolfgang, "Abolish the Juvenile Court System," 2(10) *California Lawyer* 12–13 (1982); E. van den Haag, *Punishing Criminals* (New York: Basic Books, Inc.), 1975; W. Arnold, "Race and Ethnicity Relative to Other Factors in Juvenile Court Dispositions," 77 *American Journal of Sociology* 211–222 (1971); B. Boland and J. Q. Wilson, "Age, Crime and Punishment," 51 *The Public Interest* 22–34 (1978).

3. M. Gardner, "Punitive Juvenile Justice: Some Observations on a Recent Trend," 10 *International Journal of Law and Psychiatry* 129–151 (1987), at p. 131–132.

4. Institute of Judicial Administration/American Bar Association (IJA/ABA) Joint Commission on Juvenile Justice Standards, Standards Relating to Disposition (1980). Also see: F. McCarthy, "Delinquency Dispositions under the Juvenile Justice Standards: The Consequences of a Change of Rationale," 52 *New York University Law Review* 1093–1119 (1977). McCarthy states, "...the standards advocate as the principal aim of the juvenile justice system the effective punishment of juveniles whose conduct endangers public safety" at p. 1094.

5. S. Fox, "The Reform of the Juvenile Court: The Child's Right to Punishment," 25 *Juvenile Justice* 2–9 (1974), at p. 2.

6. M. Norman and L. Gillespie, "Changing Horses: Utah's Shift in Adjudicating Serious Juvenile Offenders," 12 *Journal of Contemporary Law* 85–98 (1986), at p. 85.

7. For example, see: R. Dawson, "The Third Justice System: The New Juvenile-Criminal System of Determinate Sentencing for the Youthful Violent Offender in Texas," 19 *St. Mary's Law Journal* 943–1016(1988); Note, "The Serious Young Offender under Vermont's Juvenile Law: Beyond the Reach of *Parens Patriae*," 8 *Vermont Law Review* 173–202 (1983); R. McNally, "Juvenile Court: An Endangered Species," 47 *Federal Probation* 32–37 (1983).

8. For example, see: B. Feld, "The Juvenile Court Meets the Principle of the Offense: Legislative Changes in Juvenile Waiver Statutes," 78 *Journal of Criminal Law and Criminology* 471–533 (1987); C. Rudman, E. Hartstone, J. Pagan, and M. Moore, "Violent Youth in Adult Court: Process and Punishment," 32 *Crime and Delinquency* 75–96 (1986).

9. Dawson (1988), supra, note 7.

10. Feld (1988), *supra*, note 1.

11. M. K Becker, "Washington State's New Juvenile Code: An Introduction," 14 *Gonzaga Law Review* 289–312 (1979), at p. 308.

12. Washington Revised Codes, Section 13.40.010(2)(c)–(d).

13. Maine Revised Statutes Annotated, Title 15, Section 3002.1(c).

14. California Welfare and Institutions Code, Section 202.

15. *Id.*

16. Minnesota Statutes, Section 260.011(2).

17. For example, see: McCarthy (1977), *supra*, note 4.
18. For example, see: M. Gardner (1987), *supra,* note 3.
19. For example, see: S. Winner and M. Keller, "The Penal Model of Juvenile Justice: Is Juvenile Court Delinquency Jurisdiction Obsolete?" 52 *New York University Law Review* 1120–1135 (1977).
20. For example, see: C. Springer, *Justice for Juveniles,* U.S. Department of Justice, Office of Juvenile Justice and Delinquency Prevention, Washington, D.C., April 1986.
21. For example, see: M. Gardner, "The Right of Juvenile Offenders to Be Punished: Some Implications of Treating Kids as Persons," 68 *Nebraska Law Review* 182–215 (1989).
22. For example, see: B. Benda and D. Waite, "A Proposed Determinate Sentencing Model in Virginia: An Empirical Evaluation," 39(1) *Juvenile and Family Court Journal* 55–71 (1988).
23. G. Melton, "Taking *Gault* Seriously: Toward a New Juvenile Court," 68 *Nebraska Law Review* 146–181 (1989), at p. 151.
24. C. McGee, "Measured Steps Toward Clarity and Balance in the Juvenile Justice System," 40(3) *Juvenile and Family Court Journal* 1–23 (1989), at p. 16.
25. Gardner (1989), *supra,* note 21 at p. 185.
26. *Id.* at p. 184.
27. For example, see: A. von Hirsch, *Doing Justice* (New York: Hill and Wang, 1976).
28. R. Barnum, "The Development of Responsibility: Implications for Juvenile Justice," in Francis X. Hartman (ed.), *From Children to Citizens,* 1987, p. 74. Also see: McGee (1989), *supra,* note 24, at p. 16. He states, "Sometimes punishment alone is enough....A young petit thief might *learn* lesson enough by a sentence including a few days of incarceration and an additional restitution order."
29. McGee (1989), *supra,* note 24, at p. 16.
30. Fox, *supra,* note 5.
31. von Hirsch (1976), *supra,* note 27.
32. *People v. Olivas,* 17 Cal.3d 236, 551 P.2d 375 (1976).
33. California Welfare and Institutions Code, Section 726(c).
34. D. Maloney, D. Romig, and T. Armstrong, "Juvenile Probation: The Balanced Approach," 39(3) *Juvenile and Family Court Journal* 5–8 (1988), at p. 6.
35. *Id.*
36. *Id.*
37. IJA/ABA Standards (1980), *supra,* note 4, at p. 19 note 5, (quoting Cohen, Position Paper, Juvenile Justice Standards Project, No. 18, 1974).
38. F. Zimring, *The Changing Legal World of Adolescence.* New York: The Free Press, (1982), at p. 95–96.
39. Melton (1989), *supra,* note 23 at p. 178.
40. Gardner (1989), *supra,* note 21, at p. 195.
41. Department of the Youth Authority. Mission Statement, Premises, Expanded Directional Statements, Sacramento, CA (1983), at p. 5.
42. *Id.*
43. *Eddings v. Oklahoma,* 455 U.S. 104 (1982), quoting from *May v. Anderson,* 345 U.S. 528, 536 (1952).
44. 455 U.S. 104, 115–116 (1982).
45. *Id* at p. 116.
46. *Thompson v. Oklahoma,* 487 U.S. 815, 835 (1988).
47. Id.

48. *In re Michael,* 423 A.2d 1180, 1183 (1981).

49. Gardner (1987), *supra,* note 3, at p. 147.

50. *State v. Q. D.,* 685 P.2d 557, 560 (1984).

51. Melton (1989), *supra,* note 23 at p. 180.

52. Florida Statutes Annotated, Section 39.001(2)(a).

53. Maloney et al. (1988), *supra,* note 34.

QUESTIONS FOR DISCUSSION

1. Why has there been a move away from attempting to rehabilitate juvenile offenders toward policies of punishment and accountability? Provide examples to support your answer.

2. Discuss the controversy surrounding the definition of "justice" in the juvenile justice system. Provide examples of how some states are handling this controversy.

3. Discuss the "infancy defense." Why is this defense particularly relevant considering that more juveniles are being remanded to adult courts?

APPLICATIONS

1. As is apparent from this article, our society has gradually moved from trying to rehabilitate juvenile offenders to remedies of increasing punishment for juvenile offenders. Do you believe that this approach will be more successful? Why? Discuss your views with other members of your class.

2. The authors suggest that policymakers "must specify exactly how the system should respond to different types of offenders and offenses." Why is this difficult, if not impossible, to accomplish in any sort of equitable fashion? Discuss.

part VI

Current Issues and Policy

A policy is a plan of action. The United States has formulated criminal justice policies by emphasizing one or more of four major goals: (1) retribution, or in modern terminology, "just deserts"; (2) deterrence; (3) incapacitation; and (4) rehabilitation. The major crises in crime policy have come about due to the fundamental lack of congruity of components that go to make up the whole known as the criminal justice system. This has lead to a non-system or an antisystem in which resources, both financial and human, are misdirected and squandered by short-term thinking based on nebulous political objectives. If, for example, law enforcement policy focuses on incapacitation, the courts on deterrence, and corrections on retribution, what are the expectations of the system as a whole? What type of offender should be incapacitated, and what type should be rehabilitated? During the last two decades, deterrence and retribution have become the leading policy platforms in criminal justice. These policies have lead to the greatest financial expenditures in history, the highest level of incarceration of any industrial nation in the world, and yet we still have unbelievable rates of violence. For example, the homicide rate in the United States is approximately 22,000 victims per year. We have teenagers literally controlling parts of our major cities, disrupting schools, neighborhoods, and even our prisons. The crime problem in the United States seems at times to be an improbable calamity, with politicians staring in the role of court jester.

Our major goal in designing public policy regarding crime should be to effectively and efficiently reduce the level of crime in our society. Focusing on violent crime and the habitual recidivists that account for the significant majority of this violence, means consistently incapacitating the offenders. In addition, nonviolent offenders must be dealt with by means that reduce the risk of them reoffending. Americans want to feel safe in their homes, neighborhoods, schools, and churches, and have mistakenly transferred responsibility for goal achievement to governments, which have become reactive rather than proactive. We believe, as do many others, that our approach to crime policy needs to be bold and simple. We must work toward reducing crime and stop allowing criminals, including organized, white-collar, governmental, and street thugs, to control our lives with fear, intimidation, and violence. The continuation of the violent crime crisis in the United States could eventually erode the rights of all citizens. To participate in a democracy, a person has obligations first and prerogatives second. The reverse has become the norm for too many, and our democracy,

365

especially our sense of liberty and freedom, is jeopardized. It is only when we demand better that we will get better. Our first and most important priority in designing public policy regarding crime must be to bring whatever resources are necessary to bear on making America a safe nation.

As you assess the articles contained in Part VI, let your imagination guide you toward nontraditional possibilities for solutions to our crime problems. There are no perfect answers or solutions to the many social problems of today. It is well overdue, however, for us as a nation to demand that crime be approached with intelligence and integrity rather than rhetoric and hyperbole. This will take changing our paradigms regarding crime and criminals. It will also mean peace of mind for the rest of us.

Policies regarding crime and criminals may be based on evidence that is more smoke and mirrors rather than objective fact. Victor E. Kappeler, Mark Blumberg, and Gary Potter approach crime and criminals as products of myth in "The Social Construction of Crime Myths." Especially important to understand are the processes and characterization of crime myths in relation to facts. Interesting processes such as the functions, media, government, and techniques of crime myths are examined to shed light on agendas that are often obscured by rhetorical clouds that have nothing to do with solutions to social problems.

Can the government solve the crime problem? In "Why Governments Don't Do What They Could to Reduce Violent Crime: The Politics of Crime," Richard Neely claims they cannot, due to powerful forces opposed to reform efforts. Basically, it will take a grass-roots effort to reform criminal justice, and this means relying less and less on the government. The more dependent we become on the government to solve any social problem, the worse the problem gets.

"A Policy Maker's Guide to Controlling Delinquency and Crime through Family Interventions," by Karen E. Wright and Kevin N. Wright is an excellent article dealing with the very core of the delinquency problem. Central to understanding delinquency is an understanding that the very early years of a child's life influence the remainder of that life. Common factors, such as how parents treat or fail to treat their children, parental supervision, marital discord, and violence, are some of the more common features of delinquency-prone youth family structure. With little doubt, policies and resources directed toward improving families holds more promise than hundreds of new facilities for delinquents. An ounce of prevention is truly worth a pound of cure.

We conclude this second edition with Elliott Currie's article "Confronting Crime: Looking Toward the Twenty-First Century." Currie asks: "Are we systematically abusing and neglecting the social environment?" Currie claims that we are afraid to look at the sources of crime and have instead concerned ourselves with the "downstream" consequences. As we have argued elsewhere, this is a continuation of the reactive approach to crime. The conservative approaches to crime and justice have escalated the social problems related to crime into a crisis leading to a collapse of public faith in the abilities of the system to deliver "justice."

chapter 25

The Social Construction of Crime Myths

Victor Kappeler • Mark Blumberg • Gary Potter

INTRODUCTION

People study social problems for a variety of reasons. The most obvious is to find solutions to society's concerns. Sometimes the solution must be sought not only in the content of the issue itself but in why a particular problem becomes more prominent than another. Many scholars in many disciplines look at the origins, diffusion, and consequences of social issues which capture the public's attention. Two very different perspectives can be used to explain the existence of a social problem. One perspective would be taken by people who have been characterized as "claimsmakers," "moral entrepreneurs," "political activists," "social pathologists," and "issue energizers" (Schoenfeld, Meier, and Griffin, 1979). These individuals have vested interests in the problem they bring to the public's attention. From their perspective. the social problem they are uncovering is real and has grave consequences. These individuals usually advocate formal social policy to address the new problem. To these individuals their social problem is real in its existence, unique in its characteristics. and grave in its social consequences.

The other perspective is taken by people who study social problems and how those problems are constructed. These people often see social problems as being constructed from collective definitions rather than from individual views and perceptions. Since social problems are collective constructions based on many individual perceptions and presentations of information, they can never truly exist in their collective and socially distorted form. These people often speak of social problems in terms of their origins and attribute the conception and definition of the problems to the mass media (Fishman, 1976), urban legend (Best and Hortuchi, 1985), group hysteria (Medalia and Larsen, 1958), ideology (Ryan,

1976), political power (Quinney, 1970), or some other often latent social force that directs public attention and shapes the definition and characteristics of emerging social problems.

We have chosen the term "myth" to describe some of the collective definitions society applies to certain crime problems. The word myth seems most appropriate to the social definition of many different kinds of criminal behavior brought to the public's attention. One common meaning of myth is a traditional story of unknown authorship, with a historical basis, serving usually to explain some event. The events of myth are based upon "exaggeration" or heightening of "ordinary" events in life. Other uses of the term carry with it the connotation of nonscientific, spoken or written fiction used as if it were a true account of some event.

The phrase "crime myth" does not stray too far from these accepted definitions. Crime myths are usually created in nonscientific forums through the telling of crime-related fictions or sensational stories. These crime fictions often take on new meanings as they are told and retold and at some point evolve into accepted truth for many people.

The fiction in crime myth comes not only from fabrication of events but from the transformation and distortion of events into social and political problems. Many of our contemporary issues of crime and justice are the product of some real event or social concern. Most crime mythology is the product of breakdowns in logic, contradiction, and distortion. As crime-related issues are debated and redebated, shaped and reshaped in public forums, they become distorted into myth.

This book focuses on the processes by which these events become distorted and are given unprecedented social consideration. Single authors of short crime-related fictions are given scant attention. Instead, we attempt to illustrate the range of social processes by which popular thought concerning a crime issue transforms the original concern into a crime problem taking on the characteristics of myth. This distortion of the reality of crime and criminal justice issues into myths emerges from a "collective," sometimes "unconscious," enterprise (Mannheim, 1936). Our inquiry concentrates on current issues in crime and justice that have reached or are near their myth potential plus the costs of myth production to society.

THE FUNCTION OF CRIME MYTHS

The study of myths in crime is not a novel or merely academic undertaking; crime myths are real in the minds of their believers and have definite social consequences. Crime myths have numerous effects on our perceptions; we may not even be conscious that they are at work. Myths tend to organize our views of crime, criminals, and the proper operation of the criminal justice system. They provide us with a conceptual framework from which to identify certain social issues as crime-related, develop our personal opinions on issues of justice, and apply ready-made solutions to social problems. The organization of views through crime myths contributes to the cataloging of crime issues into artificial distinctions between criminals, victims, crime fighters, and viable social responses to crime.

Myths also support and maintain established views of crime, criminals, and the criminal justice system, causing a tendency to rely on established views of crime and justice. Myths reinforce the current designation of conduct as criminal, supporting existing practices of crime control and providing the background assumptions for future designation of conduct as criminal. In a sense, society becomes intellectually blinded by the mythology of crime and justice. The established **conceptual framework** may not enable us to define issues accurately, to explore new solutions, or to find alternatives to existing socially constructed labels and crime control practices.

Myths tend to provide the necessary information for the construction of a "social reality of crime (Quinney, 1970)." Crime myths become a convenient mortar to fill gaps in knowledge and to provide answers to questions social science either cannot answer or has failed to address. Where science and empirical evidence have failed to provide answers to the public's crime concerns, mythology has stepped in to fill the knowledge void. Collectively, crime myths create our social reality of crime and justice. Finally, crime myths provide an outlet for emotionalism and channel emotion into action. They not only allow for interpretation of general social emotions and sentiment but direct those emotions to designated targets. Crime myths allow for social action based on emotionalism while providing justification for established views of behavior, social practice, and institutional responses to crime.

CRIMINAL MYTHMAKERS

The social construction of myths of crime and criminal justice seems to follow a series of recurrent patterns. These patterns allow for an unprecedented amount of social attention to be focused upon a few isolated criminal events or issues. This attention is promoted by intense, but often brief, mass media coverage of a select problem. Intense social concern with an issue is achieved by a variety of means. The mass media, government, law enforcement officials, interpersonal communications, and the interests of reform groups all play a major role in focusing the public's attention on select social problems. There is, if you will, a myth-producing enterprise in our society. One of the largest and most powerful mythmakers in this enterprise is the mass media.

Modern mass communication has virtually replaced traditional vehicles of communicating myth. Mass communication is a formalized and institutionalized system of conveying messages. It consists of sending messages by way of technology to large groups of people. The traditional process of communication and myth distribution, once based solely on word of mouth and later extended by the written word, has been replaced by rapid electronic-based communication. This modern mass communication system has enabled myths to spread in unprecedented numbers and with frightening speed. Over 40 years ago, Edwin H. Sutherland (1950) noted that, "Fear is produced more readily in the modern community than it was earlier in our history because of increased publicity…" (143). What were once stories restricted in dissemination to small interactive social groups are now instantly projected to millions of people internationally by the mass media. This increased ability to project myth has been coupled with an ever-decreasing circle of people who control the means and mediums of myth production. This restricted number of mythmakers has given the modern media and government almost a monopoly of the myth industry. Today, the media and government select our crime problems for us and focus our attention on social issues. The role of the individual and small social groups no longer predominates in the dissemination of modern crime mythology.

MEDIA AS MYTHMAKER

The media chooses and presents unique crime problems for public consumption. The selection of crime problems is often limited to the most bizarre or gruesome act a journalist or investigator can uncover. Incident and problem selection are driven by the competitive nature of modern media. By culling unique and fascinating issues for public exhibition, the media ensures the marketability and success (viewers and advertising dollars) of a given media production. Once an incident has been selected, it is then presented as evidence of a common, more general, and representative crime problem. The practice of using sensational stories to attract readers and increase profit is sometimes referred to as "yellow" journalism. Television news has not escaped the economic lure of sensationalism. Local stations learned "late in the 1960s, that news could make money—lots of money. By the end of the 1970s, news was frequently producing 60 percent of a station's profits...and a heavily entertainment-oriented form of programming began to evolve" (Hallin, 1990:2).

Prompted by the nature of the media industry, television and newspaper reporters focus on "hot topics" of entertainment value. In the early states of myth development, a media frenzy develops which allows for expanded coverage of isolated and unique events. Typically, the appearance of an uncritical newspaper or magazine article exploring a unique social problem starts the chain of events. The journalist has uncovered a "new" social evil. Other journalists, not wanting to be left out, jump on the bandwagon. The accounts which follow may eventually blossom into highly publicized quasidocumentaries or even movies that graphically portray the problem. Social problems reach their media-built myth potential when sensationalism reaches its height and when they are reported by tabloid-television investigators. In this fashion, isolated incidents become social issues and, through politicalization, eventually crime problems.

Media frenzies often start in single newsrooms and later spread across information mediums, giving the false impression of order and magnitude to criminal events. As Mark Fishman (1976) points out in his discussion of "crime waves":

> Journalists do not create themes merely to show an audience the appearance of order....In particular, editors selecting and organizing the day's stories need themes. Each day news editors face a glut of "raw materials" out of which they must fashion relatively few stories....The chances that an event or incident will be reported increase once it has been associated with a current theme in the news (535).

Once a theme has been set by a single newsroom, selection of newsworthy stories are based on the existing news theme. Themes then spread across communication mediums giving the impression of a crime epidemic.

While the media plays an important role in the identification and construction of crime myth, it is not the sole participant in the enterprise. Journalistic freedom of topic selection is often guided by events and influences external to the media. While the media may be guilty of not reporting an incident in the proper perspective, the media is not solely to blame for sensational reporting. Unfortunately, **repugnant** crimes do occur. Some events which are blown out of proportion warrant public attention. Each myth area considered in this book also contains legitimate cause for public concern. We will return to the media's role in constructing crime myths later.

GOVERNMENT AS MYTHMAKER

There are other methods beyond the naturally occurring bizarre and unusual crimes captured by the media that begin the myth construction process. These sometimes contrived or directed government events help alert the media to a new "hot topic." In some cases, the directed information helps refocus a media frenzy. Harold Pepinsky and Paul Jesilow (1985) opened their book *Myths That Cause Crime* with a powerful statement: "The sooner we recognize that criminal justice is a state-protected racket, the better" (10). In the context of crime myth, as used here, this means that the government has a vested interest in maintaining the existing social definition of crime and extending this definition to groups and behaviors that are perceived to be a threat to the existing social order. Similarly, the government has an interest in seeing that the existing criminal justice system's response to crime is not significantly altered in purpose or function. While some "system tinkering." (Kraska, 1985) is permissible, major change in the system's response to crime is never implemented. We build more prisons, mete out longer prison terms, reinstate the death penalty, and move more offenders through the criminal justice system at faster speeds, but all these changes are intellectually bonded by a punishment/control philosophy.

The government secures its interest in identifying crime and criminals and maintaining the established criminal justice system by promoting crime myths. Since the government can control, direct, and mold messages, it is one of the most powerful mythmakers in the crime production enterprise. The government can suppress information for national security reasons; it can punish "obscenity"; it can reward the media for presenting official versions of crime myths. Compelling messages and rewarding the mass media for myth presentation is frequently done under the guise of "public service announcements" and press briefings.

The government functions not only as a controller and director of the mass media—it is a form of media. The government controls extensive print publication resources, commissions and funds research, operates radio stations, and exposes the television viewing audience to government-sponsored messages. Additionally, the government tunes the media in to certain crime myths by directing their attention and holding controlled press briefings. "Reporters' dependence on authorities makes them—and by extension media consumers—particularly vulnerable to deliberate attempts to mislead by governments and agencies" (Hynds, 1990:6).

The "war on drugs" is an excellent illustration of the government's role as a media starter in the myth construction enterprise. In 1990, President Bush's Administration arranged for the Drug Enforcement Administration (DEA) to conduct a high-profile drug arrest. Since public focus on the "drug war" was waning due to concern over other social problems, the administration needed an "event" to refocus public and political attention on the "drug war." Following a DEA drug bust just outside the White House, the president made a national television address concerning the drug issue. It was later learned that the DEA had to go to considerable means to persuade the drug dealer to meet the agents at their desired location—just outside the White House. Thus, as we will discuss later, the event had all the necessary characteristics for creating a crime myth.

The current administration is not unique in its willingness to create crime myths. The Bureau of Narcotics campaign against marijuana (1937) under the leadership of Harry Anslinger is another classic example of the media's dissemination of government-sponsored crime myths. The Bureau of Narcotics, wanting to expand its bureaucratic domain by adding marijuana to the list of controlled substances it was responsible for monitoring, put together a series of mythological and outrageous stories about atrocities allegedly committed by people under the influence of marijuana. These stories included the murder of a Florida family and their pet dog by a wayward son who had taken one toke of marijuana. Newspapers printed this story and others like it. Thus, the myth of the "dope fiend" was born out of the minds of law enforcement officials. The media involvement with the Bureau of Narcotics disinformation campaign continued with editorial calls for the suppression of the dangerous drug. In fact, such hysteria resulted that the Bureau's own legal counsel recommended discontinuation of the propaganda campaign. During the height of the media frenzy and while the Marijuana Tax Act of 1937 was being debated in Washington, news stories covering the testimony of leading medical experts about the relative safety of the drug and objections by the scientific community to the criminalization of marijuana were lost in the coverage of the government-created crime wave (see Galliher and Walker, 1977). Suffice it to say that whether self-initiated or governmentally generated, the media and government focus public attention on unique social problems; crime myths thus begin to take shape.

CREATING CRIME MYTHS

An occasional media or government attraction to some unique crime or problem may be beneficial in some cases. As Philip Jenkins and Daniel Katkin (1988) argue in their examination of child sexual abuse, intense media focus may produce some good even when it is based on exaggeration and distortion. Public attention and media focus on the unusual problem cannot by itself create a crime myth. In order for a myth to develop to a point where it becomes more than a social concern for a majority of citizens, it must be properly packaged and marketed. A requirement for myth production often repeated throughout this work is that for a crime problem to reach its myth potential, it must be reported to occur in "epidemic" proportion. A quantum leap must occur from uncovering an incident to depicting it as pervasive. Only by exaggerating the magnitude of the problem can public attention be sustained for prolonged periods, can fear be instilled, can calls for institutional control be made, and can public support be mustered to institute formal sanctions.

Exaggeration of the magnitude of a problem and the manufacturing of a crime myth are accomplished by several means. First, the media can suddenly focus upon crimes that it had previously ignored (Fishman, 1976). The media can collect and selectively choose crimes to present to the public. The organization of these presentations can create the image of a crime problem when they are taken out of their geographical, temporal, or social contexts. Crime myths are also created when the media fails to pursue stories beyond their initial reporting. Crimes reported to constitute a pattern may later be found unrelated or even conceptually distinct. There is, however, no requirement that the media correct their mistakes or recall their myths. Joel Best and Gerald Hortuchi's (1985) study of Halloween sadists' attacks against children found that the media greatly exaggerated its occurrence.

> There simply was no basis for Newsweek's (1975) claim that "several children had died." The newspapers attributed only two deaths to Halloween sadists. and neither case fit the image of a maniacal killer randomly attacking children. In 1970, five-year-old Kevin Toston died after eating heroin supposedly hidden in his Halloween candy. While this story received considerable publicity, newspapers gave less coverage to the follow-up report that Kevin had found the heroin in his uncle's home, not his treats....In 1974, eight-year-old Timothy O'Bryan died after eating Halloween candy contaminated with cyanide. Investigators concluded that his father had contaminated the treat....Thus, both boys' deaths were caused by family members, rather than by anonymous sadists (490).

The fear generated from exaggerating Halloween sadism not only affected the general public, but also organizations and individuals who are expected to have valid information regarding the reality of crime. Beginning in 1983, the International Association of Chiefs of Police (IACP) and the confectionery industry established, through sponsorship, a "Halloween Candy Hotline." The hotline was devised to give police departments technical assistance with suspected candy tampering cases. According to a news item by the IACP, the hotline received sixty-eight calls in 1990, but the article failed to note if any of these calls were actual tamperings (Editorial Staff, 1991:70). Although the Halloween hotline does serve as an example of a positive effect of exaggerating crime, it raises questions as to whether the nation's leading police executives are able to discern between actual crime problems and myths of crime.

How often does the media distort or exaggerate the crime problem in our society? Harry Marsh (1991) reviewed the research devoted to the study of the content of newspapers. His examination of literature from 1983 through 1988 found the following patterns:

- The vast majority of newspaper crime coverage pertains to violent or sensational crimes.
- The high percentages of violent crimes reported in the newspapers are not representative of the percentages reflected in official crime data.
- The over-emphasis of violent crimes and failure to address personal risk and prevention techniques often lead to exaggerated fears of victimization in certain segments of society.
- Newspaper coverage tends to support police views and values about crime and criminals...(67–68).

Misuse of statistics creates crime myths. Vested interests can manipulate "facts" when parties have control of information and access to channels of dissemination. As we shall see in later chapters, debates on organized crime are particularly susceptible to misuse and control of information. Statistics presented for public consumption are often clouded by broad definitions of crime that tend to group distinct behaviors, offenders, and victims into single categories giving the impression of an epidemic. In a study of the social reaction to sex crimes, Sutherland (1950) wrote, "Fear is seldom or never related to statistical trends in sex crimes.... Ordinarily, from two to four spectacular sex crimes in a few weeks are sufficient to evoke the phrase 'sex crime wave'" (144). Statistics and information often mislead the public when they are stripped from their original context and inferences are made between research studies. Causal links are often inferred or claimed between the crime myth under construction and some other more pervasive social concern. For example, in recent years the use of drugs has been linked to other crimes, high school drop-outs, decreased employee productivity (Kraska and Kappeler, 1988), the corruption of the police and contracting AIDs, as well as a multitude of other social maladies. The incidence of drug use in society may or may not have been perceived as a major social threat, but when coupled with other spin-off social problems, the perception of epidemic is ensured. In later chapters we will explore the myth-built links between drug use and other social problems.

CHARACTERIZATIONS OF CRIME MYTHS

In order for the momentum of a crime myth to be prolonged and public support for institutionalized controls to be generated, myths must be accompanied by certain characterizations. Momentum is achieved if the crime problem has traits that either instill fear or threaten the vast majority of society in some appreciable way. Not unlike Greek mythology, modern crime myths must follow certain themes for success. There must be "virtuous" heroes, "innocent" victims, and "evil" villains who pose a clear and certain threat to the audience. Only then can a crime myth reach its potential. Characterizations common among myths in crime and criminal justice include the identification and targeting of a distinct deviant population; the presence of an "innocent," "virtuous," or "helpless" victim population: and the existence of a substantial threat to established norms, values, or traditional lifestyles.

Crime myths are often built around unpopular groups in society. This targeting helps to ensure sustained support for a myth. Unpopular groups in society are particularly vulnerable as possible targets of mythical fears. Groups most vulnerable to myth targeting are those that are easily distinguishable from the dominant social group. Distinctions are often as crude as race, color, or national origin, but need not be limited to visual appearance. Minorities and immigrants have had their share of myth targeting. Differences in religious beliefs, political views, or even sexual preferences are attractive targets for mythmakers. This characterization in the construction of crime myth has been used by hate groups, proslavery advocates, supporters of prohibition, and advocates of the death penalty. The distinction has been used to develop crime control policy, enact criminal laws, and even bring nations to war.

The importance of this characterization of "difference" cannot be overstated. Scholars have observed the importance of casting groups as different for targeting purposes. In his insightful book, *Blaming the Victim,* William Ryan (1976) states:

This is a critical and essential step in the process, for difference is in itself hampering and maladaptive. The Different Ones are seen as less competent, less skilled, less knowing—in short less human. The ancient Greeks deduced from a single characteristic, a different language, that the barbarians—that is, "the babblers" who spoke a strange tongue—were wild, uncivilized, dangerous, **rapacious**, uneducated, lawless, and, indeed scarcely more than animals. [Such characterization] not infrequently justifies mistreatment, enslavement, or even extermination of the Different Ones (10).

Fear of minorities, foreigners, and differences in cultural or religious values has led to the creation of some shocking myths of organized crime. The birth of the Mafia myth in America is based on the created fear of cultural differences. The murder of New Orleans police chief David Hennessey in 1890 provides an excellent example. New Orleans was one of the cities that experienced a large influx of Italian immigrants during the end of the 19th century. Chief Hennessey was gunned down on a New Orleans street one night. As he was dying, the chief was said to have uttered the words "Dagos, Dagos." Officers later rounded up a large number of petty criminals of Italian descent and presented them before a grand jury that indicted them for the chief's murder. Since evidence of their involvement was lacking, the jury acquitted them of the charges. Acquittal did not deter the citizens of New Orleans who marched to the jail, seized the defendants (and others who were not even on trial) and killed eleven of them. This lynching and subsequent trials and acquittals of "different ones" is said to be the genesis of the American Mafia myth (Smith, 1975:27–45).

The difference requirement of the myth construction process is built into issues surrounding crime and justice. There is a convenient supply of unpopular people—those whom society labels criminal. Criminals are probably the most unpopular minority in any society, although they are difficult to identify visually aside from the undesirable conduct.

Another requirement for myth development is that "helpless" or "innocent" victims (people like ourselves) must be depicted as suffering the brunt of the newly found social evil. The more "innocents" perceived as being affected by the myth, the greater the likelihood of public attention and support for the creation of crime myths targeting unpopular groups. Women, children, heterosexual victims of AIDS, law enforcement officers killed in the line of duty, or unwitting business people who become the victims of "organized" crime are often used as the common "virtuous" victim who suffers at the hands of the unpopular deviant. Sutherland (1950) observed, "The hysteria produced by child murders is due in part to the fact that the ordinary citizen cannot understand a sex attack on a child. The ordinary citizen…concludes that sexual attack on an infant or girl of six years must be the act of a fiend or maniac. Fear is the greater because the behavior is so incomprehensible" (144).

This type of victim or the casting of victims as "innocents" allows for the implementation of stiff criminal sanctions against the deviants with accompanying feelings of moral superiority and even retributive satisfaction. It is not uncommon for the media to dwell on the virtues of the innocent victim to the exclusion of the offender (see Drechsel et al., 1980; Karmen, 1978). After all, what parents do not feel their child is either a "good student," a "likable person," or "a good boy or girl." This is not to say that innocents do not become the targets of violent crime, but rather to illustrate that media coverage of crime stories often focuses extensively on the innocent person victimized by the evil stranger. As we shall see in later chapters on child abduction and abuse, strangers are not the greatest threat to our nation's children. In the construction of crime mythology there are no "ordinary" victims or criminals.

The subjects of myths are characterized as constituting a major threat to middle class values, norms, or lifestyle. Myths of crime and justice when blended with threats to religious belief, economic systems, sexual attitudes or orientation, the traditional family, or political preference become a volatile mix. These characterizations of crime myths serve to fuel emotionalism. The fear generated by this mixture of the unpopular offender, the innocent victim. and the perceived threat to traditional lifestyle can produce a formal and even violent social response. The argument is simple; a growing menace and threatening epidemic is plaguing society. Not only is the conduct a preference of a deviant group, it is affecting innocents and constituting a threat to tradition. "If we relied solely on the evidence of the mass media, we might well believe that every few years, a particular form of immoral or criminal behavior becomes so dangerous as almost to threaten the foundation of society" (Jenkins, 1988: 1).

The idea that "normal" life might break down adds to the value of a crime myth and provides for its continued existence long after media attraction has vanished. These characterizations ensure that major social institutions become involved in the reform process, since the conduct is perceived as not only a physical threat but a substantial threat to existing social arrangements and institutions. Jenkins and Katkin's (1988) study of the McMartin school affair notes that during the investigation of the child molestation incidents, specific attention was given to parents' regrets that they had departed from traditional parenting roles by relying on alternative child care. Such a focus reinforces traditional values and allows for blame to be placed on the deviant parents rather than the absence of positive alternatives to traditional child rearing practices. "If only she had not worked outside the home," instead of "if only the government supported and monitored alternative child care industries."

Mythmaking and the characterization of crime problems as major threats to traditional values and society serve important political functions for law enforcement. Consider organized crime and vice. Leaders in the law enforcement community testifying before Congress and state legislators can present the issue in one of two ways. They can present a relatively safe myth which suggests that organized crime is a foreign conspiracy (Italians, Colombians, Jamaicans, etc.) which has invaded America and threatens the peace and security of a homogeneous and righteous society. Organized crime brings with it numerous evils. It corrupts otherwise incorruptible politicians and police; it makes people gamble away their life savings; it introduces drugs into the schools: it uses prostitutes to seduce family men. Even worse, organized crime is an intricate, highly structured foreign conspiracy which can only be eliminated with more money, more justice personnel, and more enforcement power. The myth is safe and convenient. It points to the different ones as the source of a problem, so we do not have to change our lifestyle or take responsibility for the problem. Finally, it explains why law enforcement has yet to win the war against organized crime in America. The alternative would be to expose the myth. Organized crime is an integral part of American society. It could not exist if the citizenry did not wish to have ready access to drugs, pornography, prostitution, gambling, no-questions-asked loans, or stolen goods. Many of the "crimes" of organized crime would not be important or profitable if the business community did not collaborate in money laundering, the illegal disposal of toxic wastes, and the fencing of stolen goods. Organized crime would find itself quite harried if an array of politicians, law enforcers, and others were not willing to "grease the skids" of organized crime. To uncover the myth of organized crime and vice, however, carries no bureaucratic rewards for law enforcement; it would offend people and end law enforcement careers. A rational bureaucrat or politician will find characterizing myths in terms of different ones and threats to traditional values more useful than fact.

Techniques of Myth Characterization

Mythmakers do not simply uncover crime and transmit information; they serve to structure reality by selecting and characterizing events—thereby cultivating images of crime (Lang and Lang, 1969; Gerbner, 1972; Schoenfeld, Meier, and Griffin, 1979). The characterization of criminal events into myth is largely a process of bias and distortion. This distortion is often an unintended consequence of the process by which information is collected, processed, and prepared for dissemination by mass media. Research on the media, the news particularly, concludes that misrepresentation and distortion is not an uncommon practice (see Marsh, 1991:72).

The collection of crime events for public presentation is often shaped by reporters' perceptions. Journalistic accounts are rarely the product of actual observation; when they are, they are often conducted by reporters largely untrained in field research. More often than not, reporting of crime is based on secondhand information a reporter gleans from witnesses. The process of listening and interviewing witnesses and crime victims invites bias. Frequently, the wrong questions are asked, essential questions are omitted, and sensationalism becomes the reporter's focus. After all, journalists are in competition when creating a product for audience consumption. The untrained observer or journalist who is driven by the competitive nature of the modern mass media may selectively observe or interview with the end product in mind. Outcome and conclusion may already have been drawn before the investigator begins collecting information. Thus, from the selection and first investigation of a criminal event. there is the possibility of distortion, bias, and sensationalism.

Following a journalist's selection of a topic and initial investigation of a potential media story, the reporter's observation must make a transformation to communicable material. It must be written for dissemination or presentation. In this process of moving from observation to presentation, several problems arise. First, there is the possibility of selective memory or even the injection of personal preference by the reporter. Forgotten statements or observations may later be recalled by the journalist in the process of constructing a crime story. As information is recalled, initially insignificant observations may take on new meaning as the story unfolds. Second, after initial drafts of the presentation are constructed, they must be edited. In this editorial process a story can change considerably. Reports are often edited by a series of people who are guided by numerous constraints. Editorial constraints often include the time available to present a story, the page space available, and the marketability of the final product. The audience and editorial ideology also influence decisions. This process requires persons often unassociated with the initial crime to make judgments about what should be said or what should be shown. Editorial decisions are not always made in conjunction with the advice of the original observer.

The selection of which stories eventually appear in the news is based upon the ordering of stories into media themes. Fishman (1976) notes that:

> The selection of news on the basis of themes is one ideological production of crime news....This procedure requires that an incident be stripped of the actual context of its occurrence so that it may be relocated in a new, symbolic context: the news theme. Because newsworthiness is based on themes, the attention devoted to an event may exceed its importance. relevance, or timelessness were these qualities determined with reference to some theory of society....Thus, something becomes a "serious type of crime" on the basis of what is going on inside newsrooms, not outside them (536).

Finally, after the presentation of a story there is the possibility of selective observation and retention on the part of the audience. Many will only remember the bizarre or hideous part of a communication to the exclusion of other information. While media attention with crime myth is often short-lived, the images created by intense media focus may linger in the minds of those exposed to them.

There are, however, other techniques used in the manipulation of information and the construction of crime myths. There is a rich history of research and literature on the use of propaganda by the media and government. Propaganda is a technique for influencing social action based on intentional distortions and manipulation of communications. While not all media and government presentation, or even a majority of it, is a conscious attempt at propaganda, many crime myths are the product of propaganda techniques. "One important point to remember is that objective reporting is a myth. Every reporter brings to the story his/her own biases and world view. Each reporter has to make choices in writing the story: what to include, what to leave out, what sources to use. A few well-placed adjectives, a few uses of 'alleged' or 'so-called' can cast a definite ideological twist" (Hynds, 1990:5). These techniques tend to shape the presentation of a crime, create images for the uncritical audience, and promote social reaction. Some of the most common techniques employed by the media and government officials for characterizing crime myths include:

- *Creating criminal stereotypes.* This practice amounts to presenting crime as a uni-dimensional and non-changing event. Certain phrases such as "crime against the elderly, child abduction," "street crime," and "organized crime" group wide varieties of behavior into single categories that have been previously characterized by the media. The use of stereotyped phrases links broad and popular conceptions of crime to diverse criminal behavior. For example, "organized" crime often creates the image of large "well-structured" groups of foreign-born individuals who engage solely in criminal enterprise.

- *Presentation of opinion as fact.* This practice involves injecting personal opinion into media presentations without a factual basis. Phrases that contain such opinions that are presented as fact might include: "the police are doing all they can to prevent this crime" or the "community is in a state of panic."

- *Speaking through sources.* This activity involves collecting opinions of others that closely match the proponent's viewpoint on a given issue. A reporter may select people to interview on the basis of how well their opinion fits the theme of the story.

- *Biased attribution and labeling.* Value-loaded terminology is used to characterize crime, criminals, or victims. A serial murderer may "stalk" the victim; a group of individuals may be referred to as a "crime family"; or a group of youths may become a "gang" that "preys" on "unsuspecting" victims.

- *Selective presentation of fact.* Presenting certain facts to the exclusion of others strengthens a biased argument. To emphasize the issue of child abduction, a proponent could cite that thousands of children are missing each year without presenting the fact that the vast majority of children are runaways.

- *Information-management.* The editorial process by which a particular news story is shaped and selected for presentation to the exclusion of other stories is one way to manage information. Presenting stories about sensational crimes like serial murder, crack babies, and child abduction to the exclusion of stories on corporate crime, securities fraud, and other more common crime are examples of the results of such management.

- *Undocumented sources of authority.* Vague references including statements like "many police officials feel" or "many people are saying" without specific reference to who is saying what and what constitutes "many" is a misleading reference to authority.

- *Stripping fact from its context.* A variation of the characteristic above is using facts or statements of authorities taken from the actual context in which they were made to support a particular position or injecting facts that are unrelated to the issue. A media presentation on drug abuse that focuses on statistics about the high school dropout rate without considering whether or not there is an empirical link between the two is stripping fact from its original context.

- *Selective interviewing.* A final method of portraying a position as more solid than the facts indicate is interviewing one or two authorities on a topic and presenting their remarks as the generalized expert opinion on a given topic. For example, interviewing one or two criminologists and giving the audience the impression that those views are reflective of the criminological community.

In the chapters that follow. we will address specific myths of crime and criminal justice. Each myth or series of myths presented in this text differ in the fashion in which they rely on these practices and other characterizations to create a crime myth.

ON ANALYZING CRIME MYTHS

There are no traditional or standard crime myths. Myths have at their origin unique events that may or may not be noticed by the mythmakers in society. A criminal event or series of events cannot become a myth unless a sufficient number of people contribute to its transformation. The story that is conceived but never told does not become an issue or a crime myth. Crime myths are unique in that they are a product of the social, political and economic atmosphere of a time. That is to say that the audience must be ready or made ready to accept a crime myth. A criminal event that has the potential for becoming a crime myth at one given moment may not be a viable myth at another point in time.

As mentioned earlier, mythmakers are varied and their roles are not static. Sometimes the government is the mythmaker and the media responds to the official myth. Other times the government responds to the myths created by the media or special interest groups. These varied mythmakers and shifting roles all make crime myths unique. Crime myths also differ in their purposes and consequences. Some myths result in the criminalization of behavior while others die quietly without social or political response. Some myths serve the interests of powerful groups in society or serve a needed social function, while others serve no useful social purpose.

The uniqueness of the origins, detection, construction, and consequence of crime myths does not lend itself well to traditional criminological analysis. There are no master keys or magic statistical bullets to understanding and solving all crime myths. There is no blanket sociological theory that explains the development and purpose of all crime myths. Each crime myth requires individualized treatment and analysis. Such a situation is an invitation for criticism. It is, however, also a strength. Wedding oneself to a particular theory, perspective, or method of knowing is like relying on a single sense to describe a garden of flowers. This work is grounded in a variety of perspectives and supports its numerous contentions with varying means of understanding. We shall leave it to the reader to judge whether we have described a rose or merely wandered into the bramble bush.

REFERENCES

BEST, J. AND HORTUCHI, G. T. (1985). The Razor and the Apple: The Social Construction of Urban Legends. *Social Problems*. 32:488–99.

DRECHSEL, R., NENEBURG, K. AND ABORISADE, B. (1980). Community Size and Newspaper Reporting of Local Courts. *Journal Quarterly*. 57:71–8.

EDITORIAL STAFF (1991). Halloween Candy Hotline. *Police Chief*. (September):70

FISHMAN, M. (1976). Crime Waves as Ideology. *Social Problems*. 25:531–43.

GALLIHER, J. AND WALKER, A. (1977). The Puzzle of the Social Origins of the Marijuana Tax Act of 1937. *Social Problems*. 24:371–73.

GERBNER, G. (1972). Communication and Social Environment. *Scientific American*. 227: 153–60.

HALLIN, D. (1990). Whatever Happened to the News? *Media & Values*. 50:2–4.

HYNDS, P. (1990). Balance Bias with Critical Questions. *Media & Values*. 50:5–7.

JENKINS P. (1988). Myth and Murder: The Serial Killer Panic of 1983–5. *Criminal Justice Research Bulletin*. 3:1–7.

JENKINS, P. AND KATKIN, D. (1988). Protecting Victims of Child Sexual Abuse: A Case for Caution. *Prison Journal*. 58(2):25–35.

KARMEN, A. (1978). How Much Heat? How Much Light: Coverage of New York City's Blackout and Looting in the Print Media. *In Deviance and Mass Media*. Winick, C. (ed.). Beverly Hills, CA: Sage Publications.

Kraska, P. B. (1985). Personal Communication. Sam Houston State University, Huntsville, TX.

Kraska, P. B. and Kappeler, V. E. (1988). Police On-duty Drug Use: A Theoretical and Descriptive Examination. *American Journal of Police.* 7: 1–26.

Lang, K. and Lang, G. E. (1969). *Television and Politics.* Chicago: Quadrangle Books.

Mannheim, K. (1936). *Ideology and Utopia.* New York: Harcourt, Brace and World. Inc.

Marsh, H. L. (1991). A Comparative Analysis of Crime Coverage in Newspapers in the United States and Other Countries From 1960–1989: A Review of the Literature. *Journal of Criminal Justice,* 19(4):67–79.

Medalia, N. Z. and Larsen, O. N. (1958). Diffusion and Belief in a Collective Delusion: The Seattle Windshield Pitting Epidemic. *American Sociological Review.* 23: 180–86.

Pepinsky, H. E. and Jesilow, P. (1985). *Myths That Cause Crime.* 2nd ed. Cabin John, MD: Seven Locks Press.

Pfohl, S. J. (1977). The Discovery of Child Abuse. *Social Problems.* 24:310–23.

Quinney, R. (1970). *The Social Reality of Crime.* Boston: Little, Brown and Company.

Ryan, W. (1976). *Blaming the Victim.* New York: Vintage Books.

Schoenfeld, A. C., Meier. R. F., and Griffin, R. J. (1979). Constructing a Social Problem: The Press and the Environment. *Social Problems* 27:38–61.

Smith, D. (1975). *The Mafia Mystique.* New York: Basic Books.

Sutherland, E. H. (1950). The Diffusion of Sexual Psychopath Laws. *American Journal of Sociology.* 56: 142–48.

QUESTIONS FOR DISCUSSION

1. According to this article, who are the two major contributors to myths about crime? Provide examples to support your answer.

2. For a crime myth to gain momentum, the myth must be accompanied by certain characterizations. Explain and cite examples.

3. List and discuss several of the most common techniques used by the media and the government for perpetuating crime myths.

APPLICATIONS

1. During the next week or two, read the local newspaper and clip out articles about crime in which the government or media have perpetuated a crime myth. Can you identify any of the specific techniques that were enumerated in this article? Discuss these with the other members of your class.

2. What is likely to happen if the media and the government continue to perpetuate crime myths? Write a brief essay expressing your opinion. Read and discuss your essays with the other members of your class.

Why Governments Don't Do What They Could to Reduce Violent Crime

The Politics of Crime

Richard Neely

Through at least the past decade, no public problem has worried Americans more persistently than crime. When people are asked in opinion surveys to list the problems that concern them most, the threat of crime typically comes at or near the top of the list. But when the same people list the issues on which they'll decide which candidate to vote for, crime usually comes behind half-a-dozen other subjects. The explanation they offer most frequently is that a candidate's statements about crime are unimportant—no one can do much about the problem.

What is misguided about this attitude is that it is possible to do something about crime. Although the evidence lacks scientific precision, certain facts of criminal-law enforcement are clear:

In many big cities, where the limit on crime is the presence of the police (as opposed to family members, watchful neighbors, and the like, who limit crime elsewhere), more officers on the streets or in the subways means fewer criminals who dare to act. But in courtrooms, most accused criminals go free because the system cannot afford to have it any other way. Everyone involved in the criminal courts is overtaxed, from the policemen, who must take time off the beat to testify, to the prosecutors, who need to dispose of cases as quickly as possible, to the judges, who know as they make their sentencing decisions that the prisons are already overcrowded. The result of this pressure is the plea-bargain, in which a man who faces, for example, a ten-year sentence with a three-year minimum term if convicted of armed robbery will instead plead guilty to grand larceny and end up serving one year in jail.

Many people complain that plea-bargaining returns criminals to the streets, but few have considered the statistics that lie behind this practice. There are nearly 104,000 felony arrests in New York City every year. New York City has facilities for only about 5,000 full-blown jury trials per year, so it is forced to do what nearly all city courts must: find some way to dispose of the surplus, usually through plea-bargaining or dropped charges.

Many of the people thereby freed undoubtedly belong in jail, and the crime rate would undoubtedly fall if they were imprisoned. All that is required is money—for police, prosecutors, judges, and jails.

Why, then have we not taken steps we know would have some effect? The answers are complicated, but chief among them is that for every proposal that might be made to reduce crime, there is a powerful, organized interest that opposes it. These obstructive groups often include the most influential force of all, the middle-class interests that so frequently complain about the threat of crime.

This problem is intimately connected with the general difficulties of American courts, but not the courts as they are usually conceived. When lay people speak of the courts, they often mean judges and attendant judicial staffs of clerks and secretaries. However, the term "courts" must be expanded when we talk of criminal law to encompass all of the supporting agencies that either feed criminals to the judges or receive them after conviction. When courts are understood in this way, it becomes clear that improving their operations can be costly. Doubling the number of policemen and prosecutors would spare many people the costs they now bear as victims of crime, but it would increase the costs many others would pay in taxes.

As is often the case, the people who stand to gain the most from this protection are the ones with the least say about how public money is spent. The primary victims of crime pay the lowest taxes. Most victims of crime live in ghettos or declining working-class neighborhoods, and they work at low-wage jobs in places such as all-night diners or gas stations, which are easy to rob. But the taxpayers who would bear the cost of better protection for these victims are themselves seldom victims—they are instead large corporations with privately retained security forces, or middle-class taxpayers who live in well-protected neighborhoods and send their children to safe neighborhood schools or private schools.

Although it might not seem in the interest of the middle class to pay for increased enforcement, the cost of crime in the United States runs to hundreds of billions of dollars every year—much more than increased enforcement would cost. Shoplifting alone accounts for a loss of between 3 and 7 percent of all merchandise inventoried for sale by large chain stores, which means we all pay 3 to 7 percent more for our routine dry-goods purchases.

Moreover, criminal courts and their supporting agencies—unlike most government operations—actually generate revenue. At the simplest level, traffic courts and magistrate courts make more money from fees and fines than it costs to operate them. When state or local business regulations are enforced, the fines **augment** the treasury. Low crime rates also contribute to a desirable climate for industry, commerce, and residences, which in turn means higher property values and a stronger tax base. Lack of funding for the courts must be something more than just a reflection of overall budget constraints; while budget considerations do play a part, underfunding is often deliberate, purposeful, and unrelated to the budget.

One simple example should illustrate the point. Cheating on federal and state income taxes is pervasive in all classes of society; except among the compulsively honest, cheating usually occurs in direct proportion to opportunity. Why, then do we not expand the Internal Revenue Service and its state counterparts? Every new revenue agent pays his salary and overhead at least eight times. The answer is that we do not really want **Rhadamanthine** enforcement of the tax laws. As long as the IRS is overworked and understaffed, everyone except the **scrupulously** honest will enact his own personal tax-reform program. The IRS's understaffing also guarantees that all but the most flagrant evaders will escape with a payment of back taxes and possibly a civil penalty.

Overworked United States attorneys cannot spend their time arguing every questionable deduction in tax court. The IRS will challenge a businessman's deductions, only to cede most of its points at settlement conferences. The mediocre enforcement of the tax codes stems not only from the IRS's lack of staff but also from a lack of U.S. attorneys, U.S. district court judges, and court-of-appeals judges. Without an increase in the personnel of supporting agencies, there is a limit to the effectiveness of new IRS agents, but there is no question that such an increase will bring in more money than it costs.

Since more rigorous enforcement will inspire a higher level of "voluntary" compliance, it must be obvious that some people out there do not want better enforcement. I am probably one. I actually do pay every cent I owe in taxes, and since I am a public official, I get audited about every four years. Notwithstanding my annoyance with those who cheat, I do not want to be audited more than once every four years, because it is a nuisance. Quite frankly, I prefer to let my neighbor cheat a little rather than be bothered with a yearly audit.

Most people probably feel as I do about forgiving their neighbors' tax trespasses in return for minimal personal harassment by Uncle Sam, but a similar philosophy of live and let live does not exist about violent crime. Why, then, do we not double the number of cops and courts?

The reason is both ideological and financial. Policemen, in my experience, are by nature bullies as well as heroes, and the smaller the police force, the more policemen tend to exhibit the characteristics of heroes rather than bullies. But the more policemen who are "cracking down on crime," the greater the likelihood that individual citizens will suffer abuse of their civil liberties. Work in any bureaucracy tends to expand to fill the time allocated to do it. If the police are not busy with serious crime, they may meddle in such citizen activities as private poker games, where no one wants their help. Consequently, a silent, even unconscious alliance exists between pro-civil-liberties liberals, who want small police forces for ideological reasons, and conservative taxpayers, who do not want to pay the costs of what from their point of view amounts to social services for others.

My favorite illustration of the diverse alliances that oppose improvements in the criminal-justice system is the repeated failure of a bill that is perennially introduced in the West Virginia Legislature. The bill, which is introduced at the request of the state attorney general, would give the attorney general statewide prosecutorial powers. Under the current system, each West Virginia county elects a prosecutor who has absolute discretion concerning what crimes will be prosecuted in his county. The attorney general handles criminal cases on appeal, defends the state's interests in federal habeas corpus proceedings, and represents the state's agencies in civil litigation; however, the attorney general has no power to initiate prosecutions at the trial-court level in the fifty-five counties. Why should there not be a statewide prosecutorial agency, particularly since many local prosecutors are reluctant to enforce the law against their political friends?

The answer is quite simple. The position of attorney general has historically been a stepping-stone to the governorship. Since 1936, four out of ten governors held the office of attorney general immediately before their election as governor. High elected office has tended to go to media stars since the demise of well-organized political machines. Only certain types of political antics, however, attract media attention; these include crusades against political corruption and white-collar crime. Everyone who is actively involved in either business or government is aware of the public-relations value of an anti-corruption crusade, yet even the consummately honest prefer not to be bothered by one. Zealous investigations demand the production of documents, testimony by employees on company time, and a costly disruption of normal business operations. None of these costs is borne by the government; all must be home by the private sector.

The important facts are that there is less than universal support for the enforcement of most laws, for consumer fraud to drug use, and that lack of consensus about the value of some types of law enforcement is seen in the legislature's failure to establish a statewide enforcement agency.

In West Virginia's four northernmost counties, the population is composed largely of the children of Italians, Greeks, Poles, Hungarians, and other non-Anglo-Saxon peoples. The biggest illegal gambling institutions used to be the churches, which held regular, illegal bingo panics and raised significant revenues (bingo games for charitable organizations were recently legalized). Other social institutions similarly rely on slot machines and football pools; it is a way of life completely different from that of the predominantly fundamentalist southern part of the state. Local prosecutors in those counties are elected by citizens who expect a policy of **conspicuous** non-enforcement of the gambling laws, at least as they apply to churches and social clubs. The last thing on earth they want is a statewide strike force destroying their churches and clubs.

In 1977, when John D. Rockefeller IV became governor, his new chief of the state police attempted to enforce the gambling laws in the northern counties. Within a month, the state police were instructed to back off, because it became obvious that continued enforcement would anger every member of the legislature from those counties and that, in retaliation, those legislators would torpedo the governor's legislative program.

Every effort at improvement in the criminal justice system will seem either helpful or threatening, depending on the perspective of some political-interest group. Thus an increase in the number of policemen means more protection to some, more bullying to others. If, for example, the staffs of prosecuting attorneys are increased so that they can diligently prosecute armed robbers, murderers, and dope peddlers, they will also be available to **ferret** out consumer fraud, anti-trust violations, and political corruption. Since prosecuting attorneys are usually elected and, therefore, are lawyers with political ambitions, they will be tempted, as in West Virginia, to play to the press by prosecuting white-collar crime. These campaigns are middle-class morality plays that assuage the newspaper reader's sense of unrecognized merit. They are usually less attractive to the political establishment, however resolute it may be about cracking down on murder and armed robbery. Even firebrand political reformers use questionable tactics at election time, and the prospect of an elaborate enforcement bureaucracy falling into enemy hands is horrifying to politicians.

A classic example of frivolous white-collar crime prosecution took place recently in Pittsburgh. A county commissioner, who was also the county Democratic Party chairman, was charged with theft of services during his tenure as county coroner. At that time, in addition to being coroner, he owned a private laboratory, which did pathology and toxicology testing. It was alleged that he brought tissue specimens from his lab to the morgue, where they were processed by morgue employees on the county payroll, thereby "stealing" $115,000 worth of county services.

The case had all the trappings of a political trial. The defendant, Cyril H. Wecht, was highly placed in county politics, so prosecuting him would bring much publicity— adverse for Wecht, angelic for the prosecutor. Wecht had political enemies even within his own party, and some of them were involved in initiating and developing the investigation. Others used the investigation and trial as a reason to force him to withdraw from the party chairmanship. And the district attorney responsible for the prosecution, perhaps trading on the publicity it generated, was running for the state supreme court bench at the same time.

Political or not, theft of government services is not a trivial charge. But this case certainly was not one of those occasions when an expensive jury trial was warranted by any cost-benefit analysis of the "public good." Fortunately for Wecht, he was able to hire the nationally known trial lawyer Stanley Preiser to defend him. After six weeks of exhaustive testimony and with thirty-two canons of documentary evidence, the jury deliberated for ten hours and acquitted Wecht.

The investigation and trial took nearly two years and involved ten investigators and seven lawyers from the district attorney's office at one time or another. The trial lasted six weeks, and the whole affair was estimated to have cost the county about $1.5 million— more than ten times the value of the services said to have been stolen. The money spent on the trial could have bought almost forty prosecutors for a year at an annual salary of $40,000, and they each could have been prosecuting fifty violent crimes and property crimes such as murder, rape, arson, armed robbery, and larceny—the ones that affect the average citizen's life.

As long as we are talking only about the criminal courts, the questions are comparatively simple. But when we add the complications created by the civil courts, all bets are off. Devoting more money to the *criminal* courts would return economic dividends to the public, but increased funding for the entire court system has a much more mixed effect. Indeed, for certain groups, including local governments, businesses, unions, landlords, and even tenants, a better-functioning court system would be a calamity.

Consider the case of New York City, which is notorious for its long court delays. In the abstract, most New Yorkers would like to have an efficient court system so that criminals would be sent away. To the casual observer, New York's felon problem would appear easy to solve by increasing the number of policemen and prosecutors, and by expanding the court system.

The hitch, however, is that a New York trial-court judge is empowered to hear both criminal and civil cases; if the number of judges is increased, more civil cases can be heard. Of 25,589 civil cases concluded in New York City in the first forty weeks of the 1979–1980 fiscal year, 5,523 were against New York City itself. New York City has been on the verge of bankruptcy since 1975, and the policies of the Reagan Administration threaten even greater financial strains in the next two and a half years. The potential liability for New York City from the civil suits currently awaiting trail runs to billions of dollars. New York City cannot afford an efficient court system, because it would be bankrupt beyond bail-out if all these suits came to trial in one or two years.

New York is an extraordinary example, but legal-aid and other public-interest lawyers elsewhere are bringing suits challenging the standards of operation in mental hospitals, prisons, schools, and other state and local facilities. When courts take action in these areas, it can mean that local governments must spend millions or even billions of dollars they never planned to. In New Jersey, for example, the state supreme court ordered the legislature to enact an income tax to support the public schools. This required the allocation of state money to projects that judges wanted rather than to projects that the governor and the legislators wanted.

The moral of these stories is that the costs of creating more courts, along with all their supporting staff, are but a fraction of the total amount of money that an expansion of the courts will eventually involve. Typically, the entire judicial branch of government takes less than 2 percent of any state's budget. In New York City, the cost of doubling the number of judges, prosecutors, city attorneys, courtrooms, and supporting staff would be small compared with the cost of paying the judgments the new courts would render against the city.

In other parts of the United States, there are powerful private interests in the same position as New York City: they are not in the least interested in improving the efficiency of civil courts. If, for instance, litigation against insurance companies takes eight years to complete, the company has the use of its money for eight years, and can invest it during that period at between 10 and 18 percent. Furthermore, delay alone is a powerful force to inspire settlements for low sums. Since most federal and state courts are unified criminal and civil tribunals, in which any judge can hear either type of case, the positive economic effect for the general public of improved criminal courts is almost always offset by increased costs on the civil side for those who have the most political power. The public takes its accustomed beating.

If expanding the courts has varied effects, some of them welcomed and some of them abhorred by powerful political groups, the logical solution would be to separate the courts' various functions. We might create institutions that would work in areas where there is broad agreement—such as fighting violent crime—while avoiding other areas. Everyone wants violent criminals prosecuted and the streets made safe. During the 1960s and 1970s, there were numerous programs that attempted to get at the root causes of crime—slums, broken families, unemployment. While we have not abandoned these efforts, there is an increasing awareness that we do not have either the resources or the knowledge to reduce violent crime through preventive means, and this lack should not be used as an excuse for doing nothing.

New institutions will not be developed, however, until there is an organized citizen lobby that makes campaign contributions, sends out direct-mail newsletters about how elected officials perform in the area of court reform, and has representatives entering into the give-and-take of political bargaining in the committee rooms and the corridors of legislatures. Until there is such a lobby around which political support can coalesce, politically workable plans will not be generated. Since there is no active citizen lobby for court reform, and since, to the contrary, all of the day-to-day political rewards go to those who oppose court reform, the legislative branch is entirely indifferent to the courts. In fact, I cannot think of any other subject of major social concern that intrudes itself less upon the imagination of the average legislator than the courts. Yet court reform, **albeit** in simplistic terms, is the frequent subject of campaign rhetoric, which gives the illusion that politicians have some continuing interest in the subject. Sadly, the courts are usually regarded in the same light as is the Federal Reserve Board—as an institution that is to be reviled and attacked but ultimately to be left unchanged.

The history of the environmental movement suggests the direction that a citizens' movement could take. Environmental and conservation issues used to be as low a legislative priority as court reform is today. But in the early 1960s, the whole question of pollution control and conservation of unspoiled wilderness captured the imagination of the college-educated middle class. Suddenly, defense of the environment took on the aura of a religious crusade. Groups such as the Sierra Club organized on the national level, and in every state local groups developed and kept in communication with one another.

The reform of the criminal law may be ripe for the same type of crusade that the environmentalists led fifteen years ago. Most street crime is, to be sure, perpetrated upon the poor, because they must live where the criminals are. But crime has risen to a level that intrudes itself into the lives of many middle-class citizens on a daily basis. It is the middle class that has organizational and political skills, along with a spare hundred dollars to contribute to a political-action group. It was essentially the middle class that accomplished the environmental revolution.

The beginnings of a citizen lobby for better law enforcement can already be perceived. In West Virginia last year, the relatives of persons killed by drunk drivers organized themselves to make the drunk-driving penalties more severe. In general, the enforcement of the drunk-driving laws of the United States is a disgrace. But last year, the public outcry against drunk drivers was such that the West Virginia Legislature made drunk driving a serious offense, amending the law to include a no-nonsense procedure for enforcement.

West Virginia's decision to crack down on drunk driving was not unique; several other states amended their laws last year with spectacular results. In California, for example, after a new drunk-driving law went into effect, the highway death toll during the Christmas season was reduced by 50 percent over the previous year.

Drunk driving differs from other criminal questions in that it is a comparatively easily understood problem and there is no political pressure to protect drunk drivers. Although there is no pressure to protect any criminal who strikes at random, the more a criminal activity looks like a regular business—car theft, gambling, drug sales—the more criminals organize to influence the political process. Even more important in the passage of the drunk-driving laws, perhaps, was the lack of debate about what would reduce drunk driving. Everyone agreed that strict sanctions, quickly applied, would do the trick for the occasional drunk, and that permanent revocation of their licenses would keep most of the habitual drunks off the road. Like the environmental movement, the lobby against drunk driving knew just what it wanted.

By contrast, efforts within the political system to improve the criminal-justice system often stall because of the timeless debate about stricter enforcement versus elimination of the root causes of crime. The advantage of a citizen lobby seriously concerned with an improved criminal-justice system is that citizens want protection—they are content if the symptoms of the disease can be controlled, and that is probably the practical approach for the foreseeable future.

It is important to differentiate between traditional law-and-order rhetoric and real criminal-law reform. Traditional law-and-order rhetoric addresses itself primarily to the decisions of the United States Supreme Court since *Miranda v. Arizona* in 1966, when the Supreme Court began the wholesale reform of the criminal law in order to further civil rights and civil liberties. A return to police brutality, official harassment of the lower socio-economic class, and kangaroo-court summary convictions by forced guilty pleas is not my idea of criminal-law reform. It is possible to have a well-functioning system of criminal-law enforcement without the violations of personal integrity inherent in the police state. But it would be expensive.

In my estimation, a good criminal-justice system that reduces violent and petty crime to roughly one-fifth of their current level could be established with substantially less political activism than was required for environmental reform. Furthermore, the costs to the nation of criminal-law reform would be dramatically less than those of the environmental movement, although they would *all* be borne directly by the taxpayers instead of being paid for through the inflation of consumer prices, as was the case with most environmental reforms. Cleaning up the environment exacted its costs through lost jobs, higher utility bills, and more expensive automobiles. Criminal-law reform will cost higher taxes.

It is not necessary that everyone suddenly become interested in criminal-law reform. After all, the number of voters who were actively dedicated to the ecology revolution was comparatively small. Extremely effective interest groups—the National Rifle Association, for example—are comparatively small in terms of active members. It must be remembered that politicians are not concerned with influencing everyone who is eligible to vote—just the 21 to 65 percent, depending on the election, who actually come to the polls. It is the militant and not the indifferent voter who must be satisfied first.

QUESTIONS FOR DISCUSSION

1. According to Neely, why is little being done about changes in the justice system that might affect the reduction of crime?

2. Discuss the reform efforts in the courts that are outlined by the author and why there is a tremendous amount of resistance to these reforms.

3. What suggestions does the author present as to how "real" change in criminal law reform will or ideally should take place?

APPLICATIONS

1. Why is it that most victims of crime, particularly heinous crimes, have the least influence over crime control policy? Is it realistic to think that significant changes in the criminal justice system will take place when the disparity and stratification between social classes seems to be widening? Discuss.

2. Given that the processes that occur in the criminal justice system typically are not initiated until after a crime has been committed, and the criminal justice agencies are to a great extent reactive organizations, how or in what ways does the criminal justice system reduce or prevent crime? Discuss.

A Policy Maker's Guide to Controlling Delinquency and Crime through Family Interventions

Karen E. Wright • Kevin N. Wright

INTRODUCTION

Most activities aimed at controlling crime and delinquency in the United States focus on offenders. Arrest, conviction, and punishment are sought to deter and incapacitate. At best these efforts have proved to be only marginally effective. Despite various attempts to improve the success of the criminal justice system in detecting, apprehending, and bringing to justice adult and juvenile offenders, crime rates remain high.

On the basis of examinations of the association between family life and delinquency, it appears that strengthening families may be an effective method of controlling crime. Research demonstrates clearly that families contribute to the development of delinquent and criminal patterns of life. Studies conducted during the last two decades have found, with considerable consistency, that what occurs in families is related to family members' subsequent delinquent and criminal behavior (for reviews of this literature, Henggeler, 1989; Loeber and Dishion, 1983; Loeber and Stouthamer-Loeber, 1986; Snyder and Patterson, 1987). Thus, strengthening families appears to be a viable option for improving crime control.

Barry Krisberg (1991:141), president of the National Council on Crime and Delinquency, suggests that policy leaders have not heeded recent advances in criminological research. Instead he notes that they have opted to continue allocating resources to deter and incapacitate offenders, although addressing the origins of delinquent behavior among children and within families might produce more fruitful results with substantially lower human costs. Similarly, Sampson (1987b:378), a sociologist who has spent considerable time studying the relationship of family life to crime and delinquency, suggests that a

Karen E. Wright and Kevin N. Wright, "A Policy Maker's Guide to Controlling Delinquency and Crime through Family Interventions," *Justice Quarterly*, 11:(2), 189–206. Reprinted with permission of the Academy of Criminal Justice Sciences.

"coherent family policy" would be more likely to reduce crime than present policies that lead to an ever-increasing prison population.

In this paper we outline policy responses to reduce delinquency through family intervention. These actions are grouped into five categories: 1) prenatal and early childhood health care, 2) early intervention, 3) comprehensive family policy, 4) family treatment for troubled youths, and 5) parent training.

A CAUTIONARY NOTE

We caution readers not to look to family interventions as a panacea. The causes of crime are complex; even the role of family life in the etiology of criminal behavior has been shown to be multifaceted. Although family variables consistently are found to be related to delinquency, they explain only modest amounts of the variation in delinquent outcomes.

Furthermore, programs aimed at intervening in children's lives with the expectation of reducing the risks of future delinquency and criminality have not always produced the hoped-for results. Zigler, Taussig, and Black (1992:997) observe, "Few programs directed at reducing delinquent behavior have shown lasting effects." Similarly, programs intended to prevent delinquency have generally produced few long-term successes (also see Gottfredson, 1986).

Even more disturbing, at least one study (McCord, 1978) discovered harmful effects of intervention in the lives of at-risk children. The Cambridge-Somerville Youth Project was initiated in 1939 to assist delinquency-prone boys and their families. Counselors worked with the boys and their families; many of the youths received academic tutoring; a significant proportion of the boys were provided with medical and psychiatric care; and some boys, who otherwise might not have participated, were brought into community programs. Involvement in the Project lasted five years on the average. A 30-year follow-up found that men who had been in the program were more likely than a control group to have sustained criminal careers, to have mental health and alcoholism problems, to have died, to have suffered stress-related diseases, to have lower-status occupations, and to be less satisfied with their jobs.

Why, asked McCord (1978:288–89), could this well-intended program have produced such subtle and unexpected effects? One explanation is that interactions with adults who possessed a different set of values from those of their families may have produced conflicting expectations in the boys. Involvement in the program may have fostered dependency on outside assistance that persisted throughout the participants' adult lives. Furthermore, the program may have raised expectations among the boys that subsequently could not be fulfilled. Finally, participation in the program may have become a self-fulfilling prophecy: receiving help led to a self-perception of needing help.

These findings led McCord to conclude, "Intervention programs risk damaging the individuals they are designed to assist" (1978:289). Even so, she did not call for the cessation of programs for at-risk youths; instead she admonished practitioners and policy makers alike to proceed cautiously, to remain aware of potential harm of programs to children, and to evaluate outcomes.

We share McCord's concern about the risks of intervention, but, like her, we maintain a commitment to exploring new and we hope more successful practices. We are encouraged by recent advances in knowledge and findings about successful programs. In the following pages we outline several strategies for working with families that have the potential to reduce the incidence of delinquency and criminality. With one exception, the interventions do not deal directly with delinquents and their families; rather, they constitute early interventions in children's lives with the potential for lifelong educational, social, and behavioral effects.

These programs incorporate an ecological view of children and family life. Families are the first and among the most important institutions affecting children's development, but the interaction between parents and children takes place in a broader social and cultural environment. Schools, workplaces, community organizations, child care facilities, and health care systems play important roles in developmental processes. Zigler et al. (1992) state that "[b]y improving parents' interactions with these systems, and by helping them to support their child's physical, cognitive, and socioemotional development" (p. 997), programs can enhance the likelihood of competence in a variety of contexts during childhood and into later life.

PRENATAL AND EARLY CHILDHOOD HEALTH CARE

One way in which public policy can begin to support children's physical, cognitive, and socioemotional development is by ensuring that all families have access to maternal and child health care. Researchers have found considerable stability in aggressive and antisocial behavior, particularly when that behavior is extensive and begins at an early age (Huesmann et al., 1984; Loeber, 1982; Olweus, 1979). This evidence has led some researchers to postulate a predisposition toward impulsive, aggressive, and antisocial behavior which may be attributable to both genetic (Anderson, Lytton, and Romney, 1986; Lytton, 1990:693; Schulsinger, 1980) and biological factors (Loeber, 1991; Werner, 1987). Many of the biological factors can be addressed directly through adequate health care.

Growing evidence suggests that low birth weight, poor nutrition, drug and alcohol abuse during pregnancy, exposure to toxins, and various other health-related factors have profound influences on children's development. They affect intelligence, impulsiveness, and aggression, all known to be related to delinquent and criminal behavior. The National Health/Education Consortium (1991) calls for a program to provide every mother and baby with early, comprehensive, preventive health care: "Unless the commitment exists to provide adequate access to comprehensive maternity and infant care, society will be forced to contend with the care and treatment of unhealthy children who, through no fault of their own, grow up with long-term disabilities or have difficulty becoming self-supporting adults" (p. 7). Aggressive outreach programs for pregnant women at high risk of having children with developmental problems are needed to ensure adequate prenatal education and health care. Early identification of children with such problems has been shown to improve their chances for educational and social success. Waiting until they are in school may make intervention too late; early screening, diagnosis, and treatment are essential. Making sure that all children have the preventive and primary care necessary to ensure a good beginning in their developmental processes is the first step toward controlling future delinquency and criminality.

EARLY INTERVENTION

Research consistently has shown that age at onset is the single most accurate predictor of later and continued delinquency and criminality (Bell, 1977; Loeber and Dishion, 1983; Lytton, 1990; Osborn and West, 1978; Tolan, 1987; Tolan and Lorion, 1988; West and Farrington, 1977; Wolfgang, Figlio, and Sellin, 1972). Furthermore, early antisocial behavioral problems tend to be **precursors** to delinquency (Barnum, 1987; Hanson et al., 1984; Loeber, 1982; Loeber, Stouthamer-Loeber, and Green, 1987).

According to the model developed at the Oregon Social Learning Center, the developmental process leading to delinquency begins in early childhood with maladaptive parent–child interactions. The components of the reciprocal relationship are complex: "The development of the child appears to be multiply determined by what the child brings to the situation, what s/he elicits from the situation, what the environment can offer and what it does offer" (Sameroff and Seifer, 1983:12). Support for this model has been generated in recent years by numerous studies (Dishion, 1990; Dishion et al., 1991; Larzelere and Patterson, 1990; Loeber and Dishion, 1983, 1984; Patterson, 1980, 1986; Patterson and Dishion, 1985; Patterson, Dishion, and Bank, 1984; Patterson and Stouthamer-Loeber, 1984; Synder and Patterson, 1987).

Parents with a difficult child may cease functioning as parents to gain superficial peace in the home. With a particularly unruly child, the parents not only may fail to supervise but actually may come to dislike the child, adding rejection to the already problematic relationship (Loeber and Stouthamer-Loeber, 1986). Among the various aspects of family life, it appears that parental rejection is the most powerful predictor of juvenile delinquency (see Loeber and Stouthamer-Loeber, 1986). Children raised in supportive, affectionate, accepting environments tend to become self-aware adults who can formulate their own long-term goals and can pursue socially and economically fulfilling lives (Borduin, Pruitt, and Henggeler, 1986; Campbell, 1987; Cernkovich and Giordano, 1987; Fox et al., 1983; Henggeler et al., 1985; Johnson, 1987; McCord, 1979; Rodick, Henggeler, and Hanson, 1986; Smith and Walters, 1978; Tolan, 1987, 1988; Tolan and Lorion, 1988). In contrast, children of harsh, unloving, overcritical, and authoritarian parents often become self-absorbed as adults. Their impulsiveness can lead to violence and substance abuse (Bandura and Walters, 1959; Chollar, 1987; Glueck and Glueck, 1950; Gray-Ray and Ray, 1990; Kroupa, 1988; Loeber and Dishion, 1984; McCord, 1983; Nye, 1958; Pfouts, Scholper, and Henley, 1981; Simons, Robertson and Downs, 1989; Stouthamer-Loeber and Loeber, 1986).

As a child grows older and spends more time outside the home, negative behaviors learned at home are likely to appear in other settings. In school, the child's antisocial disposition may interfere with learning and often will cause the child to be disliked by peers. The failing, disliked, and antisocial child will gravitate toward peers and social settings that reinforce his or her behavior, which in turn may further encourage the child's antisocial actions (Patterson, 1982). As the child or adolescent participates or engages in more frequent antisocial behavior while associating increasingly with antisocial peers, his or her bond to conventional society will grow weaker (Hanson et al., 1984; LaGrange and White, 1985; Matsueda, 1982; Matsueda and Heimer, 1987; Paternoster, 1988; Smith and

Paternoster, 1987; Steinberg and Silverberg, 1986). The weakening of this bond may be an initial cause of delinquency; continued and/or increased delinquent acts may become their own indirect cause as they further weaken the youth's bond to family, school, and conventional beliefs (Thornberry, 1987:876).

Longitudinal research is beginning to show that early identification of at-risk children and intervention in this process in their lives may hold great promise in preventing future delinquent behavior and criminality (Tremblay et al., 1991; Zigler et al., 1992). Staff members at the Oregon Social Learning Center have developed a procedure called "Multiple gating" to identify potentially troublesome children. The procedure uses teachers' and parents' reports to identify children likely to have later adjustment and conduct problems. This system has identified 56 percent of later delinquents (Loeber, Dishion, and Patterson, 1984).

Once at-risk children have been identified, interventions in the maladaptive parent–child interactions are needed. This step may involve training parents in effective child management practices; in some cases, respite may be needed for parents of particularly unruly children. Preservation of effective parental supervision, the development of social skills, and maintenance of bonds with conventional society become the goals of intervention as the children begin school.

Zigler et al. (1992) have identified four exemplary early intervention programs: the Perry Preschool Project, the Syracuse University Family Development Research Program, the Yale Child Welfare Research Program, and the Houston Parent–Child Development Center. Each of these produced long-term reductions in antisocial and aggressive behavior and delinquency. None of these four programs was started with the stated purpose of reducing delinquency; rather, the goal was to reduce the likelihood of school failure and to improve social competence. Although the programs differed, they all offered multifaceted interventions including educational assistance, health care, parent training and support, and other specific social services. Through early intervention they alleviated some of the risks in young children's lives, which thereby decreased the likelihood of future delinquency and criminality. According to Zigler and his colleagues, "the effects of successful experiences early in childhood snowballed to generate further success in school and other social contexts; the programs enhanced physical health and aspects of personality such as motivation and sociability, helping the child to adapt better to later social expectations; and family support, education and involvement in intervention improved parents' childrearing skills and thus altered the environment where children were raised" (1992:1002).

COMPREHENSIVE FAMILY POLICY

Research consistently has found that inadequate supervision is a key variable in predicting delinquency (Cernkovich and Giordano, 1987; Fischer, 1984; Laub and Sampson, 1988; Loeber and Stouthamer-Loeber, 1986; Loeber, Weiher, and Smith, 1991; McCord, 1979; Snyder and Patterson, 1987; Van Voorhis et al., 1988; Wilson, 1987). The elements necessary for effective parental supervision include the following actions: notice what the child is doing, monitor the activities over long periods, model social skills, state house rules clearly, consistently provide punishment for transgressions, provide reinforcement for conformity, and negotiate disagreement so that conflicts and crises do not escalate (Patterson, 1980:81). Monitoring children involves awareness of their companions, whereabouts, and free-time activities. It also includes appropriate communication, the child's accountability to the parents, and the amount of time spent with parents (Larzelere and Patterson, 1990). Monitoring becomes increasingly important as the child progresses into adolescence, when adequate supervision allows parents to influence the child's selection of friends and activities, to express disapproval, and to sanction antisocial and delinquent behavior (Snyder and Patterson, 1987:227).

Some analysts advocate enhancing social services through a coherent family policy. The basis for this suggestion is that inadequate housing, a lack of income, and an inability to obtain adequate day care create stress and make it difficult to function effectively as parents and supervise children adequately.

Single-parent families have been identified as particularly in need of a comprehensive family policy. Because most of these families, and particularly those at highest risk of producing delinquents, are headed by women, the needs of mother-only families are of special interest.

A review of 50 studies on family structure and delinquency revealed that delinquency was 10 to 15 percent more prevalent in single-parent than in two-parent families (Wells and Rankin, 1991:87). Experts generally agree that nothing is inherently pathological about single parenthood, but that the situation **predisposes** a set of conditions that may contribute to delinquency, such as greater autonomy for the adolescent (Dornbusch et al., 1985; Steinberg and Silverberg, 1986), less parental control (Matsueda, 1982; Steinberg, 1986; Van Voorhis et al., 1988), increased susceptibility to peer pressure (Henggeler, 1989:48), and poorer economic conditions (Morash and Rucker, 1989:83). Furthermore, because their economic status is often poor, mother-only families may live in higher-crime neighborhoods; these may contribute to higher rates of delinquency because of increased exposure to criminal influences (Felson, 1986; Felson and Cohen, 1980; Sampson, 1986a, 1986b, 1987a).

The Education and Human Service Consortium, composed of representatives from organizations such as the Center for Law and Social Policy, the Children's Defense Fund, the National Alliance of Business, the National Alliance of Secondary School Principals, and the U.S. Conference of Mayors, believes that the current system of social services fails children for five reasons: (1) services are crisis-oriented; (2) the system separates the problems of children and of families into categories that do not take into account the interrelated causes and solutions; (3) communication among service agencies is lacking; (4) specialized agencies cannot easily produce comprehensive solutions to complex problems; and (5) existing services are not funded adequately. The Consortium calls for comprehensive delivery of a wide variety of preventive, treatment, and support services, including techniques to ensure that children and families actually receive the services they need. The focus must be on empowering the entire family (Melaville and Blank, 1991).

Research has verified the beneficial effect of increased services. The provision of a coordinated set of medical and social services, including day care, had a significant impact on women and their children 10 years later. In comparison with a control group, the mothers receiving coordinated assistance were more likely to be self-supporting, had attained more education, and had smaller families. Their children performed better academically (Seitz, Rosenbaum, and Apfel, 1985). The evaluators did not compare the delinquency rates of children from supported and from unsupported families; the variables they measured, however, have been linked to delinquency prevention.

In today's economically and socially stressful world, it has become increasingly difficult for all parents, not only those who are single or poor, to supervise their children adequately, to remain active participants in their children's lives, and to be nurturing and supportive care-givers. The availability of high-quality child care—day care for preschool children and after-school care for school-age youths—is essential to assist parents in supervising their children.

FAMILY TREATMENT FOR TROUBLED YOUTHS

We have shown that when parents are harsh, unloving, overcritical, and authoritarian, healthy development is impeded, and children's risk of delinquency increase. Furthermore, inadequate supervision increases the chances of delinquent behavior.

Growing up in homes with considerable conflict, marital discord, and violence also seems to increase the risks of eventual delinquent and/or criminal behavior. Witnessing violence in the home yields a consistent but modest association with delinquency (Widom, 1989:22; also see Bach-y-Rita and Veno, 1974; Borduin et al., 1986; Gove and Crutchfield, 1982; Hanson et al., 1984; Hartstone and Hansen, 1984; Hetherington, Stouwie, and Ridberg, 1971; Koski, 1988; Lewis et al., 1979; Mann et al., 1990; McCord, 1979, 1988b, 1990; Richards, Berk, and Forster, 1979; Roff and Wirt, 1985; Sendi and Blomgren, 1975; Simcha-Fagan et al., 1975; Sorrells, 1977; Straus, Gelles, and Steinmetz, 1981; Tolan, 1987; Tolan and Lorion, 1988; West and Farrington, 1973). Moreover, being abused as a child increases the risk of becoming an abusive parent, a delinquent, or a violent adult criminal. Not only do abused children manifest more aggressive and more problematic behavior at early ages; research also shows that these children are not likely to outgrow the aggressive patterns as they mature (Widom, 1989; also see Howing et al., 1990; Koski, 1988; Lane and Davis, 1987).

Dysfunctional families—those experiencing high levels of disorganization, conflict, dominance, hostility, lack of warmth, and authoritarian disciplinary style—do not allow children to gain insight and understanding into how their misbehavior might hurt others. In such negative family conditions, children cannot develop conventional moral reasoning with roots in acceptance of mutual expectations, positive social intentions, belief in and maintenance of the social system, and acceptance of motives that include duties and respect. Delinquency can be anticipated when children or adolescents cannot see other people's perspective and lack empathy for other people's circumstances (Arbuthnot, Gordon, and Jurkovic, 1987).

Fortunately, research has identified elements of family life which may shield children from otherwise harmful circumstances. Competent mothers—those who are self-confident, consistently nonpunitive, and affectionate, and who have leadership skills—tend to protect children from **criminogenic** influences (Lytton, 1990; McCord, 1986, 1991). Similarly, the presence of one caring parent buffers children against the effect of rejection by the other parent (Minty, 1988). In homes with high marital discord, the presence of one parent who maintains a warm, positive relationship with the children buffers them from conduct disorders (Rutter, 1978). Although the children of alcoholic fathers are more likely than others to become alcoholics, the chances of becoming alcoholic are diminished if their mothers did not demonstrate approval or respect for the fathers (McCord, 1988a). Furthermore, having a close sibling or being involved in teen sports provides social support that buffers abused children from becoming delinquent (Kruttschmitt, Ward, and Sheble, 1987).

These findings suggest that even in the face of adverse family conditions, resistance to delinquency is possible. Henggeler et al. (1986) report a successful treatment experiment that used the family-ecological approach for inner-city juvenile offenders and their families. This method addressed the multidimensional nature of behavioral problems, exploring individual deficits such as poor social and problem-solving skills, inappropriate child and family interactions, and problematic transactions with extrafamilial systems such as the peer group and the school. Therapy was individualized, and focused on the most important determinants of each child's problem behavior. Observation revealed that parent-child interactions became warmer and more affectionate with treatment. In turn, parents reported a decline in their children's conduct problems, immature behavior, and association with delinquents.

Potentially the most effective response to delinquent behavior is not to treat the individual delinquent as personally responsible for his or her action, as is currently the predominant response in juvenile justice. Rather, it may lie in a more holistic strategy aimed at both the child and the family. A wide array of treatment programs has been designed to reduce family and child disorders (Hawkins et al., 1988). Teaching parents how to manage older delinquent children is one of the most promising approaches (Bank et al., 1991; Greenwood and Zimring, 1985).

TRAINING IN PARENTING

Children learn to be parents from their parents. When children grow up in families where positive parental practices are modeled, they learn how to care properly for their own children. When children are raised by harsh, rejecting, and violent parents, however, inadequate and ineffective parenting may be transmitted from one generation to the next. Even individuals who were raised in caring and supportive family situations, when confronted with an impulsive or overactive child, may find it difficult to maintain effective parenting practices, particularly when they have only limited coping resources because of their familial or economic situation and when they live in relative social isolation. For people who lack parenting skills, training is a promising method for preventing delinquency. There are two possible points of intervention: in one, parents are taught how to manage difficult children; the other consists of training young people in how to be effective parents.

Programs designed for parents try to improve family management skills by teaching parents to monitor their children's behaviors, to use moderate and consistent discipline of inappropriate behavior, and to reward desired behaviors. Most of the systematic research involves programs for parents of young children with conduct problems. Four experimental tests of such programs (Karoly and Rosenthal, 1977; Martin, 1977; Patterson, Chamberlain, and Reid, 1982; Walters and Gilmore, 1973) substantiated significant reductions in problem behaviors among preadolescent children. An experimental study of a parent training program for families of serious delinquents found that the treatment group committed fewer serious crimes than the experimental group during the treatment year and spent less time in institutions. The benefits of the program, however, reportedly were achieved at substantial emotional cost to the staff (Bank et al., 1991).

Another group that might benefit from training in parental skills consists of adolescents who may lack effective role models, such as children in institutional and foster care, youths whose families are under the supervision of a family court, pregnant teenagers who choose to keep their babies, and delinquents. Some experts advocate parent training for all high school students (Farrington and West, 1981).

CONCLUSIONS

Delinquent youths do not experience a set of common events that lead to delinquency; rather, multiple pathways steer some youths to inappropriate behavior. Some adolescents run away because of a bad situation in the home; some parents push their children out; some teenagers leave for the thrill; still others escape from overprotective parents (Huizinga, Esbensen, and Weiher, 1991:84–85). The same apparently is true for delinquents: no certain or direct pathway emerges for all children growing up at risk (Huizinga et al., 1991).

In the lives of children most at risk of becoming delinquent, however, some or all of the following circumstances may be operating: 1) they receive little love, affection, or warmth, and are physically or emotionally rejected and/or abandoned by their parents; 2) they are inadequately supervised by parents who fail to teach them right and wrong, who do not monitor their whereabouts, friends, or activities, and who discipline them erratically and harshly; and 3) they grow up in homes with considerable conflict, marital discord, and perhaps even violence (Farrington, 1990:94; Leitenberg, 1987). Families at greatest risk of delinquency are those suffering from limited coping resources, social isolation, and (among parents) poor child-rearing skills (Loeber and Stouthamer-Loeber, 1986:97). The presence of any one of these family circumstances increases the chances of raising a delinquent child. The presence of more than one factor increases the odds further (Farrington, 1990; Farrington et al., 1988; Kruttschmitt et al., 1987; Loeber and Stouthamer-Loeber, 1986; Lytton, 1990; McCord, 1990; Minty, 1988).

In this paper we have advocated five strategies for strengthening families to reduce the factors in children's lives that place them at higher risk of delinquency and criminality: 1) prenatal and early childhood health care, 2) early intervention, 3) comprehensive family policy, 4) family treatment for troubled youths, and 5) parent training. Traditional approaches to juvenile delinquency attempt to control behavior after it has become entrenched. The five strategies offered here differ in that they attempt to prevent delinquent behavior before it begins by altering the family circumstances that lead to it. The goal of this approach is not delinquency prevention as such but the development of socially competent adults. Delinquency prevention simply becomes a by-product of that process.

We have presented these five strategies separately, but attention to all five is needed. A healthy start in life is essential for educational and social success. Parent-child relations in early childhood begin the process by which children develop healthy self-concepts, confidence, motivation, and sociability. Children who are prepared socially and academically when they begin school will be more successful and will interact more positively with teachers and peers; this point, too, has implications for continued successful development into adolescence and adulthood. Parents who have adequate social and economic support clearly would be more able to function effectively as parents than individuals who are stressed and alienated by their social and economical disadvantages and isolation. Furthermore, child-rearing skills are not a given. Some parents had successful role models, but those raised by harsh, unloving, overcritical, and authoritarian parents never had the opportunity to acquire the skills they need for effective child rearing.

To meet these requirements demands a comprehensive rather than a narrow approach. The current fragmentation in social services impedes the provision of integrated preventive approaches. Furthermore, because child development is an ongoing process, intervention also must be ongoing. It would be naive to expect a program that briefly influences children's development to alter the course of their lives. If families in fact play significant roles in the developmental processes that lead to delinquency, isn't it time to intervene systematically and comprehensively in those processes which serve as the root causes of delinquency?

REFERENCES

ANDERSON, K. E., H. LYTTON, AND D. M. ROMNEY. (1986). "Mothers' Interactions with Normal and Conduct-Disordered Boys: Who Affects Whom?" *Developmental Psychology* 22(5):604–609.

ARBUTHNOT, J., D. A. GORDON, AND G. J. JURKOVIC. (1987). "Personality." In H. C. Quay (ed.), *Handbook of Juvenile Delinquency*, pp. 139–183. New York: Wiley.

BACH-Y-RITA, G. AND A. VENO. (1974). "Habitual Violence: A Profile of 62 Men." *American Journal of Psychiatry* 131:1015–1017.

BANDURA, A. AND R. H. WALTERS. (1959). *Adolescent Aggression.* New York: Ronald Press.

BANK, L., J. H. MARLOWE, J. B. REID, G. R. PATTERSON, AND M. R. WEINROTT. (1991). "A Comparative Evaluation of Parent-Training Interventions for Families of Chronic Delinquents." *Journal of Abnormal Child Psychology* 19:15–33.

BARNUM, B. (1987). "Biomedical Problems in Juvenile Delinquency: Issues in Diagnosis and Treatment." In J. Q. Wilson and G. C. Loury (eds.), *From Children to Citizens.* Vol. 3: *Families, Schools and Delinquency Prevention*, pp. 51–84. New York: Springer-Verlag.

BELL, R. Q. (1977). "Socialization Findings Re-examined." In R. Q. Bell and R. V. Harper (eds.), *Child Effects on Adults*, pp. 53–84. Hillsdale, N.J.: Erlbaum.

BORDUIN, C. M., J. A. PRUITT, AND S. W. HENGGELER. (1986). "Family Interactions in Black, Lower-Class Families with Delinquent and Nondelinquent Adolescent Boys." *Journal of Genetic Psychology* 147(3):333–42.

CAMPBELL, A. (1987). "Self-Reported Delinquency and Home Life: Evidence from a Sample of British Girls." *Journal of Youth and Adolescence* 16(2):167–77.

CERNKOVICH, S. A. AND P. C. GIORDANO. (1987). "Family Relationships and Delinquency." *Criminology* 25(2):295–321.

CHOLLAR, S. (1987). "We Reap What We Sow." *Psychology Today* 21:12.

DISHION, T. J. (1990). "The Family Ecology of Boys' Peer Relations in Middle Childhood." *Child Development* 61:874–92.

DISHION, T. J., G. R. PATTERSON, M. STOOLMILLER, AND M. L. SKINNER. (1991). "Family, School, and Behavioral Antecedents to Early Adolescent Involvement with Antisocial Peers." *Developmental Psychology* 27(1):172–80.

DORNBUSCH, S. M., J. M. CARLSMITH, S. J. BUSHWALL, P. L. RITTER, H. LEIDERMAN, A. H. HASTORF, AND R. T. GROSS. (1985). "Single Parents, Extended Households, and the Control of Adolescents." *Child Development* 56:326–41.

FARRINGTON, D. P. (1990). "Implications of Criminal Career Research for the Prevention of Offending." *Journal of Adolescence* 13:93–113.

FARRINGTON, D. P., L. MORLEY, R. J. ST. LEDGER, AND D. J. WEST. (1988). "Are There Any Successful Men from Criminogenic Backgrounds?" *Psychiatry* 51 (May):116–30.

FARRINGTON, D. P. AND D. J. WEST. (1981). "The Cambridge Study in Delinquent Development." In S. A. Mednick and A. E. Baert (eds.), *Prospective Longitudinal Research: An Empirical Basis for Primary Prevention*, Oxford: Oxford University Press.

FELSON, M. (1986). "Linking Criminal Choices, Routine Activities, Informal Control, and Criminal Outcomes." In D. B. Cornish and R. V. Clarke (eds.), *The Reasoning Criminal: Rational Choice Perspectives on Offending*, pp. 119–28. New York: Springer-Verlag.

FELSON, M. AND L. E. COHEN. (1980). "Human Ecology and Crime: A Routine Activity Approach." *Human Ecology* 8(4):389–406.

FISCHER, D. B. (1984). "Family Size and Delinquency." *Perceptual and Motor Skills* 58:527–34.

FOX, R., A. F. TOATORI, F. MACKLIN, H. GREEN, AND T. FOX. (1983). "Socially Maladjusted Adolescents' Perceptions of Their Families." *Psychological Reports* 52:831–34.

GLUECK, S. AND E. GLUECK. (1950). *Unraveling Juvenile Delinquency*. Cambridge, Mass.: Harvard University Press.

GOTTFREDSON, D. C. (1986). "An Empirical Test of School-Based Environmental and Individual Interventions to Reduce the Risk of Delinquent Behavior." *Criminology* 24:705–31.

GOVE, W. R. AND R. D. CRUTCHFIELD. (1982). "The Family and Juvenile Delinquency." *Sociological Quarterly* 23 (Summer):301–19.

GRAY-RAY, P. AND M. C. RAY. (1990). "Juvenile Delinquency in the Black Community." *Youth and Society* 22(1):67–84.

GREENWOOD, P. W. AND F. E. ZIMRING. (1985). *One More Chance: The Pursuit of Promising Intervention Strategies for Chronic Juvenile Offenders*. Santa Monica, Calif.: RAND.

HANSON, C. L., S. W. HENGGELER, W. F. HAEFELE, AND J. D. RODICK. (1984). "Demographic, Individual, and Family Relationship Correlates of Serious and Repeated Crime among Adolescents and Their Siblings." *Journal of Consulting and Clinical Psychology* 52(4):528–38.

HARTSTONE, E. AND K. V. HANSEN. (1984). "The Violent Juvenile Offender: An Empirical Portrait." In R. A. Mathias (ed.), *Violent Juvenile Offenders: An Anthology*, pp. 83–112. San Francisco: National Council on Crime and Delinquency.

HAWKINS, J. D., J. M. JENSON, R. F. CATALANO, AND D. M. LISHNER. (1988). "Delinquency and Drug Abuse: Implications for Social Services." *Social Service Review* (June): 258–84.

HENGGELER, S. W. (1989). *Delinquency in Adolescence*. Newbury Park, CA: Sage.

HENGGELER, S. W., C. L. HANSON, C. BORDUIN, S. M. WATSON, AND M. A. BRUNK. (1985). "Mother–Son Relationships of Juvenile Felons." *Journal of Consulting and Clinical Psychology* 53(6):942–43.

HENGGELER, S. W., J. D. RODICK, C. M. BORDUIN, C. L. HANSON, S. M. WATSON, AND J. R. UREY. (1986). "Multisystemic Treatment of Juvenile Offenders: Effects on Adolescent Behavior and Family Interaction." *Development Psychology* 22(1):132–41.

HETHERINGTON, E. M., R. STOUWIE, AND E. H. RIDBERG. (1971). "Patterns of Family Interaction and Child Rearing Related to Three Dimensions of Juvenile Delinquency." *Journal of Abnormal Psychology* 77:160–76.

HOWING, P. T., J. S. WODARSKI, P. D. KURTZ, J. M. GAUDIN JR., AND E. N. HERBST. (1990). "Child Abuse and Delinquency: The Empirical and Theoretical Links." *Social Work* (May):244–49.

HUESMANN, L. R., M. M. LEFKOWITZ, L. D. ERON, AND L. O. WALDER. (1984). "Stability of Aggression over Time and Generations." *Developmental Psychology* 20(6):1120–34.

HUIZINGA, D., F. A. EBSENSEN, AND A. W. WEIHER. (1991). "Are There Multiple Paths to Delinquency?" *Journal of Criminal Law and Criminology* 82(1):83–118.

JOHNSON, R. E. (1987). "Mother's versus Father's Role in Causing Delinquency." *Adolescence* 22(86) (Summer):305–15.

KAROLY, P. AND M. ROSENTHAL. (1977). "Training Parents in Behavior Modification: Effects on Perceptions of Family Interaction and Deviant Child Behavior." *Behavior Therapy* 8:406–10.

KOSKI, P. R. (1988). "Family Violence and Nonfamily Deviance: Taking Stock of the Literature." *Marriage and Family Review* 12(1–2):23–46.

KRISBERG, B. (1991). "Are You Now or Have You Ever Been a Sociologist?" *Journal of Criminal Law and Criminology* 82(1):141–55.

KROUPA, S. E. (1988). "Perceived Parental Acceptance and Female Juvenile Delinquency." *Adolescence* 23(89) (Spring):171–85.

KRUTTSCHMITT, C., D. WARD, AND M. A. SHEBLE. (1987). "Abuse-Resistant Youth: Some Factors That May Inhibit Violent Criminal Behavior." *Social Forces* 66(2):501–19.

LAGRANGE, R. L. AND H. R. WHITE. (1985). "Age Differences in Delinquency: A Test of Theory." *Criminology* 23(1):19–45.

LANE, T. W. AND G. E. DAVIS. (1987). "Child Maltreatment and Juvenile Delinquency: Does a Relationship Exist?" In J. D. Burchard and S. N. Burchard (eds.), *Prevention of Delinquent Behavior*, pp. 122–38. Newbury Park, CA: Sage.

LARZELERE, R. E. AND G. R. PATTERSON. (1990). "Parental Management: Mediator of the Effect of Socioeconomic Status on Early Delinquency." *Criminology* 28(2):301–23.

LAUB, J. H. AND R. J. SAMPSON. (1988). "Unraveling Families and Delinquency: A Reanalysis of the Gluecks' Data." *Criminology* 26(3):355–79.

LEITENBERG, H. (1987). "Primary Prevention of Delinquency." In J. D. Burchard and S. N. Burchard (eds.), *Prevention of Delinquent Behavior*, pp. 312–31. Newbury Park, CA: Sage.

LEWIS, D. O., S. S. SHANOK, J. H. PINCUS, AND G. H. GLASER (1979). "Violent Juvenile Delinquents: Psychiatric, Neurological, Psychological, and Abuse Factors." *Journal of the American Academy of Child Psychiatry* 18:307–19.

LOEBER, R. (1982). "The Stability of Antisocial and Delinquent Child Behavior: A Review." *Child Development* 53:1431–46.

———. (1991). "Antisocial Behavior: More Enduring Than Changeable?" *Journal of the American Academy of Child and Adolescent Psychiatry* 30:393–97.

LOEBER, R. AND T. J. DISHION. (1983). "Early Predictors of Male Delinquency: A Review." *Psychological Bulletin* 94(1):68–99.

_____. (1984). "Boys Who Fight at Home and School: Conditions Influencing Cross-Setting Consistency." *Journal of Consulting and Clinical Psychology* 52(5):759–68.

LOEBER, R., T. J. DISHION, AND G. R. PATTERSON. (1984). "Multiple Gating: A Multistage Assessment Procedure for Identifying Youths at Risk for Delinquency." *Journal of Research in Crime and Delinquency* 21:7–32.

LOEBER, R. AND M. STOUTHAMER-LOEBER. (1986). "Family Factors as Correlates and Predictors of Juvenile Conduct Problems and Delinquency." In M. Tonry and N. Morris (eds.), *Crime and Justice: An Annual Review of Research*, Vol. 7, pp. 29–149. Chicago: University of Chicago Press.

LOEBER, R., M. STOUTHAMER-LOEBER, AND S. M. GREEN. (1987). "Age of Onset of Conduct Problems, Different Developmental Trajectories, and Unique Contributing Factors." Paper presented at the annual meetings of the Society for Research in Child Development, Baltimore.

LOEBER, R., A. W. WEIHER, AND C. SMITH. (1991). "The Relationship between Family Interaction and Delinquency and Substance Use." In D. Huizinga, R. Loeber, and T. P. Thornberry (eds.), *Urban Delinquency and Substance Abuse: Technical Report*, Vol. 1. Washington, D.C.: Office of Juvenile Justice and Delinquency Prevention.

LYTTON, H. (1990). "Child and Parent Effects in Boys' Conduct Disorder: A Reinterpretation." *Developmental Psychology* 26(5):683–97.

MANN, B. J., C. M. BORDUIN, S. W. HENGGELER, AND D. M. BLASKE. (1990). "An Investigation of Systemic Conceptualizations of Parent-Child Coalitions and Symptom Change." *Journal of Consulting and Clinical Psychology* 58(3):336–44.

MARTIN, B. (1977). "Brief Family Therapy Intervention: Effectiveness and the Importance of Including the Father." *Journal of Consulting and Clinical Psychology* 45:1001–10.

MATSUEDA, R. L. (1982). "Testing Control Theory and Differential Association: A Causal Modeling Approach." *American Sociological Review* 47 (August): 489–504.

MATSUEDA, R. L. AND K. HEIMER. (1987). "Race, Family Structure, and Delinquency: A Test of Differential Association and Social Control Theories." *American Sociological Review* 52 (December):826–40.

MCCORD, J. (1978). "A Thirty-Year Follow-Up of Treatment Effects." *American Psychologist* 33:284–89.

_____. (1979). "Some Child-Rearing Antecedents of Criminal Behavior in Adult Men." *Journal of Personality and Social Psychology* 37:1477–86.

_____. (1983). "A Forty Year Perspective on Effects of Child Abuse and Neglect." *Child Abuse and Neglect* 7:265–70.

_____. (1986) "Instigation and Insulation: How Families Affect Antisocial Aggression." In D. Olweus, J. Block, and M. R. Yarrow (eds.), *Development of Antisocial and Prosocial Behavior,* New York: Academic Press.

_____. (1988a). "Alcoholism: Toward Understanding Genetic and Social Factors." *Psychiatry* 51(May): 131–41.

_____. (1988b). "Parental Behavior in the Cycle of Aggression." *Psychiatry* 51(February):14–23.

_____. (1990). "Crime in Moral and Social Contexts—The American Society of Criminology, 1989 Presidential Address." *Criminology* 28(1):1–26.

_____. (1991). "Family Relationships, Juvenile Delinquency, and Adult Criminality." *Criminology* 29(3):397–418.

MELAVILLE, A. I. AND M. J. BLANK. (1991). "What It Takes: Structuring Interagency Partnerships to Connect Children and Families with Comprehensive Services." Washington, DC: Education and Human Services Consortium.

MINTY, B. (1988). "Public Care or Distorted Family Relationships: The Antecedents of Violent Crime." *Howard Journal* 27(3):172–87.

MORASH, M. AND L. RUCKER. (1989). "An Exploratory Study of the Connection of Mother's Age at Childbearing to Her Children's Delinquency in Four Data Sets." *Crime and Delinquency* 35(1):45–93.

NATIONAL HEALTH/EDUCATION CONSORTIUM. (1991). "Healthy Brain Development: Precursor to Learning." Washington, D.C.: National Commission to Prevent Infant Mortality.

NYE, F. I. (1958). *Family Relationships and Delinquent Behavior.* New York: Wiley.

OLWEUS, D. (1979). "Stability of Aggressive Reaction Patterns in Males: A Review." *Psychological Bulletin* 86(4):852–75.

OSBORN, S. G. AND D. J. WEST. (1978). "The Effectiveness of Various Predictors of Criminal Careers." *Journal of Adolescence* 1:101–17.

PATERNOSTER, R. (1988). "Examining Three-Wave Deterrence Models: A Question of Temporal Order and Specification." *Journal of Criminal Law and Criminology* 79(1):135–79.

PATTERSON, G. R. (1980). "Children Who Steal." In T. Hirschi and M. Gottfredson (eds.), *Understanding Crime: Current Theory and Research*, pp. 73–90. Beverly Hills, CA: Sage.

_____. (1982). *Coercive Family Process.* Eugene, OR: Castalia.

_____. (1986). "Performance Models for Antisocial Boys." *American Psychologist* 41(4):432–44.

PATTERSON, G. R., P. CHAMBERLAIN, AND J. B. REID. (1982). "A Comparative Evaluation of a Parent Training Program." *Behavior Therapy* 13:638–50.

PATTERSON, G. R. AND T. J. DISHION. (1985). "Contributions of Families and Peers to Delinquency." *Criminology* 23(1):63–79.

PATTERSON, G. R., T. J. DISHION, AND L. BANK. (1984). "Family Interaction: A Process Model of Deviancy Training." *Aggressive Behavior* 10:253–67.

PATTERSON, G. R. AND M. STOUTHAMER-LOEBER. (1984). "The Correlation of Family Management Practices and Delinquency." *Child Development* 55:1299–1307.

PFOUTS, J. H., J. H. SCHOLPER, AND H. C. HENLEY JR. (1981). "Deviant Behaviors of Child Victims and Bystanders in Violent Families." In R. J. Hunter and Y. E. Walker (eds.), *Exploring the Relationship between Child Abuse and Delinquency*, pp. 79–99. Montclair, NJ: Allanheld.

RICHARDS, P., R. A. BERK, AND B. FORSTER. (1979). *Crime as Play: Delinquency in a Middle Class Suburb.* Cambridge, MA: Ballinger.

RODICK, J. D., S. W. HENGGELER, AND C. L. HANSON. (1986). "An Evaluation of the Family Adaptability and Cohesion Evaluation Scales and the Circumplex Model." *Journal of Abnormal Child Psychology* 14(1):77–87.

ROFF, J. D. AND R. D. WIRT. (1985). "The Specificity of Childhood Problem Behavior for Adolescent and Young Adult Maladjustment." *Journal of Clinical Psychology* 41(4):564–71.

RUTTER, M. (1978). "Family, Area and School Influences in the Genesis of Conduct Disorders." In L. A. Hersov, M. Berger, and D. Shaffer (eds.), *Aggression and Antisocial Behavior in Childhood and Adolescence.* Oxford: Pergamon.

SAMEROFF, A. AND R. SEIFER. (1983). "Sources of Community in Parent–Child Relations." Paper presented at the meetings of the Society for Research in Child Development, Detroit, MI.

SAMPSON, R. J. (1986a). "Crime in Cities: The Effects of Formal and Informal Social Control." In A. J. Reiss, Jr. and M. Tonry (eds.), *Crime and Justice Series, Communities and Crime*, Vol. 8, pp. 271–311. Chicago: University of Chicago Press.

_____. (1986b). "Neighborhood Family Structure and the Risk of Personal Victimization." In J. M. Sampson and R. J. Byrne (eds.), *The Social Ecology of Crime*, pp. 25–46. New York: Springer.

_____. (1987a). "Does an Intact Family Reduce Burglary Risk for Its Neighbors?" *Social Science Review* 71(3):204-207.

_____. (1987b). "Urban Black Violence: The Effect of Male Joblessness and Family Disruption." *American Journal of Sociology* 93(2):348–82.

SCHULSINGER, F. (1980). "Biological Psychopathology." *Annual Review of Psychology* 31:583–606.

SEITZ, V., L. K. ROSENBAUM, AND N. H. APFEL. (1985). "Effects of Family Support Intervention: A Ten-Year Follow-Up." *Child Development* 56:376–91.

SENDI, I. B. AND P. G. BLOMGREN. (1975). "A Comparative Study of Predictive Criteria in the Predisposition of Homicidal Adolescents." *American Journal of Psychiatry* 132:423–27.

SIMCHA-FAGAN, O., T. S. LANGER, J. C. GERSTEN, AND J. G. EISENBERG. (1975). "Violent and Antisocial Behavior: A Longitudinal Study of Urban Youth." Unpublished report, Office of Child Development, Washington, DC.

SIMONS, R. L., J. F. ROBERTSON, AND W. R. DOWNS. (1989). "The Nature of the Association between Parental Rejection and Delinquent Behavior." *Journal of Youth and Adolescence* 18(3):297–310.

SMITH, D. A. AND R. PATERNOSTER. (1987). "The Gender Gap in Theories of Deviance: Issues and Evidence." *Journal of Research in Crime and Delinquency* 24(2):140–72.

SMITH, R. M. AND J. WALTERS. (1978). "Delinquent and Non-delinquent Males' Perceptions of Their Fathers." *Adolescence* 13 (Spring):21–28.

SNYDER, J. AND G. R. PATTERSON. (1987). "Family Interaction and Delinquent Behavior." In H. C. Quay (ed.), *Handbook of Juvenile Delinquency*, pp. 216–43. New York: Wiley.

SORRELLS, J. M. (1977). "Kids Who Kill." *Crime and Delinquency* 23:312–20.

STEINBERG, L. (1986). "Latchkey Children and Susceptibility to Peer Pressure: An Ecological Analysis." *Developmental Psychology* 22(4):433–39.

STEINBERG, L. AND S. B. SILVERBERG. (1986). "The Vicissitudes of Autonomy in Early Adolescence." *Child Development* 57:841–51.

STOUTHAMER-LOEBER, M. AND R. LOEBER. (1986). "Boys Who Lie." *Journal of Abnormal Child Psychology* 14:551–64.

STRAUS, M. A., R. J. GELLES, AND S. K. STEINMETZ. (1981). *Behind Closed Doors: Violence in the American Family*. Garden City, NY: Anchor.

THORNBERRY, T. P. (1987). "Toward an Interaction Theory of Delinquency." *Criminology* 25(4): 863–91.

TOLAN, P. H. (1987). "Implications of Age of Onset for Delinquency Risk." *Journal of Abnormal Psychology* 15(1):47–65.

_____. (1988). "Socioeconomic, Family, and Social Stress Correlates of Adolescent Antisocial and Delinquent Behavior." *Journal of Abnormal Child Psychology* 16(3):317–31.

TOLAN, P. H. AND R. P. LORION. (1988). "Multivariate Approaches to the Identification of Delinquency Proneness in Adolescent Males." *American Journal of Community Psychology* 16(4):547–61.

TREMBLAY, R. E., J. McCORD, H. BOILEAU, P. CHARLEBOIS, C. GAGNON, M. LEBLANC, AND S. LARIVEE. (1991). "Can Disruptive Boys Be Helped to Become Competent?" *Psychiatry* 54:148–61.

VAN VOORHIS, P., F. T. CULLEN, R. A. MATHERS, AND C. C. GARNER. (1988). "The Impact of Family Structure and Quality on Delinquency: A Comparative Assessment of Structural and Functional Factors." *Criminology* 26(2):235–61.

WALTERS, H. I. AND S. K. GILMORE. (1973). "Placebo versus Social Learning Effects on Parental Training Procedures Designed to Alter the Behavior of Aggressive Boys." *Behavior Therapy* 4:311–77.

WELLS, L. E. AND J. H. RANKIN. (1991). "Families and Delinquency: A Meta-Analysis of the Impact of Broken Homes." *Social Problems* 38(1):71–93.

WERNER, E. E. (1987). "Vulnerability and Resiliency in Children at Risk for Delinquency: A Longitudinal Study from Birth to Young Adulthood." In J. D. Burchard and S. N. Burchard (eds.), *Primary Prevention of Psychopathology*, Vol. 10: *Prevention of Delinquent Behavior*, pp. 16–43. Newbury Park, CA: Sage.

WEST, D. J. AND D. P. FARRINGTON. (1973). *Who Becomes Delinquent?* London: Heinemann.

_____. (1977). *The Delinquent Way of Life: Third Report of the Cambridge Study in Delinquent Development.* New York: Crane Russak.

WIDOM, C. S. (1989). "Does Violence Beget Violence? A Critical Examination of the Literature." *Psychological Bulletin* 106(1):3–28.

WILSON, H. (1987). "Parental Supervision Re-examined." *British Journal of Criminology* 27(3): 275–301.

WOLFGANG, M. E., R. M. FIGLIO, AND T. SELLIN. (1972). *Delinquency in a Birth Cohort.* Chicago: University of Chicago Press.

ZIGLER, E., C. TAUSSIG, AND K. BLACK. (1992). "Early Childhood Intervention: A Promising Preventative for Juvenile Delinquency." *American Psychologist* 47:997–1006.

QUESTIONS FOR DISCUSSION

1. Discuss the circumstances that may be operating in the lives of children most at risk of becoming delinquent.

2. The authors discuss five strategies for strengthening families to reduce the factors that place children at higher risk of becoming delinquent and subsequently moving into adult criminality. List and discuss these factors.

4. If the primary responsibility for preventing delinquency and producing socially competent adults belongs to parents and families, what do government and the criminal justice system have to do, ultimately, with the prevention and reduction of crime?

APPLICATIONS

1. Create a list of characteristics that describe a dysfunctional family. Can you identify any families from an earlier period of your life that were dysfunctional? What has happened since to the children raised in these families? Have the children of these families now become criminal or subsequently raised a dysfunctional family? In your opinion, how might we best break this cycle? Discuss with other members of your class.

2. In your opinion, how has the changing role of females and males affected the social organization of the family? How has the economy affected the family? Are these changes desirable? Discuss with other members of your class.

Confronting Crime
Looking toward the Twenty-First Century

Elliott Currie

We have reached what may be an important turning point in the development of criminological thought and of social policy toward crime. The "convervative revolution" in criminology has lost considerable credibility, along with the entire set of minimalist strategies toward the disadvantaged that dominated social policy throughout much of the recent past. A space has opened for the development of a "social environmental" or "human-ecological" approach to crime, which combines a variety of interventions on the individual and family level with an array of broader policies aimed at controlling the social and economic forces that place individuals, families, and communities at risk in the first place.

In this paper I'd like to talk about an agenda for social policy toward crime as we move toward the twenty-first century. I'm aware that this is a very big order, and I hasten to stress that these remarks make no pretense of being definitive; my aim is only to help spark what I hope will become a fruitful and continuing debate. But I think it's important to step back periodically and ask where we have been and where we want to go. I believe that forward look is especially important now, for unless I'm greatly mistaken, we have reached a turning point in our approach to crime in the United States. We are poised uneasily at the end of one criminological era and the beginning of a new one, and it will be up to us to define just what the new one will look like.

The last such turning point took place around the beginning of the 1970s with the emergence of what we could fairly call the "conservative" revolution in criminology. (I use "conservative" here not in the narrow political sense, but in a broader philosophical one.) The conservative revolution in criminology was only one facet of a much broader transformation in American social thought and policy generally—one with particular significance for the interconnected problems of the inner cities. It had a major impact on the way in

Elliott Currie, "Confronting Crime: Looking toward the Twenty-First Century." *Justice Quarterly* 6:(1) 5–25. Reprinted with permission of the Academy of Criminal Justice Sciences.

which we approached crime in the United States, both in theory and in practice. It dethroned social explanations of the causes of crime, cast the idea of rehabilitating offenders into the category of the antique and faintly disreputable, relegated to the margins of public disclosure the idea that social programs might help prevent crime, and simultaneously elevated some combination of deterrence and incapacitation to a central, even a commanding place in anticrime policy.

But I think that this revolution has nearly run its course. I'm not suggesting that there's no life in it at all; many of its basic themes are very much alive in some quarters, not least in the recent presidential campaign. But I believe that the conservative revolution in criminology has lost much of its *intellectual* hegemony—its power to persuade and to convince and, above all, its credibility as a guiding vision for the future. In particular, there is no longer much compelling intellectual justification for its two main and intertwined themes: the wholesale rejection of the usefulness of social intervention to prevent crime and delinquency, and the expanded use of the criminal justice system to contain the consequences of social and economic neglect and disarray.

The reason for this decline is simple: the conservative model has run up against stubborn reality. It has suffered its own version of what the British criminologist Jock Young (1988:138–141) calls the "etiological crisis," which undercut the outlook that dominated American criminology until the 1970s; the view that, with desperate simplification, I've called "liberal criminology" (Currie, 1985). By "etiological crisis" Young means that the liberal view of the causes of crime, and of appropriate remedies, was undermined by the apparent paradox that crime rates rose just when a number of things which (according to this view) ought to have reduced crime were improving substantially, at least on paper and in the aggregate. Incomes were rising; unemployment (on the national level) was falling; and we were beginning to devote significant governmental attention to social programs for the education and training of the disadvantaged. If the liberal view had been correct, conservatives argued gleefully, the crime rate should have fallen; that it did not fall opened the door to a view that blamed the rise in crime primarily on the leniency of the criminal justice system (and to a lesser extent the family and the schools) while arguing that liberal programs were at best irrelevant and at worst part of the deepening culture of permissiveness and indulgence that bred crime.

But the conservative revolution began likewise to sputter in its tracks in the mid-1980s, when it became apparent to all but the most ideologically stalwart that the model wasn't working. Despite the huge increases in incarceration in the 1970s and 1980s, the rate of criminal violence remained devastatingly high, and increased in some places; whole communities were shredded and turned nightmarish by drugs and gang violence. After all, this was one of the largest experiments in social engineering ever undertaken in the United States (though it was rarely acknowledged as such); thus its failure was an event of considerable moment. The prison population tripled nationally from the early 1970s to the present—a rate of increase that far outstripped the crime rate itself (Irwin and Austin, 1987). Yet no one needs to be reminded of the tragic, sometimes nearly incomprehensible social disintegration and violence that still confront us in the streets and homes of so many of our cities.

Jock Young calls the resulting crisis in the credibility of the conservative model the "crisis of penality." Whatever we choose to call it, it is real, and it is not confined within the narrow perimeter of public policy toward crime and criminal justice. The twilight of the conservative model of crime is only one aspect of what the conservative columnist George Will (1988) calls the "dusk" of the conservative era.

I think we should make allowances here for exaggeration. Surely there is a great deal of political steam left in the conservative revolution, and its legacy in social policy will doubtless be with us for some time. But it's certainly true that the continuing crisis in urban America has begun to undercut the intellectual foundations of the entire range of conservative social policies toward those "at risk" that emerged during the 1970s and flowered during the 1980s. We might regard this set of strategies as the social equivalent of the "let it burn" policy of the U.S. National Park Service, as practiced at Yellowstone Park and elsewhere. We withdrew services and public support from the most distressed communities and the highest-risk families and individuals in America, in the vague expectation that this would free the forces of the market economy to work their supposed magic. But it has now become widely apparent, across a broad spectrum of informed opinion, that this course of action hasn't, after all, revitalized the cities or transformed and motivated the urban underclass. On the contrary, it has exacerbated the social disintegration of the cities, and in the process it has produced another generation of increasingly damaged and alienated young people. In short, it has accelerated a human-ecological disaster of almost unprecedented proportions. Our cities are in a terrible mess; and it is no longer possible to hide that fact, or to blame it credibly on the leniency of our justice system or on the demoralizing largesse of an overactive government.

These hard realities have not been lost on those whose job it is to govern the cities or to do business in them. They have rocked the intellectual and cultural foundations of the minimalist model of the 1970s and early 1980s; and they have ushered in a period in which the conventional wisdom, the moral and conceptual language in which these issues are discussed, has begun to shift in important ways. So far this shift has taken place mainly on the symbolic level, without an accompanying commitment of resources to back it up; but that doesn't mean that it's unimportant.

Thus *Business Week* magazine, in a major cover story on what it calls the crisis of "human capital" in America, gently rebukes the neglectful social policies toward the disadvantaged of the past eight years, and warns that "the U.S. may now be entering an era when neglect of the bottom half of society begins to threaten the welfare of the entire nation" (1988:103). The magazine goes on to propose substantially increased public spending for such services as preschool education and prenatal care, as well as intensive job training for the disadvantaged young.

Nor is this an isolated statement. A recent issue of *U.S. News* and *World Report* (1988)— like *Business Week*, a magazine not noted previously for its bleeding-heart sympathies— headlined its cover story "Save the Children" and chided government for offering "too many promises, too little help." Indeed, a more activist social policy—particularly toward children and families—has emerged suddenly as something close to a "motherhood" issue, at least on the level of political rhetoric. Both presidential candidates came out for social programs to benefit children and families: George Bush called on the nation to "invest in children," and the Republican party platform called for "large" increases in funding for Head Start. Similarly, the well-known corporate policy organization, the Committee for Economic Development (1987), urges billions of dollars in new funding for Head Start, child health care, and other active public policies for high-risk children. As the economic columnist Robert Samuelson (1988) notes, "a crude consensus" has emerged; its message is that "government should do more." Even some noted criminologists of a decidedly conservative bent, who in earlier incarnations ridiculed those colleagues who imagined that government could do much of anything about the conditions affecting families and children, can now be heard to suggest that limited experiments with parenting or Head Start-type programs just might be worth exploring (Wilson, 1988).

Skepticism about the depth of some of these claims is in order, especially those claims made in the heat of a presidential election campaign. Nevertheless I believe that this shift is both real and encouraging. The climate was very different as recently as the early 1980s. If you dared to suggest in those days that early childhood education or family-support programs (much less a serious employment and training policy) might play a significant role in reducing crime and delinquency, or if you hinted that we might be able to do something constructive with young offenders in the juvenile justice system so that their life chances were slightly better when they left the system than when they entered it, you were likely to be ignored or dismissed as a naive if well-meaning peddler of the stale and discredited ideas of the 1960s. In vain you might protest that pinning historical labels on these efforts was far less important than the growing evidence that some of them *worked*.

In those days such was the power of the 1970s model that mere evidence didn't stand much of a chance. (As John Kenneth Galbraith once wrote, it is far more comforting to have a firm anchor in nonsense than to put out upon the troubled seas of thought [1970: 145].) Today, however, at the close of the 1980s, the short-lived conventional wisdom of that era—that "nothing works," that all social intervention is futile or counterproductive—begins to seem like ancient history, or a bad dream.

To sum up, I believe that a new intellectual and political space has been forced open by the widespread and often frightening failures of the neglectful strategies that came before. In this space, a new criminological vision and a new public policy toward crime may take root, even flower. Having said that, however, I'm not certain what exactly will emerge to fill that space. There is a spectrum of possibilities, not all of them pleasant.

I

One troubling possibility is that we might go backwards. We might adopt the view that the failure of our recent strategies toward crime and toward the more general problems of those "at risk" tells us that the problems are much more intractable than we had supposed—so intractable that it isn't worth the effort to do anything but contain them. In turn, we might locate the source of this intractability in the biological insufficiencies or cultural inferiorities of those who continue to fail to "make it" into the increasingly elusive mainstream of American society. We might use that explanation to justify what would amount to urban triage: an even greater withdrawal of resources from the most problematic communities and a *de facto* policy of allowing them to spiral downward still further. I don't think that will happen; I think the potential social costs are too great and too widely understood. But I don't think it's inappropriately alarmist to suggest it as a possibility. After all, it is not all that far from the strategy of omission that we have followed for some years.

More likely, I think, is a more positive and more humane approach that simply doesn't go far enough. This is what troubles me about the otherwise encouraging recent revival of interest in early intervention strategies with children and families. Again, I can't emphasize too often that I think this revival is positive and is moving in the right direction. But sometimes it seems to place too many expectations on approaches to individual and family problems which do not confront the larger social and economic context in which those problems originate. It also shares a certain quintessentially American tendency to overpromise results on essentially educational solutions to social problems. I think that the results of such programs as the Perry Preschool project (Beruetta-Clement, Schweinhart, Barnett, and Weikart, 1987) are inspiring, but they are also partial.

Similar concerns have been voiced recently by careful students and practitioners of early intervention (Woodhead, 1988; Zigler, 1987). As the British scholar Martin Woodhead has written, "Expectations are becoming narrowly focused on the apparent power of early intervention to tackle social problems single-handedly"; but since "such expectations are unlikely to be realized in practice," the long-term result could be to "undermine public sympathies toward early childhood programs" (1988: 452). A preschool on every ghetto corner won't overcome the structural disintegration of the surrounding communities—a disintegration whose sources lie well beyond the disadvantaged child and family, beyond the local community, and beyond the reach of the school, and which may well intensify in the coming decades. I think we must face squarely the unhappy fact that the level of social devastation in many American communities that have been affected most seriously by the destruction of solid adult labor markets, the retreat of preventive social services, and the flood of hard drugs is now beyond anything we've ever seen in this country; and that it will require responses of a breadth and depth we have not yet contemplated seriously in the United States. We will not address these problems effectively on the cheap, simply by trying to fix up poor kids. That's a very important part of what we need to do, but it's only a part.

II

I suggest that the approach we need toward crime in the coming decades might be called "social-environmental"—or, to resurrect an older term, "human-ecological." By that I mean a strategy which includes interventions on the level of individuals and families "at risk," but also moves beyond that level to exert social control over those larger forces which now are increasingly undermining communities and placing families at risk in the first place. Those forces are aggravating an already fundamental imbalance in our society that has enormous consequences for crime and for much else; these consequences, I believe, are confirmed increasingly by an accumulating body of empirical research. Such an approach, moreover, should raise questions not simply about *what* forces in our society need controlling, but also about *who* may decide and who is held responsible for the consequences of those decisions. If we think of the era of liberal criminology as the first stage of recent criminological thinking and consider the conservative revolution as the second, such a social-environmental vision can serve as the bedrock for a third, more sophisticated stage which both builds upon and transcends the stages that came before.

For the present, let me simply sketch out a few components of such a strategy which I believe to be most crucial. Some of these elements involve interventions on the level of families and high-risk individuals; others entail addressing more complex and longer-range issues of community stability, of political economy, and even of culture. The list is meant to be illustrative, not exhaustive; I want simply to note, in broad brush-strokes, what I think ought to be some guiding themes of a twenty-first century crime policy.

First, we should expand high-quality, intensive *early education* along the model of Head Start and the Perry Preschool project. I've just argued that these programs shouldn't be viewed as panaceas, but they do make a difference (Beruetta-Clement, et al., 1987). Indeed there is some evidence that these programs have a strong positive effect on the psychological well-being and social functioning of parents as well as of children (Parker, Piotrowski, and Peay, 1987). Yet the proportion of eligible children served by such programs is now about 18 percent (*Business Week*, 1988), and not all of those programs are good ones. I've heard no credible intellectual or fiscal argument against increasing that proportion and simultaneously raising the quality of existing programs. There is an intriguing debate about *how* early educational intervention works (Woodhead, 198), but there is little question that these programs, done properly, produce results on a variety of crucial measures of development and behavior. They're also cost-efficient. It's difficult to see how we could lose by putting more resources into them.

Second, we should expand *health and mental health services* for high-risk children and youth and for their parents, including high-quality prenatal and postnatal care. We should do this anyway, but there's reason to believe that it can be a meaningful part of a comprehensive, "ecological" strategy against crime and delinquency. The evidence is complex, but highly suggestive, that such conditions as early childhood traumas of the central nervous system, early severe psychiatric problems, and perhaps low birth weight may be implicated in some kinds of delinquency, including some of the most troubling and most destructive. (See especially the work of Dorothy O. Lewis and her colleagues [1985, 1988].) The evidence also suggests that many—perhaps most—children who most need early and intensive help to address these problems aren't getting it, with the predictable result that the problems are worked out on the bodies of other people. In their study of 14 juveniles condemned to death in the United States for especially brutal crimes, Dorothy Lewis and her colleagues conclude that these children typically are "multiply handicapped": they "tend to have suffered serious CNS injuries, or have suffered since early childhood from a multiplicity of psychotic symptoms, and to have been physically and sexually abused." At the same time, "the clinical and legal services necessary to try to uncover these vulnerabilities are *routinely unavailable* to this population of juveniles" (1988: 587, 589; emphasis added)—not to mention the services necessary even to begin to treat them.

Third, in a related vein, we need a much greater commitment to *family support programs*, especially real rather than rhetorical support for comprehensive programs against child abuse and domestic violence. The debate over the family's role in crime and delinquency has been shaped, even more strongly than most criminological issues, by the shifting ideological currents of recent years. The liberal criminology of the 1950s and 1960s tended to avoid acknowledging the family's importance as a crucible of character formation and hence as a critical area for the development of delinquency—or of "prosocial" behavior. The conservative criminology of the 1970s and 1980s revived interest in the family's role in developing character and competence, but also detached the family and its functioning from the social and economic forces that shaped it powerfully. In a third stage, social-environmental criminology for the coming century must recognize that the family is both a crucial shaping force and one that is shaped in turn by forces far larger than itself. Accordingly we will need both a genuinely pro-family economic policy at the national level (about which more below) and far greater attention to interventions at the level of individual families.

On the latter level, I'd like to see violence in the home become the kind of political issue in the twenty-first century that crime in the streets has been in the last third of the twentieth. In *Confronting Crime* (Currie, 1985), I pointed to some encouraging improvements in child-rearing skills resulting from the federally funded family-resource programs in the 1970s; to these I'd add encouraging results from innovative interventions with child-abusing families (Wolfe, 1987).

Once again, however, if the emerging empirical evidence on what we *could* do is encouraging, the level of implementation is not. In the case of child abuse in particular, it is pitifully weak: we are quite simply allowing a massive and at least partly preventable tragedy to play itself out in soul-shattering ways, on children whose other social and economic disadvantages render them both vulnerable and largely invisible. This is not only a major crime in itself, but one which tends disturbingly often to perpetuate itself as many abused children become abusive parents in their turn (Gelles and Straus, 1988). There is nothing inevitable about that progression, as the developmental psychologists Joan Kaufman and Edward Zigler (1987) remind us, but even their own best estimate suggests that about one-third of severely abused children are likely to become severely abusive parents—a rate six times that of the rest of the population (1987: 190).

All of these suggestions are aimed at preventing delinquency and crime before they happen, but we also need to take a fourth step: to reassert the importance of doing something constructive with people after they've broken the law. This common-sense idea fell out of favor, almost into oblivion, in the 1970s, despite some evidence for a more encouraging view (Cullen and Gilbert, 1982; Gendreau and Ross, 1987). But no one today can deny seriously that we could be doing much more than we have done.

On the most immediate level, we can begin to deliver more consistently the basic services that many young offenders often need. Within the juvenile justice system in particular, we should insist finally that the time when young offenders are under our care be used more constructively. We ought to consider that time as a resource, which we may use profitably to ensure that they leave a little smarter, a little healthier, a little more sober than they came in. We ought to establish a higher floor of expectations about what institutions for the young should accomplish. For now I'm not talking about remaking personalities, but simply about improving basic skills and competencies. This is particularly important in view of what some research suggests about the links between low skills and poor verbal abilities and serious delinquency (Berlin and Sum, 1988; Denno, 1986). We know how to do these things; we should do them more seriously and more consistently, so that by the year 2000 no young person is languishing idle and illiterate in any juvenile institution in the country.

Finally, we need a commitment (again, real rather than rhetorical) to accessible, non-punitive drug abuse treatment for those who need it. Like our approach to the family, our views about hard drugs have been shaped deeply, and for the most part unfortunately, by broader ideological agendas rather than by a levelheaded reading of the evidence. Liberal criminology often failed to take the drug problem seriously; occasionally, it found more to worry about in the public distress over drug abuse than in the effects of hard drugs on communities and individuals—particularly the disadvantaged, who were (and are) the chief victims of the spread of hard drugs. Conservatives put most of their money on strategies—especially interdiction and harsh mandatory sentencing—that did not work, probably cannot work, and certainly would not work in the face of the simultaneous depletion of antidrug budgets by a conservative administration.

Once again, however, things have begun to show some improvement—at least on the level of political awareness. After several years of empty rhetoric about warring on drugs, national legislation has shown a moderately encouraging tilt away from overreliance on interdiction, deterrence, and incapacitation and toward moderately serious attention to treatment and prevention. That shift, however, will remain merely symbolic without a serious commitment of funds to back it up.

Beyond the problem of financing is a deeper concern. We must take great care that in the rush to leap on the political bandwagon we do not simply throw new money at the existing treatment system. I've worked in that system, and I think we must insist that it be reformed as well as supported. We must ensure that treatment is intensive and of high quality; it must be accompanied by serious outreach to hard-to-reach abusers, by aftercare that supports abusers after they leave treatment, by advocacy in the community for their broader needs with respect to housing, health care, and employment. We've learned that it's not that hard to get people off drugs; what's hard is to *keep* them off, and that tougher goal must be a main objective of twenty-first-century drug policy.

The accumulating evidence suggests that all of these steps can be important in reducing crime and delinquency if they are taken with the necessary seriousness and intensity. They also have many other positive outcomes, which we ought to support in any case. But it will take a long, hard political effort to get the bold, creative commitment of public resources that we need in order to do any of these things well. It's easy to be abstractly in favor of more and better drug treatment or preschool education or mental health services for children; it's harder to insist that we ought to *pay* for them as well. Nevertheless, I'm convinced that the time is right for making a strong effort to develop the political momentum to put programs that we know can be effective into practice; we should seize it. Speaking very personally for a moment, I am sick of the recurrent frustration of seeing us lock up kids who have remediable problems which we know how to address—locking them up because we have no place else to put them. I'm sick of seeing whole communities besieged by drug abusers who can't find treatment. I'm sick of looking again and again at the histories of violent kids and predictably finding abusive families that we might have been able to help.

III

But we must also work on the longer-range and more complex issues without which all of these interventions on the level of families and individuals will be frustrated and compromised, issues that will become increasingly crucial in view of the economic and demographic changes that we may expect in the next century. By that time, we should finally have come to grips with the simple (but, for some, difficult-to-grasp) fact that the level of crime is a social-structural problem. It is not by accident that the United States has the highest rates of serious crime in the developed world while standing out among other industrialized societies on a host of other troubling measures: child poverty, infant mortality, inadequate public services, economic inequality. It's no exaggeration to say that we've reached a point where the future of civilized life in the cities has been imperiled by generations of social neglect and economic havoc. A great many chickens have come home to roost, and at this late hour it will be extraordinarily difficult to reverse the disintegration we've allowed to continue for so many decades.

That is only the bad news, however. The good news is that at least we've begun—although haltingly and so far not very successfully—to address some of these issues on the level of national legislation. But the tentativeness of that legislation, and the bitterness with which it is resisted, tell us how far we have to go. Here are four goals for the twenty-first century. All of them are important for many reasons, not least because they have the potential to alter the context of individual and family development in ways that promise to diminish criminality.

First, we must move to *reduce inequality and social impoverishment.*

We know that the gap between affluent and poor has been increasing in the United Sates, in part because of widening differences in earnings among people who work (Currie, Dunn, and Fogarty, 1988; Harrison, Tilly, and Bluestone, 1986). And the bare income figures understate the growth in inequality because they mask the bifurcation of social services that also is taking place—the withdrawal of the public sector from the lower 30 percent or so of the population, especially the young. We need to reverse this trend, not least because the evidence continues to grow, from both crossnational and domestic studies, that violent crime is generated by extremes of inequality, especially when coupled with excessive mobility and the fragmentation of community and family life (Avison and Loring, 1986; Brownfield, 1986). Granted, reducing inequality is a tall order, but it's not impossible. Many other nations have done it. And though we can't simply transfer their approaches to our very different social and historical context, we can learn much from their experience that is vital to our own efforts to create a more just and more secure society.

The deliberate reduction of social inequality therefore, ought to be one of the primary goals of social policy in the twenty-first century. In this country, we've barely begun to address this issue. Witness the current, fiercely fought legislative battle over efforts to restore some of the value of the minimum wage, which has fallen almost 30 percent in real terms since the early 1980s. We need to continue to press for a decent floor on earnings, but we also need to do much more: ultimately to move toward what in Scandinavia is called a "solidaristic" wage policy (Rehn, 1985)—one that raises the floor not merely from $3.35 to $4.55 an hour but enough to ensure every working adult the means to a dignified livelihood—and enough to narrow the demoralizing and criminogenic abyss between affluent and poor. Such a move should include an explicit effort—as it has in Sweden, for example—to raise women's earnings closer to those of men, in order to reduce the now-intolerable deprivations and stresses inflicted on families headed by single women in the United States.

Second, and closely related to the reduction of inequality and deprivation, we should move toward an *active labor market policy* aimed at upgrading the work available to disadvantaged Americans. I think that the evidence gives strong support for a link between poor jobs—unstable, dead-end, with low wages—and many kinds of crime. And I believe that the effects tend to accumulate when several generations remain trapped with few opportunities beyond those jobs, partly because of long-term, corrosive effects on the mediating institutions of family and community (Currie, 1985; Sviridoff and McElroy, 1985). That being the case, it's difficult to be sanguine about the much-touted high rate of job creation in recent years in the United States; it's painfully clear that increasing proportions of those jobs are low-paying (Bluestone and Harrison, 1987) and often part-time (Levitan and Conway, 1988). This kind of economic "growth" can do little or nothing to address the roots of social pathology among those now disadvantaged by low earnings and by the shattering of links to more sustaining and more stable livelihoods.

As we move toward the next century, we must acknowledge—as some European countries have long done—that a more rewarding structure of employment does not flow automatically from the operation of the private market, but requires strategic, active intervention by government. In the United States, the most critical need is for publicly supported, community-oriented job creation, particularly in providing essential public services to disadvantaged communities. Among other things, a full-scale policy to create those jobs can help us accomplish some of the key strategies I've just suggested—early education, childhood mental health services, family support programs, drug treatment for all who require it. *Without* a public policy to create community-sustaining jobs, on the other hand, it's hard to see how we could put those expanded services in place. With such a policy, we could contribute to the rebuilding of a viable economic infrastructure in "high-risk" communities; and simultaneously, we could deliver the basic reparative and socializing services without which neither social peace nor economic development in those communities will be possible.

Let me emphasize again that this task is much more difficult and more long-term than most criminologists have been willing to acknowledge. Liberal criminologists have sometimes seemed to imply that simply reflating the national economy to bring down the overall unemployment rate or launching another summer job program for ghetto kids will do the trick. It would be nice if that were so, but the evidence tells us that the problems are much deeper. Again, I can't stress too often that we are dealing now with several generations of the accumulated effects of long-term economic deprivation and social impoverishment on family and personality. I believe that there is still time to reverse those effects, but no one should underestimate how hard it will be. Conservatives, for their part, consistently have obscured the importance of the connection between inadequate labor markets and crime, in part by focusing too narrowly on the immediate effects of job loss on crime (where evidence is relatively weak) and ignoring the long-term effects of persistent labor-market disadvantage (where evidence is quite strong). By now, however, all of us should have learned that we can't have it both ways: we can't simultaneously have orderly and secure communities *and* an economy that routinely condemns some people to deepening economic insecurity, social impoverishment, and communal disruption while visibly enriching others.

Third, we should work toward a genuinely *supportive national family policy.*

We talk a great deal about this in the United States: nobody is against the family and nobody would be caught dead acknowledging that the economic and social policies they favor are *bad* for families and children. But that consensus is largely superficial, and it masks the ongoing disaster that has afflicted families, especially in the bottom 30 percent or so of the income distribution (Children's Defense Fund, 1988). As things stand now, we allow a large and perhaps growing segment of American families to remain at the mercy of an essentially destabilizing and destructive economic and social environment. I've just argued that we should put more resources into supportive programs for high-risk children and families, but if we make no simultaneous effort to control the forces that wreck families in the first place, we'll be forever stuck at the level of picking up the pieces.

In particular, as we move toward the next century, we should finally become serious about adapting the nature of work to the imperatives of family life. The United States is one of the few remaining industrialized countries that doesn't officially recognize the human, social, and even economic value of freeing time for working parents to spend with their families (Hopper and Zigler, 1988). Our traditional practice has been to squeeze every minute of paid working time out of parents in the name of private economic gain and to scream bloody murder at the rather innocuous idea that private businesses have some responsibility for this aspect of their employees' welfare. Witness the fate of our stunningly timid first effort at national legislation in this direction: the Dodd Bill, which would mandate companies to provide parents with up to 10 weeks of *unpaid* leave over two years, at the birth of a child or in the event of a child's illness (some European countries mandate a *paid* leave of up to several *months*). That bill was filibustered to temporary death in the Senate, a casualty of the view (promoted by some of the business community) that it represented unwarranted interference by government in the private economy.

The reality, of course, is that our lack of a humane national policy concerning family and work—a lack which distinguishes us from virtually every other industrialized society—amounts to a massive subsidy to private business. It requires the rest of us to pay for the social costs of the resulting strains on families and for the consequences of these strains for physical and mental health, domestic violence, and delinquency. We need to push for family leaves, and more broadly, for the idea that Americans who work have a fundamental right to sufficient family time, in order to make possible (among other things) the attentive and unharried care of the young.

Fourth, just as we should move toward assuming greater responsibility for the conditions affecting the stability and functioning of families, so we need to begin assuming greater *responsibility for the economic and social stability of local communities*. One of the great (through sometimes subtle) social disasters of the past 30 years is the extent to which the often sudden and capricious movement of capital and employment opportunities has forced families to move in order to chase jobs and income. This process has deepened and accelerated in the face of intensified international economic competition in the past several years, and has increasingly fractured the stability and the sustaining power of families and communities across the country. This means (among other things) that often there is no larger network of people available to be there when parents cannot be, to take on some of the burden of the care and supervision of the young.

This is an important, and I think deepening, change in the fundamental character of the local community in America. Sociologists have long stressed the importance of local, "informal" institutions in providing the dense network of supports and controls that can help prevent delinquency and crime, especially in communities suffering other economic disadvantages (Smith and Jarjoura, 1988). But those institutions have been eroded steadily through economic decisions made, most often, outside the community and without reference to its needs. Our first very tentative national legislation to address this issue, the provision for notification of plant closing in the recent trade bill, was initially voted by President Reagan after passing both houses of Congress. Yet, like 10 weeks of unpaid leave or a restoration of the minimum wage, it's only a single step toward recognition of the larger principle that we need to place on the national agenda: in this case, making the stability of local communities, and thereby their capacity to serve as nurturing settings for the young, a central consideration in economic decision making.

IV

Finally, a *research* agenda accompanies these policies. Without presuming to dictate what criminologists ought to study, let me offer some brief and necessarily subjective thoughts about priorities for research in the coming years. The broad emphases of criminological research, like those of criminal justice policy, are shaped in part by the subtle pressures of the dominant social attitudes of their time. In the era of the conservative ascendancy in criminology, the research balance was tipped heavily toward the issues of deterrence and incapacitation—pro or con. This research emphasis was prompted in part by an underlying pessimism—ungrounded in hard empirical evidence—about the possibility of doing anything *else* to prevent crime, either on the level of changing individual offenders or of altering the criminogenic character of the communities from which they came. We learned a great deal from that outpouring of research, much of it of enduring value, but probably by now it has probably reached a point of diminishing returns. We need a less constrained agenda for research in the coming decades: an agenda that shifts the balance toward clarifying what we might do rather than assuming at the outset that we can do very little. I see at least three priorities within that agenda, all of which are implicit in the suggestions I've just made for social policy.

First, we need much more careful research into what works with individuals "at risk." We've made an important beginning in this regard in the last several years; by now the accumulating evidence should have banished the last vestiges of the simplistic idea that nothing works. But at the same time, there have been so few solidly designed and strongly implemented efforts to intervene with high-risk people that we've barely begun to test the possibilities. There has been considerable interest of late in launching yet further studies to track the careers of children longitudinally in order to see who goes wrong. I'm more interested in developing strong programs with sufficient resources and staff to ensure "therapeutic integrity" (Gendreau and Ross, 1987) designed to keep children from going wrong to begin with and to help steer them toward a more contributive life if they break the law. We should then evaluate these programs thoroughly and creatively, and translate the results of that evaluation into ongoing improvements in the programs in order to ensure that we build on the lessons learned.

Second, and in a similar vein, we need to learn more about how to create comprehensive preventive strategies for "high-risk" *communities*. We're beginning to learn something about which programs show the most promise in regenerating severely disadvantaged neighborhoods (Curtis, 1987). Once again, however, it's obviously difficult to assess the effectiveness of community-based programs unless they are implemented with enough depth and continuity to make real evaluation possible; and that, in turn, requires a level of resources that has rarely been available in the past 15 years of minimalist social policy. Therefore a key research priority for the next decades should be the development of comprehensive community prevention programs of sufficient resource intensity and staying power to do what they set out to do, and, hence, to be capable of being evaluated meaningfully, and, given encouraging results, to be replicated.

Third, we have unduly neglected what ought to be one of our most urgent research concerns: understanding more about why some societies have low or relatively low crime rates while others, including our own, suffer such pervasive violence. One of the more curious products of criminology's recent conservative past was the idea that crime is virtually the same in all societies, or that it is more important to learn what is common in the experience of crime among the world's societies than to learn what is different. Yet the vast differences in serious crime—especially violent crime—among different societies are both inescapable and potentially enormously illuminating. And though there have been some attempts, my own included (Currie, 1985; cf. Clinard, 1978), to explore the roots of those glaring differences, much more remains to be done. Learning more about how some societies manage to avoid the extremes of violence that wrack us in the United States is critical if we want to move toward a more fruitful anticrime policy and a more secure, more humane society.

V

There is much more to be said. I've said nothing, for instance, about a serious housing policy to begin to cope with the situation of the homeless, especially homeless children, who could become a criminological time bomb in the next decades. I haven't talked much about the schools. Still, even this much amounts to a very tall order, and it engages many issues that are generally considered far beyond the customary boundaries of criminology. But that's just the point. A social policy toward crime and delinquency that has even a prayer of meeting the social and economic challenges of the next century must transcend the disciplinary and bureaucratic fragmentation that now characterizes our approach to crime, even at best. And it must begin to take seriously what most of us know already: that in human societies, as in the natural environment, things are connected to each other. What we do (or don't do) in the realm of economic policy in particular has a profound impact on the basic social institutions through which individuals are brought up healthy or damaged, compassionate or unfeeling, contributive or predatory. Making a serious attack on criminal violence, in the home as on the street, involves restoring the integrity of that social environment by harnessing our material and technological resources to ends more supportive and more sustaining of community, family, and human development.

Let me take this argument one step farther. Along with and underpinning these institutional changes, in the next century we will need accompanying changes in what we loosely and vaguely call *culture*. There are those who think deliberate cultural change is difficult, if not impossible; who invoke the idea of cultural rigidity as a way of downplaying altogether the possibility of conscious social change (Jencks, Currie, and Herrnstein, 1987). But that approach betrays a narrow and static view of culture. After all, in the last generation alone we've seen several major—even epochal—normative changes in American society: in the way we think about the social role of women, or about the status of people of color; in the way we think about our relationship to the natural environment; increasingly, too, in the way we think about health and nutrition. On all of these planes, as a culture, we are very different than when I was growing up.

By the time my own daughter is my age, toward the end of the second decade of the twenty-first century, we may hope to have fostered some comparable changes in aspects of American culture that now may seem to be set in stone: the degree of social deprivation and inequality we tolerate; the amount of violence we consider normal and acceptable in the course of child rearing or of marriage; the level of access to social and health services we deem the minimum responsibility of civilized society; the relative importance of private gain and of cooperative endeavor as esteemed personal motives, or of private economic "choice" versus the stability and socializing competence of communities and families.

Just as we have begun now—belatedly and perhaps in the nick of time—to understand that we cannot systematically spoil and neglect the natural environment, or our bodies, without destructive and self-defeating consequences, so we must come to understand that the *social* environment requires a level of sustenance and stewardship far beyond what can be provided as a residual product of economic growth. The big job for twenty-first-century criminology—and for twenty-first-century social policy generally—will be to place the integrity of the social environment firmly at the top of the political and intellectual agenda, and to keep it there.

But as the recent history of environmental policy itself attests, that goal will not be accomplished without a considerable and protracted struggle. Criminologists and criminal justice practitioners can play a very important part in that struggle by pointing out continually the many links between the problems that confront us daily and the larger forces that shape them; between economic violence and interpersonal violence; between the erosion of communal life and livelihood and the deterioration and distortion of individual personality. We cannot concern ourselves only with the "downstream" consequences of the systematic abuse and neglect of the social environment; we must be bold enough to look unflinchingly at the source.

REFERENCES

AVISON, WILLIAM R., AND PAMELA L. LORING. (1986). "Population Diversity and Cross-National Homicide Patterns: The Effects of Inequality and Heterogeneity." *Criminology* 24 (No. 4).

BERLIN, GORDON, AND ANDREW SUM. (1988). *Toward a More Perfect Union: Basic Skills, Poor Families, and Our Economic Future*. New York: Ford Foundation.

BERUETTA-CLEMENT, J. R., L. J. SCHWEINHART, W. S. BARNETT, AND D. P. WEIKART. (1987). "The Effects of Early Educational Intervention on Crime and Delinquency in Adolescence and Early Adulthood," in John D. Burchard and Sara N. Burchard (eds.), *Prevention of Delinquent Behavior*. Beverly Hills, CA: Sage.

BLUESTONE, BARRY, AND BENNETT HARRISON. (1988). "The Grim Truth about the Job Miracle." *New York Times*, February 1.

BROWNFIELD, DAVID. (1986). "Social Class and Violent Behavior." *Criminology* 24 (No. 3).

BUSINESS WEEK. (1988). "Human Capital." September 19, p. 103.

CHILDREN'S DEFENSE FUND. (1988). *Vanishing Dreams: The Growing Economic Plight of America's Young Families*. Washington, DC: Children's Defense Fund.

CLINARD, MARSHALL. (1978). *Cities with Little Crime*, Cambridge: Cambridge University Press.

COMMITTEE FOR ECONOMIC DEVELOPMENT. (1987). *Children in Need: Investment Strategies for the Educationally Disadvantaged*. New York: Committee for Economic Development.

CULLEN, FRANCIS T. AND KAREN E. GILBERT. (1982). *Reaffirming Rehabilitation*. Cincinnati, OH: Anderson.

CURRIE, ELLIOTT. (1985). *Confronting Crime: An American Challenge*. New York: Pantheon.

CURRIE, ELLIOTT, ROBERT DUNN, AND DAVID FOGARTY. (1988). "The Fading Dream: Economic Crisis and the New Inequality." In Elliott Currie and Jerome H. Skolnick (eds.), *Crisis in American Institutions*, 7th ed. Glenview, IL: Scott, Foresman/Little, Brown.

CURTIS, LYNN, ED. (1987). "Policies to Prevent Crime: Neighborhood, Family, and Employment Strategies," *Annals of the American Academy of Political and Social Science*, p. 494.

DENNO, DEBORAH. (1986). "Victim, Offender, and Situational Characteristics of Violent Crime." *Journal of Criminal Law and Criminology* 77 (No. 4, Winter).

GALBRAITH, JOHN KENNETH. (1970). *The Affluent Society*. New York: New American Library.

GELLES, RICHARD J., AND MURRAY A. STRAUSS. (1988). *Intimate Violence*. New York: Simon & Schuster.

GENDREAU, PAUL, AND ROBERT R. ROSS. (1987). "Revivification of Rehabilitation: Evidence from the 1980s." *Justice Quarterly* 4 (No. 3, September).

HARRISON, BENNETT, CHRIS TILLY, AND BARRY BLUESTONE. (1986). "Rising Inequality." In David Obey and Paul Sarbanes (eds.), *The Changing American Economy*. New York: Basil Blackwell.

HOPPER, PAULINE, AND EDWARD ZIGLER. (1988). "The Medical and Social Science Basis for a National Infant Care Leave Policy." *American Journal of Orthopsychiatry* 58 (No. 3, July).

IRWIN, JOHN, AND JAMES AUSTIN. (1987). *It's about Time: Solving America's Prison Crowding Crisis*. San Francisco: National Council on Crime and Delinquency.

Jencks, Christopher, Elliott Currie, and Richard Herrnstein. (1987). "Genes and Crime: An Exchange." *New York Review of Books*, June 11.

Kaufman, Joan, and Edward Zigler. (1987). "Do Abused Children Become Abusive Parents?" *American Journal of Orthopsychiatry* 57 (No. 2, April).

Levitan, Sara, and Elizabeth Conway. (1988). "Shortchanged by Part-Time Work." *New York Times*, February 27.

Lewis, Dorothy O., E. Moe, and L. D. Jackson. (1985). "Biopsychosocial Characteristics of Children Who Later Murder: A Prospective Study." *American Journal of Psychiatry* 142 (No. 10, October).

Lewis, D. O., J. H. Pincus, B. Bard, E. Richardson, L. S. Prichep, M. Feldman, and C. Yeager. (1988). "Neuropsychiatric, Psychoeducational, and Family Characteristics of 14 Juveniles Condemned to Death in the United States." *American Journal of Psychiatry* 145 (No. 5, May).

Parker, Faith Lamb, Chaya S. Piotrowski, and Lenore Peay. (1987). "Head Start as a Social Support for Mothers: The Psychological Benefits of Involvement." *American Journal of Orthopsychiatry* 57 (No. 2, April).

Rehn, Gosta. (1985). "Swedish Active Labor Market Policy: Retrospect and Prospect." *Industrial Relations* 24 (Winter).

Samuelson, Robert. (1988). *Newsweek*, November 14, p. 559.

Smith, Douglas A. and G. Roger Jarjoura. (1988). "Social Structure and Criminal Victimization." *Journal of Research in Crime and Delinquency* 25 (No. 1, February).

Sviridoff, Michele, and Jerome E. McElroy. (1985). *Employment and Crime: A Summary Report*. New York: Vera Institute of Justice.

U.S. News and World Report. (1988). "Save the Children." November 7.

Will, George. (1988). "The Prop. 13 Pendulum Swings Back." *Los Angeles Times*, June 5, p. 5.

Wilson, James Q. (1988). Address to Western Society of Criminology, Monterey, CA: February 26 (mimeo).

Wolfe, David A. (1987). "Child Abuse Prevention with At-Risk Parents and Children." In John D. Burchard and Sara N. Burchard (eds.), *Prevention of Delinquent Behavior*. Beverly Hills, CA: Sage.

Woodhead, Martin. (1988). "When Psychology Informs Public Policy: The Case of Early Childhood Intervention." *American Psychologist* 43 (No. 6, June).

Young, Jock. (1988). "Recent Developments in Criminology." In M. Haralambos (ed.), *Developments in Sociology*. London: Causeway.

Zigler, Edward. (1987). "Formal Schooling for Four-Year-Olds? No." *American Psychologist* 42 (March).

Questions for Discussion

1. Currie believes that the conservative model that has dominated public policy for the past twenty years is beginning to decline. What evidence does he present to support this claim?

2. What are the major components of the "social-environmental" approach presented by Currie? Provide examples of each of the major components.

3. Perhaps a bigger and more long-range problem is that of the social structure. What suggestions are made about how this structure must change for an enduring improvement in the crime problem? Cite specific examples of such changes.

4. What role should research play when formulating policies for criminal justice?

5. What cultural changes are necessary for U.S. society to realize an improvement in all social problems? Provide examples to support your answer.

APPLICATIONS

1. If we expect a significant change to occur in the social environment, as we continue to confront crime, cultural changes will be necessary at the individual level. These may include changes in morals, norms, values, attitudes, behaviors, etc. Make a list of 15 attributes of cultural change that must occur in individual people before we can hope for any broad social change. Specifically, how must you change yourself before there is any hope of bringing large-scale change to social problems, especially crime?

2. After you have completed the previous application, discuss your list with others, in your class or in small groups, explaining your rationale for each listed item. Subsequently, attempt to develop one list of changes for which there is a consensus among all class members. Are there any difficulties with trying to obtain consensus? Discuss.

Glossary of Key Terms

abdicate—to formally relinquish power or responsibility.

aberrant—deviating from what is proper or normally expected.

abhorrent—disgusting or repugnant.

accomplice—someone who aids or abets another person in committing a criminal act.

accretion—a gradual growth or increase in size.

acquittal—the judgment of a jury or judge that a person is not guilty of a crime as charged.

adjudicatory hearing—court proceeding to hear and settle a case by judicial procedure.

admixture—the act of mingling or mixing.

admonition—to give mild or kind cautionary advice.

advocacy—to provide active support of a person or cause.

aggregation—to gather into a mass or sum so as to constitute a whole product.

albeit—although; notwithstanding.

alienate—to cause someone previously friendly or affectionate to become unfriendly or indifferent; estrange.

ambit—a sphere of action or influence; the scope of one's control.

ameliorating—an act that improves or makes something better.

amenable—willing to follow advice, a suggestion, or the admonitions of an authority.

amici curiae—persons invited to advise the court on matters of law in a case to which they are not a party.

amok—a variant of the word "amuck"; when something is done in a blind and heedless manner; may be a violent frenzy.

anarchy—the absence of any kind of political authority; political disorder.

androcentric—dominated by or emphasizing a masculine interest or point of view.

anecdote—a short account of some interesting or humorous event.

anomaly—deviation from the norm or common order; abnormal.

anonymous—having an unknown or unacknowledged name.

antagonistic—when a person opposes or competes actively with another; adversarial.

antipathy—a strong feeling of aversion or opposition.

apartheid—an official policy of racial segregation; newer uses of *apartheid* can mean any formal segregation by a group or body of people.

appeased—when peace or relief is brought to a person or situation.

appellation—a name or a title; the act of naming.

argot—a specialized vocabulary or jargon used by a particular group or class of people.

425

arraignment—the procedure of being called to court to answer an indictment; formal presentment of charges against a defendant.

asceticism—the belief in renouncing the comforts of society and leading a life of austere self-discipline.

assiduously—characterizes a person who gives constant devotion or attention.

assimilation—the process whereby a person or group gradually adopts the characteristics of another culture.

assuage—to make less severe or burdensome.

atomistic—an individualized approach to problem solving.

attenuated—a reduction in strength or force; to weaken.

augment—to make greater, increase, or enlarge.

aura—a distinctive quality or air that characterizes a person or thing.

behavioristic—characterizes a psychological approach that observes and analyzes only behavioral responses to stimuli in humans; does not make assumptions about conscious or unconscious motivation but rather, the role of reinforcement and punishment.

beleaguered—being troubled or harassed by a person or situation.

bench warrant—a warrant issued by a judge or court against a person guilty of contempt or indicted for a crime.

bias—a preconceived or prejudiced belief.

bigotry—characterizes a person who is intolerantly devoted to his or her own opinions and prejudices.

brandished—to have carried, waved, or shaken a weapon aggressively toward another person.

burgeoning—sending forth new growth or expanding rapidly.

buttresses—when something gives support or strength.

canons—rules, models, or standards.

carnage—a great and bloody slaughter.

castigating—subjecting a person to severe chastisement or punishment.

causes célèbres—legal cases that excite widespread interest.

celerity—rapidity of motion or action.

chauvinistic—characterizes someone who has undue partiality or attachment to a group or place to which they belong or have belonged.

circumvented—when a person manages to get around or avoid something unpleasant using ingenuity or a strategy.

civil libertarians—persons who believe that people should be free from arbitrary government interference, particularly if such interference or intervention is not specifically part of or violates any clause of the Bill of Rights.

civil litigation—court proceeding to regulate noncriminal conflicts between persons. Civil suits are more concerned with assigning blame and awarding monetary damages or compensation than with proving intent and invoking punishment, as would be the case in a criminal proceeding.

class structure—categories of people who have been grouped together based on one or more common characteristics. A class is a stratum in a societal hierarchy. Classes may be determined by wealth, power, or prestige and other socioeconomic indicators, such as income, occupation, and educational attainment.

coalescing—growing together or uniting into a whole.

cogent—convincing; pertinent, relevant, or compelling to rational thought.

cognizant—knowledgeable of something particularly through personal experience.

cognoscente—a person who is especially knowledgeable in a particular subject.

colloquy—conversation or dialogue; a high-level serious discussion.

comeuppance—a deserved rebuke or penalty.

compendious—concise and comprehensive.

complacency—self-satisfaction accompanied by unawareness of actual dangers or deficiencies.

conceptual framework—ideas or concepts of the mind that have been logically ordered for others to observe and consider.

conceptualized—to have thought of or have interpreted something conceptually or as an idea.

concomitant—something that accompanies or is connected collaterally with something else.

connotes—to be associated with or inseparable from, as a consequence.

conspicuous—striking, noticeable, or attracting attention.

consternation—amazement or dismay that hinders or throws one into confusion.

contextual—the interrelated conditions in which something exists or occurs.

controverted—when something is disputed or opposed by reasoning.

corollaries—propositions inferred from an already proved proposition that needs little or no additional proof.

corroboration—to support with evidence or authority.

corruption of blood—the effect of an attainder that bars a person from inheriting, retaining, or transmitting any estate, rank, or title.

cosmopolitan—having a worldwide or broad view rather than a limited or provincial view of a given life experience or situation.

counterculture—a culture with values and mores that run counter or in opposition to those of established society.

counterindicators—signs, symptoms, or indices that run in opposition to an acceptable or taken-for-granted phenomenon or event.

covetous—marked by an inordinate desire for wealth or possessions or for another's wealth.

crescendo—a gradual increase.

criminal calculus—the theoretical calculation used by criminals when deciding whether the potential rewards of a particular criminal act will outweigh the potential costs of being detected and apprehended.

criminogenic—producing or encouraging criminal activity; criminal behavior sometimes thought of as being caused by biological or inherited factors.

cronyism—relationships between people that are more influential in decision making than is more objective proof or evidence.

cryptically—mysteriously; having or seeming to have a hidden or secret meaning.

culpable—meriting blame or blameworthy.

cynical—contemptuously distrustful of human nature and motives.

déclassé—fallen or lowered in class, rank, or social position.

demagogues—leaders who make use of popular prejudices and false claims and promises in order to gain power.

demographic—statistical characteristics of human populations (e.g., age, income, race/ethnicity, gender).

dereliction—an intentional abandonment or conscious neglect.

desistance—when something has been stopped or ceased from proceeding or continuing.

despotic—characteristic of someone who rules or desires to rule by exercising tyrannical power.

detainer—a writ authorizing a person or another authority to continue to hold someone in custody or in detention.

deterring—characterizing anything that inhibits, discourages, or prevents.

dictatorial—befitting to one who rules absolutely and often oppressively.

diminution—the act or process of diminishing or making less.

discretion—the quality of being discreet and responsible when making decisions.

discursive—moving from topic to topic without any perceivable order.

doctrines of attainder—rules and principles governing the lifting of civil or general rights and capacities because of criminal acts or a sentence of death.

dogmatic—characterizes a person who puts forth a point of view or tenet as authoritative without adequate grounds; typically, the person will not entertain any other point of view.

dominant culture—the commanding or controlling system of values, beliefs, norms, and ideas among a defined group of people or a society.

dualistic—characterizes theories that consider reality to be reducible to two parts or modes; for many this is considered to be a gross oversimplification of reality.

dunning—to make persistent demands for payment.

dyspeptic—characterizes someone who is dissatisfied or disgruntled.

efficacy—the power to produce an effect.

egalitarian—one who asserts or advocates the removal of inequalities among people.

egregious—distinguished or conspicuous.

Eigenwelt—in one's own world.

elitism—characterizes one who is conscious about being or belonging to an elite group; snobbery or the tendency to view those who are not members of one's own group as lesser human forms.

ellipsis—the omission of one or more words in a statement.

emaciated—characterizes a person who has become very thin or is physically wasting away.

empirical—capable of being verified or disproved by observation and experimentation.

entrepreneurs—those who organize, manage, and assume the risks of a business; taking calculated risks for potential gain.

enunciated—having made a pronounced, articulated, or proclaimed statement.

ephemeral—lasting a very short time.

epitomized—has served as a typical or ideal example.

equanimity—evenness of mind; balanced.

escapade—a breaking loose from restraints; flight from confining rules.

ethos—the distinguishing character, morals, or guiding beliefs of a person, group, or institution.

euphemistically—refers to substituting an agreeable or inoffensive expression for one that may offend or suggest something unpleasant.

exacerbate—to make more violent, bitter, or severe.

existentialists—those who believe that people must ultimately assume responsibility for acts of free will without any certain knowledge per se of what is right and wrong or good and bad.

exoneration—relieving of responsibility, obligation, or hardship.

exploitation—having made use of someone meanly and unjustly for one's own personal gain.

external validity—accuracy in the ability to generalize or infer findings from a study to a larger population.

extortion—the act or practice of obtaining money or property from a person by use of force, intimidation, or undue or illegal power.

extrication—freeing or removing something from an entanglement or difficulty.

fictionalization—characterizing a group or party that is contentious or self-seeking.

ferret—to search for or to flush out.

filicide—the killing of one's own child.

foci—the plural form of *focus;* the center or principal points of attention.

forensic science—relating to or dealing with the application of scientific knowledge or tests to legal problems or criminal investigations.

fortitude—strength of mind that enables a person to encounter danger or bear pain and adversity with courage.

fragmentary—consisting of broken, detached, or incomplete parts.

fulminating—coming on suddenly with great severity, denunciations, or menace.

Gemeinschaft—a social relationship that is spontaneous and characterized by strong reciprocal bonds of kinship and sentiment within a common tradition.

grandiloquence—using pompous or lofty language; may be a grandiose mannerism.

gregariousness—characterizes those who tend to associate with others of their own kind.

habeas corpus—any of several common-law writs issued to bring a party before a court or judge.

harangue—to address in a declaiming or ranting manner.

harried—beset by problems or harassed.

hedonistic—characterizing someone who believes that the sole or chief good or purpose in life is to maximize pleasure and minimize pain.

heinous—hateful, shocking, or abominable.

hierarchy—a classification of a group of people according to ability; economic, social, professional standing; or any defined attribute.

hijinks—boisterous antics or horseplay.

holistic—relating to a concern over whole systems rather than with the analysis, treatment, or dissection into the constituent parts.

homogeneous—of the same or closely similar kind.

hyperbole—an extravagant exaggeration.

hypothesis—the statement of a relationship between two or more variables or events that has not, as yet, been verified by empirical evidence.

ideology—visionary theorizing; often integrated assertions, theories, and aims that constitute a sociopolitical agenda.

illusory—deceptive; based on or producing an illusion.

impeccable—free from fault or blame.

impecuniousness—characterizing someone who habitually has little or no money.

imperatives—characterizes events or actions that are necessary; not to be avoided or evaded.

impunity—without fear or exemption from punishment.

incarnated—having made something manifest or comprehensible; to embody.

incongruity—characterizes something that is incompatible, disagreeing, or unsuitable.

incredulous—unwilling to accept or admit what is offered as true.

incursions—an entering into other activities.

indicators—a group of statistical values or indices that taken together characterize a given event or group.

indictment—formal written statement framed by a prosecuting attorney that charges a person with criminal offenses.

inductive—employing a system of logic that draws general conclusions from specific or particular instances.

inextricably—characterizes something that is incapable of being disentangled, untied or unlinked with something else.

innocuous—harmless or inoffensive; producing no injury.

inquisition—the act of inquiring or examination, particularly before a judge and/or a jury.

interdiction—the act of halting, hampering, or cutting off the movement of an unwanted supply or intrusion.

intone—to utter or recite something in singing tones or a monotone.

jaunty—lively or spirited in manner or appearance.

judicious—having, exercising, or characterized by sound judgment.

jurisdiction—the limit or geographical territory within which judicial authority may be exercised.

jurisprudence—a system or body of law, court decisions; science or philosophy of law.

labeling—a theory that holds that deviant behavior is not a quality of the act a person commits, but rather, a consequence of applications on the offender, by others, of rules and sanctions (nothing is inherently deviant but becomes deviant only when others apply a deviant label).

liaison—a close bond or connection.

linear causality—the relationship between two or more variables such that when one variable increases or decreases, the other variable or variables increase or decrease by the same amount; one variable is said to axiomatically cause the same changes in another variable or variables repeatedly and in the same way if given the same conditions.

litigation—carrying on a legal contest by judicial process.

maelstrom—a powerful, often violent whirlpool that pulls objects into it; often, this word is used to characterize someone's life that is turbulent or frenzied.

magnetometers—instruments used to detect the presence of a metallic object or to measure the intensity of a magnetic field.

mala prohibita—a group of behaviors that are prohibited by legal codes for the maintenance of social order; behaviors or actions viewed as wrong simply because they are against the law.

malleable—capable of being altered or controlled by outside influences.

mandate—a directive or requirement.

mayhem—needless or willful damage or violence.

melancholy—causing or tending to cause sadness or depression.

metaphor—a figure of speech in which a word or phrase literally denoting one kind of object is used in place of another to suggest a likeness or analogy between them.

milieu—the physical or social setting in which something occurs or develops.

mired—characterizing a troublesome or intractable situation; entangled or sticky.

misanthrope—a person who hates or distrusts humankind.

misogynistic—characterizing a hatred of women.

mitigating—causing something to become less harsh or hostile; to mollify or soften.

Mitwelt—with one's own contemporaries.

modus vivendi—a feasible arrangement or practical compromise.

mollify—to soothe in temper or disposition; to soften or pacify.

mongering—characterizes a person who attempts to stir up trouble or spread information that is petty or discreditable.

morass—something that traps, confuses, or impedes.

mores—the fixed morally binding customs of a particular group.

multivariate regression—a statistical procedure for calculating the relative strength or weakness of the relationship between several variables with one designated variable.

myriad—innumerable, countless, or a great number.

mysticism—vague speculation or a belief without sound basis; objectively undiscernible.

neonate—a newborn child

neutralization—the quality of something that is counteracted or is made benign; neutralization is, typically, the rationalizing that is done to justify criminal acts.

nomenclature—designation or description with a particular and agreed-upon set of terms.

normative antinomy—regular or expected unresolvable conflict or contradiction.

norms—principles or expected action binding on the members of a group and serving to guide, control, or regulate what is considered to be socially proper or acceptable behavior.

nugatory—of little or no consequence.

nullity—having the quality of being nothing; insignificant or inconsequential.

obeisance—refers to being submissive or deferent.

ombudsman—typically, a government official appointed to investigate complaints made by individuals against abuses or capricious acts of public officials.

onerous—characterizes something that is troublesome or that causes a burden.

ostensibly—by all outward appearances.

pale—deficient, feeble, or faint.

panacea—a cure-all; a remedy for all ills or problems.

pandering—catering to or exploiting the weaknesses or naiveté of others.

paradigm—a theoretical framework consisting of theories, laws, or generalizations about a given aspect of the world.

paradox—a statement that is seemingly contradictory or opposed to common sense and yet is perhaps true.

paranoia—a psychosis characterized by systematized delusions of persecution or grandeur, usually without hallucinations.

parity—the quality of being equal or equivalent.

parochially—characterizes a narrow or provincial view of a given issue.

parody—a comic or ridiculous imitation of someone or something else.

pathology—structural and functional deviations from what is considered to be normal.

patriarchal—a characteristic of a social organization where men disproportionately control a large share of power; may refer to the head of a household or to beliefs and values that control institutions of government, industry, religion, and education.

penchant—a strong and continued inclination.

per diem—a daily allowance.

perfidious—characterizes someone without faith or who is disloyal.

perfunctory—superficial, routine, or without enthusiasm.

permeate—to diffuse through or to penetrate.

perpetrator—someone who has brought about or carried out a crime or deception.

pertinent—having a clear relevance to the matter on hand or to the subject.

pervasiveness—characterizes something that covers, encompasses, or is widespread.

phenomenology—the study of the development of human consciousness and self-awareness.

phenomenon—an observable fact or event.

plea bargain—a negotiation of an agreement between a prosecutor and a defendant whereby the defendant is permitted to plead guilty to a reduced charge.

plethora—an abundance or excess.

poignant—making an impression by being direct and to the point.

polestar—a directing principle or guide.

positivistic—characterizes the theory that knowledge about the world and reality are knowable only by empirical verification or scientific proof.

post hoc—formulated after the fact.

postulate—to assume or claim to be true, existent, or necessary.

precarious—an uncertain or dubious circumstance.

precursors—preceding as predictors or antecedents of subsequent events.

predicate felon—a known or proclaimed serious criminal.

predisposes—inclined or to make susceptible in advance.

prescriptive punishment—a recommended recourse of negative sanctions to be applied.

prestige—one's standing or estimation in the minds of others; the weight or credit of other people's general opinion.

presumption—a legal inference as to the existence or truth of a fact not certainly known that is drawn from the known or proved existence of some other fact.

prima facie—true, valid, or sufficient upon one's first impression or on the surface.

proliferation—perpetually or continually increased.

promulgated—having made known or public; proclaimed.

prophylactic—tending to prevent or ward off.

proviso—a condition stipulation.

prurience—the quality of being marked by or arousing an immoderate or unwholesome interest.

puritanical morality—a moral code that is far more rigorous and confining than prevailing standards.

pursuant to—in conformity with or according to a preexisting condition.

putative—commonly accepted or supposed.

quantitative data—information that has been converted into a numerical system for analysis.

quantitative methods—mathematical and statistical techniques used to analyze a given phenomenon.

quid pro quo—something given or received for something else.

quintessential—the most typical or purest form of something.

raison d'être—reason or justification for existence.

rapacious—excessively grasping or covetous.

ratify—to approve and sanction formally.

rationalize—to rely on reason as the basis for the establishment of truth.

recidivists—persons who relapse into a previous form of behavior; especially a relapse into criminal behavior.

recognizance—an obligation of record entered into before a court or magistrate requiring the performance of an act, such as the appearance in court, which if not fulfilled will result, typically, in a monetary forfeiture.

reconcilable—able to make consistent or bring into harmony.

recrimination—a retaliatory charge or accusation.

reductionism—a procedure or theory that reduces complex data or concepts to simpler terms.

reinforced—when an event or a reward occurs that increases the likelihood that certain behaviors will continue.

reiterates—repeating or rephrasing through dialogue a previously expressed statement.

replication—the action or process of reproducing or performing a procedure more than once to verify the validity and reliability of results.

repudiating—characterizes the refusal to have anything to do with; to disown or disclaim.

repugnant—incompatible or inconsistent; distasteful or aversive.

retributive—something given in kind to compensate, especially as applies to punishment.

revocation—the act of annulling by recalling or taking back previously granted conditions or rewards.

Rhadamanthine—rigorously strict or just.

rhetoric—discourse or speech; may be insincere or grandiloquent language.

sacrosanct—most sacred or holy; immune from criticism or violation.

salience—the quality of standing out conspicuously; prominent.

salutary—producing a beneficial effect.

sanguine—characterizes someone who is confident, optimistic, or steadfast.

schema—a structured framework or plan.

scrupulous—refers to someone who acts with strict regard to what is right or proper.

self-fulfilling prophecy—becoming real or true by virtue of having been predicted or expected.

semblance—an outward and often specious appearance or show; modicum or apparent.

servile—submissive or subservient.

sine qua non—something absolutely indispensable or essential.

socioeconomic—involves a combination of social and economic factors.

solemnity—characterizes a solemn event, occasion, or condition.

solidarity—unity of a group or class that is based on common community interests, objectives, or standards.

sovereignty—supreme power, especially with regard to the political system of a nation.

spate—a sudden or strong outburst.

spiritualism—the view that the spirit is the prime element of reality.

squalid—marked by filthiness and degradation from neglect or poverty.

statistically significant—a term used to indicate that a particular value of a statistical measure would not be likely to occur by chance.

status offense—refers to an offense committed by a youth that if committed as an adult would not be illegal; illegal because of the status of being young.

status quo—the existing state of affairs.

statutory—enacted, created, or regulated by a statute or law enacted by a legislature.

stereotype—a mental picture or attitude held by an individual or group, typically about another individual or group, which is an oversimplified opinion, a prejudiced appraisal, or a critical judgment.

stigmatizing—the process of regarding or labeling someone with shame or discredit.

stoic—a person apparently indifferent or unfeeling to pleasure or pain; oblivious.

stratagems—cleverly contrived tricks or tactics for obtaining a specific end.

stridency—the quality that characterizes harsh, insistent, and discordant sound; loud, vociferous.

stymied—confronted with an obstacle; to stand in the way of.

subculture—an ethnic, regional, economic, or social group exhibiting characteristic patterns of behavior sufficient to distinguish it from others within an embracing culture or society.

subjugate—to conquer or to make submissive.

subpoena—a writ commanding a person whose name is on it to appear at an appointed time in court under a penalty for failure to comply.

sub rosa—in confidence or secretly.

substantive law—the created law that defines the rights, duties, prohibitions, and punishments that have been legislatively enacted in the society.

sufficiency—sufficient means to meet one's needs; competency.

superfluous—unnecessary, wasteful, or extravagant.

surrogate—one appointed or designated to act in place of another.

symbiotic relationship—a cooperative interaction between two persons or groups.

syndrome—a group of symptoms that occur together and characterize a particular abnormality; in psychology and the medical field the word *syndrome* is generally used to label a group of symptoms when the cause or pathology of the abnormality is unknown.

tacit—expressed or carried out without words or speech.

tenuous—having little substance or strength.

transcendence—a quality characterized by exceeding usual limits; rising above or moving beyond the typical patterns of life and thought.

tribunal—a court or forum of justice.

truant—shirking responsibility; one who stays out of school without permission.

truncheon—a club, bludgeon, or a baton.

tyrannical—characterizes someone who is an absolute ruler unrestrained by law or constitution, often acting brutally or oppressively.

Umwelt—the surroundings or environment.

unencumbered—free of being weighed down or burdened; unhindered.

unrecalcitrant—indefinite of authority; easily managed or operated; unresistant.

unsullied—unsoiled or without being tarnished or defiled.

urbane—notably polite or finished in manner.

utilitarian—marked by views or practices that hold that the real measure of anything's worth is its practical use or goal.

utopian—characterizes someone who is a visionary or believes in some far-reaching, unattainably perfect world.

vagaries—erratic, unpredictable, or extravagant notions or actions.

vagrancy—the state of a person who wanders from place to place without a fixed home or livelihood, usually considered to be a public nuisance; vagrants often engage in begging, stealing, and prostitution to obtain income.

vanguard—the forefront of an action or movement.

variables—a quantity that represents a social event or behavior that may assume any one of a set of values; attributes that can change regularly over time.

variegated—having discrete markings of color or characteristics.

vendible—capable of being sold or peddled.

venerate—to honor or regard with reverence and/or acts of devotion.

venue—the place from which a jury is drawn or in which a trial takes place.

victimologists—those who study the economic, psychological, and social impact of crime upon victims.

vigilant—watchful or attentively guarding.

vignette—a brief incident, scene, or exemplary story.

vindicates—the act of justifying, substantiating, or defending.

vindictiveness—characterizes someone who is spiteful or disposed to seek revenge.

vociferousness—characterizes someone who is marked by or given to vehement and insistent outcries.

writ of certiorari—a writ of a superior court to call up records of a lower court or a body acting in a quasi-judicial capacity.

writ of habeas corpus—any of several common law writs issued to bring a party before a judge or court.

zealotry—an excess of zeal; fanatical devotion.